Advance Praise for
Rhetorical Choices, Second Edition

"Editors of *Rhetorical Choices* spread a cultural buffet of texts for readers; there's something for everyone!"

Audrey Herbrich
Blinn College

"I am extremely pleased with *Rhetorical Choices* because it serves a dual role: it empowers me to teach at a higher pedagogical level and it empowers my students who come to college to change their lives in ways that make them better writers, better readers, and better critical thinkers."

Carlyle Van Thompson
Medgar Evers College

"*Rhetorical Choices* includes a fascinating selection of articles written with intelligence and energy."

Robert Koch
St. Louis Community College, Florissant Valley

"I find the stylistic variety and subject matter of the selections in each chapter broad and suitable for use by students with varied learning styles, from diverse cultural and ethnic backgrounds, with dissimilar interests, and of varying ages. I'm also pleased with the inclusive scope of cultural, ethnic, and gender diversity among the selected authors and the subjects of their works."

Mike Williams
New Mexico Junior College

"*Rhetorical Choices* lives up to its title in that it truly does prompt students to think about how the choices they make as writers affect their arguments. It helps them see the control they can have over their own writing."

Alexander Bruce
Florida Southern College

"The questions at the end of each selection are wonderful, and I especially like the 'Strategies for Writers' and 'Research and Writing Assignments' at the end of each chapter."

Arden Jensen
Lee University

Keith Gilyard is Professor of English at The Pennsylvania State University. He has written and lectured widely about language, literature, and education. A writing teacher for three decades his books include *Voices of the Self: A Study of Language Competence,* for which he received an American Book Award in 1992, and *Let's Flip the Script: An African American Discourse on Language, Literature, and Learning.* Long active in professional organizations, he has served on the executive committees of the National Council of Teachers of English (NCTE), the Conference on English Education (CEE), and the Conference on College Composition and Communication (CCCC). Gilyard served as Chair of CCCC in 2000.

Deborah H. Holdstein is Professor of English and Chair of the Department of English at Northern Illinois University. She is also the Editor of *College Composition and Communication,* the flagship journal of studies in composition and rhetoric. Before arriving at NIU in July of 2005, Holdstein was Professor of English and Rhetoric at Governors State University and also served as Faculty Associate for Graduate Studies and Research in the Office of the Provost

and as Chair of the Graduate Council. She has published widely in composition studies, technology and the humanities, film, and literary studies in such journals as *CCC, College English,* and *Pedagogy.* Her books include *On Composition and Computers, The Prentice-Hall Anthology of Women's Literature, Challenging Perspectives,* and *Personal Effects: The Social Character of Scholarly Writing* (coedited with David Bleich). Deborah Holdstein also serves as Director of the Consultant-Evaluator Service of the Council of Writing Program Administrators.

Charles I. Schuster is a Professor of English and a former director of the First-Year Composition Program at the University of Wisconsin-Milwaukee where he currently serves as Associate Dean of the Humanities. He has also directed the UWM Writing Center, the Freshman Scholars Program, and the Peer Mentoring Program. A former President of the Council of Writing Program Administrators, Schuster currently serves on the editorial boards of *College Composition and Communication* and the *Journal of Basic Writing* and is College Editor of Heinemann-Boynton/Cook Publishers. He has authored articles on subjects including Richard Selzer, Charles Dickens, the teaching of writing, and the theories of Mikhail Bakhtin. Co-author of *Speculations,* Schuster is also General Editor of Longman's Literature and Culture series, which publishes anthologies devoted to popular fiction, the environment, race, class, and gender. He has lived in Milwaukee since 1985.

Rhetorical Choices

A Reader for Writers

SECOND EDITION

Keith Gilyard
The Pennsylvania State University

Deborah H. Holdstein
Northern Illinois University

Charles I. Schuster
University of Wisconsin-Milwaukee

PENGUIN ACADEMICS

New York   Boston   San Francisco
London   Toronto   Sydney   Tokyo   Singapore   Madrid
Mexico City   Munich   Paris   Cape Town   Hong Kong   Montreal

Executive Editor: Lynn M. Huddon
Senior Supplements Editor: Donna Campion
Senior Marketing Manager: Sandra McGuire
Production Manager: Eric Jorgensen
Project Coordination, Text Design, and Electronic Page Makeup:
    Pre-Press Company, Inc.
Senior Cover Design Manager: Nancy Danahy
Cover Image: © Getty Images, Inc.
Senior Manufacturing Buyer: Alfred C. Dorsey
Printer and Binder: Courier Corporation
Cover Printer: Phoenix Color Corp.

For permission to use copyrighted material, grateful acknowledgment is
made to the copyright holders on pp. 643–646, which are hereby made part
of this copyright page.

Library of Congress Cataloging-in-Publication Data

Rhetorical choices: a reader for writers / [compiled by] Keith Gilyard,
    Deborah H. Holdstein, Charles I. Schuster. -- 2nd ed.
        p. cm.
    Includes index.
    ISBN 0-321-44492-2
        1. College readers. 2. English language--Rhetoric--Problems, exercises,
    etc. 3. Report writing--Problems, exercises, etc. I. Gilyard, Keith, 1952-
II. Holdstein, Deborah H., 1952- III. Schuster, Charles I.

PE1417.R478 2007
808'.0427--dc22   2006046003

Please visit us at www.ablongman.com

ISBN 0-321-44492-2

678910—V013—14 13 12 11 10

Contents

7 *Process Analysis*   343

Contents by Theme

Language Variety

Education and Opportunity

Natural World

Life and Death

Preface

We have attempted in this new edition of *Rhetorical Choices*, as we did in the first, to offer students and teachers a rigorous and compelling course of study for the teaching of writing. Writing does not happen in a vacuum. It arises from thoughtful discussion, earnest debate, honest disagreement, and reasoned analysis in response to the words, ideas, insights, and arguments of others. In its most measured form, those words and ideas come from reading, since published work allows us to work backward and forward through a text. To our way of thinking, every composition course needs to offer students good, challenging, smart reading that stimulates student thinking. It hardly matters what the reading is about: international politics, global warming, basketball, *Brokeback Mountain,* college tuition, a critique of "American Idol," the history of igneous rocks, Barbie dolls, or Oprah. The important thing is for the reading to light up the minds of students enrolled in this composition course and keep them turning pages, inviting them to think, react, discuss, and—most importantly—to write. We hope the readings in this book have that effect. Frankly, there is no other reason to publish *Rhetorical Choices*. It is the prime directive of textbooks: Do something that will make a difference.

This book was created to fulfill that purpose. In considering what we would include in this second edition, we kept all the readings that teachers told us worked well for them and their students. That also meant discarding some titles from the first edition and adding 14 new selections. Most important, we tried to assemble readings that in our experience engage students and encourage them to write. Although we believe that student writing should lie at the heart of any composition class, most instructors use readings to stimulate discussion, introduce students to potential topics for their own essays, and provide models of fine prose for them to emulate. In preparing this book, we tried to remain mindful of all three goals.

New in this edition are enriched introductions to the modes, introductions that offer explicit approaches to teaching and that illuminate the ways that modes are crafted in order to achieve specific effects. It seemed to us that one way of helping instructors—and students—in writing classes would be to discuss the modes in ways that might get played out in actual classes. Thus the introduction to each of the nine modes includes a section entitled "Approaches to Using" that specific mode. These sections provide specific instructional strategies intended to help students master that particular approach.

Our intention in writing *Rhetorical Choices* was to offer students a range of works with which they can analyze language and language users, language and culture, and language and politics. We believe that a reading text designed to foster writing should foreground the political and cultural contexts behind the readings and challenge students to respond to these texts in ways that enable their growth as writers. Typically, textbooks that stress instruction in writing methods fail to accentuate how personal, cultural, and political factors are connected to rhetorical decision making. Our goal was to bring together an array of multicultural and multigenre selections that reflect a wide range of linguistic, cultural, and political concerns. Linked to those readings are questions designed to solicit active responses about rhetorical choices and the linguistic, cultural, and political factors that writers often consider as they make those choices.

The traditional modes of discourse that organize this volume are useful strategies for analyzing, developing, and organizing writing. We decided to organize this book according to nine major modes of discourse: narration, description, definition, exemplification, classification, process analysis, comparison and contrast, cause and effect, and argument. We believe these time-honored rhetorical categories will enable students to learn how sophisticated writers write—so that they can master, in their own writing, sophisticated strategies that will serve them well as they progress through college and beyond. We also had a number of other principles to which we tried to remain true:

Modeling the Modes: In selecting which works to include in this second edition, we have tried hard to adhere to one central principle: Each selection should be one that best illustrates the mode under which it is categorized. Our hope is that students and teachers can open this book at random, read a selection, and state with a strong degree of certainty which mode is being illustrated. Clearly, some of the modes represent strategies more than genres; we are thinking here of modes like process analysis or exemplification, where the focus is more on methods of development than on an entire formal structure. Such methods, however, have become time-honored ways to teach the modes because of their usefulness within the classroom.

Familiar and Original Readings: Most of us who teach composition regularly rely on certain assignments that have proven successful time and again. In putting together the selections for this edition—a process that involved many visions and revisions—we sought to provide a rich mix of classic and contemporary titles, familiar and less familiar authors. No anthology can include everyone's favorite author or title, but we think we have brought together a rich range of authors, essays, and themes. Many of the writers represented in this collection are familiar and distinguished. Others, although less known, are worthy of wider exposure. We hope all the selections encourage both students and instructors to do additional reading by these authors and others.

Linked Themes: Whenever possible, we sought to create links among the selections. Many of them are focused on similar concerns about language use and dialect; others treat similar themes or subjects. We have tried to highlight those linkages by their placement within the chapters or by making explicit references to them in our apparatus. When selections resonate with each other, they promote more sustained discussion and often lead to richer, more deeply contextualized writing assignments.

Straight Talk: *Rhetorical Choices* is a modal reader with an edge, and that edge grows out of our commitment to develop a book that is intellectually challenging, socially aware, and sensitive to the changing nature of language and culture in this country. We have provided the kinds of teaching aids that we think will be helpful, but we did not want to patronize instructors or condescend students. This is a college reader. The selections, for the most part, are demanding and require not just reading but rereading. We think that is what most college instructors—and college students, for that matter—want out of their experience.

Questions for Responding and Writing: Following each selection, we offer instructors two sets of questions. The first, entitled "Analyzing Rhetorical Choices," asks students to examine the styles, structures, and modes, focusing particularly on the craft of writing. The second, "Writing About Issues and Contexts," invites students to think more speculatively about the topics and to relate the essays to other works and the world outside the text.

Strategies and Essay Assignments: At the end of every chapter we include two additional teaching tools. The first one is entitled "Strategies for Writers," and it offers a set of very explicit guides to writing each mode, referencing each suggestion to specific selections. Following that, we offer a final section in each chapter called "Research and Writing Assignments." In this section, we provide multiple essay assignments that call upon students to engage in further research while extending the themes and issues raised in the readings.

Ease of Use: Finally, we have put together a book that we think will work in multiple ways in multiple classrooms, without over-encumbering instructors—and students—with peripheral and extraneous supplementary materials. The focus in this text is on reading critically and then helping students to incorporate the meanings and modes into their own essays. The most important question we kept asking ourselves was "What kind of book would we want to teach in our own writing classes?" *Rhetorical Choices* is that book.

Instructor's Manual

This guide offers the features that you would expect in an instructor's manual, and some that you might not, all of them condensed into a short, easy-to-navigate text that allows you to begin planning and teaching your own course quickly. You will find chapter overviews that provide notes on each of the modes presented in the textbook, sample responses to the readings, suggested writing exercises, and syllabi and sample grading rubrics you can use or amend as you see fit. In addition, this manual presents several short statements on the big questions that all writing teachers must struggle with, no matter how much expertise they have in the field. These statements, "An Overview of Writing and Writing Instruction" and "Making Access Real: Thoughts on Integrating Communication Technologies in the Writing Classroom," lay out the ideas and commitments that undergird this textbook and manual, but also trace those big questions in ways that we hope will lead you to push the commitments you already have or even help you enter those conversations if you happen to be a new instructor.

Acknowledgments

Many people deserve to be thanked for their help, support, understanding, and forbearance in helping us publish this second edition of *Rhetorical Choices*. For her constancy and support even in the darkest days of author fatigue, Lynn Huddon deserves the Nobel Prize for editorship. In the first edition, Katharine Glynn made an immense difference in helping us discover and strengthen what was best in our own work. We are also deeply indebted to the entire team at Longman, from editorial assistants (thanks, Nicole!) to marketing, and to the production group. And we want to offer a special thank you to Christine Brovelli, Deborah Holdstein's graduate assistant at NIU, who helped immeasurably in some of the detail and intellectual work required for this new edition.

We also owe a great debt to our students. They often tested these readings and assignments, helping us to refine, reshape, and revise. And they always reminded us of the goal: to do a book that makes a difference in their daily intellectual lives. Finally, we want to thank our many professional colleagues who teach at community colleges, four-year schools, and comprehensive universities across the country. We have profited from your enthusiasm for teaching, your enlightened criticisms, your passion for the printed word, your devotion to learning, your friendship, and your support.

To the many reviewers who provided valuable feedback at many stages with both the first and second editions, our thanks to: Christopher Baker, Armstrong Atlantic State University; Dan Baldwin, Muscatine Community College; Mark Bernier, Blinn College; Alexander M. Bruce, Florida Southern College; Lisa L. Colman, Southeastern Oklahoma State University; Kathleen Dorantes, Imperial Valley College; Thomas E. Fish, Cumberland College; Raymond Foster, Scottsdale Community College; Frederic Giacobazzi, Kirtland Community College; Audrey Herbrich, Blinn College; Mary Hurst, Cuyahoga Community College; Arden Jensen, Lee University; Robert Koch, St. Louis Community College; Kimmarie Lewis, Lord Fairfax Community College; Joseph F. McCadden,

Burlington County College; Jamie Molitoris, Monmouth University; Kevin Nebergall, Kirkwood Community College; Carlyle Thompson, Medgar Evers College; Victor Uszerowicz, Miami Dade Community College; and Mike Williams, New Mexico Junior College.

KEITH GILYARD
DEBORAH H. HOLDSTEIN
CHARLES I. SCHUSTER

1

Writers, Readers, and Rhetorical Choices

We believe students succeed both in college and beyond when they have been taught to engage in rigorous analysis, thoughtful inquiry, meaningful exploration, and sophisticated written argument. That is, successful students have learned how to read challenging material, analyze it, develop their own perspectives and positions in writing, and engage in thoughtful, ongoing oral and written debates about significant issues: affirmative action, sports and morality, gender equity, individual rights versus the collective good of society. These kinds of activities, of course, typically occur in most first-year composition courses, and their importance explains why such courses are required in most universities: They enable students to succeed within their majors and to become capable citizens within society. To say this another way, learning how to read, write, analyze, argue, and engage in this kind of intellectual activity depends on knowing how to make meaningful and effective rhetorical choices. Hence the title of this book.

We understand that the word *rhetoric* often carries a pejorative implication in the popular media, but for the three of us and for many of our colleagues around the country who teach composition and literature, the word is a positive one. To learn about rhetoric is to learn about argument and persuasion. Rhetoric is the study of language in all its various uses. To be an accomplished rhetorician means knowing a subject well and being able to engage in meaningful discussion with others about it. It also means having the ability to persuade others, not through deceit or distortion but through logical analysis, presentation of facts and data, and the crafting of effective, powerful, and—yes—beautiful language. That is why the phrase "rhetorical choices" means so much to us: To be able to make such choices intelligently lies at the heart of what it means to be part of an educated citizenry.

With respect to writing—the particular concern that motivated us to create this book—the phrase "rhetorical choices" means that successful student writers learn how to pay close attention to the ways in which their language use affects others. They will become more conscious about how to craft appropriate structures and phrasing, and more able to find the kinds of factual and knowledgeable support that can persuade readers to change their minds. Through making meaningful rhetorical choices, writers can make effective arguments. This kind of mastery involves speculation by students about their roles and development as student-citizens in the context of conversations swirling around them, both on campus and in the larger culture. This is the reason that this text is a *reader* or *sourcebook*—and why its focus is on the rhetorical choices that writers make to bring readers into a thoughtful and informed conversation about issues and arguments, visions and values. It is our attempt to outline a rich discussion about a range of compelling issues for students in a college writing classroom.

This book is also a *rhetoric* in the sense that it offers selections by various writers as models of admirable writing, models that can be imitated. We do not contend that these are the only admirable models available or that imitating such models is the only way to become a successful writer. Neither proposition is true, but writers often use the writings of others to strengthen themselves as writers. They draw inspiration by experiencing the skill and genius of other accomplished authors. Often they learn how to solve problems in their own writing by seeing how published authors use perspective, structure, tone, organization, and evidence, or the ways they establish mood or tone. To do this requires that a reader learn how to read as a writer, a concept that we will develop later in this chapter. All these uses of reading work best when applied to outstanding examples of written work, the kinds of examples that we have included in this book.

Reading and analyzing models is thus an important activity for writers and at the very least serves as a means to illustrate problems, solutions, and possibilities.

Anthologies such as this tend to be organized in one of two ways: by rhetorical modes (such as this one), or by theme (see our alternative table of contents). We find that modes-oriented readers are instructive and even liberating. We are convinced that reading essays and other texts within a modal framework can help you become a more sophisticated reader and writer. For one thing, reading in this way provides clear examples centered on techniques, such as using narration to tell a story or employing comparison and contrast when examining two related subjects. Such discussions of technique are greatly enhanced when they can be anchored to specific modes of discourse, to the forms that emerge when writers engage topics passionately.

We recognize that placing essays in a particular category or mode is often arbitrary. We have organized the selections in this book according to modes primarily to highlight certain structural aspects of a particular work, not to limit or neglect its other and various strengths. In fact many, if not all, of these selections could be placed in several categories. This is part of our point. The readings selected for this book illustrate that these modes and essays are flexible, not the categorized, inviolate texts or, in the case of the modes, the impenetrable boundaries they may seem to represent. Indeed, you might well move a certain essay that is in the Argument chapter to Definition (or vice versa). For instance, Malcolm X's "My First Conk" describes a process but is also part of his autobiography, a narrative; Norman Cousins's essay, "Who Killed Benny Paret?" is both argument and an example of cause and effect. Alice Walker's "Am I Blue?" represents narration as well as description, cause and effect, and to some extent, comparison and contrast. Julia Alvarez's "Snow" can be called both description and narration. How could there be narration without description? How could there be effective arguments without exemplification? Nonetheless, using categories, or modes, provides a vehicle for you to begin to look at the texts carefully and to consider how and why a writer shaped an essay in a certain way. To think about essays, stories, and poems this way lies at the heart of rhetorical understanding, at making informed rhetorical choices as both a writer and a reader.

In addition to their rhetorical value, the modes have real-world, practical implications. Physicians must compare and contrast the relative value of different medications or sets of symptoms; travel agents describe cruise ships and define the terms of various cruise packages; attorneys must argue effectively to prosecute or defend; teachers define and explain; businesspeople must also argue, define, and compare costs; consumers' guides classify and rate products and services; and so on. Using modes can also help each of us understand that we, as readers, must be constantly teaching ourselves how to read as we undertake more and more difficult material.

Finally, this is a book based on notions of how to learn writing, on what it means to be a reader and writer both within the composition classroom and beyond. Sourcebooks and rhetorics are not objective or neutral objects that show up in classrooms on their own; they don't spring from the head of Zeus. They get there because people in various situations—authors, editors, publishers, writing program administrators, instructors—make decisions based on their notions of what ought to happen in a writing classroom. Our approach, explicit in this chapter and implied throughout this book, is that learning to write is best facilitated through a *critical perspective about language*—that is, one that suggests the subjective nature of writing and the teaching of writing. Such an approach stresses the political nature of language and instruction and welcomes the attempts of students from various literacy backgrounds to negotiate successfully the language demands of academic institutions. In addition, our approach emphasizes the importance of reading with both pleasure and understanding. If the reading and writing you do in this course are to be meaningful, it is essential to read for enjoyment and to be able to appreciate the craft of writing—that is, the kinds of rhetorical choices that these authors made as they wrote.

Further, you need to approach the readings in this book with the perspective that writing is done in various ways by different writers— that there is no one way to write, just as there is no one way to read. Thus we do not engage in talk about *the* writing process or even *the* reading process. Because there are multiple ways to read and write, we offer no one recipe for how to bake good essays. Nor do we offer any formulas for instant improvement. Our aim is to provide a rich array of possibilities, to keep things flexible, and to provide a tempting and nutritious banquet of readings that can sustain you over the entire term. What we hope you will provide is energy, commitment, and a willingness to engage thoughtfully and critically with the readings and your own writing. In other words, we think rhetorical models are important, but they need to be integrated into a curricular approach that takes advantage of the interest, artistry, and imagination of students and teachers. In the end, this book is not so much about reading within the modes as it is about gaining rhetorical power and intellectual acumen through broadened knowledge and understanding.

Ways of Learning to Write

Every classroom is driven by theories. Instructors who lecture exclusively have a theory, which they may or may not articulate, that knowledge is best created and communicated through the monologic presentation of material. Conversely, instructors who favor more student-teacher exchange believe that knowledge is best fashioned in dialogue. We feel that you, as a student, should be informed about the theories that drive instruction in your writing classes and that there should be ongoing discussions about the learning process throughout the semester. In this section, we outline some notions that we think should infuse writing classrooms, and we provide the reasons we think so. We are not saying that these are the only concepts around which courses should revolve, but our experiences tell us that these are crucial principles deserving of explicit scrutiny. By reading our thoughts about classroom instruction, you will, we hope, become absorbed in and reflective about your own learning, just as we ask you to absorb and reflect on the readings in this book.

Thinking as a Writer

It is a truth almost universally acknowledged that the more you write, the better writer you will become. More specifically, such practice will make you not only a better writer—because you will become increasingly adept at making informed rhetorical choices—but also a better thinker. The complexities of the writing process, however you demonstrate these in whatever ways of composing work for you, are exactly the qualities that foster your ability to think well. And the ability to think in complex ways demonstrates exactly what is meant by the often overused and sometimes unclearly understood term *critical thinking.*

Although many of us wish there were a simple plan, a formula, for writing, there is not. Writing is rarely easy, and perceptions of what it means to be a good writer are complicated by a kind of writing folklore: "If I were a good writer, this wouldn't be so hard." "If I were a good writer, I wouldn't have to go back and edit and revise." "If I were a good writer, this would come out right the first time." Nothing could be further from the truth. As evidenced by the revised and edited manuscripts of poet-critic John Keats, on display in the British Museum, even highly skilled and experienced writers do not expect to "get it right the first time." We have selected essays and devised questions to prompt your own critical sensibilities and help you develop your own ways of analyzing, responding, and writing.

Writing is not only a means of learning, but it is also a form of exploration—a means of taking chances and risks, both intellectual and practical. Suppose you have just read a particularly complex selection in this book. Your instructor asks you to write a paper. As you begin the paper, perhaps by jotting notes on the article, you are seized by a sense of chaos. How on earth will you write this? Yet this sense of intellectual chaos may well be for you a fully appropriate, inevitable stage of the writing process—that exploratory time when you will begin to think through the article, formulate your own response to it, argue effectively using evidence from the text, and so forth. If this is a paper to be written outside class, you might clear the kitchen table, find your favorite beverage, pace a bit, and write longhand on a yellow legal pad before turning to your computer.

Whatever the rituals of your writing process, you ultimately must commit to paper or to the cyber world your rhetorical choices, well—and responsibly—articulated. Indeed, although your writing in its various guises might well entertain, inform, describe, define—and be modeled after any of the modes we use as starting points for thinking and writing in this book—writing is most significantly a way of building trust with your readers as you analyze and argue. Yet however you get to the point at which you have your final (or as writer Ann Berthoff called it, your "best-yet") draft, the writing process rarely moves in a neat linear fashion from prewriting to writing to revising to editing. Instead, it's a messy, recursive set of acts. For instance, let's go back to that paper your instructor assigned as a response to a complex selection in this book. As you write, you might create a few draft paragraphs, and then turn back and add to them, redo a paragraph or two completely, and then decide that you'd better keep them and see if they will work well toward the end of your paper rather than at the beginning. Or you might decide that you need additional evidence from the article to make your points; once you reread the article, you discover that you want to rework yet again the paragraphs you've written. In fact, if you could see the number of drafts this chapter went through before being printed, you would be either heartened or discouraged—the former because even professional writers revise, the latter because, frankly, even for professional writers, the processes of revising and editing never quite seem to end. The risk? That your point will be far more complex than you had imagined, taking more concentration, time, and revision than you had thought; that your readers might not agree with your viewpoint, however well argued. But these are exactly the types of risks that are worth taking. The clearly articulated path, the path with direction, is far more useful than the path of least resistance.

Writing for Multiple Purposes and Audiences

Although we have implicitly encouraged you to adopt a writing process that might seem inordinately time-consuming—with time spent just sitting at your kitchen table, sipping your favorite beverage, gathering your thoughts—there will always be different occasions for writing that encourage and challenge your flexibility as a writer. This is a *good* thing. In the necessarily bumpy process that ultimately shaped this chapter, each of us drafted sections of it on our own and, on rare occasions, together (when we could be in the same room). After extensive conversations among the three of us about a particular section, one of us would immediately begin to rewrite just to "get our thoughts down." Sometimes a section seemed to fall into place immediately, while others took much longer. Then one of us would put everything together and see how, or if, the pieces fit.

As we've already noted, the writing process is more often than not anything but linear. You may find yourself adding new information as you revise; you may find yourself moving one section from the end of your paper to the middle; you may find yourself at the editing stage (often a final stage) with the first section of a paper before you even draft the next. While you may always wish for the opportunity to draft and redraft and edit and revise (in other words, for the opportunity to honor your own, inevitably idiosyncratic, writing process), this will be impossible during any number of writing situations—for instance, an hour-long, in-class essay exam. In that case, your audience is clearly the teacher, and it's your responsibility to marshal evidence from classroom discussions, readings in the textbook, and so forth to make concise, well-developed, and well-argued points in a relatively short period.

Similarly, on the job, you may not have what appears to be the luxury of working alone, drafting in a leisurely fashion. Indeed, reports in the corporate world are increasingly collaborative, requiring members of a particular working team to strike a balance among different voices, ways of writing, and ways of contributing. It is useful, therefore, for you to work with your colleagues in class to talk through your responses to particularly controversial ideas you may find in these essays. Further, despite the extensive use of e-mail on the job, employers will not accept reports that reflect the rhetorical choices popular among teenagers using Instant Messenger. Using shorthand like "CU later" or the number 4 instead of the word *for* will not impress the corporate community, where sending even brief posts with feedback on important issues must be highly literate in the conventional sense. In this way, out-of-class, on-line discussion groups with your writer-colleagues and your instructor in response to discussion questions for the essays in this book (or to brainstorm and create your own and then respond to them) will give you the opportunity to do the best you can when you must organize your thoughts, compose, and send out for feedback some writing that will become public more quickly than you'd usually prefer. It will also help you determine, as a writer, ways to meet the expectations of the often complex audiences for whom you write. Remember that a document can have a life beyond your intended audience. The same is true for e-mail. What seems to be an ephemeral, nearly invisible message sent off with the click of a mouse not only has a life of its own but is considered a form of durable communication—so much so that e-mail has long been "discoverable" as evidence in court.

Given all this, it is not surprising that instructors often emphasize the importance of analyzing the audience for your writing, often suggesting that you reach for readership beyond the teacher, beyond the classroom. For whom do we write, especially if it is not just for the instructor? It is true that assessing your readers, your possible audience, can help you anticipate potential objections to your argument and at the same time reinforce the deeply social dimension of writing.

Using Your Native Linguistic Abilities

In any given classroom, you'll find a broad spectrum of linguistic ability among students. Although it's impossible to be aware of every nuance in this regard, we favor classrooms that nurture every writer, including those who have a relatively wide gap to negotiate between native discourse and Standard Written English. Not only do we view this action as a socially just intervention into the use of dominant discourses, but we also feel that building on already existing linguistic strengths is the most viable way to encourage you and your class-mates to develop into lifelong writers *and* achieve the writing standards set by colleges and universities.

Focusing on Mechanics in Context

Part of your obligation and ultimate authority as a writer depends, as we have noted, on your communicating clearly, concisely, and responsibly. While acknowledging the power relationships in the classroom and beyond that create a dominant discourse, we believe part of that obligation involves what is often dismissed or criticized as "correctness" in punctuation and mechanics. Writers are often stymied, even blocked from writing, when they pressure themselves to try to be "correct" as they draft. Most writers will agree that even in the most expeditious forms of communication—for instance, that important e-mail response to your supervisor regarding a departmental project for which you have primary responsibility—it is wise, if not essential, to save concern for mechanics and punctuation for last, just before you print out a report or click "send" to dispatch that important e-mail.

Like it or not, we often move among "communities," and each community requires us to speak and write differently and to make different rhetorical choices. Different contexts for writing require adjustments in your word choice, sentence structure, mode, and mechanics. Especially in academic writing, too many punctuation and mechanical errors can get in the way of your readers being able to appreciate what you've done and what you hope to accomplish. To some readers, your level of correctness can, for good or ill, be an indication of your level of "conventional" education, whether or not their assessment is accurate.

The context in which you practice your knowledge of mechanics and other forms of correctness can make a difference as well. One of us recalls being quite the achiever regarding commas in the sixth grade—as long as it was in the very limited context of workbook exercises. Because it's difficult to transfer the isolated examples in a workbook to "real" writing, use an English handbook as you review your own writing. Don't assume that you're an expert in mechanics because you've scored well on a punctuation quiz or an on-line workbook.

Considering Language, Power, and Citizenship

The philosopher and theorist Mikhail Bakhtin determined that there is no language that is not connected to specific social relationships; these are, in turn, connected to larger, very powerful economic, political, and ideological systems. While we affirm the importance of writing "appropriately" for different occasions, encourage and expect mechanical correctness that matches the demands of a dominant discourse, and hold other teacherly—sometimes restrictive—views of what it means to write and to be a "good" writer, we also encourage you to question issues of language and power within your classroom and within the essays that you read and analyze from this collection (this introductory chapter included). We encourage you to determine what it means to be a writer in your class—relationships between and among your colleague-writers and the instructor, say—and what it means to be a writer in relation to these questions of language and power within your college or university and beyond.

To close out this section while continuing to stress the need for all of us to stay attuned to questions of language and power, we ask you to consider the following text about the Arctic National Wildlife Refuge that was displayed on the Web site of the U.S. Fish and Wildlife Service during the week after George W. Bush's first inauguration:

> One hundred thirty-five species of birds are known to use the area, including numerous shorebirds, waterfowl, loons, songbirds, and raptors.
>
> One notable example is the snow goose. Large numbers of snow geese, varying each year from 15,000 to more than 300,000 birds, feed on the Arctic Refuge coastal tundra for three to four weeks each fall. They feed on cottongrass and other plants to build up fat reserves in preparation for their journey south, eating as much as a third of their body weight each day. The rich vegetation of the coastal tundra enables them to increase fat reserves by 400 percent in only two to three weeks.
>
> Snow geese feed on small patches of vegetation that are widely distributed across the Refuge's coastal tundra, so a large area is necessary to meet their needs. They are extremely sensitive to disturbance, often flying away from their feeding sites when human activities occur several miles distant.

Compare this with the text that appeared on the Web site before its post-inauguration revision. The parts of the previous version that were revised or deleted are italicized:

> One hundred thirty-five species of birds are known to use the area, including numerous shorebirds, waterfowl, loons, songbirds, and raptors. *Oil development in the Arctic Refuge would result in habitat loss, disturbance, and displacement or abandonment of important nesting, feeding, molting, and staging areas.*
>
> *One species of bird that could be greatly impacted by oil development is the snow goose.* Large numbers of snow geese, varying each

year from 15,000 to more than 300,000 birds, feed on the Arctic Refuge coastal tundra for three to four weeks each fall. They feed on cottongrass and other plants to build up fat reserves in preparation for their journey south, eating as much as a third of their body weight each day. The rich vegetation of the coastal tundra enables them to increase fat reserves by 400 percent in only two to three weeks.

Snow geese feed on small patches of vegetation that are widely distributed across the Refuge's coastal tundra, so a large area is necessary to meet their needs. They are extremely sensitive to disturbance, often flying away from their feeding sites when human activities occur several miles distant. *Oil exploration and development would displace snow geese from areas that are critically important to them.*

How does the deleted text change the meaning? How do these changes affect your notions of language, power, and citizenship?

Readers and Rhetorical Choices

Because readings are the centerpiece of this book and fundamental to the courses in which they are used, we want to share our general views about reading in order to point classroom discussion in directions we think are most profitable. First, we view reading to be a constructive activity rather than one in which readers "receive" messages from texts. Language is *indexical;* that is, it suggests a range of meanings and offers a wide spectrum of rhetorical choices. Sure, sometimes the meaning of language seems both clear and unambiguous, as when E. Annie Proulx (the author of the story from which the film *Brokeback Mountain* was made) writes in *The Gourmet Gardener:*

> Older authorities believed the radish originated in China, but it was extensively grown in ancient Egypt, Greece, and Rome. The Greeks thought the radish so fine that in offerings to Apollo radishes made of gold were laid before the god, while beets rated only silver, and turnips, lead.

Even language this clear, however, cannot guarantee all readers equal access to its range of meanings in exactly the same way. For example, who are these "older authorities"? How old are they, and what kind of authority do they have? Who is Apollo, and what does Proulx mean by saying that gold radishes were "laid before" him? What is the context for these two statements about the radish? What are Proulx's purposes in writing about the radish in this way, paraphrasing classical and historical sources?

Even a single word can carry multiple meanings. Consider the word *sunset.* We could probably all agree on a technical definition that would incorporate some insight about the rotation of the earth on its axis as it orbits the sun and the sun's slow decline in the west each evening. In other words, we could pretty much agree on what the word denotes. However, if we were all asked to envision a sunset or express the associations we have with the word *sunset*, which is another way of asking what *sunset* connotes or means, we would inevitably describe different visions. We might include scenes from apartment windows, front porches, beaches, parks, cities, trains, buses, airplanes, movies, and other locations. The visions we recall would also be attached to memories, ranging from very vague to sharply specific, and might be connected to emotions—joy, defeat, sadness, renewal. The word might even trigger other associations: the strong bond of friendship or love with a specific individual or the smell of an ocean breeze off the Pacific. Some of us might simply speak of the sun setting behind the trees, while others of us might be as elaborate as novelist John Oliver Killens in *The Cotillion:*

> She felt that if her father did materialize in the deep glow of the Harlem sunset she would break into a run like in the old days when she was six and seven and eight and believed in a jolly, old, fat white man by the name of Santa Claus, and thought the whole wide world was right there on her block in Harlem, and God was great and God was good and everything was for the best, because He worked myste-riously, the Grand Magician of them all. Cars honking, racing motors, fumes belching, children screaming, cursing, squealing, laughing. She stared past the busy intersection clear across Seventh Avenue all the way west to the river where the sun was a blazing disk of fire and washing the streets with a million colors and descending slowly down between the buildings at the very end of the street, down down it was sinking slowly sinking to set afire the Hudson River. Her eyes filled up and almost overflowed at the beauty of the Harlem sunset. The tene-ments bathed in soft sweet tender shadows now. She took one long last look down toward the other end of her block. Come around the cor-ner, Daddy! Come around the corner! And I will run again to meet you. She turned toward the house. Maybe he was already home. Silently she prayed he was already in the house.

To understand all that *sunset* means in this passage, you would have to consider, at the very least, the theme of innocence and its loss, the idea of reflection amid commotion, the love of place, and the mixed emotions about faith and belief (the loss of belief in Santa Claus and the commitment to prayer). And if this passage is doing its work, it will trigger certain kinds of identification with the young girl's feelings of hope and loss, identification and understanding, shaped and colored by your own experiences. It is this range of possible meanings that makes language indexical, that makes it in a very real sense always much more than the sum of its parts.

Clearly, language conveys meaning, but at the same time, readers give shape to that meaning based on their level of attention, personal experience, reading background, ability to analyze and interpret the text, and multiple other factors. Reading is, therefore, a social act, one that is much more similar to writing than many people assume. Both emerge from interactions between self and others, self and words, self and experiences. If you understand how complicated the question of meaning can become when we are dealing with a single word or a short passage, you can appreciate how active and engaged your mental faculties must be to interpret and build knowledge from the complex texts encountered in academics and beyond. Generally, you are not merely "decoding information" from something that is fixed and stable; rather, you are negotiating an understanding that must variously take into account the writer's intentions, the meaning of words on the page, and your own perspectives.

Reading for Pleasure

Although we have offered a complex analysis of reading and the nature of interpretation, we do not want to obscure one simple and fundamental truth: You must read for pleasure in order to improve as both a reader and a writer. It hardly matters what you read—mysteries, magazines, historical novels, science fiction, romance novels—they all can be useful. Of primary importance is to read with enjoyment and understanding.

We stress this because good writers are always good readers. A good reader brings a special attention to reading along with the appropriate skills. By "special attention," we mean that good readers choose readings that stretch their understanding and enrich their abilities, readings that have to be read with full attention, not while watching TV or chatting with a friend over coffee. And by appropriate skills, we mean that good readers are constantly learning how to improve their reading abilities because they pay attention to the structures of reading: forms, patterns, meanings, rhythms, tones, suggestions, nuances—those various elements that make up the craft of writing.

As an example, let's return once again to E. Annie Proulx's *The Gourmet Gardener*, a practical guide that provides information to people who want to grow their own fruits, vegetables, and herbs. Dozens of such books can be found in the bookstore offering information, illustrations, and specific how-to advice. What sets Proulx's work apart from the mainstream, however, is her ability to present information in a way that sparks the imagination with words and phrasing that lift the subject off the page. Here, for example, is the opening of her section on that most prosaic of vegetables, cauliflower:

> Cauliflower, with its pure and saintly white florets, is really a thick, malformed flower cluster packed into a dense corymb. The undulating surface of the whole head looks like a miniature hilly landscape under snow. Few vegetables are so beautiful, and so amusing to arrange.
>
> Botanically cauliflower is classed with broccoli, though it is more tender to frost, more delicate in flavor, and a greater challenge to the gardener who wants to grow perfect heads.
>
> Cauliflower has seniority; it was known long before the more pedestrian broccoli. . . .

Proulx offers a short lyrical description of cauliflower, including the simile of a snowy landscape to describe its appearance and then briefly contrasting it with broccoli. Her use of the phrase "pure and saintly" suggests that this vegetable possesses a holy quality, but she provides a stylistic counterpoint to that interpretation by using the words *thick* and *malformed*, which imply that the cauliflower is coarse and even somewhat unnatural. That she includes the unfamiliar word *corymb* should drive us toward the dictionary, and it reminds us that we are reading the work of an expert, someone familiar with the technical botanical terms. The short second paragraph (just one sentence) provides useful information by contrasting cauliflower with its cousin, broccoli. The opening sentence of her third paragraph makes us think of cauliflower as part of an aristocratic class or as a member of a governmental body (like the House or Senate) because of the word *seniority*. Following this sentence are several pages of text that are part scientific, part historical, part descriptive, part process, and part pure gardening information all bound together in a style that constantly surprises and, Proulx hopes, delights the reader.

Reading and Relating

It should be clear by now that your becoming a better reader is integral to your ability to improve and succeed as a writer. Reading well will teach you to attend to words; to learn the ways language is shaped into meaning; to become more sensitive to the tone, mood, and nuance of language; to concentrate on complex thoughts and issues. That is, it will instruct you in how to make sound and sensitive rhetorical choices that you can apply to your own speaking and writing. It will build your intuitions, especially if you learn to read as a writer, to read not only for content and pleasure but also with an awareness of what writers do to create richness and eloquence in their prose. Writing grows out of reading and, of course, good writing becomes something intended to be read.

But there is another important dimension to reading and writing that needs to be considered because it is fundamental to success: relationship. Because relationship is invisible to the eye, most textbooks and many instructors have a difficult time talking about it, but it is fundamental to making sound rhetorical choices. Enrolling in a composition class is, after all, not usually the choice of the student; most often it is a required class or at the very least strongly recommended. Most students take it because they need it or are placed into it or can't avoid it. Those of us who teach this class start with a disadvantage that few other instructors share: Because many of our students feel they would rather be just about anywhere than in a writing class, we spend the first few weeks of the term striving to reorient our students to the pleasures and satisfactions inherent to the course. Thus many composition courses start students off with community-building activities, pleasurable readings, small-group discussions, and other forms of confidence-building activities. These are important because they help reorient students, taking away some of the sting of being in a "required" class.

This is one aspect of the "relationship" we are describing here: To succeed as a reader and writer, you must find ways to create a meaningful, productive, personal relationship with your work. You must find a way to care about a critical connection with required readings and assigned essay topics. In fact, creating this kind of relationship is intrinsic to performing any work at a high level.

All the authors included in this anthology found some way to stand in meaningful relationship with their writing, subject, language, and audience. They discovered something intrinsically satisfying in doing their research, structuring and organizing their thoughts, and putting the words down on paper. Let's examine sections of two essays to illustrate how this can be done, how reading in terms of relationship can help students discover models to form this kind of stance on their own. For starters, here is the opening to Barbara Ehrenreich's "What I've Learned from Men":

For many years I believed that women had only one thing to learn from men: how to get the attention of a waiter by some means short of kicking over the table and shrieking. Never in my life have I gotten the attention of a waiter, unless it was an off-duty waiter whose car I'd accidentally scraped in a parking lot somewhere. Men, however, can summon a maître d' just by thinking the word "coffee," and this is a power women would be well-advised to study. What else would we possibly want to learn from them? How to interrupt someone in mid-sentence as if you were performing an act of conversational euthanasia? How to drop a pair of socks three feet from an open hamper and keep right on walking? How to make those weird guttural gargling sounds in the bathroom?

But now, at mid-life, I am willing to admit that there are some real and useful things to learn from men. Not from all men—in fact, we may have the most to learn from some of the men we like the least. This realization does not mean that my feminist principles have gone soft with age: what I think women could learn from men is how to get *tough*. After more than a decade of consciousness-raising, assertiveness training, and hand-to-hand combat in the battle of the sexes, we're still too ladylike. Let me try that again—we're just too *damn* ladylike.

Ehrenreich signals her dislike of certain forms of arrogant male behavior, but she does so with a gesture of irony in which she praises overly assertive male actions. By keeping her sense of humor, Ehrenreich maintains a relationship with her subject (particularly, the male subject) that is both admiring and despising, critical and appreciative. It is a relationship that keeps her in tension with her subject. Men who act in this way are not just insensitive louts; they are insensitive louts who have a firm sense of their own power and place in the world, something women often do not have, or do not have in sufficient quantity. Women who learn this lesson may lose some of their "femininity," but they will gain increased sovereignty and will be less victimized in their everyday encounters with men (or the occasional assertive woman). It might be said that part of the pleasure of reading (and rereading) this essay is experiencing the ways Ehrenreich applies this ironic stance toward her subject.

Here is a paragraph from Michael Davitt Bell's "Magic Time," in which he discusses the importance of politeness and manners when interacting with friends and strangers who speak to him about his cancer:

> To speak of manners in the context of cancer and dying may seem jarring, even insincere, but it shouldn't. For as the great novelists of manners, the Jane Austens and the Henry Jameses, all knew, the etiquette

of communication and miscommunication, the comedy of understanding and misunderstanding, is not only deeply fascinating and entertaining but also profoundly significant. These novelists knew that once the misunderstandings have been cleared up, just before the ending, the possibility of love and of true communication has come to exist. And much more love, more interesting love, is possible than if no difficulties and misunderstandings had occurred in the first place. After all, you can't have the satisfying resolution of the ending if you don't start with conflict and crisis.

For Bell, cancer is certainly a disease he wishes he did not have, but he also recognizes that it has offered him a gift, the ability to discover what is most real and most important in his life. He finds a way to stand in relationship to his subject, cancer, so that he not only lives with it fully but also reflects on it philosophically. As does Ehrenreich, and all the authors in this book, Bell offers a complex view of his subject, one that cannot easily be characterized by a single phrase or ten-word summary. Moreover, both Bell and Ehrenreich reveal a singular truth about writing—namely, that significant subjects often lie directly before us, concealed by their seeming obviousness. Part of what it means to be a writer is to discover the extraordinary in the ordinary, the insights that can arise when we look hard at the world around us.

Getting Started

If there is one principle we would like to emphasize, it is that every composition course should be challenging, both for you the student and for your instructor. Although some students and instructors consider composition a perfunctory course, we feel differently. When the teaching of composition is centered on the ideas of language as a medium for expression, on argument in all its complexities, and on what it means to make intelligent rhetorical choices about readers and writers, texts and contexts, then it becomes a complex and exciting course, both to teach and to take.

This anthology, we hope, promotes this view. The selections we have chosen offer a range of possibilities, but we hope they always prove provocative and require more than one reading. The discussion questions are intended to promote active class discussion about topics of importance. The suggestions for writing are designed to extend those discussions through the written word, through draft after draft, which is really the only way most of us have to refine our thinking and build some precision into our composing processes.

Most of all, we hope that this book, combined with your experience in this course, makes you a more knowledgeable rhetorician, able to make the best possible choices about your writing. Writing is a primary form of expression, but it is also a primary means for reflection, the consolidation of meaning, the exploration of ideas. Writing extends thought. When done well, it produces immense satisfaction and real effects in the world.

Part and parcel of our concern with reading and instructional theory is our belief that critical reading and the accompanying discussion in a classroom community are essential preparation for citizenship in a democracy. Many of our social problems have not been resolved, and emerging perspectives, including some of yours, need to be brought to bear on these issues. Your ability to provide new insights is a function of how independently you learn to think. In an essay titled "Democratic Vistas," the poet Walt Whitman writes that "Not the book needs so much to be the complete thing, but the reader of the book does. That were to make a nation of supple and athletic minds, well-train'd, intuitive, used to depend on themselves, and not on a few coteries of writers." Like Whitman, we see criticism as an indispensable habit of mind. We have attempted, with respect to the readings in this book, to pose questions that spur you to consider aspects of language and culture that you might otherwise have ignored. At the same time, we have tried not to be overly directive, as we know your individual responses are important. We hope that your engagement with these texts, both in and out of class, will help you become more analytically inclusive, less reductive—and more creative—in your deliberations.

We wish you a productive academic experience, one that will help you make the best rhetorical choices possible, in school and beyond.

2
Narration

"I couldn't believe that . . ." *"When that happened, I was think-ing . . ."* *"What I didn't understand was . . ."* Such comments are of-ten part of conversations that follow memorable social events. Some people spend more time talking about a previous night's party, for ex-ample, than they actually spent at the affair. To truly comprehend what transpired, they need to confirm, order, or come to grips with their experiences and perceptions at a more leisurely pace. They need to construct stories, or *narratives.* As noted short story writer and University of Alabama professor Michael Martone phrases it, "In the stories we tell ourselves, we tell ourselves."

To *narrate,* then, is to structure a select group of past events or im-pressions into a coherent and presumably interesting story for listeners and readers. Narratives are often used to develop and support a formal argument. A prospective law student might be required to submit a statement of personal experience to support her application. A student might recall instances of hate crimes on campus to advance his claim that strong measures need to be taken by the administration to curb or eliminate such acts. In other instances, narratives or anecdotes may be considered entertainment, just tales to provoke wonderment or laugh-ter, to evoke fear or even sadness. Whatever the case, it is important to remember that all storytellers are *narrating subjects.* That is, all narra-tors operate out of particular histories and social contexts, and they all convey particular viewpoints. To refer to a group of people as *clients* as opposed to *students,* to all of us as *mankind* as opposed to *humankind,* or to a set of political relations as *slavery* as opposed to *enslavement* is to reflect a particular perspective. Labeling an entire language variety a *nonstandard dialect* instead of regarding it as an appropriate alternative is another example of the narrator's viewpoint. Writer Amy Tan reflects on this perspective in her essay (included in this chapter) on the language of her mother, who emigrated from China to the United States: "Like others, I have described it to people as 'broken' or 'fractured' English. But I wince when I say that. It has always bothered me that I can think of no way to describe it other than 'broken,' as if it were damaged and needed to be fixed, as if it lacked a certain wholeness and soundness."

Being keenly aware of linguistic choice is an exciting and fruitful way for you to examine texts. However, it is more than a simple exercise. Practicing such awareness helps you pay fuller attention to all elements of language use and helps you make more informed decisions about your own language choices. Tan remarks that in her writing, "I use them all—all the Englishes I grew up with." Good storytellers like Tan tend to be proficient at envisioning the audience they want to affect and are mindful of the ways in which their words may be understood. Therefore, it is important that, to the extent you can, you remain aware of all the messages your words convey. It is also important, even crucial, that you practice identifying the viewpoints in the narratives you hear and read. Becoming critical readers of narratives will help you to devote critical attention to those you produce.

The most pertinent questions about any narrative or anecdote you write will be, "What happened?" and "So what?" You will be expected to identify a situation, set the scene, unfold a worthy plot, and resolve the story in a compelling and logical way. You always tell something by what you choose to report or omit. But obviously you cannot include every single aspect related to your narrative. Therefore, select anecdotes that best contribute to making your point. You would not want to slow the pace too much by including extraneous material. If you are recounting an automobile accident, for example, mentioning the color of the traffic signals is probably more useful than dwelling on the colors of the drivers' socks.

A primary goal of all writers is to have the readers keep turning the page. It is the only way to convey the controlling idea thoroughly. If readers lose interest in your story, they will not finish it unless they are required to do so, and in those circumstances, their final impression is not likely to be favorable. A principal means of holding the attention of readers is the use of evaluation, a term employed by distinguished linguist and professor William Labov in his study of narrative. This is the way narrators embed in their stories commentary designed to elicit concern from readers (keep them from asking, so what?) and influence readers to empathize or sympathize with them. Narrators are always trying to get people to be on their side. For example, in telling a story of how you became terribly ill, reasonably requested an extension of a paper deadline, and then were denied by an inflexible instructor, the citing of the illness along with the descriptors *reasonably* and *inflexible* serves as evaluative commentary. This story is different from one in which you merely state, "I was going to miss the deadline. I asked for an extension. The instructor said no." While it is true that someone might respond compassionately toward the latter story, and toward you in any event, most readers would need evaluative commentary before they could share your perspective, care about your predicament, or see you as a victim. Although excessive moralizing can ruin your story, by supplying evaluation you create the sympathetic figure you want to project.

To create the coherent framework that is fundamental to narratives or anecdotes, you need to bear in mind several other specific techniques. Chronology is the strongest structural feature of stories, and you need to portray a clear sense of a beginning, a middle, and an end. However, it is often dramatically effective to begin a story in the middle—what is known as *in media res*, Latin for "in the middle of things." This method requires more planning, as it requires you to choose specific events and narrative moments to illustrate the point you want to make. For example, you might begin a narrative by stating: "Yesterday, I had my purse stolen—but now here it is." On the face of it, this seems like an unusual circumstance. A reader or listener's first reaction is likely to be, "Really? Tell me what happened." And you would then relate a series of narrative events: where you were when this happened, what led to this event, how the purse was stolen, how you got it back, who stole it, and whether it was returned by the thief, a stranger, or the police. When composing such a narrative, you have the freedom to re-order the chronology as needed in order to make your essay more suspenseful, or to enrich your meaning.

Another form of chronology is to present significant past scenes or moments at strategic moments. By injecting these *flashbacks* into your narrative, you can vary the pace and pattern of your writing. When inserted at key moments and for important purposes, flashbacks can explain your motivation, clarify an event, or otherwise contribute to the meaning of your essay in important ways. For example, you can imagine many stories written about the controversial presidential election of 2000 commencing with an anecdote about the close and contested outcome in Florida. A writer could then shift to describing earlier events during the election that made the vote in Florida a crucial issue.

Still another technique is a *flash-forward*. The topic of a story could be negotiations about election procedures that did not go as well as they might have in, say, the 1990s. A writer could then flash-forward—"Look what ended up happening in 2000 as a result"—before shifting back to a narrative about the earlier events. In any case, the writer must use clear transitional markers to keep the sense of order straight for readers. Such guides include words like *then, next,* and *subsequently* or phrases like "but let me not get ahead of myself" or "let me backtrack a minute." In addition to transitional devices, verb tense can help maintain a sense of sequence. The writer should use verbs in a manner that is logically consistent and promotes the overall clarity of the writing.

Although your narratives always suggest something about your own position, they do not have to be about your actions or be told in *first person*, which can be called the *I* or *we* perspective. Third-person viewpoint—*he, she, it, they*—is a common alternative. Some stories are even written in the second-person or *you* mode. Consider novelist William Styron's depiction in *Lie Down in Darkness* of a passenger who has journeyed by train from Richmond to Port Warwick:

> You get up and say good-by to the novelty salesman, who is going on across the bay by ferry, and you pull your bag from the rack and climb down off the train onto the station dock where the smell of the water is clean and refreshing after the flatulent warmth of the car and where, thirty yards away, your girl or your friends are waiting with expectant grins—"Oh there he is!"—and as you walk toward them you've already forgotten the novelty salesman forever, and the ride down. It's going to be a hot day.

Dialogue is also a key device for dramatizing narratives. To hold readers' interest, it should probably be used sparingly. To be convincing, it should be as realistic as possible, which means it captures as much as possible the rhythm, vocabulary, and syntax of the speakers represented.

Ronald Kellogg, author of *The Psychology of Writing*, reminds us that narratives are such a fundamental aspect of human consciousness, even to logico-deductive thought, that we often are blind to their importance. Practically all of us, in fact, do much storytelling all the time. Conscious awareness of narration and the skill to use its structural elements well are, as we have been trying to show, important abilities for writers to develop.

Approaches to Writing Narrative Essays

All of us have stories inside us—stories about people we know, events that have occurred, crises we have managed, idiotic or inspiring things we have done. Those stories are often the best sources for narrative essays. Another more research-based source is material we have read about historical incidents, accounts of important local events, or important people who have accomplished something wondrous or important. A third source is often overlooked: everyday life made special through a powerful, funny, or surprising narrative. If you have something to say, a point you want to make, a perspective you want to express, then even a mundane topic like how you made it from the student union to your French class in six minutes while eating lunch can be worthwhile.

The most important element of your narrative, as it is for any piece of writing, is your purpose. What do you want to accomplish in composing your narrative? What effect do you want to have on your readers? Is your narrative focused on yourself or someone else? Is your story intended to illustrate something you learned? Something you are proud of accomplishing? Something that embarrassed you? Is your narrative intended to illustrate something exotic or mundane? What emotions do you want your readers to experience as a result of reading your narrative? Once you begin to concentrate on a specific purpose or effect, you can begin to construct a narrative that is intended to realize that outcome.

Whatever subject you choose, you must keep in mind the reader's investment. Your narrative may be important to you, but it has to attract the interest of a reader. Each time you sit down to write a narrative essay, the basic question you must ask is "why would someone want to read this essay?" In other words, if this weren't an assignment that the teacher had to read, what would motivate someone to start reading and keep turning pages? Sometimes that motivation comes from the story itself. Other times it comes from the character of the writer that is revealed during the telling of the story, or the sparkling and appropriate language that the writer uses, or the unusual incident that is related. As mentioned earlier, whatever the source(s), your responsibility as a writer of narrative is to hold the reader's interest by authoring an essay that gives pleasure and satisfaction.

Once you have settled on your purpose and you have some sense of why someone would want to read your essay, you can begin to choose the specific scenes, details, and observations that you think should be in it. At the early stage of drafting, it is much more important to write freely and fully. You can try free writing about your narrative subject (write down every thought that pops into your head without stopping to reread or correct anything you wrote), brainstorming lists of thoughts and approaches, drafting an outline or developmental framework, or moving directly into the telling of the narrative. The important goal at any early stage of writing is to write—to get words down on the page without worrying whether they are the right words or the best words. Many successful writers would affirm this principle: They typically write many more words and pages than those that end up in the final draft, and many of them write early drafts that are wordy, unfocused, uninteresting, and uninspiring. It is in the rewriting and revising that ordinary essays are transformed into extraordinary ones.

Chronology

Story telling may seem a simple affair: When constructing a story or narrative essay, many writers think like the King of Hearts instructing the White Rabbit in *Alice in Wonderland*. "'Begin at the beginning,' the King said, very gravely, 'and go on till you come to the end: then stop.'" This can best be described as a temporal narrative. It uses our natural understanding of time as the underpinning structure: The author narrates events in the order they occurred. Such a narrative presumes, however, a certain pattern, one that is common in many stories, whether told, written, or enacted on stage. That order is: introduction or overview, relating of the plot, presentation of the conflict or problem, development, climax, resolution or denouement. One can see that narrative structure boiled down to its essence in the famous line of Julius Caesar: "I came, I saw, I conquered." Not all narrative essays fit within this conventional and useful framework. Sometimes authors wish to re-order their narratives to produce other effects or because the nature of their subject demands it.

Selection

Once you have some pages of prose or a rough first draft, keep expanding until you have a sense that the entire story is being told in roughly the form and chronology that you think works best. As at any early draft stage, try to get an informed opinion about what you have produced so far. A visit to your campus's Writing Center or to a peer tutor knowledgeable about writing can make a major difference at this stage. If none is available, try to find someone who will read your work and respond with a thoughtful, informed perspective.

Most important, start selecting the specific images, scenes, details, and phrasing that contribute the most to your narrative. This process of selection is not easy. Many writers, especially beginning writers, feel they must include everything, that every word is equally important. More than likely, a good bit of your first draft can and should end up on the cutting room floor. One rule of thumb is that for every 200 words of prose in a final draft, you will need to have first written 400–600 words in earlier drafts. Good writing almost always requires first an overflow of language and then a careful winnowing, a distillation that refines and focuses.

To appreciate the value of this principle, just think of someone who starts a narrative essay in the following way:

> Yesterday, which was Tuesday, I read an article for my economics class, which is in Wimsley Hall, next to the Student Union, that changed my thinking about dollars and cents or the value of money. Money is important, we all know that, but what really makes it important to you, me, and everyone? According to Bernard Lietaer, who is a former banker, money is important but very misunderstood by all of us. He thinks that we all need to spend less time immersing ourselves in the making of money, in accumulating dollars and putting them in the bank or in our wallet. Instead, he states that we need to think a lot more about what money actually means.

Now compare that rough draft opening of an essay to the following final draft opening of the same essay:

> I recently read an article for my economics class that changed my thinking about money. The article summarized the views of former banker Bernard Lietaer, who argues that we need to immerse ourselves not in making money but in thinking about the meaning of money.

If that second version is better, it is primarily because the author pared down the original so that the meaning was expressed in more clear and elegant terms.

Implicit Versus Explicit Meaning

All of the stories people tell have meaning or significance, at least to the teller. Often, however, people tell stories in order to communicate a specific message or moral. A parent or friend of the family might tell you:

"When I was in college, I spent the entire first term going out to parties, playing field hockey with my friends, and taking sailing lessons—stuff I had always dreamed of doing when I was in high school. I had a great time and thought I was doing perfectly fine in my classes, but when I received my final grades, I was stunned to see that I had earned a GPA of 1.4. That was a shock, both to me and my parents. That put me on academic probation, which increased my shame and humiliation. I realized then that college demanded enormous commitment from me, commitment to attend class, complete my homework assignments, meet with my instructors if I was having problems, go to the Writing Center for tutoring—you name it. That next academic term almost killed me, but when I went home for summer, I'd gotten a 3.2 GPA in spring, which meant I'd pulled up to a 2.3 cum GPA for the year and was off probation. Whew! That first semester's grade report was a wake-up call I never forgot."

This narrative is typical of stories that have a moral: They begin with an account of what someone did, what the consequences of those actions were, and what the person learned. Like many of the fables of Aesop or stories from the *Bible*, such stories offer an explicit meaning, usually as a "lesson learned" that is communicated directly to the reader or listener at the end of the story.

Many individuals, however, prefer not to be informed about what a story means. They would rather experience the story and draw their own lesson. Such a story is told from a more open and even ambivalent perspective and leaves the readers to sort out the meaning—or meanings—themselves. Here is a different version of the story just related about first-year college:

"College proved to be a challenge to me in many ways. My first term as a brand new freshman, I spent a lot of time enjoying myself—going out to parties, playing field hockey with my friends, and taking sailing lessons—stuff I had always dreamed of doing when I was in high school. I really and truly enjoyed myself, but my classes suffered, and when I received my final grades, I was stunned to see that I had earned a GPA of 1.4. That was a shock, both to my parents and me. That poor performance put me on academic probation, which I absolutely hated. So I knuckled down the next term. I stopped going to parties, dropped out of extracurricular activities, never went out with my friends, attended all my classes, and studied 25–30 hours a week. Not surprisingly, I pulled myself up to a 3.2. That was wonderful, but I felt like a drudge and lost most of my enthusiasm for college."

This narrative offers a different perspective, leaving the reader to puzzle out what the writer intends. Whereas it seemed to be heading toward a moral, it instead presented the reader with a more open-ended narrative that cannot (at least not so far) be summed up by a moralistic coda at the end. Many narratives offer even more implicit kinds of story telling: They narrate an event or describe a series of actions and then, when they reach a certain point, stop, leaving the reader to puzzle out the meaning. One of the finest short story writers of the late twentieth century, Raymond Carver, used that technique masterfully.

Whether you choose to make your meaning explicit or implicit depends on your purpose, your audience, the story itself, and what effects you hope to achieve in telling it. Stories that make their meaning explicit often satisfy readers who don't have to guess at what the author intends. Stories that offer an implicit meaning invite additional readings and leave readers much more room for analysis and interpretation.

Enjoy the Pleasure of Story Telling

Perhaps most important, take pleasure in the narrative you write. Story telling is one of the most ancient forms of entertainment known to civilization. Oral story telling is still a great art; it forms the basis for many famous works of literature such as Homer's *Iliad* and *Odyssey*, Mark Twain's stories, *1001 Arabian Nights*, and Kipling's "Just So" stories, as well as tales that exist along an entire spectrum, from those told by family members, to those told among Indian tribes or offered to us by literary masters such as Edgar Allan Poe, Toni Morrison, William Faulkner, and Barbara Kingsolver. Narration offers you the opportunity to explore meanings through the juxtaposition of character and event unfolding through time and space. To relate a narrative is not all that hard; to relate a narrative that can be read and reread with increased pleasure and understanding is one of the most challenging assignments you will receive in any writing class.

Annie Dillard (1945–) essayist, memoirist, poet, and novelist, is a professor emeritus at Wesleyan University. Dillard, a native of Pittsburgh, Pennsylvania, and the recipient of awards from the Guggenheim Foundation and the National Endowment for the Arts, has published widely, with works appearing in such journals and magazines as The Atlantic, Harper's Magazine, Cosmopolitan, *and* The Christian Science Monitor. *She is the author of numerous books, including* Pilgrim at Tinker Creek *(1974), for which she received the Pulitzer Prize for general nonfiction;* Teaching a Stone to Talk *(1982);* The Living *(1992);* Mornings Like This *(1996); and* For the Time Being *(1999). The selection below has been excerpted from her celebrated autobiography,* An American Childhood *(1987).*

Annie Dillard

The Chase

Some boys taught me to play football. This was fine sport. You thought up a new strategy for every play and whispered it to the others. You went out for a pass, fooling everyone. Best, you got to throw yourself mightily at someone's running legs. Either you brought him down or you hit the ground flat out on your chin, with your arms empty before you. It was all or nothing. If you hesitated in fear, you would miss and get hurt: you would take a hard fall while the kid got away, or you would get kicked in the face while the kid got away. But if you flung yourself wholeheartedly at the back of his knees—if you gathered and joined body and soul and pointed them diving fearlessly—then you likely wouldn't get hurt, and you'd stop the ball. Your fate, and your team's score, depended on your concentration and courage. Nothing girls did could compare with it.

Boys welcomed me at baseball, too, for I had, through enthusiastic practice, what was weirdly known as a boy's arm. In winter, in the snow, there was neither baseball nor football, so the boys and I threw snowballs at passing cars. I got in trouble throwing snowballs, and have seldom been happier since.

On one weekday morning after Christmas, six inches of new snow had just fallen. We were standing up to our boot tops in snow on a front yard on trafficked Reynolds Street, waiting for cars. The cars traveled Reynolds Street slowly and evenly; they were targets all but wrapped in red ribbons, cream puffs. We couldn't miss.

I was seven; the boys were eight, nine, and ten. The oldest two Fahey boys were there—Mikey and Peter—polite blond boys who lived near me on Lloyd Street, and who already had four brothers and sisters. My parents approved Mikey and Peter Fahey. Chickie McBride was there, a tough kid, and Billy Paul and Mackie Kean too, from across Reynolds, where the boys grew up dark and furious, grew up skinny, knowing, and skilled. We had all drifted from our houses that morning looking for action, and had found it here on Reynolds Street.

5　　It was cloudy but cold. The cars' tires laid behind them on the snowy street a complex trail of beige chunks like crenellated castle walls. I had stepped on some earlier; they squeaked. We could have wished for more traffic. When a car came, we all popped it one. In the intervals between cars we reverted to the natural solitude of children.

I started making an iceball—a perfect iceball, from perfectly white snow, perfectly spherical, and squeezed perfectly translucent so no snow remained all the way through. (The Fahey boys and I considered it unfair actually to throw an iceball at somebody, but it had been known to happen.)

I had just embarked on the iceball project when we heard tire chains come clanking from afar. A black Buick was moving toward us down the street. We all spread out, banged together some regular snowballs, took aim, and, when the Buick drew nigh, fired.

A soft snowball hit the driver's windshield right before the driver's face. It made a smashed star with a hump in the middle.

Often, of course, we hit our target, but this time, the only time in all of life, the car pulled over and stopped. Its wide black door opened; a man got out of it, running. He didn't even close the car door.

10　　He ran after us, and we ran away from him, up the snowy Reynolds sidewalk. At the corner, I looked back; incredibly, he was still after us. He was in city clothes: a suit and tie, street shoes. Any normal adult would have quit, having sprung us into flight and made his point. This man was gaining on us. He was a thin man, all action. All of a sudden, we were running for our lives.

Wordless, we split up. We were on our turf; we could lose ourselves in the neighborhood backyards, everyone for himself. I paused and considered. Everyone had vanished except Mikey Fahey, who was just rounding the corner of a yellow brick house. Poor Mikey, I trailed him. The driver of the Buick sensibly picked the two of us to follow. The man apparently had all day.

He chased Mikey and me around the yellow house and up a backyard path we knew by heart: under a low tree, up a bank, through a hedge, down some snowy steps, and across the grocery store's delivery driveway. We smashed through a gap in another hedge, entered a scruffy backyard and ran around its back porch and tight between houses to Edgerton Avenue; we ran across Edgerton to an alley and up our own sliding woodpile to the Halls' front yard; he kept coming. We ran up Lloyd Street and wound through mazy backyards toward the steep hilltop at Willard and Lang.

He chased us silently, block after block. He chased us silently over picket fences, through thorny hedges, between houses, around garbage cans, and across streets. Every time I glanced back, choking for breath, I expected he would have quit. He must have been as breathless as we were. His jacket strained over his body. It was an immense discovery, pounding into my hot head with every sliding, joyous step, that this ordinary adult evidently knew what I thought only children who trained at football knew: that you have to fling yourself at what you're doing, you have to point yourself, forget yourself, aim, dive.

Mikey and I had nowhere to go, in our own neighborhood or out of it, but away from this man who was chasing us. He impelled us forward; we compelled him to follow our route. The air was cold; every breath tore my throat. We kept running, block after block; we kept improvising, backyard after backyard, running a frantic course and choosing it simultaneously, failing always to find small places or hard places to slow him down, and discovering always, exhilarated, dismayed, that only bare speed could save us—for he would never give up, this man—and we were losing speed.

15　　He chased us through the backyard labyrinths of ten blocks before he caught us by our jackets. He caught us and we all stopped.

We three stood staggering, half blinded, coughing, in an obscure hilltop backyard: a man in his twenties, a boy, a girl. He had released our jackets, our pursuer, our captor, our hero: he knew we weren't going anywhere. We all played by the rules. Mikey and I unzipped our jackets. I pulled off my sopping mittens. Our tracks multiplied in the backyard's new snow. We had been breaking new snow all morning. We didn't look at each other. I was cherishing my excitement. The man's lower pants legs were wet; his cuffs were full of snow, and there was a prow of snow beneath them on his shoes and socks. Some trees bordered the little flat backyard, some messy winter trees. There was no one around: a clearing in a grove, and we the only players.

It was a long time before he could speak. I had some difficulty at first recalling why we were there. My lips felt swollen; I couldn't see out of the sides of my eyes; I kept coughing.

"You stupid kids," he began perfunctorily.

We listened perfunctorily indeed, if we listened at all, for the chewing out was redundant, a mere formality, and beside the point. The point was that he had chased us passionately without giving up, and so he had caught us. Now he came down to earth. I wanted the glory to last forever.

20   But how could the glory have lasted forever? We could have run through every backyard in North America until we got to Panama. But when he trapped us at the lip of the Panama Canal, what precisely could he have done to prolong the drama of the chase and cap its glory? I brooded about this for the next few years. He could only have fried Mikey Fahey and me in boiling oil, say, or dismembered us piecemeal, or staked us to anthills. None of which I really wanted, and none of which any adult was likely to do, even in the spirit of fun. He could only chew us out there in the Panamanian jungle, after months or years of exalting pursuit. He could only begin, "You stupid kids," and continue in his ordinary Pittsburgh accent with his normal righteous anger and the usual common sense.

If in that snowy backyard the driver of the black Buick had cut off our heads, Mikey's and mine, I would have died happy, for nothing has required so much of me since as being chased all over Pittsburgh in the middle of winter—running terrified, exhausted—by this sainted, skinny, furious red-headed man who wished to have a word with us. I don't know how he found his way back to his car.

Analyzing Rhetorical Choices

1.   Dillard provides a lot of details: the names of the boys, the color and make of the car the children hit with their snowballs, the names of the streets down which the man chases them. On the other hand, other details are withheld. For example, she does not talk about her successes or failures in actually playing football. Nor do she, Mikey, and their pursuer encounter a single person during a chase that lasted, based on her description, some half a mile and at least ten minutes. Which details in Dillard's narrative are particularly convincing to you, and which additional details would you like to see provided? What overall impression does she make on you?

2.   Dillard writes, "I got in trouble throwing snowballs, and have seldom been happier since." She also describes her pursuer as "our hero." What makes her happy and the chaser heroic? How are

these ideas developed in the essay? How are they related to the description of playing football?

3. In your view, how does Dillard's style capture the thoughts of a seven-year-old? How does the language used make her viewpoint convincing—or not?

4. Relative to the conclusion of the chase, Dillard suggests that words were anticlimactic and contributed nothing to the adventure. Actions had said it all. Yet the paradox for her is that for the experience to inform others she must use words. Whom does Dillard imagine to be her audience?

Writing About Issues and Contexts

1. An autobiography is a challenging form to write: The author must find a way to write about his or her life without being self-indulgent and in a way that interests readers. Given this selection, how well do you think Dillard succeeds?

2. Dillard writes about the effort involved in playing football: "Nothing girls did could compare with it." How do you feel about this statement? Is it a plausible statement to make about 1950s Pittsburgh? Or about now? Why?

3. "The Chase" describes a classic conflict that arises because of the acts of children and the response of one adult. In what ways, if any, are the children's actions representative of most children? In what ways are they not? In what ways, if any, are the adult's actions representative of most adults? In what ways are they not? Does the man here represent anything—other than a man whose windshield got pounded by some snowballs?

4. What impact is Dillard hoping to make with this anecdote?

Born in Roxie, Mississippi, **Richard Wright** *(1908–1960) became one of
the most important writers in American history. After childhood and
adolescence in the South, Wright moved with his family to Chicago
where he became serious about a writing career. In Chicago, he wrote
fiction, nonfiction, and poetry as a member of the John Reed Club and
an employee of the Works Progress Administration. Wright moved to
New York in 1937; he settled in Paris in 1947. Known for his powerful
descriptions of environments and their effects on people, he is best
known for the story collection* Uncle Tom's Children *(1938); the novels*
Native Son *(1940) and* The Outsider *(1953); as well as his memoir* Black
Boy *(1945). This selection is chapter 13 of* Black Boy.

Richard Wright

The Library Card

One morning I arrived early at work and went into the bank
lobby where the Negro porter was mopping. I stood at a counter and
picked up the Memphis *Commercial Appeal* and began my free reading of the press. I came finally to the editorial page and saw an article
dealing with one H. L. Mencken. I knew by hearsay that he was the
editor of the *American Mercury*, but aside from that I knew nothing
about him. The article was a furious denunciation of Mencken, concluding with one, hot, short sentence: Mencken is a fool.

I wondered what on earth this Mencken had done to call down
upon him the scorn of the South. The only people I had ever heard de-
nounced in the South were Negroes, and this man was not a Negro.
Then what ideas did Mencken hold that made a newspaper like the
Commercial Appeal castigate him publicly? Undoubtedly he must be
advocating ideas that the South did not like. Were there, then, people
other than Negroes who criticized the South? I knew that during the
Civil War the South had hated northern whites, but I had not encountered such hate during my life. Knowing no more of Mencken than I
did at that moment, I felt a vague sympathy for him. Had not the
South, which had assigned me the role of a non-man, cast at him its
hardest words?

Now, how could I find out about this Mencken? There was a
huge library near the riverfront, but I knew that Negroes were not allowed to patronize its shelves any more than they were the parks and

playgrounds of the city. I had gone into the library several times to get books for the white men on the job. Which of them would now help me to get books? And how could I read them without causing concern to the white men with whom I worked? I had so far been successful in hiding my thoughts and feelings from them, but I knew that I would create hostility if I went about this business of reading in a clumsy way.

I weighed the personalities of the men on the job. There was Don, a Jew; but I distrusted him. His position was not much better than mine and I knew that he was uneasy and insecure; he had always treated me in an offhand, bantering way that barely concealed his contempt. I was afraid to ask him to help me to get books; his frantic desire to demonstrate a racial solidarity with the whites against Negroes might make him betray me.

5   Then how about the boss? No, he was a Baptist and I had the suspicion that he would not be quite able to comprehend why a black boy would want to read Mencken. There were other white men on the job whose attitudes showed clearly that they were Kluxers or sympathizers, and they were out of the question.

There remained only one man whose attitude did not fit into an anti-Negro category, for I had heard the white men refer to him as a "Pope lover." He was an Irish Catholic and was hated by the white Southerners. I knew that he read books, because I had got him volumes from the library several times. Since he, too, was an object of hatred, I felt that he might refuse me but would hardly betray me. I hesitated, weighing and balancing the imponderable realities.

One morning I paused before the Catholic fellow's desk.

"I want to ask you a favor," I whispered to him.

"What is it?"

10   "I want to read. I can't get books from the library. I wonder if you'd let me use your card?"

He looked at me suspiciously.

"My card is full most of the time," he said.

"I see," I said and waited, posing my question silently.

"You're not trying to get me into trouble, are you, boy?" he asked, staring at me.

15   "Oh, no, sir."

"What book do you want?"

"A book by H. L. Mencken."

"Which one?"

"I don't know. Has he written more than one?"

20   "He has written several."

"I didn't know that."

"What makes you want to read Mencken?"

"Oh, I just saw his name in the newspaper," I said.

"It's good of you to want to read," he said. "But you ought to read the right things."

25   I said nothing. Would he want to supervise my reading?

"Let me think," he said. "I'll figure out something."

I turned from him and he called me back. He stared at me quizzically.

"Richard, don't mention this to the other white men," he said.

"I understand," I said. "I won't say a word."

30   A few days later he called me to him.

"I've got a card in my wife's name," he said. "Here's mine."

"Thank you, sir."

"Do you think you can manage it?"

"I'll manage fine," I said.

35   "If they suspect you, you'll get in trouble," he said.

"I'll write the same kind of notes to the library that you wrote when you sent me for books," I told him. "I'll sign your name."

He laughed.

"Go ahead. Let me see what you get," he said.

That afternoon I addressed myself to forging a note. Now, what were the names of books written by H. L. Mencken? I did not know any of them. I finally wrote what I thought would be a foolproof note: *Dear Madam: Will you please let this nigger boy*—I used the word "nigger" to make the librarian feel that I could not possibly be the author of the note—*have some books by H. L. Mencken?* I forged the white man's name.

40   I entered the library as I had always done when on errands for whites, but I felt that I would somehow slip up and betray myself. I doffed my hat, stood a respectful distance from the desk, looked as unbookish as possible, and waited for the white patrons to be taken care of. When the desk was clear of people, I still waited. The white librarian looked at me.

"What do you want, boy?"

As though I did not possess the power of speech, I stepped forward and simply handed her the forged note, not parting my lips.

"What books by Mencken does he want?" she asked.

"I don't know, ma'am," I said, avoiding her eyes.

45   "Who gave you this card?"

"Mr. Falk," I said.

"Where is he?"

"He's at work, at the M—Optical Company," I said. "I've been in here for him before."

"I remember," the woman said. "But he never wrote notes like this."

50   Oh, God, she's suspicious. Perhaps she would not let me have the books? If she had turned her back at that moment, I would have ducked out the door and never gone back. Then I thought of a bold idea.

"You can call him up, ma'am," I said, my heart pounding.

"You're not using these books, are you?" she asked pointedly.

"Oh, no, ma'am. I can't read."

"I don't know what he wants by Mencken," she said under her breath.

55   I knew now that I had won; she was thinking of other things and the race question had gone out of her mind. She went to the shelves. Once or twice she looked over her shoulder at me, as though she was still doubtful. Finally she came forward with two books in her hand.

"I'm sending him two books," she said. "But tell Mr. Falk to come in next time, or send me the names of the books he wants. I don't know what he wants to read."

I said nothing. She stamped the card and handed me the books. Not daring to glance at them, I went out of the library, fearing that the woman would call me back for further questioning. A block away from the library I opened one of the books and read a title: *A Book of Prefaces*. I was nearing my nineteenth birthday and I did not know how to pronounce the word "preface." I thumbed the pages and saw strange words and strange names. I shook my head, disappointed. I looked at the other book; it was called *Prejudices*. I knew what that word meant; I had heard it all my life. And right off I was on guard against Mencken's books. Why would a man want to call a book *Prejudices*? The word was so stained with all my memories of racial hate that I could not conceive of anybody using it for a title. Perhaps I had made a mistake about Mencken? A man who had prejudices must be wrong.

When I showed the books to Mr. Falk, he looked at me and frowned.

"That librarian might telephone you," I warned him.

60   "That's all right," he said. "But when you're through reading those books, I want you to tell me what you get out of them."

That night in my rented room, while letting the hot water run over my can of pork and beans in the sink, I opened *A Book of Prefaces* and began to read. I was jarred and shocked by the style, the clear, clean, sweeping sentences. Why did he write like that? And how did one write like that? I pictured the man as a raging demon, slashing with his pen, consumed with hate, denouncing everything American, extolling everything European or German, laughing at the weaknesses of people, mocking God, authority. What was this? I stood up, trying to realize what reality lay behind the meaning of the words . . . Yes, this man was fighting, fighting with words. He was using words as a weapon, using them as one would use a club. Could words be weapons? Well, yes, for here they were. Then, maybe, perhaps, I could use them as a weapon? No. It frightened me. I read on and what amazed me was not what he said, but how on earth anybody had the courage to say it.

Occasionally I glanced up to reassure myself that I was alone in the room. Who were these men about whom Mencken was talking so passionately? Who was Anatole France? Joseph Conrad? Sinclair Lewis, Sherwood Anderson, Dostoevski, George Moore, Gustave Flaubert, Maupassant, Tolstoy, Frank Harris, Mark Twain, Thomas Hardy, Arnold Bennett, Stephen Crane, Zola, Norris, Gorky, Bergson, Ibsen, Balzac, Bernard Shaw, Dumas, Poe, Thomas Mann, O. Henry, Dreiser, H. G. Wells, Gogol, T. S. Eliot, Gide, Baudelaire, Edgar Lee Masters, Stendhal, Turgenev, Huneker, Nietzsche, and scores of others? Were these men real? Did they exist or had they existed? And how did one pronounce their names?

I ran across many words whose meanings I did not know, and I either looked them up in a dictionary or, before I had a chance to do that, encountered the word in a context that made its meaning clear. But what strange world was this? I concluded the book with the conviction that I had somehow overlooked something terribly important in life. I had once tried to write, had once reveled in feeling, had let my crude imagination roam, but the impulse to dream had been slowly beaten out of me by experience. Now it surged up again and I hungered for books, new ways of looking and seeing. It was not a matter of believing or disbelieving what I read, but of feeling something new, of being affected by something that made the look of the world different.

As dawn broke I ate my pork and beans, feeling dopey, sleepy. I went to work, but the mood of the book would not die; it lingered, coloring everything I saw, heard, did. I now felt that I knew what the white men were feeling. Merely because I had read a book that had spoken of how they lived and thought, I identified myself with that book. I felt vaguely guilty. Would I, filled with bookish notions, act in a manner that would make the whites dislike me?

65   I forged more notes and my trips to the library became frequent. Reading grew into a passion. My first serious novel was Sinclair Lewis's *Main Street*. It made me see my boss, Mr. Gerald, and identify him as an American type. I would smile when I saw him lugging his golf bags into the office. I had always felt a vast distance separating me from the boss, and now I felt closer to him, though still distant. I felt now that I knew him, that I could feel the very limits of his narrow life. And this had happened because I had read a novel about a mythical man called George F. Babbitt.

The plots and stories in the novels did not interest me so much as the point of view revealed. I gave myself over to each novel without reserve, without trying to criticize it; it was enough for me to see and feel something different. And for me, everything was something different. Reading was like a drug, a dope. The novels created moods in which I lived for days. But I could not conquer my sense of guilt, my feeling that the white men around me knew that I was changing, that I had begun to regard them differently.

Whenever I brought a book to the job, I wrapped it in newspaper—a habit that was to persist for years in other cities and under other circumstances. But some of the white men pried into my packages when I was absent and they questioned me.

"Boy, what are you reading those books for?"

"Oh, I don't know, sir."

70   "That's deep stuff you're reading, boy."

"I'm just killing time, sir."

"You'll addle your brains if you don't watch out."

I read Dreiser's *Jennie Gerhardt* and *Sister Carrie* and they revived in me a vivid sense of my mother's suffering; I was overwhelmed. I grew silent, wondering about the life around me. It would have been impossible for me to have told anyone what I derived from these novels, for it was nothing less than a sense of life itself. All my life had shaped me for the realism, the naturalism of the modern novel, and I could not read enough of them.

Steeped in new moods and ideas, I bought a ream of paper and tried to write; but nothing would come, or what did come was flat beyond telling. I discovered that more than desire and feeling were necessary to write and I dropped the idea. Yet I still wondered how it was possible to know people sufficiently to write about them? Could I ever learn about life and people? To me, with my vast ignorance, my Jim Crow station in life, it seemed a task impossible of achievement. I now knew what being a Negro meant: I could endure the hunger. I had learned to live with hate. But to feel that there were feelings denied me, that the very breath of life itself was beyond my reach, that more than anything else hurt, wounded me. I had a new hunger.

75   In buoying me up, reading also cast me down, made me see what was possible, what I had missed. My tension returned, new, terrible, bitter, surging, almost too great to be contained. I no longer *felt* that the world about me was hostile, killing; I *knew* it. A million times I asked myself what I could do to save myself, and there were no answers. I seemed forever condemned, ringed by walls.

I did not discuss my reading with Mr. Falk, who had lent me his library card; it would have meant talking about myself and that would have been too painful. I smiled each day, fighting desperately to maintain my old behavior, to keep my disposition seemingly sunny. But some of the white men discerned that I had begun to brood.

"Wake up there, boy!" Mr. Olin said one day.

"Sir!" I answered for the lack of a better word.

"You act like you've stolen something," he said.

80   I laughed in the way I knew he expected me to laugh, but I resolved to be more conscious of myself, to watch my every act, to guard and hide the new knowledge that was dawning within me.

If I went north, would it be possible for me to build a new life then? But how could a man build a life upon vague, unformed yearnings? I wanted to write and I did not even know the English language: I bought English grammars and found them dull. I felt that I was getting a better sense of the language from novels than from grammars. I read hard, discarding a writer as soon as I felt that I had grasped his point of view. At night the printed page stood before my eyes in sleep.

Mrs. Moss, my landlady, asked me one Sunday morning:

"Son, what is this you keep on reading?"

"Oh, nothing. Just novels."

85   "What you get out of 'em?"

"I'm just killing time," I said.

"I hope you know your own mind," she said in a tone which implied that she doubted if I had a mind.

I knew of no Negroes who read the books I liked and I wondered if any Negroes ever thought of them. I knew that there were Negro doctors, lawyers, newspapermen, but I never saw any of them. When I read a Negro newspaper I never caught the faintest echo of my preoccupation in its pages. I felt trapped and occasionally, for a few days, I would stop reading. But a vague hunger would come over me for books, books that opened up new avenues of feeling and seeing, and again I would forge another note to the white librarian. Again I would read and wonder as only the naïve and unlettered can read and wonder, feeling that I carried a secret, criminal burden about with me each day.

That winter my mother and brother came and we set up housekeeping, buying furniture on the installment plan, being cheated and yet knowing no way to avoid it. I began to eat warm food and to my surprise found that regular meals enabled me to read faster. I may have lived through many illnesses and survived them, never suspecting that I was ill. My brother obtained a job and we began to save toward the trip north, plotting our time, setting tentative dates for departure. I told none of the white men on the job that I was planning to go north; I knew that the moment they felt I was thinking of the North they would change toward me. It would have made them feel that I did not like the life I was living, and because my life was completely conditioned by what they said or did, it would have been tantamount to challenging them.

90   I could calculate my chances for life in the South as a Negro fairly clearly now.

I could fight the southern whites by organizing with other Negroes, as my grandfather had done. But I knew that I could never win that way; there were many whites and there were but few blacks. They were strong and we were weak. Outright black rebellion could never win. If I fought openly I would die and I did not want to die. News of lynchings were frequent.

I could submit and live the life of a genial slave, but that was impossible. All of my life had shaped me to live by my own feelings and thoughts. I could make up to Bess and marry her and inherit the house. But that, too, would be the life of a slave; if I did that, I would crush to death something within me, and I would hate myself as much as I knew the whites already hated those who had submitted. Neither could I ever willingly present myself to be kicked, as Shorty had done. I would rather have died than do that.

I could drain off my restlessness by fighting with Shorty and Harrison. I had seen many Negroes solve the problem of being black by transferring their hatred of themselves to others with a black skin and fighting them. I would have to be cold to do that, and I was not cold and I could never be.

I could, of course, forget what I had read, thrust the whites out of my mind, forget them; and find release from anxiety and longing in sex and alcohol. But the memory of how my father had conducted himself made that course repugnant. If I did not want others to violate my life, how could I voluntarily violate it myself?

95   I had no hope whatever of being a professional man. Not only had I been so conditioned that I did not desire it, but the fulfillment of such an ambition was beyond my capabilities. Well-to-do Negroes lived in a world that was almost as alien to me as the world inhabited by whites.

What, then, was there? I held my life in my mind, in my consciousness each day, feeling at times that I would stumble and drop it, spill it forever. My reading had created a vast sense of distance between me and the world in which I lived and tried to make a living, and that sense of distance was increasing each day. My days and nights were one long, quiet, continuously contained dream of terror, tension, and anxiety. I wondered how long I could bear it.

Analyzing Rhetorical Choices

1. Wright ends his first paragraph with this sentence: "The article was a furious denunciation of Mencken, concluding with one, hot, short sentence: Mencken is a fool." After reading the quiet, reportorial description that precedes this sentence, how does this sentence affect you? What is the effect of the phrase "concluding with one, hot, short sentence"?

2. Why do you think Wright includes two fairly extended dialogues: one between him and Mr. Falk and the other between him and the librarian? What do we learn from these encounters? What is the main point Wright is trying to dramatize?

3. The author seems to claim complete ignorance of the fact that people other than Negroes criticized the South. How credible a claim do you think this is, and why is his assertion important in his narrative?

Writing About Issues and Contexts

1. Wright includes several anecdotes about literacy: forging notes to the librarian, faking the inability to read, borrowing a library card, disguising book covers. What is the relevance of these anecdotes to ideas of your own about the role of literacy in education and in the larger society?

2. Wright feels that he has, in some explicit sense, been conditioned to a specific kind of life as a Negro in the South—and that the program of reading that he undertakes changes him. Do you agree? How are most of us similarly conditioned? Do you think that the views we have of others and of ourselves are frequently determined by our culture? How so?

3. Wright makes a racial distinction between Jews and whites, criticizing Don because he identifies more with whites than with Negroes. Mr. Falk, on the other hand, is an Irish Catholic hated by white Southerners and thus a potential ally. Are the author's classifications and analysis still as relevant as they were in 1927? Explain your response, being careful to examine your assumptions closely.

4. Regarding the merit of grammar books versus novels, Wright asserts "I felt that I was getting a better sense of the language from novels than from grammars." What is your opinion of his assessment?

Austin Bunn (1973–), who holds a bachelor's from Yale University, has worked as a boat carpenter, a game designer for reality television, and a journalist for numerous publications, including The New York Times Magazine, Wired, The Advocate, the Village Voice, Salon, *and* Elle. *He is the coauthor, with film producer Christine Vachon, of the memoir* A Killer Life *(2006). The essay below first appeared in* The New York Times Magazine *in 2003.*

Austin Bunn

The Bittersweet Science

Eleven-year-old Elizabeth Hughes was, in retrospect, the ideal patient: bright, obedient, uncomplaining, and wholly unprepared to die. Born in 1907 in the New York State governor's mansion, Elizabeth was the daughter of Charles Evans Hughes, who later became a justice on the Supreme Court, ran against Woodrow Wilson in 1916, and served as secretary of state under Harding. Elizabeth had a perfectly normal, aristocratic youth until she seemed to become allergic to childhood. She would come home from friends' birthday parties with an insatiable thirst, drinking almost two quarts of water at a sitting. By winter, she had become thin, constantly hungry, and exhausted. Her body turned into a sieve: No matter how much water she drank, she was always thirsty.

In early 1919, Elizabeth's parents took her to a mansion in Morristown, New Jersey, recently christened the Physiatric Institute and run by Dr. Frederick Allen. A severe, debt-ridden clinician with a pock-marked résumé, Allen had written the authoritative account on treating her condition. He prolonged hundreds of lives and was the girl's best chance. Allen examined Elizabeth and diagnosed diabetes—her body was not properly processing her food into fuel—and told her parents what they would never tell their daughter: that her life expectancy was one year, three at the outside. Even that was a magnificent extension of previous fatality rates. "The diagnosis was like knowing a death sentence had been passed," wrote one historian. Then Dr. Allen did what many doctors at the time would have done for Elizabeth, except that this doctor was exceptionally good, if not the finest in the world, at it. He began to starve her.

The history of medicine "is like the night sky," says the historian Roy Porter in his book *The Greatest Benefit to Mankind: A Medical History of Humanity.* "We see a few stars and group them into mythic constellations. What is chiefly visible is the darkness."

Diabetes doesn't come from simply eating too much sugar; nor is it cured, as was once thought, by a little horseback riding. It is not the result of a failing kidney, overactive liver, or phlegmy disposition, though these were the authoritative answers for centuries. Diabetes happens when the blood becomes saturated with glucose, the body's main energy source, which is normally absorbed by the cells—which is to say that the pathology of diabetes is subtle and invisible, so much so that a third of the people who have it don't even know it. Until the prohibition against autopsies was gradually lifted (by 1482, the pope had informally sanctioned it), what we knew of human anatomy came through the tiny window of war wounds and calamitous gashes—and even then it took centuries for doctors to decide just what the long, lumpy organ called the pancreas actually did or, in the case of diabetes, didn't do. We like to think surgically about the history of medicine, that it moved purposefully from insight to insight, angling closer to cure. But that is only the luxury of contemporary life. Looked at over time, medicine doesn't advance as much as grope forward, with remedies—like bloodletting; quicksilver ointments; and simple, unendurable hunger—that blurred the line between treatment and torture.

5   Diabetes was first diagnosed by the Greek physician Aretaeus of Cappadocia, who deemed it a "wonderful affection . . . being a melting down of the flesh and limbs into urine." For the afflicted, "life is disgusting and painful; thirst unquenchable . . . and one cannot stop them from drinking or making water." Since the classical period forbade dissection, Porter notes, "hidden workings had to be deduced largely from what went in and what came out." An early diagnostic test was to swill urine, and to the name *diabetes,* meaning "siphon," was eventually added *mellitus,* meaning "sweetened with honey." Healers could often diagnose diabetes without the taste test. Black ants were attracted to the urine of those wasting away, drawn by the sugar content. Generations later, doctors would make a similar deduction by spotting dried white sugar spots on the shoes or pants of diabetic men with bad aim.

For the Greeks, to separate disease symptoms from individual pain while isolating them from magical causes was itself an enormous intellectual leap. "We should be really impressed with Aretaeus," says Dr. Chris Feudtner, author of the coming *Bittersweet: Diabetes,*

Insulin, and the Transformation of Illness. "He was able to spot the pattern of diabetes in a dense thicket of illness and suffering."

But for centuries, this increasing precision in disease recognition was not followed by any effective treatment—more details didn't make physicians any less helpless. At the time, they were unknowingly confusing two kinds of diabetes: Type 1, known until recently as "juvenile diabetes," which is more extreme but less common than Type 2, or "adult onset," which seems to be related to obesity and overeating. With Type 1 (what Elizabeth Hughes had), the pancreas stops secreting insulin, a hormone that instructs the body to use the sugar in the blood for energy. With Type 2, the pancreas produces insulin (at least initially), but the tissues of the body stop responding appropriately. By 1776, doctors were still just boiling the urine of diabetics to conclusively determine that they were passing sugar, only to watch their patients fall into hyperglycemic comas and die.

If dangerous levels of glucose were pumping out of diabetics, one idea was obvious: Stop it from going in. That demanded a more sophisticated understanding of food itself. In the long tradition of grotesque scientific experimentation, an insight came through a lucky break: a gaping stomach wound. In 1822, William Beaumont, a surgeon in the U.S. Army, went to the Canadian border to treat a nineteen-year-old trapper hit by a shotgun. The boy recovered, but he was left with a hole in his abdomen. According to Porter, Beaumont "took advantage of his patient's unique window" and dropped food in on a string. The seasoned beef took the longest to digest. Stale bread broke down the quickest. The digestion process clearly worked differently depending on what was eaten. Then during the 1871 siege of Paris by the Germans, a French doctor named Apollinaire Bouchardat noticed that, though hundreds were starving to death, his diabetic patients strangely improved. This became the basis for a new standard of treatment. *Mangez le moins possible,* he advised them. Eat as little as possible.

In the spring of 1919, when Elizabeth Hughes came under Dr. Allen's care, she weighed seventy-five pounds and was nearly five feet tall. For one week, he fasted her. Then he put her on an extremely low-calorie diet to eradicate sugar from her urine. If the normal caloric intake for a girl her age is between 2,200 and 2,400 calories daily, Elizabeth took in 400 to 600 calories a day for several weeks, including one day of fasting each week. Her weight, not surprisingly, plummeted. As Michael Bliss notes in his book *The Discovery of Insulin,* the Hughes family brought in a nurse to help weigh and supervise every gram of food that she ate. Desserts and bread were verboten.

"She lived on lean meat, eggs, lettuce, milk, a few fruits, tasteless bran rusks, and tasteless vegetables (boiled three times to make them almost totally carbohydrate-free)," Bliss writes. Instead of a birthday cake, she had to settle for "a hat box covered in pink and white paper with candles on it. On picnics in the summertime she had her own little frying pan to cook her omelet in while the others had chops, fresh fish, corn on the cob, and watermelon."

10　　You could say that Elizabeth Hughes was on a twisted precursor of the Zone diet: Her menu relied on proteins and fats, with the abolishment of carbohydrates like bread and pasta. In fact, Allen's maniacal scrutiny of his patients' nutrition—fasting them, weighing each meal, counting calories—was one of the first "diets" in the modern sense. At the time Elizabeth entered the clinic, being well fed was a sign of good health. But the new science of nutrition fostered the idea of weight reduction as a standard of health and not illness.

Allen's "starvation diet" was a particular cruelty. Patients came to him complaining of hunger and rapid weight loss, and Allen demanded further restrictions, further weight loss. "Yes, the method was severe; yes, many patients could not or would not follow it," writes Bliss. "But what was the alternative?" Over the years, doctors recommended opium, even heaps of sugar (which only accelerated death, but since nothing else worked, why not enjoy the moment?). But nobody had a better way than Allen to extend lives. If the fasting wasn't working and symptoms got worse, Allen insisted on more rigorous undernourishment. In his campaigns to master their disease, Allen took his patients right to the edge of death, but he justified this by pointing out that patients faced a stark choice: die of diabetes or risk "inanition," which Allen explained as "starvation due to inability to acquire tolerance for any living diet." The Physiatric Institute became a famine ward.

Some of Allen's patients survived levels of inanition not thought possible, Bliss writes. One twelve-year-old patient, blind from diabetes when he was admitted, still occasionally showed sugar in his urine. The clinic became convinced that the kid—so weak he could barely get out of bed—was somehow stealing food. "It turned out that his supposed helplessness was the very thing that gave him opportunities which other persons lacked," Allen later wrote in his book, *Total Dietary Regulation in the Treatment of Diabetes*. "Among unusual things eaten were toothpaste and birdseed, the latter being obtained from the cage of a canary which he had asked for." The staff, thinking he was pilfering food, cut his diet back and further back. The boy weighed less than forty pounds when he died from starvation.

No one explained to Elizabeth Hughes why the friends she made at Allen's clinic stopped writing her letters. Death was kept hidden, though it must have been obvious from the halls of the clinic, where rows of gaunt children stared from their beds. "It would have been unendurable if only there had not been so many others," one Allen nurse wrote. Dutifully, Elizabeth—strong enough just to read and sew—hardly ever showed sugar. Her attendant punished her severely the one time she caught her stealing turkey skin from the kitchen after Thanksgiving. Still, she was wasting away. By April 1921, thirteen years old and two years into her treatment, Elizabeth was down to fifty-two pounds and averaged 405 calories a day. In letters to her parents, she talked about getting married and what she would do on her twenty-first birthday. Reading the letters "must have been heart-breaking," writes Bliss. "Elizabeth was a semi-invalid."

In the history of illness, there are countless medicines, over time and across cultures, with varying degrees of suffering and success. There is only one kind of cure—the one that invariably, irrefutably works. Insulin is not a cure. It is a treatment, but it changed everything. In the summer of 1922, two young clinicians in Toronto named Frederick Banting and Charles Best surgically removed the pancreases from dozens of dogs, causing the dogs to "get" diabetes. They found that by injecting the dogs with a filtered solution of macerated pancreas (either the dogs' own or from calf fetuses), the glucose level in the dogs' blood dropped to normal. The researchers had discovered insulin.

15   But in August 1922, Dr. Frederick Allen had patients who could not wait, like Elizabeth. Allen left for Toronto to secure insulin. While he was gone, word leaked through his clinic about the breakthrough. Patients "who had not been out of bed for weeks began to trail weakly about, clinging to walls and furniture," wrote one nurse. "Big stomachs, skin-and-bone necks, skull-like faces . . . they looked like an old Flemish painter's depiction of a resurrection after famine. It was a resurrection, a crawling stirring, as of some vague springtime."

On the night Allen returned to the clinic, he found his patients— "silent as the bloated ghosts they looked like"—waiting in the hallway for him, wrote the nurse. "When he appeared through the open door-way, he caught the full beseeching of a hundred pair of eyes. It stopped him dead. Even now I am sure it was minutes before he spoke to them. . . . 'I think,' he said. 'I think we have something for you.'" He did, but not nearly enough. Though the results were striking—with the insulin, sugar vanished from the urine of "some of the most hopelessly severe cases of diabetes I have ever seen," wrote Allen—he did not have enough extract to treat all his patients, including Elizabeth. So her parents got her to Toronto. When Banting saw Elizabeth, she was three days away from her fifteenth birthday. She weighed forty-five pounds. He wrote: "Patient extremely emaciated . . . hair brittle and thin . . . muscles extremely wasted. . . . She was scarcely able to walk."

He started her insulin treatment immediately. The first injections cleared the sugar from her urine, and by the end of the first week, she was up to 1,220 calories a day, still without sugar. By the next, she was at 2,200 calories. Banting advised her to eat bread and potatoes, but she was incredulous. It had been three and a half years since she had them. That fall, she was one of several hundred North American diabetics pulled back from the edge. By November, she went home to her parents in Washington, and by January, she weighed 105 pounds. The same year, the thirty-one-year-old Banting won the Nobel Prize. Meanwhile, Dr. Allen, proprietor of an expensive clinic whose patients no longer needed him, went broke. Insulin was a miracle drug, resurrecting diabetics from comas and putting flesh on skeletons and, since it needed to be administered at least twice daily, it was a miracle that would be performed over and over. The era of chronic medical care had begun.

That may be the most poignant part of the history of Allen's clinic. The end of the famine of Elizabeth Hughes is really the start of another hunger: for the drugs that will keep us well for the rest of our lives. Elizabeth went to Barnard, reared three children, drank and smoked, but kept her diabetes a secret almost her entire life. She died of a heart attack in 1981, more than 43,000 injections of insulin later. But if the discovery of insulin took away the terror of diabetes, it replaced the miraculous with the routine. Healing lost one major ingredient: awe. "To think that I'll be leading a normal, healthy existence is beyond all comprehension," Elizabeth wrote to her mother, days after her first injection, in 1922. "It is simply too wonderful for words."

Analyzing Rhetorical Choices

1. Bunn is relating at least three stories at the same time: a story about diabetes and its treatment, a tale about Elizabeth Hughes's encounter with the disease, and a commentary about medicine in

general. How effective are the multiple story lines? Are they appropriate? Would your approach be similar or differ greatly?

2. The author incorporates into his narrative quotes from writers Roy Porter, Chris Feudtner, and Michael Bliss; the nurses at the Physiatric Institute; and Elizabeth Hughes herself. In your view, does this technique interfere with the story? Or does it enhance the narrative?

3. Describe the tone of Bunn's essay. How objective is he? For example, what impressions does he convey of Elizabeth, her parents, and Dr. Frederick Allen?

Writing About Issues and Contexts

1. Bunn writes, "Medicine doesn't advance as much as grope forward." Is this statement accurate in contemporary times? Are there areas of medical research that should be more advanced or sophisticated at this point than they are?

2. In some sense, Dr. Allen helped to usher in the "age of diets." Bunn observes, "The new science of nutrition fostered the idea of weight reduction as a standard of health and not illness." What is your take on the popular, seemingly never-ending discussion about diets?

3. What do you think about the popular criticism that drug companies would rather develop maintenance medicines than search for cures?

Elizabeth Alexander (1962–) was born in New York City and raised in Washington, D.C. She gives numerous poetry readings and lectures widely on literature. She has taught at the University of Chicago and currently teaches at the Cave Canem Poetry Workshop and at Yale University. Volumes of her poetry include The Venus Hottentot *(1990) and* Body of Life *(1996). "Narrative: Ali" first appeared in 1994 and is included in her collection,* Antebellum Dream Book *(2001).*

Elizabeth Alexander

Narrative: Ali

A poem in twelve rounds

1.

My head so big
they had to pry
me out. I'm sorry
Bird (is what I call
5   my mother). Cassius
Marcellus Clay,
Muhammad Ali;
you can say
my name in any
10 language, any
continent: Ali.

2.

Two photographs
of Emmett Till,
born my year,
15 on my birthday.
One, he's smiling,
happy, and the other one
is after. His mother
did the bold thing,
20 kept the casket open,

made the thousands look upon
his bulging eyes,
his twisted neck,
her lynched black boy.
25 I couldn't sleep
for thinking,
Emmett Till.

One day I went
down to the train tracks,
30 found some iron
shoe shine rests
and planted them
between the ties
and waited
35 for a train to come,
and watched the train
derail, and ran,
and after that
I slept at night.

3.

40 I need to train
around people,
hear them talk,
talk back. I need
to hear the traffic,
45 see people in
the barbershop,
people getting
shoeshines, talking,
hear them talk,
50 talk back.

4.

Bottom line: Olympic gold
can't buy a black man
a Louisville hamburger
in nineteen-sixty.
55 Wasn't even real gold.

I watched the river
drag the ribbon down,
red, white, and blue.

5.

Laying on the bed
60 praying for a wife,
in walk Sonji Roi.

Pretty little shape.
Do you like
chop suey?

65 Can I wash your hair
underneath
that wig?

Lay on the bed,
Girl. Lie
70 with me.

Shake to the east,
to the north,
south, west—

but remember,
75 remember, I need
a Muslim wife. So

Quit using lipstick.
Quit your boogaloo.
Cover up your knees

80 like a Muslim
wife, religion,
religion, a Muslim

wife. Eleven
months with Sonji,
85 first woman I loved.

6.

There's not
too many days
that pass that I
don't think
90 of how it started,
but I know
no Great White Hope
can beat
a true black champ.
95 Jerry Quarry
could have been
a movie star,
a millionaire,
a Senator,
100 a President—
he only had
to do one thing,
is whip me,
but he can't.

7. Dressing Room Visitor

105 He opened
up his shirt:
"KKK" cut
in his chest.
He dropped
110 his trousers:
latticed scars
where testicles
should be. His face
bewildered, frozen,
115 in the Alabama woods
that night in 1966
when they left him
for dead, his testicles
in a Dixie cup.
120 You a warning,
they told him,
to smart-mouth,

sassy-acting niggers,
meaning niggers
125 still alive,
meaning any nigger,
meaning niggers
like me.

8. Training

Unsweetened grapefruit juice
130 will melt my stomach down.
Don't drive if you can walk,
don't walk if you can run.
I add a mile each day
and run in eight-pound boots.

135 My knuckles sometimes burst
the glove. I let dead skin
build up, and then I peel it,
let it scar, so I don't bleed
as much. My bones
140 absorb the shock.

I train in three-minute
spurts, like rounds: three
rounds big bag, three speed
bag, three jump rope, one
145 minute breaks,
no more, no less.

Am I too old? Eat only
kosher meat. Eat cabbage,
carrots, beets, and watch
150 the weight come down:
two-thirty, two-twenty,
two-ten, two-oh-nine.

9.

Will I go
like Kid Paret,
155 a fractured

skull, a ten-day
sleep, dreaming
alligators, pork-
chops, saxophones,
160 slow grinds, funk,
fishbowls, lightbulbs,
bats, typewriters,
tuning forks, funk,
clocks, red rubber
165 ball, what you see
in that lifetime
knockout minute
on the cusp?
You could be
170 let go,
you could be
snatched back.

10. Rumble in the Jungle

Ali boma ye,
Ali boma ye,
175 means kill him, Ali,
which is different
from a whupping
which is what I give,
but I lead them chanting
180 anyway, *Ali*
boma ye, because
here in Africa
black people fly
planes and run countries.

185 I'm still making up
for the foolishness
I said when I was
Clay from Louisville,
where I learned Africans
190 lived naked in straw
huts eating tiger meat,
grunting and grinning,

swinging from vines,
pounding their chests—

195 I pound my chest but of my own accord.

11.

I said to Joe Frazier,
first thing, get a good house
in case you get crippled
so you and your family
200 can sleep somewhere. Always
keep one good Cadillac.
And watch how you dress
with that cowboy hat,
pink suits, white shoes—
205 that's how pimps dress,
or kids, and you a champ,
or wish you were, 'cause
I can whip you in the ring
or whip you in the street.
210 Now back to clothes,
wear dark clothes, suits,
black suits, like you the best
at what you do, like you
President of the World.
215 Dress like that.
Put them yellow pants away.

We dinosaurs gotta
look good, gotta sound
good, gotta be good,
220 the greatest, that's what
I told Joe Frazier,
and he said to me,
we both bad niggers.
We don't do no crawlin'.

12.

225 They called me "the fistic pariah."
They said I didn't love my country,
called me a race-hater, called me out

of my name, waited for me
to come out on a streetcar, shot at me,
230 hexed me, cursed me, wished me
all manner of ill-will,
told me I was finished.

Here I am,
like the song says,
235 *come and take me,*

"The People's Champ,"

myself,
Muhammad.

Analyzing Rhetorical Choices

1. The poet is employing the first-person point of view to tell a story about Muhammad Ali. In what ways is this an effective strategy? What might the effect have been if Alexander had given the same basic information in a third-person poem or in an essay about Ali?
2. "Rounds" three and seven feature repetition. What special effect, if any, does this have? Do you see it as an effective rhetorical device? Why or why not?
3. In round five, the poet writes "in walk Sonji Roi." In round seven, she writes, "You a warning." These are both examples of African American Vernacular English. In the first instance, the poet is adhering to a rule that allows no distinction for third-person-singular use of the verb, as required in Standard English ("in walks Sonji Roi"). The second construction is an example of *zero copula*, or the absence of a form of the helping verb *to be* (not the standard "you *are* a warning") when the action is not reoccurring or the assertion is one of all-time truth not related to reoccurring events. Do these vernacular uses of language add anything to the poem, in your view? Explain your response. What would you say about the vernacular use of language in general?
4. What is Alexander's argument about Ali? What impression is she trying to make?

Writing About Issues and Contexts

1. We get a sense of Ali's career unfolding against the backdrop of the Civil Rights movement. What is the relationship of his career to the movement? What does Alexander do to make this aspect of the narrative interesting? What do you think of Ali's advice to Joe Frazier?

2. Why is keeping the casket open, as Emmett Till's mother did, the "bold thing" and seemingly the right thing?

---

*The daughter of Chinese immigrants, **Amy Tan** (1952–) was born in Oakland, California. She grew up mainly in Northern California but finished high school in Switzerland. Once back in the United States, she studied English and linguistics, eventually earning a master's degree in linguistics from San Jose State University and taking doctoral courses at Berkeley. She worked with children with disabilities and ran her own communications business before turning to a writing career in the mid-1980s. Her novels include* The Joy Luck Club *(1989), for which she received the National Book Award;* The Kitchen God's Wife *(1991);* The Hundred Secret Senses *(1995);* The Bonesetter's Daughter *(2001); and* Saving Fish from Drowning *(2005). The essay in this chapter was first published in 1990.*

Amy Tan

Mother Tongue

I am not a scholar of English or literature. I cannot give you much more than personal opinions on the English language and its variations in this country or others.

I am a writer. And by that definition, I am someone who has always loved language. I am fascinated by language in daily life. I spend a great deal of my time thinking about the power of language—the way it can evoke an emotion, a visual image, a complex idea, or a simple truth. Language is the tool of my trade. And I use them all—all the Englishes I grew up with.

Recently, I was made keenly aware of the different Englishes I do use. I was giving a talk to a large group of people, the same talk I had already given to half a dozen other groups. The nature of the talk was about my writing, my life, and my book, *The Joy Luck Club*. The talk was going along well enough, until I remembered one major difference that made the whole talk sound wrong. My mother was in the room. And it was perhaps the first time she had heard me give a lengthy speech, using the kind of English I have never used with her. I was saying things like, "The intersection of memory upon imagination" and "There is an aspect of my fiction that relates to thus-and-thus"—a speech filled with carefully wrought grammatical phrases, burdened, it suddenly seemed to me, with nominalized forms, past perfect tenses, conditional phrases, all the forms of standard English that I had learned in school and through books, the forms of English I did not use at home with my mother.

Just last week, I was walking down the street with my mother, and I again found myself conscious of the English I was using, the English I do use with her. We were talking about the price of new and used furniture and I heard myself saying this: "Not waste money that way." My husband was with us as well, and he didn't notice any switch in my English. And then I realized why. It's because over the twenty years we've been together I've often used that same kind of English with him, and sometimes he even uses it with me. It has become our language of intimacy, a different sort of English that relates to family talk, the language I grew up with.

5   So you'll have some idea of what this family talk I heard sounds like, I'll quote what my mother said during a recent conversation which I videotaped and then transcribed. During this conversation, my mother was talking about a political gangster in Shanghai who had the same last name as her family's, Du, and how the gangster in his early years wanted to be adopted by her family, which was rich by comparison. Later, the gangster became more powerful, far richer than my mother's family, and one day showed up at my mother's wedding to pay his respects. Here's what she said in part: "Du Yusong having business like fruit stand. Like off the street kind. He is Du like Du Zong—but not Tsung-ming Island people. The local people call putong, the river east side, he belong to that side local people. That man want to ask Du Zong father take him in like become own family. Du Zong father wasn't look down on him, but didn't take seriously, until that man big like become a mafia. Now important person, very hard to inviting him. Chinese way, came only to show respect, don't stay for dinner. Respect for making big celebration, he shows up. Mean gives lots of respect Chinese custom. Chinese social life that way. If too important won't have to stay too long. He come to my wedding. I didn't see, I heard it. I gone to boy's side, they have YMCA dinner. Chinese age I was nineteen."

You should know that my mother's expressive command of English belies how much she actually understands. She reads the *Forbes* report, listens to *Wall Street Week*, converses daily with her stockbroker, reads all of Shirley MacLaine's books with ease—all kinds of things I can't begin to understand. Yet some of my friends tell me they understand 50 percent of what my mother says. Some say they understand 80 to 90 percent. Some say they understand none of it, as if she were speaking pure Chinese. But to me, my mother's English is perfectly clear, perfectly natural. It's my mother tongue. Her language, as I hear it, is vivid, direct, full of observation and imagery. That was the language that helped shape the way I saw things, expressed things, made sense of the world.

Lately, I've been giving more thought to the kind of English my mother speaks. Like others, I have described it to people as "broken" or "fractured" English. But I wince when I say that. It has always bothered me that I can think of no way to describe it other than "broken," as if it were damaged and needed to be fixed, as if it lacked a certain wholeness and soundness. I've heard other terms used, "limited English," for example. But they seem just as bad, as if everything is limited, including people's perceptions of the limited English speaker.

I know this for a fact, because when I was growing up, my mother's "limited" English limited *my* perception of her. I was ashamed of her English. I believed that her English reflected the quality of what she had to say. That is, because she expressed them imperfectly her thoughts were imperfect. And I had plenty of empirical evidence to support me: the fact that people in department stores, at banks, and at restaurants did not take her seriously, did not give her good service, pretended not to understand her, or even acted as if they did not hear her.

My mother has long realized the limitations of her English as well. When I was fifteen, she used to have me call people on the phone to pretend I was she. In this guise, I was forced to ask for information or even to complain and yell at people who had been rude to her. One time it was a call to her stockbroker in New York. She had cashed out her small portfolio and it just so happened we were going to go to New York the next week, our very first trip outside California. I had to get on the phone and say in an adolescent voice that was not very convincing, "This is Mrs. Tan."

10   And my mother was standing in the back whispering loudly, "Why he don't send me check, already two weeks late. So mad he lie to me, losing me money."

And then I said in perfect English, "Yes, I'm getting rather concerned. You had agreed to send the check two weeks ago, but it hasn't arrived."

Then she began to talk more loudly. "What he want, I come to New York tell him front of his boss, you cheating me?" And I was trying to calm her down, make her be quiet, while telling the stockbroker, "I can't tolerate any more excuses. If I don't receive the check immediately, I am going to have to speak to your manager when I'm in New York next week." And sure enough, the following week there we were in front of this astonished stockbroker, and I was sitting there red-faced and quiet, and my mother, the real Mrs. Tan, was shouting at his boss in her impeccable broken English.

We used a similar routine just five days ago, for a situation that was far less humorous. My mother had gone to the hospital for an appointment, to find out about a benign brain tumor a CAT scan had revealed a month ago. She said she had spoken very good English, her best English, no mistakes. Still, she said, the hospital did not apologize when they said they had lost the CAT scan and she had come for nothing. She said they did not seem to have any sympathy when she told them she was anxious to know the exact diagnosis, since her husband and son had both died of brain tumors. She said they would not give her any more information until the next time and she would have to make another appointment for that. So she said she would not leave until the doctor called her daughter. She wouldn't budge. And when the doctor finally called her daughter, me, who spoke in perfect English—lo and behold—we had assurances the CAT scan would be found, promises that a conference call on Monday would be held, and apologies for any suffering my mother had gone through for a most regrettable mistake.

I think my mother's English almost had an effect on limiting my possibilities in life as well. Sociologists and linguists probably will tell you that a person's developing language skills are more influenced by peers. But I do think that the language spoken in the family, especially in immigrant families which are more insular, plays a large role in shaping the language of the child. And I believe that it affected my results on achievement tests, IQ tests, and the SAT. While my English skills were never judged as poor, compared to math, English could not be considered my strong suit. In grade school I did moderately well, getting perhaps B's, sometimes B-pluses, in English and scoring perhaps in the sixtieth or seventieth percentile on achievement tests. But those scores were not good enough to override the opinion that my true abilities lay in math and science, because in those areas I achieved A's and scored in the ninetieth percentile or higher.

15   This was understandable. Math is precise; there is only one correct answer. Whereas, for me at least, the answers on English tests were always a judgment call, a matter of opinion and personal experience. Those tests were constructed around items like fill-in-the-blank sentence completion, such as, "Even though Tom was _____, Mary

thought he was _____." And the correct answer always seemed to be the most bland combinations of thoughts, for example, "Even though Tom was shy, Mary thought he was charming," with the grammatical structure "even though" limiting the correct answer to some sort of semantic opposites, so you wouldn't get answers like, "Even though Tom was foolish, Mary thought he was ridiculous." Well, according to my mother, there were very few limitations as to what Tom could have been and what Mary might have thought of him. So I never did well on tests like that.

The same was true with word analogies, pairs of words in which you were supposed to find some sort of logical, semantic relationship—for example, "*Sunset* is to *nightfall* as _____ is to _____." And here you would be presented with a list of four possible pairs, one of which showed the same kind of relationship: *red* is to *stoplight*, *bus* is to *arrival*, *chills* is to *fever*, *yawn* is to *boring*. Well, I could never think that way. I knew what the tests were asking, but I could not block out of my mind the images already created by the first pair, "*sunset* is to *nightfall*"—and I would see a burst of colors against a darkening sky, the moon rising, the lowering of a curtain of stars. And all the other pairs of words—red, bus, stoplight, boring—just threw up a mass of confusing images, making it impossible for me to sort out something as logical as saying: "A sunset precedes nightfall" is the same as "a chill precedes a fever." The only way I would have gotten that answer right would have been to imagine an associative situation, for example, my being disobedient and staying out past sunset, catching a chill at night, which turns into feverish pneumonia as punishment, which indeed did happen to me.

I have been thinking about all this lately, about my mother's English, about achievement tests. Because lately I've been asked, as a writer, why there are not more Asian Americans represented in American literature. Why are there few Asian Americans enrolled in creative writing programs? Why do so many Chinese students go into engineering? Well, these are broad sociological questions I can't begin to answer. But I have noticed in surveys—in fact, just last week—that Asian students, as a whole, always do significantly better on math achievement tests than in English. And this makes me think that there are other Asian-American students whose English spoken in the home might also be described as "broken" or "limited." And perhaps they also have teachers who are steering them away from writing and into math and science, which is what happened to me.

Fortunately, I happened to be rebellious in nature and enjoy the challenge of disproving assumptions made about me. I became an English major my first year in college, after being enrolled as premed. I started writing nonfiction as a freelancer the week after I was told by my former boss that writing was my worst skill and I should hone my talents toward account management.

But it wasn't until 1985 that I finally began to write fiction. And at first I wrote using what I thought to be wittily crafted sentences, sentences that would finally prove I had mastery over the English language. Here's an example from the first draft of a story that later made its way into *The Joy Luck Club*, but without this line: "That was my mental quandary in its nascent state." A terrible line, which I can barely pronounce.

20   Fortunately, for reasons I won't get into today, I later decided I should envision a reader for the stories I would write. And the reader I decided upon was my mother, because these were stories about mothers. So with this reader in mind—and in fact she did read my early drafts—I began to write stories using all the Englishes I grew up with: the English I spoke to my mother, which for lack of a better term might be described as "simple"; the English she used with me, which for lack of a better term might be described as "broken"; my translation of her Chinese, which could certainly be described as "watered down"; and what I imagined to be her translation of her Chinese if she could speak in perfect English, her internal language, and for that I sought to preserve the essence, but neither an English nor a Chinese structure. I wanted to capture what language ability tests can never reveal: her intent, her passion, her imagery, the rhythms of her speech and the nature of her thoughts.

Apart from what any critic had to say about my writing, I knew I had succeeded where it counted when my mother finished reading my book and gave me her verdict: "So easy to read."

Analyzing Rhetorical Choices

1.   As noted previously, Tan declares that in her writing she uses all the Englishes she grew up with. In this essay, she uses her mother's language as dialogue, which makes the dialogue realistic. Her mother's language is in a frame, however, separate from the words that are outside of quotation marks. How might Tan have used

her mother tongue in the rest of the piece? Comment on whether or not this would have been effective.

2. Tan uses anecdotes to illustrate how language prejudice operates in hospitals, education, and the business world. How persuasive do you find Tan's anecdotes?

3. Concerning English and literature, Tan writes that, because she is not a scholar, she "cannot give you much more than personal opinions." We know that Tan holds a graduate degree in language study. What is the effect, then, of her claiming not to be a scholar?

Writing About Issues and Contexts

1. Tan writes of her mother's language, "That was the language that helped shape the way I saw things, expressed things, made sense of the world." Can you give examples of how and why your native language variety influences your view of the world?

2. Tan uses her Englishes to write professionally. In your estimation, can her approach be applied in the classroom? Explain your response.

3. Tan mentions that large numbers of Chinese students go into engineering. Have you been aware of or had any personal experience with particular groups of students being steered in a specific academic direction? Why do you think this occurs?

George Orwell *(1903–1950) was the pen name of Eric Arthur Blair. He was born in India, where his father served as a British civil servant while India was under British rule. Orwell was raised and educated in England before joining the Indian Imperial Police and serving in Burma (now Myanmar), a land in Southeast Asia also under British control. As opposition to British colonialism stirred within him, he left the police and returned to Europe. He wrote prolifically and was also active politically, fighting in the Spanish Civil War against fascism. Orwell is best known for his novels* Animal Farm *(1946) and* 1984 *(1949), both warnings about the dangers of totalitarian regimes. His nonfiction has been gathered in* Collected Essays, Journalism, and Letters *(1968). The following essay was written in 1936.*

George Orwell

Shooting an Elephant

In Moulmein, in Lower Burma, I was hated by large numbers of people—the only time in my life that I have been important enough for this to happen to me. I was sub-divisional police officer of the town, and in an aimless, petty kind of way anti-European feeling was very bitter. No one had the guts to raise a riot, but if a European woman went through the bazaars alone somebody would probably spit betel juice over her dress. As a police officer I was an obvious target and was baited whenever it seemed safe to do so. When a nimble Burman tripped me up on the football field and the referee (another Burman) looked the other way, the crowd yelled with hideous laughter. This happened more than once. In the end the sneering yellow faces of young men that met me everywhere, the insults hooted after me when I was at a safe distance, got badly on my nerves. The young Buddhist priests were the worst of all. There were several thousands of them in the town and none of them seemed to have anything to do except stand on street corners and jeer at Europeans.

All this was perplexing and upsetting. For at the time I had already made up my mind that imperialism was an evil thing and the sooner I chucked up my job and got out of it the better. Theoretically—and secretly, of course—I was all for the Burmese and all against their oppressors, the British. As for the job I was doing, I hated it more bitterly than I can perhaps make clear. In a job like that you see the dirty work of Empire at close quarters. The wretched prisoners huddling in the stinking cages of the lockups, the grey, cowed faces of the long-term convicts, the scarred buttocks of the men who had been flogged with bamboos—all these oppressed me with an intolerable sense of guilt. But I could get nothing into perspective. I was young and ill-educated and I had had to think out my problems in the utter silence that is imposed on every Englishman in the East. I did not even know that the British Empire is dying, still less did I know that it is a great deal better than the younger empires that are going to supplant it. All I knew was that I was stuck between my hatred of the empire I served and my rage against the evil-spirited little beasts who tried to make my job impossible. With one part of my mind I thought of the British Raj as an unbreakable tyranny, as something clamped down, in *saecula saeculorum*,* upon the will of prostrate peoples; with another part I thought that the greatest joy in the world would be to drive a bayonet into a Buddhist priest's guts. Feelings like these are the normal by-products of imperialism; ask any Anglo-Indian official, if you can catch him off duty.

One day something happened which in a roundabout way was enlightening. It was a tiny incident in itself, but it gave me a better glimpse than I had had before of the real nature of imperialism—the real motives for which despotic governments act. Early one morning the sub-inspector at a police station the other end of the town rang me up on the phone and said that an elephant was ravaging the bazaar. Would I please come and do something about it? I did not know what I could do, but I wanted to see what was happening and I got on to a pony and started out. I took my rifle, an old .44 Winchester and much too small to kill an elephant, but I thought the noise might be useful *in terrorem*. Various Burmans stopped me on the way and told me about the elephant's doings. It was not, of course, a wild elephant, but a tame one which had gone "must."† It had been chained up, as tame elephants always are when their attack of "must" is due, but on the previous night it had broken its chain and escaped. Its mahout,‡ the only person who could manage it when it was in that state, had set out in pursuit, but had taken the wrong direction and was now twelve hours' journey away, and in the morning

---

* From the beginning of time.
† Gone beserk.
‡ Elephant handler.

the elephant had suddenly reappeared in the town. The Burmese population had no weapons and were quite helpless against it. It had already destroyed somebody's bamboo hut, killed a cow, and raided some fruit-stalls and devoured the stock; also it had met the municipal rubbish van and, when the driver jumped out and took to his heels, had turned the van over and inflicted violences upon it.

The Burmese sub-inspector and some Indian constables were waiting for me in the quarter where the elephant had been seen. It was a very poor quarter, a labyrinth of squalid bamboo huts, thatched with palm-leaf, winding all over a steep hillside. I remember that it was a cloudy, stuffy morning at the beginning of the rains. We began questioning people as to where the elephant had gone, and, as usual, failed to get any definite information. That is invariably the case in the East; a story always sounds clear enough at a distance, but the nearer you get to the scene of events the vaguer it becomes. Some of the people said that the elephant had gone in one direction, some said that he had gone in another, some professed not even to have heard of an elephant. I had almost made up my mind that the whole story was a pack of lies, when we heard yells a little distance away. There was a loud, scandalized cry of "Go away, child! Go away this instant!" and an old woman with a switch in her hand came round the corner of a hut, violently shooing away a crowd of naked children. Some more women followed, clicking their tongues and exclaiming; evidently there was something that the children ought not to have seen. I rounded the hut and saw a man's dead body sprawling in the mud. He was an Indian, a black Dravidian coolie, almost naked, and he could not have been dead many minutes. The people said that the elephant had come suddenly upon him round the corner of the hut, caught him with its trunk, put its foot on his back, and ground him into the earth. This was the rainy season and the ground was soft, and his face had scored a trench a foot deep and a couple of yards long. He was lying on his belly with arms crucified and head sharply twisted to one side. His face was coated with mud, the eyes wide open, the teeth bared and grinning with an expression of unendurable agony. (Never tell me, by the way, that the dead look peaceful. Most of the corpses I have seen looked devilish.) The friction of the great beast's foot had stripped the skin from his back as neatly as one skins a rabbit. As soon as I saw the dead man I sent an orderly to a friend's house nearby to borrow an elephant rifle. I had already sent back the pony, not wanting it to go mad with fright and throw me if it smelled the elephant.

5   The orderly came back in a few minutes with a rifle and five cartridges, and meanwhile some Burmans had arrived and told us that the elephant was in the paddy fields below, only a few hundred yards away. As I started forward practically the whole population of the quarter flocked out of the houses and followed me. They had seen the rifle and were all shouting excitedly that I was going to shoot the elephant. They had not shown much interest in the elephant when he was merely ravaging their homes, but it was different now that he was going to be shot. It was a bit of fun to them, as it would be to an English crowd; besides they wanted the meat. It made me vaguely uneasy. I had no intention of shooting the elephant—I had merely sent for the rifle to defend myself if necessary—and it is always unnerving to have a crowd following you. I marched down the hill, looking and feeling a fool, with the rifle over my shoulder and an ever-growing army of people jostling at my heels. At the bottom, when you got away from the huts, there was a metalled road and beyond that a miry waste of paddy fields a thousand yards across, not yet ploughed but soggy from the first rains and dotted with coarse grass. The elephant was standing eight yards from the road, his left side towards us. He took not the slightest notice of the crowd's approach. He was tearing up bunches of grass, beating them against his knees to clean them and stuffing them into his mouth.

I had halted on the road. As soon as I saw the elephant I knew with perfect certainty that I ought not to shoot him. It is a serious matter to shoot a working elephant—it is comparable to destroying a huge and costly piece of machinery—and obviously one ought not to do it if it can possibly be avoided. And at that distance, peacefully eating, the elephant looked no more dangerous than a cow. I thought then and I think now that his attack of "must" was already passing off; in which case he would merely wander harmlessly about until the mahout came back and caught him. Moreover, I did not in the least want to shoot him. I decided that I would watch him for a little while to make sure that he did not turn savage again, and then go home.

But at that moment I glanced around at the crowd that had followed me. It was an immense crowd, two thousand at the least and growing every minute. It blocked the road for a long distance on either side. I looked at the sea of yellow faces above the garish clothes— faces all happy and excited over this bit of fun, all certain that the elephant was going to be shot. They were watching me as they would watch a conjurer about to perform a trick. They did not like me, but with the magical rifle in my hands I was momentarily worth watching. And suddenly I realized that I should have to shoot the elephant after all. The people expected it of me and I had got to do it; I could feel their two thousand wills pressing me forward, irresistibly. And it was at this moment, as I stood there with the rifle in my hands, that I first grasped the hollowness, the futility of the white man's dominion in the East. Here was I, the white man with his gun, standing in front of the unarmed native crowd—seemingly the leading actor of the piece; but in reality I was only an absurd puppet pushed to and fro by the will of those yellow faces behind. I perceived in this moment that when the white man turns tyrant it is his own freedom that he destroys. He becomes a sort of hollow, posing dummy, the conventionalized figure of a sahib.* For it is the condition of his rule that he shall spend his life in trying to impress the "natives," and so in every crisis he has got to do what the "natives" expect of him. He wears a mask, and his face grows to fit it. I had got to shoot the elephant. I had committed myself to doing it when I sent for the rifle. A sahib has got to act like a sahib; he has got to appear resolute, to know his own mind and do definite things. To come all that way, rifle in hand, with two thousand people marching at my heels, and then to trail feebly away, having done nothing—no, that was impossible. The crowd would laugh at me. And my whole life, every white man's life in the East, was one long struggle not to be laughed at.

But I did not want to shoot the elephant. I watched him beating his bunch of grass against his knees, with the preoccupied grandmotherly air that elephants have. It seemed to me that it would be murder to shoot him. At that age I was not squeamish about killing animals, but I had never shot an elephant and never wanted to. (Somehow it always seems worse to kill a *large* animal.) Besides, there was the beast's owner to be considered. Alive, the elephant was worth at least a hundred pounds; dead, he would only be worth the value of his tusks, five pounds, possibly. But I had got to act quickly. I turned to some experienced-looking Burmans who had been there when we arrived, and asked them how the elephant had been behaving. They all said the same thing: he took no notice of you if you left him alone, but he might charge if you went too close to him.

It was perfectly clear to me what I ought to do. I ought to walk up to within, say, twenty-five yards of the elephant and test his behavior. If he charged I could shoot, if he took no notice of me it would be safe to leave him until the mahout came back. But also I knew that I

---

* An official.

was going to do no such thing. I was a poor shot with a rifle and the ground was soft mud into which one would sink at every step. If the elephant charged and I missed him, I should have about as much chance as a toad under a steamroller. But even then I was not thinking particularly of my own skin, only of the watchful yellow faces behind. For at that moment, with the crowd watching me, I was not afraid in the ordinary sense, as I would have been if I had been alone. A white man mustn't be frightened in front of "natives"; and so, in general, he isn't frightened. The sole thought in my mind was that if anything went wrong those two thousand Burmans would see me pursued, caught, trampled on, and reduced to a grinning corpse like that Indian up the hill. And if that happened it was quite probable that some of them would laugh. That would never do. There was only one alternative. I shoved the cartridges into the magazine and lay down on the road to get a better aim.

10   The crowd drew very still, and a deep, low, happy sigh, as of people who see the theatre curtain go up at last, breathed from innumerable throats. They were going to have their bit of fun after all. The rifle was a beautiful German thing with cross-hair sights. I did not then know that in shooting an elephant one would shoot to cut an imaginary bar running from ear-hole to ear-hole. I ought, therefore, as the elephant was sideways on, to have aimed straight at his ear-hole; actually I aimed several inches in front of this, thinking the brain would be further forward.

When I pulled the trigger I did not hear the bang or feel the kick—one never does when a shot goes home—but I heard the devilish roar of glee that went up from the crowd. In that instant, in too short a time, one would have thought, even for the bullet to get there, a mysterious, terrible change had come over the elephant. He neither stirred nor fell, but every line on his body had altered. He looked suddenly stricken, shrunken, immensely old, as though the frightful impact of the bullet had paralyzed him without knocking him down. At last, after what seemed a long time—it might have been five seconds, I dare say—he sagged flabbily to his knees. His mouth slobbered. An enormous senility seemed to have settled upon him. One could have imagined him thousands of years old. I fired again into the same spot. At the second shot he did not collapse but climbed with desperate slowness to his feet and stood weakly upright, with legs sagging and head drooping. I fired a third time. That was the shot that did for him. You could see the agony of it jolt his whole body and knock the last remnant of strength from his legs. But in falling he seemed for a moment to rise, for as his hind legs collapsed beneath him he seemed to tower upwards like a huge rock toppling, his trunk reaching skywards like a tree. He trumpeted, for the first and only time. And then down he came, his belly towards me, with a crash that seemed to shake the ground even where I lay.

I got up. The Burmans were already racing past me across the mud. It was obvious that the elephant would never rise again, but he was not dead. He was breathing very rhythmically with long rattling gasps, his great mound of a side painfully rising and falling. His mouth was wide open—I could see far down into the caverns of pale pink throat. I waited a long time for him to die, but his breathing did not weaken. Finally, I fired my two remaining shots into the spot where I thought his heart must be. The thick blood welled out of him like red velvet, but still he did not die. His body did not even jerk when the shots hit him, the tortured breathing continued without a pause. He was dying, very slowly and in great agony, but in some world remote from me where not even a bullet could damage him further. I felt that I had got to put an end to that dreadful noise. It seemed dreadful to see the great beast lying there, powerless to move and yet powerless to die, and not even to be able to finish him. I sent back for my small rifle and poured shot after shot into his heart and down his throat. They seemed to make no impression. The tortured gasps continued as steadily as the ticking of a clock.

In the end I could not stand it any longer and went away. I heard later that it took him half an hour to die. Burmans were bringing dahs* and baskets even before I left, and I was told they had stripped his body almost to the bones by the afternoon.

Afterwards, of course, there were endless discussions about the shooting of the elephant. The owner was furious, but he was only an Indian and could do nothing. Besides, legally I had done the right thing, for a mad elephant has to be killed, like a mad dog, if its owner fails to control it. Among the Europeans opinion was divided. The older men said I was right, the younger men said it was a damn shame to shoot an elephant for killing a coolie, because an elephant was worth more than any damn Coringhee coolie. And afterwards I was very glad that the coolie had been killed; it put me legally in the right and it gave me a sufficient pretext for shooting the elephant. I often wondered whether any of the others grasped that I had done it solely to avoid looking a fool.

---

* Knives.

Analyzing Rhetorical Choices

1. The point of Orwell's narrative is to provide insight into the "real nature of imperialism." How does Orwell do this? Consider language use, organization, and selection of details. What might a Burmese perspective be?

2. The Burmese man who was killed by the elephant is described as both crucified and devilish, terms that don't normally go together in our culture. What point do you think Orwell is making with this description?

Writing About Issues and Contexts

1. Orwell seems to be arguing, in part, that imperialism has severe effects on the imperialists themselves. What are these effects? Is it proper to speak of the rulers as victims? Why or why not? In what other situations can the power structure be said to suffer?

2. Although sympathetic to the political plight of the natives, Orwell still thinks of deriving pleasure from stabbing a Buddhist priest. How is his impulse connected to language deprivation, that is, a situation where, as Orwell describes it, there was "silence imposed on every Englishman in the East"?

A native of San Francisco, California, **Shirley Jackson** *(1919–1965) attended the University of Rochester and Syracuse University. At Syracuse, she became the fiction editor of* The Syracusan, *a campus magazine. With her future husband, critic Stanley Edgar Hyman, she cofounded a second campus publication,* The Spectre. *Jackson is widely known for her suspenseful short stories and novels. Her most famous story is "The Lottery." Her novels include* The Haunting of Hill House *(1959), which was the basis for a successful movie titled* The Haunting. *A mother of four, she also wrote memoirs about her domestic life,* Life Among the Savages *(1953) and* Raising Demons *(1957).*

Shirley Jackson

Seven Types of Ambiguity

The basement room of the bookstore seemed to be enormous; it stretched in long rows of books off into dimness at either end, with books lined in tall bookcases along the walls, and books standing in piles on the floor. At the foot of the spiral staircase winding down from the neat small store upstairs, Mr. Harris, owner and sales-clerk of the bookstore, had a small desk, cluttered with catalogues, lighted by one dirty overhead lamp. The same lamp served to light the shelves which crowded heavily around Mr. Harris' desk; farther away, along the lines of book tables, there were other dirty overhead lamps, to be lighted by pulling a string and turned off by the customer when he was ready to grope his way back to Mr. Harris' desk, pay for his purchases and have them wrapped. Mr. Harris, who knew the position of any author or any title in all the heavy shelves, had one customer at the moment, a boy of about eighteen, who was standing far down the long room directly under one of the lamps, leafing through a book he had selected from the shelves. It was cold in the big basement room; both Mr. Harris and the boy had their coats on. Occasionally Mr. Harris got up from his desk to put a meagre shovelful of coal on a small iron stove which stood in the curve of the staircase. Except when Mr. Harris got up, or the boy turned to put a book back into the shelves and take out another, the room was quiet, the books standing silent in the dim light.

Then the silence was broken by the sound of the door opening in the little upstairs bookshop where Mr. Harris kept his best-sellers and art books on display. There was the sound of voices, while both Mr. Harris and the boy listened, and then the girl who took care of the up-stairs bookshop said, "Right on down the stairs. Mr. Harris will help you."

Mr. Harris got up and walked around to the foot of the stairs, turning on another of the overhead lamps so that his new customer would be able to see his way down. The boy put his book back in the shelves and stood with his hand on the back of it, still listening.

When Mr. Harris saw that it was a woman coming down the stairs he stood back politely and said, "Watch the bottom step. There's one more than people think." The woman stepped carefully down and stood looking around. While she stood there a man came carefully around the turn in the staircase, ducking his head so his hat would clear the low ceiling. "Watch the bottom step," the woman said in a soft clear voice. The man came down beside her and raised his head to look around as she had.

5   "Quite a lot of books you have here," he said.

Mr. Harris smiled his professional smile. "Can I help you?"

The woman looked at the man, and he hesitated a minute and then said, "We want to get some books. Quite a few of them." He waved his hand inclusively. "Sets of books."

"Well, if it's books you want," Mr. Harris said, and smiled again. "Maybe the lady would like to come over and sit down?" He led the way around to his desk, the woman following him and the man walk-ing uneasily between the tables of books, his hands close to his sides as though he were afraid of breaking something. Mr. Harris gave the lady his desk chair and then sat down on the edge of his desk, shoving aside a pile of catalogues.

"This is a very interesting place," the lady said, in the same soft voice she had used when she spoke before. She was middle-aged and nicely dressed; all her clothes were fairly new, but quiet and well planned for her age and air of shyness. The man was big and hearty-looking, his face reddened by the cold air and his big hands holding a pair of wool gloves uneasily.

10   "We'd like to buy some of your books," the man said. "Some good books."

"Anything in particular?" Mr. Harris asked.

The man laughed loudly, but with embarrassment. "Tell the truth," he said, "I sound sort of foolish, now. But I don't know much about these things, like books." In the large quiet store his voice seemed to echo, after his wife's soft voice and Mr. Harris'. "We were sort of hoping you'd be able to tell us," he said. "None of this trash they turn out nowadays." He cleared this throat. "Something like Dickens," he said.

"Dickens," Mr. Harris said.

"I used to read Dickens when I was a kid," the man said. "Books like that, now, good books." He looked up as the boy who had been standing off among the books came over to them. "I'd like to read Dickens again," the big man said.

15   "Mr. Harris," the boy asked quietly.

Mr. Harris looked up. "Yes, Mr. Clark?" he said.

The boy came closer to the desk, as though unwilling to interrupt Mr. Harris with his customers. "I'd like to take another look at the Empson," he said.

Mr. Harris turned to the glass-doored bookcase immediately be-hind his desk and selected a book. "Here it is," he said, "You'll have it read through before you buy it at this rate." He smiled at the big man and his wife. "Some day he's going to come in and buy that book," he said, "and I'm going to go out of business from shock."

The boy turned away, holding the book, and the big man leaned forward to Mr. Harris. "I figure I'd like two good sets, big, like Dickens," he said, "and then a couple of smaller sets."

20   "And a copy of *Jane Eyre*," his wife said, in her soft voice. "I used to love that book," she said to Mr. Harris.

"I can let you have a very nice set of the Brontës," Mr. Harris said. "Beautiful binding."

"I want them to look nice," the man said, "but solid, for reading. I'm going to read through all of Dickens again."

The boy came back to the desk, holding the book out to Mr. Harris. "It still looks good," he said.

"It's right here when you want it," Mr. Harris said, turning back to the bookcase with the book. "It's pretty scarce, that book."

25   "I guess it'll be here a while longer," the boy said.

"What's the name of this book?" the big man asked curiously.

"*Seven Types of Ambiguity*," the boy said. "It's quite a good book."

"There's a fine name for a book," the big man said to Mr. Harris. "Pretty smart young fellow, reading books with names like that."

"It's a good book," the boy repeated.

30   "I'm trying to buy some books myself," the big man said to the boy. "I want to catch up on a few I've missed. Dickens, I've always liked his books."

"Meredith is good," the boy said. "You ever try reading Meredith?"

"Meredith," the big man said. "Let's see a few of your books," he said to Mr. Harris. "I'd sort of like to pick out a few I want."

"Can I take the gentleman down there?" the boy said to Mr. Harris. "I've got to go back anyway to get my hat."

"I'll go with the young man and look at the books, Mother," the big man said to his wife. "You stay here and keep warm."

35   "Fine," Mr. Harris said. "He knows where the books are as well as I do," he said to the big man.

The boy started off down the aisle between the book tables, and the big man followed, still walking carefully, trying not to touch anything. They went down past the lamp still burning where the boy had left his hat and gloves, and the boy turned on another lamp further down. "Mr. Harris keeps most of his sets around here," the boy said. "Let's see what we can find." He squatted down in front of the bookcases, touching the backs of the rows of books lightly with his fingers. "How do you feel about the prices?" he asked.

"I'm willing to pay a reasonable amount for the books I have in mind," the big man said. He touched the book in front of him experimentally, with one finger. "A hundred and fifty, two hundred dollars altogether."

The boy looked up at him and laughed. "That ought to get you some nice books," he said.

"Never saw so many books in my life," the big man said. "I never thought I'd see the day when I'd just walk into a bookstore and buy up all the books I always wanted to read."

40   "It's a good feeling."

"I never got a chance to read much," the man said. "Went right into the machine-shop where my father worked when I was much younger than you, and worked ever since. Now all of a sudden I find I have a little more money than I used to, and Mother and I decided we'd like to get ourselves a few things we always wanted."

"Your wife was interested in the Brontës," the boy said. "Here's a very good set."

The man leaned down to look at the books the boy pointed out. "I don't know much about these things," he said. "They look nice, all alike. What's the next set?"

"Carlyle," the boy said. "You can skip him. He's not quite what you're looking for. Meredith is good. And Thackeray. I think you'd want Thackeray; he's a great writer."

45   The man took one of the books the boy handed him and opened it carefully, using only two fingers from each of his big hands. "This looks fine," he said.

"I'll write them down," the boy said. He took a pencil and a pocket memorandum from his coat pocket. "Brontës," he said, "Dickens, Meredith, Thackeray." He ran his hand along each of the sets as he read them off.

The big man narrowed his eyes. "I ought to take one more," he said. "These won't quite fill up the bookcase I got for them."

"Jane Austen," the boy said. "Your wife would be pleased with that."

"You read all these books?" the man asked.

50   "Most of them," the boy said.

The man was quiet for a minute and then he went on, "I never got much of a chance to read anything, going to work so early. I've got a lot to catch up on."

"You're going to have a fine time," the boy said.

"That book you had a while back," the man said. "What was that book?"

"It's aesthetics," the boy said. "About literature. It's very scarce. I've been trying to buy it for quite a while and haven't had the money."

55   "You go to college?" the man asked.

"Yes."

"Here's one I ought to read again," the man said. "Mark Twain. I read a couple of his books when I was a kid. But I guess I have enough to start on." He stood up.

The boy rose too, smiling. "You're going to have to do a lot of reading."

"I like to read," the man said. "I really like to read."

60   He started back down the aisles, going straight for Mr. Harris' desk. The boy turned off the lamps and followed, stopping to get his hat and gloves. When the big man reached Mr. Harris' desk he said to his wife, "That's sure a smart kid. He knows those books right and left."

"Did you pick out what you want?" his wife asked.

"The kid has a fine list for me." He turned to Mr. Harris and went on, "It's quite an experience seeing a kid like that liking books the way he does. When I was his age I was working for four or five years."

The boy came up with the slip of paper in his hand. "These ought to hold him for a while," he said to Mr. Harris.

Mr. Harris glanced at the list and nodded. "That Thackeray's a nice set of books," he said.

65   The boy had put his hat on and was standing at the foot of the stairs. "Hope you enjoy them," he said. "I'll be back for another look at that Empson, Mr. Harris."

"I'll try to keep it around for you," Mr. Harris said. "I can't promise to hold it, you know."

"I'll just count on it's being here," the boy said.

"Thanks, son," the big man called out as the boy started up the stairs. "Appreciate your helping me."

"That's all right," the boy said.

70   "He's sure a smart kid," the man said to Mr. Harris. "He's got a great chance, with an education like that."

"He's a nice young fellow," Mr. Harris said, "and he sure wants that book."

"You think he'll ever buy it?" the big man asked.

"I doubt it," Mr. Harris said. "If you'll just write down your name and address, I'll add these prices."

Mr. Harris began to note down the prices of the books, copying from the boy's neat list. After the big man had written his name and address, he stood for a minute drumming his fingers on the desk, and then he said, "Can I have another look at that book?"

75   "The Empson?" Mr. Harris said, looking up.

"The one the boy was so interested in." Mr. Harris reached around to the bookcase in back of him and took out the book. The big man held it delicately, as he had held the others, and he frowned as he turned the pages. Then he put the book down on Mr. Harris' desk.

"If he isn't going to buy it, will it be all right if I put this in with the rest?" he asked.

Mr. Harris looked up from his figures for a minute, and then he made the entry on his list. He added quickly, wrote down the total, and then pushed the paper across the desk to the big man. While the man checked over the figures Mr. Harris turned to the woman and said, "Your husband has bought a lot of very pleasant reading."

"I'm glad to hear it," she said. "We've been looking forward to it for a long time."

80   The big man counted out the money carefully, handing the bills to Mr. Harris. Mr. Harris put the money in the top drawer of his desk and said, "We can have these delivered to you by the end of the week, if that will be all right."

"Fine," the big man said. "Ready, Mother?"

The woman rose, and the big man stood back to let her go ahead of him. Mr. Harris followed, stopping near the stairs to say to the woman, "Watch the bottom step."

They started up the stairs and Mr. Harris stood watching them until they got to the turn. Then he switched off the dirty overhead lamp and went back to his desk.

Analyzing Rhetorical Choices

1. How is this story informed by the contrasts between the middle-aged man, the circumstances of his own youth, and the life of Mr. Clark, who is the youth in the story? How do these connections develop the plot?

2. The basement room is filled with "books standing silent in dim light"—Dickens, the Brontës, Meredith, Thackeray. The "loudest" book, or the one Mr. Clark is most interested in, becomes the symbol that attracts the customer. Why does the symbol become as important as the books by Dickens and the others?

3. Jackson seems to be making a point about the need for readers to participate in the meaning-making process. They must be active in order to resolve matters that could be considered ambiguous. What do you imagine happens after the purchase of the books? What details in the story lead you to this conclusion? Why does Jackson title the story, "Seven Types of Ambiguity"?

Writing About Issues and Contexts

1. The customer equates contemporary writing with "trash." He suggests that traditional works are superior. What current debates in the arts about the new versus the old interest you? If so, what are your opinions?

2. What does literacy mean to the middle-aged couple? How does their view reflect what they think about the culture they live in? What is the nature of the woman's involvement in this anecdote?

Strategies for Writers: Narration

1. Draft a narrative or an essay in which the use of anecdotes is the dominant approach. Your instructor is part of your audience, but try to set up as wide an audience as possible. You can exchange papers with your classmates. You can also find friends, family members, and other people outside the class who may agree to read your work. Perhaps you, your classmates, and instructor can develop a class magazine. Or maybe you can make a contribution to a school or community publication. Shirley Jackson published about fifteen stories in campus magazines while she was in college. Remember that people love good tales.

2. As you prepare your draft, think of your audience and the point you want to make. Consider the readers you envision reaching, and ask yourself which types of anecdotes would appeal to them and be appropriate for your purpose. You don't necessarily have to start with a consciously forceful argument. You may aim to be fairly subtle like Jackson. Or you may declare your intention like Dillard, who writes, explaining the chase, that "*The point was* that he had chased us passionately without giving up, and so he had caught us" (emphasis added). Wright and Orwell provide detailed analysis of the anecdotes they use. Bunn quotes other writers. Whichever way you proceed, remember that your writing will reflect some perspective and leave some impression on readers in any case.

3. Decide which viewpoint you favor—first, second, or third person—and whether you will employ singular or plural. Choose whether you want to use dialogue, and consider what purpose it would serve. Select the anecdotes you want to present and their sequence. It could be helpful to make an outline of events to guide you in writing your draft. You may even want to get feedback from others about your list of anecdotes before you begin writing.

4. Read and reread your draft. Share it with your instructor, classmates, and anyone else who is willing to assist. Ask readers to interpret your piece and comment on your tone, choice of language, and selection of incidents. Evaluate how closely their interpretations match your intentions, and then consider how, if necessary, you can make your point more clear. Do you need a

more direct approach? Do you need more or fewer anecdotes? Do you need different kinds of anecdotes? Have you chosen the best sequence?

5. Pay particular attention to dialogue and linguistic diversity if they are features of your text. Are you using too much dialogue? Are certain speech varieties framed, as in Amy Tan's essay? Or are language varieties mixed throughout the narrative, a technique Orwell uses? Solicit reactions related to these matters from your instructor, classmates, and others.

6. As you revise, remind yourself of the point you are trying to make or the impression you wish the reader to form. Does your work reflect your experiences and the influence of the wider culture in the ways you wish? Does it represent your best effort to leave a mark on the thinking of others?

Research and Writing Assignments

1. In "The Chase," Annie Dillard recounts childhood rituals as well as eventful moments related to childhood patterns of behavior. Write a narrative that traces your own involvement in community rituals as a child or even at present. In the course of your narrative, explain the reasons for your participation. As does Dillard, point out significant moments of self-awareness and what they have revealed to you about yourself and others.

2. Write a narrative that relates your own discovery of Austen Bunn. Perhaps your story will begin with your response to Richard Wright's "The Library Card." Detail your own process of consulting the Internet, the library, or other sources of information. Record your own reactions to some of Bunn's or Wright's work as well as to what critics have written about these authors.

3. The essays by Amy Tan and George Orwell are largely about the difficulties—but also the possibilities—of negotiating a world that extends beyond the environment in which one is raised. For Tan and her mother, it is the literary world and U.S. culture in general; for Orwell, it is colonial Burma. Write a narrative about your experiences in an unfamiliar cultural situation. Comment on whether your experiences were positive or negative and on what strategies for negotiating this unfamiliarity, if any, you found beneficial.

4. Using Elizabeth Alexander's "Narrative: Ali" as a model, compose a short biography of someone you value, and do so in first-person narrative verse. Be sure to research your subject thoroughly, but choose the most interesting and salient details to hold your audience's interest. Further, as Alexander does, try your best to capture the voice of your subject.

5. Write a short piece of fiction that illustrates a point or issue about which you are concerned. As Shirley Jackson does in "Seven Types of Ambiguity," try to dramatize your point as much as possible by using characters and dialogue.

3

Description

Part of your job as a writer involves getting your readers to focus on the scenes or portrayals you value the most. This helps you convey your impressions of objects, people, and situations. One way of achieving your goal is to provide information that appeals to readers' sensory apparatus—their abilities to see, hear, touch, taste, and smell. When you are pursuing conscious, calculated writing of this sort, you are engaged in *description*. Consider the first sentence of Richard Wright's depiction in *12 Million Black Voices* of a certain landscape:

> The land we till is beautiful, with red and black and brown clay, with fresh and hungry smells, with pine trees and palm trees, with rolling hills and swampy delta—an unbelievably fertile land, bounded on the north by the states of Pennsylvania, Ohio, Illinois, and Indiana, on the south by the Gulf of Mexico, on the west by the Mississippi River, and on the east by the Atlantic Ocean.

This is a more vivid and compelling opening than "We farm beautiful land that is hilly with a lot of trees in the South."

Wright continues to make strong appeals to our senses as he describes the yearly cycle:

> Our southern springs are filled with quiet noises and scenes of growth. Apple buds laugh into blossom. Honeysuckles creep up the sides of houses. Sunflowers nod in the hot fields. From mossy tree to mossy tree—oak, elm, willow, aspen, sycamore, dogwood, cedar, walnut, ash, and hickory—bright green leaves jut from a million branches to form an awning that tries to shield and shade the earth. Blue and pink kites of small boys sail in the windy air.

In the summer the magnolia trees fill the countryside with sweet scent for long miles. Days are slumberous, and the skies are high and thronged with clouds that ride fast. At midday the sun blazes and bleaches the soil. Butterflies flit through the heat; wasps sing their sharp, straight lines; birds fluff and flounce, piping in querulous joy. Nights are covered with canopies sometimes blue and sometimes black, canopies that sag low with ripe and nervous stars. The throaty boast of frogs momentarily drowns out the call and counter-call of crickets.

In autumn the land is afire with color. Red and brown leaves lift and flutter dryly, becoming entangled in the stiff grass and cornstalks. Cotton is picked and ginned; cane is crushed and its juice is simmered down into molasses; yams are grubbed out of the clay; hogs are slaughtered and cured in lingering smoke; corn is husked and ground into meal. At twilight the sky is full of wild geese winging ever southward, and bats jerk through the air. At night the winds blow free.

In winter the forests resound with the bite of steel axes eating into tall trees as men gather wood for the leaden days of cold. The guns of hunters snap and crack. Long days of rain come, and our swollen creeks rush to join a hundred rivers that wash across the land and make great harbors where they feed the gulf or the sea. Occasionally the rivers leap their banks and leave new thick layers of silt to enrich the earth, and then the look of the land is garish, bleak, suffused with a first-day stillness, strangeness, and awe.

Description can be an essential element in all writing. Wright's descriptive passage, for example, serves as prelude to an explanation about exploitative economic practices. Consider, too, Annie Dillard's comment in "The Chase" about the perils of making a tackle in football: "Either you brought him down or you hit the ground flat out on your chin, with your arms empty before you." Although description can be powerful when employed in parts of an essay, it can also be the dominant pattern, as in some of the essays in this chapter, including Meredith F. Small's "Captivated" and Barry Lopez's "The Stone Horse."

Whether description is the primary or secondary focus in an essay, the key to using it effectively is the appropriate selection of details to convey a *dominant impression*. Such an impression deepens your persuasive effort and helps you obtain identification with your perspective, something you are always seeking from your audience. If description is the primary method of your work, you should establish the dominant impression early and develop it consistently with well-chosen details. If the details are too numerous and minuscule, your audience is likely to view the writing as dull, perhaps irrelevant, and may not even read it. If you are describing the joys of using a computer, for instance, you would not want to get overly technical for a general audience, though providing a plethora of technical details might be perfect for other readers.

Description is frequently categorized as *objective* or *subjective*, but these classifications can be problematic. The first term is meant to signify that the writer is dispassionately describing the characteristics of an object, person, or situation without manifesting any personal bias. A laboratory report based on a chemistry experiment might serve as an example of objective writing. In subjective writing, authors deliberately attempt to make their feelings evident; an example might be an editorializing description of a river polluted by industrial waste. Most people, however, will not be restricted to writing technical reports or totally subjective statements. In fact, the distinction is often hard to maintain. Nearly all scientific reports omit some details, an act that reveals a viewpoint, and every now and then some scientist is caught falsifying data, an offense that certainly makes an objective-sounding document subjective. Likewise, even a ranting, one-sided, negative portrayal of someone could seem totally objective to a person who happens to share that author's perspective.

To organize your descriptive essay or passage, you might brainstorm a list of sensory details and then choose those that best make your point. Your thesis might be implied, as it often is in descriptive essays, or you might state it explicitly and then develop or illustrate it with your chosen details. You could present your material chronologically, as in a narrative. Alice Walker's "Am I Blue?" is an example of this. You could even organize a particular descriptive passage into a time sequence. Consider Barry Lopez's recollection of a series of sounds coming from a nearby village:

> The first sounds from this collection of ramshackle houses in a grove of cottonwoods were the distracted dawn voices of dogs. I heard them intermingled with the cries of a rooster. Later, the high-pitched voices of children calling out to each other came disembodied through the dry desert air. Now, a little after seven, I could hear someone practicing on the trumpet, the same rough phrases over and over. I suddenly remembered how as children we had tried to get the rhythm of a galloping horse with hands against our thighs, or by fluttering our tongues against the roofs of our mouths.
>
> After the trumpet, the impatient calls of adults summoning children. Sunday morning. Wood smoke hung like a lens in the trees. The

first car starts—a cold eight-cylinder engine, of Chrysler extraction perhaps, goosed to life, then throttled back to murmur through dual mufflers, the obligato music of a shade-tree mechanic. The rote bark of mongrel dogs at dawn, the jagged outcries of men and women, an engine coming to life. Like a thousand villages from West Virginia to Guadalajara.

Another aspect of descriptive writing involves the use of a spatial principle—bottom to top, left to right, foreground and background. Walker does this, for instance, in her opening paragraph, as she describes a meadow "that appeared to run from the end of our deck [foreground] straight into the mountains [background]." Notice how writer and filmmaker Gordon Parks, in a famous 1961 *Life* photo-essay called "Flavio's Home," uses the words *between, beneath, below, under,* and *down* in his description of a shack in Brazil:

> The shack was about six by ten feet. Its grimy walls were a patchwork of misshapen boards with large gaps between them, revealing other shacks below silted against the slopes. The floor, rotting under layers of grease and dirt, caught shafts of light slanting down through spaces in the roof. A large hole in the far corner served as a toilet. Beneath that hole was the sloping mountainside.

Regardless of the organizational scheme, you would do well to use orienting language, as Parks does, to keep your readers clear about the point you are developing. Richard Wright, as we have seen, chooses the seasons as an organizing device.

Good description often relies heavily on special figures of speech such as *personification, simile,* and *metaphor*. Personification is the attributing of human qualities to nonhuman entities—apple buds laughing into blossom, sunflowers nodding, rivers leaping their banks. Simile and metaphor are comparisons of two objects that are apparently dissimilar. A simile uses *like* or *as* to make the comparison. Commenting on outboard motors, E. B. White writes that "they whined about one's ears like mosquitoes." A metaphor makes the comparison directly, as does Harriet Tubman in her description of a Civil War battle she witnessed: "And then we saw the lightning, and that was the guns. And then we heard the thunder and that was the big guns. And then we heard the rain falling and that was the drops of blood falling. And when we came to get in the crops, it was dead men that we reaped."

Successful description entails the general use of vivid imagery, stretching for lively verbs, strong adjectives, and expressive adverbs.

Alice Walker does not depict Blue as merely "eating stalks." She writes that he was "munching the dried stalks half-heartedly." Julia Alvarez uses the phrase "ominous bell" in relation to the signal for an air-raid drill.

Description is a powerful tool for relating ideas and shaping perceptions—two of your primary goals as a writer. These are also goals that you, as a human, are abundantly equipped to perform. You are more sophisticated in capturing detail than any camera invented. Barring disability, you can see and hear from any angle—and touch, taste, smell, and think.

Approaches to Writing Descriptive Essays

Most writers would agree that design is in the details. That is, writers choose which details to include and which to exclude based on their purpose, what they want to achieve, what is important to them and what they anticipate will be important to their audience. Details, examples, descriptive elements are not just added to fill up the page. They must be "meaning-full," that is, must convey significance to the entire work. Here, for example, is Gordon Parks describing a Brazilian shantytown:

> Catacumba was the name of the favela where I found Flavio da Silva. It was wickedly hot. The noon sun baked the mud-rot of the wet mountainside. Garbage and human excrement clogged the open sewers snaking down the slopes. José Gallo, a *Life* reporter, and I rested in the shade of a jacaranda tree halfway up Rio de Janeiro's most infamous deathtrap. Below and above us were a maze of shacks, but in the distance alongside the beach stood the gleaming white homes of the rich.

Parks's paragraph is worth considering in some detail (no pun intended). He uses a specific place name (Catacumba) and a Spanish word (favela) to impart his expert knowledge of this slum, revealing that he knows his facts and possesses authority as a reporter. His choice of verbs (baked, clogged), nouns (favela, mud-rot, human excrement, jacaranda tree, deathtrap), and adverbs and adjectives (wickedly hot, infamous, gleaming white) contribute immeasurably to his sense of outrage over Flavio's horrific living conditions. He uses a very short but strongly impressionistic second sentence to emphasize the heat, following that up with the resulting effect, the baking of the mud-rot on the wet mountainside. He ends this paragraph by contrasting the "maze of shacks" with the "gleaming white homes of the rich." These details and choices are not random. They express in a careful and calculated way the primary perspectives and point of view that Parks wants to convey to his readers.

Like all good writers, you must also choose specific ways of describing your subject, of providing sensory details and powerful visual images to communicate your meaning. How do you know which details to include and which to exclude? As with most fundamental questions related to teaching writing, there is no simple answer. Details should be added when they further the reader's understanding of a subject, or make an important contribution to the tone and texture of the essay. They should be added as a way of bringing your subject to life and vividly rendering it so that the reader remembers your essay, not just the subject but the way it feels—its mood, emotional valence, and intellectual impact. Remember: You are much better off with too many details than too few. If your essay gets bogged down with too many specific descriptions, it is much easier to remove them than it is to try to add more detail later, especially if your memory of your subject is fading.

As you write, include those descriptive elements that have remained visually vibrant to you. If, for example, you are writing about the beauty and impact of a neighborhood flower garden that you admire, name the flowers and describe their colors. If insects—bees, wasps, or butterflies—were present, describe what they were doing and what they looked like. Describe the sounds and smells of the garden, as well as the variegated shapes and textures of the leaves, petals, and stems. Provide some history of the plantings if you know any, such as whether the flowers are annuals or perennials, whether the flowers are native or imported. Appeal as much as possible to all five senses (seeing, hearing, tasting, smelling, touching). Try to evoke with your words the same experience you had.

If all this seems difficult, it is. Good descriptive essays are challenging. Writers spend much of their time trying to recreate experience in words through description that is fresh, sharply focused, and of importance to the subject. Your goal in writing a descriptive essay is similar to that of the great nineteenth-century writer Joseph Conrad, author of *Lord Jim, Heart of Darkness*, and many other great works of literature. As Conrad put it, "My task, which I am trying to achieve, is—by the power of the written word—to make you hear, to make you feel. It is, before all, to make you see. That—and no more. And it is everything." To make your reader hear, feel, and above all to see. Conrad's statement points the way toward writing descriptive essays.

Four Grammatical Approaches to Description

Underlying language use in English are certain fundamental principles that we call grammar. Grammar is commonly understood as a set of principles (*rules* is really not the right term) that govern how utterances are formed, how meaning gets expressed. One such principle of grammar, for example, is that meaning gets communicated when the speaker and the listener share an understanding of a noun (subject) that is linked to a verb (predicate): "My notebook (subject) fell (predicate) on the floor" or "I (subject) finally completed (predicate) my calculus problems this morning." In these examples, the primary structure is "notebook-fell" and "I-completed," although it is important to note that many grammarians consider what typically follows the verb to be part of the predicate.

Rather than get into technical explanations of grammar, however, we want to offer a few specific grammatical structures that can be of great use to writers as they develop descriptions in their essays. Of course, in order to use these structures, you need to possess some knowledge of traditional grammar. For example, you need to know the difference between a phrase and a clause, a noun and a verb, a subject and a predicate. Beyond that, you need to know how to form present and past participles from verbs in order to be comfortable composing participial and absolute phrases. Similarly you need to be able to consciously write adjectival or adverbial phrases and clauses, especially since adjectival and adverbial modifiers are often used to elaborate on subjects that you are writing about. If such grammatical terms raise the hair on the back of your neck in fear, remember that you already know and use these forms intuitively. What we encourage you to do is to use them more consciously as ways to add descriptive power to your essays. As you write, experiment with these grammatical forms, even if the experimentation at first feels awkward and uncomfortable. Writing improvement demands that you take risks, try new approaches, experiment with new forms and possibilities—and that means that you will have to make mistakes in order to improve.

1. Participles and participial phrases. A participle is the form of a verb ending with either *-ing* or a past-tense marker (most commonly *-ed*). *Looking* and *looked* are the present and past participles of the verb *look*. *Sleeping* and *slept* are the present and past participles of the verb *sleep*. It helps to know what participles are and how to create them when writing descriptive passages, because they allow you to use

participial phrases to add descriptive elements to your essay. Here, for example, is the opening of Sherman Alexie's "Father Coming Home,"

> Father coming home from work. Me, waiting on the front steps, watching him walk slowly and carefully, like half of a real Indian. The other half stumbling, carrying the black metal lunch box with maybe half a sandwich, maybe the last drink of good coffee out of the thermos, maybe the last bite of a dream.

Alexie is composing this essay in what we normally call sentence fragments, that is, sentences that lack a traditional subject-predicate relationship. Instead, he uses a present participial phrase in the first sentence, which more or less serves as a stand-in place for a regular verb. And in the rest of the passage, he uses four more participles or participial phrases, which are underlined below:

> Father <u>coming home from work</u>. Me, <u>waiting on the front steps,</u> <u>watching him walk slowly and carefully,</u> like half of a real Indian. The other half <u>stumbling,</u> <u>carrying the black metal lunch box with maybe</u> <u>half a sandwich,</u> maybe the last drink of good coffee out of the thermos, maybe the last bite of a dream.

Were you to write such sentences, you might well be chastised for using sentence fragments. Being a professional writer who has earned the trust of his readers, Alexie can employ this usage, and he does so to achieve some specific effects, which are worth discussing when you analyze this essay. Your analysis might want to compare the difference in tone and implication, for example, between "Father is coming home from work" and "Father coming home from work."

Participial phrases can add a great deal of descriptive power to essays. Here are some examples from an essay about one student's experience with nature on campus. The descriptive participles and participial phrases are underlined:

> <u>Enjoying one of the last glorious days of fall</u>, Emily decided to walk through Downer Woods. Her classes over, she had an hour before lunch. <u>Hurrying toward the north end of campus</u>, Emily pulled her hat up and her collar down, <u>making sure she would</u> not get chilled. Much as she loved the outdoors, Emily hated to be cold. <u>Rounding the corner of the health center</u>, she spied Downer Woods in the distance. As she had anticipated, the trees were changing colors, the sugar maples gorgeous in their reds and yellows. <u>Hurrying now</u>, Emily could feel her spirits starting to soar. The woods were ablaze with reds and oranges, <u>reminding her of the hillsides near her home</u>.

Notice the descriptive power that is added to this paragraph by the use of participles and participial phrases.

2. Other adjective phrases (and clauses). A simple definition of an adjective is that it is a word that modifies or adds descriptive detail to nouns and pronouns. If you were to say, "Ellen bought a new car," the word *new* would be an adjective modifying *car*. If someone else responded with, "Yes, and it is one expensive luxury item," s/he would be using two adjectives, *expensive* and *luxury*. Adjectives should not be poured into essays like salt into soup; they should be added carefully and with telling effect. Better yet, they can be added not just as individual words but rather as phrases and clauses when you need to create some descriptive power. Participial phrases are one form of adjective phrase (see section 1, above). Another is a phrase or clause that begins with an adjective, such as: "Happy to be back home, my mood changed quickly when I realized that I had two more final exams on Wednesday" or "Uncertain whether he should date a woman that had her own car and lived in a penthouse, Glen decided to take a chance and ask Ellen to go to the movies." Those opening adjectival modifiers (a phrase and a clause) present concentrated information that slides easily into the main clause of the sentence. The following passage makes good use of adjective phrases and clauses:

> I spent three days studying for my sociology final. Afraid that I would earn a C in the course, I spent a lot of time going over my class notes. Sketchy though they were, they helped guide me toward what the professor had emphasized during his lectures. The textbook, thick and imposing, intimidated me as it had always done. Bracing myself, I reviewed all the key chapters, underlining key passages and concepts. By the time the exam rolled around, I was stoked. I could have taken that exam blindfolded. Confident and certain about my grade, you can imagine my surprise when I received a final grade of C-. I discovered later that the professor based most of the exam on his lecture notes, not the assigned reading.

3. Adverbial phrases and clauses. Adverbs, many of which end in *-ly*, are words that modify verbs, adjectives, and other adverbs. In a sentence like, "Carol quickly completed her singing lessons," the word *quickly* is an adverb that modifies the verb *completed*. In a more complex sentence such as, "When I was done, my boss informed me that he was very happy with my efforts," the opening "When I was done" is an adverbial clause as is the word *very* and the

prepositional phrase "with my efforts." Without some significant amount of knowledge, you are not likely always to be able to identify adverbial phrases and clauses, but you already know how to create them as part of your spoken and written abilities. Adverbial structures often answer the questions "where?" or "when?" and they often elaborate or intensify adjectives and adjective phrases and clauses. In the following passage, adverbial words, phrases, and clauses are underlined:

> Whenever I visit my aunt and uncle, they always take me out to dinner to a four-star restaurant. It is almost always a fabulous experience. Typically, they drive two hours from their farm to Chicago, although occasionally they will make a longer trip to Indianapolis or St. Louis. They insist that I wear a suit and tie, and they invariably select an exotic cuisine for me to try. No matter what kind of food we eat, I'm invariably astounded at the quality of the food and the service.

As is clear from this example, adverbial structures occur frequently in writing, especially adverbial phrases and clauses. We encourage you to experiment with such structures in your own descriptive writing.

4. Absolute phrases. Absolute phrases are often unfamiliar to writers until they realize that they have been using them intuitively for a long time. What makes them brilliant additions to a writer's descriptive repertoire is that they have the content impact of a sentence but the grammatical structure of a phrase, so they can be added on to an independent clause without creating the dreaded run-on. What is an absolute phrase? From a grammatical standpoint, an absolute is a noun/pronoun modified by an adjectival phrase, usually a participial phrase. Sometimes absolute phrases begin with the preposition *with*, which makes them look like prepositional phrases, but if what follows that introductory *with* is a noun/pronoun modified by an adjectival phrase, it is an absolute. In the sentence below, we have underlined the three absolute phrases, all of which modify the independent clause that comprises the basic core of the sentence:

> Returning from her nine-month tour of duty, Darlene was delighted to be back home, her eyes brimming with tears as she greeted her husband and children, her mother and father standing on the porch waving gaily, the family mutt yelping repeatedly while running madly in circles.

The absolute phrases in this sentence contribute substantial content, as does the opening participial phrase. If this sentence were to be written without the absolutes, it might read something like the following:

> Returning from her nine-month tour of duty, Darlene was delighted to be back home. Her eyes brimmed with tears as she greeted her husband and children. Her mother and father stood on the porch waving gaily. Meanwhile, the family mutt yelped repeatedly while running madly in circles.

There is nothing terribly wrong with this four-sentence version except that it lacks the stylistic sophistication of the first version. The sentences are shorter, and it lacks smooth transition and overall coherence. We could try to combine the last two sentences into "Her mother and father stood on the porch waving gaily, as the family mutt yelped repeatedly while running madly in circles" but the last part of this sentence feels superfluous, as if the writer is trying to fill space, and the description of the mutt's activity doesn't have any direct connection to the parents' actions.

Absolutes take practice to create. One danger is that instead of creating absolutes, you might end up creating run-on and fused sentences, or odd descriptive fragments, with chunks of words hanging off the ends of sentences. (Note that the preceding sentence ends with an absolute phrase that begins with *with*.) One way to gain confidence in creating absolutes (as with any grammatical modification) is to examine some examples and then imitate them. Here are a few examples to start you off; we have underlined the absolute phrases so that you can identify them easily:

> The snake slid through the grass, <u>its tongue flicking in and out, its body as brown as the earth beneath our feet.</u>
>
> My sister scored the winning goal, <u>her feet moving like pistons, her head snapping forward to send the ball into the net, her teammates screaming with delight.</u>
>
> Civil war may never actually be inevitable although events can sometimes overtake common sense, <u>with both sides losing sight of the common good.</u>
>
> <u>With his parents gone to Europe, his sister away at medical school, and his friends attending colleges in distance cities,</u> Daniel felt isolated but free, <u>his decisions about the farm now entirely his own.</u>

One possible strategy is to write your descriptive essay in a simple, unadorned, direct way and then go back to it at the revision stage, adding modifying phrases and clauses whenever you have a sense that more descriptive elements are needed. If you compose in this way, try adding absolute phrases in this later stage. They can contribute substantially to your descriptive power.

A professor of anthropology at Cornell University, **Meredith F. Small** *has been a commentator on National Public Radio and writes frequently for* Discover, New Scientist, Scientific American, *and* Natural History. *She has written five books, including* What's Love Got to Do with It: The Evolution of Human Mating *(1996) and* Our Babies, Ourselves: How Biology and Culture Shape the Way We Parent *(1999). The following article was first published in the magazine* Natural History *in 2003.*

Meredith F. Small

Captivated

I'm sitting on a bench in New York City's Central Park, waiting for the zoo to open. I have spent years observing macaque monkeys in the field, but these days I only teach and write about what they do, and I miss them. So whenever I'm in Manhattan, I hang out here with the snow monkeys *(Macaca fuscata).*

I've been visiting this troop for years. I have seen them in sunshine and snow; stood in the rain and watched them lick drops of wetness off their fur; held short business meetings in front of their exhibit; forced friends to meet me here. Unbeknownst to them, these furry gray monkeys from Japan have become my primate touchstone.

On this visit it's clear and sunny, and through the entrance gates I see the macaques jumping around their island exhibit. A path of rocks breaks the surface of the retaining pond that surrounds their enclosure, and a young female hops from one to another, leapfrogging over her troopmates as she goes.

Finally the gates open, and as I approach the group, my professional observing skills click in. By the time I reach them, my training as an observer—and that touch of magic I always feel in the presence of monkeys—has locked out the world; all that matters is the movement of these animals.

5   Today I count nine adults, one juvenile, and no babies. I know that fall is breeding season, and the females are signaling their fertility with red behinds. To my right a status interaction is unfolding—a female turns her rear to another female, indicating her lower position. I lean across the rail and get into the Zen of figuring out what these monkeys already know about each other—who is related to whom, how their rank is doled out, who will mate next.

My primatological reverie is interrupted by a crowd of visitors. I hear one woman call a male "she," and I'm compelled to correct her. "It's the shape of his face," I tell her, "and his size—and those bright red testicles." But I should know better than to be so patronizing, such a know-it-all. Several years ago, on one frozen January day, I asked some of the zoo's wild-animal keepers why the snow monkeys were indoors. After all, I told them, these monkeys are accustomed to crawling through snowdrifts in their native Japan. "If the pond froze over," they patiently responded, "the monkeys would simply walk out of the zoo." Humbled, I went to see the polar bear.

When I have the monkeys to myself again, I walk up the hill behind the exhibit and lean over the granite wall overlooking their enclosure, focusing on a pair of females. One is stretched out on a rock, arms and legs splayed in relaxation. Her eyelids droop. She is at peace. The other methodically moves a hand across her partner's belly, separating each strand of hair, gently touching each exposed patch of skin. Monkeys have done this to me, sitting on my shoulders with their handlike feet pressed against my neck, picking through my hair. I know it feels like heaven.

Concentrating on the grooming females, I stretch my own arms across the wall and feel the reflected warmth of the sun seep up from the granite slab. I, too, let my eyelids droop in contentment. For a few precious minutes I pretend that I have done nothing for the past few months but watch this group, that we know each other intimately, observer and observed. Monkey noises, their barks and calls, fill my ears. The familiar, musty odor of monkey fur at close quarters fills my nostrils.

I am, once again, renewed.

Analyzing Rhetorical Choices

1. Small uses phrases like "lick drops of wetness off their fur" and "leapfrogging over her troopmates as she goes" to depict vividly the monkeys that she observes. She also conveys her impressions by using location, number, and direction, as well as sensory appeals to sound, smell, touch, and sight. Find other examples of vivid language and discuss how they add to the quality of the essay.

2. Small suggests her mood with expressions such as "feels like heaven" and "primatological reverie." How convincing is this to you as description?

Writing About Issues and Contexts

1. Can you identify with the writer's passion for her particular subject? Do you possess a similar passion regarding a hobby of your own?

2. The essay is somewhat ironic. Professor Small can be captivated by snow monkeys in Central Park only because they have been captured and held captive for her study and enjoyment. What is your opinion about the job that zoos do in exhibiting captive animals?

Fiction writer, poet, and essayist **Alice Walker** *(1944–) was born in Eatonton, Georgia. A graduate of Sarah Lawrence College, she currently resides in Mendocino, California. She has received several awards for her writing.* Her books include the novels The Third Life of Grange Copeland *(1970);* Meridian *(1976);* The Color Purple *(1982), which won the Pulitzer Prize; and* By the Light of My Father's Smile *(1998). Her poetry collections include* Her Blue Body Everything We Know: Earthling Poems *(1990). Among her essay volumes are* In Search of Our Mothers' Gardens *(1983) and* Living by the Word *(1988), from which the following essay is taken.*

Alice Walker

Am I Blue?

"Ain't these tears in these eyes tellin' you?"

For about three years my companion and I rented a small house in the country that stood on the edge of a large meadow that appeared to run from the end of our deck straight into the mountains. The mountains, however, were quite far away, and between us and them there was, in fact, a town. It was one of the many pleasant aspects of the house that you never really were aware of this.

It was a house of many windows, low, wide, nearly floor to ceiling in the living room, which faced the meadow, and it was from one of these that I first saw our closest neighbor, a large white horse, cropping grass, flipping its mane, and ambling about—not over the entire meadow, which stretched well out of sight of the house, but over the five or so fenced-in acres that were next to the twenty-odd that we had rented. I soon learned that the horse, whose name was Blue, belonged to a man who lived in another town, but was boarded by our neighbors next door. Occasionally, one of the children, usually a stocky teen-ager, but sometimes a much younger girl or boy, could be seen riding Blue. They would appear in the meadow, climb up on his back, ride furiously for ten or fifteen minutes, then get off, slap Blue on the flanks, and not be seen again for a month or more.

There were many apple trees in our yard, and one by the fence that Blue could almost reach. We were soon in the habit of feeding him apples, which he relished, especially because by the middle of summer the meadow grasses—so green and succulent since January—had dried out from lack of rain, and Blue stumbled about munching the dried stalks half-heartedly. Sometimes he would stand very still just by the apple tree, and when one of us came out he would whinny, snort loudly, or stamp the ground. This meant, of course: I want an apple.

It was quite wonderful to pick a few apples, or collect those that had fallen to the ground overnight, and patiently hold them, one by one, up to his large, toothy mouth. I remained as thrilled as a child by his flexible dark lips, huge, cubelike teeth that crunched the apples, core and all, with such finality, and his high, broad-breasted *enormity;* beside which, I felt small indeed. When I was a child, I used to ride horses, and was especially friendly with one named Nan until the day I was riding and my brother deliberately spooked her and I was thrown, head first, against the trunk of a tree. When I came to, I was in bed and my mother was bending worriedly over me; we silently agreed that perhaps horseback riding was not the safest sport for me. Since then I have walked, and prefer walking to horseback riding—but I had forgotten the depth of feeling one could see in horses' eyes.

5　I was therefore unprepared for the expression in Blue's. Blue was lonely. Blue was horribly lonely and bored. I was not shocked that this should be the case; five acres to tramp by yourself, endlessly, even in the most beautiful of meadows—and his was—cannot provide many interesting events, and once rainy season turned to dry that was about it. No, I was shocked that I had forgotten that human animals and nonhuman animals can communicate quite well; if we are brought up around animals as children we take this for granted. By the time we are adults we no longer remember. However, the animals have not changed. They are in fact *completed* creations (at least they seem to be, so much more than we) who are not likely *to* change; it is their nature to express themselves. What else are they going to express? And they do. And, generally speaking, they are ignored.

After giving Blue the apples, I would wander back to the house, aware that he was observing me. Were more apples not forthcoming then? Was that to be his sole entertainment for the day? My partner's small son had decided he wanted to learn how to piece a quilt; we worked in silence on our respective squares as I thought . . .

Well, about slavery: about white children, who were raised by black people, who knew their first all-accepting love from black women, and then, when they were twelve or so, were told they must "forget" the deep levels of communication between themselves and "mammy" that they knew. Later they would be able to relate quite calmly, "My old mammy was sold to another good family." "My old mammy was ___ ___." Fill in the blank. Many more years later a white woman would say: "I can't understand these Negroes, these blacks. What do they want? They're so different from us."

And about the Indians, considered to be "like animals" by the "settlers" (a very benign euphemism for what they actually were), who did not understand their description as a compliment.

And about the thousands of American men who marry Japanese, Korean, Filipina, and other non-English-speaking women and of how happy they report they are, "*blissfully*," until their brides learn to speak English, at which point the marriages tend to fall apart. What then did the men see, when they looked into the eyes of the women they married, before they could speak English? Apparently only their own reflections.

10   I thought of society's impatience with the young. "Why are they playing the music so loud?" Perhaps the children have listened to much of the music of oppressed people their parents danced to before they were born, with its passionate but soft cries for acceptance and love, and they have wondered why their parents failed to hear.

I do not know how long Blue had inhabited his five beautiful, boring acres before we moved into our house; a year after we had arrived—and had also traveled to other valleys, other cities, other worlds—he was still there.

But then, in our second year at the house, something happened in Blue's life. One morning, looking out the window at the fog that lay like a ribbon over the meadow, I saw another horse, a brown one, at the other end of Blue's field. Blue appeared to be afraid of it, and for several days made no attempt to go near. We went away for a week. When we returned, Blue had decided to make friends and the two horses ambled or galloped along together, and Blue did not come nearly as often to the fence underneath the apple tree.

When he did, bringing his new friend with him, there was a different look in his eyes. A look of independence, of self-possession, of inalienable *horse*ness. His friend eventually became pregnant. For months and months there was, it seemed to me, a mutual feeling between me and the horses of justice, of peace. I fed apples to them both. The look in Blue's eyes was one of unabashed "this is *it*ness."

It did not, however, last forever. One day, after a visit to the city, I went out to give Blue some apples. He stood waiting, or so I thought, though not beneath the tree. When I shook the tree and jumped back from the shower of apples, he made no move. I carried some over to him. He managed to half-crunch one. The rest he let fall to the ground. I dreaded looking into his eyes—because I had of course noticed that Brown, his partner, had gone—but I did look. If I had been born into slavery, and my partner had been sold or killed, my eyes would have looked like that. The children next door explained that Blue's partner had been "put with him" (the same expression that old people used, I had noticed, when speaking of an ancestor during slavery who had been impregnated by her owner) so that they could mate and she conceive. Since that was accomplished, she had been taken back by her owner, who lived somewhere else.

15   Will she be back? I asked.

They didn't know.

Blue was like a crazed person. Blue *was*, to me, a crazed person. He galloped furiously, as if he were being ridden, around and around his five beautiful acres. He whinnied until he couldn't. He tore at the ground with his hooves. He butted himself against his single shade tree. He looked always and always toward the road down which his partner had gone. And then, occasionally, when he came up for apples, or I took apples to him, he looked at me. It was a look so piercing, so full of grief, a look so *human*, I almost laughed (I felt too sad to cry) to think there are people who do not know that animals suffer. People like me who have forgotten, and daily forget, all that animals try to tell us. "Everything you do to us will happen to you; we are your teachers, as you are ours. We are one lesson" is essentially it, I think. There are those who never once have even considered animals' rights: those who have been taught that animals actually want to be used and abused by us, as small children "love" to be frightened, or women "love" to be mutilated and raped. . . . They are the great-grandchildren of those who honestly thought, because someone taught them this: "Women can't think," and "niggers can't faint." But most disturbing of all, in Blue's large brown eyes was a new look, more painful than the look of despair: the look of disgust with human beings, with life; the look of hatred. And it was odd what the look of hatred did. It gave him, for the first time, the look of a beast. And what that meant was that he had put up a barrier within to protect himself from further violence; all the apples in the world wouldn't change that fact.

And so Blue remained, a beautiful part of our landscape, very peaceful to look at from the window, white against the grass. Once a friend came to visit and said, looking out on the soothing view: "And it *would* have to be a *white* horse; the very image of freedom." And I thought, yes, the animals are forced to become for us merely "images" of what they once so beautifully expressed. And we are used to drinking milk from containers showing "contented" cows, whose real lives we want to hear nothing about, eating eggs and drumsticks from "happy" hens, and munching hamburgers advertised by bulls of integrity who seem to command their fate.

As we talked of freedom and justice one day for all, we sat down to steaks. I am eating misery, I thought, as I took the first bite. And spit it out.

Analyzing Rhetorical Choices

1. Which details or phrases allow you to picture Blue's physical appearance and activities in your mind's eye?
2. Which details or phrases reveal the horse's "inner state"?
3. Is Blue a symbol, and if so, of what?

Writing About Issues and Contexts

1. How do you respond to Walker's suggestion that nonhuman animals are more *completed* than we are?
2. What do you think of Walker's references to the other social issues she mentions? Are her observations and analyses persuasive?
3. What is your stance on animal rights and your response to Walker's reaction at the end of the essay?

Born in New York City, **Julia Alvarez** (1950–) was moved to the Dominican Republic shortly thereafter. She returned in 1960. She attended boarding schools and high school, going on to earn a bachelor's degree from Middlebury College and a master's degree from Syracuse University. She is currently a writer-in-residence at Middlebury College. Her titles include How the Garcia Girls Lost Their Accents (1990), In the Time of the Butterflies (1994), ¡Yo! (1997), and the poetry volumes Homecoming (1984) and The Other Side/El Otro Lado (1995). The following story is from How the Garcia Girls Lost Their Accents.

Julia Alvarez

Snow

Yolanda

Our first year in New York we rented a small apartment with a Catholic school nearby, taught by the Sisters of Charity, hefty women in long black gowns and bonnets that made them look peculiar, like dolls in mourning. I liked them a lot, especially my grandmotherly fourth grade teacher, Sister Zoe. I had a lovely name, she said, and she had me teach the whole class how to pronounce it. *Yo-lan-da.* As the only immigrant in my class, I was put in a special seat in the first row by the window, apart from the other children so that Sister Zoe could tutor me without disturbing them. Slowly, she enunciated the new words I was to repeat: *laundromat, corn flakes, subway, snow.*

Soon I picked up enough English to understand holocaust was in the air. Sister Zoe explained to a wide-eyed classroom what was happening in Cuba. Russian missiles were being assembled, trained supposedly on New York City. President Kennedy, looking worried too, was on the television at home, explaining we might have to go to war against the Communists. At school, we had air-raid drills: an ominous bell would go off and we'd file into the hall, fall to the floor, cover our heads with our coats, and imagine our hair falling out, the bones in our arms going soft. At home, Mami and my sisters and I said a rosary for world peace. I heard new vocabulary: *nuclear bomb, radioactive fallout, bomb shelter.* Sister Zoe explained how it would happen. She drew a picture of a mushroom on the blackboard and dotted a flurry of chalkmarks for the dusty fallout that would kill us all.

The months grew cold, November, December. It was dark when I got up in the morning, frosty when I followed my breath to school. One morning as I sat at my desk daydreaming out the window, I saw dots in the air like the ones Sister Zoe had drawn—random at first, then lots and lots. I shrieked, "Bomb! Bomb!" Sister Zoe jerked around, her full black skirt ballooning as she hurried to my side. A few girls began to cry.

But then Sister Zoe's shocked look faded. "Why, Yolanda dear, that's snow!" She laughed. "Snow."

5   "Snow," I repeated. I looked out the window warily. All my life I had heard about the white crystals that fell out of American skies in the winter. From my desk I watched the fine powder dust the sidewalk and parked cars below. Each flake was different, Sister Zoe had said, like a person, irreplaceable and beautiful.

Analyzing Rhetorical Choices

1. Locate phrases in addition to "like dolls in mourning" and "wide-eyed classroom" that help you imagine the setting that Alvarez portrays. How do they contribute to your understanding?

2. Alvarez closes by comparing snowflakes to individual people. What do you feel is the major point of her piece?

Writing About Issues and Contexts

1. What do you think of the classroom arrangement whereby the narrator sat apart to receive individual tutoring?

2. How does the Cold War climate of the early 1960s, as depicted by the author, compare and contrast to your sense of the international political arena today?

*Born in Mount Vernon, New York, **Elwyn Brooks White** (1899–1985) graduated from Cornell University in 1921. He enjoyed longtime associations with both* The New Yorker *and* Harper's Magazine. *A prolific essayist, his works have been collected in* One Man's Meat *(1942), where the following selection appeared,* The Points of My Compass *(1962), the* E. B. White Reader *(1966), and* Writings from *The New Yorker, 1925–1976 (1990). White also authored the children's classics* Stuart Little *(1945) and* Charlotte's Web *(1952).*

E. B. White

Once More to the Lake

One summer, along about 1904, my father rented a camp on a lake in Maine and took us all there for the month of August. We all got ringworm from some kittens and had to rub Pond's Extract on our arms and legs night and morning, and my father rolled over in a canoe with all his clothes on; but outside of that the vacation was a success and from then on none of us ever thought there was any place in the world like that lake in Maine. We returned summer after summer—always on August 1st for one month. I have since become a salt-water man, but sometimes in summer there are days when the restlessness of the tides and the fearful cold of the sea water and the incessant wind which blows across the afternoon and into the evening make me wish for the placidity of a lake in the woods. A few weeks ago this feeling got so strong I bought myself a couple of bass hooks and a spinner and returned to the lake where we used to go, for a week's fishing and to revisit old haunts.

I took along my son, who had never had any fresh water up his nose and who had seen lily pads only from train windows. On the journey over to the lake I began to wonder what it would be like. I wondered how time would have marred this unique, this holy spot— the coves and streams, the hills that the sun set behind, the camps and the paths behind the camps. I was sure that the tarred road would have found it out and I wondered in what other ways it would be desolated. It is strange how much you can remember about places like that once you allow your mind to return into the grooves which lead back. You remember one thing, and that suddenly reminds you of another thing. I guess I remembered clearest of all the early mornings, when the lake was cool and motionless, remembered how the bedroom smelled of the lumber it was made of and the wet woods whose scent entered through the screen. The partitions in the camp were thin and did not extend clear to the top of the rooms, and as I was always the first up I would dress softly so as not to wake the others, and sneak out into the sweet outdoors and start out in the canoe, keeping close along the shore in the long shadows of the pines. I remembered being very careful never to rub my paddle against the gunwale for fear of disturbing the stillness of the cathedral.

The lake had never been what you would call a wild lake. There were cottages sprinkled around the shores, and it was in farming country although the shores of the lake were quite heavily wooded. Some of the cottages were owned by nearby farmers, and you would live at the shore and eat your meals at the farmhouse. That's what our family did. But although it wasn't wild, it was a fairly large and undisturbed lake and there were places in it which, to a child at least, seemed infinitely remote and primeval.

I was right about the tar: it led to within half a mile of the shore. But when I got back there, with my boy, and we settled into a camp near a farmhouse and into the kind of summertime I had known, I could tell that it was going to be pretty much the same as it had been before—I knew it, lying in bed the first morning, smelling the bedroom, and hearing the boy sneak quietly out and go off along the shore in a boat. I began to sustain the illusion that he was I, and therefore, by simple transposition, that I was my father. This sensation persisted, kept cropping up all the time we were there. It was not an entirely new feeling, but in this setting it grew much stronger. I seemed to be living a dual existence. I would be in the middle of some simple act, I would be picking up a bait box or laying down a table fork, or I would be saying something, and suddenly it would be not I but my father who was saying the words or making the gesture. It gave me a creepy sensation.

5   We went fishing the first morning. I felt the same damp moss covering the worms in the bait can, and saw the dragonfly alight on the tip of my rod as it hovered a few inches from the surface of the water. It was the arrival of this fly that convinced me beyond any doubt that everything was as it always had been, that the years were a mirage and there had been no years. The small waves were the same, chucking the rowboat under the chin as we fished at anchor, and the boat was the same boat, the same color green and the ribs broken in the same places, and under the floor-boards the same freshwater leavings

and débris—the dead helgramite, the wisps of moss, the rusty discarded fishhook, the dried blood from yesterday's catch. We stared
silently at the tips of our rods, at the dragonflies that came and went.
I lowered the tip of mine into the water, tentatively, pensively dislodg-
ing the fly, which darted two feet away, poised, darted two feet back,
and came to rest again a little farther up the rod. There had been no
years between the ducking of this dragonfly and the other one—the
one that was part of memory. I looked at the boy, who was silently
watching his fly, and it was my hands that held his rod, my eyes
watching. I felt dizzy and didn't know which rod I was at the end of.

We caught two bass, hauling them in briskly as though they were
mackerel, pulling them over the side of the boat in a businesslike
manner without any landing net, and stunning them with a blow on
the back of the head. When we got back for a swim before lunch, the
lake was exactly where we had left it, the same number of inches from
the dock, and there was only the merest suggestion of a breeze. This
seemed an utterly enchanted sea, this lake you could leave to its own
devices for a few hours and come back to, and find that it had not
stirred, this constant and trustworthy body of water. In the shallows,
the dark, water-soaked sticks and twigs, smooth and old, were undulating in clusters on the bottom against the clean ribbed sand, and the
track of the mussel was plain. A school of minnows swam by, each
minnow with its small individual shadow, doubling the attendance, so
clear and sharp in the sunlight. Some of the other campers were in
swimming, along the shore, one of them with a cake of soap, and the
water felt thin and clear and unsubstantial. Over the years there had
been this person with the cake of soap, this cultist, and here he was.
There had been no years.

Up to the farmhouse to dinner through the teeming, dusty field,
the road under our sneakers was only a two-track road. The middle
track was missing, the one with the marks of the hooves and the
splotches of dried, flaky manure. There had always been three tracks
to choose from in choosing which track to walk in; now the choice
was narrowed down to two. For a moment I missed terribly the middle alternative. But the way led past the tennis court, and something
about the way it lay there in the sun reassured me; the tape had loos-
ened along the backline, the alleys were green with plantains and
other weeds, and the net (installed in June and removed in September)
sagged in the dry noon, and the whole place steamed with midday
heat and hunger and emptiness. There was a choice of pie for dessert,
and one was blueberry and one was apple, and the waitresses were

the same country girls, there having been no passage of time, only the illusion of it as in a dropped curtain—the waitresses were still fifteen; their hair had been washed, that was the only difference—they had been to the movies and seen the pretty girls with the clean hair.

Summertime, oh summertime, pattern of life indelible, the fade-proof lake, the woods unshatterable, the pasture with the sweetfern and the juniper forever and ever, summer without end; this was the background, and the life along the shore was the design, the cottages with their innocent and tranquil design, their tiny docks with the flag-pole and the American flag floating against the white clouds in the blue sky, the little paths over the roots of the trees leading from camp to camp and the paths leading back to the outhouses and the can of lime for sprinkling, and at the souvenir counters at the store the miniature birch-bark canoes and the post cards that showed things looking a little better than they looked. This was the American family at play, escaping the city heat, wondering whether the newcomers in the camp at the head of the cove were "common" or "nice," wondering whether it was true that the people who drove up for Sunday dinner at the farmhouse were turned away because there wasn't enough chicken.

It seemed to me, as I keep remembering all this, that those times and those summers had been infinitely precious and worth saving. There had been jollity and peace and goodness. The arriving (at the beginning of August) had been so big a business in itself, at the railway station the farm wagon drawn up, the first smell of the pineladen air, the first glimpse of the smiling farmer, and the great importance of the trunks and your father's enormous authority in such matters, and the feel of the wagon under you for the long ten-mile haul, and at the top of the last long hill catching the first view of the lake after eleven months of not seeing this cherished body of water. The shouts and cries of the other campers when they saw you, and the trunks to be unpacked, to give up their rich burden. (Arriving was less exciting nowadays, when you sneaked up in your car and parked it under a tree near the camp and took out the bags and in five minutes it was all over, no fuss, no loud wonderful fuss about trunks.)

10 Peace and goodness and jollity. The only thing that was wrong now, really, was the sound of the place, an unfamiliar nervous sound of the outboard motors. This was the note that jarred, the one thing that would sometimes break the illusion and set the years moving. In those other summertimes all motors were inboard; and when they were at a little distance, the noise they made was a sedative, an ingredient of

summer sleep. They were one-cylinder and two-cylinder engines, and some were make-and-break and some were jump-spark, but they all made a sleepy sound across the lake. The one-lungers throbbed and fluttered, and the twin-cylinder ones purred and purred, and that was a quiet sound too. But now the campers all had outboards. In the daytime, in the hot mornings, these motors made a petulant, irritable sound; at night, in the still evening when the afterglow lit the water, they whined about one's ears like mosquitoes. My boy loved our rented outboard, and his great desire was to achieve single-handed mastery over it, and authority, and he soon learned the trick of choking it a little (but not too much), and the adjustment of the needle valve. Watching him I would remember the things you could do with the old one-cylinder engine with the heavy flywheel, how you could have it eating out of your hand if you got really close to it spiritually. Motor boats in those days didn't have clutches, and you would make a landing by shutting off the motor at the proper time and coasting in with a dead rudder. But there was a way of reversing them, if you learned the trick, by cutting the switch and putting it on again exactly on the final dying revolution of the flywheel, so that it would kick back against compression and begin reversing. Approaching a dock in a strong following breeze, it was difficult to slow up sufficiently by the ordinary coasting method, and if a boy felt he had complete mastery over his motor, he was tempted to keep it running beyond its time and then reverse it a few feet from the dock. It took a cool nerve, because if you threw the switch a twentieth of a second too soon you could catch the flywheel when it still had speed enough to go up past center, and the boat would leap ahead, charging bull-fashion at the dock.

We had a good week at the camp. The bass were biting well and the sun shone endlessly, day after day. We would be tired at night and lie down in the accumulated heat of the little bedrooms after the long hot day and the breeze would stir almost imperceptibly outside and the smell of the swamp drift in through the rusty screens. Sleep would come easily and in the morning the red squirrel would be on the roof, tapping out his gay routine. I kept remembering everything, lying in bed in the mornings—the small steamboat that had a long rounded stern like the lip of a Ubangi, how quietly she ran on the moonlight sails, when the older boys played their mandolins and the girls sang and we ate doughnuts dipped in sugar, and how sweet the music was on the water in the shining night, and what it had felt like to think about girls then. After breakfast we would go up to the store and the things were in the same place—the minnows in a bottle, the plugs and spinners disarranged and pawed over by the youngsters from the boys' camp, the fig newtons and the Beeman's gum. Outside, the road was tarred and cars stood in front of the store. Inside, all was just as it had always been, except there was more Coca-Cola and not so much Moxie and root beer and birch beer and sarsaparilla. We would walk out with a bottle of pop apiece and sometimes the pop would backfire up our noses and hurt. We explored the streams, quietly, where the turtles slid off the sunny logs and dug their way into the soft bottom; and we lay on the town wharf and fed worms to the tame bass. Everywhere we went I had trouble making out which was I, the one walking at my side, the one walking in my pants.

One afternoon while we were there at that lake a thunderstorm came up. It was like the revival of an old melodrama that I had seen long ago with childish awe. The second-act climax of the drama of the electrical disturbance over a lake in America had not changed in any important respect. This was the big scene, still the big scene. The whole thing was so familiar, the first feeling of oppression and heat and a general air around camp of not wanting to go very far away. In midafternoon (it was all the same) a curious darkening of the sky, and a lull in everything that had made life tick; and then the way the boats suddenly swung the other way at their moorings with the coming of a breeze out of the new quarter, and the premonitory rumble. Then the kettle drum, then the snare, then the bass drum and cymbals, then crackling light against the dark, and the gods grinning and licking their chops in the hills. Afterward the calm, the rain steadily rustling in the calm lake, the return of light and hope and spirits, and the campers running out in joy and relief to go swimming in the rain, their bright cries perpetuating the deathless joke about how they were getting simply drenched, and the children screaming with delight at the new sensation of bathing in the rain, and the joke about getting drenched linking the generations in a strong indestructible chain. And the comedian who waded in carrying an umbrella.

When the others went swimming my son said he was going in too. He pulled his dripping trunks from the line where they had hung all through the shower, and wrung them out. Languidly, and with no thought of going in, I watched him, his hard little body, skinny and bare, saw him wince slightly as he pulled up around his vitals the small, soggy, icy garment. As he buckled the swollen belt suddenly my groin felt the chill of death.

Analyzing Rhetorical Choices

1. In your view, which instances of descriptive language or sensory details best convey the sense of setting?
2. What do you think about the absence in the essay of dialogue or commentary from White's son? How is this essay weaker or stronger for this absence?
3. How convincing is White's concluding line? Explain whether you read it literally or as a literary invention.

Writing About Issues and Contexts

1. How does White use the past to reflect on the present and the present to reflect on the past? Are there any ways that you can successfully relive the past or resist modernization? Explain your response.
2. Does White's essay remind you of anyone you know? Envision yourself having an experience similar to the one described by the author, and write about it in several paragraphs.

Sherman J. Alexie Jr. (1966–) grew up on the Spokane Indian Reservation in Wellpinit, Washington. He attended Washington State University and soon after graduating published The Business of Fancydancing: Stories and Poems *(1992), from which this selection comes. His subsequent books include a volume of poetry,* Walter Flowing Home *(1996); a collection of stories and poems,* One Stick Song *(2000); two story collections,* The Lone Ranger and Tonto Fistfight in Heaven *(1994) and* Ten Little Indians *(2003); and a novel,* Indian Killer *(1996).*

Sherman Alexie

Father Coming Home

THEN   Father coming home from work. Me, waiting on the front steps, watching him walk slowly and carefully, like half of a real Indian. The other half stumbling, carrying the black metal lunch box with maybe half a sandwich, maybe the last drink of good coffee out of the thermos, maybe the last bite of a dream.

SPOKANE   Father coming home from work five days a week. Me, waiting every day until the day he doesn't come walking home, because he cut his knee in half with a chainsaw. Me, visiting my father laying in bed in the hospital in Spokane. Both of us, watching the color television until my mother comes from shopping at Goodwill or Salvation Army, until the nurses come in telling us we have to go.

CEREMONIES   Father coming home from the hospital in a wheelchair. Me, waiting for him to stand up and teach me how to shoot free throws. Me, running up to him one day and jumping hard into his lap, forgetting about his knee. Father holding me tight against his chest, dark and muddy, squeezing his pain into my thin ribs, his eyes staying clear.

AFTER   Father coming home from the mailbox, exercising his knee again and again. Me, looking up from the floor as he's shaking his head because there is no check, no tiny miracles coming in the mail. Father bouncing the basketball, shooting lay-in after lay-in, working the knee until it bleeds along the scars. Father crying from the pain late at night, watching television. Me, pretending to be asleep. All of us listening to canned laughter.

5 INSOMNIA   Father coming home from another job interview, limping only a little but more than enough to keep hearing no, no, no. Me, eating potatoes again in the kitchen, my mother's face growing darker and darker by halves. One half still mostly beautiful, still mostly Indian, the other half something all-crazy and all-hungry. Me, waking her up in the middle of the night, telling her my stomach is empty. Her throwing me outside in my underwear and locking the door. Me, trying anything to get back in.

HOMECOMING Father coming home from drinking, after being gone for weeks. Me, following him around all the time. Him, never leaving my sight, going into the bathroom. Me, sitting outside the door, waiting, knocking on the wood every few seconds, asking him *Are you there? Are you still there?*

NOW   Father coming home finally from a part-time job. Driving a water truck for the BIA. Me, waiting on the front steps, watching him come home early every day. Him, telling my mother when they think I can't hear, he doesn't know if he's strong enough. Father telling mother he was driving the truck down Little Falls Hill, trying to downshift but his knee not strong enough to keep holding the clutch in. Me, holding my breath. Him, driving around the corner on two wheels, tons and tons of water, half-insane. Me, closing my eyes. Him, balancing, always ready to fall. Me, holding onto father with all my strength.

Analyzing Rhetorical Choices

1. How effective is the structure of "Father Coming Home"? In particular, what is your response to the flush-left subtitles and the repetition of "Father coming home. . . . Me . . ."?

2. What would you guess the narrator's age to be? In what ways, if any, is the narrator's voice appropriate?

3. How long a period do you think is represented in the piece?

Writing About Issues and Contexts

1. Do you think that the father should have taken the job with the Bureau of Indian Affairs (BIA), given his injury? Explain.
2. What conclusions or assumptions do you make about compensation, the economics, and the part-time job with the BIA?

Rachel Guido deVries (1947–) is a novelist and poet. Her works include the novel Tender Warriors *(1986) and the poetry volume* How to Sing to a Dago *(1996), from which this selection is taken.*

Rachel Guido deVries

On Alabama Ave., Paterson, NJ, 1954

At seven I dreamed again and again
of plummeting down the narrow stairs
into the arms of Mario the greenhorn
with his curly black hair. Old
5 Mrs. Pepe cleaned scungilli outside
on the porch. I watched her big hands
go in and out of the pot and thought
about her son Mario wishing he were
my pop. In the tiny flat on the third
10 floor. Pop was already bald and bellowing
rage. Mamma bit her tongue into silence
she never stopped wishing on me.

When Mamma's five sisters came over
she was happy. They talked dirty
15 in Calabrian and laughed loud. They
smacked each other on the back or
grabbed hands, smoked cigarettes and
ate the whole time, coffee cake, macaroni,
meatballs, biscotti, and fruit. Little
20 apricots sweet and delicate and yellow,
and tossed the smooth brown pits
on a blue plate, where they clattered
like dice.

Analyzing Rhetorical Choices

1. Why do you think deVries breaks the two stanzas where she does?
2. What kinds of assumptions does deVries make about her readers, given her word choices in this poem?
3. The poet closes with the imagery of apricot pits clattering like dice. Do you think that she intends the word *dice* to have social relevance as well? If so, what is she implying?

Writing About Issues and Contexts

1. Describe at least one comparable memory concerning childhood that you wish you could have changed.
2. How would you compare the domestic roles portrayed in 1954 to those of today?

Kira Salak (1971–) holds a Ph.D. in English from the University of Missouri and is a contributing editor for National Geographic Adventure. *The National Geographic Society selected her in 2005 for one of its Emerging Explorers Awards. Salak is the author of* Four Corners: One Woman's Solo Journey Into the Heart of Papua New Guinea *(2001) and* The Cruelest Journey: Six Hundred Miles to Timbuktu *(2004). In 2004, Salak won the PEN Award in Journalism and a Lowell Thomas Travel Journalism Award for environmental reporting. "The Vision Seekers" was first published in* The Sophisticated Traveler *in 2004.*

Kira Salak

The Vision Seekers

Here's the truth: I have traveled more than four thousand miles to the middle of the Peruvian Amazon to be "cured" by shamans. It's nighttime. The riverboat I'm on plies dark waters, the jungle thick on either side, emitting loud reptilian sounds that drone on like police sirens. I see no lights, no villages anywhere. My companions are Kevin, a pan-flute maker from Canada; Wendy, an acupuncturist and energetic healer from Massachusetts, and her husband, Joe, a burly carpenter who wants nothing to do with us or shamanism, who has said upward of five words so far and who busily reads *Chomsky on MisEducation* as the jungle slides by.

Hamilton Souther, our shamanic guide, sits with long, burnished legs on the guardrail of the boat. "Our greatest fear is the fear of death," he's telling us. "During the *ayahuasca* ceremony, you'll be taken to the edge of that fear, taught to surrender to it, release it." He has the classic good looks of a *Baywatch* actor. Hamilton is twenty-six years old, a native of California who has practiced shamanism for several years. His company, Blue Morpho Tours, features a "shamanic healing center" in a remote area of the Amazon. Listening to him is like listening to the newest Castaneda. He talks constantly about spirit friends and alternative realms of reality.

I discovered Blue Morpho Tours while investigating the huge variety of New Age trips offered on the Web, many stressing shamanism in various cultures as a means of reaching spiritual "transformation." Skeptical but curious, I wondered what that meant and how it worked. Not quite sure what to expect, I signed up for the trip.

Our boat ride will take fourteen hours from the Peruvian town of Iquitos, followed by another river journey to reach our destination. On the deck below, passengers' hammocks crowd together like rows of cocoons, bodies swinging and bumping into one another, frenetic guitar music rupturing the mosquito-filled night.

5 It's midday. We're all in a dugout, heading up a narrow river into the depth of the jungle. Giant butterflies with wings of blue satin fly sluggishly over the water. Nests of parakeets let off raucous squawks, rivaling the boat's motor. The sun and its sticky heat burrows into my skin, exhausting me.

In our boat are two local shamans we picked up this morning from the tiny river town of Genaro Herrerra. Don Julio, eighty-six, is widely considered by locals to be one of the greatest living shamans in the Amazon; his only baggage consists of a small woven pouch full of *mapacho* (sacred tobacco) cigars, which Peruvian shamans smoke to secure the favor of spirits. The second shaman, Don Alberto, forty-six, Hamilton's current shamanic mentor, rests on the gunwale and winces at the sun-dappled waters.

The sun vies with the clouds; large flies land painlessly on me, swelled with blood before I notice them. Joe has stuck the Chomsky book, now dogeared and smudged, in the back of his jeans. His wife, Wendy, on this trip in part to try to improve her energetic healing abilities, has her camcorder out, recording our journey up the river. Kevin, who said he chose to go on this tour to "hopefully release issues," sits silently beside me. He is middle-aged, shy, unmarried. I tell Hamilton about the inexplicable daily migraines that started in just the past year and how they leave me temporarily blind in one eye.

The motor is killed. We pass through a swamplike area of low branches into a small lagoon. High on a nearby slope sits Hamilton's healing center: a large hut made of rainforest planks and palm-leaf thatch, with the jungle imposing on all sides. A single family acts as caretakers. Hamilton introduces us to their youngest girl, Carlita, only five, a budding shaman who already knows the sacred *icaros*, or shamanic power songs. Carrying a Barbie purse around her arm, she gives us all a deep, penetrating stare that unhinges me.

Shamans don't cut down medicinal plants in the jungle without first asking the spirits' permission and giving thanks. Victor, our jungle guide, teaches us about this as he takes our group on an afternoon trek, stopping abruptly before a fresh skeleton on the ground.

10 "Bushmaster," Victor says, beaming like a proud father.

The bushmaster is the largest venomous snake in the New World. Victor has also introduced us to a large wasp whose venom kills tarantulas and incapacitates humans. And now, overhead, he taps his machete against a vine that, if severed, he says, will leak a fluid that easily burns through human flesh.

These are only a few of the dry-ground threats, which don't include the fare of the waterways: piranhas, electric eels, alligators. It's a shaman's paradise, shot full of formidable creatures and the spirits that command them.

I return to the hut with another of my migraines. Kevin and I decide to attend Hamilton's energetic healing class, Hamilton taking us on a guided visualization. The idea, he explains, is to feel connected to the earth's center and the universe. "See yourself heading to the stars," he says. "Tell me when you see the planet Mercury."

It's hard to concentrate. Joe has been lecturing Victor on the uncanny similarities between George W. Bush and Genghis Khan.

15   "Thank the emerald light for taking you to the golden arc of the sun and the eternal flame," Hamilton is saying.

I'm starting to hope that I'm not stranded in the middle of the Amazon with a bunch of lunatics. Little Carlita sits nearby, staring at us from the crook of a rocking chair. She takes slow puffs from a shaman's cigar, her eyes narrow, face expressionless.

Last night, Kevin, Wendy, and I met in the hut to participate in the first of our three shamanic ceremonies. We drank the "sacred visionary medicine" called ayahuasca, which had been prepared by Don Alberto earlier that day. Perhaps because it had been burned accidentally, we felt nothing.

Today, a new batch is being prepared, and tonight's ceremony promises to give us a real shamanic experience—whatever that will entail. Anxiety settles in my gut. "Ayahuasca" itself is the name of a jungle vine, but the word is used as shorthand for a concoction of boiled plant essences that, when drunk, allow for—as Hamilton puts it—"journeys into the realm of spirit."

Our group joins Don Alberto in collecting and preparing the fixings for the special brew. Any would-be Peruvian shaman must master an extensive knowledge of Amazonian plant species, each of which, the shamans believe, has a spirit that contributes protection or guidance to the ceremony. Don Alberto puts several different ingredients into a large cooking pot to be repeatedly boiled for the next several hours: pieces of tree bark, crushed ayahuasca, and fresh, green chacruna leaves.

20   "Once you take ayahuasca, you can meet any spirit you'd like—deceased loved ones, guardian angels, power animals," Hamilton tells us seriously. "Just call upon them, and they'll come."

"I've always wanted to meet Walt Whitman," I muse out loud.

The hour arrives—9 P.M. Having fasted for seven hours, Kevin, Wendy, and I take our seats in the middle of the hut. We each get a plastic bucket and a roll of toilet paper for wiping our faces. Shamans believe that the inevitable vomiting—"purging"—caused by the ayahuasca mixture is a physical manifestation of negative energy being dispelled from the body. The more disgorged, the better.

Hamilton, Don Alberto, and the ancient Don Julio sit before us, lighting their cigars. When they yawn, which is frequently, they make undulating sounds like horses neighing. Don Alberto blows tobacco smoke into the bottle of thick, brown ayahuasca, then whistles under his breath. Spirits, Hamilton says, are now filling the hut. All manner of wholesome, positive spirits. Don Alberto begins pouring out cups of ayahuasca, blessing our serving before we drink; the ayahuasca has the taste and consistency of Bailey's Irish Cream. The shamans are last to drink.

I wait. Ten minutes. Twenty. It looks as if the rafters of the hut are swaying. Someone extinguishes the kerosene lamp and there's complete darkness. The shamans start shaking their *shacapas,* leaf rattles, and singing loudly. I lie down, eyes closed, a pleasant vibration coursing through my body to the beat of the shamans' songs.

25   A piercing scream tears through the hut. I hear violent gurgling and retching. "Hamilton!" Wendy yells. "Get this out of my head! Make it stop!"

Hamilton stops singing for a moment. "Wendy," he says soothingly, "that's just your fear speaking. Ask God to take your fear away."

Now Kevin lets out a loud wail. "Oh, God! Help me! No! *No!*" He throws up, and I hear the loud, mysterious plop of something large landing in the bucket.

The shamans get up to perform healing songs over Kevin and Wendy, who are vomiting now. "Don't resist," Hamilton tells them. "Surrender to your fear. Surrender. Let it all out." He comes over to me. "The spirits tell me that your migraines are caused by worry energy trapped in your head. I'm going to take that energy out for you now." He puts his lips to my temple, sucking hard several times and spitting the unsavory energy over his shoulder.

I start to see geometric patterns. Colorful realms. Shapes and forms coalesce into an endless stream of beauty and perfection. An old man in a white robe walks toward me, smiling. He greets me with a long hug, kissing the top of my head. Walt Whitman!

30 Wendy and Kevin's desperate bellows retreat into distant space. The visions end. I feel an awful, painful ball of nausea in my gut and vomit prodigiously into the bucket.

Kevin has stopped screaming and sobs now. "I see angels," he chimes. "It's so beautiful."

The shamans fall silent. Don Julio announces that he's called back the spirits and ended the ceremony early because the forces were too strong for Wendy and Kevin. A light goes on. I open my eyes to see Hamilton holding Kevin in his arms like a small child. "You're back," he's cooing to him. "Welcome back."

Kevin looks around him in wonder, smiling. "I've never been so happy," he says.

We all received a day of downtime after the ceremony. Wendy had met me outside the hut, crying and distraught, and I didn't know what to do for her. Hamilton assured us that she'd soon feel better, that she was still "resisting the experience." Luckily, Victor had taken her and Joe to see some pink dolphins, which seemed to calm her. Ignoring her protestations, Kevin and I went ahead with our final scheduled ayahuasca ceremony on the last night; we both had little vomiting and our visions were pleasant ones.

35 It's almost the end of the trip. Wendy sits before Don Julio and Don Alberto, reading their palms. Joe passes me a bumper sticker: "Bush Lies—Who Dies?" I catch Kevin smiling. He initiates a conversation with me for the first time and takes out his pan flute to serenade us.

"How are you feeling today?" he asks me.

I try to be scientific about it. My migraines are completely gone, I tell him. I'm enjoying a bizarre, inexplicable feeling of happiness and peace that actually transcends my usual writer's angst.

The others leave. A few days later, on my own overnight journey back to Iquitos, I lie beside Hamilton on the roof of the riverboat and discuss what has happened. "OK," I say, "so how do I know if any of this was real?"

He chuckles knowingly, putting his hands behind his head and staring up at stars so bright that they burn afterimages on my retinas. "It doesn't matter if you think it's real or not," he says, "just as long as it works."

Analyzing Rhetorical Choices

1. Early in her essay, Salak writes of "loud reptilian sounds that drone on like police sirens." Find other examples of metaphor or simile in her work.

2. Salak takes liberties, what we often call poetic license, in her writing. For example, can butterflies really fly sluggishly? Or can sun and sticky heat burrow into one's skin? Why does Salak use such description and do you find it effective?

Writing About Issues and Contexts

1. Visit (as we have) the Blue Morpho Tours site on the Internet (*http: bluemorphotours.com*). What is your take on this and similar endeavors?

2. Why would someone reading Chomsky on miseducation have no interest in shamans? What is your view of Hamilton's statement, "Just as long as it works"?

Formerly a landscape photographer, **Barry Lopez** *(1945–) is currently regarded as one of the nation's premier nature writers. He has numerous awards, including the National Book Award in 1986 for* Arctic Dreams. *His other books include* Of Wolves and Men *(1978),* The Rediscovery of North America *(1990),* Field Notes *(1994), and* Light Action in the Caribbean *(2000). "The Stone Horse" first appeared in the writing periodical* Antaeus *in 1986.*

Barry Lopez

The Stone Horse

I

The deserts of southern California, the high, relatively cooler and wetter Mojave and the hotter, dryer Sonoran to the south of it, carry the signatures of many cultures. Prehistoric rock drawings in the Mojave's Coso Range, probably the greatest concentration of petroglyphs in North America, are at least three thousand years old. Big-game-hunting cultures that flourished six or seven thousand years before that are known from broken spear tips, choppers, and burins left scattered along the shores of great Pleistocene lakes, long since evaporated. Weapons and tools discovered at China Lake may be thirty thousand years old; and worked stone from a quarry in the Calico Mountains is, some argue, evidence that human beings were here more than 200,000 years ago.

Because of the long-term stability of such arid environments, much of this prehistoric stone evidence still lies exposed on the ground, accessible to anyone who passes by—the studious, the acquisitive, the indifferent, the merely curious. Archaeologists do not agree on the sequence of cultural history beyond about twelve thousand years ago, but it is clear that these broken bits of chalcedony, chert, and obsidian, like the animal drawings and geometric designs etched on walls of basalt throughout the desert, anchor the earliest threads of human history, the first record of human endeavor here.

Western man did not enter the California desert until the end of the eighteenth century, 250 years after Coronado brought his soldiers into the Zuni pueblos in a bewildered search for the cities of Cibola. The earliest appraisals of the land were cursory, hurried. People traveled *through* it, en route to Santa Fe or the California coastal settlements. Only miners tarried. In 1823 what had been Spain's became Mexico's, and in 1848 what had been Mexico's became America's; but the bare, jagged mountains and dry lake beds, the vast and uniform plains of creosote bush and yucca plants, remained as obscure as the northern Sudan until the end of the nineteenth century.

Before 1940 the tangible evidence of twentieth-century man's passage here consisted of very little—the hard tracery of travel corridors; the widely scattered, relatively insignificant evidence of mining operations; and the fair expanse of irrigated fields at the desert's periphery. In the space of a hundred years or so the wagon roads were paved, railroads were laid down, and canals and high-tension lines were built to bring water and electricity across the desert to Los Angeles from the Colorado River. The dark mouths of gold, talc, and tin mines yawned from the bony flanks of desert ranges. Dust-encrusted chemical plants stood at work on the lonely edges of dry lake beds. And crops of grapes, lettuce, dates, alfalfa, and cotton covered the Coachella and Imperial valleys, north and south of the Salton Sea, and the Palo Verde Valley along the Colorado.

5   These developments proceeded with little or no awareness of earlier human occupations by cultures that preceded those of the historic Indians—the Mojave, the Chemehuevi, the Quechan. (Extensive irrigation began actually to change the climate of the Sonoran Desert, and human settlements, the railroads, and farming introduced many new, successful plants into the region.)

During World War II, the American military moved into the desert in great force, to train troops and to test equipment. They found the clear weather conducive to year-round flying, the dry air and isolation very attractive. After the war, a complex of training grounds, storage facilities, and gunnery and test ranges was permanently settled on more than three million acres of military reservations. Few perceived the extent or significance of the destruction of the aboriginal sites that took place during tank maneuvers and bombing runs or in the laying out of highways, railroads, mining districts, and irrigated fields. The few who intuited that something like an American Dordogne Valley lay exposed here were (only) amateur archaeologists; even they reasoned that the desert was too vast for any of this to matter.

After World War II, people began moving out of the crowded Los Angeles basin into homes in Lucerne, Apple, and Antelope valleys in the western Mojave. They emigrated as well to a stretch of resort land at the foot of the San Jacinto Mountains that included Palm Springs, and farther out to old railroad and military towns like Twentynine Palms and Barstow. People also began exploring the desert, at first in military-surplus jeeps and then with a variety of all-terrain and off-road vehicles that became available in the 1960s. By the mid-1970s, the number of people using such vehicles for desert recreation had increased exponentially. Most came and went in innocent curiosity; the few who didn't wreaked a havoc all out of proportion to their numbers. The disturbance of previously isolated archaeological sites increased by an order of magnitude. Many sites were vandalized before archaeologists, themselves late to the desert, had any firm grasp of the bounds of human history in the desert. It was as though in the same moment an Aztec library had been discovered intact various lacunae had begun to appear.

The vandalism was of three sorts: the general disturbance usually caused by souvenir hunters and by the curious and the oblivious; the wholesale stripping of a place by professional thieves for black-market sale and trade; and outright destruction, in which vehicles were actually used to ram and trench an area. By 1980, the Bureau of Land Management estimated that probably 35 percent of the archaeological sites in the desert had been vandalized. The destruction at some places by rifles and shotguns, or by power winches mounted on vehicles, was, if one cared for history, demoralizing to behold.

In spite of public education, land closures, and stricter law enforcement in recent years, the BLM estimates that, annually, about 1 percent of the archaeological record in the desert continues to be destroyed or stolen.

II

10   A BLM archaeologist told me, with understandable reluctance, where to find the intaglio. I spread my Automobile Club of Southern California map of Imperial County out on his desk, and he traced the route with a pink felt-tip pen. The line crossed Interstate 8 and then turned west along the Mexican border.

"You can't drive any farther than about here," he said, marking a small X. "There's boulders in the wash. You walk up past them."

On a separate piece of paper he drew a route in a smaller scale that would take me up the arroyo to a certain point where I was to cross back east, to another arroyo. At its head, on higher ground just to the north, I would find the horse.

"It's tough to spot unless you know it's there. Once you pick it up . . ." He shook his head slowly, in a gesture of wonder at its existence.

I waited until I held his eye. I assured him I would not tell anyone else how to get there. He looked at me with stoical despair, like a man who had been robbed twice, whose belief in human beings was offered without conviction.

15   I did not go until the following day because I wanted to see it at dawn. I ate breakfast at four A.M. in El Centro and then drove south. The route was easy to follow, though the last section of road proved difficult, broken and drifted over with sand in some spots. I came to the barricade of boulders and parked. It was light enough by then to find my way over the ground with little trouble. The contours of the landscape were stark, without any masking vegetation. I worried only about rattlesnakes.

I traversed the stone plain as directed, but, in spite of the frankness of the land, I came on the horse unawares. In the first moment of recognition I was without feeling. I recalled later being startled, and that I held my breath. It was laid out on the ground with its head to the east, three times life size. As I took in its outline I felt a growing concentration of all my senses, as though my attentiveness to the pale rose color of the morning sky and other peripheral images had now ceased to be important. I was aware that I was straining for sound in the windless air, and I felt the uneven pressure of the earth hard against my feet. The horse, outlined in a standing profile of the dark ground, was as vivid before me as a bed of tulips.

I've come upon animals suddenly before, and felt a similar tension, a precipitate heightening of the senses. And I have felt the inexplicable but sharply boosted intensity of a wild moment in the bush, where it is not until some minutes later that you discover the source of electricity—the warm remains of a grizzly bear kill, or the still moist tracks of a wolverine.

But this was slightly different. I felt I had stepped into an unoccupied corridor. I had no familiar sense of history, the temporal structure in which to think: this horse was made by Quechan people three hundred years ago. I felt instead a headlong rush of images: people hunting wild horses with spears on the Pleistocene veld of southern California; Cortés riding across the causeway into Montezuma's Tenochtitlán; a short-legged Comanche, astride his horse like some sort of ferret, slashing through cavalry lines of young men who rode like farmers; a hoof exploding past my face one morning in a corral in Wyoming. These images had the weight and silence of stone.

When I released my breath, the images softened. My initial feeling, of facing a wild animal in a remote region, was replaced with a calm sense of antiquity. It was then that I became conscious, like an ordinary tourist, of what was before me, and thought: this horse was probably laid out by Quechan people. But when? I wondered. The first horses they saw, I knew, might have been those that came north from Mexico in 1692 with Father Eusebio Kino. But Cocopa people, I recalled, also came this far north on occasion, to fight with their neighbors, the Quechan. And *they* could have seen horses with Melchior Díaz, at the mouth of the Colorado River in the fall of 1540. So, it could be four hundred years old. (No one in fact knows.)

20   I still had not moved. I took my eyes off the horse for a moment to look south over the desert plain into Mexico, to look east past its head at the brightening sunrise, to situate myself. Then, finally, I brought my trailing foot slowly forward and stood erect. Sunlight was running like a thin sheet of water over the stony ground and it threw the horse into relief. It looked as though no hand had ever disturbed the stones that gave it its form.

The horse had been brought to life on ground called desert pavement, a tight, flat matrix of small cobbles blasted smooth by sand-laden winds. The uniform, monochromatic blackness of the stones, a patina of iron and magnesium oxides called desert varnish, is caused by long-term exposure to the sun. To make this type of low-relief ground glyph, or intaglio, the artist either selectively turns individual stones over to their lighter side or removes areas of stone to expose the lighter soil underneath, creating a negative image. This horse, about eighteen feet from brow to rump and eight feet from withers to hoof, had been made in the latter way, and its outline was bermed at certain points with low ridges of stone a few inches high to enhance its three-dimensional qualities. (The left side of the horse was in full profile; each leg was extended at 90 degrees to the body and fully visible, as though seen in three-quarter profile.)

I was not eager to move. The moment I did I would be back in the flow of time, the horse no longer quivering in the same way before me. I did not want to feel again the sequence of quotidian events—to be drawn off into deliberation and analysis. A human being, a four-footed animal, the open land. That was all that was present—and a "thoughtless" understanding of the very old desires bearing on this particular animal: to hunt it, to render it, to fathom it, to subjugate it, to honor it, to take it as a companion.

What finally made me move was the light. The sun now filled the shallow basin of the horse's body. The weighted line of the stone berm created the illusion of a mane and the distinctive roundness of an equine belly. The change in definition impelled me. I moved to the left, circling past its rump, to see how the light might flesh the horse out from various points of view. I circled it completely before squatting on my haunches. Ten or fifteen minutes later I chose another view. The third time I moved, to a point near the rear hooves, I spotted a stone tool at my feet. I stared at it a long while, more in awe than disbelief, before reaching out to pick it up. I turned it over in my left palm and took it between my fingers to feel its cutting edge. It is always difficult, especially with something so portable, to rechannel the desire to steal.

I spent several hours with the horse. As I changed positions and as the angle of the light continued to change I noticed a number of things. The angle at which the pastern carried the hoof away from the ankle was perfect. Also, stones had been placed within the image to suggest at precisely the right spot the left shoulder above the foreleg. The line that joined thigh and hock was similarly accurate. The muzzle alone seemed distorted—but perhaps these stones had been moved by a later hand. It was an admirably accurate representation, but not what a breeder would call perfect conformation. There was the suggestion of a bowed neck and an undershot jaw, and the tail, as full as a winter coyote's, did not appear to be precisely to scale.

25   The more I thought about it, the more I felt I was looking at an individual horse, a unique combination of generic and specific detail. It was easy to imagine one of Kino's horses as a model, or a horse that ran off from one of Coronado's columns. What kind of horses would these have been? I wondered. In the sixteenth century the most sought-after horses in Europe were Spanish, the offspring of Arabian stock and Barbary horses that the Moors brought to Iberia and bred to the older, eastern European strains brought in by the Romans. The model for this horse, I speculated, could easily have been a palomino, or a descendant of horses trained for lion hunting in North Africa.

A few generations ago, cowboys, cavalry quartermasters, and draymen would have taken this horse before me under consideration and not let up their scrutiny until they had its heritage fixed to their satisfaction. Today, the distinction between draft and harness horses is arcane knowledge, and no image may come to mind for a blue roan or a claybank horse. The loss of such refinement in everyday conversation leaves me unsettled. People praise the Eskimo's ability to distinguish among forty types of snow but forget the skill of others who routinely differentiate between overo and tobiano pintos. Such distinctions are made for the same reason. You have to do it to be able to talk clearly about the world.

For parts of two years I worked as a horse wrangler and packer in Wyoming. It is dim knowledge now; I would have to think to remember if a buckskin was a kind of dun horse. And I couldn't throw a double-diamond hitch over a set of panniers—the packer's basic tie-down—without guidance. As I squatted there in the desert, however, these more personal memories seemed tenuous in comparison with the sweep of this animal in human time. My memories had no depth. I thought of the Hittite cavalry riding against the Syrians 3,500 years ago. And the first of the Chinese emperors, Ch'in Shih Huang, buried in Shensi Province in 210 B.C. with thousands of life-size horses and soldiers, a terra-cotta guardian army. What could I know of what was in the mind of whoever made this horse? Was there some racial memory of it as an animal that had once fed the artist's ancestors and then disappeared from North America? And then returned in this strange alliance with another race of men?

Certainly, whoever it was, the artist had observed the animal very closely. Certainly the animal's speed had impressed him. Among the first things the Quechan would have learned from an encounter with Kino's horses was that their own long-distance runners—men who could run down mule deer—were no match for this animal.

From where I squatted I could look far out over the Mexican plain. Juan Bautista de Anza passed this way in 1774, extending El Camino Real into Alta California from Sinaloa. He was followed by others, all of them astride the magical horse; *gente de razón*, the people of reason, coming into the country of *los primitivos*. The horse, like the stone animals of Egypt, urged these memories upon me. And as I drew them up from some forgotten corner of my mind—huge horses carved in the white chalk downs of southern England by an Iron Age people; Spanish horses rearing and wheeling in fear before alligators in Florida—the images seemed tethered before me. With this sense of proportion, a memory of my own—the morning I almost lost my face to a horse's hoof—now had somewhere to fit.

30   I rose up and began to walk slowly around the horse again. I had taken the first long measure of it and was now looking for a way to depart, a new angle of light, a fading of the image itself before the rising sun, that would break its hold on me. As I circled, feeling both heady and serene at the encounter, I realized again how strangely

vivid it was. It had been created on a barren bajada between two arroyos, as nondescript a place as one could imagine. The only plant life here was a few wands of ocotillo cactus. The ground beneath my shoes was so hard it wouldn't take the print of a heavy animal even after a rain. The only sounds I heard here were the voices of quail.

The archaeologist had been correct. For all its forcefulness, the horse is inconspicuous. If you don't care to see it you can walk right past it. That pleases him, I think. Unmarked on this bleak shoulder of the plain, the site signals to no one; so he wants no protective fences here, no informative plaque, to act as beacons. He would rather take a chance that no motorcyclist, no aimless wanderer with a flair for violence and a depth of ignorance, will ever find his way here.

The archaeologist had given me something before I left his office that now seemed peculiar—an aerial photograph of the horse. It is widely believed that an aerial view of an intaglio provides a fair and accurate depiction. It does not. In the photograph the horse looks somewhat crudely constructed; from the ground it appears far more deftly rendered. The photograph is of a single moment, and in that split second the horse seems vaguely impotent. I watched light pool in the intaglio at dawn; I imagine you could watch it withdraw at dusk and sense the same animation I did. In those prolonged moments its shape and so, too, its general character changed—noticeably. The living quality of the image, its immediacy to the eye, was brought out by the light-in-time, not, at least here, in the camera's frozen instant.

Intaglios, I thought, were never meant to be seen by gods in the sky above. They were meant to be seen by people on the ground, over a long period of shifting light. This could even be true of the huge figures on the Plain of Nazca in Peru, where people could walk for the length of a day beside them. It is our own impatience that leads us to think otherwise.

This process of abstraction, almost unintentional, drew me gradually away from the horse. I came to a position of attention at the edge of the sphere of its influence. With a slight bow I paid my respects to the horse, its maker, and the history of us all, and departed.

III

35   A short distance away I stopped the car in the middle of the road to make a few notes. I could not write down what I was thinking when I was with the horse. It would have seemed disrespectful, and it would have required another kind of attention. So now I patiently drained my

memory of the details it had fastened itself upon. The road I'd stopped on was adjacent to the All American Canal, the major source of water for the Imperial and Coachella valleys. The water flowed west placidly. A disjointed flock of coots, small, dark birds with white bills, was paddling against the current, foraging in the rushes.

I was peripherally aware of the birds as I wrote, the only movement in the desert, and of a series of sounds from a village a half-mile away. The first sounds from this collection of ramshackle houses in a grove of cottonwoods were the distracted dawn voices of dogs. I heard them intermingled with the cries of a rooster. Later, the high-pitched voices of children calling out to each other came disembodied through the dry desert air. Now, a little after seven, I could hear someone practicing on the trumpet, the same rough phrases played over and over. I suddenly remembered how as children we had tried to get the rhythm of a galloping horse with hands against our thighs, or by fluttering our tongues against the roofs of our mouths.

After the trumpet, the impatient calls of adults summoning children. Sunday morning. Wood smoke hung like a lens in the trees. The first car starts—a cold eight-cylinder engine, of Chrysler extraction perhaps, goosed to life, then throttled back to murmur through dual mufflers, the obligato music of a shade-tree mechanic. The rote bark of mongrel dogs at dawn, the jagged outcries of men and women, an engine coming to life. Like a thousand villages from West Virginia to Guadalajara.

I finished my notes—where was I going to find a description of the horses that came north with the conquistadors? Did their manes come forward prominently over the brow, like this one's, like the forelocks of Blackfeet and Assiniboin men in nineteenth-century paintings? I set the notes on the seat beside me.

The road followed the canal for a while and then arced north, toward Interstate 8. It was slow driving and I fell to thinking how the desert had changed since Anza had come through. New plants and animals—the MacDougall cottonwood, the English house sparrow, the chukar from India—have about them now the air of the native-born. Of the native species, some—no one knows how many—are extinct. The populations of many others, especially the animals, have been sharply reduced. The idea of a desert impoverished by agricultural poisons and varmint hunters, by off-road vehicles and military operations, did not seem as disturbing to me, however, as this other horror, now that I had been those hours with the horse. The vandals, the few who crowbar rock art off the desert's walls, who dig up graves, who punish the ground that holds intaglios, are people who devour history. Their self-centered scorn, their disrespect for ideas and images beyond their ken, create the awful atmosphere of loose ends in which totalitarianism thrives, in which the past is merely curious or wrong.

40   I thought about the horse sitting out there on the unprotected plain. I enumerated its qualities in my mind until a sense of its vulnerability receded and it became an anchor for something else. I remembered that history, a history like this one, which ran deeper than Mexico, deeper than the Spanish, was a kind of medicine. It permitted the great breadth of human expression to reverberate, and it did not urge you to locate its apotheosis in the present.

Each of us, individuals and civilizations, has been held upside down like Achilles in the River Styx. The artist mixing his colors in the dim light of Altamira; an Egyptian ruler living still now, wrapped in his byssus, stored against time in a pyramid; the faded Dorset culture of the Arctic; the Hmong and Samburu and Walbiri of historic time; the modern nations. This great, imperfect stretch of human expression is the clarification and encouragement, the urging and the reminder, we call history. And it is inscribed everywhere in the face of the land, from the mountain passes of the Himalayas to a nameless bajada in the California desert.

Small birds rose up in the road ahead, startled, and flew off. I prayed no infidel would ever find that horse.

Analyzing Rhetorical Choices

1. How would you describe Lopez's tone in this essay, and what is your reaction to it?
2. How effective are the rather lengthy sections about history, especially in the first section of the essay?
3. Lopez includes a number of key metaphors and descriptions of setting. Which ones seem to work particularly well?

Writing About Issues and Contexts

1. How, in your view, could we strike the best balance between the preservation of historical artifacts and modern demands for space to build, for example, military facilities?

2. Are there sites/sights that you would leave home at four o'clock in the morning to visit? Describe at least one or two, and connect these to the essay.

3. What similarities, if any, do you see between Lopez's essay and those by Alice Walker and E. B. White?

Strategies for Writers: Description

1. Practice writing essays, vignettes, or poems in which you focus on description. Challenge yourself to find highly expressive verbs and modifiers. Strive to come up with metaphors that convey your ideas most vividly.

2. Share your efforts with students, instructors, family, and friends. Ask specifically about their reactions to your images. Note other feedback as well. Consider all responses as you revise.

3. Study E. B. White's extended simile comparing a thunderstorm to an old melodrama. Write an extended simile on a subject of interest to you.

4. Try to give an animal, perhaps your pet, a personality the way Alice Walker does Blue.

5. Like Lopez in the presence of the stone horse, contemplate an object or place and try to record a "headlong rush of images."

6. Reread some of the selections in this chapter, concentrating on identifying the sensory details. Add descriptions involving senses not referred to in specific passages. For example, deVries does not include details about taste. What might such details be?

7. Prepare your work for additional sharing or publication. Proofread with attention to elements such as word omissions, spelling, punctuation, and grammar. If necessary, solicit help from a style manual and people willing to help in this process.

Research and Writing Assignments

1. Follow the example of Alice Walker's "Am I Blue?" and consider a color or other characteristic—red, yellow, hunger, thirst, or ambition. Write a descriptive passage that illustrates a specific point, perspective, or personality by exploring the characteristic in detail. Push yourself to produce as many relevant appeals to the senses as you can.

2. As you have read, Julia Alvarez, Rachel Guido deVries, and Sherman Alexie provide descriptive sketches that also function as tales about coming of age amid social and political tensions. Write a descriptive essay that reflects your own childhood

understanding of family or wider social issues. Emphasize any dramatic learning episodes that you recall, such as Yolanda's introduction to snow.

3. In "Once More to the Lake," the author returns to an important scene of his youth and has a revelation. If possible, return to a significant scene of your childhood and describe it in detail. In any event, write about a site you once frequented and reveal any new insights you may now have that are associated with the place.

4. Research or visit a location that is unfamiliar to you and write an essay about it. As Barry Lopez does in "The Stone Horse," incorporate descriptive details to give readers a full sense of the geography.

4
Definition

Definition is one of the most basic ways that individuals learn, especially when encountering a new or specialized language or confronting unfamiliar words and concepts. This is true for children but is just as important for college students confronted with unfamiliar words and concepts. An instructor or textbook might state, "At that stage, Metterlink's ideas were still inchoate," or "Let's hope that the United States is able to resile from its current position on global warming." Without a definition of key words, these sentences are confusing. Likewise, without consulting a bound or on-line dictionary, it is probably difficult for many readers to understand the following, admittedly pretentious, sentence: "Her indefatigable desire to resort to eponymous references produced holophrastic results that left me intellectually enervated and downright morose." Making sense of this statement requires an understanding of word definitions and the ability to put those definitions together to create coherent understanding.

At its most fundamental level, definition is about understanding words and being able to infuse spoken and written sentences with meaning. It is a transaction between writer and reader that is accomplished through words and text. Many people have been guilty at one time or another of reading complex passages of prose and guessing wrongly at the meanings of words, or misusing words and concepts in their own writing and speaking—because they were unwilling to consult a dictionary or reference book. Anyone who makes this kind of mistake might well be considered . . . gormless. (Note: If you are interested in the play of word definitions, you might want to subscribe to a free on-line service known as Wordsmith, located at *http://www.wordsmith.org*, or check out "Says You!" at *http://www. wgbh.org/radio/saysyou.*)

Uncovering the definitions of individual words, however, is not quite so simple as looking them up in a dictionary or receiving one of them a day from an on-line service. Word meanings are deeply embedded in a social/political/economic context. That is, without getting too heavily into theory, words gather meaning depending on how they are used, by whom, and setting and context. One of the clearest examples of this can be found in Maggie Balistreri's brief but puckish book, *The Evasion English Dictionary* (2003). Balistreri found herself increasingly annoyed that certain common words and phrases were being used to evade meaning rather than state meaning: "It is, for example, harder to look somebody in the eye and say 'I am unproductive' than it is to say 'I feel unproductive.'" Balistreri then selects some examples and illustrates them. One extended set of definitions concerns the word *like*, one of the more common expressions, especially among certain west coast populations, teens, and devotees of Alicia Silverstone's *Clueless*. Here are three of Balistreri's definitions of *like* (there are ten overall definitions of this one word in the book):

The vague *like* (Translation—"thereabouts"):

There were like, a thousand screaming vans

It was written like, two hundred years ago.

The betrayer *like* (Translation—"I lie"):

I was so upset I cried for like, three days.

You bring up a good point, and I like, totally sympathize with you; however

The apology *like* (Translation—"Sorry, I'm inarticulate"):

I was like, wow.

It was so interesting; it was like, I can't explain it. You know what I mean?

Try to come up with the other seven meanings of the word *like*, based on the common expressions in which it occurs.

Important though word definition is—and it is fundamental to reading and writing—the focus in this chapter is on a mode of writing called extended definition. Extended definition occurs when a writer chooses to define a complex subject, usually because it is significant to a general readership and also interests the writer. Perhaps a better way to think about extended definition is to label it as a specific kind of explanation, one that takes on difficult and abstract concepts and offers an improved understanding of them. Thus definition as a mode of writing is essential to improving understanding and communication because it establishes the meaning of a term, concept, or idea almost always by connecting it to a larger context.

Typically the most successful extended definition essays arise when the writer chooses from among a variety of possibilities to explore a subject and then shares the result with an audience. For example, a class focusing on protest movements or political history might engage in an extended discussion about the concept of free speech. One of their first questions is likely to be "What is free speech?" In order to answer this question, which obviously entails a definition essay of some kind, students will probably need to trace this right back to its origin, namely the First Amendment, which guarantees free speech to all Americans. Defining free speech in terms of the First Amendment leads to a further challenge, however, since this short, succinct statement leaves ample room for interpretation:

The First Amendment

Congress shall make no law respecting an establishment of religion, or prohibiting the free exercise thereof; or abridging the freedom of speech, or of the press; or the right of the people peaceably to assemble, and to petition the government for a redress of grievances.

Is advocating violent revolution protected by the First Amendment? How about hate speech? Or racist expressions? Or detailed explanations of how to make homemade incendiary devices? Debates about the meaning of the First Amendment—in essence, its extended definition—continue to this day. Does the First Amendment protect the speech in high school newspapers? Do public school teachers have the right to assign controversial textbooks to their students? Do school libraries have the right to offer such books to their patrons? How about the intertwined and competing voices of pro-life or pro-choice advocates; are all forms of their speech protected? Should college students be required to observe a speech code, authorized by the school administration, while in class, in their dormitories, or on university grounds? Is hate speech protected under any circumstances? What exactly is hate speech? For that matter, what exactly does the First Amendment protect and what lies outside its bounds?

These or similar questions will inevitably arise when you attempt an extended definition essay on the First Amendment. Indeed, the schools, the U.S. Congress, and the courts wrestle with these and similar questions about First Amendment rights on a regular basis. A seemingly simple statement in the U.S. Constitution, indeed the very first amendment, requires continuous definition and redefinition. Your responsibility as a writer is to find a similar kind of important, complex, compelling term or concept to define.

Approaches to Writing Extended Definition Essays

The most important prerequisite when writing an extended definition essay is to find a worthy subject. This obvious advice (after all, when would you want to write an essay on an unworthy subject?) is hard to follow. If you are assigned to define a word or concept, your first response is likely to be that each topic you discover is unavailable to you: "everyone knows what a 'natural disaster' is" or "there is nothing to say about 'greening the earth' that is new to anyone" or "writing about 'national security' is just too complex for a three- or four-page essay." The key to finding a suitable subject is to find something about which you have some passion: computer gaming, freestyle swimming, civil rights, television sitcoms, urban politics, community revitalization programs. Choosing a subject to define demands that you be intellectually and emotionally charged by the challenge of completing this assignment. That requires that you feel commitment to define your term because this work is important to you; then the trick (though usually not a difficult trick) is to write your essay in such a way that you also communicate this importance to your reader.

Without this intellectual and passionate commitment to your subject, you will lack the energy to do the necessary research required to write an extended definition essay. That research is what will produce information that is new to you, and more important, new to your reader. As with virtually every essay you will ever write, thorough and sound research is the key to good writing. Discover facts and information that are new to you. Discover stories and examples that illustrate your subject. Discover what you know—and what you need to know to complete this assignment. Keep a careful record of your research, noting sources so that you can cite them as needed in your final draft. As you read, write down additional sources cited so that you consult them and get a fuller picture of the term or concept that you are defining. Stand back from your research occasionally to reflect on what you have done, whether it is germane, and what more you think is needed as you write. Be mindful of your due date:

Sometimes research can get so enveloping that you suddenly discover an essay is due and all you have ready is a thick sheaf of notes, quotes, and references.

Walk Around Your Subject

Let's say, to choose just one example, that you decide to write an extended definition essay about recycling. As you engage in your research, you discover that the topic is too large; you are beginning to feel overwhelmed by its complexity. If so, it is time to walk around your subject; that is, to stand back from your topic, reflect on its importance, and look at it from a variety of perspectives. Focus specifically on the three major elements of the rhetorical triangle: the writer, the reader, and the subject. Ask yourself why the subject is important to you. What made you choose it? Why would someone else care? What kinds of information, history, stories, facts, or examples will best illustrate your subject and most affect your reader? What does the subject itself demand if it is to be explained, understood, enlightened? Some subjects almost cry out for personal anecdotes and stories ("pet sitting" or "being a big sister"); others seem to urge writers to take on a more scientific or factual approach ("inflation" or "editorial writing"); while still others might profit from a blended approach that melds formal analysis with personal anecdote ("potholes" or "the fall harvest"). The most important contribution you can make to your own writing is to continuously reflect on your writing from the multiple perspectives of writer, reader, subject. That is what "walking around your subject" means.

Think About What, When, Why, and How

To anchor this discussion of approaches to writing an extended definition essay, let's assume that you have decided to write an extended definition essay about "the ideal breakfast food—the pancake," a food that you adore and that you eat regularly. It is a subject about which you have some passion (at least the passion to eat them) and you think the choice of "the pancake" as subject is original and even a bit clever, but you are stalled when it comes to writing about pancakes. Once you actually sit down to write, the subject seems both ordinary and even a bit silly; you worry that your instructor will dismiss the subject of "the pancake" as unworthy of an essay. Even so, it is a topic you can't get out of your head, and you are determined to try to write about it for your extended definition, even as you worry about not knowing much about this subject and about whether you can sustain an entire essay.

One approach to getting started is to ask "what," "when," "why," and "how" questions about your subject, no matter what it is. Those questions will help you determine whether your chosen topic can be the subject of an essay, and they will guide you toward the kinds of research and structure that will make your subject come alive for both you and your readers. You might, therefore, ask the following kinds of questions:

What is the meaning of breakfast? What is the word's etymology?

How important is breakfast in terms of health and nutrition?

What foods are the best to eat at breakfast?

What is the history of breakfast over the last 50 years in America?

What kinds of breakfasts are served internationally?

What are the most popular foods to eat at breakfast?

When did Americans start to eat pancakes at breakfast?

What exactly is a pancake?

What is its history? Who invented it? Where did it come from?

When did the pancake become popular?

What is its nutritional value? Is it recommended as part of a healthy diet?

What different kinds of pancakes are there? How are they served?

Why do you love to eat pancakes?

What are the most popular pancakes?

How do the various ingredients interact to form pancakes?

What do pancakes look like/taste like in other countries?

What is the difference between a pancake and a crepe?

What about pancakes that are eaten as side dishes to regular meals (i.e., potato pancakes)? Are they really pancakes?

When did Americans start eating maple syrup with breakfast pancakes? What is the history of pancakes and syrup?

How do people value pancakes? Do they evoke particular family gatherings and sentimental occasions? Do pancakes contribute to social cohesion? Do they become part of our ritualized behavior?

Not all these questions are relevant, but many of them will lead you toward a fuller understanding of the meaning(s) of breakfast and the particular meaning(s) of pancakes as a breakfast food. Similar questions can be asked about any meaningful term or concept, spurring your thinking and research methods so that you can get started writing.

Consider Past, Present, Future

In a similar fashion, you can use the three aspects of time to help expand your thinking about your subject. Some subjects, especially those that have changed over time, are particularly well suited to this method of analysis. For example, let's say that you decide to write about Social Security, a topic very much in the news of late. Using this method, you could ask:

When was Social Security created? Why?

What was its purpose(s)?

How does Social Security work? Whom does it benefit?

Does Social Security benefit the same kinds of people today as in the past?

Why is Social Security funding less secure now than in the past?

What are some of the proposals for changing Social Security?

How will they affect the future of this program?

These and other questions might spur you to examine a subject as it moves through time, or you might just focus on its history, or examine its history briefly and then analyze how it works in the present.

Use the Specific to Illustrate the Abstract

Readers thrive on details and examples. Few of us can understand generalities and abstractions, even once we know a great deal about a field or discipline. One of the dangers of writing in the definition mode is that the writer can veer off into generalities or use an overly technical or pretentious vocabulary in an attempt to impress readers or simply to express vague truths. Either approach is a mistake. One of the great challenges of writing a definition essay is to blend general and specific, abstract and concrete. In some of the other modes (narration, comparison/contrast, description, to name just three) the mode itself steers a writer toward the use of details. Definition essays, however, push writers toward generalizing, and this is dangerous.

You need constantly to remain vigilant to the need for examples and the use of specifics. As recommended repeatedly in this book, effective writers use general statements to make large and important points, and then illustrate and exemplify those assertions by including details, anecdotes, facts, and other specific kinds of information that are pertinent and anchor the essay. An essay about pancakes, for example, might include excerpts from a cookbook devoted to the creation of that American staple, while an extended definition about Social Security might be exemplified in one section by a statistical analysis of the effect of this program in ameliorating poverty among the working poor. Few effective extended definition essays focus exclusively on the abstract, nor do they consist only of specific examples. Readers need to know the important assertions that you are putting forward, and they need those assertions to be supported by specific examples.

Stay Focused

Do not get distracted by the research discoveries you make or by digressions into intriguing subjects that are only tangentially related to your primary assignment. Keep in mind that an extended definition essay must always be focused on definition, on expanding the readers' understanding of the word or concept you have chosen. One way to maintain this focus is to write out your primary purpose on a sheet of paper, tape it above your writing desk, and use it to remind you of what the intention of this essay is.

When writing a definition essay, writers usually focus immediate attention directly on the word or concept being defined, making a declaration early on that they will be "defining X" or "explaining the meaning of X." Thus most extended definition essays do not keep the reader in suspense regarding their primary purpose. In "The Holocaust," for example, Bruno Bettelheim makes clear from the outset that he will define the word *Holocaust*, just as Gretel Ehrlich signals her interest in defining *men* by the very choice of her title. This makes sense, since we usually read extended definition essays because we are intrigued by the word or concept being defined. Because we can look up the word or concept in a reference book, what we are looking for in a definition essay is something more. That "more" is the unique perspective that a writer can bring to the act of writing. Successful definition essays give readers the meaning of a term—but in ways that reflect the particular and personal point of view of the writer. That is the reason writers attempt a definition essay: to give their own personal shape and flavor to the meaning of a word, a concept, a thing, or a place. We see this in all the essays in this section, from Lisa Kanae's definition of *pidgin*, which she ties to the concrete example of her brother, to Judy Brady's "I Want a Wife" and Gloria Naylor's "The Meanings of a Word."

Provide Original and Compelling Information

The bane of any extended definition essay is stale information, dull observations, and obvious statements. If you are defining what it means to be a college student, chances are your readers don't need you to spend a lot of time describing how you have to study for tests or learn to be more mature and independent. Those insights may well be true, but they are what most students would say most of the time. Instead, your essay might focus on the need to make significant and personal connections with faculty, or on the importance of engaging in research activities with professors in your major. Such subjects are more likely to interest readers because they offer a more original and compelling perspective.

Of course, what may be original and compelling to you may be a yawner for your reader. How can you tell? Writing is always about trial and error, and what you must be able to do is to try out your draft on readers: students in your class, a tutor in the writing center, your instructor during office hours—that is, with readers that will give you an honest, thoughtful, careful reading of your work.

Begin with a Focusing Statement; End with Summary Observations

In general, anyone who offers you a formula for writing a specific kind of essay is probably making a mistake. The most famous formula in composition is the five-paragraph theme: Write a thesis statement in paragraph one; illustrate that thesis with three examples in three paragraphs; and end the essay with a summary paragraph that rephrases what you said in paragraph one. Formalized prescriptions such as this can be useful for very beginning writers, but writers can become too dependent on them and often tend to pour their contents into this one form, regardless of what kind of development the subject needs to succeed with readers.

Definition essays, however, often have two characteristics. As noted earlier, many of them begin with some kind of opening statement in the first few paragraphs that introduces the reader explicitly to the word, term, or concept that is being defined. Elie Wiesel begins his essay with the key term he wants to define, *fanaticism*, while Lisa Kanae takes a more indirect approach using narrative and collage to assemble different aspects of the word's meaning. Many definition essays send an explicit message to readers—in essence, telling the reader fairly early what word or concept is being defined—but others offer indirect approaches to the meaning of a word.

Definition essays usually end with a conclusion or summary statement about the term—what it is the writer wants the reader to learn, what specific conclusion has been reached. Wiesel wants to remind us that "memory may be our most powerful weapon against fanaticism," Ehrlich that cowboys are complex beings who contain opposing qualities. Both essays reveal two different but related ways to conclude; both remind the reader at the end of the major thrust of the essay, restating the primary message.

Readers want to know what a word or concept means, and they especially want a definition essay to have relevance to their own lives and experiences. Successful definition essays place their definitions within a larger framework, contextualizing them within a specific and knowable setting. Readers best understand words and concepts when they are defined in terms of local culture, history, neighborhood, school, disciplines, politics, and so forth. A writer might try to define the word *creativity* in general terms, but the essay will best succeed if the author considers creativity in light of writing a particular poem, developing a new software application, or discovering an original concept about social conformity and individual choice. Grounding a definition in a specific context can provide the relevance readers crave and allow the writer to make use of specific examples and particulars that hold a definition essay within everyday reality.

Judy Brady (1937–) was born in San Francisco, California, where she currently lives. She earned a bachelor of fine arts degree in painting from the University of Iowa in 1962 and resists calling herself a writer. Although she refers to herself as "a disenfranchised (and fired) house-wife, now secretary," Brady writes a regular column for the Women's Cancer Research Center and in 1991 published the anthology 1 in 3: Women with Cancer Confront an Epidemic. *Her most popular essay, "I Want a Wife," first appeared in the spring 1972 issue of* Ms. *magazine.*

Judy Brady
I Want a Wife

I belong to that classification of people known as wives. I am A Wife. And, not altogether incidentally, I am a mother.

Not too long ago a male friend of mine appeared on the scene fresh from a recent divorce. He had one child, who is, of course, with his ex-wife. He is looking for another wife. As I thought about him while I was ironing one evening, it suddenly occurred to me that I, too, would like to have a wife. Why do I want a wife?

I would like to go back to school so that I can become economically independent, support myself, and, if need be, support those dependent upon me. I want a wife who will work and send me to school. And while I am going to school I want a wife to take care of my children. I want a wife to keep track of the children's doctor and dentist appointments. And to keep track of mine, too. I want a wife to make sure my children eat properly and are kept clean. I want a wife who will wash the children's clothes and keep them mended. I want a wife who is a good nurturant attendant to my children, who arranges for their schooling, makes sure that they have an adequate social life with their peers, takes them to the park, the zoo, etc. I want a wife who takes care of the children when they are sick, a wife who arranges to be around when the children need special care, because, of course, I cannot miss classes at school. My wife must arrange to lose time at work and not lose the job. It may mean a small cut in my wife's income from time to time, but I guess I can tolerate that. Needless to say, my wife will arrange and pay for the care of the children while my wife is working.

I want a wife who will take care of *my* physical needs. I want a wife who will keep my house clean. A wife who will pick up after my children, a wife who will pick up after me. I want a wife who will keep my clothes clean, ironed, mended, replaced when need be, and who will see to it that my personal things are kept in their proper place so that I can find what I need the minute I need it. I want a wife who cooks the meals, a wife who is a *good* cook. I want a wife who will plan the menus, do the necessary grocery shopping, prepare the meals, serve them pleasantly, and then do the cleaning up while I do my studying. I want a wife who will care for me when I am sick and sympathize with my pain and loss of time from school. I want a wife to go along when our family takes a vacation so that someone can continue to care for me and my children when I need a rest and change of scene.

5   I want a wife who will not bother me with rambling complaints about a wife's duties. But I want a wife who will listen to me when I feel the need to explain a rather difficult point I have come across in my course of studies. And I want a wife who will type my papers for me when I have written them.

I want a wife who will take care of the details of my social life. When my wife and I are invited out by my friends, I want a wife who will take care of the babysitting arrangements. When I meet people at school that I like and want to entertain, I want a wife who will have the house clean, will prepare a special meal, serve it to me and my friends, and not interrupt when I talk about things that interest me and my friends. I want a wife who will have arranged that the children are fed and ready for bed before my guests arrive so that the children do not bother us. I want a wife who takes care of the needs of my guests so that they feel comfortable, who makes sure that they have an ashtray, that they are passed the hors d'oeuvres, that they are offered a second helping of the food, that their wine glasses are replenished when necessary, that their coffee is served to them as they like it. And I want a wife who knows that sometimes I need a night out by myself.

I want a wife who is sensitive to my sexual needs, a wife who makes love passionately and eagerly when I feel like it, a wife who makes sure that I am satisfied. And, of course, I want a wife who will not demand sexual attention when I am not in the mood for it. I want a wife who assumes the complete responsibility for birth control, because I do not want more children. I want a wife who will remain sexually faithful to me so that I do not have to clutter up my intellectual life with jealousies. And I want a wife who understands that *my* sexual needs may entail more than strict adherence to monogamy. I must, after all, be able to relate to people as fully as possible.

If, by chance, I find another person more suitable as a wife than the wife I already have, I want the liberty to replace my present wife with another one. Naturally, I will expect a fresh new life; my wife will take the children and be solely responsible for them so that I am left free.

When I am through with school and have a job, I want my wife to quit working and remain at home so that my wife can more fully and completely take care of a wife's duties.

10   My God, who *wouldn't* want a wife?

Analyzing Rhetorical Choices

1. What is the effect of Brady's opening sentence, "I belong to that classification of people known as wives"? Why do you think she uses the phrase "classification of people"?

2. Why does Brady keep repeating "I want a wife"? What effect(s) does this phrase have as a consequence of its being continually repeated?

3. Comment on Brady's use of italics in this essay. In what ways is it effective, distracting, or overly dramatic?

Writing About Issues and Contexts

1. In what ways, if any, is Brady's essay an accurate definition of a wife? In what ways, if any, is it a distortion?

2. If Brady is accurate in describing a wife, what is a husband? Define one in several paragraphs, imitating Brady's style or any other that you deem appropriate.

Elaine Potter Richardson (1949–) was born in St. John's, Antigua, which was then a British colony in the Caribbean. She came to the United States in 1966 at the age of 17; a fictional account of her experience growing up and leaving home can be found in her novel, Annie John *(1985). After working in a variety of jobs, including as a nanny, she began writing for the "Talk of the Town" section of* The New Yorker *magazine and assumed the literary name of* **Jamaica Kincaid,** *by which she is best known today. Kincaid has published many books, primarily focused on her family experiences, including* Lucy *(1990) and* The Autobiography of My Mother *(1996). She has also published an angry account of colonization,* A Small Place *(1988). She lives in Vermont with her husband, son, and daughter.*

Jamaica Kincaið

Girl

Wash the white clothes on Monday and put them on the stone heap; wash the color clothes on Tuesday and put them on the clothesline to dry; don't walk barehead in the hot sun; cook pumpkin fritters in very hot sweet oil; soak your little clothes right after you take them off; when buying cotton to make yourself a nice blouse, be sure that it doesn't have gum on it, because that way it won't hold up well after a wash; soak salt fish overnight before you cook it; is it true that you sing benna in Sunday school?; always eat your food in such a way that it won't turn someone else's stomach; on Sundays try to walk like a lady and not like the slut you are so bent on becoming; don't sing benna in Sunday school; you mustn't speak to wharf-rat boys, not even to give directions; don't eat fruits on the street—flies will follow you; *but I don't sing benna on Sundays at all and never in Sunday school;* this is how to sew on a button; this is how to make a button-hole for the button you have just sewed on; this is how to hem a dress when you see the hem coming down and so to prevent yourself from looking like the slut I know you are so bent on becoming; this is how you iron your father's khaki shirt so that it doesn't have a crease; this is how you iron your father's khaki pants so that they don't have a crease; this is how you grow okra—far from the house, because okra tree harbors red ants; when you are growing dasheen, make sure it gets plenty of water or else it makes your throat itch when you are eating it; this is how you sweep a corner; this is how you sweep a whole house; this is how you sweep a yard; this is how you smile to someone you don't like too much; this is how you smile to someone you don't like at all; this is how you smile to someone you like completely; this is how you set a table for tea; this is how you set a table for dinner; this is how you set a table for dinner with an important guest; this is how you set a table for lunch; this is how you set a table for breakfast; this is how to behave in the presence of men who don't know you very well, and this way they won't recognize immediately the slut I have warned you against becoming; be sure to wash every day, even if it is with your own spit; don't squat down to play marbles—you are not a boy, you know; don't pick people's flowers—you might catch something; don't throw stones at blackbirds, because it might not be a blackbird at all; this is how to make a bread pudding; this is how to make doukona; this is how to make pepper pot; this is how to make a good medicine for a cold; this is how to make a good medicine to throw away a child before it even becomes a child; this is how to catch a fish; this is how to throw back a fish you don't like, and that way something bad won't fall on you; this is how to bully a man; this is how a man bullies you; this is how to love a man, and if this doesn't work there are other ways, and if they don't work don't feel too bad about giving up; this is how to spit up in the air if you feel like it, and this is how to move quick so that it doesn't fall on you; this is how to make ends meet; always squeeze bread to make sure it's fresh; *but what if the baker won't let me feel the bread?*; you mean to say that after all you are really going to be the kind of woman who the baker won't let near the bread?

Analyzing Rhetorical Choices

1. Who is the speaker of this essay? Who is speaking in italics? How would you characterize the interaction, however slight, of these two speakers?

2. Why do you think Kincaid wrote this essay all as one sentence? What effect does this form have on you, as reader? Evaluate its effectiveness (or ineffectiveness).

Writing About Issues and Contexts

1. Who is this "girl"? Who does the speaker want her to be?
2. According to this essay, how would you define the ideal girl? What kinds of traits and values does she have?
3. Evaluate the advice being given here, in terms of how valuable it is to a girl, especially one growing up within a very hierarchical and traditional island society such as Antigua's.

Jonathan Rauch (1960–) is a native of Phoenix, Arizona. After graduating from Yale University, he worked at the Winston-Salem Journal *in North Carolina, for the* National Journal, *and as a correspondent for* The Atlantic Monthly. *Rauch's articles have appeared in the* New Republic, *the* Economist, Harper's, U. S. News & World Report, *the* New York Times, *the* Wall Street Journal, *the* Washington Post, *and the* Los Angeles Times, *among other publications. His books include* Kindly Inquisitors: The New Attacks on Free Thought *(1993),* Government's End: Why Washington Stopped Working *(1999), and* Gay Marriage: Why It Is Good for Gays, Good for Straights, and Good for America *(2004). "Caring for Your Introvert" was first published in* The Atlantic Monthly *in 2003.*

Jonathan Rauch

Caring for Your Introvert

Do you know someone who needs hours alone every day? Who loves quiet conversations about feelings or ideas, and can give a dynamite presentation to a big audience, but seems awkward in groups and maladroit at small talk? Who has to be dragged to parties and then needs the rest of the day to recuperate? Who growls or scowls or grunts or winces when accosted with pleasantries by people who are just trying to be nice?

If so, do you tell this person he is "too serious," or ask if he is okay? Regard him as aloof, arrogant, rude? Redouble your efforts to draw him out?

If you answered yes to these questions, chances are that you have an introvert on your hands—and that you aren't caring for him properly. Science has learned a good deal in recent years about the habits and requirements of introverts. It has even learned, by means of brain scans, that introverts process information differently from other people (I am not making this up). If you are behind the curve on this important matter, be reassured that you are not alone. Introverts may be common, but they are also among the most misunderstood and aggrieved groups in America, possibly the world.

I know. My name is Jonathan, and I am an introvert.

5   Oh, for years I denied it. After all, I have good social skills. I am not morose or misanthropic. Usually. I am far from shy. I love long

conversations that explore intimate thoughts or passionate interests. But at last I have self-identified and come out to my friends and colleagues. In doing so, I have found myself liberated from any number of damaging misconceptions and stereotypes. Now I am here to tell you what you need to know in order to respond sensitively and supportively to your own introverted family members, friends, and colleagues. Remember, someone you know, respect, and interact with every day is an introvert, and you are probably driving this person nuts. It pays to learn the warning signs.

What is introversion? In its modern sense, the concept goes back to the 1920s and the psychologist Carl Jung. Today it is a mainstay of personality tests, including the widely used Myers-Briggs Type Indicator. Introverts are not necessarily shy. Shy people are anxious or frightened or self-excoriating in social settings; introverts generally are not. Introverts are also not misanthropic, though some of us do go along with Sartre as far as to say "Hell is other people at breakfast." Rather, introverts are people who find other people tiring.

Extroverts are energized by people, and wilt or fade when alone. They often seem bored by themselves, in both senses of the expression. Leave an extrovert alone for two minutes and he will reach for his cell phone. In contrast, after an hour or two of being socially "on," we introverts need to turn off and recharge. My own formula is roughly two hours alone for every hour of socializing. This isn't antisocial. It isn't a sign of depression. It does not call for medication. For introverts, to be alone with our thoughts is as restorative as sleeping, as nourishing as eating. Our motto: "I'm OK, you're OK—in small doses."

How many people are introverts? I performed exhaustive research on this question, in the form of a quick Google search. The answer: about 25 percent. Or: just under half. Or—my favorite—"a minority in the regular population but a majority in the gifted population."

Are introverts misunderstood? Wildly. That, it appears, is our lot in life. "It is very difficult for an extrovert to understand an introvert," write the education experts Jill D. Burruss and Lisa Kaenzig. (They are also the source of the quotation in the previous paragraph.) Extroverts are easy for introverts to understand, because extroverts spend so much of their time working out who they are in voluble, and frequently inescapable, interaction with other people. They are as inscrutable as puppy dogs. But the street does not run both ways. Extroverts have little or no grasp of introversion. They assume that company, especially their own, is always welcome. They cannot imagine why someone would need to be alone; indeed, they often take umbrage at the suggestion. As often as I have tried to explain the matter to extroverts, I have never sensed that any of them really understood. They listen for a moment and then go back to barking and yipping.

10   *Are introverts oppressed?*   I would have to say so. For one thing, extroverts are overrepresented in politics, a profession in which only the garrulous are really comfortable. Look at George W. Bush. Look at Bill Clinton. They seem to come fully to life only around other people. To think of the few introverts who did rise to the top in politics—Calvin Coolidge, Richard Nixon—is merely to drive home the point. With the possible exception of Ronald Reagan, whose fabled aloofness and privateness were probably signs of a deep introverted streak (many actors, I've read, are introverts, and many introverts, when socializing, feel like actors), introverts are not considered "naturals" in politics.

Extroverts therefore dominate public life. This is a pity. If we introverts ran the world, it would no doubt be a calmer, saner, more peaceful sort of place. As Coolidge is supposed to have said, "Don't you know that four-fifths of all our troubles in this life would disappear if we would just sit down and keep still?" (He is also supposed to have said, "If you don't say anything, you won't be called on to repeat it." The only thing a true introvert dislikes more than talking about himself is repeating himself.)

With their endless appetite for talk and attention, extroverts also dominate social life, so they tend to set expectations. In our extrovertist society, being outgoing is considered normal and therefore desirable, a mark of happiness, confidence, leadership. Extroverts are seen as bighearted, vibrant, warm, empathic. "People person" is a compliment. Introverts are described with words like "guarded," "loner," "reserved," "taciturn," "self-contained," "private"—narrow, ungenerous words, words that suggest emotional parsimony and smallness of personality. Female introverts, I suspect, must suffer especially. In certain circles, particularly in the Midwest, a man can still sometimes get away with being what they used to call a strong and silent type; introverted women, lacking that alternative, are even more likely than men to be perceived as timid, withdrawn, haughty.

Are introverts arrogant? Hardly. I suppose this common misconception has to do with our being more intelligent, more reflective, more independent, more level-headed, more refined, and more sensitive than extroverts. Also, it is probably due to our lack of small talk, a lack that extroverts often mistake for disdain. We tend to think before talking, whereas extroverts tend to think *by* talking, which is why their meetings never last less than six hours. "Introverts," writes a perceptive fellow named Thomas P. Crouser, in an online review of a recent book called *Why Should Extroverts Make All the Money?* (I'm not making *that* up, either), "are driven to distraction by the semi-internal dialogue extroverts tend to conduct. Introverts don't outwardly complain, instead roll their eyes and silently curse the darkness." Just so.

The worst of it is that extroverts have no idea of the torment they put us through. Sometimes, as we gasp for air amid the fog of their 98-percent-content-free talk, we wonder if extroverts even bother to listen to themselves. Still, we endure stoically, because the etiquette books—written, no doubt, by extroverts—regard declining to banter as rude and gaps in conversation as awkward. We can only dream that someday, when our condition is more widely understood, when perhaps an Introverts' Rights movement has blossomed and borne fruit, it will not be impolite to say "I'm an introvert. You are a wonderful person and I like you. But now please shush."

15 *How can I let the introvert in my life know that I support him and respect his choice?* First, recognize that it's not a choice. It's not a lifestyle. It's an *orientation*. Second, when you see an introvert lost in thought, don't say "What's the matter?" or "Are you all right?" Third, don't say anything else, either.

Analyzing Rhetorical Choices

1. How literally do you read Rauch's essay? Are some sections to be taken more seriously than others? For example, Coolidge and Nixon presided over two of the most problematic presidencies of the twentieth century, which does not seem to be a good argument on behalf of introverts.

2. Rauch claims that he is not making up the data about brain scans but does not reveal the sources of the data. Does this fact diminish his argument for you, or is the argument persuasive nonetheless?

3. The author uses the terms *come out* and *orientation*, making explicit parallels to the gay rights movement. Does this approach help or hamper his presentation?

Writing About Issues and Contexts

1. Are you also behind the curve on introverts? Are you one? Do you know any that you are treating poorly?
2. Are introverts among the most aggrieved groups or oppressed groups in America? What is your evidence?
3. Discuss the gender issue. Do female introverts suffer more, as Rauch suspects?

Born in Vienna, Austria, **Bruno Bettelheim** *(1903–1990) survived the
Holocaust and came to the United States in 1939, becoming a natural-
ized citizen in 1944. From 1944–1973 he served as a professor of psychology at the University of Chicago. Drawing on his own experiences in
the concentration camps and the horrific experiences of the children he
witnessed there, Bettelheim became one of the world's leading authorities
on childhood emotional disorders. His groundbreaking books on this
subject include* Love Is Not Enough: The Treatment of Emotionally
Disturbed Children *(1950),* Dialogues with Mothers *(1962), and* The
Uses of Enchantment: The Meaning and Importance of Fairy Tales
*(1976). Bettelheim died in 1990, committing suicide after a long illness.
The selection that follows is excerpted from a much longer essay in the
book* Surviving and Other Essays *(1979).*

Bruno Bettelheim

The Holocaust

To begin with, it was not the hapless victims of the Nazis who
named their incomprehensible and totally unmasterable fate the
"holocaust." It was the Americans who applied this artificial and
highly technical term to the Nazi extermination of the European Jews.
But while the event when named as mass murder most foul evokes the
most immediate, most powerful revulsion, when it is designated by a
rare technical term, we must first in our minds translate it back into
emotionally meaningful language. Using technical or specially created
terms instead of words from our common vocabulary is one of the
best-known and most widely used distancing devices, separating the
intellectual from the emotional experience. Talking about "the holocaust" permits us to manage it intellectually where the raw facts,
when given their ordinary names, would overwhelm us emotionally—
because it was catastrophe beyond comprehension, beyond the limits
of our imagination, unless we force ourselves against our desire to extend it to encompass these terrible events.

This linguistic circumlocution began while it all was only in the
planning stage. Even the Nazis—usually given to grossness in language and action—shied away from facing openly what they were up
to and called this vile mass murder "the final solution of the Jewish
problem." After all, solving a problem can be made to appear like an

honorable enterprise, as long as we are not forced to recognize that the solution we are about to embark on consists of the completely un-provoked, vicious murder of millions of helpless men, women, and children. The Nuremberg judges of these Nazi criminals followed their example of circumlocution by coining a neologism out of one Greek and one Latin root: genocide. These artificially created techni-cal terms fail to connect with our strongest feelings. The horror of murder is part of our most common human heritage. From earliest in-fancy on, it arouses violent abhorrence in us. Therefore in whatever form it appears we should give such an act its true designation and not hide it behind polite, erudite terms created out of classical words.

To call this vile mass murder "the holocaust" is not to give it a special name emphasizing its uniqueness which would permit, over time, the word becoming invested with feelings germane to the event it refers to. The correct definition of *holocaust* is "burnt offering." As such, it is part of the language of the psalmist, a meaningful word to all who have some acquaintance with the Bible, full of the richest emotional connotations. By using the term "holocaust," entirely false associations are established through conscious and unconscious con-notations between the most vicious of mass murders and ancient ritu-als of a deeply religious nature.

Using a word with such strong unconscious religious connota-tions when speaking of the murder of millions of Jews robs the vic-tims of this abominable mass murder of the only thing left to them: their uniqueness. Calling the most callous, most brutal, most horrid, most heinous mass murder a burnt offering is a sacrilege, a profana-tion of God and man.

5   Martyrdom is part of our religious heritage. A martyr, burned at the stake, is a burnt offering to his god. And it is true that after the Jews were asphyxiated, the victims' corpses were burned. But I believe we fool ourselves if we think we are honoring the victims of system-atic murder by using this term, which has the highest moral connota-tions. By doing so, we connect for our own psychological reasons what happened in the extermination camps with historical events we deeply regret, but also greatly admire. We do so because this makes it easier for us to cope; only in doing so we cope with our distorted im-age of what happened, not with the events the way they did happen.

By calling the victims of the Nazis martyrs, we falsify their fate. The true meaning of *martyr* is: "One who voluntarily undergoes the penalty of death for refusing to renounce his faith" (*Oxford English Dictionary*). The Nazis made sure that nobody could mistakenly think that their victims were murdered for their religious beliefs. Renouncing their faith would have saved none of them. Those who had converted to Christianity were gassed, as were those who were atheists, and those who were deeply religious Jews. They did not die for any conviction, and certainly not out of choice.

Millions of Jews were systematically slaughtered, as were untold other "undesirables," not for any convictions of theirs, but only because they stood in the way of the realization of an illusion. They neither died for their convictions, nor were they slaughtered because of their convictions, but only in consequence of the Nazis' delusional belief about what was required to protect the purity of their assumed superior racial endowment, and what they thought necessary to guarantee them the living space they believed they needed and were entitled to. Thus while these millions were slaughtered for an idea, they did not die for one.

Millions—men, women, and children—were processed after they had been utterly brutalized, their humanity destroyed, their clothes torn from their bodies. Naked, they were sorted into those who were destined to be murdered immediately, and those others who had a short-term usefulness as slave labor. But after a brief interval they, too, were to be herded into the same gas chambers into which the others were immediately piled, there to be asphyxiated so that, in their last moments, they could not prevent themselves from fighting each other in vain for a last breath of air.

To call these most wretched victims of a murderous delusion, of destructive drives run rampant, martyrs or a burnt offering is a distortion invented for our comfort, small as it may be. It pretends that this most vicious of mass murders had some deeper meaning; that in some fashion the victims either offered themselves or at least became sacrifices to a higher cause. It robs them of the last recognition which could be theirs, denies them the last dignity we could accord them: to face and accept what their death was all about, not embellishing it for the small psychological relief this may give us.

10   We could feel so much better if the victims had acted out of choice. For our emotional relief, therefore, we dwell on the tiny minority who did exercise some choice: the resistance fighters of the Warsaw ghetto, for example, and others like them. We are ready to overlook the fact that these people fought back only at a time when everything was lost, when the overwhelming majority of those who had been forced into the ghettos had already been exterminated without resisting. Certainly those few who finally fought for their survival

and their convictions, risking and losing their lives in doing so, deserve our admiration; their deeds give us a moral lift. But the more we dwell on these few, the more unfair are we to the memory of the millions who were slaughtered—who gave in, did not fight back—because we deny them the only thing which up to the very end remained uniquely their own: their fate.

Analyzing Rhetorical Choices

1. How would you describe the diction and sentence structure in this selection? Choose some specific words and sentences that you find challenging and offer definitions and paraphrases.

2. What etymological information does Bettelheim provide in this selection? Why does he do this?

3. How does Bettelheim express his outrage at the different terms used to describe the victims of the Nazis? What alternative description would you suggest to describe these victims that would be true to the spirit of Bettelheim's essay?

Writing About Issues and Contexts

1. Does this essay define? If so, what exactly does it define and what are the essential terms of its central definition?

2. What is wrong with using the word *holocaust* to describe the destruction of the Nazis' victims? What are the potential political effects of "linguistic circumlocution"? What is wrong with the word *martyr*?

3. Bettelheim writes, "Millions of Jews were systematically slaughtered, as were untold other 'undesirables,' not for any convictions of theirs, but only because they stood in the way of the realization of an illusion." What does he mean by this? What does he mean by the word *illusion* here?

Lisa Linn Kanae (1960–) was born in Honolulu, Hawai'i. At the age of 30, she decided to return to college and complete a bachelor's degree and then earn a master's in English from the University of Hawai'i at Manoa, where she was the recipient of the 1999 Patricia Sumei Saiki Creative Writing Award; 1998 Academy of American Poets Harold Taylor Prize; 1997–1998 Red Mandarin and Lady Yi-suen Shen Scholarship Award; and the 1996–1997 Hemingway Award for Creative Nonfiction. Kanae's prose and poetry is published in 'Oiwi: A Native Hawaiian Journal, Bamboo Ridge Press publications, Hybolics, and Tinfish. She currently teaches English composition and literature courses at Kapi'olani Community College on the island of O'ahu. "Pidgin" is an excerpt from Kanae's memoir essay, Sista Tongue (2001), which weaves the social history of Hawai'i Creole English with personal experience and general attitudes toward dialect and language.

Lisa Kanae

Pidgin

Editor's Note: The unusual typographic features of this essay in the pages that follow are not a mistake. Lisa Kanae expresses her meaning in Sista Tongue *both in terms of the explicit meanings of words and the implicit meanings of graphic design. As closely as possible, we have tried to remain true to the appearance of the pages as they were originally printed; thus the pages that follow approximate the format of the book as it was originally printed. Cover and book design are by Kristin Kaleinani Gonzales, a native Hawai'ian, who earned her bachelor's in fine arts degree from the University of Hawai'i at Manoa and much of whose artwork examines the complex meanings of identity and culture.*

Wendell Johnson, Professor of Speech Pathology and Psychology,
University of Iowa and editor of Speech Handicapped School Children,
writes that self-expression, self-communication, and communication
between the speaker and other persons are the fundamental purposes of
speech. According to Professor Johnson,

> a speech disorder occurs when all of the
> basic functions of speech are affected to
> some degree and, in certain cases, one
> function may be more seriously disturbed
> than another (6).

My little bradda not mento, so you betta stop teasing him all da time jus cuz you tink you can talk more betta dan him. Jus cuz you can go one regula-kine school—not da special-kine school whea da teacha clamp one rula-looking kine ting on your tongue.

Wot? You no believe me?

I saw yum fo real kine. I promise! I dunno why da teacha did dat to him. Jus cuz my litto bradda get hard time fo talk no mean he stupid. He no can— was dat word again—arteekcolate? My fadda tease him all da time. Call him "short tongue." Sometimes Popo Lum, da landlady downstairs, talk to Harold-Boy like he deaf and dumb or something.

Sheeze.

He only four years old, try.

Articulation: when tongue, jaw, teeth, lips, and palate alter the air stream coming from the vocal cords creating sounds, which make up syllables, which make up words. The most important structure of articulation is the tongue, which is responsible for effecting the changes in the mouth basic to the production of all but a few sounds. The tongue is so essential to human speech, languages are often referred to as "tongues" (Hanson 1–9).

I hold my madda's hand everytime da school bus from da special school come fo take Harold-Boy away. Insai dat bus get funny-kine looking childrens. E, I bet dey hate for talk too. One boy look like he stay wearing one bird cage ova his head. Only his eyes move. Get one girl wit magnifying glasses—da kine for kill ants—strap to her head. She get metal sticks stuck to her legs too. Get one nodda girl who no can stay still. She use to pull out her hair beefo da bus driva wen force her for wear white seat belts across her chest and her legs. And get one supa skinny boy, he just stare at my bradda.

"Wot you looking at?" I yell.

"Badda you?"

Da skinny boy no say nutting. Gala gala drips from his crooked lip. His collar stay all wet.

"Be good now," I tell my little bradda. "Bum-bye wen you come home we go watch cartoon, kay?"

The body of the tongue is shaped like a broad-based anvil; the body is what we see when we look into the mouth. The body of the tongue is divided into four parts: the tip, the blade, the front, and the back. What we cannot see when we look into the mouth is the tongue's root. (Hanson 1–9)

Creole languages are primarily born out of necessity. In his 1936 article, "The Competition of Languages in Hawaii," Dr. John E. Reinecke, whose scholarly work has contributed to the scientific study of Creole languages, defines a Creole dialect by describing its function in plantation communities:

> **A Creole dialect is a greatly simplified, makeshift form of a European language which has arisen in master-servant situations on a large scale between European employers and (usually) non-European laborers. It is especially common in plantation regions, and is necessary where the laborers are drawn from several linguistic groups.** *(7)*

Reinecke points out that the formation of a Creole language met the need for a "medium of communication between members of non-English speaking groups" (Reinecke 105).

In many cases, plantation labor populations were so ethnically diverse that a Creole language became the only feasible means of communication between the different ethnic groups—

—a common tongue of the working class.

This lingua franca was not only used between groups of multi-ethnic laborers, it was also used between the laborers and the plantation "masters." Reinecke writes that it would be impossible for the plantation "master" to become proficient in every language of the ethnically diverse labor groups; therefore Creole was also used as a "language of command" (18) because "masters rarely deign to learn the speech of the servile population" (18).

Plantation "masters" used Creole languages to create class stratification between "master" and "servant" laborer. Creole languages were also used to enforce and maintain that class stratification by keeping the laborer ignorant of the "master's" ruling class language. Joseph Vendryes, author of *Language: A Linguistic Introduction to History* writes **Creoles were once considered the speech of "inferior beings** . . . a subordinate class whose superiors have never troubled nor desired to make them speak any language correctly "** (Vendryes qtd. in Reinecke 18).

At firs my madda was supa worried dat Harold-Boy neva start talking da same time as me and my cousin dem. Now she stay mo worried, because he no can talk like everybody else. But, not like everybody in dis house talk good English. My madda, she every time tell me,

"you not going get one good job if you no can talk good English. People going tink you stupid."

Stupid?

Gee, no wonda she stay all
hu-hu about Harold-Boy.
Me, at leese I can talk. But
Harold-Boy . . . das one
different story. He get
one—watchoo call—one
speech impedment. Das why
dey treat him like he mento.
Piss me off.

My litto bradda no belong on dat bus wit all dose handicap freaks.

There is a general understanding among listeners of a language that identifies whether a sound comes within what is considered normal limits or whether we sense something is wrong or misarticulated. This impression of misarticulation may be generally referred to as baby talk, lazy tongue movement, or any other variety of descriptive terms that imply the listener has some trouble understanding what is being said (Rousey 34).

Only me can undahstand wot Harold-Boy trying fo say.

Itah, itah: sister.

Wuh-yol: world.

Too-too-, too-too: Popeye da Sailor Man.

Harold-Boy smile up wen Popeye squeeze da can, eat da spinach, beat up Brutus. Harold-Boy, he make oojee kine face wen Olive Oil like kiss Popeye all ova, and he love to sing along wit da Popeye song.

You like undahstand my bradda or wot?

Try let him sing.

What kind of social implications does a "language of command" created for "master-servant" environments have upon the descendants of that "servile population," especially when those descendants continue to use an evolved form of that Creole generations later—after the plantation has closed down, and the laborer is revered as an ancestor? Today, half of the State of Hawai'i's population of approximately one million people speaks Hawai'i Creole English (HCE) (Romaine 527).

I am one voice out of that one million.

Analyzing Rhetorical Choices

1. How do you respond to the structure of the two opening paragraphs? What is your response to the radical shift in tone and formality, and to the lack of transition between the first two paragraphs?
2. How does the speaker choose to characterize herself and her brother, Harold-Boy? How do you respond to her statement that "My litto bradda no belong on dat bus wit all dose handicap freaks"?
3. Kanae writes in two different versions of English, Pidgin and Standard. Which is more effective? Why? How does the creative spelling of Pidgin affect you as a reader?
4. Why do you think Kanae uses the various kinds of spacing and typefaces? How do they affect you as a reader?

Writing About Issues and Contexts

1. According to Kanae, what is Pidgin? How does it function socially among the populations that speak it?
2. At one point in *Sista Tongue*, Kanae exemplifies what she means by Pidgin by writing, "Go bus out da pidgin wen trying fo get one kama'aina discount from da local guy or gal behind da rent-a-car counta. Garrans da haole tourist at da same counta going pay mo money fo rent one car." What does this passage mean? How would you interpret it socially in terms of what it says about relations among Pidgin speakers and between Pidgin and non-Pidgin speakers?
3. Is the narrator's mother correct when she says, "you not going get one good job if you no can talk good English. People going tink you stupid"? Analyze this statement in terms of your own insights and experiences, writing a balanced assessment of its accuracy.
4. Interpret the title, *Sista Tongue*. What are the implications of this title in relation to the author? The subject? You the reader?

Gloria Naylor (1950–) was born in New York City, graduated from Brooklyn College in 1981, and went on to receive her master's in African American literature at Yale. Naylor has written numerous works, including five interconnected novels: The Women of Brewster Place *(1982), for which she received an American Book Award for best new novel;* Linden Hills *(1985);* Mama Day *(1988);* Bailey's Café *(1992); and* The Men of Brewster Place *(1998). In 1989,* The Women of Brewster Place *was adapted as a television miniseries starring Oprah Winfrey. The following essay was published in 1986.*

Gloria Naylor

The Meanings of a Word

Language is the subject. It is the written form with which I've managed to keep the wolf away from the door and, in diaries, to keep my sanity. In spite of this, I consider the written word inferior to the spoken, and much of the frustration experienced by novelists is the awareness that whatever we manage to capture in even the most transcendent passages falls far short of the richness of life. Dialogue achieves its power in the dynamics of a fleeting moment of sight, sound, smell, and touch.

I'm not going to enter the debate here about whether it is language that shapes reality or vice versa. That battle is doomed to be waged whenever we seek intermittent reprieve from the chicken and egg dispute. I will simply take the position that the spoken word, like the written word, amounts to a nonsensical arrangement of sounds or letters without a consensus that assigns "meaning." And building from the meanings of what we hear, we order reality. Words themselves are innocuous; it is the consensus that gives them true power.

I remember the first time I heard the word *nigger*. In my third-grade class, our math tests were being passed down the rows, and as I handed the papers to a little boy in back of me, I remarked that once again he had received a much lower mark than I did. He snatched his test from me and spit out that word. Had he called me a nymphomaniac or a necrophiliac, I couldn't have been more puzzled. I didn't know what a nigger was, but I knew that whatever it meant, it was something he shouldn't have called me. This was verified when I raised my hand, and in a loud voice repeated what he had said and watched the teacher scold him for using a "bad" word. I was later to go home and ask the inevitable question that every black parent must face—"Mommy, what does 'nigger' mean?"

And what exactly did it mean? Thinking back, I realize that this could not have been the first time the word was used in my presence. I was part of a large extended family that had migrated from the rural South after World War II and formed a close-knit network that gravitated around my maternal grandparents. Their ground-floor apartment in one of the buildings they owned in Harlem was a weekend mecca for my immediate family, along with countless aunts, uncles, and cousins who brought along assorted friends. It was a bustling and open house with assorted neighbors and tenants popping in and out to exchange bits of gossip, pick up an old quarrel, or referee the ongoing checkers game in which my grandmother cheated shamelessly. They were all there to let down their hair and put up their feet after a week of labor in the factories, laundries, and shipyards of New York.

5   Amid the clamor, which could reach deafening proportions—two or three conversations going on simultaneously, punctuated by the sound of a baby's crying somewhere in the back rooms or out on the street—there was still a rigid set of rules about what was said and how. Older children were sent out of the living room when it was time to get into the juicy details about "you-know-who" up on the third floor who had gone and gotten herself "p·r·e·g·n·a·n·t!" But my parents, knowing that I could spell well beyond my years, always demanded that I follow the others out to play. Beyond sexual misconduct and death, everything else was considered harmless for our young ears. And so among the anecdotes of the triumphs and disappointments in the various workings of their lives, the word *nigger* was used in my presence, but it was set within contexts and inflections that caused it to register in my mind as something else.

In the singular, the word was always applied to a man who had distinguished himself in some situation that brought their approval for his strength, intelligence, or drive:

"Did Johnny really do that?"

"I'm telling you, that nigger pulled in $6,000 of overtime last year. Said he got enough for a down payment on a house."

When used with a possessive adjective by a woman—"my nigger"— it became a term of endearment for husband or boyfriend. But it could be more than just a term applied to a man. In their mouths it became the pure essence of manhood—a disembodied force that channeled their past history of struggle and present survival against the odds into a victorious statement of being: "Yeah, that old foreman found out quick enough—you don't mess with a nigger."

10   In the plural, it became a description of some group within the community that had overstepped the bounds of decency as my family defined it: Parents who neglected their children, a drunken couple who fought in public, people who simply refused to look for work, those with excessively dirty mouths or unkempt households were all "trifling niggers." This particular circle could forgive hard times, unemployment, the occasional bout of depression—they had gone through all of that themselves—but the unforgivable sin was lack of self-respect.

A woman could never be a *nigger* in the singular, with its connotation of confirming worth. The noun *girl* was its closest equivalent in that sense, but only when used in direct address and regardless of the gender doing the addressing. *Girl* was a token of respect for a woman. The one-syllable word was drawn out to sound like three in recognition of the extra ounce of wit, nerve or daring that the woman had shown in the situation under discussion.

"G·i·r·l, stop. You mean you said that to his face?"

But if the word was used in a third-person reference or shortened so that it almost snapped out of the mouth, it always involved some element of communal disapproval. And age became an important factor in these exchanges. It was only between individuals of the same generation, or from an older person to a younger (but never the other way around), that "girl" would be considered a compliment.

I don't agree with the argument that use of the word *nigger* at this social stratum of the black community was an internalization of racism. The dynamics were the exact opposite: the people in my grandmother's living room took a word that whites used to signify worthlessness or degradation and rendered it impotent. Gathering there together, they transformed *nigger* to signify the varied and complex human beings they knew themselves to be. If the word was to disappear totally from the mouths of even the most liberal of white society, no one in that room was naive enough to believe it would disappear from white minds. Meeting the word head-on, they proved it had absolutely nothing to do with the way they were determined to live their lives.

15   So there must have been dozens of times that the word *nigger* was spoken in front of me before I reached the third grade. But I didn't

"hear" it until it was said by a small pair of lips that had already learned it could be a way to humiliate me. That was the word I went home and asked my mother about. And since she knew that I had to grow up in America, she took me in her lap and explained.

Analyzing Rhetorical Choices

1. Analyze Naylor's opening paragraph in terms of formality, shifts in tone, parallel structure, alliteration, and other stylistic uses of language.
2. Naylor seems intent on shocking the reader with her opening sentence of the third paragraph. In what ways is this sentence an effective opening to the rest of the essay?
3. Why does Naylor additionally define the term *girl?* How does this contribute to the essay? Are there affectionate terms like *girl* in your everyday language that are specific to your cultural experience? If so, list several of them and use them in sentences that express this affection.

Writing About Issues and Contexts

1. How does Naylor's opening paragraph relate to the topic she analyzes? Offer your own view whether "Words themselves are innocuous; it is the consensus that gives them true power."
2. Naylor writes that "the word *nigger* was used in my presence, but it was set within contexts and inflections that caused it to register in my mind as something else." What does she mean by this? What is registered in her mind when the word *nigger* is used within her family setting?
3. Is the use of this word by blacks themselves "an internalization of racism"? Are similar derogatory terms used by other ethnic groups? Why or why not?

   How can we make sense of the "negative" terms that members of a particular ethnicity or subculture may use when referring to themselves?

Born in Santa Barbara, California, **Gretel Ehrlich** *(1946–) attended Bennington College, UCLA Film School, and the New School for Social Research. She has written numerous books, including* Heart Mountain *(1988),* Islands, the Universe, Home *(1991),* A Match to the Heart *(1994),* This Cold Heaven: Seven Seasons in Greenland *(2001), and most recently,* The Future of Ice *(2004). In addition to her career as a writer, Ehrlich has worked as a ranch hand, sheepherder, and documentary film-maker for the Public Broadcasting System. Her essays about being a sheepherder in Wyoming came together to form the book* The Solace of Open Spaces *(1985), which was five years in the making. The collection of 12 essays, which includes "About Men," won awards from the American Academy of Arts and Letters and the Whiting Foundation.*

Gretel Ehrlich

About Men

When I'm in New York but feeling lonely for Wyoming I look for the Marlboro ads in the subway. What I'm aching to see is horseflesh, the glint of a spur, a line of distant mountains, brimming creeks, and a reminder of the ranchers and cowboys I've ridden with for the last eight years. But the men I see in those posters with their stern, humorless looks remind me of no one I know here. In our hellbent earnestness to romanticize the cowboy we've ironically disesteemed his true character. If he's "strong and silent" it's because there's probably no one to talk to. If he "rides away into the sunset" it's because he's been on horseback since four in the morning moving cattle and he's trying, fifteen hours later, to get home to his family. If he's "a rugged individualist" he's also part of a team: ranch work is teamwork and even the glorified open-range cowboys of the 1880s rode up and down the Chisholm Trail in the company of twenty or thirty other riders. Instead of the macho, trigger-happy man our culture has perversely wanted him to be, the cowboy is more apt to be convivial, quirky, and softhearted. To be "tough" on a ranch has nothing to do with conquests and displays of power. More often than not, circumstances—like the colt he's riding or an unexpected blizzard—are overpowering him. It's not toughness but "toughing it out" that counts. In other words, this macho, cultural artifact the cowboy has become is simply a man who possesses resilience, patience, and an instinct for survival.

"Cowboys are just like a pile of rocks—everything happens to them. They get climbed on, kicked, rained and snowed on, scuffed up by wind. Their job is 'just to take it,'" one old-timer told me.

A cowboy is someone who loves his work. Since the hours are long—ten to fifteen hours a day—and the pay is $30 he has to. What's required of him is an odd mixture of physical vigor and maternalism. His part of the beef-raising industry is to birth and nurture calves and take care of their mothers. For the most part his work is done on horseback and in a lifetime he sees and comes to know more animals than people. The iconic myth surrounding him is built on American notions of heroism: the index of a man's value as measured in physical courage. Such ideas have perverted manliness into a self-absorbed race for cheap thrills. In a rancher's world, courage has less to do with facing danger than with acting spontaneously—usually on behalf of an animal or another rider. If a cow is stuck in a boghole he throws a loop around her neck, takes his dally (a half hitch around the saddle horn), and pulls her out with horsepower. If a calf is born sick, he may take her home, warm her in front of the kitchen fire, and massage her legs until dawn. One friend, whose favorite horse was trying to swim a lake with hobbles on, dove under water and cut her legs loose with a knife, then swam her to shore, his arm around her neck lifeguard-style, and saved her from drowning. Because these incidents are usually linked to someone or something outside himself, the westerner's courage is selfless, a form of compassion.

The physical punishment that goes with cowboying is greatly underplayed. Once fear is dispensed with, the threshold of pain rises to meet the demands of the job. When Jane Fonda asked Robert Redford (in the film *Electric Horseman*) if he was sick as he struggled to his feet one morning, he replied, "No, just bent." For once the movies had it right. The cowboys I was sitting with laughed in agreement. Cowboys are rarely complainers; they show their stoicism by laughing at themselves.

If a rancher or cowboy has been thought of as a "man's man"—laconic, hard-drinking, inscrutable—there's almost no place in which the balancing act between male and female, manliness and femininity, can be more natural. If he's gruff, handsome, and physically fit on the outside, he's androgynous at the core. Ranchers are midwives, hunters, nurturers, providers, and conservationists all at once. What we've interpreted as toughness—weathered skin, calloused hands, a squint in the eye and a growl in the voice—only masks the tenderness inside. "Now don't go telling me these lambs are cute," one rancher warned me the first day I walked into the football-field-sized lambing sheds. The next thing I knew he was holding a black lamb. "Ain't this little rat good-lookin'?"

5   So many of the men who came to the West were southerners—men looking for work and a new life after the Civil War—that chivalrousness and strict codes of honor were soon thought of as western traits. There were very few women in Wyoming during territorial days, so when they did arrive (some as mail-order brides from places like Philadelphia) there was a stand-offishness between the sexes and a formality that persists now. Ranchers still tip their hats and say, "Howdy, ma'am" instead of shaking hands with me.

Even young cowboys are often evasive with women. It's not that they're Jekyll and Hyde creatures—gentle with animals and rough on women—but rather, that they don't know how to bring their tenderness into the house and lack the vocabulary to express the complexity of what they feel. Dancing wildly all night becomes a metaphor for the explosive emotions pent up inside, and when these are, on occasion, released, they're so battery-charged and potent that one caress of the face or one "I love you" will peal for a long while.

The geographical vastness and the social isolation here make emotional evolution seem impossible. Those contradictions of the heart between respectability, logic, and convention on the one hand, and impulse, passion, and intuition on the other, played out wordlessly against the paradisical beauty of the West, give cowboys a wide-eyed but drawn look. Their lips pucker up, not with kisses but with immutability. They may want to break out, staying up all night with a lover just to talk, but they don't know how and can't imagine what the consequences will be. Those rare occasions when they do bare themselves result in confusion. "I feel as if I'd sprained my heart," one friend told me a month after such a meeting.

My friend Ted Hoagland wrote, "No one is as fragile as a woman but no one is as fragile as a man." For all the women here who use "fragileness" to avoid work or as a sexual ploy, there are men who try to hide theirs, all the while clinging to an adolescent dependency on women to cook their meals, wash their clothes, and keep the ranch house warm in winter. But there is true vulnerability in evidence here. Because these men work with animals, not machines or numbers, because they live outside in landscapes of torrential beauty, because they are confined to a place and a routine embellished with awesome variables, because calves die in the arms that pulled others into life, because they go to the mountains as if on a pilgrimage to find out what makes a herd of elk tick, their strength is also a softness, their toughness, a rare delicacy.

Analyzing Rhetorical Choices

1. Why do you think Ehrlich begins her essay by describing the Marlboro man? Why do you think she focuses exclusively on the cowboy?

2. What does Ehrlich accomplish with her series of "if" sentences in the opening paragraph? How is this contrastive pattern continued through the rest of the paragraph and generally through the essay?

3. Explain the meaning and rhetorical power of Ehrlich's statement, "If he's gruff, handsome, and physically fit on the outside, he's androgynous at the core."

4. Write an analysis of Ehrlich's last paragraph. What stylistic devices does she use, and how effective are they?

Writing About Issues and Contexts

1. What qualities are associated with the cowboy? How has the popular image of the cowboy "disesteemed his truest character"?

2. Ehrlich attempts to redefine the cowboy in order to reclaim him from the romantic image that can be found in most popular media. Describe the ways this essay deals with cowboys. In what ways is it realistic? Romantic? Honest? Idealistic?

3. Ehrlich writes, "Their lips pucker up, not with kisses but with immutability." What does she mean by this? How is this statement central to her definition of the cowboy?

An eloquent spokesperson for compassionate understanding and human rights, **Elie Wiesel** *(1928–) was born in Sighet, Romania, and grew up in a world that centered on family, religious study, community, and God. All this came crashing down when, at the age of 16, his village was destroyed and he was deported to Auschwitz along with his father. Wiesel survived internment and was liberated in April 1945, four months after his father perished. An account of his experiences can be found in his extremely powerful book* Night *(1958), in which he states, "Never shall I forget those moments which murdered my God and my soul and turned my dreams to dust. Never shall I forget these things, even if I am condemned to live as long as God Himself. Never." Wiesel was appointed chair of the President's Commission on the Holocaust and in 1985 was awarded the Congressional Gold Medal of Achievement. In 1986, he was awarded the Nobel Peace Prize for his life's work speaking and writing about the catastrophic effects of hatred and prejudice.*

Elie Wiesel

How Can We Understand Their Hatred?

Fanaticism today is not a nice word; it carries an unpleasant connotation. But in ancient times, fanatics enjoyed a more favorable reaction from the public. They were linked to religion and, more specifically, to religious experience. In the Bible, Pinhas was praised for slaying a sinner. The Prophet Elijah was admired as an extreme opponent of the wicked Queen Jezebel. Later, in Islam, *fana* (meaning the annihilation of the will) described the Sufi's desire to attain ecstasy in his union with the divine.

Today, in our modern language, fanaticism refers to excessive behavior, uncritical political opinions, ethnic zeal and religious bigotry. How did this come to be?

Previous centuries suffered from tribal and religious wars and from national extremism, but our last century was ravaged mainly by ideological and secular hatred. Nazism and communism moved fanaticism to unprecedented dimensions—dimensions future historians may term as absolute. Stalin used Terror just as Hitler used Death to oppress tens of millions of people: Never have man-made ideologies introduced so much evil into society; never have they given Death so much power.

Early in my own life, I experienced the consequences of fanaticism. On Sept. 11, like so many others throughout the world, I saw its terrible consequences again. Glued for days to the television, I witnessed unthinkable acts of terror. How, I asked myself, after the last century's horrors, could fanaticism still hold sway?

5   On reflection, I believe that fanaticism appeals to people for a variety of reasons. But on the deepest level, fanaticism is seductive because it makes the fanatic feel less alone.

The fanatic fails to understand that the tragedy of man is that, in essential matters, we are each condemned to be alone—we can never break out of the "self." How does one cease being one's own jailer? By becoming each other's prisoner. The fanatic thinks he can tear down the walls of his cell by joining other fanatics. No need to think—the Party does the thinking for him, and the deciding for him.

The fanatic is stubborn, obstinate, dogmatic: Everything for him is black or white, curse or blessing, friend or foe—and nothing in between. He has no taste for or interest in nuances. Does he seek clarity? Driven by irrational impulses, he wants everything to be visible and necessarily clear.

The fanatic simplifies matters: He is immune to doubt and to hesitation. Intellectual exercise is distasteful, and the art and beauty of dialogue alien to him. Other people's ideas or theories are of no use to him. He is never bothered by difficult problems: A decree or a bullet solves them . . . immediately. The fanatic feels nothing but disdain toward intellectuals who spend precious time analyzing, dissecting, debating philosophical notions and hypotheses. What matters to the fanatic is the outcome—not the way leading there.

And more: The fanatic derides and hates tolerance, which he perceives as weakness, resignation or submission. That is why he despises women: Their tenderness is to him a sign of passivity. The fanatic's only interest is domination by fear and terror. Violence is his favorite language—a vulgar language filled with obscenities: He doesn't speak, he shouts; he doesn't listen, he is too busy yelling; he doesn't think, he doesn't want *anyone* to think.

10   In other words, the fanatic, intoxicated with hatred, tries to reduce everybody to his own size.

He has a goal and is ready to pay any price to achieve it. Or more precisely: He is ready to make *others* pay any price in order to achieve it.

The fanatic feels important, for he presumes being capable of altering—and dominating—the course of history. Using the obscure power of hatred, he feels he can—and must—take charge of man's fate. Working in the dark, forever involved in plots and counterplots, he thinks his mission is to abolish the present state of affairs and replace it with his own system. No wonder that he, the human failure, now feels proud and superior.

The fanatic who kills in God's name makes his God a murderer.

Let me conclude with this thought:

15   Of all the "isms" produced by the past centuries, fanaticism alone survives. We have witnessed the downfall of Nazism, the defeat of fascism and the abdication of communism. But fanaticism is still alive. And it is spreading fast. As horrible as it may sound, racial hatred, anti-Semitism and bin Laden terrorism are popular and still glorified in certain communities.

How can the fanatics be brought back to moral sanity? How can the killers and suicide warriors be disarmed?

If there is a simple answer, I do not know it. All I know is that, as we embark on this newest century, we cannot continue to live with fanaticism—and only we ourselves can stem it.

How are we to do this?

We must first fight indifference.

20   Indifference to evil is the enemy of good, for indifference is the enemy of everything that exalts the honor of man. We fight indifference through education; we diminish it through compassion. The most efficient remedy? Memory.

To remember means to recognize a time other than the present; to remember means to acknowledge the possibility of a dialogue. In recalling an event, I provoke its rebirth in me. In evoking a face, I place myself in relationship to it. In remembering a landscape, I oppose it to the walls that imprison me. The memory of an ancient joy or defeat is proof that nothing is definitive, nor is it irrevocable. To live through a catastrophe is bad; to forget it is worse.

And so, as we move forward from Sept. 11, let us continue to remember. For memory may be our most powerful weapon against fanaticism.

Analyzing Rhetorical Choices

1. Why does Wiesel turn to the Bible for his early account of fanaticism? How does that strengthen his rhetorical position?
2. Analyze the following sentence of Wiesel's in terms of its stylistic effectiveness: "Stalin used Terror just as Hitler used Death to oppress tens of millions of people: Never have man-made ideologies introduced so much evil into society; never have they given Death so much power."
3. Wiesel divides his essay into three parts. What does each part do? How well do they relate to each other?

Writing About Issues and Contexts

1. According to Wiesel, what is fanaticism? How has the meaning of the word, in terms of social acceptance, changed over time?
2. What is the appeal of fanaticism? Are you fanatical about something, and if so, what? Is fanaticism always bad? What connotations does it convey?
3. What argument is Wiesel attempting to make about remembrance and relationship? Why does he argue that memory "may be our most powerful weapon against fanaticism"? Offer your response.

One of the most celebrated writers in the United States, **Cynthia Ozick** *(1928–) was born in New York City to immigrant Russian Jews. Her uncle, Abraham Regelson, who was a well-regarded poet, inspired her to become a writer. Ozick earned a bachelor's from New York University and a master's from Ohio State University. She has since received awards from the Guggenheim Foundation, the National Endowment for the Arts, and the American Academy of Arts and Letters, as well as several honorary doctorates. Her books include the novels* Trust *(1966),* The Cannibal Galaxy *(1983),* The Messiah of Stockholm *(1987), and* Heir to the Glimmering World *(2004); the story collections* The Pagan Rabbit *(1971),* Levitation *(1982), and* The Shawl *(1996); and the essay volumes* Art & Ardor *(1983),* Metaphor & Memory *(1989), and* Quarrel & Quandary *(2000). The following essay first appeared in* The New Yorker *in 2003.*

Cynthia Ozick
What Helen Keller Saw

Suspicion stalks fame; incredulity stalks great fame. At least three times—at the ages of eleven, twenty-three, and fifty-two—Helen Keller was assaulted by accusation, doubt, and overt disbelief. She was the butt of skeptics and the cynosure of idolaters. Mark Twain compared her to Joan of Arc, and pronounced her "fellow to Caesar, Alexander, Napoleon, Homer, Shakespeare and the rest of the immortals." Her renown, he said, would endure a thousand years.

It has, so far, lasted more than a hundred, while steadily dimming. Fifty years ago, even twenty, nearly every ten-year-old knew who Helen Keller was. "The Story of My Life," her youthful autobiography, was on the reading lists of most schools, and its author was popularly understood to be a heroine of uncommon grace and courage, a sort of worldly saint. Much of that worshipfulness has receded. No one nowadays, without intending satire, would place her alongside Caesar and Napoleon; and, in an era of earnest disabilities legislation, who would think to charge a stone-blind, stone-deaf woman with faking her experience?

Yet as a child she was accused of plagiarism, and in maturity of "verbalism"—substituting parroted words for firsthand perception. All this came about because she was at once liberated by language and in bondage to it, in a way few other human beings can fathom.

The merely blind have the window of their ears, the merely deaf listen through their eyes. For Helen Keller there was no ameliorating "merely"; what she suffered was a totality of exclusion. The illness that annihilated her sight and hearing, and left her mute, has never been diagnosed. In 1882, when she was four months short of two years, medical knowledge could assert only "acute congestion of the stomach and brain," though later speculation proposes meningitis or scarlet fever. Whatever the cause, the consequence was ferocity—tantrums, kicking, rages—but also an invented system of sixty simple signs, intimations of intelligence. The child could mimic what she could neither see nor hear: putting on a hat before a mirror, her father reading a newspaper with his glasses on. She could fold laundry and pick out her own things. Such quiet times were few. Having discovered the use of a key, she shut up her mother in a closet. She overturned her baby sister's cradle. Her wants were physical, impatient, helpless, and nearly always belligerent.

She was born in Tuscumbia, Alabama, fifteen years after the Civil War, when Confederate consciousness was still inflamed. Her father, who had fought at Vicksburg, called himself a "gentleman farmer," and edited a small Democratic weekly until, thanks to political influence, he was appointed a United States marshal. He was a zealous hunter who loved his guns and his dogs. Money was usually short; there were escalating marital angers. His second wife, Helen's mother, was younger by twenty years, a spirited woman of intellect condemned to farmhouse toil. She had a strong literary side (Edward Everett Hale, the New Englander who wrote "The Man Without a Country," was a relative) and read seriously and searchingly. In Charles Dickens's "American Notes," she learned about Laura Bridgman, a deaf-blind country girl who was being educated at the Perkins Institution for the Blind, in Boston. Ravaged by scarlet fever at the age of two, she was even more circumscribed than Helen Keller—she could neither smell nor taste. She was confined, Dickens said, "in a marble cell, impervious to any ray of light, or particle of sound," lost to language beyond a handful of words unidiomatically strung together.

5   News of Laura Bridgman ignited hope—she had been socialized into a semblance of personhood, while Helen remained a small savage—and hope led, eventually, to Alexander Graham Bell. By then, the invention of the telephone was well behind him, and he was tenaciously committed to teaching the deaf to speak intelligibly. His wife was deaf; his mother had been deaf. When the six-year-old Helen was brought to him, he took her on his lap and instantly calmed her by letting her feel

the vibrations of his pocket watch as it struck the hour. Her responsiveness did not register in her face; he described it as "chillingly empty." But he judged her educable, and advised her father to apply to Michael Anagnos, the director of the Perkins Institution, for a teacher to be sent to Tuscumbia.

Anagnos chose Anne Mansfield Sullivan, a former student at Perkins. "Mansfield" was her own embellishment; it had the sound of gentility. If the fabricated name was intended to confer an elevated status, it was because Annie Sullivan, born into penury, had no status at all. At five, she contracted trachoma, a disease of the eye. Three years on, her mother died of tuberculosis and was buried in potter's field—after which her father, a drunkard prone to beating his children, deserted the family. The half-blind Annie was tossed into the poorhouse at Tewksbury, Massachusetts, among syphilitic prostitutes and madmen. Decades later, recalling its "strangeness, grotesqueness and even terribleness," Annie Sullivan wrote, "I doubt if life or for that matter eternity is long enough to erase the terrors and ugly blots scored upon my mind during those dismal years from 8 to 14."

She was rescued from Tewksbury by a committee investigating its spreading notoriety, and was mercifully transferred to Perkins. She learned Braille and the manual alphabet—finger positions representing letters—and, at the Massachusetts Eye and Ear Infirmary, underwent two operations, which enabled her to read almost normally, though the condition of her eyes was fragile and inconsistent over her lifetime. After six years, she graduated from Perkins as class valedictorian. But what was to become of her? How was she to earn a living? Someone suggested that she might wash dishes or peddle needlework. "Sewing and crocheting are inventions of the devil," she sneered. "I'd rather break stones on the king's highway than hem a handkerchief."

She went to Tuscumbia instead. She was twenty years old and had no experience suitable for what she would encounter in the despairs and chaotic defeats of the Keller household. The child she had come to educate threw cutlery, pinched, grabbed food off dinner plates, sent chairs tumbling, shrieked, struggled. She was strong, beautiful but for one protruding eye, unsmiling, painfully untamed: virtually her first act on meeting the new teacher was to knock out one of her front teeth. The afflictions of the marble cell had become inflictions. Annie demanded that Helen be separated from her family; her father could not bear to see his ruined little daughter disciplined. The teacher and her recalcitrant pupil retreated to a cottage on the grounds of the main house, where Annie was to be the sole authority.

What happened then and afterward she chronicled in letter after letter, to Anagnos and, more confidingly, to Mrs. Sophia Hopkins, the Perkins housemother who had given her shelter during school vacations. Mark Twain saw in Annie Sullivan a *writer:* "How she stands out in her letters!" he exclaimed. "Her brilliancy, penetration, originality, wisdom, character and the fine literary competencies of her pen—they are all there." Jubilantly, she set down the progress, almost hour by hour, of an exuberant deliverance far more remarkable than Laura Bridgman's frail and inarticulate release. Annie Sullivan's method, insofar as she recognized it formally as a method, was pure freedom. Like any writer, she wrote and wrote and wrote, all day long: words, phrases, sentences, lines of poetry, descriptions of animals, trees, flowers, weather, skies, clouds, concepts—whatever lay before her or came usefully to mind. She wrote not on paper with a pen but with her fingers, spelling rapidly into the child's alert palm. Mimicking unknowable configurations, Helen spelled the same letters back—but not until a connection was effected between finger-wriggling and its referent did mind break free.

10   This was, of course, the fabled incident at the well pump, when Helen suddenly understood that the pecking at her hand was inescapably related to the gush of cold water spilling over it. "Somehow," the adult Helen Keller recollected, "the mystery of language was revealed to me." In the course of a single month, from Annie's arrival to her triumph in bridling the household despot, Helen had grown docile, affectionate, and tirelessly intent on learning from moment to moment. Her intellect was fiercely engaged, and when language began to flood it she rode on a salvational ark of words.

To Mrs. Hopkins, Annie wrote ecstatically:

> Something within me tells me that I shall succeed beyond my dreams. . . . I know that [Helen] has remarkable powers, and I believe that I shall be able to develop and mould them. I cannot tell how I know these things. I had no idea a short time ago how to go to work; I was feeling about in the dark; but somehow I know now, and I know that I know. I cannot explain it; but when difficulties arise, I am not perplexed or doubtful. I know how to meet them; I seem to divine Helen's peculiar needs. . . .
>
> Already people are taking a deep interest in Helen. No one can see her without being impressed. She is no ordinary child, and people's interest in her education will be no ordinary interest. Therefore let us be exceedingly careful in what we say and write about her. . . . My beautiful Helen shall not be transformed into a prodigy if I can help it.

At this time, Helen was not yet seven years old, and Annie was being paid twenty-five dollars a month.

The public scrutiny Helen Keller aroused far exceeded Annie's predictions. It was Michael Anagnos who first proclaimed her to be a miracle child—a young goddess. "History presents no case like hers," he exulted. "As soon as a slight crevice was opened in the outer wall of their twofold imprisonment, her mental faculties emerged full-armed from their living tomb as Pallas Athene from the head of Zeus." And again: "She is the queen of precocious and brilliant children, Emersonian in temper, most exquisitely organized, with intellectual sight of unsurpassed sharpness and infinite reach, a true daughter of Mnemosyne." Annie, the teacher of a flesh-and-blood child, protested: "His extravagant way of saying [these things] rubs me the wrong way. The simple facts would be so much more convincing!" But Anagnos's glorifications caught fire: one year after Annie had begun spelling into her hand, Helen Keller was celebrated in newspapers all over America and Europe. When her dog was inadvertently shot, an avalanche of contributions poured in to replace it; unprompted, she directed that the money be set aside for the care of an impoverished deaf-blind boy at Perkins. At eight, she was taken to visit President Cleveland at the White House, and in Boston was introduced to many of the luminaries of the period: Oliver Wendell Holmes, John Greenleaf Whittier, Edward Everett Hale, and Bishop Phillips Brooks (who addressed her puzzlement over the nature of God). At nine, she wrote to Whittier, saluting him as "Dear Poet":

> I thought you would be glad to hear that your beautiful poems make me very happy. Yesterday I read "In School Days" and "My Playmate," and I enjoyed them greatly. . . . It is very pleasant to live here in our beautiful world. I cannot see the lovely things with my eyes, but my mind can see them all, and so I am joyful all the day long.
>
> When I walk out in my garden I cannot see the beautiful flowers, but I know that they are all around me; for is not the air sweet with their fragrance? I know too that the tiny lily-bells are whispering pretty secrets to their companions else they would not look so happy. I love you very dearly, because you have taught me so many lovely things about flowers and birds, and people.

Her dependence on Annie for the assimilation of her immediate surroundings was nearly total, but through the raised letters of Braille she could be altogether untethered: books coursed through her. In childhood, she was captivated by "Little Lord Fauntleroy," Frances Hodgson Burnett's story of a sunnily virtuous boy who melts a crusty old man's heart; it became a secret template of her own character as she hoped she might always manifest it—not sentimentally but in full awareness of dread. She was not deaf to Caliban's wounded cry: "You taught me language, and my profit on't/Is, I know how to curse." Helen Keller's profit was that she knew how to rejoice. In young adulthood, she seized on Swedenborgian spiritualism. Annie had kept away from teaching any religion at all: she was a down-to-earth agnostic whom Tewksbury had cured of easy belief. When Helen's responsiveness to bitter social deprivation later took on a worldly strength, leading her to socialism, and even to unpopular Bolshevik sympathies, Annie would have no part of it, and worried that Helen had gone too far. Marx was not in Annie's canon. Homer, Virgil, Shakespeare, and Milton were: she had Helen reading "Paradise Lost" at twelve.

But Helen's formal schooling was widening beyond Annie's tutelage. With her teacher at her side—and the financial support of such patrons as John Spaulding, the Sugar King, and Henry Rogers, of Standard Oil—Helen spent a year at Perkins, and then entered the Wright-Humason School, in New York, a fashionable academy for deaf girls; she was its single deaf-blind pupil. She was also determined to learn to speak like other people, but her efforts could not be readily understood. Speech was not her only ambition: she intended to go to college. To prepare, she enrolled in the Cambridge School for Young Ladies, where she studied mathematics, German, French, Latin, and Greek and Roman history. In 1900, she was admitted to Radcliffe (then an "annex" to Harvard), still with Annie in attendance. Despite Annie's presence in every class, diligently spelling the lecture into Helen's hand, and wearing out her troubled eyes as she transcribed text after text into the manual alphabet, no one thought of granting her a degree along with Helen: the radiant miracle outshone the driven miracle worker. It was not uncommon for Annie Sullivan to play second fiddle to Helen Keller, or to be charged with being Helen's jailer, or harrier, or ventriloquist. During examinations at Radcliffe, Annie was not permitted to be in the building. Otherwise, Helen relied on her own extraordinary memory and on Annie's lightning fingers. Luckily, a second helper soon turned up: he was John Macy, a twenty-five-year-old English instructor at Harvard, a writer and editor, a fervent socialist, and, eventually, Annie Sullivan's husband, eleven years her junior.

15   At Radcliffe, Helen became a writer. Charles Townsend Copeland—
Harvard's illustrious Copey, a professor of rhetoric—had encouraged
her (as she put it to him in a grateful letter) "to make my own observations and describe the experiences peculiarly my own. Henceforth I am
resolved to be myself, to live my own life and write my own thoughts."
Out of this came "The Story of My Life," the autobiography of a twenty-
one-year-old, published while she was still an undergraduate. It began as
a series of sketches for the *Ladies' Home Journal*; the fee was three thousand dollars. John Macy described the laborious process:

> When she began work at her story, more than a year ago, she set
> up on the Braille machine about a hundred pages of what she called
> "material," consisting of detached episodes and notes put down as
> they came to her without definite order or coherent plan. . . . Then
> came the task where one who has eyes to see must help her. Miss
> Sullivan and I read the disconnected passages, put them into chrono-
> logical order, and counted the words to be sure the articles should be
> the right length. All this work we did with Miss Keller beside us, refer-
> ring everything, especially matters of phrasing, to her for revision. . . .
>   Her memory of what she had written was astonishing. She re-
> membered whole passages, some of which she had not seen for many
> weeks, and could tell, before Miss Sullivan had spelled into her hand
> a half-dozen words of the paragraphs under discussion, where they
> belonged and what sentences were necessary to make the connec-
> tions clear.

This method of collaboration continued throughout Helen Keller's
professional writing life; yet within these constraints the design and the
sensibility were her own. She was a self-conscious stylist. Macy remarked that she had the courage of her metaphors—he meant that she
sometimes let them carry her away—and Helen herself worried that
her prose could now and then seem "periwigged." To the contemporary ear, there is too much Victorian lace and striving uplift in her ca-
dences; but the contemporary ear is scarcely entitled, simply by being
contemporary, to set itself up as judge—every period is marked by a
prevailing voice. Helen Keller's earnestness is a kind of piety. It is as if
Tennyson and the transcendentalists had together got hold of her typewriter. At the same time, she is embroiled in the whole range of human
perplexity—except, tellingly, for irony. She has no "edge," and why
should she? Irony is a radar that seeks out the dark side; she had darkness enough. She rarely knew what part of her mind was instinct and
what part was information, and she was cautious about the difference.
"It is certain," she wrote, "that I cannot always distinguish my own

thoughts from those I read, because what I read becomes the very substance and texture of my mind. . . . It seems to me that the great difficulty of writing is to make the language of the educated mind express
our confused ideas, half feelings, half thoughts, where we are little
more than bundles of instinctive tendencies." She who had once been
incarcerated in the id did not require Freud to instruct her in its inchoate presence.

"The Story of My Life," first published in 1903, is being honored
in its centenary year by two new reissues, one from the Modern
Library, edited and with a preface by James Berger, and the other from
W. W. Norton, edited by Roger Shattuck with Dorothy Herrmann;
Shattuck also supplies a thoughtful foreword and afterword. Much else
accompanies the Keller text: Macy's ample contribution to the original
edition, as well as Annie's indelible reports and Helen's increasingly impressive letters from childhood on. All these elements together make up
at least a partial biography, though they do not take us into Helen
Keller's astonishing future as world traveller and energetic advocate for
the blind. (Two full biographies, "Helen Keller: A Life," by Dorothy
Herrmann, and "Helen and Teacher," by Joseph P. Lash, flesh out her
long and active life.) Macy was able to write about Helen nearly as au-
thoritatively as Annie, but also (in private) more skeptically: after his
marriage, the three of them, a feverishly literary crew, set up housekeeping in rural Wrentham, Massachusetts. Macy soon discovered that
he had married not just a woman, and a moody one at that, but the in-
frastructure of a public institution. As Helen's secondary amanuensis,
he continued to be of use until the marriage foundered—on his profli-
gacy with money, on Annie's irritability (she scorned his uncompromising socialism), and, finally, on his accelerating alcoholism.

Because Macy was known to have assisted Helen in the preparation of "The Story of My Life," the insinuations of control that often
assailed Annie landed on him. Helen's ideas, it was suggested, were
really Macy's; he had transformed her into a "Marxist propagandist."
It was true that she sympathized with his political bent, but she had
arrived at her views independently. The charge of expropriation, of
both thought and idiom, was old, and dogged her at intervals during
her early and middle years: she was a fraud, a puppet, a plagiarist.
She was false coin. She was "a living lie."

Helen Keller was eleven when these words were first hurled at her by
an infuriated Michael Anagnos. What brought on this defection was
a little story she had written, called "The Frost King," which she

sent him as a birthday present. In the voice of a highly literary children's narrative, it recounts how the "frost fairies" cause the seasons turning:

> When the children saw the trees all aglow with brilliant colors they clapped their hands and shouted for joy, and immediately began to pick great bunches to take home. "The leaves are as lovely as the flowers!" cried they, in their delight.

20   Anagnos—doubtless clapping his hands and shouting for joy—immediately began to publicize Helen's newest accomplishment. "The Frost King" appeared both in the Perkins alumni magazine and in another journal for the blind, which, following Anagnos, unhesitatingly named it "without parallel in the history of literature." But more than a parallel was at stake; the story was found to be nearly identical to "The Frost Fairies," by Margaret Canby, a writer of children's books. Anagnos was humiliated, and fled headlong from adulation to excoriation. Feeling personally betrayed and institutionally discredited, he arranged an inquisition for the terrified Helen, standing her alone in a room before a jury of eight Perkins officials and himself, all mercilessly cross-examining her. Her mature recollection of Anagnos's "court of investigation" registers as pitiably as the ordeal itself:

> Mr. Anagnos, who loved me tenderly, thinking that he had been deceived, turned a deaf ear to the pleadings of love and innocence. He believed, or at least suspected, that Miss Sullivan and I had deliberately stolen the bright thoughts of another and imposed them on him to win his admiration. . . . As I lay in my bed that night, I wept as I hope few children have wept. I felt so cold, I imagined I should die before morning, and the thought comforted me. I think if this sorrow had come to me when I was older, it would have broken my spirit beyond repairing.

She was defended by Alexander Graham Bell, and by Mark Twain, who parodied the whole procedure with a thumping hurrah for plagiarism, and disgust for the egotism of "these solemn donkeys breaking a little child's heart with their ignorant damned rubbish! . . . A gang of dull and hoary pirates piously setting themselves the task of disciplining and purifying a kitten that they think they've caught filching a chop!" Margaret Canby's tale had been spelled to Helen perhaps three years before, and lay dormant in her prodigiously retentive memory; she was entirely oblivious of reproducing phrases not her own. The scandal Anagnos had precipitated left a lasting bruise. But it was also the beginning of a psychological, even a metaphysical, clarification that Helen refined and ratified as she grew older, when similar, if subtler, suspicions cropped up in the press. "The Story of My Life" was attacked in *The Nation* not for plagiarism in the usual sense but for the purloining of "things beyond her powers of perception with the assurance of one who has verified every word. . . . One resents the pages of second-hand description of natural objects." The reviewer blamed her for the sin of vicariousness. "All her knowledge," he insisted, "is hearsay knowledge."

It was almost a reprise of the Perkins tribunal: she was again being confronted with the charge of inauthenticity. Anagnos's rebuke—"Helen Keller is a living lie"—regularly resurfaced, in the form of a neurologist's or a psychologist's assessment, or in the reservations of reviewers. A French professor of literature, who was himself blind, determined that she was "a dupe of words, and her aesthetic enjoyment of most of the arts is a matter of auto-suggestion rather than perception." A *New Yorker* interviewer complained, "She talks bookishly. . . . To express her ideas, she falls back on the phrases she has learned from books, and uses words that sound stilted, poetical metaphors."

But the cruellest appraisal of all came, in 1933, from Thomas Cutsforth, a blind psychologist. By this time, Helen was fifty-two, and had published four additional autobiographical volumes. Cutsforth disparaged everything she had become. The wordless child she once was, he maintained, was closer to reality than what her teacher had made of her through the imposition of "word-mindedness." He objected to her use of images such as "a mist of green," "blue pools of dog violets," "soft clouds tumbling." All that, he protested, was "implied chicanery" and "a birthright sold for a mess of verbiage." He criticized

> the aims of the educational system in which [Helen Keller] has been confined during her whole life. Literary expression has been the goal of her formal education. Fine writing, regardless of its meaningful content, has been the end toward which both she and her teacher have striven. . . . Her own experiential life was rapidly made secondary, and it was regarded as such by the victim. . . . Her teacher's ideals became her ideals, her teacher's likes became her likes, and whatever emotional activity her teacher experienced she experienced.

For Cutsforth—and not only for him—she was the victim of language rather than its victorious master. She was no better than a copy; whatever was primary, and thereby genuine, had been stamped out. As for Annie, while here she was pilloried as her pupil's victimizer, elsewhere she was pitied as a woman cheated of her own life by having sacrificed it to serve another. Either Helen was Annie's slave or Annie was Helen's.

25   Helen knew what she saw. Once, having been taken to the uppermost viewing platform of what was then the tallest building in the world, she defined her condition:

> I will concede that my guides saw a thousand things that escaped me from the top of the Empire State Building, but I am not envious. For imagination creates distances that reach to the end of the world. . . . There was the Hudson—more like the flash of a sword-blade than a noble river. The little island of Manhattan, set like a jewel in its nest of rainbow waters, stared up into my face, and the solar system circled about my head!

Her rebuttal to word-mindedness, to vicariousness, to implied chicanery and the living lie, was inscribed deliberately and defiantly in her images of "sword-blade" and "rainbow waters." The deaf-blind person, she wrote, "seizes every word of sight and hearing, because his sensations compel it. Light and color, of which he has no tactual evidence, he studies fearlessly, believing that all humanly knowable truth is open to him." She was not ashamed of talking bookishly: it meant a ready access to the storehouse of history and literature. She disposed of her critics with a dazzling apothegm—"The bulk of the world's knowledge is an imaginary construction"—and went on to contend that history itself "is but a mode of imagining, of making us see civilizations that no longer appear upon the earth." Those who ridiculed her rendering of color she dismissed as "spirit-vandals" who would force her "to bite the dust of material things." Her idea of the subjective onlooker was broader than that of physics, and while "red" may denote an explicit and measurable wavelength in the visible spectrum, in the mind it varies from the bluster of rage to the reticence of a blush: physics cannot cage metaphor.

She saw, then, what she wished, or was blessed, to see, and rightly named it imagination. In this she belongs to a broader class than that narrow order of the deaf-blind. Her class, her tribe, hears what no healthy ear can catch and sees what no eye chart can quantify. Her common language was not with the man who crushed a child for memorizing what the fairies do, or with the carpers who scolded her for the crime of a literary vocabulary. She was a member of the race of poets, the Romantic kind; she was close cousin to those novelists who write not only what they do not know but what they cannot possibly know.

And though she was early taken in hand by a writerly intelligence, it was hardly in the power of the manual alphabet to pry out a writer who was not already there. Laura Bridgman stuck to her lacemaking, and with all her senses intact might have remained a needlewoman. John Macy believed finally that between Helen and Annie there was only one genius—his wife. In the absence of Annie's inventiveness and direction, he implied, Helen's efforts would show up as the lesser gifts they were. This did not happen. Annie died, at seventy, in 1936, four years after Macy; they had long been estranged. Depressed, obese, cranky, and inconsolable, she had herself gone blind. Helen came under the care of her secretary, Polly Thomson, a loyal but unliterary Scotswoman: the scenes she spelled into Helen's hand never matched Annie's quicksilver evocations.

Even as Helen mourned the loss of her teacher, she flourished. With the assistance of Nella Henney, Annie Sullivan's biographer, she continued to publish journals and memoirs. She undertook gruelling visits to Japan, India, Israel, Europe, Australia, everywhere championing the disabled and the dispossessed. She was indefatigable until her very last years, and died in 1968, weeks before her eighty-eighth birthday.

30   Yet the story of her life is not the good she did, the panegyrics she inspired, or the disputes (genuine or counterfeit? victim or victimizer?) that stormed around her. The most persuasive story of Helen Keller's life is what she said it was: "I observe, I feel, I think, I imagine." She was an artist. She imagined.

"Blindness has no limiting effect upon mental vision," she argued again and again. "My intellectual horizon is infinitely wide. The universe it encircles is immeasurable." And, like any writer making imagination's mysterious claims before the material-minded, she had cause to cry out, "Oh, the supercilious doubters!"

Nevertheless, she was a warrior in a vaster and more vexing conflict. Do we know only what we see, or do we see what we somehow already know? Are we more than the sum of our senses? Does a picture—whatever strikes the retina—engender thought, or does thought create the picture? Can there be subjectivity without an object to glance off? Theorists have their differing notions, to which the ungraspable organism that is Helen Keller is a retort. She is not an advocate for one side or the other in the ancient debate concerning the nature of the real. She is not a philosophical or neurological or therapeutic topic: She stands for enigma; there lurks in her still the angry child who demanded to be understood yet could not be deciphered. She refutes those who cannot perceive, or do not care to value, what is hidden from sensation: collective memory, heritage, literature.

Helen Keller's lot, it turns out, was not unique. "We work in the dark," Henry James affirmed, on behalf of his own art; and so did she. It was the same dark. She knew her Wordsworth: "Visionary power / Attends the motions of the viewless winds, / Embodied in the mystery of words: / There, darkness makes abode." She vivified Keats's phantom theme of negative capability, the poet's oarless casting about for the hallucinatory shadows of desire. She fought the debunkers who, for the sake of a spurious honesty, would denude her of landscape and return her to the marble cell. She fought the literalists who took imagination for mendacity, who meant to disinherit her, and everyone, of poetry. Her legacy, after all, is an epistemological marker of sorts: proof of the real existence of the mind's eye.

In one respect, though, she was as fraudulent as the cynics charged. She had always been photographed in profile; this hid her disfigured left eye. In maturity, she had both eyes surgically removed and replaced with glass—an expedient known only to her intimates. Everywhere she went, her sparkling blue prosthetic eyes were admired for their living beauty and humane depth.

Analyzing Rhetorical Choices

1. Ozick opens by informing the reader of the three occasions when Helen Keller was "assaulted by accusation, doubt, and overt disbelief." However, the specifics are not revealed to the reader until much later in the essay. What are the advantages and disadvantages of this approach?

2. The author provides profiles of other people who were involved in Keller's life to flesh out the essay. Are there additional people that Ozick should have profiled? Are there any experiences that she could have omitted without diminishing her essay?

3. Ozick concludes the essay on an ironic note, revealing Keller was indeed fraudulent in the sense that her "sparkling blue prosthetic eyes were admired for their living beauty and humane depth." Why do you think Ozick opted for this ending?

Writing About Issues and Contexts

1. Is Ozick correct that Keller's fame has faded and that younger students, of your generation perhaps, do not know much about her? If so, why do you feel this has happened?

2. Should Annie Sullivan indeed have been awarded a college degree along with Helen Keller? What alternative routes to a college degree might you support?

3. What is your response to the set of questions that Ozick poses near the end: "Do we know only what we see, or do we see what we somehow already know? Are we more than the sum of our senses? Does a picture—whatever strikes the retina—engender thought, or does thought create the picture? Can there be subjectivity without an object to glance off?"

Strategies for Writers: Definition

1. Jamaica Kincaid takes a very simple word, *girl*, and redefines it, as does Judy Brady with the word *wife*. What they have done is to choose a term for which there is no universally accepted meaning and write an extended definition. What problems do you anticipate if you attempt similarly to define a simple term? What level of specificity does this type of definition require?

2. A related assignment is to define a word that carries with it great potential for controversy. Gloria Naylor's essay, for example, is called "The Meanings of a Word," and she talks about the racially sensitive word *nigger*. Would a white person be able to write an essay defining *nigger*? Can a male define the word *woman* or a woman define the word *man* without invoking controversy? How can you best develop a definition for potentially controversial words like these that carry such problematic meanings in many contexts? What kinds of assurances can you provide your reader that you are proceeding with intelligence and sensitivity?

3. When does defining become stereotyping or dangerous? When is it liberating?

4. Extended definition can embrace other modes and be used in the service of argument. For instance, Lisa Kanae extends her definition of *pidgin* by using forms of narration and ultimately arguing a distinct point of view. While her essay is purportedly a definition of *pidgin*, its purpose is ultimately to change people's minds about language. Good definition is always argument. How will you shape your essay to ostensibly define yet ultimately argue? For what purpose?

5. Definition can be used to extend our understanding and sympathy towards a particular group or class, as Ehrlich does in "About Men" and as Wiesel does in "How Can We Understand Their Hatred?" Will your essay extend sympathy, understanding, enlightenment—in other words, how will you go beyond mere definition toward compelling your readers to re-vision the term or concept you define?

Research and Writing Assignments

1. In their essays, Judy Brady, Jamaica Kincaid, and Gretel Ehrlich choose to consider some aspect of what it means to be defined

in terms of gender—that is, the various constructions of maleness or femaleness that get created within cultural life. Thus Brady defines what it means to be a traditional wife, Kincaid a traditional girl within Antiguan society, and Ehrlich redefines the traditional understanding of a cowboy. In an essay that makes explicit use of some of the strategies exhibited in these three essays, define a significant aspect of gendered identity. Some possible topics include scientist, husband, friend, baby, grandparent, boy, athlete.

2. Cynthia Ozick uses information about others, including written excerpts, to help define the life of Helen Keller for a contemporary audience. Choose a significant historical figure in order to narrate and define his or her life. Following Ozick's example, use autobiographical and secondary material, if possible, while still keeping the project fairly brief.

3. The kinds of language that people use in everyday interactions can have devastating effects, as the essays by Lisa Kanae and Gloria Naylor (and the poems by Countee Cullen in the following chapter) make clear. As the mother in "Pidgin" says with unintended irony, "You not going get one good job if you no can talk good English. People going tink you stupid." In an essay that incorporates library research by at least two sociolinguists, such as William Labov and John Reinecke Jr., offer your informed perspective on dialect, language use, and social interaction. Your essay can explore your own personal (neighborhood) dialect, analyze words or phrases specific to your culture or community, or consider the principle of "correctness" in speaking and writing. Whatever approach you take, your essay needs to consider the idea that the inability to use "good English" makes people "tink you stupid."

4. Bruno Bettelheim and Elie Wiesel focus on the importance of memory as a way to understand the present as well as the past. Their essays put us in mind of the aphorism, "To ignore history is to be doomed to repeat it." Choose a term such as *patriotism*, *heroism*, or *leadership* and define it, using some U.S. historical accounts to support your definition. How do we understand the term now? How was it understood previously? What kinds of tensions and conflicts exist in our understanding of this word as it is used in public debates since September 11, 2001?

5. Autobiography can be a powerful form, especially when it centers on trying to discover an insight or uncover an individual

"truth" that is of real significance to the author—and the audience. We see this principle made clear in the essays by Lisa Kanae and a number of authors in this book, including Annie Dillard, Richard Wright, Richard Rodriguez, and Frank McCourt. Write an autobiographical essay that centers on a complex issue, problem, or experience that has meaning not only to you but to a more general audience as well. Use Kanae's essay as a model, and in a postscript to your essay, explain how it influenced your writing.

5

Exemplification

What exactly is exemplification? It is the use of details and examples within writing: specific facts, anecdotes, scenes, statistics, research, and information that illustrate, or exemplify, the subject. Writers use it constantly to inject appropriate details into their writing so that their subjects and arguments are anchored in reality. Exemplifying often allows writers to make their subjects vivid, to encourage readers to see, smell, and experience the subject. As a strategy, it often becomes almost intuitive for writers: They offer a generalization and follow it with examples; they put forward a thesis and then offer specific support for it; they make an observation and support it with citations and information. Thus the pattern is a general statement followed by details and examples. The details and examples might be as short as a sentence or as long as several pages, depending on what the writer feels is necessary to explain the subject or make it appear vividly on the page.

One of the most important aspects of exemplifying is selection: determining what kinds of details and examples are needed, where and how they will be used within the writing. There is no magic formula for deciding which examples to include or how many there should be. You are undoubtedly familiar with people who are so laconic that they provide virtually no exemplification, so little in fact that it is almost impossible to understand what they are talking about. On the other end of the spectrum are people who give so many details and facts that you are overwhelmed with minutiae and often so bored that you stop listening. Both extremes have negative consequences, and as a writer, you depend on your readers (instructors, students, peers, supervisors, and colleagues) to help you find the middle path: including details that enrich the writing, inform your readers, and keep them turning pages.

Exemplification is especially important when introducing an unfamiliar word, subject, or concept, which is the primary purpose that leads most writers to exemplify their subjects. Larry Good, a composer and humor columnist, describes the annoying problem of having an "ear worm," a problem that has nothing to do with worms at all. To clarify what he means and to add some sizzle to his prose, Good illustrates his short essay with a variety of song lyrics and other forms of exemplification that add to the humor he uses in describing a problem that most people have experienced at one time or another.

I am one of those people who has an internal tape of music that plays constantly in my head. It is a condition that strikes millions of Americans . . . who were subjected to a lot of television in the sixties. It can cause disorientation, an inability to concentrate, and absolute ridicule.

I have approached perfect strangers from behind, in the frozen foods section at City Market, unwittingly humming the Bee Gees "If I can't have you, I don't want nobody, baby, if I can't have you, woh-oo-oh . . . oh." Out loud!

That is why I don't appreciate the constant barrage of low-grade musical "entertainment" that we are all subjected to in nearly all public places now. I am entirely too susceptible to it. Whatever is playing on my internal tape machine starts fighting with the DMX in the room, and invariably the stupidest of the two musics wins. I may enter the shop with a safe and pleasant orchestral arrangement of Beethoven's Waldstein Sonata pulsing in my brain, but I leave the store five minutes later with an internal shriek of "She-ree, Sher-ar-ar-eee, bay-yay-bee (Sherry ba-bee)" which I can expect to repeat hundreds, or even thousands, of times.

What causes this? How can I make it stop? Can I harness this freakish talent so that I can play back music that I would like to hear, instead of music I don't ever want to hear again? These are just a few obvious questions that come to mind with regard to this freakish malady. There is a German word for this—*ohrwarm*—literally translated it means "ear worm."

The ear worm is like a radio station that plays a skipping record, but you can't turn it off, and you can't change the station. I used to wonder why I so often found myself humming "America, the Beautiful" until I realized that every time I turn on my computer printer, it begins a rough version of the melody, and so the ear worm attempts to finish the song. All day. There are plenty of causes, but there are no cures.

The most damnable of ear worms are the one-liners, where you don't know what the next phrase is, or what the words are. Something like the theme from "Happy Days" once you get past "1 o'clock, 2 o'clock, 3 o'clock rock." See what I mean? Sometimes, if you can figure out how it ends, the ear worm will go away. For example, if afflicted with "Sherry Baby" by Frankie Valli and the Four Seasons, you have to know that the falsetto shrieking will resolve with "Sher-ree, won't you come out tonight." It takes a special kind of doctor to treat this sort of affliction.

My wife thinks it is funny to deliberately sneak up on me and sing mellifluous snippets like "Here's a story . . . of a man named Brady. . . ." She has no idea of the mental cruelty involved in such an act. Before I can stop her the damage is done, and the whole Brady Bunch song circles my brain, complete with the Hollywood Squares style television graphic and the wrap-up horn line at the end. "Ba-dum, pa-dum, bum." These are obvious causes, but sometimes secondary suggestions are rewarded with a full-fledged ear worm. The mail cart pulls away from my curb, and suddenly my internal radio is playing "Hey, just a minute, wait a minute, Mister Postman (look at me—Oh, Yeah) is there a package, or a letter for me?" and on and on.

The ear worm can switch from the Beatles' version to the Carpenters' version without pausing. The ear worm doesn't require that I know the lyrics of a piece of music. The ear worm is satisfied with amorphous syllabic onomatopoeia. But I'm not. Is it a package? A letter? A card? Is it "Just-a-minute, wait-a-minute"? or two "wait-a-minutes"? Aurgh. The thing is driving me crazy. This must be what my brain does when I'm not using it. But I know others suffer just as I do.

There has been a dirge-like tune parading through my head for about two years now, one I can't identify or kill, and though as a musician, I could take this as divine inspiration, it's just not. As a musician, I recognize a lifeless pedantic melody when I hear one, and this melodic blurb doesn't deserve any further musical setting to unleash it on the world.

There are certain melodies that are built from natural elements. Songs like the theme from "Close Encounters" which, in four notes defines the tonal system we use in Western music, are somehow linked to the natural order of things, to physics and acoustics and harmony and melody. So, I could see running around with a bad case of "Close Encounters of the Third Kind" or even a "Pachelbel Canon," and understand that this was just nature at work on my inner muse.

But this doesn't explain today's ear worm "well, twiddle-dee-dee, and twiddle-dee-dum, look out Baby, 'cause here I come." It's crazy. Help.

Larry Good finds a way to make his ear worm concept both familiar and highly individual by carefully selecting precise details, musical groups, and lyrics to exemplify the ear worm. Incorporating specifics such as the sound of "Sherry Baby," his wife's cruelly inflicting an ear worm on him, and the illuminating explanation of the significance of the theme from the film *Close Encounters of the Third Kind* light up this essay and help secure it in our memories.

Ear worms aside, certain academic disciplines and scholarly subjects create expectations about the level of detail that a piece of writing needs. Historians, for example, mainly focus on facts and details; exemplification is their primary method of establishing historical perspective and persuading readers that their accounts have genuine validity. Philosophers, on the other hand, usually focus on abstract principles that defy exemplification; thus philosophical writing, by its very nature, must use less exemplification than do the writings of other academic disciplines. A philosophy essay that has the same amount of exemplification as a history essay is not likely to succeed as well. Different disciplines, purposes, audiences, and expectations shape the ways exemplification is used by various writers, including the writers represented in this chapter.

Examine, for a moment, the opening paragraph of the David Brooks selection. Brooks starts with an assertion—that we may talk about diversity but we don't live it in our neighborhoods. His way of driving that point home is to ask if a neighborhood exists in which "a black Pentecostal minister lives next to a white anti-globalization activist, who lives next to an Asian short-order cook, who lives next to a professional golfer, who lives next to a postmodern-literature professor and a cardiovascular surgeon." Brooks's way to demonstrate the truth of his assertion is to offer a hypothetical example, one that he knows is not true and thus proves his point. He then goes on to offer other specific examples that expand our understanding of his primary thesis about the lack of diversity in this country.

One of the most overlooked reasons a writer uses exemplification is to discover more information about the subject and to gauge when to begin writing. No matter what you are writing about, you must be in command of your subject; you must always know more about your subject than your reader does and more than you include in your essay. The extra, unused material serves as the foundation on which you stand so that your treatment of your subject is just beyond the reach of your readers. If you sit down to write without having this wealth of details, statistics, and particulars at your command, you are not likely to write a successful essay that informs and intrigues your readers. To possess that wealth of knowledge, you must build up your factual resources, as Diane Ackerman does so she can write with authority about the vagaries of taste and appetite.

Years ago, the famous comic duo of Bob and Ray created a radio skit in which Bob interviewed Ray, with Ray assuming the persona of an amateur historian who had just published a massive history of the United States. Their interview went something like the following:

Bob: This is a long history that you have written here. It must be about 1,300 pages long.

Ray: Yes, I have tried to be comprehensive and include every possible subject so that I could tell the complete history of this great country.

Bob: I certainly appreciate that, but I notice that a few mistakes have crept into your book.

Ray: Really?

Bob: Yes. For example, you state that the first President of the United States and the Father of Our Country was Lyndon Johnson.

Ray: Oh, is that a mistake?

Bob: Yes, it is. The person you are referring to is George Washington. A little later in the book you state that the American Civil War began in 1973.

Ray: I thought it did begin somewhere around then.

Bob: No, it began in 1860.

Ray: Well, in a book this size, you can expect a few errors to creep in now and again.

Bob: But don't you agree that these are major errors? For example, you also state that the country directly to the south of us is France. But the country located south of us is Mexico.

Ray: Well, aren't you doing a bit of nitpicking now? Anybody can make a mistake like that!

One of the aspects of this humorous interview is how unperturbed Ray's character is about all the errors he has committed. And he is wholly unaware of how these errors completely undermine his authority and credibility as an author. Anyone who thinks that Lyndon Johnson is the Father of Our Country or that the Civil War began in

1973 cannot be trusted as a historian. Any writer who exemplifies, carefully checking sources and facts, goes a long way toward writing effectively.

An author in command of his or her facts can establish a great deal of credibility with readers. Diane Ackerman does exactly this in her account of human tastes and culinary preferences. Few readers are likely to know, for example, the extraordinary range of foods that humans eat—from cow's blood and deep-fried songbirds to rats and decaying cucumbers (commonly called pickles). Ackerman's mastery of facts and details—the way she uses exemplification to surprise and amaze—persuades readers that she is in complete control of her subject and thus an authority whom they can confidently trust.

Writers must find ways to prove their expertise to their readers, and one of the best ways to accomplish this goal is through exemplification. By including important details, significant facts and statistics, appropriate quotations from knowledgeable authorities and the like, you can establish meaningful credibility and put yourself in a position to enlarge the perspective of all your readers. No matter what mode of writing you employ—narration, process, comparison/contrast, argumentation—exemplification is a critical and constitutive element of your success as a writer.

Approaches to Using Exemplification Essays

In many ways, there is no single entity called an "exemplification essay," although the skills of exemplifying written work can be practiced in a concentrated way. What we have gathered in this chapter are essays that usefully exemplify exemplification, so to speak. As you read through this book or any other, however, you will see that most essays use details, facts, narrative examples, and other forms of exemplification to support, illustrate, and solidify their purposes. What most writers have to learn is why, when, how, and how much to deploy these examples.

Those decisions are never easy ones. For example, if you are writing about Abraham Lincoln, is it important to explain to readers that he was president of the United States during the Civil War, and then explain what a president of the United States is and does? Your first response might be that such information is completely unnecessary, since everyone knows who Lincoln was and what a president does. Your decision about how much to explain and provide examples and details, however, depends on your audience. If you are writing to eight-year-olds in a third grade class, recent immigrants to America, or international students living in an eastern European country, the answer may well be yes. Considered in this light, choosing why, when, and how to exemplify is a complex, rhetorical decision that depends, like so many choices in writing, on your understanding of your rhetorical context.

Using Exemplification to Define Purpose

Many books on writing ask high school and college students to explain the purpose of their writing in one or two sentences called *topic sentences*. That is a useful exercise, because anyone who writes ought to be able to explain the purpose of his or her essay. Many writers, however, choose to explain their purpose in writing by offering readers a series of examples or particular details that in many ways have the same effect as dropping stones in a still pond: They concentrate a splash in one area but then ripple outward. Here, for example, is how Frederick Erickson, a noted anthropologist, explained his purpose in writing about literacy in 1984:

> Literacy, as *being lettered*, has to do with strategy and prestige. This prestige is partly due to the strategic power that comes from mastery of an information communication system. This prestige also is derived from values of aesthetics and moral virtue which mask the issue of power. Indeed, in 17th century English, to be *lewd* is not to be sexually unrestrained, but to be unlettered. It is only later in English usage that lewdness took on sexual connotations, which gradually became the main usage. . . .
>
> As an anthropologist my main questions about literacy and numeracy are these: Given that for approximately 5 million years human societies have managed to rear their young so that almost every one in the society was able to master the knowledge and skills necessary for survival, why does this not happen in modern societies with schools? Or does it happen—do schools teach what is necessary, but define and measure achievement in such ways that it looks as if large proportions of the school population fail? Why is it that when we know that the cognitive operations necessary to learn to speak a language are mastered by almost every child by age 5, many of those same children seem unable to learn to read in school, even though the cognitive complexity of learning to read, at least at the early stages, is so much less than that required to learn to speak? Why can a child make change successfully at the grocery store and fail to do those same arithmetic operations correctly when presented with a math worksheet in the classroom? In current public discourse about literacy, are we talking

about knowledge and skill in decoding letters, or are we talking about being "lettered" as a marker of social class status and cultural capital? Do we see the school diploma mainly as evidence of mastery of knowledge and skill in literacy in the literal and narrow sense of the term?

. . . In short, the relations between the manifest curriculum of school subject matter—literacy and numeracy in the narrow sense—and the hidden curriculum of social sorting and ranking are an issue of central interest for the social sciences, as well as for the educators and citizens. "Literacy, Reasoning, and Civility," *Review of Research in Education*, 54 (1984), 525–46

Erickson uses a series of particular assertions and facts as rhetorical questions to shape his purpose in writing this essay. What he wants to know is whether the real issue in school learning is not mastery of reading, writing, and numeracy skills but rather how issues of "social sorting and ranking" affect teacher effectiveness and student performance. Even though this essay was written 21 years ago, the issues it raises by means of exemplifying its purpose remain relevant for everyone who cares about educating children.

Using Exemplification to Stimulate Your Reader's Interest

Details, narrative anecdotes, short factual accounts, and other forms of exemplification can ignite a reader's interest. They work best, however, when they illustrate an essential element of your subject, some central theme that you wish to develop in your essay. In his excellent biography of the great populist politician, Huey Long, T. Harry Williams opens chapter one with the following narrative exemplification:

The story seems too good to be true—but people who should know swear that it is true. The first time that Huey P. Long campaigned in rural, Latin, Catholic south Louisiana, the local boss who had him in charge said at the beginning of the tour: "Huey, you ought to remember one thing in your speeches today. You're from north Louisiana, but now you're in south Louisiana. And we got a lot of Catholic voters down here." "I know," Huey answered. And throughout the day in every small town Long would begin by saying: "When I was a boy, I would get up at six o'clock in the morning on Sunday, and I would hitch our old horse up to the buggy and I would take my Catholic grandparents to mass. I would bring them home, and at ten o'clock I would hitch the old horse up again, and I would take my Baptist grandparents to church." The effect of the anecdote on the audiences was obvious, and on the way back to Baton Rouge that night the local leader said admiringly: "Why, Huey, you've been holding out on us. I didn't know you had any Catholic grandparents." "Don't be a damn fool," replied Huey. "We didn't even have a horse."

Williams opens with this anecdote, this method of exemplifying Long's character, because he wants to show Long's creativity, unscrupulousness, cynicism, humor, and sharp-edged political skills. The story has an additional effect on most readers. It makes them intrigued with Long and want to keep turning pages to read more.

Exemplification that spurs readers to keep turning pages does not have to take the form of a narrative. Many facts, details, statistics, and the like can provide an important context for a subject and draw readers forward into the text. In his essay on literacy, Frederick Erickson at one point paraphrases the research of two individuals and states that in conflictual situations, "individuals who speak different dialects will speak progressively more broad forms of that dialect as interaction proceeds and conflict escalates." His point is that cultural difference can be not only a source of conflict but also the end result. His use of a specific research finding exemplifies his larger point about literacy and social context, and because it underscores a surprising and little known insight, it keeps the reader's motivation high.

Using Exemplification to Provide Context

Perhaps one of the most important functions of exemplification is that it provides context for your writing. By that we mean that exemplifying your subject allows readers to understand more fully what you mean, how your subject relates to their own experience, how others have thought or written about it. By including particular examples in your writing, you provide your readers with signposts that point the way toward your explicit and implicit meanings.

Here, for example, are two paragraphs from Steven Pinker's important book, *The Language Instinct*. Since so much of our focus in this book is on language and language use, it is appropriate we think to exemplify exemplification with writing from a book about language. In this short excerpt from chapter one, Pinker explains why language is "the preeminent trait" of the human species:

Language is so tightly woven into human experience that it is scarcely possible to imagine life without it. Chances are that if you find two or more people together anywhere on earth, they will soon be exchanging words. When there is no one to talk with, people talk to themselves, to their dogs, even to their plants. In our social relations, the race is not to the swift but to the verbal—the spellbinding orator, the silver-tongued seducer, the persuasive child who wins the battle of wills against a brawnier parent. Aphasia, the loss of language following brain injury, is devastating, and in severe cases family members may feel that the whole person is lost forever. . . .

Most educated people already have opinions about language. They know that it is man's most important cultural invention, the quintessential example of his capacity to use symbols, and a biologically unprecedented event irrevocably separating him from other animals. They know that language pervades thought, with different languages causing their speakers to construe reality in different ways. They know that children learn to talk from role models and caregivers. They know that grammatical sophistication used to be nurtured in the schools, but sagging educational standards and the debasement of popular culture have led to a frightening decline in the ability of the average person to construct a grammatical sentence. They also know that English is a zany, logic-defying tongue, in which one drives on a parkway and parks in a driveway, plays at a recital and recites at a play. They know that English spelling takes such wackiness to even greater heights—George Bernard Shaw complained that *fish* could just as sensibly be spelled *ghoti* (*gh* as in *tough*, *o* as in *women*, *ti* as in *nation*)—and that only institutional inertia prevents the adoption of a more rational spell-it-like-it-sounds system.

Pinker's use of exemplification is . . . well, exemplary. His examples are brief but trenchant: when two people come together, language results; the ubiquity of language; the power of language ability to help individuals succeed; the identification of language with personality and human identity; the loss of grammar education from the schools; and the zaniness of English spelling, with the particular use of the example from George Bernard Shaw. Pinker's details and examples create the context for his discussion of language as a basic, human instinct, something that is not so much taught as it is created from within the human mind.

We offer Pinker as one example of exemplification exemplified. Almost all good writing, irrespective of mode, benefits from your knowledge, your ability to bring in details and specifics that signal your purpose, stimulate your reader's interest, and anchor your writing within a meaningful context. Those examples should derive naturally from the research you do and the knowledge you bring to your subject. They should never be extraneous details or irrelevant notes that are included to show off your erudition; that kind of ostentatious demonstration of knowledge will grow tiresome to your readers in a hurry.

Ian Frazier (1951–) is a native of Cleveland, Ohio, and currently resides in Montclair, New Jersey. After graduating from Harvard University, where he served on the staff of the Harvard Lampoon, *he embarked upon a professional writing career. His books include* Dating Your Mom *(1986),* Great Plains *(1989),* Family *(1994),* Coyote v. Acme *(1996),* On the Rez *(2000), and* Gone to New York *(2005). "If Memory Doesn't Serve" was first published in* The Atlantic Monthly *in 2004.*

Ian Frazier

If Memory Doesn't Serve

Among the cruelest tricks life plays is the way it puts the complicated part at the end, when the brain is declining into simplicity, and the simple part at the beginning, when the brain is fresh and has memory power to spare. As a boy I had only a few things to keep track of. There was one place, the small town where I lived; two pro sports, baseball and football; three TV channels; four sequential seasons, as yet unmixed by global warming; five kids in my neighborhood to play with; and so on. In no category did the number of entries go much above a dozen or two. I didn't meet people and have to remember their names, because everybody I ran into I already knew. With my extra, leftover memory I preserved pointless conversations, nonsense phrases my brother made up, remarks by adults they later claimed they hadn't said, and incidental data such as the farthest point up our street from which it was possible to run and still catch the school bus.

Since then my memory has been required to hold gigantically much more, the bulk of it so dull. Feats of adult remembering often conform to the "negative Disneyland" rule of grown-up pleasures: that is, it is fun, of a sort, suddenly to remember where you left the registration stickers for your car, but only in comparison to the trip to the Department of Motor Vehicles you would have to make if you didn't. I sometimes nearly crumble in self-pity at the mnemonic brainbusters life hands me. An example: a few years ago the friends my young son usually played with were Joshua, Rhys, and Julian. No memory problems there—each interesting and lively boy easily matched with his name in my mind. The mothers of the boys, however, were (respectively) Georgeanne, Geraldine, and Gabrielle. To a person whose days of high-detail remembering are gone, those are essentially the same name. When greeting someone, it is not enough to know that her name begins with a G. I held this unfair complicatedness against each of them and acted put-upon and odd around them.

Does anyone remember the name of Russ Nixon, catcher for the Cleveland Indians in 1958? Once I spent lonely hours trying to remember it, and when morning came and I could call a friend who knew, I understood what had happened. My friend spoke and the name emerged, good as new, from the later Nixon overlays that had hidden it. The brain has only so many slots, and by the time you reach fifty they have become cluttered and full. I'm sure most of us have a small place in our brains containing the following four items:

1. H. G. Wells
2. George Orwell
3. Orson Welles
4. Orson Bean

They cluster together through some unknown law of the synapses. The first two are easy to confuse because both are thirties-era, English, and science-fictiony (*The Time Machine, Nineteen Eighty-four*). The second and third blend because George Orwell and Orson Welles, as names, sound like made-up, roman-à-clef versions of each other. Also, Welles did a famous hoax radio broadcast of Wells's *War of the Worlds,* a confusing event in itself. And then you have Orson Bean, who is in there probably just to round out the conjugation, or through one of those comic mishaps he used to get into in his roles as an actor. Sometimes when I have a spare moment I take each name out, consider it, link it to the proper person, recall each one's face and biography, and then put all the names back in place in my mind. I believe this is a basically healthy exercise, like flossing.

Then, if I'm feeling like it, or if I'm still lying awake, I run through a few more calisthenics to keep myself sharp. AA is not the same as Triple A—a fact I learn and relearn at car-rental counters when I ask for an AA discount. Michael Moore, the activist author and documentary filmmaker, once made a movie called *Roger and Me,* partly about Roger Smith, then the president of General Motors. Consequently, it is quite natural to slip up and refer to Michael Moore as Roger Moore. The two are different, however; Roger Moore is a suave-seeming English movie actor who used to play James Bond, a couple of James Bonds ago. And speaking of that, I am me, and not James Bond's creator, Ian Fleming, the late English intelligence officer and author of spy thrillers. Twice now while I've been on book tours the person introducing me to the audience at a reading has said, "And now, please join me in welcoming Ian Fleming." After the second time I took to carrying a copy of *Goldfinger*, just to be ready, but so far it hasn't happened again.

5   Jamie Bassett was my son's third-grade teacher; Diana Tackett was my daughter's second-grade teacher. Kathy York was my daughter's third-grade teacher; Drury Thorp was my son's second-grade teacher. (Drury Thorp is related to the humorist Robert Benchley, who still has his own slot in my mind.) Ashanti is not the same as Beyoncé; the former is a popular singer who recently appeared on the cover of a New York newspaper carrying a handbag printed with a greatly enlarged photograph of her own face; the latter is a popular singer who has won several Grammy Awards and who performed the national anthem at the 2004 Super Bowl—the Janet Jackson one. Russell Means and Dennis Banks were both leaders of the American Indian Movement back in the seventies; I am prone to refer to either or both as Russell Banks, who is neither, but a well-known novelist. Victor Klemperer, the German writer, kept a detailed two-volume journal of his days in Dresden during World War II, and has been called "the great diarist of the Holocaust"; Werner Klemperer is the American television and movie actor who played Colonel Klink on the TV series *Hogan's Heroes*. (Remarkably, Werner and Victor were cousins.)

Suddenly a nagging thought occurs to me: there is Ashanti, and there is Beyoncé . . . but wasn't there a third in that category? Yes. There was another like them—another young, model-beautiful black woman singer usually referred to by a single name. She has recently disappeared over the music-scene horizon. Her big hit song was "The Boy Is Mine." She sang it as a duet with somebody. I saw the video of it many times. In it she did a lot of vogueing, hand gestures, framing her face with her fingers, and so forth. I used to do a lip-sync imitation of her, using the same gestures but ending with one of my own, which was to lift my baseball cap above my head twice with both hands. I showed my imitation often to my teenage daughter and her friends, embarrassing her. What was that singer's name? It was . . . Brandy! Thank you, memory. Ashanti, Beyoncé, and Brandy.

Jamie Bassett, Diana Tackett; Drury Thorp, Kathy York. The names of elementary school teachers have a strange power to evoke the past. Ashanti, Beyoncé, Brandy. I am slightly afraid there's yet another in that category I've forgotten about, but I won't worry over it now. Russell Means (AIM), Russell Banks (novelist), Dennis Banks

(AIM). Victor Klemperer, diarist of the Holocaust; Werner Klemperer, actor who played Colonel Klink. When I have all the names straight, maybe I will get to sleep.

F. Scott Fitzgerald, whom I confuse with nobody, once said that the measure of a first-rate intellect is its ability to hold two contradictory ideas at the same time. I believe this may be one of those profound sayings that fall apart if you examine them closely. Holding two contradictory ideas simultaneously is a stunt that millions of minds pull off every day. A fifth of the people on the planet believe that their spouse is both the most wonderful person alive and the biggest disaster that ever happened to them; many of the inhabitants, sophisticated or not, of New York and Los Angeles will affirm in a single conversation that theirs is both the best and the worst city in the world. In fact, holding contradictory ideas simultaneously is a snap, because they are so distinct, and thus unlikely to interpenetrate dizzyingly with each other and swap themselves around.

A better gauge of mental subtlety, it seems to me, is whether you can retain ideas that are very similar but also different. For example, can you simultaneously think of, while noting the differences between, the dancer/actresses Rita Moreno and Chita Rivera? If you can accomplish that, try upping the ante by adding the actresses Carmen Miranda and Ida Lupino. Now see if you can hold all four in your mind simultaneously. The world of TV and movies offers many such tests. It takes all my mind's agility to hold at once the actresses Sarah Jessica Parker and Jennifer Aniston. The first step is not to think about Sarah Michelle Gellar or Sally Jessy Raphael, because that will only confuse things. Sarah Jessica Parker and Jennifer Aniston are both young, blond, beautiful, and wise-cracking but vulnerable. Both were in successful TV series that just ended. The first is married to Matthew Broderick, the second to Brad Pitt. Sarah has wavy hair; Jennifer's is straight. Thinking of one somehow makes it almost impossible to think of the other. Both are in the news a lot, which allows more chances to practice.

10 Then there are Charles Durning and Brian Dennehy (Wilford Brimley being the confusing third in that category); Fernando Lamas and Ricardo Montalban (José Ferrer, ditto); Norman Fell and Jack Klugman; Van Heflin and Red Buttons; Swoosie Kurtz and Stockard Channing; Wally Cox and Don Knotts . . . My only advice about untangling the whole Lee Majors/William Shatner/Chad Everett/Robert Wagner/Robert Conrad/William Conrad nexus is: don't go there. As

actors from old TV series recede in time, memory conflates them into a single ur-TV star. Recently I've found that even the movie stars Robert De Niro and Al Pacino are starting to blur together in my mind.

The other day, while cleaning the house, I pointed to the dustpan in the corner of the living room and asked my daughter, "Could you please bring me the spatula?" She asked, "You mean the dustpan?" I replied—taking a page from her book—"Whatever." A dustpan and a spatula really are a lot alike. Why use a separate word for each object? "Dustpan" is drab and colorless, whereas "spatula" is a poetic-sounding creation that just rolls off the tongue. Also, "spatula" has a venerable history as a comic keyword, like "rutabaga" and "Buick" and "schnauzer." So why not call both objects "spatula"? That's the decision I've made. "Spatula" might not be quite accurate when applied to a dustpan, but for most practical purposes it's close enough. As you get older, you don't want to waste time on tiny details.

On the other hand, you don't want to become so carried away with "spatula" that you repeat it over and over to yourself as you lie in bed late at night. It's a perfect example of the kind of word that, if repeated often enough, will make you insane.

If despair is a sin (and it is—it's an aspect of the deadly sin of sloth), the virtuous person must resist it, and all tendencies likely to lead to it. Torturing the mind with minutiae is one of those. Originally, I seem to recall, America took pride in its plainspoken rejection of all the pomp and foofaraw of corrupt, overcomplicated Europe. Now America is complication itself. Look down the table at the public library where people plug in their laptops, and see the heaped-up entanglements of cables and wires. Try to read the pamphlet in six-point type that your new phone carrier sends you when you change long-distance service. Go to the supermarket to buy an ordinary item for your spouse. The other day at the A&P I noticed a man lost in thought in front of a bank of different kinds of brownie mix. Then he took out his cell phone and made a call: "Hi, babe . . . You wanted Triple Chunk? Okay . . . I thought you said Triple *Fudge* Chunk." At some point the brain, in order to avoid despair, begins to shut down.

My son, who is eleven, has a memory like wet cement. Occurrences leave impressions on it and are there to stay—clear, manifest, close at hand. Like apparently all children today, he has an effortless affinity with gadgetry that exhausts me just to look at it. I call him when I want some advanced appliance turned off or on. Even more useful is his ability to replay data he has observed. Ask him what we were talking about before we started talking about what we're talking about now, and he knows. He always retrieves the thread of a conversation in a manner that's matter-of-fact or bored.

15   For me, however, the feeling at these moments is a vast and happy relief. When you've been trying to remember something and you suddenly remember it, the mental pleasure is keen. Not remembering eats at you, but remembering soothes and resoothes. I imagine that feeling might be what heaven is like. You pop through to the other side, and suddenly every question you have wondered about for years and then given up on is answered. The fate of an object lost in childhood, the names of people met only once at a cocktail party, the difference between William Conrad and Robert Conrad—every answer coming to you in a limpid rush of enlightenment, as if you'd known it all along.

Analyzing Rhetorical Choices

1. What are the author's major claims? Is each major claim supported with sufficient examples? Which additional examples could you add?

2. Frazier is known for his humorous tone. Is such humor an effective device from your viewpoint as a reader?

3. Remembering everything, Frazier asserts, might be what heaven is like. Meredith F. Small uses virtually the same description in "Captivated" (Chapter 3). What phrase might you offer instead of the "feels like heaven" cliché?

Writing About Issues and Contexts

1. Is the complicated part of life really at the end? After consulting some additional reading about memory, explain your view on the subject. Is the ability to recall the same thing as memory?

2. Generate a list of categories that confuse you. Do you think that writing about them will help you keep things straight in the future?

A reporter for the major newspaper in Portland, the Oregonian, **Emily Tsao** *(1973–) is a journalist and former chapter president of the Asian American Journalists Association. Educated at Yale University, Tsao is active in the leadership development of journalists and is a staunch advocate for human rights and equal opportunity. She has written, "Stereotypes affect us all. It is only when we work to change perceptions that true progress can begin." Originally published in the* Washington Post, *the following essay has been widely reprinted.*

Emily Tʃao

Thoughts of an Oriental Girl

I am an Oriental girl. Excuse me, I forgot to use my politically correct dictionary. Let me rephrase that. I am an Asian-American woman. Yes, that sounds about right. Excuse me again; I mean politically correct.

When I first stepped onto the campus scene last year, I, like many other anxious freshmen, wanted to fit in. I wanted to wear the right clothes, carry the right bookbag and, most important, say the right things. Speaking to upperclassmen, however, I realized that I had no command of the proper "PC" language.

Girls, it became clear, were to be called women. Freshmen who were girls were to be called freshwomen. Mixed groups of both sexes were to be labeled freshpeople, and upperclassmen were to be referred to as upperclasspeople. Orientals were to be called Asian Americans, blacks were to be called African Americans and Hispanics Latinos.

To me, most of this seemed pointless. Being called a girl doesn't bother me. I'm 18 years old. My mom is a woman. I'm her kid. I don't expect her to refer to me as a woman.

5   I have always referred to my female friends as girls, and still do. I want my boyfriend to call me his girlfriend, not his woman friend.

My friends and I refer to the male students at college as boys or guys. Never men. Kevin Costner and Robert Redford are men. Men don't drink themselves sick at keg parties every weekend, ask Dad for money, or take laundry home to Mom.

For 12 years in high school and grade school, the female students were always girls and the males were boys. Why does going to college with these same peers suddenly make me a woman and the boys men? I certainly don't feel much older or wiser than I did last year. When people refer to me as a woman, I turn around to see who might be standing behind me.

Another fad now is for people to spell women with a "y" in place of the "e"—"womyn." These people want to take the "men" out of "women." Next perhaps they'll invent "femyle."

I've always been gender conscious with my language when it seemed logical. In third grade I referred to the mailman as a mailperson because our mail was sometimes delivered by a woman. I don't think I ever said mailwoman, though, because it just didn't sound right.

10 From elementary through high school, I told people I was Chinese, and if I wanted to refer to all Asians, I used the word "Orientals." I guess I was young and foolish and didn't know any better.

At college I was told that the proper label for me was Asian American, that "Oriental" was a word to describe furniture, not people. But what is the difference? All Asians are still being clumped together, even though each group—Chinese, Korean, Japanese, Indians, Vietnamese and Filipinos, to name just a few—comes from a different country with a different language and culture.

The new "PC" term to describe Asian Americans and all other minorities is "people of color." The reason, I am told, is that the "minority" population has grown to be the majority. But even if that's true, the phrase seems contradictory. Since many African Americans no longer want to be referred to as blacks, why should the term for minorities once again refer to skin color? The same is true for Asians, most of whom find the label "yellow" more offensive than Oriental. And isn't white also a color?

As long as we're throwing out all the old labels, why not replace "white" with "European American." Wasps could be EAASPs (European-American Anglo Saxon Protestants). Well, maybe not. Minority groups want new labels to give themselves a more positive image, but unless the stereotypes disappear as well, is it really going to help very much?

Look at the word "sophomore," which comes from Greek roots meaning "wise fool." PC-conscious sophomores ought to revolt against this offensive phrase. I, however, will not be among them. Changing the word won't make me any smarter, humbler or wiser.

Analyzing Rhetorical Choices

1. How does Tsao establish a conversational tone? Why do you think she does this, and how does it affect you as a reader?

2. What kinds of details and examples does Tsao include to reinforce her irritation at the PC (politically correct) nature of the "campus scene"?

Writing About Issues and Contexts

1. In what ways does Tsao attempt to counteract stereotypical views of Asian Americans, or should we say Oriental men and women? Explain whether you think she succeeds in this effort.

2. Is Tsao correct in writing that "Minority groups want new labels to give themselves a more positive image, but unless the stereotypes disappear as well, is it really going to help very much?" Offer your own response to this statement.

3. Is the kind of language use that Tsao critiques a form of falsification? Why does the college culture create this new vocabulary? Do you consider it a form of PC behavior that overcompensates for the implicit racist, sexist, and classist opinions that can be found among many Americans, even those on college campuses?

Born in Waukegan, Illinois, **Diane Ackerman** *(1948–) graduated from*
Pennsylvania State University in 1970 and earned her M.F.A., M.A.,
and Ph.D. from Cornell University. In addition to having worked as
a social worker in New York City and as a government researcher at
Pennsylvania State University, Ackerman has taught at many universities,
including the University of Pittsburgh, Washington University, Ohio
University, and New York University. She is a staff writer for The New
Yorker *and has participated in many readings, residencies, and work-*
shops. A published poet as well as an accomplished nonfiction writer,
Ackerman's books include The Moon by Whale Light: And Other
Adventures among Bats, Penguins, Crocodilians, and Whales *(1991), A*
Natural History of Love *(1994), and* The Rarest of the Rare: Vanishing
Animals, Timeless Worlds *(1995). The following excerpt is from* A
Natural History of the Senses, *published in 1990.*

Diane Ackerman

The Vagaries of Taste

The Omnivore's Picnic

You have been invited to dinner at the home of extraterrestrials,
and asked to bring friends. Being considerate hosts, they first inquire
if you have any dietary allergies or prohibitions, and then what sort
of food would taste good to you. What do humans eat? they ask.
Images cascade through your mind, a cornucopia of plants, animals,
minerals, liquids, and solids, in a vast array of cuisines. The Masai enjoy drinking cow's blood. Orientals eat stir-fried puppy. Germans eat
rancid cabbage (sauerkraut), Americans eat decaying cucumbers
(pickles), Italians eat whole deep-fried songbirds, Vietnamese eat fer-
mented fish dosed with chili peppers, Japanese and others eat fungus
(mushrooms), French eat garlic-soaked snails. Upper-class Aztecs ate
roasted dog (a hairless variety named *xquintli,* which is still bred in
Mexico). Chinese of the Chou dynasty liked rats, which they called
"household deer," and many people still do eat rodents, as well as
grasshoppers, snakes, flightless birds, kangaroos, lobsters, snails, and
bats. Unlike most other animals, which fill a small yet ample niche in
the large web of life on earth, humans are omnivorous. The Earth offers perhaps 20,000 edible plants alone. A poor season for eucalyptus

will wipe out a population of koala bears, which have no other food source. But human beings are Nature's great ad libbers and revisers. Diversity is our delight. In time of drought, we can ankle off to a new locale, or break open a cactus, or dig a well. When plagues of locusts destroy our crops, we can forage on wild plants and roots. If our herds die, we find protein in insects, beans, and nuts. Not that being an omnivore is easy. A koala bear doesn't have to worry about whether or not its next mouthful will be toxic. In fact, eucalyptus is highly poisonous, but a koala has an elaborately protective gut, so it just eats eucalyptus, exactly as its parents did. Cows graze without fear on grass and grain. But omnivores are anxious eaters. They must continually test new foods to see if they're palatable and nutritious, running the risk of inadvertently poisoning themselves. They must take chances on new flavors, and, doing so, they frequently acquire a taste for something offbeat that, though nutritious, isn't the sort of thing that might normally appeal to them—chili peppers (which Columbus introduced to Europe), tobacco, alcohol, coffee, artichokes, or mustard, for instance. When we were hunter-gatherers, we ate a great variety of foods. Some of us still do, but more often we add spices to what we know, or find at hand, *for variety,* as we like to say. Monotony isn't our code. It's safe, in some ways, but in others it's more dangerous. Most of us prefer our foods cooked to the steaminess of freshly killed prey. We don't have ultrasharp carnivore's teeth, but we don't need them. We've created sharp tools. We do have incisor teeth for slicing fruits, and molars for crushing seeds and nuts, as well as canines for ripping flesh. At times, we eat nasturtiums and pea pods and even the effluvia from the mammary glands of cows, churned until it curdles, or frozen into a solid and attached to pieces of wood.

Our hosts propose a picnic, since their backyard is a meadow lit by two suns, and they welcome us and our friends. Our Japanese friend chooses the appetizer: sushi, including shrimp still alive and wriggling. Our French friend suggests a baguette, or better still croissants, which have an unlikely history, which he insists on telling everyone: To celebrate Austria's victory against the invading Ottoman Turks, bakers created pastry in the shape of the crescent on the Turkish flag, so that the Viennese could devour their enemies at table as they had on the battlefield. Croissants soon spread to France and, during the 1920s, traveled with other French ways to the United States. Our Amazonian friend chooses the main course—nuptial kings and queens of leaf-cutter ants, which taste like walnut butter, followed by roasted turtle and sweet-fleshed piranha. Our German friend insists that we include some spaetzle and a loaf of darkest pumpernickel bread, which gets its name from the verb *pumpern,* "to break wind," and *Nickel,* "the devil," because it was thought to be so hard to digest that even the devil would fart if he ate it. Our Tasaday friend wants some natek, a starchy paste his people make from the insides of caryota palm trees. The English cousin asks for a small platter of potted ox tongues, very aged blue cheese, and, for dessert, trifle—whipped cream and slivered almonds on top of a jam-and-custard pudding thick with sherry-soaked ladyfingers.

To finish our picnic lunch, our Turkish friend proposes coffee in the Turkish style—using a mortar and pestle to break up the beans, rather than milling them. To be helpful, he prepares it for us all, pouring boiling water over coffee grounds through a silver sieve into a pot. He brings this to a light boil, pours it through the sieve again, and offers us some of the clearest, brightest coffee we've ever tasted. According to legend, he explains, coffee was discovered by a ninth-century shepherd, who one day realized that his goats were becoming agitated whenever they browsed on the berries of certain bushes. For four hundred years, people thought only to chew the berries. Raw coffee doesn't brew into anything special, but in the thirteenth century someone decided to roast the berries, which releases a pungent oil and the mossy-bitter aroma now so familiar to us. Our Indian friend passes round cubes of sugar, which we are instructed to let melt on the tongue as we sip our coffee, and our minds roam back to the first recorded instance of sugar, in the Atharvaveda, a sacred Hindu text from 800 B.C., which describes a royal crown made of glittering sugar crystals. Then he circulates a small dish of coriander seeds, and we pinch a few in our fingers, set them on our tongues, and feel our mouths freshen from the aromatic tang. A perfect picnic. We thank our hosts for laying on such a splendid feast, and invite them to our house for dinner next. "What do jujubarians eat?" we ask.

· · ·

The Bloom of a Taste Bud

Seen by scanning electron microscope, our taste buds look as huge as volcanoes on Mars, while those of a shark are beautiful mounds of pastel-colored tissue paper—until we remember what they're used for. In reality, taste buds are exceedingly small. Adults have about 10,000, grouped by theme (salt, sour, sweet, bitter), at various sites in the mouth. Inside each one, about fifty taste cells busily relay information to a neuron, which will alert the brain. Not much tasting happens in the center of the tongue, but there are also incidental taste buds on the palate, pharynx, and tonsils, which cling like bats to the damp, slimy limestone walls of a cave. Rabbits have 17,000 taste buds, parrots only about 400, cows 25,000. What are they tasting? Maybe a cow needs that many to enjoy a relentless diet of grass.

5   At the tip of the tongue, we taste sweet things; bitter things at the back; sour things at the sides; and salty things spread over the surface, but mainly up front. The tongue is like a kingdom divided into principalities according to sensory talent. It would be as if all those who could see lived to the east, those who could hear lived to the west, those who could taste lived to the south, and those who could touch lived to the north. A flavor traveling through this kingdom is not recognized in the same way in any two places. If we lick an ice cream cone, a lollipop, or a cake-batter-covered finger, we touch the food with the tip of the tongue, where the taste buds for sweetness are, and it gives us an extra jolt of pleasure. A cube of sugar under the tongue won't taste as sweet as one placed *on* the tongue. Our threshold for bitter is the lowest. Because the taste buds for bitter lie at the back of the tongue; as a final defense against danger they can make us gag to keep a substance from sliding down the throat. Some people do, in fact, gag when they take quinine, or drink coffee for the first time, or try olives. Our taste buds can detect sweetness in something even if only one part in two hundred is sweet. Butterflies and blowflies, which have most of their taste organs on their front feet, need only step in a sweet solution to taste it. Dogs, horses, and many other animals have a sweet tooth, as we do. We can detect saltiness in one part in 400, sourness in one part in 130,000, but bitterness in as little as one part in 2,000,000. Nor is it necessary for us to recognize poisonous things as tasting different from one another; they just taste bitter. Distinguishing between bitter and sweet substances is so essential to our lives that it has burst through our language. Children, joy, a trusted friend, a lover all are referred to as "sweet." Regret, an enemy, pain, disappointment, a nasty argument all are referred to as "bitter." The "bitter pill" we metaphorically dread is likely to be poison.

Taste buds got their name from the nineteenth-century German scientists Georg Meissner and Rudolf Wagner, who discovered mounds made up of taste cells that overlap like petals. Taste buds wear out every week to ten days, and we replace them, although not as frequently over the age of forty-five—our palates really do become jaded as we get older. It takes a more intense taste to produce the same level of sensation, and children have the keenest sense of taste. A baby's mouth has many more taste buds than an adult's, with some even dotting the cheeks. Children adore sweets partly because the tips of their tongues, more sensitive to sugar, haven't yet been blunted by years of gourmandizing or trying to eat hot soup before it cools. A person born without a tongue, or who has had his tongue cut out, still can taste. Brillat-Savarin tells of a Frenchman in Algeria who was punished for an attempted prison escape by having "the forepart of his tongue . . . cut off clear to the ligament." Swallowing was difficult and tiring for him, although he could still taste fairly well, "but very sour or bitter things caused him unbearable pain."

Just as we can smell something only when it begins to evaporate, we can taste something only when it begins to dissolve, and we cannot do that without saliva. Every taste we can imagine—from mangoes to hundred-year-old eggs—comes from a combination of the four primary tastes plus one or two others. And yet we can distinguish between tastes with finesse, as wine-, tea-, cheese- and other professional tasters do. The Greeks and Romans, who were sophisticated about fish, could tell just by tasting one what waters it came from. As precise as our sense of taste is, illusions can still surprise us. For example, MSG doesn't taste saltier than table salt, but it really contains much more sodium. One of its ingredients, glutamate, blocks our ability to taste it as salty. A neurologist at the Albert Einstein College of Medicine once tested the amount of MSG in a bowl of wonton soup in a Chinese restaurant in Manhattan, and he found 7.5 grams of MSG, as much sodium as one should limit oneself to in an entire day.

After brushing our teeth in the morning, orange juice tastes bitter. Why? Because our taste buds have membranes that contain fatlike phospholipids, and toothpastes contain a detergent that breaks down fat and grease. So the toothpaste first assaults the membranes with its detergent, leaving them raw; then chemicals in the toothpaste, such as formaldehyde, chalk, and saccharin, cause a sour taste when they mix with the citric and ascorbic acids of orange juice. Chewing the leaves of the asclepiad (a relative of the milkweed) makes one's ability to taste sweetness vanish. Sugar would taste bland and gritty. When Africans chew a berry they call "miraculous fruit," it becomes impossible to taste anything sour: lemons taste sweet, sour wine tastes sweet, rhubarb tastes sweet. Anything off-puttingly sour suddenly becomes delicious. A weak enough solution of salt tastes sweet to us, and some people salt melons to enhance the sweet flavor. Lead and beryllium salts can taste treacherously sweet, even though they're poisonous and we ought to be tasting them as bitter.

No two of us taste the same plum. Heredity allows some people to eat asparagus and pee fragrantly afterward (as Proust describes in *Remembrance of Things Past*), or eat artichokes and then taste any drink, even water, as sweet. Some people are more sensitive to bitter tastes than others and find saccharin appalling, while others guzzle diet sodas. Salt cravers have saltier saliva. Their mouths are accustomed to a higher sodium level, and foods must be saltier before they register as salty. Of course, everyone's saliva is different and distinctive, flavored by diet, whether or not they smoke, heredity, perhaps even mood.

10   How strange that we acquire tastes as we grow. Babies don't like olives, mustard, hot pepper, beer, fruits that make one pucker, or coffee. After all, coffee is bitter, a flavor from the forbidden and dangerous realm. To eat a pickle, one risks one's common sense, overrides the body's warning with sheer reason. *Calm down, it's not dangerous,* the brain says, it's novel and interesting, a change, an exhilaration.

Smell contributes grandly to taste. Without smell, wine would still dizzy and lull us, but much of its captivation would be gone. We often smell something before we taste it, and that's enough to make us salivate. Smell and taste share a common airshaft, like residents in a high rise who know which is curry, lasagna, or Cajun night for their neighbors. When something lingers in the mouth, we can smell it, and when we inhale a bitter substance—a nasal decongestant, for example—we often taste it as a brassiness at the back of the throat. Smell hits us faster: It takes 25,000 times more molecules of cherry pie to taste it than to smell it. A head cold, by inhibiting smell, smothers taste.

We normally chew about a hundred times a minute. But, if we let something linger in our mouth, feel its texture, smell its bouquet, roll it around on the tongue, then chew it slowly so that we can hear its echoes, what we're really doing is savoring it, using several senses in a gustatory free-for-all. A food's flavor includes its texture, smell, temperature, color, and painfulness (as in spices), among many other features. Creatures of sound, we like some foods to titillate our hearing more than others. There's a gratifying crunch to a fresh carrot stick, a seductive sizzle to a broiling steak, a rumbling frenzy to soup coming to a boil, an arousing bunching and snapping to a bowl of breakfast cereal. "Food engineers," wizards of subtle persuasion, create products to assault as many of our senses as possible. Committees put a lot of thought into the design of fast foods. As David Bodanis points out with such good humor in *The Secret House,* potato chips are:

> an example of total destruction foods. The wild attack on the plastic wrap, the slashing and tearing you have to go through is exactly what the manufacturers wish. For the thing about crisp foods is that they're louder than non-crisp ones. . . . Destructo-packaging sets a favorable mood. . . . Crisp foods have to be loud in the upper register. They have to produce a high-frequency shattering; foods which generate low-frequency rumblings are crunchy, or slurpy but not crisp. . . .

Companies design potato chips to be too large to fit into the mouth, because in order to hear the high-frequency crackling you need to keep your mouth open. Chips are 80 percent air, and each time we bite one we break open the air-packed cells of the chip, making that noise we call "crispy." Bodanis asks:

> How to get sufficiently rigid cell walls to twang at these squeaking harmonics? Starch them. The starch granules in potatoes are identical to the starch in stiff shirt collars . . . whitewash . . . is . . . near identical in chemical composition. . . . All chips are soaked in fat. . . . So it's a shrapnel of flying starch and fat that produces the conical air-pressure wave when our determined chip-muncher finally gets to finish her chomp.

These are high-tech potato chips, of course, The original potato chip was invented in 1853 by George Crum, a chef at Moon Lake Lodge in Saratoga Springs, New York, who became so angry when a guest demanded thinner and thinner French fries that he sliced them laughably thin (he thought) and fried them until they were varnish-brown. The guest loved them, envious fellow guests requested them, word spread, and ultimately Crum started up his own restaurant, which specialized in potato chips.

The mouth is what keeps the prison of our bodies sealed up tight. Nothing enters for help or harm without passing through the mouth, which is why it was such an early development in evolution. Every slug, insect, and higher animal has a mouth. Even one-celled animals like paramecia have mouths, and the mouth appears immediately in human embryos. The mouth is more than just the beginning of the long pipeline to the anus: It's the door to the body, the place where we greet the world, the parlor of great risk. We use our mouths for other things—language, if we're human; drilling tree bark if we're a woodpecker; sucking blood if we're a mosquito—but the mouth mainly holds the tongue, a thick mucous slab of muscle, wearing minute cleats as if it were an athlete.

Analyzing Rhetorical Choices

1. What is the effect of Ackerman's use of the second-person and third-person plural in this reading? What kinds of relationships do these usages create between reader and text and between reader and author?

2. One characteristic of Ackerman's style is her tendency to elaborate on meanings and terms. She tells us about the different culinary habits of Jews, Malays, Catholics, Anglicans, and Egyptians. She informs us about the number of taste buds on a human tongue and then the number on the tongue of a rabbit, a parrot, and a cow. She writes that the mouth "is more than just the beginning of the long pipeline to the anus: It's the door to the body, the place where we greet the world, the parlor of great risk." Is this technique effective? Why or why not? How does it affect you as a reader?

3. Select at least five uses of metaphors or similes in this selection and discuss them in terms of their originality, descriptive qualities, and rhetorical effectiveness.

4. Evaluate Ackerman's use of exemplification. How well is it integrated into the text? What kinds of sources does she draw upon? Consider as well whether she includes the appropriate amount of information for you as reader, and state your reasoning.

Writing About Issues and Contexts

1. Do you agree that "taste is largely social"? How does Ackerman support this understanding of "taste"? Provide at least one example from your own experience that either validates or undercuts this concept.

2. What is the significance of taste for human beings? What kinds of meanings and values does it have for us, according to Ackerman?

3. How has taste influenced our use of language? Cite specific instances that Ackerman describes along with several examples of your own in which concepts of taste have entered into everyday speaking.

A native of Louisville, Kentucky, **Countee** *(pronounced "Count-ay")* **Cullen** *(1903–1946) was born Countee LeRoy Porter but took the name of Frederick Cullen, the Harlem reverend who adopted the 15-year-old boy. Cullen earned academic honors at his high school where he was also elected vice-president of his class and served as editor of the school newspaper. Subsequently, he won poetry prizes as an undergraduate at New York University and earned a master's degree from Harvard in 1926. A poet, playwright, essayist, columnist, and children's writer, his published works include* Color *(1925) and* Copper Sun *(1927). A key figure in the Harlem Renaissance, Cullen received an award from the National Association for the Advancement of Colored People (NAACP) for "distinguished achievement in literature by a Negro" in 1927 and was awarded a prestigious Guggenheim Fellowship to write poetry in France from 1928 to 1930.*

Countee Cullen

For a Lady I Know

She even thinks that up in heaven
Her class lies late and snores,
While poor black cherubs rise at seven
To do celestial chores.

Incident

Once riding in old Baltimore,
Heart-filled, head-filled with glee,
I saw a Baltimorean
Keep looking straight at me.

5 Now I was eight and very small,
And he was no whit bigger,
And so I smiled, but he poked out
His tongue, and called me, "Nigger."

I saw the whole of Baltimore
10 From May until December;
Of all the things that happened there
That's all that I remember.

Analyzing Rhetorical Choices

1. How does the formal simplicity of these two poems contribute to their emotional power? Consider the meter, the rhyme, and the four-line stanzas in your response.
2. Why does Cullen mention the phrase "her class" in "For a Lady I Know"? What effect does the word *celestial* have on the reader, in terms of its placement and complexity, compared with the other words in this poem?
3. Explain the implication of each title. How do they contribute to the overall effect of each poem?

Writing About Issues and Contexts

1. How do these poems reflect different aspects of racial discrimination?
2. How do these two poems relate to the essays later in this chapter by Henry Louis Gates, Jr., and Amy Wang? How do they relate to Gloria Naylor's essay in Chapter 4?
3. Why is it significant that the Baltimorean in "Incident" is so small and young?

Toni Cade Bambara (1939–1995) was a distinguished writer, lecturer, and civil rights activist. Born in New York City, Bambara attended Queens College and City College in New York City, and she also studied theater, mime, dance, film, and linguistics at eight other institutions in Europe and America. Committed to social change through political action, she worked as a welfare investigator, a community organizer, a literacy instructor, a college professor, and a director of plays and films. She is perhaps best known for her collections of short stories including Gorilla, My Love *(1972, and source of this selection) and* The Sea Birds Are Still Alive *(1977). Her novel* The Salt Eaters *(1980) is still read and taught widely; it has been described as "an incantation, poem-drunk, myth-happy, mud-caked, jazz-ridden, prodigal in meanings."*

Toni Cade Bambara

The Lesson

Back in the days when everyone was old and stupid or young and foolish and me and Sugar were the only ones just right, this lady moved on our block with nappy hair and proper speech and no makeup. And quite naturally we laughed at her, laughed the way we did at the junk man who went about his business like he was some big-time president and his sorry-ass horse his secretary. And we kinda hated her too, hated the way we did the winos who cluttered up our parks and pissed on our handball walls and stank up our hallways and stairs so you couldn't halfway play hide-and-seek without a goddamn gas mask. Miss Moore was her name. The only woman on the block with no first name. And she was black as hell, cept for her feet, which were fish-white and spooky. And she was always planning these boring-ass things for us to do, us being my cousin, mostly, who lived on the block cause we all moved North the same time and to the same apartment then spread out gradual to breathe. And our parents would yank our heads into some kinda shape and crisp up our clothes so we'd be presentable for travel with Miss Moore, who always looked like she was going to church, though she never did. Which is just one of the things the grownups talked about when they talked behind her back like a dog. But when she came calling with some sachet she'd sewed up or some gingerbread she'd made or some book, why then they'd all be too embarrassed to turn her down and we'd get handed over all spruced up. She'd been to college and said it was only right that she should take responsibility for the young ones' education, and she not even related by marriage or blood. So they'd go for it. Specially Aunt Gretchen. She was the main gofer in the family. You got some ole dumb shit foolishness you want somebody to go for, you send for Aunt Gretchen. She been screwed into the go-along for so long, it's a blood-deep natural thing with her. Which is how she got saddled with me and Sugar and Junior in the first place while our mothers were in a la-de-da apartment up the block having a good ole time.

So this one day, Miss Moore rounds us all up at the mailbox and it's puredee hot and she's knockin herself out about arithmetic. And school suppose to let up in summer I heard, but she don't never let up. And the starch in my pinafore scratching the shit outta me and I'm really hating this nappy-head bitch and her goddamn college degree. I'd much rather go to the pool or to the show where it's cool. So me and Sugar leaning on the mailbox being surly, which is a Miss Moore word. And Flyboy checking out what everybody brought for lunch. And Fat Butt already wasting his peanut-butter-and-jelly sandwich like the pig he is. And Junebug punchin on Q.T.'s arm for potato chips. And Rosie Giraffe shifting from one hip to the other waiting for somebody to step on her foot or ask her if she from Georgia so she can kick ass, preferably Mercedes'. And Miss Moore asking us do we know what money is, like we a bunch of retards. I mean real money, she say, like it's only poker chips or monopoly papers we lay on the grocer. So right away I'm tired of this and say so. And would much rather snatch Sugar and go to the Sunset and terrorize the West Indian kids and take their hair ribbons and their money too. And Miss Moore files that remark away for next week's lesson on brotherhood, I can tell. And finally I say we oughta get to the subway cause it's cooler and besides we might meet some cute boys. Sugar done swiped her mama's lipstick, so we ready.

So we heading down the street and she's boring us silly about what things cost and what our parents make and how much goes for rent and how money ain't divided up right in this country. And then she gets to the part about we all poor and live in the slums, which I don't feature. And I'm ready to speak on that, but she steps out in the street and hails two cabs just like that. Then she hustles half the crew in with her and hands me a five-dollar bill and tells me to calculate 10 percent tip for the driver. And we're off. Me and Sugar and Junebug and Flyboy hangin out the window and hollering to everybody, putting lipstick on each other cause Flyboy a faggot anyway, and making farts with our sweaty armpits. But I'm mostly trying to figure how to spend this money. But they all fascinated with the meter ticking and Junebug starts laying bets to how much it'll read when Flyboy can't hold his breath no more. Then Sugar lays bets as to how much it'll be when we get there. So I'm stuck. Don't nobody want to go for my plan, which is to jump out at the next light and run off to the first bar-b-que we can find. Then the driver tells us to get the hell out cause we there already. And the meter reads eighty-five cents. And I'm stalling to figure out the tip and Sugar say give him a dime. And I decide he don't need it as bad as I do, so later for him. But then he tries to take off with Junebug's foot still in the door so we talk about his mama something ferocious. Then we check out that we on Fifth Avenue and everybody dressed up in stockings. One lady in a fur coat, hot as it is. White folks crazy.

"This is the place," Miss Moore say, presenting it to us in the voice she uses at the museum. "Let's look in the windows before we go in."

5   "Can we steal?" Sugar asks very serious like she's getting the ground rules squared away before she plays. "I beg your pardon," say Miss Moore, and we fall out. So she leads us around the windows of the toy store and me and Sugar screamin, "This is mine, that's mine, I gotta have that, that was made for me, I was born for that," till Big Butt drowns us out.

"Hey, I'm going to buy that there."

"That there? You don't even know what it is, stupid."

"I do so," he say punchin on Rosie Giraffe. "It's a microscope."

"Whatcha gonna do with a microscope, fool?"

10   "Look at things."

"Like what, Ronald?" ask Miss Moore. And Big Butt ain't got the first notion. So here go Miss Moore gabbing about the thousands of bacteria in a drop of water and the somethinorother in a speck of blood and the million and one living things in the air around us is invisible to the naked eye. And what she say that for? Junebug go to town on that "naked" and we rolling. Then Miss Moore ask what it cost. So we all jam into the window smudgin it up and the price tag say $300. So then she ask how long'd take for Big Butt and Junebug to save up their allowances. "Too long," I say. "Yeh," adds Sugar, "outgrown it by that time." And Miss Moore say no, you never outgrow learning instruments. "Why, even medical students and interns and," blah, blah, blah. And we ready to choke Big Butt for bringing it up in the first damn place.

"This here costs four hundred eighty dollars," say Rosie Giraffe. So we pile up all over her to see what she pointin out. My eyes tell me it's a chunk of glass cracked with something heavy, and different-color inks dripped into the splits, then the whole thing put into a oven or something. But for $480 it don't make sense.

"That's a paperweight made of semi-precious stones fused together under tremendous pressure," she explains slowly, with her hands doing the mining and all the factory work.

"So what's a paperweight?" ask Rosie Giraffe.

15   "To weigh paper with, dumbbell," say Flyboy, the wise man from the East.

"Not exactly," say Miss Moore, which is what she say when you warm or way off too. "It's to weigh paper down so it won't scatter and make your desk untidy." So right away me and Sugar curtsy to each other and then to Mercedes who is more the tidy type.

"We don't keep paper on top of the desk in my class," say Junebug, figuring Miss Moore crazy or lyin one.

"At home, then," she say. "Don't you have a calendar and a pencil case and a blotter and a letter-opener on your desk at home where you do your homework?" And she know damn well what our homes look like cause she nosys around in them every chance she gets.

"I don't even have a desk," say Junebug. "Do we?"

20   "No. And I don't get no homework neither," says Big Butt.

"And I don't even have a home," say Flyboy like he do at school to keep the white folks off his back and sorry for him. Send this poor kid to camp posters, is his specialty.

"I do," says Mercedes. "I have a box of stationery on my desk and a picture of my cat. My godmother bought the stationery and the desk. There's a big rose on each sheet and the envelopes smell like roses."

"Who wants to know about your smelly-ass stationery," say Rosie Giraffe fore I can get my two cents in.

"It's important to have a work area all your own so that . . ."

25   "Will you look at this sailboat, please," say Flyboy, cuttin her off and pointin to the thing like it was his. So once again we tumble all over each other to gaze at this magnificent thing in the toy store which is just big enough to maybe sail two kittens across the pond if you strap them to the posts tight. We all start reciting the price tag like we in assembly. "Hand-crafted sailboat of fiberglass at one thousand one hundred ninety-five dollars."

"Unbelievable," I hear myself say and am really stunned. I read it again for myself just in case the group recitation put me in a trance. Same thing. For some reason this pisses me off. We look at Miss Moore and she lookin at us, waiting for I dunno what.

"Who'd pay all that when you can buy a sailboat set for a quarter at Pop's, a tube of glue for a dime, and a ball of string for eight cents? It must have a motor and a whole lot else besides," I say. "My sailboat cost me about fifty cents."

"But will it take water?" say Mercedes with her smart ass.

"Took mine to Alley Pond Park once," say Flyboy. "String broke. Lost it. Pity."

30   "Sailed mine in Central Park and it keeled over and sank. Had to ask my father for another dollar."

"And you got the strap," laugh Big Butt. "The jerk didn't even have a string on it. My old man wailed on his behind."

Little Q.T. was staring hard at the sailboat and you could see he wanted it bad. But he too little and somebody'd just take it from him. So what the hell. "This boat for kids, Miss Moore?"

"Parents silly to buy something like that just to get all broke up," say Rosie Giraffe.

"That much money it should last forever," I figure.

35   "My father'd buy it for me if I wanted it."

"Your father, my ass," say Rosie Giraffe getting a chance to finally push Mercedes.

"Must be rich people shop here," say Q.T.

"You are a very bright boy," say Flyboy. "What was your first clue?" And he rap him on the head with the back of his knuckles, since Q.T. the only one he could get away with. Though Q.T. liable to come up behind you years later and get his licks in when you half expect it.

"What I want to know is," I says to Miss Moore though I never talk to her, I wouldn't give the bitch that satisfaction, "is how much a real boat costs? I figure a thousand'd get you a yacht any day."

40   "Why don't you check that out," she says, "and report back to the group?" Which really pains my ass. If you gonna mess up a perfectly good swim day least you could do is have some answers. "Let's go in," she say like she got something up her sleeve. Only she don't lead the way. So me and Sugar turn the corner to where the entrance is, but when we get there I kinda hang back. Not that I'm scared, what's there to be afraid of, just a toy store. But I feel funny, shame. But what I got to be shamed about? Got as much right to go in as

anybody. But somehow I can't seem to get hold of the door, so I step away for Sugar to lead. But she hangs back too. And I look at her and she looks at me and this is ridiculous. I mean, damn, I have never ever been shy about doing nothing or going nowhere. But then Mercedes steps up and then Rosie Giraffe and Big Butt crowd in behind and shove, and next thing we all stuffed into the doorway with only Mercedes squeezing past us, smoothing out her jumper and walking right down the aisle. Then the rest of us tumble in like a glued-together jigsaw done all wrong. And people lookin at us. And it's like the time me and Sugar crashed into the Catholic church on a dare. But once we got in there and everything so hushed and holy and the candles and the bowin and the handkerchiefs on all the drooping heads, I just couldn't go through with the plan. Which was for me to run up to the altar and do a tap dance while Sugar played the nose flute and messed around in the holy water. And Sugar kept givin me the elbow. Then later teased me so bad I tied her up in the shower and turned it on and locked her in. And she'd be there till this day if Aunt Gretchen hadn't finally figured I was lyin about the boarder takin a shower.

Same thing in the store. We all walkin on tiptoe and hardly touchin the games and puzzles and things. And I watched Miss Moore who is steady watchin us like she waitin for a sign. Like Mama Drewery watches the sky and sniffs the air and takes note of just how much slant is in the bird formation. Then me and Sugar bump smack into each other, so busy gazing at the toys, 'specially the sailboat. But we don't laugh and go into our fat-lady bump-stomach routine. We just stare at that price tag. Then Sugar run a finger over the whole boat. And I'm jealous and want to hit her. Maybe not her, but I sure want to punch somebody in the mouth.

"Whatcha bring us here for, Miss Moore?"

"You sound angry, Sylvia. Are you mad about something?" Givin me one of them grins like she tellin a grown-up joke that never turns out to be funny. And she's lookin very closely at me like maybe she plannin to do my portrait from memory. I'm mad, but I won't give her that satisfaction. So I slouch around the store being very bored and say, "Let's go."

Me and Sugar at the back of the train watchin the tracks whizzin by large then small then gettin gobbled up in the dark. I'm thinkin about this tricky toy I saw in the store. A clown that somersaults on a bar then does chin-ups just cause you yank lightly at his leg. Cost $35. I could see me askin my mother for a $35 birthday clown. "You wanna who that costs what?" she'd say, cocking her head to the side to get a better view of the hole in my head. Thirty-five dollars and the whole household could go visit Granddaddy Nelson in the country. Thirty-five dollars would pay for the rent and the piano bill too. Who are these people that spend that much for performing clowns and $1000 for toy sailboats? What kinda work they do and how they live and how come we ain't in on it? Where we are is who we are, Miss Moore always pointin out. But it don't necessarily have to be that way, she always adds then waits for somebody to say that poor people have to wake up and demand their share of the pie and don't none of us know what kind of pie she talkin about in the first damn place. But she ain't so smart cause I still got her four dollars from the taxi and she sure ain't gettin it. Messin up my day with this shit. Sugar nudges me in my pocket and winks.

45   Miss Moore lines us up in front of the mailbox where we started from, seem like years ago, and I got a headache for thinkin so hard. And we lean all over each other so we can hold up under the draggy-ass lecture she always finishes us off with at the end before we thank her for borin us to tears. But she just looks at us like she readin tea leaves. Finally she say, "Well, what do you think of F. A. O. Schwarz?"

Rosie Giraffe mumbles, "White folks crazy."

"I'd like to go there again when I get my birthday money," says Mercedes, and we shove her out the pack so she has to lean on the mailbox by herself.

"I'd like a shower. Tiring day," say Flyboy.

Then Sugar surprises me by sayin, "You know, Miss Moore, I don't think all of us here put together eat in a year what that sailboat costs." And Miss Moore lights up like somebody goosed her. "And?" she say, urging Sugar on. Only I'm standin on her foot so she don't continue.

50   "Imagine for a minute what kind of society it is in which some people can spend on a toy what it would cost to feed a family of six or seven. What do you think?"

"I think," say Sugar pushing me off her feet like she never done before, cause I whip her ass in a minute, "that this is not much of a democracy if you ask me. Equal chance to pursue happiness means an equal crack at the dough, don't it?" Miss Moore is besides herself and I am disgusted with Sugar's treachery. So I stand on her foot one more time to see if she'll shove me. She shuts up, and Miss Moore looks at me, sorrowfully I'm thinkin. And somethin weird is goin on, I can feel it in my chest.

"Anybody else learn anything today?" lookin dead at me. I walk away and Sugar has to run to catch up and don't even seem to notice when I shrug her arm off my shoulder.

"Well, we got four dollars anyway," she says.

"Uh hunh."

55 "We could go to Hascombs and get half a chocolate layer and then go to the Sunset and still have plenty money for potato chips and ice cream sodas."

"Uh hunh."

"Race you to Hascombs," she say.

We start down the block and she gets ahead which is O.K. by me cause I'm going to the West End and then over to the Drive to think this day through. She can run if she want to and even run faster. But ain't nobody gonna beat me at nuthin.

Analyzing Rhetorical Choices

1. Why do you think Bambara chose to write this story in African American Vernacular English (AAVE)? How is its effectiveness enhanced by the language used to narrate this event?

2. Although Sylvia speaks and narrates in AAVE, Miss Moore does not: she speaks in what many call Standard English. What contrast gets established between the way Sylvia talks and the way Miss Moore talks? What points are driven home by this contrast?

3. Describe how Bambara uses details and specific descriptions to establish the grounds of her argument, and how the story itself is an example of exemplification.

Writing About Issues and Contexts

1. This story is told by Sylvia in a form known as a dramatic monologue. How would you describe Sylvia as she reveals herself in telling this story? How would you describe her values, her neighborhood, and her expectations about herself and her friends?

2. Why does Miss Moore take the kids to F. A. O. Schwarz on Fifth Avenue in New York City, perhaps the most expensive toy store in America? What "lesson" does she have in mind?

3. After seeing the sailboat and its $1,195 price tag, Sylvia and Miss Moore have an exchange in which Miss Moore says, "You sound angry, Sylvia. Are you mad about something?" Is Sylvia mad, and

if so, what is she mad about? Why would Miss Moore wish to make her angry?

4. What is the relationship between Miss Moore and the kids on the block, and between Miss Moore and the other adults in the neighborhood? Does her relationship with Sylvia alter during their visit to F. A. O. Schwarz, and if so how?

5. What is the significance of the last two lines of the story? Do they refer only to a race between Sugar and Sylvia, or to some kind of life lesson? Given Sylvia's final comment in this story, what kind of future would you envision for her?

A well-known academic in African American studies, **Henry Louis Gates, Jr.** *(1950–) was born in Keyser, West Virginia, and earned his bachelor's degree from Yale University and his Ph.D. from the University of Cambridge in England. From 1970 to 1971, he served as a general anesthetist at Anglican Mission Hospital in Kilimatinde, Tanzania; in the early 1970s, he also served as a staff reporter and correspondent for the* Times *(London). Gates went on to become director of undergraduate Afro-American studies at Yale and now serves as the head of the African American department at Harvard University. Gates is the general editor of* The Norton Anthology of African-American Literature *and* The Encyclopedia Africana. *His works include* The Signifying Monkey: Towards a Theory of Afro-American Literary Criticism *(1988),* Colored People: A Memoir *(1994),* Thirteen Ways of Looking at a Black Man *(1997), and* Wonders of the African World *(1999). This essay first appeared in* Sports Illustrated.

Henry Louis Gates, Jr.

Delusions of Grandeur

Standing at the bar of an all-black VFW post in my hometown of Piedmont, W.Va., I offered five dollars to anyone who could tell me how many African-American professional athletes were at work today. There are 35 million African-Americans, I said.

"Ten million!" yelled one intrepid soul, too far into his cups.

"No way . . . more than 500,000," said another.

"You mean *all* professional sports," someone interjected, "including golf and tennis, but not counting the brothers from Puerto Rico?" Everyone laughed.

5   "Fifty thousand, minimum," was another guess.

Here are the facts:

There are 1,200 black professional athletes in the U.S.

There are 12 times more black lawyers than black athletes.

There are 2-1/2 times more black dentists than black athletes.

10   There are 15 times more black doctors than black athletes.

Nobody in my local VFW believed these statistics; in fact, few people would believe them if they weren't reading them in the pages of *Sports Illustrated.* In spite of these statistics, too many African-American youngsters still believe that they have a much better chance of becoming another Magic Johnson or Michael Jordan than they do of matching the achievements of Baltimore Mayor Kurt Schmoke or neurosurgeon Dr. Benjamin Carson, both of whom, like Johnson and Jordan, are black.

In reality, an African-American youngster has about as much chance of becoming a professional athlete as he or she does of winning the lottery. The tragedy for our people, however, is that few of us accept that truth.

Let me confess that I love sports. Like most black people of my generation—I'm 40—I was raised to revere the great black athletic heroes and I never tired of listening to the stories of triumph and defeat that, for blacks, amount to a collective epic much like those of the ancient Greeks: Joe Louis's demolition of Max Schmeling; Satchel Paige's dazzling repertoire of pitches; Jesse Owens's in-your-face performance in Hitler's 1936 Olympics; Willie Mays's over-the-shoulder basket catch; Jackie Robinson's quiet strength when assaulted by racist taunts; and a thousand other grand tales.

Nevertheless, the blind pursuit of attainment in sports is having a devastating effect on our people. Imbued with a belief that our principal avenue to fame and profit is through sport, and seduced by a win-at-any-cost system that corrupts even elementary school students, far too many black kids treat basketball courts and football fields as if they were classrooms in an alternative school system. "O.K., I flunked English," a young athlete will say. "But I got an A plus in slam-dunking."

15   The failure of our public schools to educate athletes is part and parcel of the schools' failure to educate almost everyone. A recent survey of the Philadelphia school system, for example, stated that "more than half of all students in the third, fifth and eighth grades cannot perform minimum math and language tasks." One in four middle school students in that city fails to pass to the next grade each year. It is a sad truth that such statistics are repeated in cities throughout the nation. Young athletes—particularly young black athletes—are especially ill-served. Many of them are functionally illiterate, yet they are passed along from year to year for the greater glory of good old Hometown High. We should not be surprised to learn, then, that only 26.6% of black athletes at the collegiate level earn their degrees. For every successful educated black professional athlete, there are thousands of dead and wounded. Yet young blacks continue to aspire to careers as athletes, and it's no wonder why; when the University of

North Carolina recently commissioned a sculptor to create archetypes of its student body, guess which ethnic group was selected to represent athletes?

Those relatively few black athletes who do make it in the professional ranks must be prevailed upon to play a significant role in the education of all of our young people, athlete and nonathlete alike. While some have done so, many others have shirked their social obligations: to earmark small percentages of their incomes for the United Negro College Fund; to appear on television for educational purposes rather than merely to sell sneakers; to let children know the message that becoming a lawyer, a teacher or a doctor does more good for our people than winning the Super Bowl; and to form productive liaisons with educators to help forge solutions to the many ills that beset the black community. These are merely a few modest proposals.

A similar burden falls upon successful blacks in all walks of life. Each of us must strive to make our young people understand the realities. Tell them to cheer Bo Jackson but to emulate novelist Toni Morrison or businessman Reginald Lewis or historian John Hope Franklin or Spelman College president Johnetta Cole—the list is long.

Of course, society as a whole bears responsibility as well. Until colleges stop using young blacks as cannon fodder in the big-business wars of so-called nonprofessional sports, until training a young black's mind becomes as important as training his or her body, we will continue to perpetuate a system akin to that of the Roman gladiators, sacrificing a class of people for the entertainment of the mob.

Analyzing Rhetorical Choices

1. What kinds of proof does Gates offer to support his argument about the importance of education for black youth? How would you describe the effectiveness of the exemplification Gates uses to build his case?

2. Why does Gates open with the scene in the bar? Evaluate its effectiveness.

3. Why was it important to Gates to publish this article in *Sports Illustrated?*

4. Evaluate the rhetorical devices that Gates uses in his final two paragraphs. How do those devices help him end the article with emphasis?

Writing About Issues and Contexts

1. Gates argues that in addition to African Americans themselves, "society as a whole bears responsibility" for black youth's focus on sports rather than education. Evaluate this argument in at least two paragraphs of reasoned analysis that offers a thoughtful perspective on individual choice and societal values.

2. How can we change the way schools educate youth, especially black youth, regarding sports and success? Use evidence from the essay as well as from your own experience.

3. Gates mentions famous blacks—both athletes and nonathletes. Are all these names equally familiar? How does their familiarity among the general public (or lack of it) support his argument?

A native of Pittsburgh, **Amy Wang** *(1969–) is the daughter of Chinese parents who emigrated to the United States. A graduate of Cornell University in 1990, she earned a master's degree in journalism from the well-known Columbia University School of Journalism in 1993. That same year she published this personal account in the Sunday magazine of the* Philadelphia Inquirer *while working there as a copy editor. Wang currently holds the position of assistant bureau chief for* The Oregonian. *She, her husband, and son live in Portland, Oregon.*

Amy Wang

The Same Difference

It was on my way home that the moment of truth swept by— again.

There we were, a friend and I, heading north on the Pennsylvania Turnpike to central New York to visit my parents. Somehow our conversation had parted the curtains before my childhood memories, and before I knew it, I was telling him about an incident I have never quite forgotten.

As I spoke, it was almost as if my adult self were back in Pittsburgh, watching; strange how in my memory the sun is always glinting through a bright haze on that day. The trees are bare, or nearly so, with dark branches that reach out to splinter the sun's rays. I am walking alone, down a white concrete sidewalk littered with leaves, twigs, buckeyes. School is out for the day, and everyone is going home.

From behind come shouts, and I turn to see a group of children from school. A moment passes, and I realize they are shouting at me. I listen for several seconds before the words whip into clarity:

5   Chink! Hey, chink! Chinky chinky chink!

They are running. I am frozen, my heart the only part of me moving, and it is pounding. Then one of them stoops, picks up a twig and hurls it at me. It lands short, a foot away on the sidewalk. Then I turn, still blocks from home, and run. The twigs keep coming, clattering close behind as the others shout and follow. As I run, I think of the steep steps to the front door and despair.

But when I reach the steps and turn around, only silence follows. And when my mother answers the doorbell's ring, she sees only her daughter, cheeks a little flushed, waiting to be let in. Almost instinctively, I know I must not tell her. It would only hurt her, and there is nothing she can do. Besides, it is nothing I want to discuss.

"Wow," he said. "And you were in sixth grade when this happened?"

"Six," I said. "I was 6 when this happened. I was in first grade."

10   He was clearly appalled, his eyes in far focus as he tried to understand how such a thing could happen to a small child. I was concentrating on the road, but even a sidelong glance showed he did not, could not, quite understand. And it was then that I felt the familiar stab of disappointment: the realization that no matter how long we traveled together, we would always be on parallel roads, moving on either side of a great divide. I would never know his assurance as he made his way through a world where his skin color was an assumption, and he would never know my anxiety as I made my way through a world where my skin color was an anguish.

We were silent, and after a while he fell asleep. "Wake me up when we get to Allentown," he had said as he drifted off, and we both smiled, remembering a classmate who had once padded an expense account for profit by driving from New York to Allentown and back twice in two days.

The thought of the old mill town triggered memories of another old mill town, where I had gotten my first job out of college. It was at the local newspaper, working nights on the copy desk. Our shifts ended at 1 A.M., and I often drove home through deserted streets, the hush broken only by the whir of an occasional street-cleaning machine or the clanking of a distant garbage truck. The other drivers on the streets at that hour seemed just as weary, just as intent on getting to bed.

In such an atmosphere I often dream, and so to this day a shadowy, slowed-down quality suffuses the memory of turning my head and looking out the side window one night just in time to see an old red Dodge draw up in the next lane at a traffic light. Inside, four young white crewcut men dressed in denim and flannel strain toward me, their faces distorted with hate, their mouths twisted with invective. Our windows are closed, so I am spared their actual words, but their frenzied pantomime leaves little to be imagined.

When the light turns green I pull away hastily, but they cruise alongside for the next few blocks. By the time they tire of me and swing into a left turn, I am seething with fear and rage. I wait until they are committed to the turn, then raise my middle finger. One of them looks back for a final insult, sees my gesture, and gapes—but only for a moment. He turns, and I know he is screaming at the driver to turn back. I gun it.

15   They never come after me, and I make it home alive. Numb, I crawl into bed. It is only after I lie down that I realize how they might have hurt me, the four of them with their huge Dodge against my tiny Nissan, and I begin to shake. As my mind tumbles, the phone rings. For a moment I think it is them, and then logic returns. I answer, and it is my boyfriend, calling from Boston. I tell him what happened, melting into tears. He is sympathetic, but then he asks: "How do you know they weren't yelling at you because you were a woman?"

I don't, of course, but that is not the point. His whiteness rushes through the line with the very question. "It doesn't matter," I tell him, and suddenly I can't stand to hear his voice. I tell him I don't want to discuss it anymore, and hang up.

Somewhere along Route 79 in New York he said, "This is beautiful." I smiled, remembering the years I spent in Finger Lakes country: middle school, high school, college. Here were trees I had climbed, hills I had sledded down, malls I knew by heart; here were roads that led to memories and people who knew my history.

And it was because I had to come back here that another He was able to betray me. It was during the first summer I spent away from home, working at a magazine in New York. Picture now a pavilion on the grounds of a quiet country club where the staff is enjoying the annual company picnic, and there I am by the jukebox, hovering over the glassed-in 45s as a light mist dampens the grass. As The Contours wail "Do You Love Me," I sway to the beat, attracting a stranger's eyes. In a moment he is introducing himself; in an hour he is sitting by me in the bus taking us back to the city; in a week he is asking me out to dinner.

I am no longer thinking clearly. On my last day at the magazine, he watches as I clean out my desk, then asks me, in a low but urgent tone, not to forget him. He tells me he wants my address, and a sudden foreboding chill nearly stuns me with its iciness, sending shivers through my hand as I write out the address and phone number. Then I ask for his address and phone number. I do not think to ask him not to forget me.

20   Weeks go by without a word, and then one night, I know. The chill comes back: For days I hate white men, all of them, they all bear the blame for his misdeed. But I have known too many good ones for

my fury to last, and finally I am forced to admit that I have been a fool, and that this time, at least, it had nothing to do with race.

"It could have happened to anyone," a (white male) friend tells me. "It happens to everyone."

I am not immediately consoled. But time goes on, and finally, so do I.

By the time we pulled into my parents' driveway, it was nearly dinnertime. I sprang out, glad to stretch, and bounded into the house, but he was slow to follow, and I had discarded my shoulder bag and greeted everyone by the time he finally appeared in the doorway. I went to introduce him, wondering why he was hanging back. Then he raised his eyes to mine as he came up the stairs, and I realized he was nervous: He was in my world now, and he was finally getting an inkling of what I went through every day.

Payback time. At last.

25   Then my mother was there, smiling and shaking his hand, and my father was right behind her, also smiling.

"Welcome," he said.

For a moment, I could see the horizon, where parallel lines sometimes seem to meet.

Analyzing Rhetorical Choices

1. Wang exemplifies her essay by using three examples. How effective are they? Do you end up being persuaded to her point of view about racial hatred? Explain in an extended paragraph.
2. How effective is the device of the car trip? How does it help Wang to write this essay? Is the trip believable? Persuasive?

Writing About Issues and Contexts

1. After the first incident that Wang describes, she is tempted to inform her mother about being harassed by the children but she writes that "instinctively, I know I must not tell her. It would only hurt her, and there is nothing she can do. Besides, it is nothing I want to discuss." Why do you think she feels this way? Offer an analysis of whether she should have spoken to her mother or not, and why.
2. Wang reports that the four young men "never come after me, and I make it home alive." Is she overreacting? How do you read this statement?

3. What is the effect of Wang's statement after being chased home that "when I reach the steps and turn around, only silence follows"?

4. Why does Wang include her friend's misstatement in which he remarks that she was in sixth grade? What does this say about him and about general perceptions that some Americans have about racial discrimination?

Born in Butte, Montana, **Barbara Ehrenreich** *(1941–) was educated at Reed College and went on to earn a Ph.D. from Rockefeller University. A self-described socialist and feminist, Ehrenreich has written about student unrest on campus, health care, and most recently, the working poor, particularly women. Her work has been selected for the National Magazine Award, the Ford Foundation Award for Humanistic Perspectives on Contemporary Issues, and the* Los Angeles Times *Book Award, among others. Ehrenreich was also awarded a prestigious Guggenheim Fellowship in 1987. She has published many books, including* Fear of Falling: The Inner Life of the Middle Class *(1989),* The Snarling Citizen: Essays *(1995), and* Nickel and Dimed: On (Not) Getting By in America *(2001). Her essays have been published in many magazines including* Radical America, Nation, Esquire, Vogue, *the* New Republic, The New York Times Magazine, Mother Jones, *and* Ms., *where this essay first appeared.*

Barbara Ehrenreich

What I've Learned from Men

For many years I believed that women had only one thing to learn from men: how to get the attention of a waiter by some means short of kicking over the table and shrieking. Never in my life have I gotten the attention of a waiter, unless it was an off-duty waiter whose car I'd accidentally scraped in a parking lot somewhere. Men, however, can summon a maître d' just by thinking the word "coffee," and this is a power women would be well-advised to study. What else would we possibly want to learn from them? How to interrupt someone in mid-sentence as if you were performing an act of conversational euthanasia? How to drop a pair of socks three feet from an open hamper and keep right on walking? How to make those weird guttural gargling sounds in the bathroom?

But now, at mid-life, I am willing to admit that there are some real and useful things to learn from men. Not from all men—in fact, we may have the most to learn from some of the men we like the least. This realization does not mean that my feminist principles have gone soft with age: what I think women could learn from men is how to get *tough*. After more than a decade of consciousness-raising, assertiveness training, and hand-to-hand combat in the battle of the sexes, we're still too ladylike. Let me try that again—we're just too *damn* ladylike.

Here is an example from my own experience, a story that I blush to recount. A few years ago, at an international conference held in an exotic and luxurious setting, a prestigious professor invited me to his room for what he said would be an intellectual discussion on matters of theoretical importance. So far, so good. I showed up promptly. But only minutes into the conversation—held in all-too-adjacent chairs— it emerged that he was interested in something more substantial than a meeting of minds. I was disgusted, but not enough to overcome 30-odd years of programming in ladylikeness. Every time his comments took a lecherous turn, I chattered distractingly; every time his hand found its way to my knee, I returned it as if it were something he had misplaced. This went on for an unconscionable period (as much as 20 minutes); then there was a minor scuffle, a dash for the door, and I was out—with nothing violated but my self-esteem. I, a full-grown feminist, conversant with such matters as rape crisis counseling and sexual harassment at the workplace, had behaved like a ninny—or, as I now understand it, like a lady.

The essence of ladylikeness is a persistent servility masked as "niceness." For example, we (women) tend to assume that it is our responsibility to keep everything "nice" even when the person we are with is rude, aggressive, or emotionally AWOL. (In the above ex-ample, I was so busy taking responsibility for preserving the veneer of "niceness" that I almost forgot to take responsibility for myself.) In conversations with men, we do almost all the work: sociologists have observed that in male-female social interactions it's the woman who throws out leading questions and verbal encouragements ("So how did you *feel* about that?" and so on) while the man, typically, says "Hmmmm." Wherever we go, we're perpetually smiling—the on-cue smile, like the now-outmoded curtsy, being one of our cul-ture's little rituals of submission. We're trained to feel embarrassed if we're praised, but if we see a criticism coming at us from miles down the road, we rush to acknowledge it. And when we're feeling aggres-sive or angry or resentful, we just tighten up our smiles or turn them into rueful little moues. In short, we spend a great deal of time acting like wimps.

5 For contrast, think of the macho stars we love to watch. Think, for example, of Mel Gibson facing down punk marauders in "The Road Warrior" . . . John Travolta swaggering his way through the

early scenes of "Saturday Night Fever". . . or Marlon Brando shrugging off the local law in "The Wild One." Would they simper their way through tight spots? Chatter aimlessly to keep the conversation going? Get all clutched up whenever they think they might—just might—have hurt someone's feelings? No, of course not, and therein, I think, lies their fascination for us.

The attraction of the "tough guy" is that he has—or at least seems to have—what most of us lack, and that is an aura of power and control. In an article, feminist psychiatrist Jean Baker Miller writes that "a woman's using self-determined power for herself is equivalent to selfishness [and] destructiveness"—an equation that makes us want to avoid even the appearance of power. Miller cites cases of women who get depressed just when they're on the verge of success—and of women who do succeed and then bury their achievement in self-deprecation. As an example, she describes one company's periodic meetings to recognize outstanding salespeople: when a woman is asked to say a few words about her achievement, she tends to say something like, "Well, I really don't know how it happened. I guess I was just lucky this time." In contrast, the men will cheerfully own up to the hard work, intelligence, and so on, to which they owe their success. By putting herself down, a woman avoids feeling brazenly powerful and potentially "selfish"; she also does the traditional lady's work of trying to make everyone else feel better ("She's not really so smart, after all, just lucky").

So we might as well get a little tougher. And a good place to start is by cutting back on the small acts of deference that we've been programmed to perform since girlhood. Like unnecessary smiling. For many women—waitresses, flight attendants, receptionists—smiling is an occupational requirement, but there's no reason for anyone to go around grinning when she's not being paid for it. I'd suggest that we save our off-duty smiles for when we truly feel like sharing them, and if you're not sure what to do with your face in the meantime, study Clint Eastwood's expressions—both of them.

Along the same lines, I think women should stop taking responsibility for every human interaction we engage in. In a social encounter with a woman, the average man can go 25 minutes saying nothing more than "You don't say?" "Izzat so?" and, of course, "Hmmmm." Why should we do all the work? By taking so much responsibility for making conversations go well, we act as if we had much more at stake in the encounter than the other party—and that gives him (or her) the power advantage. Every now and then, we deserve to get more out of a conversation than we put into it: I'd suggest not offering information you'd rather not share ("I'm really terrified that my sales plan won't work") and not, out of sheer politeness, soliciting information you don't really want ("Wherever did you get that lovely tie?"). There will be pauses, but they don't have to be awkward for *you*.

It is true that some, perhaps most, men will interpret any decrease in female deference as a deliberate act of hostility. Omit the free smiles and perky conversation-boosters and someone is bound to ask, "Well, what's come over *you* today?" For most of us, the first impulse is to stare at our feet and make vague references to a terminally ill aunt in Atlanta, but we should have as much right to be taciturn as the average (male) taxi driver. If you're taking a vacation from smiles and small talk and some fellow is moved to inquire about what's "bothering" you, just stare back levelly and say, the international debt crisis, the arms race, or the death of God.

10   There are all kinds of ways to toughen up—and potentially move up—at work, and I leave the details to the purveyors of assertiveness training. But Jean Baker Miller's study underscores a fundamental principle that anyone can master on her own. We can stop acting less capable than we actually are. For example, in the matter of taking credit when credit is due, there's a key difference between saying "I was just lucky" and saying "I had a plan and it worked." If you take the credit you deserve, you're letting people know that you were confident you'd succeed all along, and that you fully intend to do so again.

Finally, we may be able to learn something from men about what to do with anger. As a general rule, women get irritated: men get *mad*. We make tight little smiles of ladylike exasperation; they pound on desks and roar. I wouldn't recommend emulating the full basso profundo male tantrum, but women do need ways of expressing justified anger clearly, colorfully, and, when necessary, crudely. If you're not just irritated, but *pissed off*, it might help to say so.

I, for example, have rerun the scene with the prestigious professor many times in my mind. And in my mind, I play it like Bogart. I start by moving my chair over to where I can look the professor full in the face. I let him do the chattering, and when it becomes evident that he has nothing serious to say, I lean back and cross my arms, just to let him know that he's wasting my time. I do not smile, neither do I nod encouragement. Nor, of course, do I respond to his blandishments with apologetic shrugs and blushes. Then, at the first flicker of lechery, I stand up and announce coolly, "All right, I've had enough of this crap." Then I walk out—slowly, deliberately, confidently. Just like a man.

Or—now that I think of it—just like a woman.

Analyzing Rhetorical Choices

1. Is the title of this essay ironic? If so, in what ways? How does the title prepare us for what Ehrenreich is going to say, both on a first reading and on subsequent readings?

2. Ehrenreich closes her first paragraph with a series of rhetorical questions. Extend that paragraph by developing four more rhetorical questions that satirize male behavior and build toward a final, climactic question that completes the paragraph with a crescendo.

3. Describe Ehrenreich's tone, and cite at least three examples from the essay that reinforce that tone. How does the tone, and the perspective that underlies it, keep you interested in the essay?

4. Ehrenreich uses the first-person plural in this essay. How effective is this? Is she in danger of alienating male readers who might pick up *Ms.* magazine and read her essay? Explain whether you think this is a risk worth taking.

Writing About Issues and Contexts

1. Ehrenreich identifies her principles as "feminist." What does she mean by that? What are "feminist principles"?

2. According to Ehrenreich, what is the "essence of ladylikeness"? What examples does she offer to help her describe ladylike behavior? Comment on whether you think her definition is appropriate today and explain your reasoning.

3. Ehrenreich's prime example, the one that is the departure point for this essay, describes her interaction with a prestigious professor who engages in overtly lecherous behavior. How does this example establish a framework for the entire essay?

*David Brooks (1961–) was born in Toronto and grew up in New York
City. After graduating from the University of Chicago, he has been
a correspondent for* The Atlantic Monthly, *a contributing editor of*
Newsweek, *a senior editor of the* Weekly Standard, *and a political ana-
lyst for the* NewsHour with Jim Lehrer. *A prominent conservative voice,
his books include* Bobos in Paradise: The New Upper Class and How
They Got There *(2000) and* On Paradise Drive: How We Live Now (And
Always Have) in the Future Tense *(2004).* "People Like Us" *was first
published in* The Atlantic Monthly *in 2003.*

David Brooks

People Like Us

Maybe it's time to admit the obvious. We don't really care about diversity all that much in America, even though we talk about it a great
deal. Maybe somewhere in this country there is a truly diverse neighborhood in which a black Pentecostal minister lives next to a white
anti-globalization activist, who lives next to an Asian short-order cook,
who lives next to a professional golfer, who lives next to a postmodern-
literature professor and a cardiovascular surgeon. But I have never been
to or heard of that neighborhood. Instead, what I have seen all around
the country is people making strenuous efforts to group themselves
with people who are basically like themselves.

Human beings are capable of drawing amazingly subtle social
distinctions and then shaping their lives around them. In the
Washington, D.C., area Democratic lawyers tend to live in suburban
Maryland, and Republican lawyers tend to live in suburban Virginia.
If you asked a Democratic lawyer to move from her $750,000 house
in Bethesda, Maryland, to a $750,000 house in Great Falls, Virginia,
she'd look at you as if you had just asked her to buy a pickup truck
with a gun rack and to shove chewing tobacco in her kid's mouth. In
Manhattan the owner of a $3 million SoHo loft would feel out of
place moving into a $3 million Fifth Avenue apartment. A West
Hollywood interior decorator would feel dislocated if you asked him
to move to Orange County. In Georgia a barista from Athens would
probably not fit in serving coffee in Americus.

It is a common complaint that every place is starting to look the
same. But in the information age, the late writer James Chapin once

told me, every place becomes more like itself. People are less often tied down to factories and mills, and they can search for places to live on the basis of cultural affinity. Once they find a town in which people share their values, they flock there, and reinforce whatever was distinctive about the town in the first place. Once Boulder, Colorado, became known as congenial to politically progressive mountain bikers, half the politically progressive mountain bikers in the country (it seems) moved there; they made the place so culturally pure that it has become practically a parody of itself.

But people love it. Make no mistake—we are increasing our happiness by segmenting off so rigorously. We are finding places where we are comfortable and where we feel we can flourish. But the choices we make toward that end lead to the very opposite of diversity. The United States might be a diverse nation when considered as a whole, but block by block and institution by institution it is a relatively homogeneous nation.

5   When we use the word "diversity" today we usually mean racial integration. But even here our good intentions seem to have run into the brick wall of human nature. Over the past generation reformers have tried heroically, and in many cases successfully, to end housing discrimination. But recent patterns aren't encouraging: according to an analysis of the 2000 census data, the 1990s saw only a slight increase in the racial integration of neighborhoods in the United States. The number of middle-class and upper-middle-class African-American families is rising, but for whatever reasons—racism, psychological comfort—these families tend to congregate in predominantly black neighborhoods.

In fact, evidence suggests that some neighborhoods become more segregated over time. New suburbs in Arizona and Nevada, for example, start out reasonably well integrated. These neighborhoods don't yet have reputations, so people choose their houses for other, mostly economic reasons. But as neighborhoods age, they develop personalities (that's where the Asians live, and that's where the Hispanics live), and segmentation occurs. It could be that in a few years the new suburbs in the Southwest will be nearly as segregated as the established ones in the Northeast and the Midwest.

Even though race and ethnicity run deep in American society, we should in theory be able to find areas that are at least culturally diverse. But here, too, people show few signs of being truly interested in building diverse communities. If you run a retail company and you're thinking of opening new stores, you can choose among dozens of consulting firms that are quite effective at locating your potential customers. They can do this because people with similar tastes and preferences tend to congregate by ZIP code.

The most famous of these precision marketing firms is Claritas, which breaks down the U.S. population into sixty-two psycho-demographic clusters, based on such factors as how much money people make, what they like to read and watch, and what products they have bought in the past. For example, the "suburban sprawl" cluster is composed of young families making about $41,000 a year and living in fast-growing places such as Burnsville, Minnesota, and Bensalem, Pennsylvania. These people are almost twice as likely as other Americans to have three-way calling. They are two and a half times as likely to buy Light n' Lively Kid Yogurt. Members of the "towns & gowns" cluster are recent college graduates in places such as Berkeley, California, and Gainesville, Florida. They are big consumers of DoveBars and *Saturday Night Live*. They tend to drive small foreign cars and to read *Rolling Stone* and *Scientific American*.

Looking through the market research, one can sometimes be amazed by how efficiently people cluster—and by how predictable we all are. If you wanted to sell imported wine, obviously you would have to find places where rich people live. But did you know that the sixteen counties with the greatest proportion of imported-wine drinkers are all in the same three metropolitan areas (New York, San Francisco, and Washington, D.C.)? If you tried to open a motor-home dealership in Montgomery County, Pennsylvania, you'd probably go broke, because people in this ring of the Philadelphia suburbs think RVs are kind of uncool. But if you traveled just a short way north, to Monroe County, Pennsylvania, you would find yourself in the fifth motor-home-friendliest county in America.

10   Geography is not the only way we find ourselves divided from people unlike us. Some of us watch Fox News, while others listen to NPR. Some like David Letterman, and others—typically in less urban neighborhoods—like Jay Leno. Some go to charismatic churches; some go to mainstream churches. Americans tend more and more often to marry people with education levels similar to their own, and to befriend people with backgrounds similar to their own.

My favorite illustration of this latter pattern comes from the first, noncontroversial chapter of *The Bell Curve*. Think of your twelve closest friends, Richard J. Herrnstein and Charles Murray write. If you had chosen them randomly from the American population, the

odds that half of your twelve closest friends would be college graduates would be six in a thousand. The odds that half of the twelve
would have advanced degrees would be less than one in a million.
Have any of your twelve closest friends graduated from Harvard,
Stanford, Yale, Princeton, Caltech, MIT, Duke, Dartmouth, Cornell,
Columbia, Chicago, or Brown? If you chose your friends randomly
from the American population, the odds against your having four or
more friends from those schools would be more than a billion to one.

Many of us live in absurdly unlikely groupings, because we have
organized our lives that way.

It's striking that the institutions that talk the most about diversity
often practice it the least. For example, no group of people sings the
diversity anthem more frequently and fervently than administrators at
just such elite universities. But elite universities are amazingly undi-
verse in their values, politics, and mores. Professors in particular are
drawn from a rather narrow segment of the population. If faculties reflected the general population, 32 percent of professors would be registered Democrats and 31 percent would be registered Republicans.
Forty percent would be evangelical Christians. But a recent study of
several universities by the conservative Center for the Study of Popular
Culture and the American Enterprise Institute found that roughly 90
percent of those professors in the arts and sciences who had registered
with a political party had registered Democratic. Fifty-seven professors
at Brown were found on the voter-registration rolls. Of those, fifty-
four were Democrats. Of the forty-two professors in the English, history, sociology, and political-science departments, all were Democrats.
The results at Harvard, Penn State, Maryland, and the University of
California at Santa Barbara were similar to the results at Brown.

What we are looking at here is human nature. People want to be
around others who are roughly like themselves. That's called community. It probably would be psychologically difficult for most Brown
professors to share an office with someone who was pro-life, a member of the National Rifle Association, or an evangelical Christian. It's
likely that hiring committees would subtly—even unconsciously—
screen out any such people they encountered. Republicans and evangelical Christians have sensed that they are not welcome at places like
Brown, so they don't even consider working there. In fact, any registered Republican who contemplates a career in academia these days is
both a hero and a fool. So, in a semi-self-selective pattern, brainy people with generally liberal social mores flow to academia, and brainy
people with generally conservative mores flow elsewhere.

15 The dream of diversity is like the dream of equality. Both are based on ideals we celebrate even as we undermine them daily. (How many times have you seen someone renounce a high-paying job or pull his child from an elite college on the grounds that these things are bad for equality?) On the one hand, the situation is appalling. It is appalling that Americans know so little about one another. It is appalling that many of us are so narrow-minded that we can't tolerate a few people with ideas significantly different from our own. It's appalling that evangelical Christians are practically absent from entire professions, such as academia, the media, and filmmaking. It's appalling that people should be content to cut themselves off from everyone unlike themselves.

The segmentation of society means that often we don't even have arguments across the political divide. Within their little validating communities, liberals and conservatives circulate half-truths about the supposed awfulness of the other side. These distortions are believed because it feels good to believe them.

On the other hand, there are limits to how diverse any community can or should be. I've come to think that it is not useful to try to hammer diversity into every neighborhood and institution in the United States. Sure, Augusta National should probably admit women, and university sociology departments should probably hire a conservative or two. It would be nice if all neighborhoods had a good mixture of ethnicities. But human nature being what it is, most places and institutions are going to remain culturally homogeneous.

It's probably better to think about diverse lives, not diverse institutions. Human beings, if they are to live well, will have to move through a series of institutions and environments, which may be individually homogeneous but, taken together, will offer diverse experiences. It might also be a good idea to make national service a rite of passage for young people in this country: it would take them out of their narrow neighborhood segment and thrust them in with people unlike themselves. Finally, it's probably important for adults to get out of their own familiar circles. If you live in a coastal, socially liberal neighborhood, maybe you should take out a subscription to *The Door,* the evangelical humor magazine; or maybe you should visit Branson, Missouri. Maybe you should stop in at a megachurch. Sure, it would be superficial familiarity, but it beats the iron curtains that now separate the nation's various cultural zones.

Look around at your daily life. Are you really in touch with the broad diversity of American life? Do you care?

Analyzing Rhetorical Choices

1. In the first paragraph, Brooks includes an ethnic descriptor for some types—black Pentecostal minister, white anti-globalization activist, Asian short-order cook. Then he drops the ethnic labels—professional golfer, postmodern-literature professor, cardiovascular surgeon. What is the effect of this switch?

2. Brooks keeps writing in the conditional. In other words, he focuses on his ideas about what people *would* do. Are these claims an effective form of argument?

3. Throughout the essay, Brooks uses *we*: We don't really care about diversity . . . we are increasing our happiness, and so forth. As a reader, do you feel included as part of *we* or is this technique unconvincing?

Writing About Issues and Contexts

1. Is it truly human nature, as the author suggests, for people to want to be around others like themselves? Has the author provided sufficient evidence in your view? What evidence could you provide for or against the proposition?

2. Brooks argues, "In fact, any registered Republican who contemplates a career in academia these days is both a hero and a fool." Do you agree with the author? How do you think most students would respond?

3. In his last paragraph, Brooks invites, "Look around at your daily life. Are you really in touch with the broad diversity of American life? Do you care?" What is your response to Brooks's questions?

Strategies for Writers: Exemplification

1. Exemplifying is a way of making your essay richer and more particular; it also can help you create structure and provide a way to develop your essay, as you can see in Ian Frazier's "If Memory Doesn't Serve." It is also a way of making appropriate choices that are rhetorically embedded—that is, choices about data and other specifics that serve your purposes as a writer and are strategically chosen and placed. Look over the draft of your most current essay. Are your examples well chosen? Well developed? Well placed?

2. How is exemplification a part of argument? It certainly involves the choice of appropriate examples to make your case, and it can be called a "type" of argument, a strategy for developing it. Like description, the choice of appropriate details associated with exemplification is crucial to the success of your writing. Exchange your drafts with your classmates; discover whether or not your readers find your details appropriate and useful for your purpose. Review your own draft to see if you immerse your reader in details as does Diane Ackerman. Compare your work to her "The Vagaries of Taste," and revise to elaborate on any details that need enhancement. Remember, however, that you are the final judge of whether or not the examples you use are appropriate and adequate for your writing.

3. David Brooks and Emily Tsao provide details that are unusual and sometimes startling. Exchange drafts with your classmates. Are there ways in which you can take generally good, acceptable examples and make them unusual—even startling—and yet appropriate for your purpose?

4. Countee Cullen has centered each of his two poems on one specific detail. Select one of these details and make it the subject of an essay. With your classmates, brainstorm lists that help you extend your example. At the same time, notice how definition, narration, and other ways of organizing your writing that we discuss in this volume might be appropriate for your work in this instance.

5. Another way to use examples is through research. If you decide to use secondary materials, your credibility depends on your citing your sources carefully and appropriately. This is often done by means of footnotes in academic essays, but notice

the ways that Ackerman acknowledges her sources in "The Vagaries of Taste."

6. Exemplification places a high value on directness. Some cultures, however, not only value being indirect more than they do being direct but also consider indirectness a virtue. Discuss and debate this issue with your classmates. To what extent are we obliged to take on the styles of the dominant culture? Why or why not?

Research and Writing Assignments

1. David Brooks's "People Like Us" uses a series of examples, some speculative, to present his case. Following Brooks's model, write an essay about a political or social issue that concerns you, using a series of your own observations about contemporary politics or culture.

2. Diane Ackerman writes about taste with a strong sense of wonder and pleasure. Using her essay as a model, write an essay that uses the same kind of detail and specificity to explain one of the following everyday activities: sighing, hiccupping, laughing, or yawning. Whatever subject you choose, you will have to do some extensive research (as Ackerman did) to write an essay that conveys new and interesting information.

3. A common theme of several selections in this chapter is explicit expressions of racial discrimination. Countee Cullen, Toni Cade Bambara, and Amy Wang offer various perspectives drawn primarily from childhood, from Cullen's memory of childhood hatred to Wang's memories of anti-Chinese and anti-Asian prejudice. In an essay, examine the complex roots of childhood prejudice. How do children of different ethnicities, who grow up in different neighborhoods, or who practice different customs and religions learn to hate each other? What sociological or tribal purposes does such prejudice serve? What is the relation between childhood prejudice and education, and between childhood prejudice and social class? Since few of us wish to remain "prejudiced," how can we realistically overcome it? This is a subject that is best suited to library research so you can include informed perspectives from respected researchers and scholars in your essay. For instance, you might want to investi-

gate a 2002 study of children in Northern Ireland, which was designed to trace the roots of Catholic/Protestant prejudice.

4. Both Toni Cade Bambara and Barbara Ehrenreich center their essays on the notion of lessons and learning, and both feature narrative. Write your own nonfictional narrative account of an experience you had that taught you something valuable or significant. Be sure to include specific details so the experience can come alive in the reader's imagination. For added effect, try to leave the "lesson" implicit. That is, don't end your narrative essay with a "moral," but tell about something in such a way that your readers can draw their own conclusions about why this event was something that made a significant impact on you.

5. In his essay, Henry Louis Gates, Jr., offers an assessment of the false promise that professional athletics holds out to black youth and the destructive consequences of this false promise. Does athletics offer many students (of most any ethnicity or gender) the hope of a rich and glorious livelihood? Choose a high school or college athlete and interview that individual to see what his or her personal aspirations are in relation to a professional sports career. Then present that information in the form of an essay that features direct quotations from your interview. Your essay can be in the form of either a profile of the student you interview or an essay that analyzes this complex issue and uses your interview as a source for exemplification.

6

Classification

In many ways, our first analytic understanding of the world comes to us through classification. We learn how to identify specific traits and characteristics and from them form general categories of understanding. For example, through intuitive observation, we identify one of our parents as Mom and the other as Dad. Soon after, based on these individual definitions, we make a greater intellectual leap and classify adults in similar roles as mothers or fathers. Ultimately, we meet and interact with other individuals, classifying them as siblings, aunts and uncles, friends, teachers, strangers, and so on. Classifying becomes a way of organizing the world, of putting people, places, and things into meaningful categories so that we can understand them better, relate them to one another, distinguish them more clearly.

This is not a simple or simplistic process. To classify demands keen observational powers, the ability to compare and contrast, strong cognitive skills, and a great deal of judgment. Hurried and unsophisticated attempts at classifying can betray us. If we are hasty or uninformed, we put things into incorrect categories and make judgments that can lead to false generalizations, stereotyping, and reductive thinking. By classifying without doing sufficient research and analysis, we may well overlook key qualities and force subjects into categories in which they do not belong. "That song has a West Coast feel to it," someone might say without realizing that the song comes out of the Austin country music scene. Or in a vain attempt to display vast knowledge, someone might tell everyone, incorrectly, that a scallop is not a mollusk, a telling mistake in classification for those familiar with the movie *Barbershop*.

When done well, classification gives us a powerful way to understand the world. It compels us to look at objects both microscopically (details, specifics, individual traits) and macroscopically (common qualities, general similarities, overarching frameworks). To illustrate how important and how complex classification can be, here is an example from science, a discipline deeply dependent on classification. Chemistry, physics, geology, and biology classify information in ways that allow scientists to understand basic principles and practices. The study of insects is a prime example. At the elementary school level, most kids are interested in insects, or what they call "bugs," fascinated, and sometimes repelled, by beetles, wasps, ants, butterflies, and spiders. But are these all insects? What is the best method for explaining what an insect is, and isn't? The answer, according to elementary school teacher Nancy Goslin—who has put her lesson plan on a Web site, *http://www.successlink.org/gti/gti_lesson.asp?lid=3869*— is to understand how insects get classified. According to Goslin, who paraphrases good science to simplify the process a bit for elementary students, insects have five characteristics:

1. An exoskeleton
2. Three pairs of legs
3. One pair of antennae
4. Compound eyes
5. Many adults have wings

If every insect has an external skeleton, six legs, one pair of antennae, compound eyes, and (frequently) wings, then yes, beetles, wasps, ants, and butterflies are all insects. But a spider, which has eight legs and no wings, is not. In fact, spiders have other characteristics that place them within the class known as Arachnida, which includes scorpions, mites, and ticks. Making these kinds of classifications helps us better understand the world around us.

At a much more advanced level, scientists make more refined distinctions within this class known as Insecta. It includes more than 25 orders—for instance, Coleoptera (beetles) and Lepidoptera (moths and butterflies)—and within these orders, it is possible to make further refinements and classify an insect according to its family, genus, or species. For elementary school students, a basic understanding of insect classification is sufficient, but those who specialize in the field of entomology (the study of the class Insecta) have to know much more to analyze insects according to their proper classification. They are more likely to use the following complex classificatory scheme:

Insect Classification

Apterygota (wingless insects)
- Thysanura—bristletails
- Diplura—two-tailed bristletails
- Protura—proturans
- Collembola—springtails

Pterygota (winged insects)

Exopterygota (insects with partial metamorphosis)
- Ephemeroptera—mayflies
- Odonata—dragonflies
- Plecoptera—stoneflies
- Orthoptera—crickets and grasshoppers
- Dermaptera—earwigs
- Dictyoptera—cockroaches
- Psocoptera—booklice and barklice
- Mallophaga—biting lice
- Anoplura—sucking lice
- Hemiptera—true bugs
- Thysanoptera—thrips

Endopterygota (insects with complete metamorphosis)
- Neuroptera—lacewings, alderflies, and snakeflies
- Mecoptera—scorpion flies
- Lepidoptera—butterflies and moths
- Trichoptera—caddis flies
- Diptera—true flies
- Siphonaptera—fleas
- Hymenoptera—ants, bees, wasps
- Coleoptera—beetles

What this much more sophisticated and exacting classificatory scheme tells us is that some insects have wings and others do not, and that one of the major distinctions among insects is differentiating those that completely metamorphose (change radically from a larva to an adult, such as from a caterpillar to a moth) and those that metamorphose partially, like aphids and dragonflies. It also tells us that there is a great variety of insects and invites us to study them based on their differences and similarities, according to which they are placed within classifications. Moreover, refined as this taxonomy is, it still leaves scientists room for debate and disagreement. On his Web site (*http://www.bombus.freeserve.co.uk/classification.htm*), the author of these particular categories states, "Some classifications now place Diplura, Protura, and Collembola outside the class Insecta." Are springtails insects? It looks like the scientific jury is still out.

Like entomologists, everyone engages in sophisticated forms of classification: when deciding how to organize a music collection or when categorizing friends according to their most obvious personality traits. When you read a short piece of writing, you classify it by deciding whether it is a short story, journalistic narrative, magazine article, or scholarly essay. To classify in these ways requires two kinds of knowledge: knowledge of the specific features of the subject and knowledge about the general kinds of categories into which individual subjects might be placed. Thus classifying requires both inductive and deductive kinds of thinking (see Chapter 10 for a brief definition of these terms).

One danger of classifying is binary thinking—the natural tendency to classify things into opposites: right/left, up/down, good/bad, smart/dumb, moral/immoral. Our physical orientation in the world often encourages us toward binary thinking, since we have two eyes, two arms, a front and a back. Much of the time, however, binaries are reductive and false, especially when it comes to complex analysis. Most individuals are neither smart nor dumb but exhibit a range of intellectual abilities. Most people, like most countries in the world, are neither moral nor immoral, neither good nor evil; they behave morally in some respects and less morally in others. Meaningful classification requires sophisticated analysis and the creation of thoughtful categories that reflect the complexity of the subject.

Done well, classification is an extremely useful organizational strategy. For instance, you might consider the various kinds of learning that you have experienced and which are most effective, or the types of activities that best contribute to charitable work in your particular community and the outcomes of these activities. Classification can also be a useful strategy for explaining complex legal and emotional relationships. You might, for example, analyze the various classifications about race according to current (and past) U.S. census practices. Or how cities and geographic regions get classified in terms of whether they are most or least segregated. Or how gemstones are categorized and what those categories mean, both within the jewelry industry and to you personally. Depending on your purpose and audience, you will decide on the most informative and insightful ways to classify so as to best serve your readers.

As you read and analyze the essays in this section, you will notice that some are explicit classification essays, while others reveal their dependence on classification more subtly. Compare, for instance, the ironies and complexities of the lists of categories from *Harper's Magazine* with the William Zinsser essay, "College Pressures," and Malcolm Gladwell's "Big and Bad." As a strategy for organizing an essay, classification—as is the case with all the modes in this book—does not follow lockstep patterns. Rather, it is a way of thinking about a subject that gets expressed in purpose, form, and evidence. The key to successful classification is logical consistency combined with subtle and supple analysis. Classification is never appropriate if it results in easy and formulaic categories and reductive thinking. Both the writer and the reader need to apply classification so that they both discover new insights or a fresh way of looking at the familiar.

Approaches to Writing Classification Essays

First of all, to write a successful classification essay, choose an appropriate subject that suits your purpose. Not all subjects and purposes can be used with this approach, since it depends upon analyzing a subject that can be broken down into two or more parts. Were you to decide to write an essay on the devastating consequences of the 1918 influenza epidemic, a subject much in the news as we work on this edition of *Rhetorical Choices*, your essay might well take the form of a narrative or descriptive essay. Those two modes might well make sense, but more than likely you would not wish to describe the epidemic by using classification. Classifying the influenza would offer little insight into the subject; most medical doctors and other knowledgeable experts agree that it was one of the worst such outbreaks since the development of modern medicine. In writing about influenza, however, you might well make some supplementary use of the mode of classification, since the flu virus can take one of three forms (known as A, B, or C) and an outbreak of flu can be characterized as endemic, epidemic, or pandemic. This supplementary use might take the form of a paragraph or two within a larger essay that is narrative, descriptive, or definitional.

A more appropriate subject to be analyzed within the mode of classification is one that must be broken down into its constituent parts in order to be clearly understood. You might, for example, decide to write about the different kinds of bats that exist in the world, from fruit bats to vampire bats. One way to categorize them is from small to large; another way is to distinguish between those that are carnivorous and those that are vegetarian. Your method of classification will depend upon the purpose of your essay. Similarly, you might choose to write about modern media, beginning with two large classifications, analog and digital, and then breaking them down further within each category. Thus the most important goal in writing a classification essay is to find a subject worthy of describing in terms of its various components and then doing so in such a way that you develop a purpose that will hold your—and your readers'—interest.

Choose a Suitable Subject

It makes most sense to write a classification essay when your subject is complex and can be separated into subcategories that help inform the reader of your subject's meaning. Such subjects can be challenging to locate, especially ones about which you care enough so that writing an essay makes sense to you and to your readers. For example, you receive a classification assignment and are not sure what to write. After some thought, you decide to write an essay about investing, especially since you are interested in how you might invest some of your income once you graduate from college. After talking to a Writing Center tutor, you realize that "investment" is too broad a subject, so you narrow your focus to one aspect of investing, namely mutual funds. After doing some research, you discover there are three main kinds of mutual funds: money market funds, bond funds, and stock funds. In your essay, you will have to define what each of these funds is, and in researching that subject you learn that each of these funds can be broken down into subcategories. For example, the primary kinds of bond funds are municipal bond funds, corporate bond funds, mortgage-backed security funds, and U.S. Government bond funds. Each of these funds offers investors a different kind of portfolio and different kinds of risks, and as you analyze their similarities and differences, you also simultaneously elaborate and refine your classification system.

Classification as a mode works best when writing about subjects that are substantial in scope but can be best understood when broken down into their component parts. The subject should be worthy of interest. It would make little sense to analyze the different kinds of rubber bands (thick, medium, and narrow, or red, yellow, brown, and blue). Most people don't care enough about rubber bands to read an entire classification essay on them, but they often do care about subjects such as mutual funds, synthetic and natural fibers, or the different kinds of courts in the United States and what their various functions are. Choosing a worthy subject is essential when writing a classification essay.

Exemplify

Once you start writing, whether your subject is as mundane as grading cuts of beef or as arcane as valuing antique dolls, you will need to place the various components along a spectrum or range (of age, quality, density, complexity, etc.). Once you have discovered a subject, you will need to understand it well enough to be able to offer illustrative examples. Exemplification is often the key to a successful classification essay because it anchors your insights with specific illustrations. If your subject is a worthy one, it will require an analysis into its constituent parts, and typically you will need to provide illustrations, examples, and appropriate details for those parts to be understood. Classifying only makes sense if each of the categories is well defined, well depicted, and well developed. Of course, you will want also to be sure that your essay offers information and insights beyond the obvious. After all, if the reader already knows what you will write, there is no reason for anyone to read it.

Selections from *Harper's Magazine*

[Nomenclature]

Begun This Clone War Has

From Flybase, a database of fruit-fly genes maintained by a consortium of research institutions. The genes were named by the researchers who discovered them. Convention suggests that if the genes' human counterparts are discovered, they will be given the same names.

aloof
always early
amontillado
bang senseless
bang sensitive
bride of sevenless
brother of odd with entrails
   limited
bumper-to-bumper
clootie dumpling
couch potato
crack
crossbronx
currant bun
Daughter killer
daughter of sevenless
Deadpan
deathknell
Dinty
disco-related
dog of glass
effete
eggroll
enoki mushroom
escargot
ether a go-go

faint sausage
fear-of-intimacy
fuzzy onions
genghis khan
glass bottom boat
Godzilla
Grunge
gut feeling
helter-skelter
he's not interested
hoi-polloi
I'm not dead yet
In dunce
inebriated
jekyll and hyde
just odd knobs
ken and barbie
king tubby
klingon
ladybird early
ladybird late
lemming
Lesbian
long island expressway
maelstrom
Malvolio

members only
mozzarella
naked cuticle
nanking
okra
out at first
oxen
pacman
papillote
pentagon
pugilist
quagmire
quick-to-court
redtape
Revolute
roadkill
rolling stone
sawtooth

scab
scott of the antarctic
scruin like at the midline
sevenless
Sex lethal
shank
similar to Deadpan
singles bar
slamdance
spotted dick
stranded at second
super sex combs
Thor
thousand points of light
Trailer hitch
vibrator
viking

Bill Gates Is. . .

The following descriptions of Microsoft chairman Bill Gates are taken from the 33,867 public comments received by the U.S. Justice Department concerning its proposed settlement with Microsoft. The department is required by law to solicit and publish public comments, and to respond to each one, before reaching a final settlement.

a brave boy and son of his parents
a brilliant man
a businessman's role model
a cash cow
a champion
a character
a Communist
a crook and a liar
a Dem
a deserving man
a driven man
a fair and honest man

a fine example of what a person can achieve with determination
and hard work
a genius
a genius just like Edison or Ford
a genius nerd
a great inventor
a guy who made good and has been punished for his success
a lawyer's son
a man with a vision and the fortitude to make it happen
a patriot
a perfect example of folks who make a difference in our lives,
and how to improve ourselves!!
a pioneer
a prince of a person
a SELF-MADE person
a shrewd businessman if nothing else
a smart man
a terrorist that doesn't use bullets
a tough competitor
a true American
a true American hero
a true businessman
a very successful man
a wolf in sheep fur
aggressive
an absolute genius
an American
an American patriot
an angel compared to Ken Lay
an excellent businessman
an icon of the American dream
constantly coming up with better ideas for working-class people
essentially amoral
EVIL
generous
involved in some world-domination scheme
just a genius
laughing at the Justice Department
living the American dream
making a mockery of the Court
my hero!
no angel
no better than a criminal
no crook
no genius but a fantastic POKER PLAYER!

no idiot
not a criminal
not a terrorist
not being nominated for Sainthood
not for freedom and innovation
not interested in quality product
not John Galt
not one of my personally favorite people
not Osama bin Laden
not the bad guy
not to be trusted
now more powerful than George Bush
obviously more powerful than the government!
one of the greatest leaders in the history of our capitalist country
one of the major contributors to our economy
one of the true heroes of this country
really afraid of face-to-face or shoulder-to-shoulder competition
reminiscent of earlier American giants like Thomas Edison
right again
sneering inwardly
someone who this country should be very proud of
subject to the provisions of U.S.C. Title 18 Section 96
telling YOU what YOU are going to do
the "Alexander the Great" of product development and marketing
THE ANTICHRIST!!!!
the best businessman ever to walk the Earth
the best of the best!
the computer world's version of a Bin Laden
the J. P. Morgan of his generation
the most respected nonpolitical world leader
the Patron Saint of Computers
the richest man in the world
the smartest (excluding myself of course) man in the U.S.A.
the ultimate capitalist pig
the why we are here from the beginning
Tony Blair's friend
too arrogant by far
totally unacceptable
truly a giver
truly a unique individual
very generous with his money
what America is about
wonderful for giving people such great software
wrong, wrong, wrong, wrong, wrong!!!!!!!!!!

[Roster]

Have a Huang and a Smile

From a list of brands owned by Coca-Cola, published on the Coca-Cola Web site.

Alive
American
Beverly
Bimbo
Bimbo Break
BonAqua
Bori Bori
Bright and Early
Burn
Chippewa
Chivalry
Chotto Kaoru
Chuhai
Cocoteen
Cresta-Ko
DESCA
diet Kia Ora-Ko
Emblem
Eva
Fruktime
Georgia
Gold Spot
Hachimittu
Huang
Inca Kola
Jesus
Jolly Juice
Juggy

Kuli
Lilt
Love Body
Miami
Nevada
New Vegitabeta
Ok
Old Colony-Ko
Pulp
Pump
Qoo
Riwa
Seiryusabo
Shock
Simba
Smart
Squirt-Ko
Supa
Tian Yu Di
Tiky-Ko
Thums Up
Urge
Vegitabeta
Wannabe
Woorijip
Youki
Water Salad
Wilkins

Analyzing Rhetorical Choices

1. These various selections from *Harper's Magazine* reveal different types of naming and classifying. Why did the editors of *Harper's* title each section as they did?

2. In the first piece, "Nomenclature" is placed in brackets. What effect does this have? Why is the title of the piece "Begun This Clone War Has"? What about the piece called "Have a Huang and a Smile" and its bracketed label, "Roster"? How do the lists of names become categories as well? To what effect?

Writing About Issues and Contexts

1. How does the first piece, "Nomenclature," suggest various attitudes toward cloning, the ostensible subject of the section? Select several of the categories or names that you think are the most interesting. What connotative or political effects do these various categories for fruit flies have? What implications might there be for the human genes that will be similarly named?

2. Similarly, "Bill Gates Is . . ." refers to its list of names as "descriptions." How, too, are they categories? To what effect? What seem to be the varieties of ways to describe or categorize the various aspects of Bill Gates as a person and businessman?

3. How does the larger category of "brand names" change depending on cultural contexts, and how might they reflect culture? See if you can, through research, find out which names of soft drinks have been developed into actual products. Why, for instance, does "water salad" as a type or category of beverage seem inappropriate for sale in the United States?

Born in Minneapolis, Minnesota, **Peggy Orenstein** *(1961–) received a degree in English from Oberlin College and served in various editorial positions for publications such as* Mother Jones, 7 Days, Manhattan, inc., *and* Esquire. *Orenstein is a frequent contributor to both* The New York Times Magazine *and the* Los Angeles Times. *Orenstein is an advocate of women's rights whose work addresses topics ranging from female sexuality, to reproduction, to breast cancer. Her book* Schoolgirls: Young Women, Self-Esteem, and the Confidence Gap *(1994) was named a* New York Times *"Notable Book of the Year."* Flux *(2000), Orenstein's second book, explores the choices regarding sexuality, career, education, and motherhood that must be made by women between the ages of 25 and 45. "Where Have All the Lisas Gone?" originally appeared in the July 4, 2003, edition of* The New York Times Magazine.

Peggy Orenstein

Where Have All the Lisas Gone?

According to the official Popular Baby Names Web site, the name we are considering for our daughter, to be born later this summer, was in the Top 200 for her sex last year. It was less popular than Molly but more so than Abby. This has me worried. It seems perched at a precarious point from which it could, without warning, rocket into overuse. Witness Chloe, which has shot from 184 to 24 since 1991. Call out the name in your local Gymboree, and four little heads will whip around.

Popular Baby Names, which is operated by the Social Security Administration, ranks the 1,000 most common boys' and girls' names since 1900 (www.ssa.gov/OACT/babynames/). You can also look up a specific name and track its status over time (an activity that, I warn you, is an Internet addict's sinkhole). The site, started seven years ago, was initially the side project of a government actuary named Michael Shackleford. Michael reigned as the No. 1 boys' name for thirty-five years beginning in 1964, after about a decade of duking it out with David and Robert. It was unseated by Jacob in 1999.

Shackleford grew up, with no small amount of bitterness, in a multiple-Michael world. He hoped that by publishing the list, parents-to-be would see that his name (and other common names) were shopworn and choose something more original. (Shackleford, incidentally, quit the Social Security Administration in 2000 and moved to Las Vegas, where he has become a gambling consultant known as the Wizard of Odds. His own children are named Melanie, No. 88, and Aidan, No. 63.)

Perennials like Michael or Sarah are not, to my mind, the nub of the issue. They don't explain why so many people seeking more adventurous names seem to hit upon the same ones. Why did I recently receive birth announcements from three couples who had never met, who lived as distant from one another as Maine, Minnesota, and California, yet who had all named their sons Leo? How to account for the sudden spate of Natalies?

5   I am not so smug as to think myself immune to first-name zeitgeist. A few years ago, I developed a sudden affection for Julia, which now hovers at 31, and then for Hannah, which is No. 3. Although I have never personally met a Madison (2), I have watched friends seduced by the seeming novelty of Alyssa (12), Olivia (10), and Dylan (24 among boys), only to discover that their children are destined to spend life with the initials of their last names appended to their first.

While my husband doesn't seem concerned—at least judged by the excessive eye rolling when I bring up another contender—I've trawled the Social Security site for clues to the potential future of "our" name. I've sifted through message boards on pregnancy sites to see if it has cropped up among other moms-to-be. I've checked a site that polls users to determine a name's image based on continuums of ambition, attractiveness, and athleticism. I've even looked on the Kabalarian Philosophy site, which, using a supposed mathematical principle, analyzes the "power" hidden in more than 500,000 names. None of that, however, explained what I really want to know: how a particular name becomes popular and whether it's inevitable, like it or not, that my husband and I will choose the next Kayla (19).

Pamela Redmond Satran and Linda Rosenkrantz have built their empire on the backs of people like me. Their eight books, including the classic *Beyond Jennifer & Jason, Madison & Montana*, have sold more than a million copies; a new volume, the pared-down and pointedly titled *Cool Names*, will be published next month. Like *Jennifer & Jason*, it is part advice manual, part pop sociology text. Avoiding the deadly (and useless) dictionary format, it divides names into sections. There's the safe Hot Cool (Polly, Harry); the famous Cool Cool (Charlize, Keanu); the retro Pre-Cool Cool (Beata, Lazarus); and the

New Cool, which encompasses, among other things, constellations (Elara, Orion). The express purpose is to help jittery parents-to-be separate current favorites from what's about to break big from what the daring among them can pioneer.

The duo read the baby-name tea leaves of preschool class lists, maternity wards, and birth announcements. They also consult the Social Security site, though Satran warns of a critical glitch: It doesn't combine alternative spellings. In 1998, for instance, Kaitlyn was way down at 36. But if you totted up the Katelyns, Caitlins, Caitlyns, Kaitlins, Katelynns, Katlyns, Kaitlynns, Katelins, Caitlynns, Katlins, Katlynns, and Kaytlyns, that name would have easily bested the No. 1-ranked Emily. Like any kind of forecasting, though, from predicting cargo pants to recognizing that we're about to have an orange moment, picking the next Grace (15) is as much art as science. "We look at all the lists," Satran says. "We look at movie stars' names and what they're naming their children. We look at names that cut across several trends at once. But after that, it's just instinct."

Satran and Rosenkrantz have a pretty solid record of prognosticating, particularly on groups of names. They sounded the alarm on the use of places (Paris, Sierra, Asia) as first names in 1988, years before that trend slid from mainstream to cliché. A friend named her daughter London, Satran remembers, which caught her attention. A short time later, she heard about a baby boy named after a Pennsylvania town. She then met a Holland and heard about a Dakota. Those encounters dovetailed with an uptick of androgynous names for girls. By the time Alec Baldwin and Kim Basinger named their daughter Ireland, Satran and Rosenkrantz knew that place names were firmly on the map.

10   Names weren't always subject to fashion. About half of all boys in Raleigh Colony were named John, Thomas, or William, and more than half of newborn girls in the Massachusetts Bay Colony were named Mary, Elizabeth, or Sarah. Even in the twentieth century, John, William, James, and Robert were, in some combination, the top three names for boys for more than fifty years. Among girls, Mary held on to No. 1 for forty-six years, when it was supplanted for six years by Linda, fought its way back for another nine, then succumbed to the juggernaut of Lisa.

These days, even a popular name isn't especially prevalent: Though the name was ranked fourth, there were only about 16,300 Emmas born last year. Sell-by dates are shorter too, at least for girls. Only three of today's Top 10 names (Sarah, Samantha, and Ashley) survived since 1990.

With boys—well, there's Michael. Parents continue to be more conventional with their sons, more conscious of tradition and generational continuity. Girls' names are more likely to be chosen for style and beauty. That makes them both more interesting to track and more vulnerable to sounding passé, the human equivalent of bragging about your new pashmina.

The Harvard sociologist Stanley Lieberson first bumped up against the fashion quotient of names in the 1960s. Believing they were bucking convention, he and his wife named their eldest daughter Rebecca, only to discover a few years later that she was part of a pack. How had that happened? The marketplace, after all, has no interest in what we name our children; no corporation profits if you choose Kaylee over Megan. That makes names one of the rare measures of collective taste.

Lieberson, the author of *A Matter of Taste: How Names, Fashions and Culture Change,* insists that names generally rise and fall independent of larger cultural or historical events. Consider the resurgence of biblical names. "They came back like gangbusters in the late twentieth century," Lieberson says. "There was speculation that it was related to a resurgence of religion. But people who use Old Testament names are, if anything, less religious in their behavior than those who don't. It's just fashion."

15   Naming styles, Lieberson says, are usually variations on what came before, moving forward predictably, the way lapels get wider and wider until they reach a peak and switch direction. He calls this "the ratchet effect." Take Old Testament names. In 1916, Ruth, for no obvious reason, was the only one to crack the Top 20 for girls. After it crested, it was replaced by Judith in 1940, then Deborah in 1950. By the late 1980s, there were three Old Testament names among the top slots: Rachel, Sarah, and Rebecca. Now it's Hannah, Abigail, and Sarah, with Leah (90 and holding) as the only potential replacement. Perhaps after a hundred years, girls' biblical names have ratcheted as far as they can go.

Sometimes, Lieberson explains, rather than a concept, it's just a sound that catches hold: the "a" at the end of girls' names (Emma, Hannah, Mia, Anna), or the hard "k" at the beginning (Kylie, Kaylee, Caitlin, Courtney). That breakthrough sound undulates outward, in a kind of jazz riff, gradually mutating. So the "djeh" sound in Jennifer begat Jenna and Jessica, but Jennifer also begat Heather and Amber, which share its suffix. (Before Jennifer, the only commonly used "er" name was Esther, which was never a favorite.) Those names went on to spawn waves of their own. African-American parents, who are more likely than other groups to invent names for their daughters—again, less often for their sons—recently became enamored with "meek": Jameeka, Camika, Mikayla. (Remember the legendary three "meeks" of the Tennessee Lady Vols basketball team—Tamika Catchings, Chamique Holdsclaw, Semeka Randall?)

But why does "a" or "djeh" or "meek" appeal in the first place? Why not the "th" in Ethel and Thelma (or Ruth!) or the final "s" in Gladys and Lois? That's harder to explain. "My speculation would be that a sound like the final 'a,' which did not used to be particularly popular, probably broke through as a variation on some existing name," Lieberson says, "and then it developed its own life."

That's not to say that external forces are irrelevant. Race clearly influences naming. So does class, especially among whites. Lieberson found that highly educated mothers are more likely to give daughters names that connote strength (Elizabeth or Catherine as opposed to Tiffany or Crystal). Yet, when it comes to boys, the trend reverses, with the more bookish moms going for Julian over Chuck.

That's the problem with the Popular Baby Names site: With no nuance, no dissection by demographic, it can get you only so far. For instance, Satran and Rosenkrantz recently polled upscale nursery schools in Manhattan and Berkeley, California. Among that crowd, Charlottes (206) and Rubys (210) ran rampant, but it was a desert for Savannahs (40).

20   After a couple of hours of my relentless quizzing, Satran (whose own children are named Rory, Joseph, and Owen) suggested that some people become a tad obsessed by their quest for originality. While it may evoke a particular theoretical profile (Bambi, anyone?), there is no definitive evidence that a name affects an individual child's popularity, mental health, or achievement level. "There are people who want to sell the idea that your name is your destiny," Satran says. "Names aren't your destiny any more than your shoes are." She pauses, then adds, "Well, OK, maybe your shoes are your destiny."

On the other hand, when she recently advised a friend that Maya was becoming overexposed, it made no difference. Sometimes people fall in love with a name and don't want to believe it's played out. Or they're comforted by something that's a touch more common—not everyone wants to be a trendsetter, not even those who say they do.

"There's this ideal," Satran says, "not just in names but other things that have to do with style, that you should make a personal statement. But the fact is that most people are not that adventurous.

They say they want individual style but they pick their furniture at
Pottery Barn. So if you tell them you're going to name your child
Matilda, they'll say, 'That's awful.' But if you say Sophia or Lily or
any of the names that I'm totally sick of, they'll say, 'That's such a
beautiful name.'"

Even pros like Satran and Rosenkrantz are occasionally blindsided
by a name, as when Trinity leapfrogged to 74 after the release of *The
Matrix*. Popular culture is an oft-cited launching pad for naming fads—
soap operas most famously (Kayla, Hunter, Caleb, and Ashley all
zoomed upward after star turns on daytime dramas). Still, the effect is
not as direct as it may seem. Buffy, despite a fanatic cult devotion to the
vampire slayer, has not breached the Top 1,000 (although Willow has
been climbing modestly since 1998). Aaliyah surged after the singer's
death, but Diana barely budged after the Princess of Wales died.

A closer look finds that Trinity was already on the upswing, from
951 in 1993 to 555 five years later. "Riding the curve," as Lieberson
calls it, is often the true explanation behind a pop-name phenomenon.
A name (or a sound sequence) is in the air, albeit marginally so; because of that, it's used for a character or happens to be that of a high-
profile performer (like Jada, 78). That, in turn, catapults the name
forward, seemingly out of nowhere.

25   Bringing us back to the improbable popularity of Madison: It
first hit the Top 1,000 in the 1980s and it was, unlike Trinity, probably a pure media event originating in the film *Splash*. Recall that,
while struggling to choose a name, Daryl Hannah's mermaid strolls
onto a certain Manhattan street, et voilà.

Still, Madison? No. 2? How in the name of good taste did that happen? Satran points to a confluence of trends: Madison came along at a
time when place names and surnames (McKenzie, Morgan) as first
names were hot, as well as the related androgynous names for girls
(Taylor, Sydney) and the Ralph Lauren, faux horsey-set names (Peyton,
Kendall). Then there's Lieberson's phonetic wave theory. In this case,
Madeline (56) may have begun to grow tired while Madison sounded
just a little fresher. So when Madison finally sinks, who will replace her?

On a hunch, I typed another New York place name into the
Popular Baby Names site: Brooklyn. Sure enough, it has vaulted from
755 to 155 since 1991. Then I tried expanding in a different direction
on the sound chain from Madeline and discovered that Adeline was
inching up as well. Given those trends, it would not be as random as
it would appear if, a few years from now, Adelaide and Portland, two
seemingly unrelated names, were both in the Top 10.

Now I was getting somewhere. A few nights later, I saw a film that took place around 1900, a mother lode of contemporary names for both sexes. One character was Annabelle. That sounded jaunty. I liked it. But what was its appeal? Then I recalled the current popularity of the Isabella/Isabel/Isabelle chain (14, 84, 112) not to mention Anna (20) and Ella (92). Lovely names all, but they've been done. That made me suspicious. As it turned out, Annabelle was rising with a bullet (from 984 to 330 in seven years, while Annabella went from 963 to 722 in just one). The following week I spied it monogrammed on a sleeping bag in the Pottery Barn Kids catalog. Annabelle was off my list.

Michael aside, overuse usually spells the end of a name, at least for a while. Names also lose luster when they become tied to a particular era. If you really want to ensure your baby girl will be unique among her peers, name her Barbara, Nancy, Karen, or Susan. Or Peggy. Those sound like the names of middle-aged women because— guess what?—they are.

30   But names are often resurrected when the generation that bears them dies out. Although our mothers may joke that the play group made up of Max, Rose, Sam, and Sophie sounds like the roster of a convalescent home, contemporary parents find those names charming. Doubtless, today's Brittany will name her daughter Delores.

Or maybe she'll call her Remember. Satran claims that the next big trend will be word names. Colors, for example (she just heard of a baby Cerulean), or words that resonate with the parents' values or professions like Integrity or Story. "There's been a street-level thing happening for a while with names like Destiny and Genesis," she says. "They weren't mainstream, but they were there. The tipping point came when Christie Brinkley, who is very visible, named her daughter Sailor because she and her husband liked to sail. Parents are increasingly looking for names that are different and also looking for names with personal meaning. Word names are a natural place to go. It's virgin territory. Our grandchildren will have names we don't even think of as names now."

Satran expects to see a fad in heroes' last names as first names (Monet, Koufax) as well as futuristic or Asian-sounding names borrowed from video games (Vyce, Ajuki). Among African-American parents, she says, the coming thing will be idiosyncratic punctuation accelerated by the singer India.Arie and the singer Brandy, who recently named her daughter Sy'rai.

Which brings me back to the name we are considering for our daughter. We're not, as it turns out, willing to saddle her with something as outré as Minerva. And Zazie or Tallulah are just trying too hard. Our name, as the experts would predict, is a sideways hop rather than a radical leap from names that have recently been stylish. So yes, it could take off. Still, it's a little softer, a little more free-spirited than its precursors, not the sort of name you'd imagine for a future Wall Street gunner. But that suits me fine: I ditched the East Coast fifteen years ago for the sunny iconoclasm of Northern California and a life that has become far less conventional than I once imagined. I want my daughter's name, and, I suppose, her life, to reflect that.

I hesitantly asked Satran's opinion, realizing that, like the mother of Maya, I might refuse to heed it. Had we accidentally picked the next Zoe? "Nope," she said. "I think you're safe."

35   So what is it? I can only respond with Satran's parting piece of advice: "Don't tell anyone the name before the baby is born. Do you really need to know about the girl with that name someone hated in fourth grade?"

She's right. Besides, I don't want to start a trend.

Analyzing Rhetorical Choices

1. In addition to classification, what rhetorical modes does Orenstein use to make her argument? Are her arguments successful? Explain your position.

2. What is Orenstein's tone in the essay? What particular words or phrases does Orenstein use to set the tone?

3. In her discussion of why a name becomes popular, Orenstein organizes naming styles into several different categories. What are some of these categories? What elements define the categories?

Writing About Issues and Contexts

1. Analyze Orenstein's claim that girls' names are "more vulnerable to sounding passé." Why does the same claim not hold true for boys' names? What comparisons can be made between the trends of girls' names and those of boys' names?

2. According to the article, why is it important that a child's name be distinct—but not too distinct? In what ways might distinct names become stigmatized or classified as stereotypes?

3. Consider Orenstein's discussion of naming styles and the influence of popular media and "larger cultural and historical events." What are some trends associated with this influence? What characterizes these trends?

Judith Viorst (1936–) has written in a wide variety of forms. Her style is marked not only by depth of emotion but also humor. She is well-known for her several books for children, including Alexander and the Terrible, Horrible, No Good, Very Bad Day *(1972) and* Sad Underwear and Other Complications *(1995). For many years, she has written a column in* Redbook. *She has published books of humorous verse, including* How Did I Get to Be Forty and Other Little Atrocities *(1976), as well as novels, such as* Murdering Mr. Monti: A Merry Little Tale of Sex and Violence *(1994). The following essay appeared in* Redbook *in 1977.*

Judith Viorst

Friends, Good Friends— and Such Good Friends

Women are friends, I once would have said, when they totally love and support and trust each other, and bare to each other the secrets of their souls, and run—no questions asked—to help each other, and tell harsh truths to each other (no, you can't wear that dress unless you lose ten pounds first) when harsh truths must be told.

Women are friends, I once would have said, when they share the same affection for Ingmar Bergman, plus train rides, cats, warm rain, charades, Camus, and hate with equal ardor Newark and Brussels sprouts and Lawrence Welk and camping.

In other words, I once would have said that a friend is a friend all the way, but now I believe that's a narrow point of view. For the friendships I have and the friendships I see are conducted at many levels of intensity, serve many different functions, meet different needs and range from those as all-the-way as the friendship of the soul sisters mentioned above to that of the most nonchalant and casual playmates.

Consider these varieties of friendship:

5   1. Convenience friends. These are women with whom, if our paths weren't crossing all the time, we'd have no particular reason to be friends: a next-door neighbor, a woman in our car pool, the mother of one of our children's closest friends or maybe some mommy with whom we serve juice and cookies each week at the Glenwood Co-op Nursery.

Convenience friends are convenient indeed. They'll lend us their cups and silverware for a party. They'll drive our kids to soccer when we're sick. They'll take us to pick up our car when we need a lift to the garage. They'll even take our cats when we go on vacation. As we will for them.

But we don't, with convenience friends, ever come too close or tell too much; we maintain our public face and emotional distance. "Which means," says Elaine, "that I'll talk about being overweight but not about being depressed. Which means I'll admit being mad but not blind with rage. Which means that I might say that we're pinched this month but never that I'm worried sick over money."

But which doesn't mean that there isn't sufficient value to be found in these friendships of mutual aid, in convenience friends.

2. Special-interest friends. These friendships aren't intimate, and they needn't involve kids or silverware or cats. Their value lies in some interest jointly shared. And so we may have an office friend or a yoga friend or a tennis friend or a friend from the Women's Democratic Club.

10 "I've got one woman friend," says Joyce, "who likes, as I do, to take psychology courses. Which makes it nice for me—and nice for her. It's fun to go with someone you know and it's fun to discuss what you've learned, driving back from the classes." And for the most part, she says, that's all they discuss.

"I'd say that what we're doing is *doing* together, not being to-gether," Suzanne says of her Tuesday-doubles friends. "It's mainly a tennis relationship, but we play together well. And I guess we all need to have a couple of playmates."

I agree.

My playmate is a shopping friend, a woman of marvelous taste, a woman who knows exactly *where* to buy *what,* and furthermore is a woman who always knows beyond a doubt what one ought to be buying. I don't have the time to keep up with what's new in eye-shadow, hemlines and shoes and whether the smock look is in or finished already. But since (oh, shame!) I care a lot about eye-shadow, hemlines and shoes, and since I don't *want* to wear smocks if the smock look is finished, I'm very glad to have a shopping friend.

3. Historical friends. We all have a friend who knew us when . . . maybe way back in Miss Meltzer's second grade, when our family lived in that three-room flat in Brooklyn, when our dad was out of

work for seven months, when our brother Allie got in that fight where they had to call the police, when our sister married the endodontist from Yonkers and when, the morning after we lost our virginity, she was the first, the only, friend we told.

15   The years have gone by and we've gone separate ways and we've little in common now, but we're still an intimate part of each other's past. And so whenever we go to Detroit we always go to visit this friend of our girlhood. Who knows how we looked before our teeth were straightened. Who knows how we talked before our voice got un-Brooklyned. Who knows what we ate before we learned about artichokes. And who, by her presence, puts us in touch with an earlier part of ourself, a part of ourself it's important never to lose.

"What this friend means to me and what I mean to her," says Grace, "is having a sister without sibling rivalry. We know the texture of each other's lives. She remembers my grandmother's cabbage soup. I remember the way her uncle played the piano. There's simply no other friend who remembers those things."

4. Crossroads friends. Like historical friends, our crossroads friends are important for *what was*—for the friendship we shared at a crucial, now past, time of life. A time, perhaps, when we roomed in college together; or worked as eager young singles in the Big City together; or went together, as my friend Elizabeth and I did, through pregnancy, birth and that scary first year of new motherhood.

Crossroads friends forge powerful links, links strong enough to endure with not much more contact than once-a-year letters at Christmas. And out of respect for those crossroads years, for those dramas and dreams we once shared, we will always be friends.

5. Cross-generational friends. Historical friends and cross-generational friends seem to maintain a special kind of intimacy—dormant but always ready to be revived—and though we may rarely meet, whenever we do connect, it's personal and intense. Another kind of intimacy exists in the friendships that form across generations in what one woman calls her daughter-mother and her mother-daughter relationships.

20   Evelyn's friend is her mother's age—"but I share so much more than I ever could with my mother"—a woman she talks to of music, of books and of life. "What I get from her is the benefit of her experience. What she gets—and enjoys—from me is a youthful perspective. It's a pleasure for both of us."

I have in my own life a precious friend, a woman of 65 who has lived very hard, who is wise, who listens well; who has been where I am and can help me understand it; and who represents not only an ultimate ideal mother to me but also the person I'd like to be when I grow up.

In our daughter role we tend to do more than our share of self-revelation; in our mother role we tend to receive what's revealed. It's another kind of pleasure—playing wise mother to a questing younger person. It's another very lovely kind of friendship.

6. Part-of-a-couple friends. Some of the women we call our friends we never see alone—we see them as part of a couple at couples' parties. And though we share interests in many things and respect each other's views, we aren't moved to deepen the relationship. Whatever the reason, a lack of time or—and this is more likely—a lack of chemistry, our friendship remains in the context of a group. But the fact that our feeling on seeing each other is always, "I'm *so* glad she's here" and the fact that we spend half the evening talking together says that this too, in its own way, counts as a friendship.

(Other part-of-a-couple friends are the friends that came with the marriage, and some of these are friends we could live without. But sometimes, alas, she married our husband's best friend; and sometimes, alas, she *is* our husband's best friend. And so we find ourself dealing with her, somewhat against our will, in a spirit of what I'll call *reluctant* friendship.)

25   7. Men who are friends. I wanted to write just of women friends, but the women I've talked to won't let me—they say I must mention man-woman friendships too. For these friendships can be just as close and as dear as those that we form with women. Listen to Lucy's description of one such friendship:

"We've found we have things to talk about that are different from what he talks about with my husband and different from what I talk about with his wife. So sometimes we call on the phone or meet for lunch. There are similar intellectual interests—we always pass on to each other the books that we love—but there's also something tender and caring too."

In a couple of crises, Lucy says, "he offered himself for talking and for helping. And when someone died in his family he wanted me there. The sexual, flirty part of our friendship is very small, but *some*—just enough to make it fun and different." She thinks—and I agree—that the sexual part, though small, is always *some,* is always there when a man and a woman are friends.

It's only in the past few years that I've made friends with men, in the sense of a friendship that's *mine,* not just part of two couples. And achieving with them the ease and the trust I've found with women friends has value indeed. Under the dryer at home last week, putting on mascara and rouge, I comfortably sat and talked with a fellow named Peter. Peter, I finally decided, could handle the shock of me minus mascara under the dryer. Because we care for each other. Because we're friends.

8. There are medium friends, and pretty good friends, and very good friends indeed, and these friendships are defined by their level of intimacy. And what we'll reveal at each of these levels of intimacy is calibrated with care. We might tell a medium friend, for example, that yesterday we had a fight with our husband. And we might tell a pretty good friend that this fight with our husband made us so mad that we slept on the couch. And we might tell a very good friend that the reason we got so mad in that fight that we slept on the couch had something to do with that girl who works in his office. But it's only to our very best friends that we're willing to tell all, to tell what's going on with that girl in his office.

30   The best of friends, I still believe, totally love and support and trust each other, and bare to each other the secrets of their souls, and run—no questions asked—to help each other, and tell harsh truths to each other when they must be told.

But we needn't agree about everything (only 12-year-old girl friends agree about *everything*) to tolerate each other's point of view. To accept without judgment. To give and to take without ever keeping score. And to *be* there, as I am for them and as they are for me, to comfort our sorrows, to celebrate our joys.

Analyzing Rhetorical Choices

1. How does Viorst delineate her categories of friendship? What appears to be her purpose in this essay?
2. Are there other modes besides classification at work in this essay? What are they? What purpose might they serve?
3. What is Viorst's tone in this essay? What effect does it have on the reader? What words or phrases create this particular tone?

Writing About Issues and Contexts

1. Discuss the differences in friendships between and among men and women based on Viorst's essay. Using her essay as a starting point, discuss these issues in terms of your experience, possibly comparing and contrasting her views with yours.

2. What does it mean to "calibrate with care" the level of intimacy in friendships and other relationships? Do you find the description applicable to your experience?

Canadian writer **Margaret Atwood** *(1939–) has written numerous volumes of poetry, including her first,* Double Persephone *(1961), and novels, including* The Edible Woman *(1969),* Cat's Eye *(1988),* The Robber
Bride *(1993), and her most celebrated,* The Handmaid's Tale *(1986).
Atwood graduated from the University of Toronto in 1961 and earned
her master's degree at Radcliffe College in 1962. Also a critic and
teacher, Atwood's work focuses on feminist issues.* The Handmaid's Tale
*is a futuristic satire, which, like her other work, features intelligent,
strong women. The essay "Pornography" grew, in part, from Atwood's
research for her 1981 novel,* Bodily Harm.

Margaret Atwood
Pornography

When I was in Finland a few years ago for an international writers'
conference, I had occasion to say a few paragraphs in public on the subject of pornography. The context was a discussion of political repression, and I was suggesting the possibility of a link between the two. The
immediate result was that a male journalist took several large bites out
of me. Prudery and pornography are two halves of the same coin, said
he, and I was clearly a prude. What could you expect from an Anglo-
Canadian? Afterward, a couple of pleasant Scandinavian men asked me
what I had been so worked up about. All "pornography" means, they
said, is graphic depictions of whores, and what was the harm in that?

Not until then did it strike me that the male journalist and I had
two entirely different things in mind. By "pornography," he meant
naked bodies and sex. I, on the other hand, had recently been doing
the research for my novel *Bodily Harm,* and was still in a state of
shock from some of the material I had seen, including the Ontario
Board of Film Censors' "outtakes." By "pornography," I meant
women getting their nipples snipped off with garden shears, having
meat hooks stuck into their vaginas, being disemboweled; little girls
being raped; men (yes, there are some men) being smashed to a pulp
and forcibly sodomized. The cutting edge of pornography, as far as I
could see, was no longer simple old copulation, hanging from the
chandelier or otherwise: it was death, messy, explicit and highly sadis-
tic. I explained this to the nice Scandinavian men. "Oh, but that's just
the United States," they said. "Everyone knows they're sick." In their

country, they said, violent "pornography" of that kind was not permitted on television or in movies; indeed, excessive violence of any kind was not permitted. They had drawn a clear line between erotica, which earlier studies had shown did not incite men to more aggressive and brutal behavior toward women, and violence, which later studies indicated did.

Some time after that I was in Saskatchewan, where, because of the scenes in *Bodily Harm*, I found myself on an open-line radio show answering questions about "pornography." Almost no one who phoned in was in favor of it, but again they weren't talking about the same stuff I was, because they hadn't seen it. Some of them were all set to stamp out bathing suits and negligees, and, if possible, any depictions of the female body whatsoever. God, it was implied, did not approve of female bodies, and sex of any kind, including that practiced by bumble-bees, should be shoved back into the dark, where it belonged. I had more than a suspicion that *Lady Chatterley's Lover*, Margaret Laurence's *The Diviners*, and indeed most books by most serious modern authors would have ended up as confetti if left in the hands of these callers.

For me, these two experiences illustrate the two poles of the emotionally heated debate that is now thundering around this issue. They also underline the desirability and even the necessity of defining the terms. "Pornography" is now one of those catchalls, like "Marxism" and "feminism," that have become so broad they can mean almost anything, ranging from certain verses in the Bible, ads for skin lotion and sex texts for children to the contents of Penthouse, Naughty '90s postcards and films with titles containing the word *Nazi* that show vicious scenes of torture and killing. It's easy to say that sensible people can tell the difference. Unfortunately, opinions on what constitutes a sensible person vary.

5   But even sensible people tend to lose their cool when they start talking about this subject. They soon stop talking and start yelling, and the name-calling begins. Those in favor of censorship (which may include groups not noticeably in agreement on other issues, such as some feminists and religious fundamentalists) accuse the others of exploiting women through the use of degrading images, contributing to the corruption of children, and adding to the general climate of violence and threat in which both women and children live in this society; or, though they may not give much of a hoot about actual women and children, they invoke moral standards and God's supposed aversion to "filth," "smut" and deviated *perversion,* which may mean ankles.

The camp in favor of total "freedom of expression" often comes out howling as loud as the Romans would have if told they could no longer have innocent fun watching the lions eat up Christians. It too may include segments of the population who are not natural bedfellows: those who proclaim their God-given right to freedom, including the freedom to tote guns, drive when drunk, drool over chicken porn and get off on videotapes of women being raped and beaten, may be waving the same anticensorship banner as responsible liberals who fear the return of Mrs. Grundy, or gay groups for whom sexual emancipation involves the concept of "sexual theatre." *Whatever turns you on* is a handy motto, as is *A man's home is his castle* (and if it includes a dungeon with beautiful maidens strung up in chains and bleeding from every pore, that's his business).

Meanwhile, theoreticians theorize and speculators speculate. Is today's pornography yet another indication of the hatred of the body, the deep mind-body split, which is supposed to pervade Western Christian society? Is it a backlash against the women's movement by men who are threatened by uppity female behavior in real life, so like to fantasize about women done up like outsize parcels, being turned into hamburger, kneeling at their feet in slavelike adoration or sucking off guns? Is it a sign of collective impotence, of a generation of men who can't relate to real women at all but have to make do with bits of celluloid and paper? Is the current flood just a result of smart marketing and aggressive promotion by the money men in what has now become a multibillion-dollar industry? If they were selling movies about men getting their testicles stuck full of knitting needles by women with swastikas on their sleeves, would they do as well, or is this penchant somehow peculiarly male? If so, why? Is pornography a power trip rather than a sex one? Some say that those ropes, chains, muzzles and other restraining devices are an argument for the immense power female sexuality still wields in the male imagination: you don't put these things on dogs unless you're afraid of them. Others, more literary, wonder about the shift from the 19th-century Magic Women or Femme Fatale image to the lollipop-licker, airhead or turkey-carcass treatment of women in porn today. The proporners don't care much about theory: they merely demand product. The antiporners don't care about it in the final analysis either: there's dirt on the street, and they want it cleaned up, now.

It seems to me that this conversation, with its *You're-a-prude/ You're-a-pervert* dialectic, will never get anywhere as long as we continue to think of this material as just "entertainment." Possibly we're deluded by the packaging, the format: magazine, book, movie, the-atrical presentation. We're used to thinking of these things as part of the "entertainment industry," and we're used to thinking of ourselves as free adult people who ought to be able to see any kind of "enter-tainment" we want to. That was what the First Choice pay-TV debate was all about. After all, it's only entertainment, right? Entertainment means fun, and only a killjoy would be antifun. What's the harm?

This is obviously the central question: *What's the harm?* If there isn't any real harm to any real people, then the antiporners can tsk-tsk and/or throw up as much as they like, but they can't rightfully expect more legal controls or sanctions. However, the no-harm position is far from being proven.

10   (For instance, there's a clear-cut case for banning—as the federal government has proposed—movies, photos and videos that depict children engaging in sex with adults: real children are used to make the movies, and hardly anybody thinks this is ethical. The possibilities for coercion are too great.)

To shift the viewpoint, I'd like to suggest three other models for looking at "pornography"—and here I mean the violent kind.

Those who find the idea of regulating pornographic materials re-pugnant because they think it's Fascist or Communist or otherwise not in accordance with the principles of an open democratic society should consider that Canada has made it illegal to disseminate material that may lead to hatred toward any group because of race or religion. I sug-gest that if pornography of the violent kind depicted these acts being done predominantly to Chinese, to blacks, to Catholics, it would be off the market immediately, under the present laws. Why is hate literature illegal? Because whoever made the law thought that such material might incite real people to do real awful things to other real people. The human brain is to a certain extent a computer: garbage in, garbage out. We only hear about the extreme cases (like that of American multimur-derer Ted Bundy) in which pornography has contributed to the death and/or mutilation of women and/or men. Although pornography is not the only factor involved in the creation of such deviance, it certainly has upped the ante by suggesting both a variety of techniques and the social acceptability of such actions. Nobody knows yet what effect this stuff is having on the less psychotic.

Studies have shown that a large part of the market for all kinds of porn, soft and hard, is drawn from the 16-to-21-year-old population of young men. Boys used to learn about sex on the street, or (in Italy, according to Fellini movies) from friendly whores, or, in more genteel surroundings, from girls, their parents, or, once upon a time, in school, more or less. Now porn has been added, and sex education in the schools is rapidly being phased out. The buck has been passed, and boys are being taught that all women secretly like to be raped and that real men get high on scooping out women's digestive tracts.

Boys learn their concept of masculinity from other men: is this what most men want them to be learning? If word gets around that rapists are "normal" and even admirable men, will boys feel that in order to be normal, admirable and masculine they will have to be rapists? Human beings are enormously flexible, and how they turn out depends a lot on how they're educated, by the society in which they're immersed as well as by their teachers. In a society that advertises and glorifies rape or even implicitly condones it, more women get raped. It becomes socially acceptable. And at a time when men and the traditional male role have taken a lot of flak and men are confused and casting around for an acceptable way of being male (and, in some cases, not getting much comfort from women on that score), this must be at times a pleasing thought.

15   It would be naïve to think of violent pornography as just harmless entertainment. It's also an educational tool and a powerful propaganda device. What happens when boy educated on porn meets girl brought up on Harlequin romances? The clash of expectations can be heard around the block. She wants him to get down on his knees with a ring, he wants her to get down on all fours with a ring in her nose. Can this marriage be saved?

Pornography has certain things in common with such addictive substances as alcohol and drugs: for some, though by no means for all, it induces chemical changes in the body, which the user finds exciting and pleasurable. It also appears to attract a "hard core" of habitual users and a penumbra of those who use it occasionally but aren't dependent on it in any way. There are also significant numbers of men who aren't much interested in it, not because they're undersexed but because real life is satisfying their needs, which may not require as many appliances as those of users.

For the "hard core," pornography may function as alcohol does for the alcoholic: tolerance develops, and a little is no longer enough. This may account for the short viewing time and fast turnover in porn theatres. Mary Brown, chairwoman of the Ontario Board of Film Censors, estimates that for every one mainstream movie requesting entrance to Ontario, there is one porno flick. Not only the quantity consumed but the quality of explicitness must escalate, which may account for the growing violence: once the big deal was breasts, then it was genitals, then copulation, then that was no longer enough and the hard users had to have more. The ultimate kick is death, and after that, as the Marquis de Sade so boringly demonstrated, multiple death.

The existence of alcoholism has not led us to ban social drinking. On the other hand, we do have laws about drinking and driving, excessive drunkenness and other abuses of alcohol that may result in injury or death to others.

This leads us back to the key question: what's the harm? Nobody knows, but this society should find out fast, before the saturation point is reached. The Scandinavian studies that showed a connection between depictions of sexual violence and increased impulse toward it on the part of male viewers would be a starting point, but many more questions remain to be raised as well as answered. What, for instance, is the crucial difference between men who are users and men who are not? Does using affect a man's relationship with actual women, and, if so, adversely? Is there a clear line between erotica and violent pornography, or are they on an escalating continuum? Is this a "men versus women" issue, with all men secretly siding with the proporners and all women secretly siding against? (I think not; there *are* lots of men who don't think that running their true love through the Cuisinart is the best way they can think of to spend a Saturday night, and they're just as nauseated by films of someone else doing it as women are.) Is pornography merely an expression of the sexual confusion of this age or an active contributor to it?

20 Nobody wants to go back to the age of official repression, when even piano legs were referred to as "limbs" and had to wear pantaloons to be decent. Neither do we want to end up in George Orwell's *1984*, in which pornography is turned out by the State to keep the proles in a state of torpor, sex itself is considered dirty and the approved practise is only for reproduction. But Rome under the emperors isn't such a good model either.

If all men and women respected each other, if sex were considered joyful and life-enhancing instead of a wallow in germ-filled glop, if everyone were in love all the time, if, in other words, many people's lives were more satisfactory for them than they appear to be now, pornography might just go away on its own. But since this is obviously not happening, we as a society are going to have to make some informed and responsible decisions about how to deal with it.

Analyzing Rhetorical Choices

1. Might there be any particular purpose for Atwood's beginning the essay with a personal story? What effect does this have?
2. What are Atwood's "models" for categorizing pornography? Are they effective? Explain. How do the classifications advance Atwood's argument?

Writing About Issues and Contexts

1. Analyze whether Atwood, in her central argument, seems to value one type of solution over another. Discuss why this might be so.
2. What are the distinctions between acceptable and unacceptable pornography that Atwood describes? Given your reading, observations, and experience, do you agree or disagree? Be sure to back up your points of view.
3. Is Atwood's essay unfair to men? Is the essay realistic? Unduly pessimistic? Read her essay closely to back up your points, and find appropriate evidence—or categories—of your own to either substantiate Atwood or to refute her.

---

*William Zinsser (1922–) was born in New York City and graduated in
1944 from Princeton University. He is particularly well known for his
books on writing, including* On Writing Well: An Informal Guide to
Writing Nonfiction *(its 30th anniversary edition was published in 2006).
He has also worked at the now-defunct* New York Herald Tribune *and
was a writer for* Life *magazine and the* New York Times. *Zinsser has
also written works on baseball and other aspects of life in the United
States. "College Pressures" appeared in 1979 and was written for*
Country Journal *magazine. Interestingly, the difficult economic times
affecting college students when this essay was published are similar to
those affecting college students as this volume goes to press.*

William Zinsser

College Pressures

Dear Carlos: I desperately need a dean's excuse for my chem
midterm which will begin in about 1 hour. All I can say is that I totally
blew it this week. I've fallen incredibly, inconceivably behind.

Carlos: Help! I'm anxious to hear from you. I'll be in my room
and won't leave it until I hear from you. Tomorrow is the last day
for. . . .

Carlos: I left town because I started bugging out again. I stayed up
all night to finish a take home make-up exam and am typing it to
hand in on the 10th. It was due on the 5th. P.S. I'm going to the dentist. Pain is pretty bad.

Carlos: Probably by Friday I'll be able to get back to my studies.
Right now I'm going to take a long walk. This whole thing has taken
a lot out of me.

5   Carlos: I'm really up the proverbial creek. The problem is I really
bombed the history final. Since I need that course for my major. . . .

Carlos: Here follows a tale of woe. I went home this weekend,
had to help my Mom, & caught a fever so didn't have much time to
study. My professor. . . .

Carlos: Aargh! Nothing original but everything's piling up at
once. To be brief, my job interview. . . .

Hey Carlos, good news! I've got mononucleosis.

Who are these wretched supplicants, scribbling notes so laden
with anxiety, seeking such miracles of postponement and balm? They
are men and women who belong to Bradford College, one of the

twelve residential colleges at Yale University, and the messages are just a few of the hundreds that they left for their dean, Carlos Hortas—often slipped under his door at 4 A.M.—last year.

10   But students like the ones who wrote those notes can also be found on campuses from coast to coast—especially in New England and at many other private colleges across the country that have high academic standards and highly motivated students. Nobody could doubt that the notes are real. In their urgency and their gallows humor they are authentic voices of a generation that is panicky to succeed.

My own connection with the message writers is that I am master of Bradford College. I live in its Gothic quadrangle and know the students well. (We have 485 of them.) I am privy to their hopes and fears—and also to their stereo music and their piercing cries in the dead of night ("Does anybody *ca-a-are?*"). If they went to Carlos to ask how to get through tomorrow, they come to me to ask how to get through the rest of their lives.

Mainly I try to remind them that the road ahead is a long one and that it will have more unexpected turns than they think. There will be plenty of time to change jobs, change careers, change whole attitudes and approaches. They don't want to hear such liberating news. They want a map—right now—that they can follow unswervingly to career security, financial security, Social Security, and, presumably, a prepaid grave.

What I wish for all students is some release from the clammy grip of the future. I wish them a chance to savor each segment of their education as an experience in itself and not as a grim preparation for the next step. I wish them the right to experiment, to trip and fall, to learn that defeat is as instructive as victory and is not the end of the world.

My wish, of course, is naive. One of the few rights that America does not proclaim is the right to fail. Achievement is the national god, venerated in our media—the million-dollar athlete, the wealthy executive—and glorified in our praise of possessions. In the presence of such a potent state religion, the young are growing up old.

15   I see four kinds of pressure working on college students today: economic pressure, parental pressure, peer pressure, and self-induced pressure. It is easy to look around for villains—to blame the colleges for charging too much money, the professors for assigning too much work, the parents for pushing their children too far, the students for driving themselves too hard. But there are no villains, only victims.

"In the late 1960s," one dean told me, "the typical question that I got from students was 'Why is there so much suffering in the world?'"

or 'How can I make a contribution?' Today it's 'Do you think it would look better for getting into law school if I did a double major in history and political science, or just majored in one of them?'" Many other deans confirmed this pattern. One said: "They're trying to find an edge—the intangible something that will look better on paper if two students are about equal."

Note the emphasis on looking better. The transcript has become a sacred document, the passport to security. How one appears on paper is more important than how one appears in person. *A* is for Admirable and *B* is for Borderline, even though, in Yale's official system of grading, *A* means "excellent" and *B* means "very good." Today, looking very good is no longer good enough, especially for students who hope to go on to law school or medical school. They know that entrance into the better schools will be an entrance into the better law firms and better medical practices where they will make a lot of money. They also know that the odds are harsh. Yale Law School, for instance, matriculates 170 students from an applicant pool of 3,700; Harvard enrolls 550 from a pool of 7,000.

It's all very well for those of us who write letters of recommendation for our students to stress the qualities of humanity that will make them good lawyers or doctors. And it's nice to think that admission officers are really reading our letters and looking for the extra dimension of commitment or concern. Still, it would be hard for a student not to visualize these officers shuffling so many transcripts studded with *A*s that they regard a *B* as positively shameful.

The pressure is almost as heavy on students who just want to graduate and get a job. Long gone are the days of the "gentleman's C," when students journeyed through college with a certain relaxation, sampling a wide variety of courses—music, art, philosophy, classics, anthropology, poetry, religion—that would send them out as liberally educated men and women. If I were an employer I would rather employ graduates who have this range and curiosity than those who narrowly pursued safe subjects and high grades. I know countless students whose inquiring minds exhilarate me. I like to hear the play of their ideas. I don't know if they're getting *A*s or *C*s, and I don't care. I also like them as people. The country needs them, and they will find satisfying jobs. I tell them to relax. They can't.

20   Nor can I blame them. They live in a brutal economy. Tuition, room, and board at most private colleges now comes to at least $7,000, not counting books and fees. This might seem to suggest that the colleges are getting rich. But they are equally battered by inflation.

Tuition covers only 60 percent of what it costs to educate a student, and ordinarily the remainder comes from what colleges receive in endowments, grants, and gifts. Now the remainder keeps being swallowed by cruel costs—higher every year—of just opening the doors. Heating oil is up. Insurance is up. Postage is up. Health-premium costs are up. Everything is up. Deficits are up. We are witnessing in America the creation of a brotherhood of paupers—colleges, parents, and students, joined by the common bond of debt.

Today it is not unusual for a student, even if he works part time at college and full time during the summer, to accrue $5,000 in loans after four years—loans that he must start to repay within one year after graduation. Exhorted at commencement to go forth into the world, he is already behind as he goes forth. How could he not feel under pressure throughout college to prepare for this day of reckoning? I have used "he" incidentally, only for brevity. Women at Yale are under no less pressure to justify their expensive education to themselves, their parents, and society. In fact, they are probably under more pressure. For although they leave college superbly equipped to bring fresh leadership to traditionally male jobs, society hasn't yet caught up with this fact.

Along with economic pressure goes parental pressure. Inevitably, the two are deeply intertwined.

I see many students taking pre-medical courses with joyless tenacity. They go off to their labs as if they were going to the dentist. It saddens me because I know them in other corners of their life as cheerful people.

"Do you want to go to medical school?" I ask them.

25   "I guess so," they say, without conviction, or "Not really."

"Then why are you going?"

"Well, my parents want me to be a doctor. They're paying all this money and . . ."

Poor students, poor parents. They are caught in one of the oldest webs of love and duty and guilt. The parents mean well; they are trying to steer their sons and daughters toward a secure future. But the sons and daughters want to major in history or classics or philosophy—subjects with no "practical" value. Where's the payoff on the humanities? It's not easy to persuade such loving parents that the humanities do indeed pay off. The intellectual faculties developed by studying subjects like history and classics—an ability to synthesize and relate, to weigh cause and effect, to see events in perspective—are just the faculties that make creative leaders in business or almost any general field.

Still, many fathers would rather put their money on courses that point toward a specific profession—courses that are pre-law, pre-medical, pre-business, or, as I sometimes heard it put, "pre-rich."

But the pressure on students is severe. They are truly torn. One part of them feels obliged to fulfill their parents' expectations; after all, their parents are older and presumably wiser. Another part tells them that the expectations that are right for their parents are not right for them.

30   I know a student who wants to be an artist. She is very obviously an artist and will be a good one—she has already had several modest exhibits. Meanwhile she is growing as a well-rounded person and taking humanistic subjects that will enrich the inner resources out of which her art will grow. But her father is strongly opposed. He thinks that an artist is a "dumb" thing to be. The student vacillates and tries to please everybody. She keeps up with her art somewhat furtively and takes some of the "dumb" courses her father wants her to take— at least they are dumb courses for her. She is a free spirit on a campus of tense students—no small achievement in itself—and she deserves to follow her muse.

Peer pressure and self-induced pressure are also intertwined, and they begin almost at the beginning of freshman year.

"I had a freshman student I'll call Linda," one dean told me, "who came in and said she was under terrible pressure because her roommate, Barbara, was much brighter and studied all the time. I couldn't tell her that Barbara had come in two hours earlier to say the same thing about Linda."

The story is almost funny—except that it's not. It's symptomatic of all the pressures put together. When every student thinks every other student is working harder and doing better, the only solution is to study harder still. I see students going off to the library every night after dinner and coming back when it closes at midnight. I wish they could sometimes forget about their peers and go to a movie. I hear the clacking of typewriters in the hours before dawn. I see the tension in their eyes when exams are approaching and papers are due: "*Will I get everything done?*"

Probably they won't. They will get sick. They will get "blocked." They will sleep. They will oversleep. They will bug out. *Hey Carlos, help!*

35   Part of the problem is that they do more than they are expected to do. A professor will assign five-page papers. Several students will start writing ten-page papers to impress him. Then more students will

write ten-page papers, and a few will raise the ante to fifteen. Pity the poor student who is still just doing the assignment.

"Once you have twenty or thirty percent of the student population deliberately overexerting," one dean points out, "it's bad for everybody. When a teacher gets more and more effort from his class, the student who is doing normal work can be perceived as not doing well. The tactic works, psychologically."

Why can't the professor just cut back and not accept longer papers? He can, and he probably will. But by then the term will be half over and the damage done. Grade fever is highly contagious and not easily reversed. Besides, the professor's main concern is with his course. He knows his students only in relation to the course and doesn't know that they are also overexerting in their other courses. Nor is it really his business. He didn't sign up for dealing with the student as a whole person and with all the emotional baggage the student brought along from home. That's what deans, masters, chaplains, and psychiatrists are for.

To some extent this is nothing new: a certain number of professors have always been self-contained islands of scholarship and shyness, more comfortable with books than with people. But the new pauperism has widened the gap still further, for professors who actually like to spend time with students don't have as much time to spend. They also are overexerting. If they are young, they are busy trying to publish in order not to perish, hanging by their fingernails onto a shrinking profession. If they are old and tenured, they are buried under the duties of administering departments—as departmental chairmen or members of committees—that have been thinned out by the budgetary axe.

Ultimately it will be the students' own business to break the circles in which they are trapped. They are too young to be prisoners of their parents' dreams and their classmates' fears. They must be jolted into believing in themselves as unique men and women who have the power to shape their own future.

40   "Violence is being done to the undergraduate experience," says Carlos Hortas. "College should be open-ended: at the end it should open many, many roads. Instead, students are choosing their goal in advance, and their choices narrow as they go along. It's almost as if they think that the country has been codified in the type of jobs that exist—that they've got to fit into certain slots. Therefore, fit into the best-paying slot."

"They ought to take chances. Not taking chances will lead to a life of colorless mediocrity. They'll be comfortable. But something in the spirit will be missing."

I have painted too drab a portrait of today's students, making them seem a solemn lot. That is only half of their story; if they were so dreary I wouldn't so thoroughly enjoy their company. The other half is that they are easy to like. They are quick to laugh and to offer friendship. They are not introverts. They are usually kind and are more considerate of one another than any student generation I have known.

Nor are they so obsessed with their studies that they avoid sports and extracurricular activities. On the contrary, they juggle their crowded hours to play on a variety of teams, perform with musical and dramatic groups, and write for campus publications. But this in turn is one more cause of anxiety. There are too many choices. Academically, they have 1,300 courses to select from; outside class they have to decide how much spare time they can spare and how to spend it.

This means that they engage in fewer extracurricular pursuits than their predecessors did. If they want to row on the crew and play in the symphony they will eliminate one; in the '60s they would have done both. They also tend to choose activities that are self-limiting. Drama, for instance, is flourishing in all twelve of Yale's residential colleges as it never has before. Students hurl themselves into these productions—as actors, directors, carpenters, and technicians—with a dedication to create the best possible play, knowing that the day will come when the run will end and they can get back to their studies.

45   They also can't afford to be the willing slave of organizations like the *Yale Daily News*. Last spring at the one-hundredth anniversary banquet of that paper—whose past chairmen include such once and future kings as Potter Stewart, Kingman Brewster, and William F. Buckley, Jr.—much was made of the fact that the editorial staff used to be small and totally committed and that "newsies" routinely worked fifty hours a week. In effect they belonged to a club; Newsies is how they defined themselves at Yale. Today's student will write one or two articles a week, when he can, and he defines himself as a student. I've never heard the word Newsie except at the banquet.

If I have described the modern undergraduate primarily as a driven creature who is largely ignoring the blithe spirit inside who keeps trying to come out and play, it's because that's where the crunch is, not only at Yale but throughout American education. It's why I think we should all be worried about the values that are nurturing a generation so fearful of risk and so goal-obsessed at such an early age.

I tell students that there is no one "right" way to get ahead—that each of them is a different person, starting from a different point and bound for a different destination. I tell them that change is a tonic and that all the slots are not codified nor the frontiers closed. One of my ways of telling them is to invite men and women who have achieved success outside the academic world to come and talk informally with my students during the year. They are heads of companies or ad agencies, editors of magazines, politicians, public officials, television magnates, labor leaders, business executives, Broadway producers, artists, writers, economists, photographers, scientists, historians—a mixed bag of achievers.

I ask them to say a few words about how they got started. The students assume that they started in their present profession and knew all along that it was what they wanted to do. Luckily for me, most of them got into their field by a circuitous route, to their surprise, after many detours. The students are startled. They can hardly conceive of a career that was not pre-planned. They can hardly imagine allowing the hand of God or chance to nudge them down some unforeseen trail.

Analyzing Rhetorical Choices

1. Analyze Zinsser's ways of classifying and creating his categories and their effectiveness. How are the categories, as Zinsser says, "intertwined"? How does that help or hinder the essay?

2. Zinsser's writing often reveals his journalistic background. Where, in particular, is this evident? Read the essay closely, looking at paragraphs, word choices, and the like. What function, for instance, do his one-sentence paragraphs serve?

3. Analyze the effectiveness of the introduction, the "notes to Carlos." What is your response as you read these notes?

4. What assumptions does Zinsser seem to make about his audience? On what type of readership would this essay have the greatest impact?

Writing About Issues and Contexts

1. Is there too much pressure on today's college students? Compare your views with Zinsser's.

2. Zinsser outlines the various forms of anxiety that plague students. Why does Zinsser suggest that women might feel greater pressure than do men?

3. Zinsser's essay was published in 1979. To what extent is it still relevant today? Explain your point of view.

4. "[Students] ought to take chances. Not taking chances will lead to a life of colorless mediocrity." How do you respond to this statement?

*A winner of numerous awards, including the prestigious National Endowment for the Arts Fiction Award, **Gloria Anzaldúa** (1942–) is described as a "Chicana dyke-feminist, tejana patlache poet, writer, and cultural theorist" from the Rio Grande Valley of south Texas. She has taught at a variety of colleges and universities. Her best-known book,* Borderlands/La Frontera: The New Mestiza *(1987), from which this piece is taken, combines several genres—poetry (in both Spanish and English), memoir, and nonfiction prose. Anzaldúa has also written a children's book,* Friends from the Other Side/Amigos del otro lado *(1993). In addition, she has edited* Making Face, Making Soul/Haciendo Caras: Creative and Critical Perspectives by Women of Color *(1990), which features essays on identity, feminism, racism, and multiple literacies.*

Gloria Anzaldúa

How to Tame a Wild Tongue

"We're going to have to control your tongue," the dentist says, pulling out all the metal from my mouth. Silver bits plop and tinkle into the basin. My mouth is a motherlode.

The dentist is cleaning out my roots. I get a whiff of the stench when I gasp. "I can't cap that tooth yet, you're still draining," he says.

"We're going to have to do something about your tongue," I hear the anger rising in his voice. My tongue keeps pushing out the wads of cotton, pushing back the drills, the long thin needles. "I've never seen anything as strong or as stubborn," he says. And I think, how do you tame a wild tongue, train it to be quiet, how do you bridle and saddle it? How do you make it lie down?

> Who is to say that robbing a people of its language is less violent than war?
>
> —*Ray Gwyn Smith*

I remember being caught speaking Spanish at recess—that was good for three licks on the knuckles with a sharp ruler. I remember being sent to the corner of the classroom for "talking back" to the Anglo teacher when all I was trying to do was tell her how to pronounce my name. "If you want to be American, speak 'American.' If you don't like it, go back to Mexico where you belong."

5   "I want you to speak English. *Pa' hallar buen trabajo tienes que vaber hablar el inglés bien. Qué vale toda tu educación si todavía hablas inglés con un* 'accent,'"[1] my mother would say, mortified that I spoke English like a Mexican. At Pan American University, I, and all Chicano students were required to take two speech classes. Their purpose: to get rid of our accents.

Attacks on one's form of expression with the intent to censor are a violation of the First Amendment. *El Anglo con cara de inocente nos arrancó la lengua.*[2] Wild tongues can't be tamed, they can only be cut out.

Overcoming the Tradition of Silence

Abogadas, escupimos el oscuro.
Peleando con nuestra propia sombra
el silencio nos sepulta.[3]

En boca cerrada no entran moscas. "Flies don't enter a closed mouth" is a saying I kept hearing when I was a child. *Ser habladora* was to be a gossip and a liar, to talk too much. *Muchachitas bien criadas,*[4] well-bred girls don't answer back. *Es una falta de respeto*[5] to talk back to one's mother or father. I remember one of the sins I'd recite to the priest in the confession box the few times I went to confession: talking back to my mother, *hablar pa' 'tras, repelar.*[6] *Hocicona, repelona, chismosa,*[7] having a big mouth, questioning, carrying tales are all signs of being *mal criada.*[8] In my culture they are all words that are derogatory if applied to women—I've never heard them applied to men.

The first time I heard two women, a Puerto Rican and a Cuban, say the word *"nosotras,"*[9] I was shocked. I had not known the word

---

[1] "In order to find a good job, you have to know how to speak English well. Of what value is your education if you still speak English with an 'accent.'"

[2] The Anglo with an innocent face tore our tongue out.

[3] "Choked, we spit out darkness / Fighting with our own shadow / The silence buries us."

[4] Well-bred little girls.

[5] It is not respectful.

[6] To talk back, to argue.

[7] Chatterer, arguer, gossip.

[8] Ill-bred girl.

[9] We (fem.).

existed. Chicanas use *nosotros*[10] whether we're male or female. We are robbed of our female being by the masculine plural. Language is a male discourse.

> And our tongues have become
> dry the wilderness has
> dried out our tongues and
> we have forgotten speech.
>
> —*Irena Klepfisz*

Even our own people, other Spanish speakers *nos quieren poner candados en la boca.*[11] They would hold us back with their bag of *reglas de academia.*[12]

> *Oyé como ladra: el lenguaje de la frontera*[13]
> *Quien tiene boca se equivoca.*[14]
>
> —*Mexican saying*

10   "*Pocho,* cultural traitor, you're speaking the oppressor's language by speaking English, you're ruining the Spanish language," I have been accused by various Latinos and Latinas. Chicano Spanish is considered by the purist and by most Latinos deficient, a mutilation of Spanish.

But Chicano Spanish is a border tongue which developed naturally. Change, *evolución, enriquecimiento de palabras nuevas por invención o adopción* have created variants of Chicano Spanish, *un nuevo lenguaje. Un lenguaje que corresponde a un modo de vivir.*[15] Chicano Spanish is not incorrect, it is a living language.

For a people who are neither Spanish nor live in a country in which Spanish is the first language; for a people who live in a country in which English is the reigning tongue but who are not Anglo; for a people who cannot entirely identify with either standard (formal, Castillian) Spanish nor standard English, what recourse is left to them but to create their own language? A language which they can connect their identity to, one capable of communicating the realities and values true to themselves—a language with terms that are neither

---

[10]We (masc.).

[11]Want to put locks on our mouths.

[12]Academic rules.

[13]Hear how the dog barks: language of the frontier.

[14]"He who has a mouth makes mistakes."

[15]Evolution, enrichment of new words through invention and adoption . . . a new language. A language that corresponds to a way of life.

español ni inglés,[16] but both. We speak a patois, a forked tongue, a variation of two languages.

Chicano Spanish sprang out of the Chicanos' need to identify ourselves as a distinct people. We needed a language with which we could communicate with ourselves, a secret language. For some of us, language is a homeland closer than the Southwest—for many Chicanos today live in the Midwest and the East. And because we are a complex, heterogeneous people, we speak many languages. Some of the languages we speak are:

1. Standard English
2. Working class and slang English
3. Standard Spanish
4. Standard Mexican Spanish
5. North Mexican Spanish dialect
6. Chicano Spanish (Texas, New Mexico, Arizona and California have regional variations)
7. Tex-Mex
8. *Pachuco* (called *caló*)

My "home" tongues are the languages I speak with my sister and brothers, with my friends. They are the last five listed, with 6 and 7 being closest to my heart. From school, the media and job situations, I've picked up standard and working class English. From Mamagrande Locha and from reading Spanish and Mexican literature, I've picked up Standard Spanish and Standard Mexican Spanish. From *los recién llegados,* Mexican immigrants, and *braceros,*[17] I learned the North Mexican dialect. With Mexicans I'll try to speak either Standard Mexican Spanish or the North Mexican dialect. From my parents and Chicanos living in the Valley, I picked up Chicano Texas Spanish, and I speak it with my mom, younger brother (who married a Mexican and who rarely mixes Spanish with English), aunts and older relatives.

15   With Chicanas from *Nuevo México* or *Arizona* I will speak Chicano Spanish a little, but often they don't understand what I'm saying. With most California Chicanas I speak entirely in English (unless I forget). When I first moved to San Francisco, I'd rattle off something in Spanish, unintentionally embarrassing them. Often it is only with another Chicana *tejana*[18] that I can talk freely.

---

[16]Spanish nor English.
[17]*Los recién llegados:* recent arrivals; *braceros:* laborers.
[18]Texan (fem.).

Words distorted by English are known as anglicisms or *pochismos.* The *pocho* is an anglicized Mexican or American of Mexican origin who speaks Spanish with an accent characteristic of North Americans and who distorts and reconstructs the language according to the influence of English. Tex-Mex, or Spanglish, comes most naturally to me. I may switch back and forth from English to Spanish in the same sentence or in the same word. With my sister and my brother Nune and with Chicano *tejano* contemporaries I speak in Tex-Mex.

From kids and people my own age I picked up *Pachuco. Pachuco* (the language of the zoot suiters) is a language of rebellion, both against Standard Spanish and Standard English. It is a secret language. Adults of the culture and outsiders cannot understand it. It is made up of slang words from both English and Spanish. *Ruca* means girl or woman, *vato* means guy or dude, *chale* means no, *simón* means yes, *churro* is sure, talk is *periquiar, pigionear* means petting, *que gacho* means how nerdy, *ponte águila* means watch out, death is called *la pelona.* Through lack of practice and not having others who can speak it, I've lost most of the *Pachuco* tongue.

Chicano Spanish

Chicanos, after 250 years of Spanish/Anglo colonization have developed significant differences in the Spanish we speak. We collapse two adjacent vowels into a single syllable and sometimes shift the stress in certain words such as *maíz/maiz, cohete/cuete.*[19] We leave out certain consonants when they appear between vowels: *lado/lao, mojado/mojao.*[20] Chicanos from South Texas pronounce *f* as *j* as in *jue (fue).*[21] Chicanos use "archaisms," words that are no longer in the Spanish language, words that have been evolved out. We say *semos, truje, haiga, ansina,* and *naiden.*[22] We retain the "archaic" *j,* as in *jalar,*[23] that derives from an earlier *h* (the French *halar* or the

---

[19]*Maiz:* corn; *cohete:* rocket.
[20]*Lado:* side; *mojado:* wet.
[21]Went.
[22]*Semos:* we are; *truje:* brought; *haiga:* there is; *ansina:* that (adj.); *naiden:* nobody.
[23]To pull.

Germanic *halon* which was lost to standard Spanish in the 16th century), but which is still found in several regional dialects such as the one spoken in South Texas. (Due to geography, Chicanos from the Valley of South Texas were cut off linguistically from other Spanish speakers. We tend to use words that the Spaniards brought over from Medieval Spain. The majority of the Spanish colonizers in Mexico and the Southwest came from Extremadura—Hernán Cortés was one of them—and Andalucía. Andalucians pronounce *ll* like a *y*, and their *d*'s tend to be absorbed by adjacent vowels: *tirado*[24] becomes *tirao*. They brought *el lenguaje popular, dialectos y regionalismos.*)[25]

Chicanos and other Spanish speakers also shift *ll* to *y* and *z* to *s*. We leave out initial syllables, saying *tar* for *estar, toy* for *estoy, hora* for *ahora* (*cubanos* and *puertorriqueños*[26] also leave out initial letters of some words). We also leave out the final syllable such as *pa* for *para*. The intervocalic *y*, the *ll* as in *tortilla, ella, botella*, gets replaced by *tortia* or *tortiya, ea, botea*. We add an additional syllable at the beginning of certain words: *atocar* for *tocar, agastar* for *gastar*. Sometimes we'll say *lavaste las vacijas*, other times *lavates* (substituting the *ates* verb endings for the *aste*).[27]

20   We use anglicisms, words borrowed from English: *bola* from ball, *carpeta* from carpet, *máchina de lavar* (instead of *lavadora*) from washing machine. Tex-Mex argot, created by adding a Spanish sound at the beginning or end of an English word such as *cookiar* for cook, *watchar* for watch, *parkiar* for park, and *rapiar* for rape, is the result of the pressures on Spanish speakers to adapt to English.

We don't use the word *vosotros/as* or its accompanying verb form. We don't say *claro* (to mean yes), *imagínate*, or *me emociona*,[28] unless we picked up Spanish from Latinas, out of a book, or in a classroom. Other Spanish-speaking groups are going through the same, or similar, development in their Spanish.

---

[24]Thrown.

[25]Popular language, dialects, and regionalism.

[26]*Estar:* to be; *estoy:* I am; *ahora:* now; *cubanos, puertorriqueños:* Cubans, Puerto Ricans.

[27]*Para:* for; *trotilla, ella, botella:* tortilla, she, bottle; *tocar:* to touch; *gastar:* to spend; *lavaste las vacijas:* did you wash the dishes (*vacijas* is Texan).

[28]*Vosotros/as:* you (plural, formal); *imagínate:* imagine; *me emociona:* I am moved.

Linguistic Terrorism

Deslenguadas. Somos los del español deficiente.[29] We are your linguistic nightmare, your linguistic aberration, your linguistic *mestisaje*, the subject of your *burla*. Because we speak with tongues of fire we are culturally crucified. Racially, culturally and linguistically *somos huérfanos*[30]—we speak an orphan tongue.

Chicanas who grew up speaking Chicano Spanish have internalized the belief that we speak poor Spanish. It is illegitimate, a bastard language. And because we internalize how our language has been used against us by the dominant culture, we use our language differences against each other.

Chicana feminists often skirt around each other with suspicion and hesitation. For the longest time I couldn't figure it out. Then it dawned on me. To be close to another Chicana is like looking into the mirror. We are afraid of what we'll see there. *Pena.* Shame. Low estimation of self. In childhood we are told that our language is wrong. Repeated attacks on our native tongue diminish our sense of self. The attacks continue throughout our lives.

Chicanas feel uncomfortable talking in Spanish to Latinas, afraid of their censure. Their language was not outlawed in their countries. They had a whole lifetime of being immersed in their native tongue; generations, centuries in which Spanish was a first language, taught in school, heard on radio and TV, and read in the newspaper.

25   If a person, Chicana or Latina, has a low estimation of my native tongue, she also has a low estimation of me. Often with *mexicanas y latinas* we'll speak English as a neutral language. Even among Chicanas we tend to speak English at parties or conferences. Yet, at the same time, we're afraid the other will think we're *agringadas*[31] because we don't speak Chicano Spanish. We oppress each other trying to out-Chicano each other, vying to be the "real" Chicanas, to speak like Chicanos. There is no one Chicano language just as there is no one Chicano experience. A monolingual Chicana whose first language is English or Spanish is just as much a Chicana as one who speaks several variants of Spanish. A Chicana from Michigan or Chicago or Detroit is just as much a Chicana as one from the southwest. Chicano Spanish is as diverse linguistically as it is regionally.

---

[29]Loose tongues. We are those with deficient Spanish.

[30]*Mestisaje:* hybrid; *burla:* joke; *somos huérfanos:* we are orphans.

[31]Foreigners, like "gringos."

By the end of this century, Spanish speakers will comprise the biggest minority group in the U.S., a country where students in high schools and colleges are encouraged to take French classes because French is considered more "cultured." But for a language to remain alive it must be used. By the end of this century English, and not Spanish, will be the mother tongue of most Chicanos and Latinos.

So, if you want to really hurt me, talk badly about my language. Ethnic identity is twin skin to linguistic identity—I am my language. Until I can take pride in my language, I cannot take pride in myself. Until I can accept as legitimate Chicano Texas Spanish, Tex-Mex and all the other languages I speak, I cannot accept the legitimacy of myself. Until I am free to write bilingually and to switch codes without having always to translate, while I still have to speak English or Spanish when I would rather speak Spanglish, and as long as I have to accommodate the English speakers rather than having them accommodate me, my tongue will be illegitimate.

I will no longer be made to feel ashamed of existing. I will have my voice: Indian, Spanish, white. I will have my serpent's tongue—my woman's voice, my sexual voice, my poet's voice. I will overcome the tradition of silence.

> My fingers
> move sly against your palm
> Like women everywhere, we speak in code . . .
> —*Melanie Kaye/Kantrowitz*

Analyzing Rhetorical Choices

1. Reread the opening of the essay. What are the various metaphorical ways in which Anzaldúa speaks of her tongue, or specifically, of her "wild tongue"? What purpose does this serve in the essay?
2. Why would this essay be included in a section on classification or perhaps, as implied by the title, process? What are the various categories that Anzaldúa sets up, not only to explain the various languages spoken by her people but also to argue her essay?
3. What is Anzaldúa's rhetorical purpose in using Spanish that she translates—and, more importantly, sometimes does not translate? Should editors provide translations of the Spanish words? What are the consequences of these choices?
4. Who are the audiences for this essay? What is the basis for your analysis and conclusion?

Writing About Issues and Contexts

1. In your view, what are the tensions that exist between the desire to be a "distinct people," as Anzaldúa claims for Chicanos and Chicanas, and the larger pull toward various types of assimilation? Consider whether there are some immigrant groups for whom distinction is often a stigma. If you believe such groups exist, why do you think they feel stigmatized?

2. As Anzaldúa has written, "So if you want to really hurt me, talk badly about my language." Why does speaking against someone's use of language create such a negative effect? How would you characterize the relationship between language and personal identity?

When Time *magazine started its new "Computers" section in 1982,*
Philip Elmer-DeWitt *(1949–) became its first writer. In fact, he was
among the few on the staff who was experienced with technology. As the
senior editor for technology, Elmer-DeWitt has written on various issues,
including genetics, cloning, and pornography in cyberspace. The following essay appeared in* Time *in 1994.*

Philip Elmer-DeWitt

Bards of the Internet

One of the unintended side effects of the invention of the telephone was that writing went out of style. Oh, sure, there were still
full-time scribblers—journalists, academics, professional wordsmiths.
And the great centers of commerce still found it useful to keep on
hand people who could draft a memo, a brief, a press release or a contract. But given a choice between picking up a pen or a phone, most
folks took the easy route and gave their fingers—and sometimes their
mind—a rest.

Which makes what's happening on the computer networks all the
more startling. Every night, when they should be watching television,
millions of computer users sit down at their keyboards; dial into
CompuServe, Prodigy, America Online or the Internet; and start typing—E-mail, bulletin-board postings, chat messages, rants, diatribes,
even short stories and poems. Just when the media of McLuhan were
supposed to render obsolete the medium of Shakespeare, the online
world is experiencing the greatest boom in letter writing since the
eighteenth century.

"It is my overwhelming belief that e-mail and computer confer-
encing is teaching an entire generation about the flexibility and utility
of prose," writes Jon Carroll, a columnist at the San Francisco
Chronicle. Patrick Nielsen Hayden, an editor at Tor Books, compares
electronic bulletin boards with the "scribblers' compacts" of the late
eighteenth and early nineteenth centuries, in which members passed
letters from hand to hand, adding a little more at each turn. David
Sewell, an associate editor at the University of Arizona, likens
netwriting to the literary scene Mark Twain discovered in San
Francisco in the 1860s, "when people were reinventing journalism by
grafting it onto the tall-tale folk tradition." Others hark back to Tom

Paine and the Revolutionary War pamphleteers, or even to the Elizabethan era, when, thanks to Gutenberg, a generation of English writers became intoxicated with language.

But such comparisons invite a question: If online writing today represents some sort of renaissance, why is so much of it so awful? For it can be very bad indeed: sloppy, meandering, puerile, ungrammatical, poorly spelled, badly structured and at times virtually content free. "HEY!!!!" reads an all-too-typical message on the Internet, "I THINK METALLICA IZ REEL KOOL DOOD!!!!"

5   One reason, of course, is that E-mail is not like ordinary writing. "You need to think of this as 'written speech,'" says Gerard Van der Leun, literary agent based in Westport, Connecticut, who has emerged as one of the preeminent stylists on the Net. "These things are little more considered than coffeehouse talk and a lot less considered than a letter. They're not to have and hold; they're to fire and forget." Many online postings are composed "live" with the clock ticking, using rudimentary word processors on computer systems that charge by the minute and in some cases will shut down without warning when an hour runs out.

That is not to say that with more time every writer on the Internet would produce sparkling copy. Much of the fiction and poetry is second-rate or worse, which is not surprising given that the barriers to entry are so low. "In the real world," says Mary Anne Mohanraj, a Chicago-based poet, "it takes a hell of a lot of work to get published, which naturally weeds out a lot of the garbage. On the Net, just a few keystrokes sends your writing out to thousands of readers."

But even among the reams of bad poetry, gems are to be found. Mike Godwin, a Washington-based lawyer who posts under the pen name "mnemonic," tells the story of Joe Green, a technical writer at Cray Research who turned a moribund discussion group called rec.arts.poems into a real poetry workshop by mercilessly critiquing the pieces he found there. "Some people got angry and said if he was such a god of poetry, why didn't he publish his poems to the group?" recalls Godwin. "He did, and blew them all away." Green's *Well Met in Minnesota,* a mock-epic account of a face-to-face meeting with a fellow network scribbler, is now revered on the Internet as a classic. It begins, "The truth is that when I met Mart I was dressed as the *Canterbury Tales.* Rather difficult to do as you might suspect, but I wanted to make a certain impression."

The more prosaic technical and political discussion groups, meanwhile, have become so crowded with writers crying for attention that a

Darwinian survival principle has started to prevail. "It's so competitive that you have to work on your style if you want to make any impact," says Jorn Barger, a software designer in Chicago. Good writing on the Net tends to be clear, vigorous, witty and above all brief. "The medium favors the terse," says Crawford Kilian, a writing teacher at Capilano College in Vancouver, British Columbia. "Short paragraphs, bulleted lists, and one-liners are the units of thought here."

Some of the most successful netwriting is produced in computer conferences, where writers compose in a kind of collaborative heat, knocking ideas against one another until they spark. Perhaps the best examples of this are found on the WELL, a Sausalito, California, bulletin board favored by journalists. The caliber of discussion is often so high that several publications—including the *New York Times* and the *Wall Street Journal*—have printed excerpts from the WELL.

10   Curiously, what works on the computer networks isn't necessarily what works on paper. Netwriters freely lace their prose with strange acronyms and "smileys," the little faces constructed with punctuation marks and intended to convey the winks, grins and grimaces of ordinary conversations. Somehow it all flows together quite smoothly. On the other hand, polished prose copied onto bulletin boards from books and magazines often seems long-winded and phony. Unless they adjust to the new medium, professional writers can come across as self-important blowhards in debates with more nimble networkers. Says Brock Meeks, a Washington-based reporter who covers the online culture for *Communications Daily:* "There are a bunch of hacker kids out there who can string a sentence together better than their blue-blooded peers simply because they log on all the time and write, write, write."

There is something inherently democratizing—perhaps even revolutionary—about the technology. Not only has it enfranchised thousands of would-be writers who otherwise might never have taken up the craft, but it has also thrown together classes of people who hadn't had much direct contact before: students, scientists, senior citizens, computer geeks, grassroots (and often blue-collar) bulletin-board enthusiasts and most recently the working press.

"It's easy to make this stuff look foolish and trivial," says Tor Books Nielsen Hayden. "After all, a lot of everyone's daily life is foolish and trivial. I mean, really, smileys? Housewives in Des Moines who log on as VIXEN?"

But it would be a mistake to dismiss the computer-message boards or to underestimate the effect a lifetime of dashing off E-mail will have on a generation of young writers. The computer networks may not be Brook Farm or the Globe Theatre, but they do represent, for millions of people, a living breathing life of letters. One suspects that the Bard himself, confronted with the Internet, might have dived right in and never logged off.

Analyzing Rhetorical Choices

1. Why would Elmer-DeWitt begin an essay about the Internet with the telephone? What larger lesson might he be trying to communicate?

2. How does Elmer-DeWitt classify various writers on the Internet? For what purpose? How are they—or are they not—"bards"?

3. What seems to be Elmer-DeWitt's own attitude about writing on the Internet? Examine his argument closely (is it inductive or deductive?), using examples to demonstrate your points.

Writing About Issues and Contexts

1. What is the downside of the Chicago-based poet's well-intended statement that "On the Net, just a few keystrokes sends your writing out to thousands of readers"? How could Internet writing be both "awful" and yet have created a "renaissance"?

2. Do you agree with Elmer-DeWitt's statement that "There is something inherently democratizing—perhaps even revolutionary—about the technology"? Is the author somewhat dismissive of some who partake in this "democracy"?

3. How has the Internet changed since this essay was published in 1994? What differences does the essay's age make—or not—to some of the arguments Elmer-DeWitt makes?

4. In your view, how have e-mail and other forms of cyberwriting—the abbreviations of instant messaging, for instance—changed the ways people write? Have these hindered, helped, or merely provided different occasions for writing? Use the essay and evidence of your own to demonstrate your points.

*Born in England, **Malcolm Gladwell** (1963–) grew up in Canada and in 1984 graduated with a degree in history from the University of Toronto. Gladwell was a reporter for the* Washington Post, *first as a science writer and then as a New York City bureau chief, serving the newspaper from 1987 to 1996. Gladwell's most recent book,* Blink: The Power of Thinking Without Thinking *(2005), was a* New York Times *number one best-seller. "Your mind takes about two seconds to jump to a series of conclusions," says Gladwell; the book is an exploration of what happens in our minds during those seconds. In 2005, Gladwell was named one of* Time *magazine's 100 Most Influential People. Since leaving the* Post, *he has been a staff writer for* The New Yorker, *in which this article was published in 2004.*

Malcolm Gladwell

Big and Bad

In the summer of 1996, the Ford Motor Company began building the Expedition, its new, full-sized S.U.V., at the Michigan Truck Plant, in the Detroit suburb of Wayne. The Expedition was essentially the F-150 pickup truck with an extra set of doors and two more rows of seats—and the fact that it was a truck was critical. Cars have to meet stringent fuel-efficiency regulations. Trucks don't. The handling and suspension and braking of cars have to be built to the demanding standards of drivers and passengers. Trucks only have to handle like, well, trucks. Cars are built with what is called unit-body construction. To be light enough to meet fuel standards and safe enough to meet safety standards, they have expensive and elaborately engineered steel skeletons, with built-in crumple zones to absorb the impact of a crash. Making a truck is a lot more rudimentary. You build a rectangular steel frame. The engine gets bolted to the front. The seats get bolted to the middle. The body gets lowered over the top. The result is heavy and rigid and not particularly safe. But it's an awfully inexpensive way to build an automobile. Ford had planned to sell the Expedition for thirty-six thousand dollars, and its best estimate was that it could build one for twenty-four thousand—which, in the automotive industry, is a terrifically high profit margin. Sales, the company predicted, weren't going to be huge. After all, how many Americans could reasonably be expected to pay a twelve-thousand-dollar premium for what was essentially a dressed-up truck? But Ford executives decided that the Expedition would be a highly profitable niche product. They were half right. The "highly profitable" part turned out to be true. Yet, almost from the moment Ford's big new S.U.V.s rolled off the assembly line in Wayne, there was nothing "niche" about the Expedition.

Ford had intended to split the assembly line at the Michigan Truck Plant between the Expedition and the Ford F-150 pickup. But, when the first flood of orders started coming in for the Expedition, the factory was entirely given over to S.U.V.s. The orders kept mounting. Assembly-line workers were put on sixty- and seventy-hour weeks. Another night shift was added. The plant was now running twenty-four hours a day, six days a week. Ford executives decided to build a luxury version of the Expedition, the Lincoln Navigator. They bolted a new grille on the Expedition, changed a few body pancls, added some sound insulation, took a deep breath, and charged forty-five thousand dollars—and soon Navigators were flying out the door nearly as fast as Expeditions. Before long, the Michigan Truck Plant was the most profitable of Ford's fifty-three assembly plants. By the late nineteen-nineties, it had become the most profitable factory of any industry in the world. In 1998, the Michigan Truck Plant grossed eleven billion dollars, almost as much as McDonald's made that year. Profits were $3.7 billion. Some factory workers, with overtime, were making two hundred thousand dollars a year. The demand for Expeditions and Navigators was so insatiable that even when a blizzard hit the Detroit region in January of 1999—burying the city in snow, paralyzing the airport, and stranding hundreds of cars on the freeway—Ford officials got on their radios and commandeered parts bound for other factories so that the Michigan Truck Plant assembly line wouldn't slow for a moment. The factory that had begun as just another assembly plant had become the company's crown jewel.

In the history of the automotive industry, few things have been quite as unexpected as the rise of the S.U.V. Detroit is a town of engineers, and engineers like to believe that there is some connection between the success of a vehicle and its technical merits. But the S.U.V. boom was like Apple's bringing back the Macintosh, dressing it up in colorful plastic, and suddenly creating a new market. It made no sense to them. Consumers said they liked four-wheel drive. But the overwhelming majority of consumers don't need four-wheel drive. S.U.V. buyers said they liked the elevated driving position. But when, in focus groups, industry marketers probed further, they heard things that left them rolling their eyes. As Keith Bradsher writes in "High and Mighty"—perhaps the most important book about Detroit since Ralph Nader's "Unsafe at Any Speed"—what consumers said was "If the vehicle is up high, it's easier to see if something is hiding underneath or lurking behind it." Bradsher brilliantly captures the mixture of bafflement and contempt that many auto executives feel toward the customers who buy their S.U.V.s. Fred J. Schaafsma, a top engineer for General Motors, says, "Sport-utility owners tend to be more like 'I wonder how people view me,' and are more willing to trade off flexibility or functionality to get that." According to Bradsher, internal industry market research concluded that S.U.V.s tend to be bought by people who are insecure, vain, self-centered, and self-absorbed, who are frequently nervous about their marriages, and who lack confidence in their driving skills. Ford's S.U.V. designers took their cues from seeing "fashionably dressed women wearing hiking boots or even work boots while walking through expensive malls." Toyota's top marketing executive in the United States, Bradsher writes, loves to tell the story of how at a focus group in Los Angeles "an elegant woman in the group said that she needed her full-sized Lexus LX 470 to drive up over the curb and onto lawns to park at large parties in Beverly Hills." One of Ford's senior marketing executives was even blunter: "The only time those S.U.V.s are going to be off-road is when they miss the driveway at 3 A.M."

The truth, underneath all the rationalizations, seemed to be that S.U.V. buyers thought of big, heavy vehicles as safe: they found comfort in being surrounded by so much rubber and steel. To the engineers, of course, that didn't make any sense, either: if consumers really wanted something that was big and heavy and comforting, they ought to buy minivans, since minivans, with their unit-body construction, do much better in accidents than S.U.V.s. (In thirty-five-m.p.h. crash test, for instance, the driver of a Cadillac Escalade—the G.M. counterpart to the Lincoln Navigator—has a sixteen-per-cent chance of a life-threatening head injury, a twenty-per-cent chance of a life-threatening chest injury, and a thirty-five-per-cent chance of a leg injury. The same numbers in a Ford Windstar minivan—a vehicle engineered from the ground up, as opposed to simply being bolted onto a pickup-truck frame—are, respectively, two per cent, four per cent, and one per cent.) But this desire for safety wasn't a rational calculation. It was a *feeling*. Over the past decade, a number of major automakers in America have relied on the services of a French-born cultural anthropologist, G. Clotaire Rapaille, whose speciality is getting beyond the rational—

what he calls "cortex"—impressions of consumers and tapping into their deeper, "reptilian" responses. And what Rapaille concluded from countless, intensive sessions with car buyers was that when S.U.V. buyers thought about safety they were thinking about something that reached into their deepest unconscious. "The No. 1 feeling is that everything surrounding you should be round and soft, and should give," Rapaille told me. "There should be air bags everywhere. Then there's this notion that you need to be up high. That's a contradiction, because the people who buy these S.U.V.s know at the cortex level that if you are high there is more chance of a rollover. But at the reptilian level they think that if I am bigger and taller I'm safer. You feel secure because you are higher and dominate and look down. That you can look down is psychologically a very powerful notion. And what was the key element of safety when you were a child? It was that your mother fed you, and there was warm liquid. That's why cupholders are absolutely crucial for safety. If there is a car that has no cupholder, it is not safe. If I can put my coffee there, if I can have my food, if everything is round, if it's soft, and if I'm high, then I feel safe. It's amazing that intelligent, educated women will look at a car and the first thing they will look at is how many cupholders it has." During the design of Chrysler's PT Cruiser, one of the things Rapaille learned was that car buyers felt unsafe when they thought that an outsider could easily see inside their vehicles. So Chrysler made the back window of the PT Cruiser smaller. Of course, making windows smaller—and thereby reducing visibility—makes driving *more* dangerous, not less so. But that's the puzzle of what has happened to the automobile world: feeling safe has become more important than actually being safe.

5 One day this fall, I visited the automobile-testing center of Consumers Union, the organization that publishes *Consumer Reports*. It is tucked away in the woods, in south-central Connecticut, on the site of the old Connecticut Speedway. The facility has two skid pads to measure cornering, a long straightaway for braking tests, a meandering "handling" course that winds around the back side of the track, and an accident-avoidance obstacle course made out of a row of orange cones. It is headed by a trim, white-haired Englishman named David Champion, who previously worked as an engineer with Land Rover and with Nissan. On the day of my visit, Champion set aside two vehicles: a silver 2003 Chevrolet TrailBlazer—an enormous five-thousand-pound S.U.V.—and a shiny blue two-seater Porsche Boxster convertible.

We started with the TrailBlazer. Champion warmed up the Chevrolet with a few quick circuits of the track, and then drove it hard through the twists and turns of the handling course. He sat in the bucket seat with his back straight and his arms almost fully extended, and drove with practiced grace: every movement smooth and relaxed and unhurried. Champion, as an engineer, did not much like the TrailBlazer. "Cheap interior, cheap plastic," he said, batting the dashboard with his hand. "It's a little bit heavy, cumbersome. Quiet. Bit wallowy, side to side. Doesn't feel that secure. Accelerates heavily. Once it gets going, it's got decent power. Brakes feel a bit spongy." He turned onto the straightaway and stopped a few hundred yards from the obstacle course.

Measuring accident avoidance is a key part of the Consumers Union evaluation. It's a simple setup. The driver has to navigate his vehicle through two rows of cones eight feet wide and sixty feet long. Then he has to steer hard to the left, guiding the vehicle through a gate set off to the side, and immediately swerve hard back to the right, and enter a second sixty-foot corridor of cones that are parallel to the first set. The idea is to see how fast you can drive through the course without knocking over any cones. "It's like you're driving down a road in suburbia," Champion said. "Suddenly, a kid on a bicycle veers out in front of you. You have to do whatever it takes to avoid the kid. But there's a tractor-trailer coming toward you in the other lane, so you've got to swing back into your own lane as quickly as possible. That's the scenario."

Champion and I put on helmets. He accelerated toward the entrance to the obstacle course. "We do the test without brakes or throttle, so we can just look at handling," Champion said. "I actually take my foot right off the pedals." The car was now moving at forty m.p.h. At that speed, on the smooth tarmac of the raceway, the TrailBlazer was very quiet and we were seated so high that that the road seemed somehow remote. Champion entered the first row of cones. His arms tensed. He jerked the car to the left. The TrailBlazer's tires squealed. I was thrown toward the passenger-side door as the truck's body rolled, then thrown toward Champion as he jerked the TrailBlazer back to the right. My tape recorder went skittering across the cabin. The whole maneuver had taken no more than a few seconds, but it felt as if we had been sailing into a squall. Champion brought the car to a stop. We both looked back: the TrailBlazer had hit the cone at the gate. The kid on the bicycle was probably dead. Champion shook his head. "It's very rubbery. It slides a lot. I'm not getting much communication back from the steering wheel. It feels really ponderous, clumsy. I felt a little bit of tail swing."

I drove the obstacle course next. I started at the conservative speed of thirty-five m.p.h. I got through cleanly. I tried again, this time at thirty-eight m.p.h., and that small increment of speed made a dramatic difference. I made the first left, avoiding the kid on the bicycle. But, when it came time to swerve back to avoid the hypothetical oncoming eighteen-wheeler, I found that I was wrestling with the car. The protests of the tires were jarring. I stopped, shaken. "It wasn't going where you wanted it to go, was it?" Champion said. "Did you feel the weight pulling you sideways? That's what the extra weight that S.U.V.s have tends to do. It pulls you in the wrong direction." Behind us was a string of toppled cones. Getting the TrailBlazer to travel in a straight line, after that sudden diversion, hadn't been easy. "I think you took out a few pedestrians," Champion said with a faint smile.

10   Next up was the Boxster. The top was down. The sun was warm on my forehead. The car was low to the ground; I had the sense that if I dangled my arm out the window my knuckles would scrape on the tarmac. Standing still, the Boxster didn't feel safe: I could have been sitting in a go-cart. But when I ran it through the handling course I felt that I was in perfect control. On the straightaway, I steadied the Boxster at forty-five m.p.h., and ran it through the obstacle course. I could have balanced a teacup on my knee. At fifty m.p.h., I navigated the left and right turns with what seemed like a twitch of the steering wheel. The tires didn't squeal. The car stayed level. I pushed the Porsche up into the mid-fifties. Every cone was untouched. "Walk in the park!" Champion exclaimed as we pulled to a stop.

Most of us think that S.U.V.s are much safer than sports cars. If you asked the young parents of America whether they would rather strap their infant child in the back seat of the TrailBlazer or the passenger seat of the Boxster, they would choose the TrailBlazer. We feel that way because in the TrailBlazer our chances of surviving a collision with a hypothetical tractor-trailer in the other lane are greater than they are in the Porsche. What we forget, though, is that in the TrailBlazer you're also much more likely to hit the tractor-trailer because you can't get out of the way in time. In the parlance of the automobile world, the TrailBlazer is better at "passive safety." The Boxster is better when it comes to "active safety," which is every bit as important.

Consider the set of safety statistics compiled by Tom Wenzel, a scientist at Lawrence Berkeley National Laboratory, in California, and Marc Ross, a physicist at the University of Michigan. The numbers are expressed in fatalities per million cars, both for drivers of particular models and for the drivers of the cars they hit. (For example, in the first case, for every million Toyota Avalons on the road, forty Avalon drivers die in car accidents every year, and twenty people die in accidents involving Toyota Avalons.) The numbers below have been rounded:

Make/Model	Type	Driver Deaths	Other Deaths	Total
Toyota Avalon	large	40	20	60
Chrysler Town & Country	minivan	31	36	67
Toyota Camry	mid-size	41	29	70
Volkswagen Jetta	subcompact	47	23	70
Ford Windstar	minivan	37	35	72
Nissan Maxima	mid-size	53	26	79
Honda Accord	mid-size	54	27	82
Chevrolet Venture	minivan	51	34	85
Buick Century	mid-size	70	23	93
Subaru Legacy/Outback	compact	74	24	98
Mazda 626	compact	70	29	99
Chevrolet Malibu	mid-size	71	34	105
Chevrolet Suburban	S.U.V.	46	59	105
Jeep Grand Cherokee	S.U.V.	61	44	106
Honda Civic	subcompact	84	25	109
Toyota Corolla	subcompact	81	29	110
Ford Expedition	S.U.V.	55	57	112
GMC Jimmy	S.U.V.	76	39	114
Ford Taurus	mid-size	78	39	117
Nissan Altima	compact	72	49	121
Mercury Marquis	large	80	43	123
Nissan Sentra	subcompact	95	34	129
Toyota 4Runner	S.U.V.	94	43	137
Chevrolet Tahoe	S.U.V.	68	74	141

Make/Model	Type	Driver Deaths	Other Deaths	Total
Dodge Stratus	mid-size	103	40	143
Lincoln Town Car	large	100	47	147
Ford Explorer	S.U.V.	88	60	148
Pontiac Grand Am	compact	118	39	157
Toyota Tacoma	pickup	111	59	171
Chevrolet Cavalier	subcompact	146	41	186
Dodge Neon	subcompact	161	39	199
Pontiac Sunfire	subcompact	158	44	202
Ford F-Series	pickup	110	128	238

Are the best performers the biggest and heaviest vehicles on the road? Not at all. Among the safest cars are the midsize imports, like the Toyota Camry and the Honda Accord. Or consider the extraordinary performance of some subcompacts, like the Volkswagen Jetta. Drivers of the tiny Jetta die at a rate of just forty-seven per million, which is in the same range as drivers of the five-thousand-pound Chevrolet Suburban and almost half that of popular S.U.V. models like the Ford Explorer or the GMC Jimmy. In a head-on crash, an Explorer or a Suburban would crush a Jetta or a Camry. But, clearly, the drivers of Camrys and Jettas are finding a way to avoid head-on crashes with Explorers and Suburbans. The benefits of being nimble—of being in an automobile that's capable of staying out of trouble—are in many cases greater than the benefits of being big.

I had another lesson in active safety at the test track when I got in the TrailBlazer with another Consumers Union engineer, and we did three emergency-stopping tests, taking the Chevrolet up to sixty m.p.h. and then slamming on the brakes. It was not a pleasant exercise. Bringing five thousand pounds of rubber and steel to a sudden stop involves lots of lurching, screeching, and protesting. The first time, the TrailBlazer took 146.2 feet to come to a halt, the second time 151.6 feet, and the third time 153.4 feet. The Boxster can come to a complete stop from sixty m.p.h. in about 124 feet. That's a difference of about two car lengths, and it isn't hard to imagine any number of scenarios where two car lengths could mean the difference between life and death.

* * *

15 The S.U.V. boom represents, then, a shift in how we conceive of safety—from active to passive. It's what happens when a larger number of drivers conclude, consciously or otherwise, that the extra thirty feet that the TrailBlazer takes to come to a stop don't really matter, that the tractor-trailer will hit them anyway, and that they are better off treating accidents as inevitable rather than avoidable. "The metric that people use is size," says Stephen Popiel, a vice-president of Millward Brown Goldfarb, in Toronto, one of the leading automotive market-research firms. "The bigger something is, the safer it is. In the consumer's mind, the basic equation is, If I were to take this vehicle and drive it into this brick wall, the more metal there is in front of me the better off I'll be."

This is a new idea, and one largely confined to North America. In Europe and Japan, people think of a safe car as a nimble car. That's why they build cars like the Jetta and the Camry, which are designed to carry out the driver's wishes as directly and efficiently as possible. In the Jetta, the engine is clearly audible. The steering is light and precise. The brakes are crisp. The wheelbase is short enough that the car picks up the undulations of the road. The car is so small and close to the ground, and so dwarfed by other cars on the road, that an intelligent driver is constantly reminded of the necessity of driving safely and defensively. An S.U.V. embodies the opposite logic. The driver is seated as high and far from the road as possible. The vehicle is designed to overcome its environment, not to respond to it. Even four-wheel drive, seemingly the most beneficial feature of the S.U.V., serves to reinforce this isolation. Having the engine provide power to all four wheels, safety experts point out, does nothing to improve braking, although many S.U.V. owners erroneously believe this to be the case. Nor does the feature necessarily make it safer to turn across a slippery surface: that is largely a function of how much friction is generated by the vehicle's tires. All it really does is improve what engineers call tracking—that is, the ability to accelerate without slipping in perilous conditions or in deep snow or mud. Champion says that one of the occasions when he came closest to death was a snowy day, many years ago, just after he had bought a new Range Rover. "Everyone around me was slipping, and I was thinking, *Yeahhh*. And I came to a stop sign on a major road, and I was driving probably twice as fast as I should have been, because I could. I had traction. But I also weighed probably twice as much as most cars. And I still had only four brakes and four tires on the road. I slid right across a four-lane road." Four-wheel drive robs the driver of feedback. "The car driver whose wheels spin once or twice while backing out of the driveway knows that the road is slippery," Bradsher writes. "The SUV driver who navigates the driveway and street without difficulty until she tries to brake may not find out that the road is slippery until it is too late." Jettas are safe because they make their drivers feel unsafe. S.U.V.s are unsafe because they make their drivers feel safe. That feeling of safety isn't the solution; it's the problem.

Perhaps the most troublesome aspect of S.U.V. culture is its attitude toward risk. "Safety, for most automotive consumers, has to do with the notion that they aren't in complete control," Popiel says. "There are unexpected events that at any moment in time can come out and impact them—an oil patch up ahead, an eighteen-wheeler turning over, something falling down. People feel that the elements of the world out of their control are the ones that are going to cause them distress."

Of course, those things really aren't outside a driver's control: an alert driver, in the right kind of vehicle, can navigate the oil patch, avoid the truck, and swerve around the thing that's falling down. Traffic-fatality rates vary strongly with driver behavior. Drunks are 7.6 times more likely to die in accidents than non-drinkers. People who wear their seat belts are almost half as likely to die as those who don't buckle up. Forty-year-olds are ten times less likely to get into accidents than sixteen-year-olds. Drivers of minivans, Wenzel and Ross's statistics tell us, die at a fraction of the rate of drivers of pickup trucks. That's clearly because minivans are family cars, and parents with children in the back seat are less likely to get into accidents. Frank McKenna, a safety expert at the University of Reading, in England, has done experiments where he shows drivers a series of videotaped scenarios—a child running out the front door of his house and onto the street, for example, or a car approaching an intersection at too great a speed to stop at the red light—and asks people to press a button the minute they become aware of the potential for an accident. Experienced drivers press the button between half a second and a second faster than new drivers, which, given that car accidents are events measured in milliseconds, is a significant difference. McKenna's work shows that, with experience, we all learn how to exert some degree of control over what might otherwise appear to be uncontrollable events. Any conception of safety that revolves entirely around the vehicle, then, is incomplete. Is the Boxster safer than the TrailBlazer? It depends on who's behind the wheel. In the hands of, say, my very respectable and prudent middle-aged mother, the Boxster is by far the safer car. In my hands, it probably isn't. On the open road, my reaction to the Porsche's extraordinary road manners and the sweet, irresistible wail of its engine would be to drive much faster than I should. (At the end of my day at Consumers Union, I parked the Boxster, and immediately got into my own car to drive home. In my mind, I was still at the wheel of the Boxster. Within twenty minutes, I had a two-hundred-and-seventy-one-dollar speeding ticket.) The trouble with the S.U.V. ascendancy is that it excludes the really critical component of safety: the driver.

In psychology, there is a concept called learned helplessness, which arose from a series of animal experiments in the nineteen-sixties at the University of Pennsylvania. Dogs were restrained by a harness, so that they couldn't move, and then repeatedly subjected to a series of electrical shocks. Then the same dogs were shocked again, only this time they could easily escape by jumping over a low hurdle. But most of them didn't; they just huddled in the corner, no longer believing that there was anything they could do to influence their own fate. Learned helplessness is now thought to play a role in such phenomena as depression and the failure of battered women to leave their husbands, but one could easily apply it more widely. We live in an age, after all, that is strangely fixated on the idea of helplessness: we're fascinated by hurricanes and terrorist acts and epidemics like SARS—situations in which we feel powerless to affect our own destiny. In fact, the risks posed to life and limb by forces outside our control are dwarfed by the factors we can control. Our fixation with helplessness distorts our perceptions of risk. "When you feel safe, you can be passive," Rapaille says of the fundamental appeal of the S.U.V. "Safe means I can sleep. I can give up control. I can relax. I can take off my shoes. I can listen to music." For years, we've all made fun of the middle-aged man who suddenly trades in his sedate family sedan for a shiny red sports car. That's called a midlife crisis. But at least it involves some degree of engagement with the act of driving. The man who gives up his sedate family sedan for an S.U.V. is saying something far more troubling—that he finds the demands of the road to be overwhelming. Is acting out really worse than giving up?

20 On August 9, 2000, the Bridgestone Firestone tire company announced one of the largest product recalls in American history. Because of mounting concerns about safety, the company said, it was replacing some fourteen million tires that had been used primarily on

the Ford Explorer S.U.V. The cost of the recall—and of a follow-up replacement program initiated by Ford a year later—ran into billions of dollars. Millions more were spent by both companies on fighting and settling lawsuits from Explorer owners, who alleged that their tires had come apart and caused their S.U.V.s to roll over. In the fall of that year, senior executives from both companies were called to Capitol Hill, where they were publicly berated. It was the biggest scandal to hit the automobile industry in years. It was also one of the strangest. According to federal records, the number of fatalities resulting from the failure of a Firestone tire on a Ford Explorer S.U.V., as of September, 2001, was two hundred and seventy-one. That sounds like a lot, until you remember that the total number of tires supplied by Firestone to the Explorer from the moment the S.U.V. was introduced by Ford, in 1990, was fourteen million, and that the average life span of a tire is forty-five thousand miles. The allegation against Firestone amounts to the claim that its tires failed, with fatal results, two-hundred and seventy-one times in the course of six hundred and thirty billion vehicle miles. Manufacturers usually win prizes for failure rates that low. It's also worth remembering that during that same ten-year span almost half a million Americans died in traffic accidents. In other words, during the nineteen-nineties hundreds of thousands of people were killed on the roads because they drove too fast or ran red lights or drank too much. And, of those, a fair proportion involved people in S.U.V.s who were lulled by their four-wheel drive into driving recklessly on slick roads, who drove aggressively because they felt invulnerable, who disproportionately killed those they hit because they chose to drive trucks with inflexible steel-frame architecture, and who crashed because they couldn't bring their five-thousand-pound vehicles to a halt in time. Yet, out of all those fatalities, regulators, the legal profession, Congress, and the media chose to highlight the .0005 per cent that could be linked to an alleged defect in the vehicle.

But should that come as a surprise? In the age of the S.U.V., this is what people worry about when they worry about safety—not risks, however commonplace, involving their own behavior but risks, however rare, involving some unexpected event. The Explorer was big and imposing. It was high above the ground. You could look down on other drivers. You could see if someone was lurking behind or beneath it. You could drive it up on someone's lawn with impunity. Didn't it seem like the safest vehicle in the world?

Analyzing Rhetorical Choices

1. Who is the audience for Gladwell's essay? What type of audience would be most influenced by the essay?
2. How does Gladwell use social-scientific evidence to classify his categories? In what ways does this evidence support his argument?
3. Analyze the final line of Gladwell's essay: "Didn't it seem like the safest vehicle in the world?" What is the effect of ending the essay with a rhetorical question? What other questions are implied by this question?

Writing About Issues and Contexts

1. Why are S.U.V.s not as popular in countries other than the United States? What economic and social implications surround this trend of unpopularity? (And consider the exception: the sudden popularity of S.U.V.s in Saudi Arabia, despite rising gasoline prices elsewhere in the world.)
2. Gladwell states "feeling safe has become more important than actually being safe." In light of recent scientific research, why do some people continue to risk their own safety and the safety of others in order to fulfill a seemingly false sense of security?
3. Comment on the statement that "S.U.V.s tend to be bought by people who are insecure, vain, self-centered, and self-absorbed, who are frequently nervous about their marriages, and who lack confidence in their driving skills." What evidence can you give in support of this statement? Is there evidence to the contrary?

Strategies for Writers: Classification

1. Classifying is a natural function of the human mind. However, to classify can also be to stereotype. When is classification positive? When is it negative? How have you classified the people in this class? In this book? In this discussion group? How do you classify your professors? Compare notes with your classmates. Are their classifications as accurate as yours? Are there equally valid—or invalid—ways to type the same thing?

2. Review the essays and questions in this chapter. Which essays seem to use classification most effectively and appropriately? Which, in your view, are less effective? Why?

3. How do you classify the varieties of your educational experience? Compare your categories to those of Zinsser in "College Pressures."

4. Classification is also tied to comparison and contrast and definition. How could Margaret Atwood's essay on pornography also be considered definition? Are there other ways to classify pornography that might depart from Atwood's essay?

5. Judith Viorst created eight categories to describe friends. Each category is distinguished by the level of intimacy of the friendship, and each is clearly defined. The essay focuses on categories and their definitions, with the comparison and contrast of each category implied rather than made explicit. Find a key term or concept and provide various degrees of categories and definitions, developing an essay that echoes the strategies used by Viorst.

Research and Writing Assignments

1. As noted elsewhere in this chapter, to classify is also to define. Philip Elmer-DeWitt classifies, in complex ways, the various permutations of cyberspace and, by implication, the various types of literacy attributed to (or needed by) those participating in Internet-based activities. In addition to the importance of access to computers and the Internet for such participation, extend Elmer-DeWitt's classifications to delineate the types of literacies necessary for full participation in technologically based activities. What assumptions do you make in deciding on the names of your classifications?

2. Gloria Anzaldúa's "How to Tame a Wild Tongue" and Malcolm Gladwell's "Big and Bad" use more subtle forms of classification than do other entries in this chapter. For instance, Anzaldúa's essay might well fit into the chapter on process, if we look merely at its title. Gladwell's "classifying" comes about more by implication than by direct naming of categories. Compare these two apparently disparate essays, looking closely at their differing ways of classifying and the other rhetorical strategies the authors use to make their arguments. How does each author cross the boundaries of rhetorical strategies to create an effective essay?

3. Using your discretion as you research this complex and controversial topic, find appropriate counterarguments to Margaret Atwood's way of classifying and defining pornography. Find at least two other writers who address the topic, looking closely at the assumptions behind their ways of classifying pornography and the ways in which they make their arguments, comparing and contrasting them with Atwood's. How do these writers use classification as effective rhetorical strategies, if they do? Which are more effective? Less effective? Why?

4. How do Judith Viorst and Peggy Orenstein classify with different goals and for different purposes? Viorst delineates the varieties within the category of friendship; Orenstein adds new categories to the ways of classifying baby names. Using research on techniques other writers might use to "classify" similar topics, examine how Viorst and Orenstein either expand or limit the effectiveness of classification as a rhetorical strategy for argument.

5. Using William Zinsser's "College Pressures" as your starting point, examine the Web sites of several universities, making sure to include several highly competitive and less competitive institutions. How do these schools classify themselves, their students, and the presumed experience of students on campus? What do these institutions reveal about themselves, directly and perhaps inadvertently? Additionally, how do these relate to the "college pressures" revealed by Zinsser?

7
Process Analysis

Writers choose to compose in the mode of process analysis because they are motivated by the need to explain. Often they possess a specific expertise and are asked to teach what they know to a more general public. Some process essays provide explanations that focus on *how*—how to dress for success, how to get from one place to another, how to hit a curve ball, how to assemble a doll collection. Such essays are, in essence, narratives of instruction intended to teach a lesson or a set of skills. Sometimes, however, writers choose to describe a more subtle process, namely the process of discovery. Writers with this purpose in mind are concerned less about offering a set of directions and more about describing a process of personal development that leads to increased insight and understanding—about specific life goals, social circumstances, the nature of experience.

Both kinds of essays fit in the process analysis mode because both are temporal in nature; that is, they both can be used to describe a process that has a beginning, middle, and end. That means that a process analysis essay tells a story, sometimes quite literally, and often resembles a work of narrative, although its primary purpose is always to explain how to do something or how to achieve a specific objective. Perhaps the best way to describe a process analysis essay is to say that it has a highly applied-use value and wants to teach us a lesson we can follow.

Writing process analysis essays may seem easy at first blush, but it is a challenging mode to do well. For example, you have probably purchased a bicycle, computer desk, or DVD player that came in a box labeled "Assembly Required" and then attempted to follow the enclosed instructional manual. Sometimes the instructions guide you effortlessly through the process; other times they probably frustrated and befuddled you. Usually, the failure can be traced to the writer lacking necessary information, assuming knowledge on the part of the consumer, or omitting key steps and information. Occasionally, the writing is bad—paragraphs lack focus and transition, steps are poorly described, the order of assembly is incorrect, the syntax is snarled. Efficient and clear instructions are not easy to write. More and more companies are employing professional writers to do this work, and these writers must find a way to describe complex processes in precise language so that those with little or no knowledge can follow them.

Examples of process analysis can be found everywhere. A quick Internet search of the best-selling books in America reveals titles like *How to Make Enduring Friendships, How to Make Love Like a Porn Star, How to Make Your Own Organic Cosmetics,* and *How to Make a Killing on Wall Street.* Such titles fill countless pages of publishers' catalogs. Television and radio shows abound informing people how to live a healthy life, how to solve cat and dog behavior problems, how to lose weight, how to shop on-line. All are examples of process analysis.

Interested in driving from Little Rock, Arkansas, to Austin, Texas, but don't know the route? No problem. Just log onto the Internet, do a quick search, and download a map and directions. The Yahoo! map opposite offers a relatively simple example of process analysis, but even this task requires a comprehensive knowledge of roads and routes along with the ability to compose in a clear and organized fashion.

It is worth noting that this map has certain features that can be found in many process analysis essays. First, it includes illustrations, a helpful feature not always feasible when writing an academic essay. Visual aids, when appropriate, can be a great help to readers and are a useful form of exemplification. Second, the map signals its purpose clearly from the beginning, indicating that it is a Yahoo! map describing how to get from Little Rock to Austin. Third, the directions are clear, explicit, and logically organized, citing specific turning directions, streets, and mileage indicators. Finally, the map includes a cautionary statement about its own veracity, advising users to "do a reality check and make sure the road still exists"—a statement that, surprisingly, is not intended for comic effect. Since even the best-

Yahoo! Maps

Maps | Driving Directions

Starting from:	❶ Little Rock, AR Save Address	
Arriving at:	❷ Austin, TX Save Address	Get Reverse Directions
Distance:	514.1 miles	Approximate Travel Time: 7 hours 54 mins

📧 Email Directions   🖨 Printable Version   ☐ Text Only Driving Directions

Full Route

Destination · Interactive Map

© 2003 Yahoo! Inc © 2002 Navigation Technologies

Directions	Miles	
1. Start on **STATE CAPITOL**	0.1	↑
2. Bear Left on a local road	0.0	↰
3. Turn Right on **MARTIN LUTHER KING JR DR**	0.1	↱
4. Turn Left on **W 7TH ST**	0.4	↰
5. Turn Right on **S CHESTER ST**	0.2	↱
6. Take the **I-630 EAST** ramp	0.2	↱
7. Merge on **I-630 EAST**	1.1	↑
8. Take the **I-30 WEST** exit towards **TEXARKANA**, exit #139B	0.3	↱
9. Merge on **I-30 WEST**	1.6	↱
10. Continue on **I-30 WEST/I-440 WEST**	0.4	↑
11. Continue on **I-30 WEST**	303.2	↑
12. Take the **I-635 SOUTH** exit, exit #56B	1.0	↑
13. Merge on **I-635 SOUTH**	8.4	↱
14. Continue on **I-20 WEST**	11.9	↑
15. Take the **I-35E SOUTH** exit towards **WACO**, exit #467B	0.9	↱
16. Merge on **I-35E SOUTH**	46.7	↱
17. Take the **I-35 SOUTH** exit	0.5	↑
18. Merge on **I-35 SOUTH**	136.3	↰
19. Take the **8TH - 3RD STS** exit, exit #234B	0.1	↱
20. Continue on **N I-35**	0.3	↰
21. Turn Right on **E 4TH ST**	0.4	↱
22. Turn Right on **BRAZOS ST**	0.1	↱

Distance: 514.1 miles Approximate Travel Time: 7 hours 54 mins

When using any driving directions or map, it's a good idea to do a reality check and make sure the road still exists, watch out for construction, and follow all traffic safety precautions. This is only to be used as an aid in planning.

described process analysis can end in failure (accidents happen and cannot always be prevented), it is useful to remain aware of one's fallibility when offering instructions to others.

Process analysis essays come in many styles, tones, and levels of difficulty. Many are direct, informational, and written in a fairly "neutral" tone and style. Middle Tennessee State University offers its students a short process analysis on the Wesley Foundation Web site (*http://www.mtsu.edu/~wesleyfo/roommates.html*). The focus is on getting along with your roommate.

Roommate: Friend or Foe?

Living with a roommate can be a great experience.
But it can also be a horror story.

Maybe it's your first time away from home. Most likely, it is the first time you have lived with someone who isn't a family member.
While it is possible to get along well from the start with your roommate, not many find it so easy. Often, living with a roommate requires work.

There is no easy formula for living with roommates. Below are some suggestions from those who gone through dorm life:

- When you first move in, try to reach agreement with your roommate about these things: housekeeping; telephone: cost and use; shared expenses; visiting hours; sleeping hours: reconciling the early bird with the night owl; space: closet, study, personal; borrowing: clothes, books, personal property; playing music: type, volume, hours.
- Clear communication from the start. Be aware of what bugs you and let your roommate know.
- Keep communicating. If your roommate does something that irritates you, tell your roomie, not the person across the hall.
- Maintain a sense of humor.
- Do things with your roommate outside of the room. Going to a movie may help remind you that your roommate is human.
- Don't expect people to know how you are feeling—tell them.
- Go into dorm living with a realistic attitude. Resign yourself to the fact that concessions will have to be made.
- Respect your roommate as a person and respect their stuff.
- Don't take all comments personally.
- If things aren't going well, talk to your residence advisor or campus ministry folks.

- Remember, not everyone can get along with everyone else. If the situation gets bad, get out. Check on policies about moving to a different room.
- After all, the above suggestions are easier said than done. Godspeed! Keep the faith.
- Lastly, keep in mind that living with a previously total stranger is an adventure where the outcome is largely up to you. You may find that your roommate is indeed a foe. However, you may make a friend who becomes a lifelong confidant. Above all, learning to get along with a roommate is a valuable education for marriage and family life.

This Web document is practical and obviously intended for students, with its informal word choice, breezy practicality, and upbeat tone. The list of suggestions it enumerates could be reformulated into an informative process analysis essay about roommate relationships or refashioned into a more tongue-in-cheek essay about "surviving a roommate" or "how to persuade a roommate to bunk elsewhere so that you end up with a single room"!

Humor can be an effective device when writing process analysis, as seen in the following Web column by two well-known public radio personalities, Tom and Ray Magliozzi, whose call-in show is featured on many public radio stations. This October 1999 exchange, which can be found at their Web site *(http://www.cartalk.com/content/ columns)*, is transcribed from one of the many phone calls they receive and answer on the air and is an example of how sound advice can be offered with a humorous tone.

Dear Tom and Ray:

My '97 Honda Civic EX recently developed a new feature: The blue windshield washer solution has been colonized by some pink slime that smells like somebody's unwashed gym clothes. My microbiologist co-worker says that there are some forms of microbial life that can live in alcohol-containing solutions, like wiper fluid. My husband was trying to figure out how to remove the reservoir to clean it out, but it looks like it won't come out unless we take the bumper off first. Is there an easy way to clean out this container?—Elaine

Tom: Sure. With a garden hose.

Ray: You CAN take the whole reservoir out without actually removing the bumper, but you need to remove the inner fender liner, and that's a pain in the butt, too. So the hose is the tool of choice here.

Tom: The windshield-washer reservoir is a closed system. There's the tank, a little pump and a rubber tube that carries the liquid to the windshield. That's it. So you won't harm or contaminate anything else by sticking the garden hose in there.

Ray: Pop off the top, stick the hose in there and let it overflow for 5 or 10 minutes. While you're doing that, use the windshield washer a few times to clean out the rubber tubes, too.

Tom: Then put a little bit of bleach in the water—along with a couple of expired penicillin tablets from your medicine cabinet—and let it sit. A day or two later, give the thing a scrub with one of those long-handled kitchen pot scrubbers, and put the hose in it again.

Ray: And when you're all done, you can siphon out the bulk of the water and fill it back up with soapy blue stuff.

Tom: And if the microbes come back after that, call the Centers for Disease Control and Prevention in Atlanta. Tell them you're willing to donate a reservoir of rare microbes to science, but they'll have to come and swap out your windshield-washer container for you if they want them.

The Magliozzi brothers' transcript illustrates that an explanation of a particular process often includes additional helpful information—in this case, the structure of the washer reservoir. Whenever writing process analysis essays, a useful rule-of-thumb is that you should know much more about your subject than you end up including in the essay. Writers who exhaust all their knowledge almost certainly do not yet possess sufficient knowledge to do the best possible job. The Magliozzi brothers possess so much knowledge about car repair that they make accurate diagnoses of most problems based on conversations with the cars' owners over the telephone.

Approaches to Writing Process Analysis Essays

As is clear, process analysis essays offer many opportunities to experiment with tone, format, and structure. They also require a careful and perceptive analysis of purpose and audience. Do you want primarily to offer an explicit description of a process as exemplified by the Frederick Douglass essay, or do you prefer to offer an account of a process of discovery, as does Fan Shen? Both essays use descriptions of process to open up significant subjects including identity, subjectivity, and cultural difference. In terms of audience, do your readers already possess information so that you can write more technically about your subject? Do they have specific needs and interests? Why would they want to read your process analysis? What benefit(s) would they receive?

It is also worth noting that visualization can be very important when writing process analysis. More than most other modes, process analysis asks writers to place themselves within very specific settings, to get situated within the procedures or stages being described. Whether explaining how to get a conk (Malcolm X) or learning how to say nothing in 500 words (Paul Roberts), process analysis writers need to be able to place themselves within the situations they are describing and write so that the reader can visualize them. At times it may be helpful to close your eyes and imagine the context in as much detail as possible. Ultimately, the best process analysis essays are those that invite us to relive the experience in some thoughtful and productive way.

Plan Your Essay

More than most other modes, process analysis requires a clear, organized, focused approach to your subject. You will want to write by using all or most of the following steps:

1. Choose a subject that is complex and sustains your interest. Sure, you can write an essay about how to apply mascara, but it is doubtful that many people will need to read it. If you find that subject compelling, you will likely need to find some way to make it more worthwhile, such as writing about how to apply mascara on a windy day or choosing the best mascara for your complexion and facial features.

2. Research your subject in depth. Process analysis demands extensive knowledge. You should do enough research that you do not use it all in your essay. That way you'll know that you have done so much research that you have gone beyond what is needed in the essay itself.

3. Develop a logical plan for presenting your process. Most process analysis essays are highly organized and take the reader through the process in a clear, sensible manner. If you are describing how to carve a swan out of ice, you would not want to begin halfway through stage four, shaping the beak. In fact, you might want to begin with the design, then move on to how to create a sufficiently large block of ice, and so forth.

4. Make sure you have included everything essential. Sometimes the challenge of writing process analysis is that you know your subject so well, you leave out important information. One of the best

ways to check for this problem is to read your essay to an attentive listener who knows nothing about the process you are describing. If that person understands you, chances are your essay is both clear and complete.

5. Include sensible transitions. Since process analysis can often be divided into specific stages ("do this first, do this next, then this"), the essay can at times lack smoothness and subtle coherence. One way to resolve this problem is to include appropriate transitional phrases and clauses, such as "once that is completed," or "after having devoured the last 35 fried chicken wings."

6. As always, edit for errors and omissions. You should always complete your draft several days before it is due so that you can take it to the Writing Center, share it with a careful reader, and have time to proofread, edit, or revise as needed. Rushed essays that land on the instructor's desk hot off the printer are almost always incomplete, sloppy, or otherwise not yet ready.

Frederick Douglass (1818–1895) was born into slavery in Maryland. Although severely beaten for several attempts to escape, he finally succeeded in 1838 and fled to Massachusetts, where he became an agent and spokesman for the Massachusetts Anti-Slavery League. He lectured on slavery in Great Britain, where money was collected for his freedom, whereupon he took the last name of Douglass. Considered the first African American to gain national stature, Douglass edited an abolitionist paper, The North Star, *from 1847 to 1860, and was among those to convince President Abraham Lincoln to issue the Emancipation Proclamation. "Learning to Read and Write" comes from Douglass's autobiography,* Narrative of the Life of Frederick Douglass, An American Slave *(1845).*

Frederick Douglass

Learning to Read and Write

I lived in Master Hugh's family about seven years. During this time, I succeeded in learning to read and write. In accomplishing this, I was compelled to resort to various stratagems. I had no regular teacher. My mistress, who had kindly commenced to instruct me, had, in compliance with the advice and direction of her husband, not only ceased to instruct, but had set her face against my being instructed by anyone else. It is due, however, to my mistress to say of her, that she did not adopt this course of treatment immediately. She at first lacked the depravity indispensable to shutting me up in mental darkness. It was at least necessary for her to have some training in the exercise of irresponsible power, to make her equal to the task of treating me as though I were a brute.

My mistress was, as I have said, a kind and tender-hearted woman; and in the simplicity of her soul she commenced, when I first went to live with her, to treat me as she supposed one human being ought to treat another. In entering upon the duties of a slaveholder, she did not seem to perceive that I sustained to her the relation of a mere chattel, and that for her to treat me as a human being was not only wrong, but dangerously so. Slavery proved as injurious to her as it did to me. When I went there, she was a pious, warm, and tender-hearted woman. There was no sorrow or suffering for which she had not a tear. She had bread for the hungry, clothes for the naked, and comfort for every mourner that came within her reach. Slavery soon proved its ability to divest her of these heavenly qualities. Under its influence, the tender heart became stone, and the lamb-like disposition gave way to one of tiger-like fierceness. The first step in her downward course was in her ceasing to instruct me. She now commenced to practise her husband's precepts. She finally became even more violent in her opposition than her husband himself. She was not satisfied with simply doing as well as he had commanded; she seemed anxious to do better. Nothing seemed to make her more angry than to see me with a newspaper. She seemed to think that here lay the danger. I have had her rush at me with a face made all up of fury, and snatch from me a newspaper, in a manner that fully revealed her apprehension. She was an apt woman; and a little experience soon demonstrated, to her satisfaction, that education and slavery were incompatible with each other.

From this time I was most narrowly watched. If I was in a separate room any considerable length of time, I was sure to be suspected of having a book, and was at once called to give an account of myself. All this, however, was too late. The first step had been taken. Mistress, in teaching me the alphabet, had given me the *inch,* and no precaution could prevent me from taking the *ell.*

The plan which I adopted, and the one by which I was most successful, was that of making friends of all the little white boys whom I met in the street. As many of these as I could, I converted into teachers. With their kindly aid, obtained at different times and in different places, I finally succeeded in learning to read. When I was sent on errands, I always took my book with me, and by going one part of my errand quickly, I found time to get a lesson before my return. I used also to carry bread with me, enough of which was always in the house, and to which I was always welcome; for I was much better off in this regard than many of the poor white children in our neighborhood. This bread I used to bestow upon the hungry little urchins, who, in return, would give me that more valuable bread of knowledge. I am strongly tempted to give the names of two or three of those little boys, as a testimonial of the gratitude and affection I bear them; but prudence forbids;—not that it would injure me, but it might embarrass them; for it is almost an unpardonable offence to teach slaves to read in this Christian country. It is enough to say of the dear little fellows, that they lived on Philpot Street, very near Durgin and Bailey's shipyard. I used to talk this matter of slavery over with them. I would sometimes say to them, I wished I could be as free as they would be when they got to be men. "You will be free as soon as you are twenty-one, *but I am a slave for life!* Have not I as good a right to be free as you have?" These words used to trouble them; they would express for me the liveliest sympathy, and console me with the hope that something would occur by which I might be free.

5   I was now about twelve years old, and the thought of being *a slave for life* began to bear heavily upon my heart. Just about this time, I got hold of a book entitled "The Columbian Orator." Every opportunity I got, I used to read this book. Among much of other interesting matter, I found in it a dialogue between a master and his slave. The slave was represented as having run away from his master three times. The dialogue represented the conversation which took place between them, when the slave was retaken the third time. In this dialogue, the whole argument in behalf of slavery was brought forward by the master, all of which was disposed of by the slave. The slave was made to say some very smart as well as impressive things in reply to his master—things which had the desired though unexpected effect; for the conversation resulted in the voluntary emancipation of the slave on the part of the master.

In the same book, I met with one of Sheridan's mighty speeches on and in behalf of Catholic emancipation. These were choice documents to me. I read them over and over again with unabated interest. They gave tongue to interesting thoughts of my own soul, which had frequently flashed through my mind, and died away for want of utterance. The moral which I gained from the dialogue was the power of truth over the conscience of even a slaveholder. What I got from Sheridan was a bold denunciation of slavery, and a powerful vindication of human rights. The reading of these documents enabled me to utter my thoughts, and to meet the arguments brought forward to sustain slavery; but while they relieved me of one difficulty, they brought on another even more painful than the one of which I was relieved. The more I read, the more I was led to abhor and detest my enslavers. I could regard them in no other light than a band of successful robbers, who had left their homes, and gone to Africa, and stolen us from our homes, and in a strange land reduced us to slavery. I loathed them as being the meanest as well as the most wicked of men. As I read and contemplated the subject, behold! that very discontentment which Master Hugh had predicted would follow my learning to read had already come, to torment and sting my soul to unutterable anguish. As I writhed under it, I would at times feel that learning to read had been a curse rather than a blessing. It had given me a view of my wretched condition, without the remedy. It opened my eyes to the horrible pit, but to no ladder upon which to get out. In moments of agony, I envied my fellow-slaves for their stupidity. I have often wished myself a beast. I preferred the condition of the meanest reptile to my own. Any thing, no matter what, to get rid of thinking! It was this everlasting thinking of my condition that tormented me. There was no getting rid of it. It was pressed upon me by every object within sight or hearing, animate or inanimate. The silver trump of freedom had roused my soul to eternal wakefulness. Freedom now appeared, to disappear no more forever. It was heard in every sound, and seen in every thing. It was ever present to torment me with a sense of my wretched condition. I saw nothing without seeing it, I heard nothing without hearing it, and felt nothing without feeling it. It looked from every star, it smiled in every calm, breathed in every wind, and moved in every storm.

I often found myself regretting my own existence, and wishing myself dead; and but for the hope of being free, I have no doubt but that I should have killed myself, or done something for which I should have been killed. While in this state of mind, I was eager to hear anyone speak of slavery. I was a ready listener. Every little while, I could hear something about the abolitionists. It was some time before I found what the word meant. It was always used in such connections as to make it an interesting word to me. If a slave ran away and succeeded in getting clear, or if a slave killed his master, set fire to a barn, or did any thing very wrong in the mind of a slaveholder, it was spoken of as the fruit of *abolition*. Hearing the word in this connection very often, I set about learning what it meant. The dictionary afforded me little or no help. I found it was "the act of abolishing," but then I did not know what was to be abolished. Here I was perplexed. I did not dare to ask any one about its meaning, for I was satisfied that it was something they wanted me to know very little about. After a patient waiting, I got one of our city papers, containing an account of the number of petitions from the north, praying for the abolition of slavery in the District of Columbia, and of the slave trade between the States. From this time I understood the words *abolition* and *abolitionist,* and always drew near when that word was spoken, expecting to hear something of importance to myself and fellow-slaves. The light broke in upon me by degrees. I went one day down on the wharf of Mr. Waters; and seeing two Irishmen unloading a scow of stone, I went, unasked, and helped them. When we had finished, one of them came to me and asked me if I were a slave. I told him I was.

He asked, "Are ye a slave for life?" I told him that I was. The good Irishman seemed to be deeply affected by the statement. He said to the other that it was a pity so fine a little fellow as myself should be a slave for life. He said it was a shame to hold me. They both advised me to run away to the north; that I should find friends there, and that I should be free. I pretended not to be interested in what they said, and treated them as if I did not understand them; for I feared they might be treacherous. White men have been known to encourage slaves to escape, and then, to get the reward, catch them and return them to their masters. I was afraid that these seemingly good men might use me so; but I nevertheless remembered their advice, and from that time I resolved to run away. I looked forward to a time at which it would be safe for me to escape. I was too young to think of doing so immediately; besides, I wished to learn how to write, as I might have occasion to write my own pass. I consoled myself with the hope that I should one day find a good chance. Meanwhile, I would learn to write.

The idea as to how I might learn to write was suggested to me by being in Durgin and Bailey's ship-yard, and frequently seeing the ship carpenters, after hewing, and getting a piece of timber ready for use, write on the timber the name of that part of the ship for which it was intended. When a piece of timber was intended for the larboard side, it would be marked thus—"L." When a piece was for the starboard side, it would be marked thus—"S." A piece for the larboard side forward, would be marked thus—"L. F." When a piece was for starboard side forward, it would be marked thus—"S. F." For larboard aft, it would be marked thus—"L. A." For starboard aft, it would be marked thus—"S. A." I soon learned the names of these letters, and for what they were intended when placed upon a piece of timber in the ship-yard. I immediately commenced copying them, and in a short time was able to make the four letters named. After that, when I met with any boy who I knew could write, I would tell him I could write as well as he. The next word would be, "I don't believe you. Let me see you try it." I would then make the letters which I had been so fortunate as to learn, and ask him to beat that. In this way I got a good many lessons in writing, which it is quite possible I should never have gotten in any other way. During this time, my copy-book was the board fence, brick wall, and pavement; my pen and ink was a lump of chalk. With these, I learned mainly how to write. I then commenced and continued copying the Italics in Webster's Spelling Book, until I could make them all without looking on the book. By this time, my little Master Thomas had gone to school, and learned how to write, and had written over a number of copy-books. These had been brought home, and shown to some of our near neighbors, and then laid aside. My mistress used to go to class meeting at the Wilk Street meetinghouse every Monday afternoon, and leave me to take care of the house. When left thus, I used to spend the time in writing in the spaces left in master Thomas's copy-book, copying what he had written. I continued to do this until I could write a hand very similar to that of Master Thomas. Thus, after a long, tedious effort for years, I finally succeeded in learning how to write.

Analyzing Rhetorical Choices

1. Douglass's essay is written in a style characteristic of a great many works by highly literate authors in the nineteenth century. How would you describe that style? What makes it easy or challenging to read? How effective is it in terms of the way it represents the ethos of Douglass?

2. Douglass often adopts a strategy known as antithesis, in which he places two terms close together within a sentence or paragraph for the sake of creating a contrast. Select at least four instances of antithesis, and offer your own paraphrase of what he is saying. In a short paragraph, comment on the rhetorical effectiveness of this device.

3. Douglass writes, "I am strongly tempted to give the names of two or three of those little boys, as a testimonial of the gratitude and affections I bear them; but prudence forbids;—not that it would injure me, but it might embarrass them; for it is almost an unpardonable offence to teach slaves to read in this Christian country." Offer a critique of this sentence in terms of its structure and tone.

Writing About Issues and Contexts

1. How is it possible that "Slavery proved as injurious to [his mistress] as it did to [Douglass]"? (Consider how this is similar to the observations made by Orwell in "Shooting an Elephant" in Chapter 2.) What does this statement tell us about Douglass's view of human nature?

2. How does Douglass support his contention that "education and slavery were incompatible with each other"?

3. Compare Douglass's essay with the following essay by Kenneth M. Stampp, in which Stampp describes the process by which slaves are made "to stand in fear." How might Douglass's statement about education and slavery being incompatible apply to Stampp's essay?

4. It might be said that Douglass manipulates many of the people around him to learn how to read. Is this manipulation positive? Is it justified?

Kenneth M. Stampp (1912–) was born in Milwaukee, Wisconsin, and is the author of many noted works in history, including And the War Came *(1950),* The Peculiar Institution: Slavery in the Ante-Bellum South *(1956), and* The Causes of the Civil War *(1959). He is professor emeritus at the University of California at Berkeley, and has taught at Oxford University and the University of Munich. A recipient of many awards including two Guggenheim Fellowships, Stampp earned his Ph.D. from the University of Wisconsin in 1942. This essay comes from* The Peculiar Institution.

Kenneth M. Stampp

To Make Them Stand in Fear

A wise master did not take seriously the belief that Negroes were natural-born slaves. He knew better. He knew that Negroes freshly imported from Africa had to be broken to bondage; that each succeeding generation had to be carefully trained. This was no easy task, for the bondsman rarely submitted willingly. Moreover, he rarely submitted completely. In most cases there was no end to the need for control—at least not until old age reduced the slave to a condition of helplessness.

Masters revealed the qualities they sought to develop in slaves when they singled out certain ones for special commendation. A small Mississippi planter mourned the death of his "faithful and dearly beloved servant" Jack: "Since I have owned him he has been true to me in all respects. He was an obedient trusty servant. . . . I never knew him to steal nor lie and he ever set a moral and industrious example to those around him. . . . I shall ever cherish his memory." A Louisiana sugar planter lost a "very valuable Boy" through an accident: "His life was a very great one. I have always found him willing and obedient and never knew him to fail to do anything he was put to do." These were "ideal" slaves, the models slaveholders had in mind as they trained and governed their workers.

How might this ideal be approached? The first step, advised those who wrote discourses on the management of slaves, was to establish and maintain strict discipline. An Arkansas master suggested the adoption of the "Army Regulations as to the discipline in Forts." "They must obey at all times, and under all circumstances, cheerfully and with alacrity," affirmed a Virginia slaveholder. "It greatly impairs the happiness of a negro, to be allowed to cultivate an insubordinate temper. Unconditional submission is the only footing on which slavery should be placed. It is precisely similar to the attitude of a minor to his parent, or a soldier to his general." A South Carolinian limned a perfect relationship between a slave and his master: "that the slave should know that his master is to govern absolutely, and he is to obey implicitly. That he is never for a moment to exercise either his will or judgment in opposition to a positive order."

The second step was to implant in the bondsmen themselves a consciousness of personal inferiority. They had "to know and keep their places," to "feel the difference between master and slave," to understand that bondage was their natural status. They had to feel that African ancestry tainted them, that their color was a badge of degradation. In the country they were to show respect for even their master's nonslaveholding neighbors; in the towns they were to give way on the streets to the most wretched white man. The line between the races must never be crossed, for familiarity caused slaves to forget their lowly station and to become "impudent."

5   Frederick Douglass explained that a slave might commit the offense of impudence in various ways: "in the tone of an answer; in answering at all; in not answering; in the expression of countenance; in the motion of the head; in the gait, manner and bearing of the slave." Any of these acts, in some subtle way, might indicate the absence of proper subordination. "In a well regulated community," wrote a Texan, "a negro takes off his hat in addressing a white man. . . . Where this is not enforced, we may always look for impudent and rebellious negroes."

The third step in the training of slaves was to awe them with a sense of their master's enormous power. The only principle upon which slavery could be maintained, reported a group of Charlestonians, was the "principle of fear." In his defense of slavery James H. Hammond admitted that this, unfortunately, was true but put the responsibility upon the abolitionists. Antislavery agitation had forced masters to strengthen their authority: "We have to rely more and more on the power of fear. . . . We are determined to continue masters, and to do so we have to draw the reign tighter and tighter day by day to be assured that we hold them in complete check." A North Carolina mistress, after subduing a troublesome domestic, realized that it was essential "to make them stand in fear"!

In this the slaveholders had considerable success. Frederick Douglass believed that most slaves stood "in awe" of white men; few could free themselves altogether from the notion that their masters were "invested with a sort of sacredness." Olmsted saw a small white girl stop a slave on the road and boldly order him to return to his plantation. The slave fearfully obeyed her command. A visitor in Mississippi claimed that a master, armed only with a whip or cane, could throw himself among a score of bondsmen and cause them to "flee with terror." He accomplished this by the "peculiar tone of authority" with which he spoke. "Fear, awe, and obedience . . . are interwoven into the very nature of the slave."

The fourth step was to persuade the bondsmen to take an interest in the master's enterprise and to accept his standards of good conduct. A South Carolina planter explained: "The master should make it his business to show his slaves, that the advancement of his individual interest, is at the same time an advancement of theirs. Once they feel this, it will require but little compulsion to make them act as it becomes them." Though slaveholders induced only a few chattels to respond to this appeal, these few were useful examples for others.

The final step was to impress Negroes with their helplessness, to create in them "a habit of perfect dependence" upon their masters. Many believed it dangerous to train slaves to be skilled artisans in the towns, because they tended to become self-reliant. Some thought it equally dangerous to hire them to factory owners. In the Richmond tobacco factories they were alarmingly independent and "insolvent." A Virginian was dismayed to find that his bondsmen, while working at an iron furnace, "got a habit of roaming about and *taking care of themselves.*" Permitting them to hire their own time produced even worse results. "No higher evidence can be furnished of its baneful effects," wrote a Charlestonian, "than the unwillingness it produces in the slave, to return to the regular life and domestic control of the master."

10 A spirit of independence was less likely to develop among slaves kept on the land, where most of them became accustomed to having their master provide their basic needs, and where they might be taught that they were unfit to look out for themselves. Slaves then directed their energies to the attainment of mere "temporary ease and enjoyment." "Their masters," Olmsted believed, "calculated on it in them—do not wish to cure it—and by constant practice encourage it."

Here, then, was the way to produce the perfect slave: accustom him to rigid discipline, demand from him unconditional submission, impress upon him his innate inferiority, develop in him a paralyzing fear of white men, train him to adopt the master's code of good be-havior, and instill in him a sense of complete dependence. This, at least, was the goal.

But the goal was seldom reached. Every master knew that the av-erage slave was only an imperfect copy of the model. He knew that some bondsmen yielded only to superior power—and yielded reluc-tantly. This complicated his problem of control.

Analyzing Rhetorical Choices

1. How do you interpret the tone of Stampp's opening, "A wise mas-ter did not take seriously the belief that Negroes were natural-born slaves. He knew better."
2. Stampp thoroughly describes a process. What is his point in doing so? How does his objective, factual tone reinforce the overall in-tention?
3. Stampp follows almost an identical format paragraph by para-graph. Describe the format, and comment on the overall rhetori-cal effectiveness of this kind of structural repetition.

Writing About Issues and Contexts

1. Compare this essay to Frederick Douglass's "Learning to Read and Write." How does the Douglass essay reinforce Stampp's analysis?
2. Why is the psychological control of slaves so significant to the process Stampp enumerates? How is keeping slaves on the planta-tion equally significant? Why?
3. Is the kind of training that Stampp details a kind of brainwashing? Is it similar to the kind of training that military recruits or politi-cal converts experience? Describe the similarities and differences between teaching someone how to be "a slave" and teaching some-one how to be a soldier, a patriot, or even an extremely obedient child.

Fan Shen (1955–) was a Red Guard, a farm hand, a Barefoot Doctor, and an electrician before attending college after studying high school courses on his own. He received his bachelor's from Lanzhou University in China, master's from University of Nebraska-Lincoln, and Ph.D. from Marquette University. A bilingual writer, he has published numerous articles in both English and Chinese, and his latest work, "Gang of One: Memoirs of a Red Guard," was named "Editor's Choice for 2004" by Booklist. Fan Shen now teaches English as a professor at Rochester Community and Technical College in Minnesota.

Fan Shen

The Classroom and the Wider Culture: Identity as a Key to Learning English Composition

One day in June 1975, when I walked into the aircraft factory where I was working as an electrician, I saw many large-letter posters on the walls and many people parading around the workshops shouting slogans like "Down with the word 'I'!" and "Trust in masses and the Party!" I then remembered that a new political campaign called "Against Individualism" was scheduled to begin that day. Ten years later, I got back my first English composition paper at the University of Nebraska-Lincoln. The professor's first comments were: "Why did you always use 'we' instead of 'I'?" and "Your paper would be stronger if you eliminated some sentences in the passive voice." The clashes between my Chinese background and the requirements of English composition had begun. At the center of this mental struggle, which has lasted several years and is still not completely over, is the prolonged, uphill battle to recapture "myself."

In this paper I will try to describe and explore this experience of reconciling my Chinese identity with an English identity dictated by the rules of English composition. I want to show how my cultural background shaped—and shapes—my approaches to my writing in English and how writing in English redefined—and redefines—my *ideological* and *logical* identities. By "ideological identity" I mean the system of values that I acquired (consciously and unconsciously) from my social and cultural background. And by "logical identity" I mean the natural (or Oriental) way I organize and express my thoughts in writing. Both had to be modified or redefined in learning English composition. Becoming aware of the process of redefinition of these different identities is a mode of learning that has helped me in my efforts to write in English, and, I hope, will be of help to teachers of English composition in this country. In presenting my case for this view, I will use examples from both my composition courses and literature courses, for I believe that writing papers for both kinds of courses contributed to the development of my "English identity." Although what I will describe is based on personal experience, many Chinese students whom I talked to said that they had had the same or similar experiences in their initial stages of learning to write in English.

Identity of the Self: Ideological and Cultural

Starting with the first English paper I wrote, I found that learning to compose in English is not an isolated classroom activity, but a social and cultural experience. The rules of English composition encapsulate values that are absent in, or sometimes contradictory to, the values of other societies (in my case, China). Therefore, learning the rules of English composition is, to a certain extent, learning the values of Anglo-American society. In writing classes in the United States I found that I had to reprogram my mind, to redefine some of the basic concepts and values that I had about myself, about society, and about the universe, values that had been imprinted and reinforced in my mind by my cultural background, and that had been part of me all my life.

Rule number one in English composition is: Be yourself. (More than one composition instructor has told me, "Just write what *you* think.") The values behind this rule, it seems to me, are based on the principle of protecting and promoting individuality (and private property) in this country. The instruction was probably crystal clear to students raised on these values, but, as a guideline of composition, it was not very clear or useful to me when I first heard it. First of all, the image or meaning that I attached to the word "I" or "myself" was, as I found out, different from that of my English teacher. In China, "I" is always subordinated to "We"—be it the working class, the Party, the country, or some other collective body. Both political pressure and literary tradition require that "I" be somewhat hidden or buried in writings and speeches; presenting the "self" too obviously would give people the impression of being disrespectful of the Communist Party in political writings and boastful in scholarly writings. The word "I" has often been identified with another "bad" word, "individualism," which has become a synonym for selfishness in China. For a long time the words "self" and "individualism" have had negative connotations in my mind, and the negative force of the words naturally extended to the field of literary studies. As a result, even if I had brilliant ideas, the "I" in my papers always had to show some modesty by not competing with or trying to stand above the names of ancient and modern authoritative figures. Appealing to Mao or other Marxist authorities became the required way (as well as the most "forceful" or "persuasive" way) to prove one's point in written discourse. I remember that in China I had even committed what I can call "reversed plagiarism"—here, I suppose it would be called "forgery"—when I was in middle school: willfully attributing some of my thoughts to "experts" when I needed some arguments but could not find a suitable quotation from a literary or political "giant."

5   Now, in America, I had to learn to accept the words "I" and "self" as something glorious (as Whitman did), or at least something not to be ashamed of or embarrassed about. It was the first and probably biggest step I took into English composition and critical writing. Acting upon my professor's suggestion, I intentionally tried to show my "individuality" and to "glorify" "I" in my papers by using as many "I's" as possible—"I think," "I believe," "I see"—and deliberately cut out quotations from authorities. It was rather painful to hand in such "pompous" (I mean immodest) papers to my instructors. But to an extent it worked. After a while I became more comfortable with only "the shadow of myself." I felt more at ease to put down *my* thoughts without looking over my shoulder to worry about the attitudes of my teachers or the reactions of the Party secretaries, and to speak out as "bluntly" and "immodestly" as my American instructors demanded.

But writing many "I's" was only the beginning of the process of redefining myself. Speaking of redefining myself is, in an important sense, speaking of redefining the word "I." By such a redefinition I mean not only the change in how I envisioned myself, but also the change in how *I* perceived the world. The old "I" used to embody only one set of values, but now it had to embody multiple sets of values. To be truly "myself," which I knew was a key to my success in learning English composition, meant *not to be my Chinese self* at all.

That is to say, when I write in English I have to wrestle with and abandon (at least temporarily) the whole system of ideology which previously defined me in myself. I had to forget Marxist doctrines (even though I do not see myself as a Marxist by choice) and the Party lines imprinted in my mind and familiarize myself with a system of capitalist/bourgeois values. I had to put aside an ideology of collectivism and adopt the values of individualism. In composition as well as in literature classes, I had to make a fundamental adjustment: If I used to examine society and literary materials through the microscopes of Marxist dialectical materialism and historical materialism, I now had to learn to look through the microscopes the other way around, i.e., to learn to look at and understand the world from the point of view of "idealism." (I must add here that there are American professors who use a Marxist approach in their teaching.)

The word "idealism," which affects my view of both myself and the universe, is loaded with social connotations, and can serve as a good example of how redefining a key word can be a pivotal part of redefining my ideological identity as a whole.

To me, idealism is the philosophical foundation of the dictum of English composition: "Be yourself." In order to write good English, I knew that I had to be myself, which actually meant not to be my Chinese self. It meant that I had to create an English self and be *that* self. And to be that English self, I felt, I had to understand and accept idealism the way a Westerner does. That is to say, I had to accept the way a Westerner sees himself in relation to the universe and society. On the one hand, I knew a lot about idealism. But on the other hand, I knew nothing about it. I mean I knew a lot about idealism through the propaganda and objections of its opponent, Marxism, but I knew little about it from its own point of view. When I thought of the word "materialism"—which is a major part of Marxism and in China has repeatedly been "shown" to be the absolute truth—there were always positive connotations, and words like "right," "true," etc., flashed in my mind. On the other hand, the word "idealism" always came to me with the dark connotations that surround words like "absurd," "illogical," "wrong," etc. In China "idealism" is depicted as a ferocious and ridiculous enemy of Marxist philosophy. Idealism, as the simplified definition imprinted in my mind had it, is the view that the material world does not exist: that all that exists is the mind and its ideas. It is just the opposite of Marxist dialectical materialism which sees the mind as a product of the material world. It is not too difficult to see that idealism, with its idea that mind is of primary importance, provides a philosophical foundation for the Western emphasis on the value of individual human minds, and hence individual human beings. Therefore, my final acceptance of myself as of primary importance—an importance that overshadowed that of authority figures in English composition—was, I decided, dependent on an acceptance of idealism.

My struggle with idealism came mainly from my efforts to understand and to write about works such as Coleridge's *Biographia Literaria* and Emerson's "Over-Soul." For a long time I was frustrated and puzzled by the idealism expressed by Coleridge and Emerson—given their ideas, such as "I think, therefore I am" (Coleridge obviously borrowed from Descartes) and "the transparent eyeball" (Emerson's view of himself)—because in my mind, drenched as it was in dialectical materialism, there was always a little voice whispering in my ear "You are, therefore you think." I could not see how human consciousness, which is not material, could create apples and trees. My intellectual conscience refused to let me believe that the human mind is the primary world and the material world secondary. Finally, I had to imagine that I was looking at a world with my head upside down. When I imagined that I was in a new body (born with the head upside down) it was easier to forget biases imprinted in my subconsciousness about idealism, the mind, and my former self. Starting from scratch, the new inverted self—which I called my "English Self" and into which I have transformed myself—could understand and *accept* with ease, idealism as "the truth" and "himself" (i.e., my English Self) as the "creator" of the world.

10   Here is how I created my new "English Self." I played a "game" similar to ones played by mental therapists. First I made a list of (simplified) features about writing associated with my old identity (the Chinese Self), both ideological and logical, and then beside the first list I added a column of features about writing associated with my new identity (the English Self). After that I pictured myself getting out of my old identity, the timid, humble, modest Chinese "I," and creeping into my new identity (often in the form of a new skin or a mask), the confident, assertive, and aggressive English "I." The new "Self" helped me to remember and accept the different rules of Chinese and English composition and the values that underpin these rules. In a sense, creating an English Self is a way of reconciling my old cultural values with the new values required by English writing, without losing the former.

An interesting structural but not material parallel to my experiences in this regard has been well described by Min-zhan Lu in her important article, "From Silence to Words: Writing as Struggle" (*College English* 49 [April 1987]: 437–48). Min-zhan Lu talks about struggles between two selves, an open self and a secret self, and between two discourses, a mainstream Marxist discourse and a bourgeois discourse her parents wanted her to learn. But her struggle was different from mine. Her Chinese self was severely constrained and suppressed by mainstream cultural discourse, but never interfused with it. Her experiences, then, were not representative of those of the majority of the younger generation who, like me, were brought up on only one discourse. I came to English composition as a Chinese person, in the fullest sense of the term, with a Chinese identity already fully formed.

Identity of the Mind: Illogical and Alogical

In learning to write in English, besides wrestling with a different ideological system, I found that I had to wrestle with a logical system very different from the blueprint of logic at the back of my mind. By "logical system" I mean two things: the Chinese way of thinking I used to approach my theme or topic in written discourse, and the Chinese critical/logical way to develop a theme or topic. By English rules, the first is illogical, for it is the opposite of the English way of approaching a topic; the second is alogical (nonlogical), for it mainly uses mental pictures instead of words as a critical vehicle.

The Illogical Pattern

In English composition, an essential rule for the logical organization of a piece of writing is the use of a "topic sentence." In Chinese composition, "from surface to core" is an essential rule, a rule which means that one ought to reach a topic gradually and "systematically" instead of "abruptly."

The concept of a topic sentence, it seems to me, is symbolic of the values of a busy people in an industrialized society, rushing to get things done, hoping to attract and satisfy the busy reader very quickly. Thinking back, I realized that I did not fully understand the virtue of the concept until my life began to rush at the speed of everyone else's in this country. Chinese composition, on the other hand, seems to embody the values of a leisurely paced rural society whose inhabitants have the time to chew and taste a topic slowly. In Chinese composition, an introduction explaining how and why one chooses this topic is not only acceptable, but often regarded as necessary. It arouses the reader's interest in the topic little by little (and this is seen as a virtue of composition) and gives him/her a sense of refinement. The famous Robert B. Kaplan "noodles" contrasting a spiral Oriental thought process with a straight-line Western approach ("Cultural Thought Patterns in Inter-Cultural Education," *Readings on English as a Second Language*, Ed. Kenneth Croft, 2nd ed., Winthrop, 1980, 403–10) may be too simplistic to capture the preferred pattern of writing in English, but I think they still express some truth about Oriental writing. A Chinese writer often clears the surrounding bushes before attacking the real target. This bush-clearing pattern in Chinese writing goes back two thousand years to Kong Fuzi (Confucius). Before doing anything, Kong says in his *Luen Yu (Analects)*, one first needs to call things by their proper names (expressed by his phrase "Zheng Ming"). In other words, before touching one's main thesis, one should first state the "conditions" of composition: how, why, and when the piece is being composed. All of this will serve as a proper foundation on which to build the "house" of the piece. In the two thousand years after Kong, this principle of composition was gradually formalized (especially through the formal essays required by imperial examinations) and became known as "Ba Gu," or the eight-legged essay. The logic of Chinese composition, exemplified by the eight-legged essay, is like the peeling of an onion: Layer after layer is removed until the reader finally arrives at the central point, the core.

15   *Ba Gu* still influences modern Chinese writing. Carolyn Matalene has an excellent discussion of this logical (or illogical) structure and its influence on her Chinese students' efforts to write in English ("Contrastive Rhetoric: An American Writing Teacher in China," *College English 47* [November 1985]: 789–808). A recent Chinese textbook for composition lists six essential steps (factors) for writing a narrative essay, steps to be taken in this order: time, place, character, event, cause, and consequence (*Yuwen Jichu Zhishi Liushi Jiang [Sixty Lessons on the Basics of the Chinese Language]*, Ed. Beijing Research Institute of Education, Beijing Publishing House, 1981, 525–609). Most Chinese students (including me) are taught to follow this sequence in composition.

The straightforward approach to composition in English seemed to me, at first, illogical. One could not jump to the topic. One had to walk step by step to reach the topic. In several of my early papers I found that the Chinese approach—the bush-clearing approach—persisted, and I had considerable difficulty writing (and in fact understanding) topic sentences. In what I deemed to be topic sentences, I grudgingly gave out themes. Today, those papers look to me like Chinese papers with forced or false English openings. For example, in a narrative paper on a trip to New York, I wrote the forced/false topic sentence, "A trip to New York in winter is boring." In the next few paragraphs, I talked about the weather, the people who went with me, and so on, before I talked about what I learned from the trip. My real thesis was that one could always learn something even on a boring trip.

The Alogical Pattern

In learning English composition, I found that there was yet another cultural blueprint affecting my logical thinking. I found from my early papers that very often I was unconsciously under the influence of a Chinese critical approach called the creation of "yijing," which is totally non-Western. The direct translation of the word "yijing" is: yi, "mind or consciousness," and jing, "environment." An ancient approach which has existed in China for many centuries and is still the subject of much discussion, yijing is a complicated concept that defies a universal definition. But most critics in China nowadays seem to agree on one point, that yijing is the critical approach that separates Chinese literature and criticism from Western literature and criticism. Roughly speaking, yijing is the process of creating a pictorial environment while reading a piece of literature. Many critics in China believe that yijing is a creative process of inducing oneself, while reading a piece of literature or looking at a piece of art, to create mental pictures, in order to reach a unity of nature, the author, and the reader. Therefore, it is by its very nature both creative and critical. According to the theory, this nonverbal, pictorial process leads directly to a higher ground of beauty and morality. Almost all critics in China agree that yijing is not a process of logical thinking—it is not a process of moving from the premises of an argument to its conclusion, which is the foundation of Western criticism. According to yijing, the process of criticizing a piece of art or literary work has to involve the process of creation on the reader's part. In yijing, verbal thoughts and pictorial thoughts are one. Thinking is conducted largely in pictures and then "transcribed" into words. (Ezra Pound once tried to capture the creative aspect of yijing in poems such as "In a Station of the Metro." He also tried to capture the critical aspect of it in his theory of imagism and vorticism, even though he did not know the term "yijing.") One characteristic of the yijing approach to criticism, therefore, is that it often includes a description of the created mental pictures on the part of the reader/critic and his/her mental attempt to bridge (unite) the literary work, the pictures, with ultimate beauty and peace.

In looking back at my critical papers for various classes, I discovered that I unconsciously used the approach of yijing, especially in some of my earlier papers when I seemed not yet to have been in the grip of Western logical critical approaches. I wrote, for instance, an essay entitled "Wordsworth's Sound and Imagination: The Snowdon Episode." In the major part of the essay I described the pictures that flashed in my mind while I was reading passages in Wordsworth's long poem, *The Prelude*.

> I saw three climbers (myself among them) winding up the mountain in silence "at the dead of night," absorbed in their "private thoughts." The sky was full of blocks of clouds of different colors, freely changing their shapes, like oily pigments disturbed in a bucket of water. All of a sudden, the moonlight broke the darkness "like a flash," lighting up the mountain tops. Under the "naked moon," the band saw a vast sea of mist and vapor, a silent ocean. Then the silence was abruptly broken, and we heard the "roaring of waters, torrents, streams/Innumerable, roaring with one voice" from a "blue chasm," a fracture in the vapor of the sea. It was a joyful revelation of divine truth to the human mind: the bright, "naked" moon sheds the light of "higher reasons" and "spiritual love" upon us; the vast ocean of mist looked like a thin curtain through which we vaguely saw the infinity of nature beyond; and the sounds of roaring waters coming out of the chasm of vapor cast us into the boundless spring of imagination from the depth of the human heart. Evoked by the divine light from above, the human spring of imagination is joined by the natural spring and becomes a sustaining source of energy, feeding "upon infinity" while transcending infinity at the same time. . . .

Here I was describing my own experience more than Wordsworth's. The picture described by the poet is taken over and developed by the reader. The imagination of the author and the imagination of the reader are thus joined together. There was no "because" or "therefore" in the paper. There was little *logic*. And I thought it was (and it is) criticism. This seems to me a typical (but simplified) example of the yijing approach. (Incidentally, the instructor, a kind professor, found the paper interesting, though a bit "strange.")

I am not saying that such a pattern of "alogical" thinking is wrong—in fact some English instructors find it interesting and acceptable—but it is very non-Western. Since I was in this country to learn the English language and English literature, I had to abandon Chinese "pictorial logic," and to learn Western "verbal logic."

If I Had to Start Again

20   The change is profound: Through my understanding of new meanings of words like "individualism," "idealism," and "I," I began to accept the underlying concepts and values of American writing, and by learning to use "topic sentences" I began to accept a new logic. Thus, when I write papers in English, I am able to obey all the general rules of English composition. In doing this I feel that I am writing through, with, and because of a new identity. I welcome the change, for it has added a new dimension to me and to my view of the world. I am not saying that I have entirely lost my Chinese identity. In fact I feel that I will never lose it. Any time I write in Chinese, I resume my old identity, and obey the rules of Chinese composition such as "Make the 'I' modest," and "Beat around the bush before attacking the central topic." It is necessary for me to have such a Chinese identity in order to write authentic Chinese. (I have seen people who, after learning to write in English, use English logic and sentence patterning to write Chinese. They produce very awkward Chinese texts.) But when I write in English, I imagine myself slipping into a new "skin," and I let the "I" behave much more aggressively and knock the topic right on the head. Being conscious of these different identities has helped me to reconcile different systems of values and logic, and has played a pivotal role in my learning to compose in English.

Looking back, I realize that the process of learning to write in English is in fact a process of creating and defining a new identity and balancing it with the old identity. The process of learning English composition would have been easier if I had realized this earlier and consciously sought to compare the two different identities required by the two writing systems from two different cultures. It is fine and perhaps even necessary for American composition teachers to teach about topic sentences, paragraphs, the use of punctuation, documentation, and so on, but can anyone design exercises sensitive to the ideological and logical differences that students like me experience—and design them so they can be introduced at an early stage of an English composition class? As I pointed out earlier, the traditional advice "Just be yourself" is not clear and helpful to students from Korea, China, Vietnam, or India. From "Be yourself" we are likely to hear either "Forget your cultural habit of writing" or "Write as you would write in your own language." But neither of the two is what the instructor meant or what we want to do. It would be helpful if he or she pointed out the different cultural/ideological connotations of the word "I," the connotations that exist in a group-centered culture and an individual-centered culture. To sharpen the contrast, it might be useful to design papers on topics like "The Individual vs. The Group: China vs. America" or "Different 'I's' in Different Cultures."

Carolyn Matalene mentioned in her article (789) an incident concerning American businessmen who presented their Chinese hosts with gifts of cheddar cheese, not knowing that the Chinese generally do not like cheese. Liking cheddar cheese may not be essential to writing English prose, but being truly accustomed to the social norms that stand behind ideas such as the English "I" and the logical pattern of English composition—call it "compositional cheddar cheese"—is essential to writing in English. Matalene does not provide an "elixir" to help her Chinese students like English "compositional cheese," but rather recommends, as do I, that composition teachers not be afraid to give foreign students English "cheese," but to make sure to hand it out slowly, sympathetically, and fully realizing that it tastes very peculiar in the mouths of those used to a very different cuisine.

Analyzing Rhetorical Choices

1. How does Shen create a rhetorical ethos through his writing that speaks with authority and connects with the reader?

2. Shen cites many writers and texts in his effort to describe the process of his becoming literate in English. Do these sources contribute to the persuasiveness of his account? How do you assess their effectiveness?

3. Given what Shen writes about "ideological identity," is this essay composed more from a Chinese or from an American "identity"? Explain your response and what the difference is between the two in terms of rhetorical choices made by the writer. In responding, explain why you think he includes so much about Chinese ways of composing.

Writing About Issues and Contexts

1. Shen believes that "Rule number one in English composition is: Be yourself." Do you believe that this is the case? Why or why not? What assumptions lie behind Shen's statement? Is this a helpful concept for American-born students? Why or why not?

2. What do you think of Shen's view of the topic sentence? How does his discussion explain his cultural perspectives? How might it help you articulate yours?

3. Do you agree that "the process of learning to write in English is in fact a process of creating and defining a new identity and balancing it with the old identity"? Is this as true for native speakers as it is for nonnative speakers of English?

*One of eight children, **Malcolm Little** (1925–1965) was born in Omaha, Nebraska. Driven out of Nebraska by the Ku Klux Klan because of preaching a form of black nationalism, Malcolm's father moved the family to Michigan; there, when Malcolm was six, the Reverend Earl Little was murdered. Malcolm ultimately ended up in foster homes and, though he did well in school, was discouraged from pursuing his dream of becoming a lawyer. He ended up in prison for burglary, and as an inmate engaged in an intensive self-education program. Greatly influenced by the writings of Elijah Muhammad, founder of the group now known as the Nation of Islam, Malcolm X became a well-known member, an adherent of Islam, and a disciple of its leader. In 1963, he left the group, then known as the Black Muslims, and founded a competing organization. In 1964 he narrated his life story to Alex Haley (author of* Roots) *and that account was published in 1965 as* The Autobiography of Malcolm X, *an excerpt of which follows here. Malcolm X was assassinated in 1965 by three men, reputedly followers of the Black Muslim leader, Elijah Muhammad.*

Malcolm X

My First Conk

Shorty soon decided that my hair was finally long enough to be conked. He had promised to school me in how to beat the barber shops' three- and four-dollar price by making up congolene, and then conking ourselves.

I took the little list of ingredients he had printed out for me, and went to a grocery store, where I got a can of Red Devil lye, two eggs, and two medium-sized white potatoes. Then at a drugstore near the poolroom, I asked for a large jar of vaseline, a large bar of soap, a large-toothed comb and a fine-toothed comb, one of those rubber hoses with a metal spray-head, a rubber apron, and a pair of gloves.

"Going to lay on that first conk?" the drugstore man asked me. I proudly told him, grinning, "Right!"

Shorty paid six dollars a week for a room in his cousin's shabby apartment. His cousin wasn't at home. "It's like the pad's mine, he spends so much time with his woman," Shorty said. "Now, you watch me—"

5   He peeled the potatoes and thin-sliced them into a quart-sized Mason fruit jar, then started stirring them with a wooden spoon as he gradually poured in a little over half the can of lye. "Never use a metal spoon; the lye will turn it black," he told me.

A jelly-like, starchy-looking glop resulted from the lye and potatoes, and Shorty broke in the two eggs, stirring real fast—his own conk and dark face bent down close. The congolene turned pale-yellowish. "Feel the jar," Shorty said. I cupped my hand against the outside, and snatched it away. "Damn right, it's hot, that's the lye," he said. "So you know it's going to burn when I comb it in—it burns bad. But the longer you can stand it, the straighter the hair."

He made me sit down, and he tied the string of the new rubber apron tightly around my neck, and combed up my bush of hair. Then, from the big vaseline jar, he took a handful and massaged it hard all through my hair and into the scalp. He also thickly vaselined my neck, ears and forehead. "When I get to washing out your head, be sure to tell me anywhere you feel any little stinging," Shorty warned me, washing his hands, then pulling on the rubber gloves, and tying on his own rubber apron. "You always got to remember that any congolene left in burns a sore into your head."

The congolene just felt warm when Shorty started combing it in. But then my head caught fire.

I gritted my teeth and tried to pull the sides of the kitchen table together. The comb felt as if it was raking my skin off.

10   My eyes watered, my nose was running. I couldn't stand it any longer; I bolted to the washbasin. I was cursing Shorty with every name I could think of when he got the spray going and started soap lathering my head.

He lathered and spray-rinsed, lathered and spray-rinsed, maybe ten or twelve times, each time gradually closing the hot-water faucet, until the rinse was cold, and that helped some.

"You feel any stinging spots?"

"No," I managed to say. My knees were trembling.

"Sit back down, then. I think we got it all out okay."

15   The flame came back as Shorty, with a thick towel, started drying my head, rubbing hard. *Easy, man, easy!* " I kept shouting.

"The first time's always worst. You get used to it better before long. You took it real good, homeboy. You got a good conk."

When Shorty let me stand up and see in the mirror, my hair hung down in limp, damp strings. My scalp still flamed, but not as badly; I could bear it. He draped the towel around my shoulders, over my rubber apron, and began again vaselining my hair.

I could feel him combing, straight back, first the big comb, then the fine-tooth one.

Then, he was using a razor, very delicately, on the back of my neck. Then, finally, shaping the sideburns.

20   My first view in the mirror blotted out the hurting. I'd seen some pretty conks, but when it's the first time, on your *own* head, the transformation, after the lifetime of kinks, is staggering.

The mirror reflected Shorty behind me. We both were grinning and sweating. And on top of my head was this thick, smooth sheen of shining red hair—real red—as straight as any white man's.

How ridiculous I was! Stupid enough to stand there simply lost in admiration of my hair now looking "white," reflected in the mirror in Shorty's room. I vowed that I'd never again be without a conk, and I never was for many years.

This was my first really big step toward self-degradation: when I endured all of that pain, literally burning my flesh to have it look like a white man's hair. I had joined that multitude of Negro men and women in America who are brainwashed into believing that the black people are "inferior"—and white people "superior"—that they will even violate and mutilate their God-created bodies to try to look "pretty" by white standards.

Look around today, in every small town and big city, from two-bit catfish and soda-pop joints into the "integrated" lobby of the Waldorf-Astoria, and you'll see conks on black men. And you'll see black women wearing these green and pink and purple and red and platinum-blonde wigs. They're all more ridiculous than a slapstick comedy. It makes you wonder if the Negro has completely lost his sense of identity, lost touch with himself.

25   You'll see the conk worn by many, many so-called "upper class" Negroes, and, as much as I hate to say it about them, on all too many Negro entertainers. One of the reasons that I've especially admired some of them, like Lionel Hampton and Sidney Poitier, among others, is that they have kept their natural hair and fought to the top. I admire any Negro man who has never had himself conked, or who has had the sense to get rid of it—as I finally did.

I don't know which kind of self-defacing conk is the greater shame—the one you'll see on the heads of the black so-called "middle class" and "upper class," who ought to know better, or the one you'll see on the heads of the poorest, most downtrodden, ignorant black men. I mean the legal-minimum-wage ghetto-dwelling kind of Negro, as I was when I got my first one. It's generally among these poor fools that you'll see a black kerchief over the man's head, like Aunt Jemima; he's trying to make his conk last longer, between trips to the barbershop. Only for special occasions is this kerchief-protected conk exposed—to show off how "sharp" and "hip" its owner is. The ironic thing is that I have never heard any woman, white or black, express any admiration for a conk. Of course, any white woman with a black man isn't thinking about his hair. But I don't see how on earth a black woman with any race pride could walk down the street with any black man wearing a conk—the emblem of his shame that he is black.

To my own shame, when I say all of this, I'm talking first of all about myself—because you can't show me any Negro who ever conked more faithfully than I did. I'm speaking from personal experience when I say of any black man who conks today, or any white-wigged black woman, that if they gave the brains in their heads just half as much attention as they do their hair, they would be a thousand times better off.

Analyzing Rhetorical Choices

1. Describe the process for getting a conk. In what ways does this process describe another process that has little to do with straightening hair? How can the "simple" process of hair straightening convey this larger meaning?

2. Why do you think Malcolm X informs the reader that "you can't show me any Negro who ever conked more faithfully than I did"? How does this statement influence the reader's perception of Malcolm X in terms of his overall argument about conking?

3. Comment on Malcolm X's use of irony and understatement. What effects do these have on you as a reader?

4. What impression of Malcolm X is conveyed by this excerpt? What aspects of his language and story evoke your sense of the man?

Writing About Issues and Contexts

1. When Malcolm X refers to the conk as a "self-defacing" shame, he evokes a strong history of internalized oppression on the part of African Americans. What does he mean?

2. When he writes of "the black so-called 'middle class' and 'upper class,'" why does Malcolm X use the term *so-called* and put the

words *middle class* and *upper class* in quotation marks? Why did Malcolm X view the African American middle and upper classes as "so-called" classes? Explain ways in which this situation may or may not have changed since Malcolm X wrote these words.

3. Malcolm X describes the process of conking, but he does so in the form of a story rather than as a set of instructions. Why do you think he chooses this method of deploying this mode?

4. What implicit statement does Malcolm X make when he writes: "And on top of my head was this thick, smooth sheen of shining red hair—real red—as straight as any white man's"?

Born in England, the daughter of a baron and baroness, **Jessica Mitford**
*(1917–1996) rebelled against her rich and conservative parents, coming
to the United States at the age of 21 and living out the rest of her life in
this country, at first working in sales and as a bartender. She did not begin her writing career until she was 38 years old. Called "Queen of the
Muckrackers" by* Time *magazine, Mitford's notoriety as an investigative
reporter was solidified with the book from which the following excerpt is
taken. Titled* The American Way of Death *(1963), it offered a witty and
brilliant attack on the funeral industry in the United States. The book
horrified its readers—and angered those in the funeral industry. Mitford's
other books include an analysis of prisons,* Kind and Usual Punishment
(1973), and a critique of the business of giving birth, The American Way
of Birth *(1992).*

Jessica Mitford

The American Way of Death

Embalming is indeed a most extraordinary procedure, and one
must wonder at the docility of Americans who each year pay hundreds of millions of dollars for its perpetuation, blissfully ignorant of
what it is all about, what is done, how it is done. Not one in ten thousand has any idea of what actually takes place. Books on the subject
are extremely hard to come by. They are not to be found in most libraries or bookshops.

In an era when huge television audiences watch surgical operations in the comfort of their living rooms, when, thanks to the ani-
mated cartoon, the geography of the digestive system has become familiar territory even to the nursery school set, in a land where the
satisfaction of curiosity about almost all matters is a national pastime,
the secrecy surrounding embalming can, surely, hardly be attributed
to the inherent gruesomeness of the subject. Custom in this regard has
within this century suffered a complete reversal. In the early days of
American embalming, when it was performed in the home of the deceased, it was almost mandatory for some relative to stay by the embalmer's side and witness the procedure. Today, family members who
might wish to be in attendance would certainly be dissuaded by the

funeral director. All others, except apprentices, are excluded by law from the preparation room.

A close look at what does actually take place may explain in large measure the undertaker's intractable reticence concerning a procedure that has become his major *raison d'être*. Is it possible he fears that public information about embalming might lead patrons to wonder if they really want this service? If the funeral men are loath to discuss the subject outside the trade, the reader may, understandably, be equally loath to go on reading at this point. For those who have the stomach for it, let us part the formaldehyde curtain. . . .

The body is first laid out in the undertaker's morgue—or rather, Mr. Jones is reposing in the preparation room—to be readied to bid the world farewell.

5   The preparation room in any of the better funeral establishments has the tiled and sterile look of a surgery, and indeed the embalmer-restorative artist who does his chores there is beginning to adopt the term "dermasurgeon" (appropriately corrupted by some mortician-writers as "demisurgeon") to describe his calling. His equipment, consisting of scalpels, scissors, augers, forceps, clamps, needles, pumps, tubes, bowls, and basin, is crudely imitative of the surgeon's, as is his technique, acquired in a nine- or twelve-month post-high-school course in an embalming school. He is supplied by an advanced chemical industry with a bewildering array of fluids, sprays, pastes, oils, powders, creams, to fix or soften tissue, shrink or distend it as needed, dry it here, restore the moisture there. There are cosmetics, waxes, and paints to fill and cover features, even plaster of Paris to replace entire limbs. There are ingenious aids to prop and stabilize the cadaver: a Vari-Pose Head Rest, the Edwards Arm and Hand Positioner, the Repose Block (to support the shoulders during the embalming), and the Throop Foot Positioner, which resembles an old-fashioned stocks.

Mr. John H. Eckles, president of the Eckles College of Mortuary Science, thus describes the first part of the embalming procedure: "In the hands of a skilled practitioner, this work may be done in a comparatively short time and without mutilating the body other than by slight incision—so slight that it scarcely would cause serious inconvenience if made upon a living person. It is necessary to remove the blood, and doing this not only helps in the disinfecting, but removes the principal cause of disfigurements due to discoloration."

Another textbook discusses the all-important time element: "The earlier this is done, the better, for every hour that elapses between death and embalming will add to the problems and complications encountered. . . . ."Just how soon should one get going on the embalming? The author tells us, "On the basis of such scanty information made available to this profession through its rudimentary and haphazard system of technical research, we must conclude that the best results are to be obtained if the subject is embalmed before life is completely extinct—that is, before cellular death has occurred. In the average case, this would mean within an hour after somatic death." For those who feel that there is something a little rudimentary, not to say haphazard, about this advice, a comforting thought is offered by another writer. Speaking of fears entertained in early days of premature burial, he points out, "One of the effects of embalming by chemical injection, however, has been to dispel fears of live burial." How true; once the blood is removed, chances of live burial are indeed remote.

To return to Mr. Jones, the blood is drained out through the veins and replaced by embalming fluid pumped in through the arteries. As noted in *The Principles and Practices of Embalming,* "every operator has a favorite injection and drainage point—a fact which becomes a handicap only if he fails or refuses to forsake his favorites when conditions demand it." Typical favorites are the carotid artery, femoral artery, jugular vein, subclavian vein. There are various choices of embalming fluid. If Flextone is used, it will produce a "mild, flexible rigidity. The skin retains a velvety softness, the tissues are rubbery and pliable. Ideal for women and children." It may be blended with B. and G. Products Company's Lyf-Lyk tint, which is guaranteed to reproduce "nature's own skin texture . . . the velvety appearance of living tissue." Suntone comes in three separate tints: Suntan; Special Cosmetic Tint, a pink shade "especially indicated for young female subjects"; and Regular Cosmetic Tint, moderately pink.

About three to six gallons of a dyed and perfumed solution of formaldehyde, glycerin, borax, phenol, alcohol, and water is soon circulating through Mr. Jones, whose mouth has been sewn together with a "needle directed upward between the upper lip and gum and brought out through the left nostril," with the corners raised slightly "for a more pleasant expression." If he should be buck-toothed, his teeth are cleaned with Bon Ami and coated with colorless nail polish. His eyes, meanwhile, are closed with flesh-tinted eye caps and eye cement.

10   The next step is to have at Mr. Jones with a thing called a trocar. This is a long, hollow needle attached to a tube. It is jabbed into the abdomen, poked around the entrails and chest cavity, the contents of which are pumped out and replaced with "cavity fluid." This done, and the hole in the abdomen sewn up, Mr. Jones's face is heavily creamed

(to protect the skin from burns which may be caused by leakage of the chemicals), and he is covered with a sheet and left unmolested for a while. But not for long—there is more, much more, in store for him. He has been embalmed, but not yet restored, and the best time to start restorative work is eight to ten hours after embalming, when the tissues have become firm and dry.

The object of all this attention to the corpse, it must be remembered, is to make it presentable for viewing in an attitude of healthy repose. "Our customs require the presentation of our dead in the semblance of normality . . . unmarred by the ravages of illness, disease or mutilation," says Mr. J. Sheridan Mayer in his *Restorative Art*. This is rather a large order since few people die in the full bloom of health, unravaged by illness and unmarked by some disfigurement. The funeral industry is equal to the challenge: "In some cases the gruesome appearance of a mutilated or disease-ridden subject may be quite discouraging. The task of restoration may seem impossible and shake the confidence of the embalmer. This is the time for intestinal fortitude and determination. Once the formative work is begun and affected tissues are cleaned or removed, all doubts of success vanish. It is surprising and gratifying to discover the results which may be obtained."

The embalmer, having allowed an appropriate interval to elapse, returns to the attack, but now he brings into play the skill and equipment of sculptor and cosmetician. Is a hand missing? Casting one in plaster of Paris is a simple matter. "For replacement purposes, only a cast of the back of the hand is necessary; this is within the ability of the average operator and is quite adequate." If a lip or two, a nose or an ear should be missing, the embalmer has at hand a variety of restorative waxes with which to model replacements. Pores and skin texture are simulated by stippling with a little brush, and over this cosmetics are laid on. Head off? Decapitation cases are rather routinely handled. Ragged edges are trimmed, and head joined to torso with a series of splints, wires and sutures. It is a good idea to have a little something at the neck—a scarf or high collar—when time for viewing comes. Swollen mouth? Cut out tissue as needed from inside the lips. If too much is removed, the surface contour can easily be restored by padding with cotton. Swollen necks and cheeks are reduced by removing tissue through vertical incisions made down each side of the neck. "When the deceased is casketed, the pillow will hide the suture incisions . . . as an extra precaution against leakage, the suture may be painted with liquid sealer."

The opposite condition is more likely to present itself—that of emaciation. His hypodermic syringe now loaded with massage cream, the embalmer seeks out and fills the hollowed and sunken areas by injection. In this procedure the backs of the hands and fingers and the underchin area should not be neglected.

Positioning the lips is a problem that recurrently challenges the ingenuity of the embalmer. Closed too tightly, they tend to give a stern, even disapproving expression. Ideally, embalmers feel, the lips should give the impression of being ever so slightly parted, the upper lip protruding slightly for a more youthful appearance. This takes some engineering, however, as the lips tend to drift apart. Lip drift can sometimes be remedied by pushing one or two straight pins through the inner margin of the lower lip and then inserting them between the two front upper teeth. If Mr. Jones happens to have no teeth, the pins can just as easily be anchored in his Armstrong Face Former and Denture Replacer. Another method to maintain lip closure is to dislocate the lower jaw, which is then held in its new position by a wire run through holes which have been drilled through the upper jaws at the midline. As the French are fond of saying, *il faut souffrir pour être belle.*[1]

15   If Mr. Jones has died of jaundice, the embalming fluid will very likely turn him green. Does this deter the embalmer? Not if he has intestinal fortitude. Masking pastes and cosmetics are heavily laid on, burial garments and casket interiors are color-correlated with particular care, and Jones is displayed beneath rose-colored lights. Friends will say, "How *well* he looks." Death by carbon monoxide, on the other hand, can be rather a good thing from an embalmer's viewpoint: "One advantage is the fact that this type of discoloration is an exaggerated form of a natural pink coloration." This is nice because the healthy glow is already present and needs but little attention.

The patching and filling completed, Mr. Jones is now shaved, washed, and dressed. Cream-based cosmetic, available in pink, flesh, suntan, brunette, and blonde, is applied to his hands and face, his hair is shampooed and combed (and, in the case of Mrs. Jones, set), his hands manicured. For the horny-handed son of toil special care must be taken; cream should be applied to remove ingrained grime, and the nails cleaned. "If he were not in the habit of having them manicured in life, trimming and shaping is advised for better appearance—never questioned by kin."

Jones is now ready for casketing (this is the present participle of the verb "to casket"). In this operation his right shoulder should be

---

[1]It is necessary to suffer to be beautiful.

depressed slightly "to turn the body a bit to the right and soften the appearance of lying flat on the back." Positioning the hands is a matter of importance, and special rubber positioning blocks may be used. The hands should be cupped slightly for a more lifelike, relaxed appearance. Proper placement of the body requires a delicate sense of balance. It should lie as high as possible in the casket, yet not so high that the lid, when lowered, will hit the nose. On the other hand, we are cautioned, placing the body too low "creates the impression that the body is in a box."

Jones is next wheeled into the appointed slumber room where a few last touches may be added—his favorite pipe placed in his hand or, if he was a great reader, a book propped into position. (In the case of little Master Jones a Teddy bear may be clutched.) Here he will hold open house for a few days, visiting hours 10 A.M to 9 P.M.

Analyzing Rhetorical Choices

1. How well does Mitford illustrate the process of embalming?
2. What is the tone of this excerpt? What aspects of Mitford's language use indicate this? How does it provide counterpoint to the subject of the essay? What is the effect of this contrast?
3. Mitford makes use of many technical terms in her process analysis. How effective are these citations? How do they influence your perception of her authority in terms of describing embalming?
4. Why does Mitford name the corpse? How does this rhetorical decision affect your response to the essay?

Writing About Issues and Contexts

1. How does Mitford's essay implicate the reader—and the consumer—in the practices of embalming? For what purpose?
2. Comment on the ways in which the funeral industry takes advantage of consumers, according to Mitford. What is the effect of "kin" rarely questioning an embalmer's techniques? How does Mitford illustrate that funerals are not for the dead but for those who survive? Why?
3. Is Mitford guilty of insensitivity in writing this essay? Is she demonstrating insufficient regard for both the funeral industry and the grieving survivors? Offer your views in a response that attacks or defends Mitford's account.

*Paul Roberts (1917–1967) was an English professor with a speciali-
zation in linguistics. Educated at San Jose State University and the
University of California at Berkeley, Roberts taught at San Jose State
and Cornell University and directed the Center for American Studies
in Rome. His textbooks, which were well known to anyone attending
high school or college in the 1950s and 1960s, include* Understanding
Grammar *(1954) and his best-known work,* Understanding English
(1958), from which this excerpt is taken.

Paul Roberts

How to Say Nothing
in 500 Words

Nothing About Something

It's Friday afternoon, and you have almost survived another week
of classes. You are just looking forward dreamily to the weekend
when the English instructor says: "For Monday you will turn in a
five-hundred-word composition on college football."

Well, that puts a good big hole in the weekend. You don't have
any strong views on college football one way or the other. You get
rather excited during the season and go to all the home games and
find it rather more fun than not. On the other hand, the class has been
reading Robert Hutchins in the anthology and perhaps Shaw's
"Eighty-Yard Run," and from the class discussion you have got the
idea that the instructor thinks college football is for the birds. You are
no fool, you. You can figure out what side to take.

After dinner you get out the portable typewriter that you got for
high school graduation. You might as well get it over with and enjoy
Saturday and Sunday. Five hundred words is about two double-
spaced pages with normal margins. You put in a sheet of paper, think
up a title, and you're off:

Why College Football Should Be Abolished

College football should be abolished because it's bad for the
school and also bad for the players. The players are so busy practicing that they don't have any time for their studies.

This, you feel, is a mighty good start. The only trouble is that it's only thirty-two words. You still have four hundred and sixty-eight to go, and you've pretty well exhausted the subject. It comes to you that you do your best thinking in the morning, so you put away the typewriter and go to the movies. But the next morning you have to do your washing and some math problems, and in the afternoon you go to the game. The English instructor turns up too, and you wonder if you've taken the right side after all. Saturday night you have a date, and Sunday morning you have to go to church. (You shouldn't let English assignments interfere with your religion.) What with one thing and another, it's ten o'clock Sunday night before you get out the typewriter again. You make a pot of coffee and start to fill out your views on college football. Put a little meat on the bones.

Why College Football Should Be Abolished

In my opinion, it seems to me that college football should be abolished. The reason why I think this to be true is because I feel that football is bad for the colleges in nearly every respect. As Robert Hutchins says in his article in our anthology in which he discusses college football, it would be better if the colleges had race horses and had races with one another, because then the horses would not have to attend classes. I firmly agree with Mr. Hutchins on this point, and I am sure that many other students would agree too.

One reason why it seems to me that college football is bad is that it has become too commercial. In the olden times when people played football just for the fun of it, maybe college football was all right, but they do not play football just for the fun of it now as they used to in the old days. Nowadays college football is what you might call a big business. Maybe this is not true at all schools, and I don't think it is especially true here at State, but certainly this is the case at most colleges and universities in America nowadays, as Mr. Hutchins points out in his very interesting article. Actually the coaches and alumni go around to the high schools and offer the high school stars large salaries to come to their colleges and play football for them. There was one case where a high school star was offered a convertible if he would play football for a certain college.

Another reason for abolishing college football is that it is bad for the players. They do not have time to get a college education, because they are so busy playing football. A football player has to practice every afternoon from three to six, and then he is so tired that he can't concentrate on his studies. He just feels like dropping off to sleep after dinner, and then the next day he goes to his classes without having studied and maybe he fails the test.

(Good ripe stuff so far, but you're still a hundred and fifty-one words from home. One more push.)

> Also I think college football is bad for the colleges and the universities because not very many students get to participate in it. Out of a college of ten thousand students only seventy-five or a hundred play football, if that many. Football is what you might call a spectator sport. That means that most people go to watch it but do not play it themselves.

(Four hundred and fifteen. Well, you still have the conclusion, and when you retype it, you can make the margins a little wider.)

> These are the reasons why I agree with Mr. Hutchins that college football should be abolished in American colleges and universities.

5   On Monday you turn it in, moderately hopeful, and on Friday it comes back marked "weak in content" and sporting a big "D."

This essay is exaggerated a little, not much. The English instructor will recognize it as reasonably typical of what an assignment on college football will bring in. He knows that nearly half of the class will contrive in five hundred words to say that college football is too commercial and bad for the players. Most of the other half will inform him that college football builds character and prepares one for life and brings prestige to the school. As he reads paper after paper all saying the same thing in almost the same words, all bloodless, five hundred words dripping out of nothing, he wonders how he allowed himself to get trapped into teaching English when he might have had a happy and interesting life as an electrician or a confidence man.

Well, you may ask, what can you do about it? The subject is one on which you have few convictions and little information. Can you be expected to make a dull subject interesting? As a matter of fact, this is precisely what you are expected to do. This is the writer's essential task. All subjects, except sex, are dull until somebody makes them interesting. The writer's job is to find the argument, the approach, the angle, the wording that will take the reader with him. This is seldom easy, and it is particularly hard in subjects that have been much discussed: College Football, Fraternities, Popular Music, Is Chivalry Dead?, and the like. You will feel that there is nothing you can do with such subjects except repeat the old bromides. But there are some things you can do which will make your papers, if not throbbingly alive, at least less insufferably tedious than they might otherwise be.

Avoid the Obvious Content

Say the assignment is college football. Say that you've decided to be against it. Begin by putting down the arguments that come to your mind: it is too commercial, it takes the students' minds off their studies, it is hard on the players, it makes the university a kind of circus instead of an intellectual center, for most schools it is financially ruinous. Can you think of any more arguments just off hand? All right. Now when you write your paper, *make sure that you don't use any of the material on this list.* If these are the points that leap to your mind, they will leap to everyone else's too, and whether you get a "C" or a "D" may depend on whether the instructor reads your paper early when he is fresh and tolerant or late, when the sentence "In my opinion, college football has become too commercial," inexorably repeated, has brought him to the brink of lunacy.

Be against college football for some reason or reasons of your own. If they are keen and perceptive ones, that's splendid. But even if they are trivial or foolish or indefensible, you are still ahead so long as they are not everybody else's reasons too. Be against it because the colleges don't spend enough money on it to make it worth while, because it is bad for the characters of the spectators, because the players are forced to attend classes, because the football stars hog all the beautiful women, because it competes with baseball and is therefore un-American and possibly Communist inspired. There are lots of more or less unused reasons for being against college football.

10 Sometimes it is a good idea to sum up and dispose of the trite and conventional points before going on to your own. This has the advantage of indicating to the reader that you are going to be neither trite nor conventional. Something like this:

> We are often told that college football should be abolished because it has become too commercial or because it is bad for the players. These arguments are no doubt very cogent, but they don't really go to the heart of the matter.

Then you go to the heart of the matter.

Take the Less Usual Side

One rather simple way of getting interest into your paper is to take the side of the argument that most of the citizens will want to avoid. If the assignment is an essay on dogs, you can, if you choose, explain that dogs are faithful and lovable companions, intelligent, useful as guardians of the house and protectors of children, indispensable in police work—in short, when all is said and done, man's best friends. Or you can suggest that those big brown eyes conceal, more often than not, a vacuity of mind and an inconstancy of purpose; that the dogs you have known most intimately have been mangy, ill-tempered brutes, incapable of instruction; and that only your nobility of mind and fear of arrest prevent you from kicking the flea-ridden animals when you pass them on the street.

Naturally, personal convictions will sometimes dictate your approach. If the assigned subject is "Is Methodism Rewarding to the Individual?" and you are a pious Methodist, you have really no choice. But few assigned subjects, if any, will fall in this category. Most of them will lie in broad areas of discussion with much to be said on both sides. They are intellectual exercises and it is legitimate to argue now one way and now another, as debaters do in similar circumstances. Always take the side that looks to you hardest, least defensible. It will almost always turn out to be easier to write interestingly on that side.

This general advice applies where you have a choice of subjects. If you are to choose among "The Value of Fraternities" and "My Favorite High School Teacher" and "What I Think About Beetles," by all means plump for the beetles. By the time the instructor gets to your paper, he will be up to his ears in tedious tales about the French teacher at Bloombury High and assertions about how fraternities build character and prepare one for life. Your views on beetles, whatever they are, are bound to be a refreshing change.

Don't worry too much about figuring out what the instructor thinks about the subject so that you can cuddle up with him. Chances are his views are no stronger than yours. If he does have convictions and you oppose them, his problem is to keep from grading you higher than you deserve in order to show he is not biased. This doesn't mean that you should always cantankerously dissent from what the instructor says; that gets tiresome too. And if the subject assigned is "My Pet Peeve," do not begin, "My pet peeve is the English instructor who assigns papers on 'my pet peeve.'" This was still funny during the War of 1812, but it has sort of lost its edge since then. It is in general good manners to avoid personalities.

Slip Out of Abstraction

15   If you will study the essay on college football . . . you will perceive that one reason for its appalling dullness is that it never gets down to particulars. It is just a series of not very glittering generalities: "football

is bad for the colleges," "it has become too commercial," "football is a big business," "it is bad for the players," and so on. Such round phrases thudding against the reader's brain are unlikely to convince him, though they may well render him unconscious.

If you want the reader to believe that college football is bad for the players, you have to do more than say so. You have to display the evil. Take your roommate, Alfred Simkins, the second-string center. Picture poor old Alfy coming home from football practice every evening, bruised and aching, agonizingly tired, scarcely able to shovel the mashed potatoes into his mouth. Let us see him staggering up to the room, getting out his econ textbook, peering desperately at it with his good eye, falling asleep and failing the test in the morning. Let us share his unbearable tension as Saturday draws near. Will he fail, be demoted, lose his monthly allowance, be forced to return to the coal mines? And if he succeeds, what will be his reward? Perhaps a slight ripple of applause when the third-string center replaces him, a moment of elation in the locker room if the team wins, of despair if it loses. What will he look back on when he graduates from college? Toil and torn ligaments. And what will be his future? He is not good enough for pro football, and he is too obscure and weak in econ to succeed in stocks and bonds. College football is tearing the heart from Alfy Simkins and, when it finishes with him, will callously toss aside the shattered hulk.

This is no doubt a weak enough argument for the abolition of college football, but it is a sight better than saying, in three or four variations, that college football (in your opinion) is bad for the players.

Look at the work of any professional writer and notice how constantly he is moving from the generality, the abstract statement, to the concrete example, the facts and figures, the illustration. If he is writing on juvenile delinquency, he does not just tell you that juveniles are (it seems to him) delinquent and that (in his opinion) something should be done about it. He shows you juveniles being delinquent, tearing up movie theatres in Buffalo, stabbing high school principals in Dallas, smoking marijuana in Palo Alto. And more than likely he is moving toward some specific remedy, not just a general wringing of the hands.

It is no doubt possible to be *too* concrete, too illustrative or anecdotal, but few inexperienced writers err this way. For most the soundest advice is to be seeking always for the picture, to be always turning general remarks into seeable examples. Don't say, "Sororities teach girls the social graces." Say "Sorority life teaches a girl how to carry on a conversation while pouring tea, without sloshing the tea into the saucer." Don't say, "I like certain kinds of popular music very much." Say, "Whenever I hear Gerber Spinklittle play 'Mississippi Man' on the trombone, my socks creep up my ankles."

Get Rid of Obvious Padding

20   The student toiling away at his weekly English theme is too often tormented by a figure: five hundred words. How, he asks himself, is he to achieve this staggering total? Obviously by never using one word when he can somehow work in ten.

He is therefore seldom content with a plain statement like "Fast driving is dangerous." This has only four words in it. He takes thought, and the sentence becomes:

> In my opinion, fast driving is dangerous.

Better, but he can do better still:

> In my opinion, fast driving would seem to be rather dangerous.

If he is really adept, it may come out:

> In my humble opinion, though I do not claim to be an expert on this complicated subject, fast driving, in most circumstances, would seem to be rather dangerous in many respects, or at least so it would seem to me.

Thus four words have been turned into forty, and not an iota of content has been added.

Now this is a way to go about reaching five hundred words, and if you are content with a "D" grade, it is as good a way as any. But if you aim higher, you must work differently. Instead of stuffing your sentences with straw, you must try steadily to get rid of the padding, to make your sentences lean and tough. If you are really working at it, your first draft will greatly exceed the required total, and then you will work it down, thus:

> It is thought in some quarters that fraternities do not contribute as much as might be expected to campus life.
> Some people think that fraternities contribute little to campus life.

> The average doctor who practices in small towns or in the country must toil night and day to heal the sick.
> Most country doctors work long hours.

> When I was a little girl, I suffered from shyness and embarrassment in the presence of others.
> I was a shy little girl.

> It is absolutely necessary for the person employed as a marine fireman to give the matter of steam pressure his undivided attention at all times.
> The fireman has to keep his eye on the steam gauge.

You may ask how you can arrive at five hundred words at this rate. Simply. You dig up more real content. Instead of taking a couple of obvious points off the surface of the topic and then circling warily around them for six paragraphs, you work in and explore, figure out the details. You illustrate. You say that fast driving is dangerous, and then you prove it. How long does it take to stop a car at forty and at eighty? How far can you see at night? What happens when a tire blows? What happens in a head-on collision at fifty miles an hour? Pretty soon your paper will be full of broken glass and blood and headless torsos, and reaching five hundred words will not really be a problem.

Call a Fool a Fool

Some of the padding in freshman themes is to be blamed not on anxiety about the word minimum but on excessive timidity. The student writes, "In my opinion, the principal of my high school acted in ways that I believe every unbiased person would have to call foolish." This isn't exactly what he means. What he means is, "My high school principal was a fool." If he was a fool, call him a fool. Hedging the thing about with "in-my-opinion's" and "it-seems-to-me's" and "as-I-see-it's" and "at-least-from-my-point-of-view's" gains you nothing. Delete these phrases whenever they creep into your paper.

25   The student's tendency to hedge stems from a modesty that in other circumstances would be commendable. He is, he realizes, young and inexperienced, and he half suspects that he is dopey and fuzzy-minded beyond the average. Probably only too true. But it doesn't help to announce your incompetence six times in every paragraph. Decide what you want to say and say it as vigorously as possible, without apology and in plain words.

Linguistic diffidence can take various forms. One is what we call *euphemism*. This is the tendency to call a spade "a certain garden implement" or women's underwear "unmentionables." It is stronger in some eras than others and in some people than others but it always operates more or less in subjects that are touchy or taboo: death, sex, madness, and so on. Thus we shrink from saying "He died last night" but say instead "passed away," "left us," "joined his Maker," "went to his reward." Or we try to take off the tension with a lighter cliché: "kicked the bucket," "cashed in his chips," "handed in his dinner pail." We have found all sorts of ways to avoid saying *mad:* "mentally ill," "touched," "not quite right upstairs," "feeble-minded," "innocent," "simple," "off his trolley," "not in his right mind." Even such a now plain word as *insane* began as a euphemism with the meaning "not healthy."

Modern science, particularly psychology, contributes many polysyllables in which we can wrap our thoughts and blunt their force. To many writers there is no such thing as a bad schoolboy. Schoolboys are maladjusted or unoriented or misunderstood or in need of guidance or lacking in continued success toward satisfactory integration of the personality as a social unit, but they are never bad. Psychology no doubt makes us better men or women, more sympathetic and tolerant, but it doesn't make writing any easier. Had Shakespeare been confronted with psychology, "To be or not to be" might have come out "To continue as a social unit or not to do so. That is the personality problem. Whether 'tis a better sign of integration at the conscious level to display a psychic tolerance toward the maladjustments and repressions induced by one's lack of orientation in one's environment or—" But Hamlet would never have finished the soliloquy.

Writing in the modern world, you cannot altogether avoid modern jargon. Nor, in an effort to get away from euphemism, should you salt your paper with four-letter words. But you can do much if you will mount guard against those roundabout phrases, those echoing polysyllables that tend to slip into your writing to rob it of its crispness and force.

Beware of the Pat Expression

Other things being equal, avoid phrases like "other things being equal." Those sentences that come to you whole, or in two or three doughy lumps, are sure to be bad sentences. They are no creation of yours but pieces of common thought floating in the community soup.

30   Pat expressions are hard, often impossible, to avoid, because they come too easily to be noticed and seem too necessary to be dispensed with. No writer avoids them altogether, but good writers avoid them more often than poor writers.

By "pat expressions" we mean such tags as "to all practical intents and purposes," "the pure and simple truth," "from where I sit," "the time of his life," "to the ends of the earth," "in the twinkling of an eye," "as sure as you're born," "over my dead body," "under cover of darkness," "took the easy way out," "when all is said and done," "told him time and time again," "parted the best of friends," "stand up and be counted," "gave him the best years of her life," "worked her fingers to the bone." Like other clichés, these expressions were once forceful. Now we should use them only when we can't possibly think of anything else.

Some pat expressions stand like a wall between the writer and thought. Such a one is "the American way of life." Many student writers feel that when they have said that something accords with the American way of life or does not they have exhausted the subject. Actually, they have stopped at the highest level of abstraction. The American way of life is the complicated set of bonds between a hundred and eighty million ways. All of us know this when we think about it, but the tag phrase too often keeps us from thinking about it.

So with many another phrase dear to the politician: "this great land of ours," "the man in the street," "our national heritage." These may prove our patriotism or give a clue to our political beliefs, but otherwise they add nothing to the paper except words.

Colorful Words

The writer builds with words, and no builder uses a raw material more slippery and elusive and treacherous. A writer's work is a constant struggle to get the right word in the right place, to find that particular word that will convey his meaning exactly, that will persuade the reader or soothe him or startle or amuse him. He never succeeds altogether—sometimes he feels that he scarcely succeeds at all—but such successes as he has are what make the thing worth doing.

35 There is no book of rules for this game. One progresses through everlasting experiment on the basis of ever-widening experience. There are few useful generalizations that one can make about words as words, but there are perhaps a few.

Some words are what we call "colorful." By this we mean that they are calculated to produce a picture or induce an emotion. They are dressy instead of plain, specific instead of general, loud instead of soft. Thus, in place of "Her heart beat," we may write "Her heart *pounded, throbbed, fluttered, danced*." Instead of "He sat in his chair," we may say, "He *lounged, sprawled, coiled.*" Instead of "It was hot," we may say, "It was *blistering, sultry, muggy, suffocating, steamy, wilting.*"

However, it should not be supposed that the fancy word is always better. Often it is as well to write "Her heart beat" or "It was hot" if that is all it did or all it was. Ages differ in how they like their prose. The nineteenth century liked it rich and smoky. The twentieth has usually preferred it lean and cool. The twentieth-century writer, like all writers, is forever seeking the exact word, but he is wary of sounding feverish. He tends to pitch it low, to understate it, to throw it away. He knows that if he gets too colorful, the audience is likely to giggle.

See how this strikes you: "As the rich, golden glow of the sunset died away along the eternal western hills, Angela's limpid blue eyes looked softly and trustingly into Montague's flashing brown ones, and her heart pounded like a drum in time with the joyous song surging in her soul." Some people like that sort of thing, but most modern readers would say, "Good grief," and turn on the television.

Colored Words

Some words we would call not so much colorful as colored—that is, loaded with associations, good or bad. All words—except perhaps structure words—have associations of some sort. We have said that the meaning of a word is the sum of the contexts in which it occurs. When we hear a word, we hear with it an echo of all the situations in which we have heard it before.

40   In some words, these echoes are obvious and discussable. The word *mother*, for example, has, for most people, agreeable associations. When you hear *mother* you probably think of home, safety, love, food, and various other pleasant things. If one writes, "She was like a mother to me," he gets an effect which he would not get in "She was like an aunt to me." The advertiser makes use of the associations of *mother* by working it in when he talks about his product. The politician works it in when he talks about himself.

So also with such words as *home, liberty, fireside, contentment, patriot, tenderness, sacrifice, childlike, manly, bluff, limpid.* All of these words are loaded with favorable associations that would be rather hard to indicate in a straightforward definition. There is more than a literal difference between "They sat around the fireside" and "They sat around the stove." They might have been equally warm and happy around the stove, but *fireside* suggests leisure, grace, quiet tradition, congenial company, and *stove* does not.

Conversely, some words have bad associations. *Mother* suggests pleasant things, but *mother-in-law* does not. Many mothers-in-law are heroically lovable and some mothers drink gin all day and beat their children insensible, but these facts of life are beside the point. The thing is that *mother* sounds good and *mother-in-law* does not.

Or consider the word *intellectual*. This would seem to be a complimentary term, but in point of fact it is not, for it has picked up associations of impracticality and ineffectuality and general dopiness. So also with such words as *liberal, reactionary, Communist, socialist, capitalist, radical, schoolteacher, truck driver, undertaker, operator, salesman, huckster, speculator.* These convey meanings on the literal level, but beyond that—sometimes, in some places—they convey contempt on the part of the speaker.

The question of whether to use loaded words or not depends on what is being written. The scientist, the scholar, try to avoid them; for the poet, the advertising writer, the public speaker, they are standard equipment. But every writer should take care that they do not substitute for thought. If you write, "Anyone who thinks that is nothing but a Socialist (or Communist or capitalist)," you have said nothing except that you don't like people who think that, and such remarks are effective only with the most naïve readers. It is always a bad mistake to think your readers more naïve than they really are.

Colorless Words

45   But probably most student writers come to grief not with words that are colorful or those that are colored but with those that have no color at all. A pet example is *nice*, a word we would find it hard to dispense with in casual conversation but which is no longer capable of adding much to a description. Colorless words are those of such general meaning that in a particular sentence they mean nothing. Slang adjectives, like *cool* ("That's real cool") tend to explode all over the language. They are applied to everything, lose their original force, and quickly die.

Beware also of nouns of very general meaning, like *circumstances, cases, instances, aspects, factors, relationships, attitudes, eventualities,* etc. In most circumstances you will find that those cases of writing which contain too many instances of words like these will in this and other aspects have factors leading to unsatisfactory relationships with the reader resulting in unfavorable attitudes on his part and perhaps other eventualities, like a grade of "D." Notice also what "etc." means. It means "I'd like to make this last longer, but I can't think of any more examples."

Analyzing Rhetorical Choices

1. Roberts actually describes two processes in this essay: one that he thinks will result in a poor essay and one that he thinks will result in a better one. Are both processes described clearly and vividly? Why do you think he chooses to describe both ways of composing an essay?

2. Roberts addresses the reader directly as "you" at the opening of this essay and he reverts to it frequently throughout the remainder. But he also shifts to first-person plural (*we* and *us*) and to third-person singular *(the writer)* and the largely impersonal *one* elsewhere. Describe the effects these various shifts have on you as you read. Why do you think he keeps shifting his perspective?

3. Describe Roberts's tone and illustrate your answer by citing a number of specific word choices and phrasing that he adopts.

Writing About Issues and Contexts

1. What do you think of Roberts's contention that "the difference between a 'C' or a 'D' may depend on who grades the paper"? How does Roberts implicate both students and teachers? Write a short statement, agreeing or disagreeing with Roberts's statement.

2. Students seem to hold certain assumptions about writing, according to Roberts. What are they? Explain whether these assumptions make sense to you.

3. Discuss Roberts's use of *color* in relation to words (colorless, colorful, and so forth). How do they relate to his advice to students?

Charles Johnson (1948–) was born in Evanston, Illinois, where as a teenager he began his career as a political cartoonist. Johnson's success as a cartoonist led to a public television series in 1971 called "Charlie's Pad," which he created, hosted, and coproduced. While attending Southern Illinois University, Johnson studied with John Gardner, literary theorist and novelist. Johnson's first novel, Faith and the Good Thing *(1974), was published while he was pursuing his doctoral degree in phenomenology and literary aesthetics at the State University of New York at Stony Brook. Johnson's historical novel,* Middle Passage *(1990), the story of a freed slave who journeys back to Africa, was the winner of the 1990 National Book Award. "Dr. King's Refrigerator" was originally published in* Dr. King's Refrigerator and Other Bedtime Stories *(2005), a collection of Johnson's short stories.*

Charles Johnson

Dr. King's Refrigerator

In September, the year of Our Lord 1954, a gifted young minister from Atlanta named Martin Luther King Jr. accepted his first pastorate at the Dexter Avenue Baptist Church in Montgomery, Alabama. He was twenty-five-years old, and in the language of the academy he took his first job when he was ABD at Boston University's School of Theology—All But Dissertation—which is a common and necessary practice for scholars who have completed their coursework and have families to feed. If you are offered a job when still in graduate school, you snatch it, and if all goes well, you finish the thesis that first year of your employment when you are in the thick of things, trying mightily to prove—in Martin's case—to the staid, high-toned laity at Dexter that you really are worth the $4,800 salary they are paying you. He had, by the way, the highest-paying job of any minister in the city of Montgomery, and the expectations for his daily performance—as a pastor, husband, community leader, and the son of Daddy King—were equally high.

But what few people tell the eager ABD is how completing the doctorate from a distance means wall-to-wall work. There were always meetings with the local NAACP, ministers' organizations, and church committees; or, failing that, the budget and treasury to balance; or, failing that, the sick to visit in their homes, the ordination of deacons to preside over, and a new sermon to write every week. During that first year away from Boston, he delivered forty-six sermons to his congregation, and twenty sermons and lectures at other colleges and churches in the South. And, dutifully, he got up every morning at 5:30 to spend three hours composing the thesis in his parsonage, a white frame house with a railed-in front porch and two oak trees in the yard, after which he devoted another three hours to it late at night, in addition to spending sixteen hours each week on his Sunday sermons.

On the Wednesday night of December first, exactly one year before Rosa Parks refused to give up her bus seat, and after a long day of meetings, writing memos and letters, he sat entrenched behind a roll-top desk in his cluttered den at five minutes past midnight, smoking cigarettes and drinking black coffee, wearing an old fisherman's knit sweater, his desk barricaded in by books and piles of paperwork. Naturally, his in-progress dissertation, "A Comparison of the Conceptions of God in the Thinking of Paul Tillich and Henry Nelson Wieman," was itching at the edge of his mind, but what he really needed this night was a theme for his sermon on Sunday. Usually by Tuesday Martin at least had a sketch, by Wednesday he had his research and citations—which ranged freely over five thousand years of eastern and western philosophy—compiled on note cards, and by Friday he was writing his text on a pad of lined yellow paper. Put bluntly, he was two days behind schedule.

A few rooms away, his wife was sleeping under a blue corduroy bedspread. For an instant he thought of giving up work for the night and climbing into sheets warmed by her body, curling up beside this heartbreakingly beautiful and very understanding woman, a graduate of the New England Conservatory of Music, who had sacrificed her career back East in order to follow him into the Deep South. He remembered their wedding night on June 18 a year ago, in Perry County, Alabama, and how the insanity of segregation meant that he and his new bride could not stay in a hotel operated by whites. Instead they spent their wedding night at a black funeral home and had no honeymoon at all. Yes, he probably should join her in their bedroom. He wondered if she resented how his academic and theological duties took him away from her and their home (many an ABD's marriage ended before the dissertation was done)—work like that infernal, unwritten sermon, which hung over his head like the sword of Damocles.

5   Weary, feeling guilty, he pushed back from his desk, stretched out his stiff spine, and decided to get a midnight snack.

Now, he knew he shouldn't do that, of course. He often told friends that food was his greatest weakness. His ideal weight in college was 150 pounds, and he was aware that, at five feet, seven inches tall, he should not eat between meals. His bantam weight ballooned easily. Moreover, he'd read somewhere that the average American will in his (or her) lifetime eat 60,000 pounds of food. To Martin's ethical way of thinking, consuming that much tonnage was downright obscene, given the fact that there was so much famine and poverty throughout the rest of the world. He made himself a promise—a small prayer—to eat just a little, only enough tonight to replenish his tissues.

He made his way cautiously through the dark seven-room house, his footsteps echoing on the hardwood floors as if he were in a swimming pool, scuffing from the smoke-filled den to the living room, where he circled round the baby grand piano his wife practiced on for church recitals, then past her choices in decorations—two African masks on one wall and West Indian gourds on the mantle above the fireplace—to the kitchen. There, he clicked on the overhead light and drew open the door to their refrigerator.

Scratching his stomach, he gazed—and gazed—at four well-stocked shelves of food. He saw a Florida grapefruit and a California orange. On one of the middle shelves he saw corn and squash, both native to North America, and introduced by Indians to Europe in the fifteenth century through Columbus. To the right of that, his eyes tracked bright yellow slices of pineapple from Hawaii, truffles from England, and a half-eaten Mexican tortilla. Martin took a step back, cocking his head to one side, less hungry now than curious about what his wife had found at public market and stacked inside their refrigerator without telling him.

He began to empty the refrigerator and the heavily packed food cabinets, placing everything on the table and kitchen counter and, when those were filled, on the flower-printed linoleum floor, taking things out slowly at first, his eyes squinted, scrutinizing each item like an old woman on a fixed budget at the bargain table in a grocery store. Then he worked quickly, bewitched, chuckling to himself as he tore apart his wife's tidy, well-scrubbed, Christian kitchen. He removed all the beryline olives from a thick glass jar and held each one up to the light, as if perhaps he'd never really seen an olive before, or seen one so clearly. Of one thing he was sure: no two olives were the same. Within fifteen minutes, Martin stood surrounded by a galaxy of food.

10   From one corner of the kitchen floor to the other, there were popular American items such as pumpkin pie and hot dogs, but also

heavy, sour-sweet dishes like German sauerkraut and schnitzel right beside Tibetan rice, one of the staples of the Far East, all sorts of spices, and the macaroni, spaghetti, and ravioli favored by Italians. There were bricks of cheese and wine from French vineyards, coffee from Brazil, and from China and India black and green teas that probably had been carried from fields to faraway markets on the heads of women or the backs of donkeys, horses, and mules.

All of human culture, history, and civilization scrolled at his feet, and he had only to step into his kitchen to discover it. No one people or tribe, living in one place on this planet, could produce the endless riches for the palate that he'd just pulled from his refrigerator. He looked around the disheveled room, and he saw in each succulent fruit, each loaf of bread, and each grain of rice a fragile, inescapable network of mutuality in which all earthly creatures were codependent, integrated, and tied in a single garment of destiny. He recalled Exodus 25:30, and realized that all this before him was showbread. From the floor Martin picked up a Golden Delicious apple, took a bite from it, and instantly he prehended the haze of heat from summers past, the roots of the tree from which the fruit was taken, the cycles of sun and rain and seasons, the earth and even those who tended the orchard. Then he slowly put the apple down, feeling not so much hunger now as a profound indebtedness and thanksgiving—to everyone and everything in Creation. For was not he too the product of infinite causes and the full, miraculous orchestration of Being stretching back to the beginning of time?

At that moment his wife came into the disaster area that was their kitchen, half asleep, wearing blue slippers and an old housecoat over her nightgown. When she saw what her philosopher husband had done, she said *Oh!* and promptly disappeared from the room. A moment later she was back, having composed herself, though her voice was barely above a whisper: "Are you all right?"

"Of course I am! I've never felt better!" he said. "The whole universe is inside our refrigerator!"

She blinked. "Really? You don't mean that, do you? Honey, have you been drinking? I've told you time and again that orange juice and vodka you like so much isn't good for you, and if anyone at church smells it on your breath . . ."

15   "If you must know, I was hard at work on my thesis an hour ago. I didn't drink a drop of anything—except coffee."

"Well, that explains," she said.

"No, you don't understand! I was trying to write my speech for Sunday, but—but—I couldn't think of anything, and I got hungry . . ."

She stared at food heaped on the floor. "This hungry?"

"Well, no." His mouth wobbled, and now he was no longer thinking about the metaphysics of food but instead how the mess he'd made must look through her eyes. And, more important, how *he* must look through her eyes. "I think I've got my sermon, or at least something I might use later. It's so obvious to me now!" He could tell by the tilt of her head and the twitching of her nose that she didn't think any of this was obvious at all. "When we get up in the morning, we go into the bathroom, where we reach for a sponge provided for us by a Pacific Islander. We reach for soap created by a Frenchman. The towel is provided by a Turk. Before we leave for our jobs, we are beholden to more than half the world."

20   "Yes, dear." She sighed. "I can see that, but what about my kitchen? You *know* I'm hosting the Ladies' Prayer Circle today at eight o'clock. That's seven hours from now. Please tell me you're going to clean up everything before you go to bed."

"But I have a sermon to write! What I'm saying—trying to say—is that whatever affects one directly affects all indirectly!"

"Oh, yes, I'm sure all this is going to have a remarkable effect on the Ladies' Prayer Circle . . ."

"Sweetheart . . ." He held up a grapefruit and a head of lettuce. "I had a revelation tonight. Do you know how rare that is? Those things don't come easy. Just ask Meister Eckhart or Martin Luther—you know Luther experienced enlightenment on the toilet, don't you? Ministers only get maybe one or two revelations in a lifetime. But you made it possible for me to have a vision when I opened the refrigerator." All at once, he had a discomforting thought. "How much did you spend for groceries last week?"

"I bought extra things for the Ladies' Prayer Circle," she said. "Don't ask how much and I won't ask why you've turned the kitchen inside out." Gracefully, like an angel, or the perfect wife in the Book of Proverbs, she stepped toward him over cans and containers, plates of leftovers and bowls of chili. She placed her hand on his cheek, like a mother might do with her gifted and exasperating child, a prodigy who had just torched his bedroom in a scientific experiment. Then she wrapped her arms around him, slipped her hands under his sweater, and gave him a kiss. Stepping back, she touched the tip of his nose with her finger and turned to leave. "Don't stay up too late," she said. "Put everything back before it spoils. And come to bed—I'll be waiting."

25   Martin watched her leave and said, "Yes, dear," still holding a very spiritually understood grapefruit in one hand and an onto-

logically clarified head of lettuce in the other. He started putting back everything on the shelves, deciding as he did so that while his sermon could wait until morning, his new wife definitely should not.

Analyzing Rhetorical Choices

1. How does Johnson's story fit into the mode of process analysis? What process is he describing? Do you think that he is describing more than one process? Why or why not?

2. Why does Johnson frame his story around King's day-to-day routine? How does this narrative framework influence the stylistic effect of the story?

3. Paying particular attention to word choice and word patterns, comment on the passage where Johnson describes the contents of the Kings' refrigerator and cupboards. What is the rhetorical effectiveness of the listing of these contents in such detail?

Writing About Issues and Contexts

1. Consider the statement that "whatever affects one directly affects all indirectly." What is meant by this statement? What examples can you give to support this theory that what affects one person affects all people?

2. Analyze the following passage

    All of human culture, history, and civilization scrolled at his feet, and he had only to step into his kitchen to discover it. No one people or tribe, living in one place on this planet, could produce the endless riches for the palate that he'd just pulled from his refrigerator.

    What is the significance of King's discovery? What are the larger implications of this discovery?

3. If process analysis can properly be described as a "narrative of instruction," how do you analyze the process that King experiences? What lessons does King learn? What lessons does Johnson impart to the reader?

Strategies for Writers: Process Analysis

1. As you have seen in "My First Conk" and "Dr. King's Refrigerator," a process analysis can both describe a material event and signify a larger meaning about social, political, economic, or cultural values. In discussion with your classmates, determine how the process you plan to describe can take on significant meaning beyond the basic process itself. You may find as you do so that you are developing a narrative or the beginning of an implied argument.

2. Try to visualize the process you plan to describe, then describe it in specific visual terms to your classmates. You may consider spatial arrangements just as you would for description. How does description enhance your process? Use the experience of talking to your classmates to help you structure your draft. Once you have the process analysis written, try it out on your colleagues, asking them to help you develop a clear and well-illustrated explanation of the process you have chosen to describe.

3. The readings in this chapter show that process analyses are rarely neutral. For instance, Kenneth M. Stampp delineates, step-by-step, the process by which someone is able to dehumanize someone else and reinforce the master/slave relationship. Can you write a similarly ironic process description that represents a particular perspective that you believe in?

4. Process analysis often expresses a perspective and a sense of one's relationships with others along with relevant, clear detail. Douglass accomplishes this in "Learning to Read and Write." He also suggests that to keep slaves illiterate was also to define them as subhuman; the process of learning to read becomes a process of creating humanity. How does process interact with definition in this essay, where to define slavery as subhuman is part of the process of maintaining slavery—and where slavery is also dependent on withholding the process of literacy? How do these issues also relate to the Stampp essay?

5. As you write your process analysis, clarify your own perspective or evaluation of your subject, as Paul Roberts does in "How to Say Nothing in 500 Words." What do you imply by what you write?

6. Perhaps more than most modes, process analysis requires careful attention to detail and a high degree of accuracy so that the reader can understand the process being described or evaluated. Notice how carefully Paul Roberts and Fan Shen structure their processes and the wealth of exemplification each of them includes. As you write, be sure to include useful detail, and check your accuracy. Errors of fact, typographical errors, and other forms of careless writing erode a reader's confidence in any writer.

Research and Writing Assignments

1. For Douglass, learning how to read was also learning how to be free, how to engage the world as a citizen and not a slave. Explore a similar process of learning how to be literate, either your own or someone else's, and write an essay that describes that process and what it meant. To do the necessary research for this essay, you may want to speak to your family members about your own literacy development, or contact a community literacy center or a public library so that you can research the literacy development of someone else.

2. How does a person become enslaved? Certainly both Frederick Douglass and Kenneth M. Stampp consider various elements of how that process occurs, with Douglass writing from the perspective of the slave and Stampp from the slave owner. Is slavery a condition of mind as much as a condition of body? What are the psychological and physiological changes that must occur for someone to be enslaved? In an essay that draws upon research, analyze the process of enslavement. If you do not wish to write about the enslavement of African Americans, consider other forms of "capturing" and holding people within relationships that erase their individual wills, such as religious cults, spousal abuse, or domestic workers who are purchased by wealthy families.

3. Malcolm X and Fan Shen delineate the ways in which minorities often feel they must make compromises to fit into the dominant culture. Compare and contrast the various perspectives in these essays about whether those who do not consider themselves "mainstream" need to compromise individual

qualities in order to become "assimilated." As part of your focus, you might want to consider Fan Shen's statement that "Rule number one in English composition is: Be yourself." Can those who identify themselves as part of a "minority" remain true to this advice and yet also be part of the mainstream?

4. In his story "Dr. King's Refrigerator," Charles Johnson quotes Dr. King as saying "I had a revelation tonight. Do you know how rare that is? Those things don't come easy." Johnson's narrative focuses on the possibility that the routine of our daily life, such as looking in the refrigerator for a late-night snack, can lead us to a spiritual discovery. Drawing on the story by Johnson, as well as any additional research you can do, write an essay that describes a specific process of discovery. What implicit and explicit processes of your own have the potential to lead you on a journey of discovery? What choices have you made that have resulted in an important spiritual, emotional, or intellectual discovery? Consider Johnson's proposal that discovery can happen just about anywhere at any time; we just have to open ourselves up to the possibility of the experience.

5. Jessica Mitford writes about embalming as "an extraordinary procedure." In explicit detail, she reveals a process that is hidden to most eyes and that we might not usually think about. Using Mitford as your model, select another process about which one usually does not write, and "unwrap" and reveal it (using, if you wish, Mitford's directness, adroit use of detail, and possibly even her wry sense of humor). Write about a process that you can share with both your teacher and your classmates—one that is uncommon and unusual but something that can be written about in an open forum.

6. Paul Roberts offers us specific advice about how to write an essay. Using Roberts as a departure point, describe your own composing process. Do not feel that you have to agree or disagree with Roberts. Instead, create an ethnographic analysis of your own actions, writing rhythms, false starts, genuine patterns, and ultimate successes. What kinds of activities enable you to write well? What kinds of challenges and crises do you confront when you write? In your essay, include, as Roberts does, as much exemplification as possible so as to help your reader visualize what you do, why you do it, what works, and what doesn't.

8

Comparison and Contrast

Many decisions you make, including those that have brought you to this point as a college student, are based on the similarities and differences you consider. You have most likely pondered the prospects of life with a college degree and the prospects of life without one. You have probably thought about the merits of the school you attend relative to those of other institutions. In addition, you have probably thought about the likenesses and distinctions among majors, schedules, and instructors. You have already seen how the use of *comparison* (likeness) and *contrast* (distinction) is frequently crucial to clarifying issues, making an argument, arriving at a decision, or establishing a framework for discussion.

As with all writing techniques, comparison and contrast should serve the purpose you have set for a particular piece of writing. At times you will be asked explicitly—usually on an exam—to compare and contrast people, practices, and ideas. In such cases, comparison and contrast would be the primary pattern of development, and the similarities and differences you write about would often be related to a clearly defined thesis. If asked to compare and contrast the Kennedy inauguration with the first Clinton inauguration, you could assert that the Clinton inauguration in 1993 was a deliberate attempt to imitate Kennedy's 1961 inauguration. You could then comment on such elements as the political situations, the similar sound bites in each inaugural address, the almost identical length of the speeches, and the participation in each ceremony of a poet from the incoming president's home state.

When you have been assigned the task of writing about how two things are the same or different, the reason for using comparison and contrast will be evident. For example, Jodi Kantor was probably asked to review two boxing memoirs, and "Wham! Bam! Thanks a Bunch!" was the result. In other instances, however, you will need to convey clearly the purpose of the comparison and contrast. Poet and cultural critic Quincy Troupe, for instance, uses comparison and contrast in his memoir *Miles and Me* to account for the cool music and demeanor of legendary trumpeter and East St. Louis native Miles Davis. After writing about the great drum and bugle corps marching bands of St. Louis and East St. Louis, which incorporate German traditions and African American innovations, Troupe continues his description:

> These bands developed a style of playing the bugle, later transferred to the cornet and trumpet, that became known as the St. Louis "running" style. Pioneered by Eddie Randall, Levi Madison, Harold "Shorty" Baker, and Clark Terry (Miles' first real mentor in trumpet style) and perfected by Miles (who, in his youth, had played in several East St. Louis marching bands), it was characterized by musical ideas, chords, and notes strung together in a continuous blowing, dialoging manner, akin to a fast-talking conversationalist. (Trumpeter Lester Bowie, from St. Louis, provides an example of this style today.)
>
> This distinctive St. Louis sound was connected to the great trumpet tradition of New Orleans by the musicians who traveled on the riverboats shuttling up and down the Mississippi. But where New Orleans trumpet players employed a hotter, bigger, brassier style (as exemplified by Buddy Bolden, Freddie Keppard, Louis Armstrong, Al Hirt, Wynton Marsalis, Nicholas Payton, and Terrence Blanchard), the St. Louis style was generally cooler, more subtle and conversational (although it, too, could be hot and brassy at times).
>
> The different styles came out of different cultures. New Orleans is a lively city with a coastal culture heavily influenced by the French, Spanish, Native American, and African peoples. With its Mardi Gras, Congo Square, African ring dance, Voodoo Queen Marie Laveau, African drumming, Cajun fiddling, and Creole cooking, the culture of the Crescent City is thoroughly intermingled like a great big pot of gumbo or jambalaya.
>
> St. Louis, on the other hand, is a city founded by the French but controlled by Germans. And although many other ethnic groups (French, Italians, Jews, Hungarians, Native Americans, and African Americans) have had an impact, the culture is pervasively German. It is

more Calvinistic than Catholic, more marching band than Mardi Gras. It is a culture where a show of emotion is considered uncouth, almost uncivilized. Thus, a much more restrained musical culture developed among St. Louis blacks, one that took a much cooler approach. The one city-wide parade, the Veil Prophet Parade, was for nearly one hundred years a whites-only event. (The parade and ball were finally integrated in the 1970s.) Such parades were sedate, dull affairs. I witnessed many and never saw anyone dance with any saints or speak to any spirits. Blacks had the Annie Malone Parade to get by on, but even this was no joyous, celebratory affair; rather, it was cool and laid back. If New Orleans is gumbo and jambalaya, St. Louis is chitterlings, barbecue, mashed potatoes and gravy. That Miles grew up in this cooler musical milieu is reflected in his approach to music and in the man himself.

While Troupe acknowledges some similarity between the St. Louis sound and the New Orleans trumpet tradition, he highlights the contrast between the two. He thus explains why one culture—St. Louis—could produce a Miles Davis when it did, while another culture—New Orleans—could not. The line of reasoning could be represented as follows: lively mix of French, Spanish, Native American, and African cultures→Catholic→Mardi Gras→emotional, openly celebratory→a culture that can be likened to gumbo or jambalaya→local models, like Louis Armstrong and Al Hirt, who play the "hot, brassy" style→thus no Miles Davis, *but* pervasive German influence in the St. Louis area→Calvinistic→restrained marching bands→African American musical innovation that emphasized coolness→a culture that can be likened to mashed potatoes and gravy→local models, like Eddie Randall and Clark, who play the "running" style→Miles Davis. It is a given that Miles's tremendous individual talent is an essential part of the equation.

Troupe's analysis is richly detailed and contains relevant points of contrast. When writing an essay in the comparison-and-contrast mode, you might find it useful to brainstorm a list of the features that seem relevant to exploring your topic. You could then cluster those features into pairs or groups, eliminating any that do not readily help your case. For instance, people might on average be a little taller, or shorter, in St. Louis than in New Orleans, but that would not have helped Troupe develop his point about the respective trumpet traditions.

Whether you brainstorm and cluster features in advance of writing a first draft or mainly generate comparisons as you develop your essay, you will want to settle on a dominant pattern of presentation. The two patterns are generally referred to as the subject-by-subject and point-by-point methods, respectively, though most writing reflects some mixture of the two. In the subject-by-subject method, you describe all the relevant features of one subject before you describe the features of a second or subsequent subjects. Troupe, for instance, could have finished his description of the St. Louis musical style and culture before mentioning New Orleans. In other words, his organization might have been as follows:

Subject A—The St. Louis Trumpet Style

1. Characteristics of the sound
2. Notable musicians
3. History
4. Development
5. Surrounding culture

Subject B—The New Orleans Trumpet Style

1. Characteristics of the sound
2. Notable musicians
3. History
4. Development
5. Surrounding culture

Because the overall analysis is fairly brief, such a choice may not have affected his readers. However, if Troupe had used a dozen pages to explain one set of phenomena followed by a dozen pages to explain the other group of experiences, then the reading would have taken on a different quality. Because of the limitations of memory, it is virtually impossible for us to keep all the points of comparison and contrast in mind when reading lengthy pieces. Thus, if your goal as a writer is to leave only a general impression of similarity and difference, a subject-by-subject comparison may be the appropriate technique. On the other hand, if your goal is to create sharper images of comparison and contrast, the point-by-point method would better suit your needs. The point-by-point method is closer to what Troupe actually used. Although not entirely precise, his presentation can be represented in the following way:

Point A—The trumpet styles of St. Louis and New Orleans are related, yet different

1. Connected because of musicians' travel along the Mississippi River
2. Different characteristics of the two sounds
3. Notable musicians who exemplify the two sounds

Point B—The styles evolved from different cultures

1. Different ethnic contributions and influences
2. Different secular rituals and dominant religious influences
3. Different degrees of outward expressiveness

Of course, you should experiment with these types of arrangements, as Troupe undoubtedly has, to come up with what you feel works best for a particular piece. In this chapter, the subject-by-subject method is dominant in the pieces by Bruce Catton and R. A. Hudson. The point-by-point technique is illustrated well by Bharati Mukherjee, Jodi Kantor, and Deborah Tannen.

As you develop an essay using comparison and contrast, you will want to use appropriate transitional words or phrases to keep your readers oriented. The longer the piece of writing, the more important is the use of such devices. Words such as *similarly, likewise,* and *however* are often used as markers. Common phrases include "in the same vein," "on the other hand," and various constructions using the word *more* (for example, "more marching band than Mardi Gras").

A special type of comparison worth mentioning is the *analogy.* This is when one thing is explained in terms of another. In an extended analogy, Bart Giamatti, former commissioner of Major League baseball, explains sport in terms of work:

> The basis of sport is work. Running, jumping, lifting, pushing, bending, pulling, planting the legs, and using the back—these exertions are essential to physical labor and to athletic competition. The closeness of a given game to the rituals and effort of work invests the game with dignity; without that proximity to labor, the game would merely be a release from work instead of a refinement of it. The radical difference between work and game, however, occurs when limits or rules are imposed on this labor, patterns which acknowledge that this new work, this sport is not a matter of life and death. Whereas, that work, the work of your back and arms, in field or mill, on ship or in forest, was crucial to your survival, and to the survival of those dependent on you, this work is different; it is delimited, separate, independent, a refinement of reality but distinct. This work is fully as serious and difficult as real work, but this unreal work is not coextensive with life. This work of sport, usually but not always at some predetermined point, will have an end. It will be over, not to begin again with the sun. This work, unlike that real work, does not sustain life in any immediate and practical way, such as providing food; but this unreal serious work does sustain life in the sense that it makes life bearable. It allows all of us to go back renewed to whatever real work we do, perhaps to go back for a moment redeemed.

For Giamatti, sport is not really *like* work in a way that would bear simple comparison; it is connected to work in an integral way. Sport is not the *opposite* of work; it is a version of it. Through effective comparison and contrast, Giamatti evokes the power of the subject, revealing sport in its complexities, its levels of connection with the larger world.

Approaches to Writing Comparison/ Contrast Essays

Writing a comparison/contrast essay emerges from thinking in oppositions, that is, thinking in binary terms. What do we mean by that? Binary thinking is in many ways foundational to western thought. We see it in a myriad of contexts: good vs. bad, love vs. hate, moral vs. immoral, up vs. down, courage vs. fear, inner vs. outer, man vs. woman, flat vs. round. We see the same kind of binary thinking in the debates about what it means to be natural vs. unnatural, whether high school science classes should teach evolution vs. intelligent design, and whether our politicians should promote republican vs. democratic governmental policies. Binary thinking is so ingrained in the ways we converse, write, and conceive of the world in western countries that it can be difficult to imagine other ways of thinking and behaving.

Two forms of binary thinking tend to prevail (ooops—another binary formulation!). The most familiar expression of binary thinking is Hegelian in nature and posits that Position A (a thesis) should be opposed by Position B (an antithesis), and that out of that interaction will emerge a better, more informed Position C (a synthesis). This kind of binary thinking should be familiar, since it speaks to progress and a belief that out of contending voices comes consensus, agreement, and improved understanding. A second form of binary thinking, however, presupposes that opposition does not lead to synthesis but rather that such opposition is an end in itself. This kind of thinking can be found in a good bit of eastern philosophy such as Buddhism and Taoism, where we see that the principles of yin and yang, for example, though oppositional, are each necessary for the other's existence. This more dialectical or dialogical expression of binarism can also be traced back to ancient thought, and it leads to conclusions that are often more balanced and tentative, since the various contending views are unreconcilable.

Whichever approach you take, binary thinking is at the heart of comparison/contrast essay writing, for this mode requires you to consider one subject in relation to another. Of course, not every comparison makes sense: Most of us would not be interested in reading an essay that compares live oak trees to hand lotion. There may be something interesting and valuable in such an essay, but the two subjects are so unlike as to make a meaningful essay all but impossible. Thus the first step in writing a successful comparison/contrast essay is to search for subjects that mutually inform one another and allow you to engage in productive analysis. Suppose, for example, you decide to write about energy, an issue much in the news. Some possible topics include:

- Should we increase production of oil and natural gas or should we focus more on fuel conservation?
- Should we begin gas and oil exploration of the Arctic National Wildlife Refuge or invest in wind or solar power technologies?
- Which is a better way to address our electric power energy problems: coal burning or nuclear power plants?
- What are the pros and cons of creating federal legislation outlawing all motorized vehicles that do not get at least 30 miles per gallon for in-city driving?

Each of these topics allows you to start thinking in binary terms by posing two alternatives. In researching and then writing your essay, you might begin holding one view and then discover that you have changed your mind to the other point of view or even decided that both make sense for different reasons.

The Danger of Dichotomizing

As is clear from the above discussion, finding a subject that allows you to think in binary terms is essential to writing a comparison/contrast essay. Your subject must offer clear similarities and dissimilarities, and you must be able to illuminate it in important and compelling ways by writing about it within this mode. One of the most tempting but least useful approaches to such subjects is to succumb to dichotomizing. Dichotomies are oppositional ways of thinking, and most of the time, dichotomizing leads to oversimplification and the demonization of one of your choices.

Let's say, for example, that you decide to write about whether to eat meat or be a vegetarian. If you have strong feelings about the virtues of meat eating and the silliness, even stupidity, of being a vegetarian, it will be very hard for you to write about the virtues of vegetarianism. Likewise, if you consider meat eating immoral, unethical, cruel, and utterly irrelevant nutrition and culinary pleasure, you will struggle to write about why some people want to eat a lamb chop. Dichotomized thinking leads to oversimplification and superficial analysis. It can be effective if you are trying for a humorous or satirical approach to a subject, but those kinds of essays can be dangerous unless you clearly signal your intention. Jonathan Swift's famous bitterly satirical solution to the problem of Irish poverty in his essay, "A Modest Proposal" (1729), signals its intentions in obvious ways, but it is still misread by students in literature classes, who end up thinking that Swift is vicious and utterly immoral. Daniel Defoe's ironic pamphlet, "The Shortest Way with Dissenters" (1702), caused such an uproar that the authorities imprisoned him. Satirizing one side of an argument is a long and venerable literary tradition, but you want to make sure that you signal your real intentions in some subtle but significant way.

Limiting and Developing Your Subject

As with every essay, you need to control your subject so that you can write about it in useful ways in a composition that is appropriate to the context of first-year composition. Bruce Catton's treatment of Grant and Lee is an excellent example of an essay that limits its subject while making the reader aware of broader implications. Catton could have chosen to contrast attitudes in the North with attitudes in the South during 1864, but such a subject would require at least a chapter if not an entire book. Instead, he concentrates on the two generals and uses them as examples of each side's traditions and values. In your essay, you too will need to find a subject that has significance and can be developed within an essay of 400 to 1,000 words, depending on the assignment.

Often you can find that subject only by doing research in an area that interests you, taking notes, drafting a paragraph or two, and testing out various possibilities. You may make a false start or two, but that's understandable. For example, you may decide to write about contrasting aesthetic styles, and after some research you start outlining some of those differences, as follows:

Aesthetic styles

Art, Clothes, Home Furnishings

- What I like: wood, rich colors, carving, lots of objects, varying textures, dark rather than light

- What I don't like: stark, black and white, straight lines, metal (chrome), smooth surfaces

After some thought, you decide to contrast two styles in terms of interior design: Victorian vs. Danish, the elaborate vs. the minimalist, discussing why you prefer one over the other. Unfortunately, you need to do a good bit more research about both, and as you do so, the amount of information begins to get overwhelming. Rather than abandon the subject, you decide to narrow it further and focus on two living rooms, one with a strong Victorian emphasis, the other done primarily in Danish style, concentrating on furniture choices. That kind of process is typical for writing a comparison/contrast essay. It may even eventuate in your coming to a deeper appreciation of the virtues of minimalism in room design, so that you end up deciding that the Danish style needs to be incorporated in surprising ways within your Victorian motif.

Once you have chosen and limited your subject, you will need to do enough research so that you can write knowledgeably about it. Comparison/contrast essays demand that you know your subject thoroughly. A good rule of thumb is to know much more about your topic than you include in your essay. That way you get to choose what is important and try varying ways to organize your information, testing which way works best. Thus you may decide to write the first half of your essay about Victorian style and the second half about Danish style, or you may decide to write a paragraph about Victorian style followed by a paragraph about Danish style. Or you may organize your essay visually, beginning with overall impressions of one style and then the other, followed by a contrasting analysis of five specific spaces (entrance, sofa with easy chairs, fireplace, large window, open sitting/talking area). Having plenty of information, observations, and details allows you increased understanding and flexibility in choosing what and how you will write about your subject.

Bruce Catton (1899–1978) was born in Petoskey, Michigan, and attended Oberlin College. A Navy veteran who served during World War I, he had notable careers in both civil service and journalism. He served on the War Production Board and worked for the departments of Commerce and the Interior. In addition, he was the longtime senior editor of American Heritage. *A Civil War expert, he published several books on the conflict, including* Mr. Lincoln's Army *(1951) and* A Stillness at Appomattox *(1953), which won a Pulitzer Prize and National Book Award. The essay in this chapter was first published in a collection of essays by noted historians titled* The American Story *(1956).*

Bruce Catton

Grant and Lee: A Study in Contrasts

When Ulysses S. Grant and Robert E. Lee met in the parlor of a modest house at Appomattox Court House, Virginia, on April 9, 1865, to work out the terms for the surrender of Lee's Army of Northern Virginia, a great chapter in American life came to a close, and a great new chapter began.

These men were bringing the Civil War to its virtual finish. To be sure, other armies had yet to surrender, and for a few days the fugitive Confederate government would struggle desperately and vainly, trying to find some way to go on living now that its chief support was gone. But in effect it was all over when Grant and Lee signed the papers. And the little room where they wrote out the terms was the scene of one of the poignant, dramatic contrasts in American history.

They were two strong men, these oddly different generals, and they represented the strengths of two conflicting currents that, through them, had come into final collision.

Back of Robert E. Lee was the notion that the old aristocratic concept might somehow survive and be dominant in American life.

5   Lee was tidewater Virginia, and in his background were family, culture, and tradition . . . the age of chivalry transplanted to a New World which was making its own legends and its own myths. He embodied a way of life that had come down through the age of knighthood and the English country squire. America was a land that was be-

ginning all over again, dedicated to nothing much more complicated than the rather hazy belief that all men had equal rights and should have an equal chance in the world. In such a land Lee stood for the feeling that it was somehow of advantage to human society to have pronounced inequality in the social structure. There should be a leisure class, backed by ownership of land; in turn, society itself should be keyed to the land as the chief source of wealth and influence. It would bring forth (according to this ideal) a class of men with a strong sense of obligation to the community; men who lived not to gain advantage for themselves, but to meet the solemn obligations which had been laid on them by the very fact that they were privileged. From them the country would get its leadership; to them it could look for the higher values—of thought, of conduct, of personal deportment—to give it strength and virtue.

Lee embodied the noblest elements of this aristocratic ideal. Through him, the landed nobility justified itself. For four years, the Southern states had fought a desperate war to uphold the ideals for which Lee stood. In the end, it almost seemed as if the Confederacy fought for Lee; as if he himself was the Confederacy . . . the best thing that the way of life for which the Confederacy stood could ever have to offer. He had passed into legend before Appomattox. Thousands of tired, underfed, poorly clothed Confederate soldiers, long since past the simple enthusiasm of the early days of the struggle, somehow considered Lee the symbol of everything for which they had been willing to die. But they could not quite put this feeling into words. If the Lost Cause, sanctified by so much heroism and so many deaths, had a living justification, its justification was General Lee.

Grant, the son of a tanner on the Western frontier, was everything Lee was not. He had come up the hard way and embodied nothing in particular except the eternal toughness and sinewy fiber of the men who grew up beyond the mountains. He was one of a body of men who owed reverence and obeisance to no one, who were self-reliant to a fault, who cared hardly anything for the past but who had a sharp eye for the future.

These frontier men were the precise opposites of the tidewater aristocrats. Back of them, in the great surge that had taken people over the Alleghenies and into the opening Western country, there was a deep, implicit dissatisfaction with a past that had settled into grooves. They stood for democracy, not from any reasoned conclusion about the proper ordering of human society, but simply because they had grown up in the middle of democracy and knew how it worked. Their society might have privileges, but they would be privileges each man had won for himself. Forms and patterns meant nothing. No man was born to anything, except perhaps to a chance to show how far he could rise. Life was competition.

Yet along with this feeling had come a deep sense of belonging to a national community. The Westerner who developed a farm, opened a shop, or set up in business as a trader, could hope to prosper only as his own community prospered—and his community ran from the Atlantic to the Pacific and from Canada down to Mexico. If the land was settled, with towns and highways and accessible markets, he could better himself. He saw his fate in terms of the nation's own destiny. As its horizons expanded, so did his. He had, in other words, an acute dollars-and-cents stake in the continued growth and development of his country.

10   And that, perhaps, is where the contrast between Grant and Lee becomes most striking. The Virginia aristocrat, inevitably, saw himself in relation to his own region. He lived in a static society which could endure almost anything except change. Instinctively, his first loyalty would go to the locality in which that society existed. He would fight to the limit of endurance to defend it, because in defending it he was defending everything that gave his own life its deepest meaning.

The Westerner, on the other hand, would fight with an equal tenacity for the broader concept of society. He fought so because everything he lived by was tied to growth, expansion, and a constantly widening horizon. What he lived by would survive or fall with the nation itself. He could not possibly stand by unmoved in the face of an attempt to destroy the Union. He would combat it with everything he had, because he could only see it as an effort to cut the ground out from under his feet.

So Grant and Lee were in complete contrast, representing two diametrically opposed elements in American life. Grant was the modern man emerging; beyond him, ready to come on the stage, was the great age of steel and machinery, of crowded cities and a restless burgeoning vitality. Lee might have ridden down from the old age of chivalry, lance in hand, silken banner fluttering over his head. Each man was the perfect champion of his cause, drawing both his strengths and his weaknesses from the people he led.

Yet it was not all contrast, after all. Different as they were—in background, in personality, in underlying aspiration—these two great soldiers had much in common. Under everything else, they were marvelous fighters. Furthermore, their fighting qualities were really very much alike.

Each man had, to begin with, the great virtue of utter tenacity and fidelity. Grant fought his way down the Mississippi Valley in spite of acute personal discouragement and profound military handicaps. Lee hung on in the trenches at Petersburg after hope itself had died. In each man there was an indomitable quality . . . the born fighter's refusal to give up as long as he can still remain on his feet and lift his two fists.

15   Daring and resourcefulness they had, too; the ability to think faster and move faster than the enemy. These were the qualities which gave Lee the dazzling campaigns of Second Manassas and Chancellorsville and won Vicksburg for Grant.

Lastly, and perhaps greatest of all, there was the ability, at the end, to turn quickly from war to peace once the fighting was over. Out of the way these two men behaved at Appomattox came the possibility of a peace of reconciliation. It was a possibility not wholly realized, in the years to come, but which did, in the end, help the two sections to become one nation again . . . after a war whose bitterness might have seemed to make such a reunion wholly impossible. No part of either man's life became him more than the part he played in this brief meeting in the McLean house at Appomattox. Their behavior there put all succeeding generations of Americans in their debt. Two great Americans, Grant and Lee—very different, yet under everything very much alike. Their encounter at Appomattox was one of the great moments of American history.

Analyzing Rhetorical Choices

1. Catton largely relies on the subject-by-subject technique to contrast and compare Grant and Lee. In which ways do you find this pattern of comparison and contrast effective?
2. Catton uses the adjective *great* to describe both an era that was ending and one that was beginning. Does *great* seem appropriate to you as a description of both eras? Explain your response.
3. Although Catton asserts that Grant and Lee were of different backgrounds, aspirations, and personalities, he does not detail how their personalities differed. What information about the personalities of the two generals do you think would have improved the author's analysis?

Writing About Issues and Contexts

1. Although slavery is not mentioned in the text, how might your knowledge of its existence shape your response to Catton's essay?
2. A significant number of soldiers who became invested in and fought for the Confederacy were, in fact, Northerners who had relocated. How does this fact affect your response to Catton's portrayal of Lee?
3. In what ways do succeeding generations remain indebted to Grant and Lee?

A *native of Calcutta, India,* **Bharati Mukherjee** *(1940–) grew up in India and Europe. She received a bachelor's degree from the University of Calcutta and a master's from the University of Baroda.* Mukherjee *came to the United States in 1961 to pursue a degree at the University of Iowa and has resided since in the United States or Canada. She currently holds the rank of distinguished professor of English at the University of California at Berkeley. Her books include* The Tiger's Daughter *(1972),* Darkness *(1985),* Jasmine *(1989),* The Holder of the World *(1993),* Leave It to Me *(1997), and* Desirable Daughters *(2002). The following article originally appeared in the* New York Times *in 1996.*

Bharati Mukherjee

Two Ways to Belong in America

This is a tale of two sisters from Calcutta, Mira and Bharati, who have lived in the United States for some 35 years, but who find themselves on different sides in the current debate over the status of immigrants. I am an American citizen and she is not. I am moved that thousands of long-term residents are finally taking the oath of citizenship. She is not.

Mira arrived in Detroit in 1960 to study child psychology and pre-school education. I followed her a year later to study creative writing at the University of Iowa. When we left India, we were almost identical in appearance and attitude. We dressed alike, in saris; we expressed identical views on politics, social issues, love, and marriage in the same Calcutta convent-school accent. We would endure our two years in America, secure our degrees, then return to India to marry the grooms of our father's choosing.

Instead, Mira married an Indian student in 1962 who was getting his business administration degree at Wayne State University. They soon acquired the labor certifications necessary for the green card of hassle-free residence and employment.

Mira still lives in Detroit, works in the Southfield, Mich., school system, and has become nationally recognized for her contributions in the fields of pre-school education and parent-teacher relationships. After 36 years as a legal immigrant in this country, she clings passionately to her Indian citizenship and hopes to go home to India when she retires.

5   In Iowa City in 1963, I married a fellow student, an American of Canadian parentage. Because of the accident of his North Dakota birth, I bypassed labor-certification requirements and the race-related "quota" system that favored the applicant's country of origin over his or her merit. I was prepared for (and even welcomed) the emotional strain that came with marrying outside my ethnic community. In 33 years of marriage, we have lived in every part of North America. By choosing a husband who was not my father's selection, I was opting for fluidity, self-invention, blue jeans and T-shirts, and renouncing 3,000 years (at least) of caste-observant, "pure culture" marriage in the Mukherjee family. My books have often been read as unapologetic (and in some quarters overenthusiastic) texts for cultural and psychological "mongrelization." It's a word I celebrate.

Mira and I have stayed sisterly close by phone. In our regular Sunday morning conversations, we are unguardedly affectionate. I am her only blood relative on this continent. We expect to see each other through the looming crises of aging and ill health without being asked. Long before Vice President Gore's "Citizenship U.S.A." drive, we'd had our polite arguments over the ethics of retaining an overseas citizenship while expecting the permanent protection and economic benefits that come with living and working in America.

Like well-raised sisters, we never said what was really on our minds, but we probably pitied one another. She, for the lack of structure in my life, the erasure of Indianness, the absence of an unvarying daily core. I, for the narrowness of her perspective, her uninvolvement with the mythic depths or the superficial pop culture of this society. But, now, with the scapegoating of "aliens" (documented or illegal) on the increase, and the targeting of long-term legal immigrants like Mira for new scrutiny and new self-consciousness, she and I find ourselves unable to maintain the same polite discretion. We were always unacknowledged adversaries, and we are now, more than ever, sisters.

"I feel used," Mira raged on the phone the other night. "I feel manipulated and discarded. This is such an unfair way to treat a person who was invited to stay and work here because of her talent. My employer went to the I.N.S. and petitioned for the labor certification. For over 30 years, I've invested my creativity and professional skills into the improvement of *this* country's pre-school system. I've obeyed all the rules, I've paid my taxes, I love my work, I love my students, I love the friends I've made. How dare America now change its rules in midstream? If America wants to make new rules curtailing benefits of legal immigrants, they should apply only to immigrants who arrive after those rules are already in place."

To my ears, it sounded like the description of a long-enduring, comfortable yet loveless marriage, without risk or recklessness. Have we the right to demand, and to expect, that we be loved? (That, to me is the subtext of the arguments by immigration advocates.) My sister is an expatriate, professionally generous and creative, socially courteous and gracious, and that's as far as her Americanization can go. She is here to maintain an identity, not to transform it.

10   I asked her if she would follow the example of others who have decided to become citizens because of the anti-immigration bills in Congress. And here, she surprised me. "If America wants to play the manipulative game, I'll play it, too," she snapped. "I'll become a U.S. citizen for now, then change back to Indian when I'm ready to go home. I feel some kind of irrational attachment to India that I don't to America. Until all this hysteria against legal immigrants, I was totally happy. Having my green card meant I could visit any place in the world I wanted to and then come back to a job that's satisfying and that I do very well."

In one family, from two sisters alike as peas in a pod, there could not be a wider divergence of immigrant experience. America spoke to me—I married it—I embraced the demotion from expatriate aristocrat to immigrant nobody, surrendering those thousands of years of "pure culture," the saris, the delightfully accented English. She retained them all. Which of us is the freak?

Mira's voice, I realize, is the voice not just of the immigrant South Asian community but of an immigrant community of the millions who have stayed rooted in one job, one city, one house, one ancestral culture, one cuisine, for the entirety of their productive years. She speaks for greater numbers than I possibly can. Only the fluency of her English and the anger, rather than fear, born of confidence from her education, differentiate her from the seamstresses, the domestics, the technicians, the shop owners, the millions of hard-working but effectively silenced documented immigrants as well as their less fortunate "illegal" brothers and sisters.

Nearly 20 years ago, when I was living in my husband's ancestral homeland of Canada, I was always well-employed but never allowed to feel part of the local Quebec or larger Canadian society. Then, through a Green Paper that invited a national referendum on the unwanted side effects of "nontraditional" immigration, the Government officially turned against its immigrant communities, particularly those from South Asia.

I felt then the same sense of betrayal that Mira feels now. I will never forget the pain of that sudden turning, and the casual racist outbursts the Green Paper elicited. That sense of betrayal had its desired effect and drove me, and thousands like me, from the country.

15   Mira and I differ, however, in the ways in which we hope to interact with the country that we have chosen to live in. She is happier to live in America as expatriate Indian than as an immigrant American. I need to feel like a part of the community I have adopted (as I tried to feel in Canada as well). I need to put roots down, to vote and make the difference that I can. The price that the immigrant willingly pays, and that the exile avoids, is the trauma of self-transformation.

Analyzing Rhetorical Choices

1. Concerning her relationship with Mira, Mukherjee writes, "Like well-raised sisters, we never said what really was on our minds. . . ." In your view, how much does this description help to explain their relationship?

2. Regarding Mira's complaint about proposed immigration rules, Mukherjee suggests that "it sounded like the description of a long-enduring, comfortable yet loveless marriage, without risk or restlessness." Do you agree with her analogy? Is there another way you would describe Mira's position?

Writing About Issues and Contexts

1. How would you answer the author's question, "which one of us is the freak?"

2. Do you agree with Mira's position or Bharati's? Is there a middle ground between the two?

3. How does Mukherjee's last sentence take on added significance after the events of September 11, 2001?

Following a brief stint at Harvard Law School and a year as an aide to Rudolph Giuliani, **Jodi Kantor** *(1976–) became an editor at* Slate, *the most popular on-line magazine with more than two million visitors per month. In March 2003, she was made the Arts & Leisure editor of the* New York Times. *The following is a review of* The Boxer's Heart *by Kate Sekules and* Looking for a Fight *by Lynn Snowden Picket.*

Jodi Kantor

Wham! Bam! Thanks a Bunch!

Two Memoirs by Women Who Took Up Boxing and Became Dangerous

Most memoirs describe their authors' getting bruised in some way, but the new ones by Kate Sekules and Lynn Snowden Picket are satisfyingly literal about it. Both women took up boxing as a hobby, and the books describe how they bled their way from neophytes to confirmed pugilists.

If you were just glancing over their books, Sekules and Picket would look like twins: both edit or write for glossy magazines, trained at Gleason's Gym in Brooklyn and took up boxing in the mid-1990's, when they were in their mid-30's. But their differences begin with their respective attractions to the ring. Sekules, bored with Manhattan's aerobics-industrial complex, is simply looking for a new workout. She enumerates various traumas that might account for her desire to box—a comically wussy athletic education, a lingering case of the body-image blues. But in listing them, she sounds more like an actor searching for a character's motivation than someone truly brimming with fury. Meanwhile, Picket is every bit as angry as the title of her book suggests. She has just suffered through a humiliating divorce—her husband had been cheating—and plans to avenge herself in the ring: "I'm full of rage and I want to beat someone up. I want to know what it is to have physical power over men. I want to inspire fear. I want to matter," she says.

Each alights at Gleason's Gym, the storied training ground of fighters from Jake LaMotta to Larry Holmes, and immediately swoons over its warped mirrors, bloodstained canvases and general air of sweaty antiglamour. At first, there's something laughably Bobo-ish about these well-heeled women—Sekules is an editor at Food & Wine magazine, while Picket bids on art at Sotheby's—venturing to Brooklyn to find their inner grit among the tough-guy habitués of Gleason's. But Sekules is appealingly self-aware about the project: "There is no doubt that part of what I'm falling in love with is the thing my very presence here will help subvert; that is, boxing as it used to seem—an arcane testosterone ghetto, photogenic and roman-tic, adoringly treated in black-and-white by Scorsese in *Raging Bull* or Bruce Weber in *Broken Noses*."

Arrivistes they may be, but dilettantes they're not. Before long, Sekules and Picket are each sparring regularly, and they acquire the pur-pled knuckles, blackened eyes and bloody noses to prove it. Sparring—which is part workout, part scrimmage—has its own etiquette, and some of the books' best moments come as Sekules and Picket puzzle over how to hit hard enough to be taken seriously, but not so aggres-sively as to turn casual challenges into all-out slugfests. This calculation is made even trickier by their sex: the men they face are reluctant to hit a woman, but even more reluctant to be beaten by one.

5   As they work their way toward their first real bouts, the authors provide a steady flow of vivid anecdotes, from Picket's account of how sudden stops in the ring eventually knock a boxer's toenails off, to Sekules's description of how, before her pro debut, the local boxing commissioner demands "visual evidence" that she is really female. Both are graceful sportswriters, but Picket's small, grating tic of relay-ing superfluous details—in particular, what she's wearing—often inter-feres both with her narrative and her desire to be taken seriously. And whereas Picket expresses little contact with or affinity for fellow women fighters, Sekules gives us a sense of women's boxing as a thriv-ing movement. Her comrades include Jill Matthews, a punk rocker and rabbi's daughter; Karyn Kusama, director of the recent film *Girlfight;* and Lucia Rijker, a champion fighter and practicing Buddhist. (But not Lynn Snowden Picket. If the authors' paths crossed, neither mentions it.)

Sekules also includes a rousing history of female boxing, stretch-ing from the earliest recorded bout in 1722 to Christy Martin's 1996 fight against Deirdre Gogarty on the Mike Tyson-Frank Bruno under-card, which upstaged the men's match, providing a symbolic rebuke to Tyson, who had just finished serving time for rape. This interest in other women fighters, past and present, provides welcome context for Sekules's own quest and keeps her solipsism quotient in check.

If Sekules and Picket are any example, women boxers still have much to prove. The writers are mistaken for battered women by well-meaning strangers, Picket is propositioned by her trainer and Sekules is sought out by guys looking for sadomasochistic kinks. Sekules makes more of these insults, interspersing her story with frequent asides on gender, sports and violence. But the action in the gym is so much more effectively rendered, and the subtext already so rich and pronounced, that these reflections feel windy and superfluous. "Women are born with a lightning rod, and whether we honor it or not, it is the feminine principle, a subcutaneous awareness of connect-edness," writes the otherwise reliable Sekules.

In the end, Sekules seems to get from boxing what she came for: a stronger body and sense of self, as well as a gymload of new friends. Picket, on the other hand, picks up some nasty habits. For one thing, she can no longer keep her hands to herself. She slugs a hapless guy who accidentally sloshes beer on her at a fight; a teenager who startles her in Central Park; and her boyfriend's brother, after he jokingly lands a sucker punch on her at a party. Worse, she punches a stranger who brings his young son to Gleason's one day and shouts out uninvited instructions as she spars. Brushing away contrition about hitting him in front of his son, she chortles: "Never tell a woman what to do if she happens to be wearing boxing gloves."

Ironically, when Picket really does need to defend herself, she can't: after her nose is bloodied by an overaggressive sparring partner, Picket drags her slight-bodied, sensitive boyfriend to the gym and threatens to dump him if he doesn't defend her honor by threatening her assailant. Instead of making her feel powerful, boxing eventually makes her paranoid and panicky, even fearful that "someone's out there, waiting to beat me up." Finally, during her first real bout, a revelation hits her: "This is like getting into a car accident for sport," she thinks, and a little more than 10 pages later she's quit boxing entirely. Picket finishes her book by solemnly itemizing the brain damage that the sport can inflict. She declares her boxing project "ludicrous and deranged," and claims that had she known then what she does now, she never would have stepped into the ring in the first place.

10   Which would have been a shame. Sekules and Picket may not belong beside A. J. Liebling and Norman Mailer in the boxing writer hall of fame, but their girl-next-door approaches are still absorbing.

These writers bridge the gap between the fans who find boxing thrilling and the detractors who find it senselessly brutal by showing us how one can become the other. And who has ever watched a boxing match without wondering what it would be like to participate? Reading about Muhammad Ali and the other greats doesn't quite satisfy this urge; while we want to know and understand them, few of us could ever see ourselves in their boots. For those of us, male or female, who will never get in the ring, these books provide an idea of how we might perform there and what it might do to us.

Analyzing Rhetorical Choices

1. Kantor's essay is a combination of the subject-by-subject and point-by-point techniques. Are the lines of argument, the notions of comparisons and contrasts, kept clear enough for you? Support your response.

2. Does Kantor's selection of details or anecdotes create interest on your part in the books she reviews? If so, why?

3. What is your response to such phrases as "testosterone ghetto," "Manhattan's aerobics-industrial complex," and "solipsism quotient"? Whom does she envision as her audience?

Writing About Issues and Contexts

1. How do you feel about what, according to this article, motivates these women to box?

2. Kantor disagrees with Sekules's idea of a feminine principle. Do you agree with Sekules or Kantor? Explain your choice.

3. Assuming that you were going to pick only one of these books to read, which one would you choose? Why do you make that choice?

Cornel West (1953–) is a professor of African American Studies at Princeton University. A native of Tulsa, Oklahoma, he received his undergraduate degree from Harvard and graduate degrees from Princeton. He has taught at several universities, including Harvard and Yale. His research interests include African American critical thought, social theory, modern and postmodern philosophy and literature, and the future of black youth. One of the nation's most popular lecturers, West's books include Beyond Eurocentrism and Multiculturalism *(1993),* Race Matters *(1993), and* The Cornel West Reader *(1999). The selection that follows is from* Jews and Blacks: A Dialogue on Race, Religion, and Culture in America, *which he coauthored with Michael Lerner in 1995.*

Cornel West
Blacks and Jews

Why are Blacks and Jews in the United States the most unique and fascinating people in modern times? Why have both groups contributed so disproportionately to the richness and vitality in American life? Can we honestly imagine what twentieth-century American democracy would be like without the past and present doings and sufferings of Blacks and Jews? What forms will progressive politics take, if any, with escalating tensions between these two historically liberal groups?

When historians look back on the emergence, development, and decline of American civilization, they obviously will note its distinctive features—constitutional democracy and precious liberties (with its class, gender, and especially racial constraints), material prosperity, technological ingenuity, ethnic and regional diversity, market-driven yet romantic popular culture, relative lack of historical consciousness, and an obsession with progress in the future. Yet these historians would miss much if they failed to acknowledge and examine the two most extraordinary peoples in U.S. history—people of African descent and people of Jewish origins and persuasion. Needless to say, all people are, in some significant sense, extraordinary. But Blacks and Jews stand out in a glaring manner.

Both Jews and Blacks are a pariah people—a people who had to make and remake themselves as outsiders on the margins of American society and culture. Both groups assumed that the status quo was unjust and therefore found strategies to survive and thrive against the odds. Both groups defined themselves as a people deeply shaped by America but never *fully* a part of America. Both groups appealed to biblical texts and relied on communal bonds to sustain themselves—texts that put a premium on justice, mercy, and solidarity with the downtrodden, and bonds shot through with a deep distrust, suspicion, even paranoia, toward the powerful and privileged. Both groups have been hated and despised peoples who find it difficult, if not impossible, to fully overcome group insecurity and anxiety as well as truly be and love themselves as individuals and as a people. Wearing the masks, enduring petty put-downs, and coping with subtle insults remains an everyday challenge for most Blacks and some Jews in America.

Both groups are the most modern of modern people in that they have created new and novel ways of life, innovative and improvisational modes of being in the world. Their entree into modernity as degraded Others—dishonored slaves (Blacks) and devalued non-Christians (Jews)—forced them to hammer out the most un-American yet modern of products—tragicomic dispositions toward reality that put sadness, sorrow, and suffering at the center of their plights and predicaments. This tragicomic character of the Black and Jewish experiences in modernity—coupled with a nagging moral conscience owing to undeniable histories of underdog status and unusual slavery-to-freedom narratives in authoritative texts—haunts both groups.

5   And what Blacks and Jews have done with their intelligence, imagination, and ingenuity is astounding. Twentieth-century America—a century that begins only a generation after the emancipation of penniless, illiterate, enslaved Africans and the massive influx of poor Eastern European Jewish immigrants—is unimaginable without the creative breakthroughs and monumental contributions of Blacks and Jews. At the very highest levels of achievement, we have Louis Armstrong and Aaron Copland, Duke Ellington and Leonard Bernstein, John Coltrane and George Gershwin, Sarah Vaughan and Irving Berlin, Toni Morrison and Saul Bellow, W. E. B. Du Bois and Hannah Arendt, Romare Bearden and Jackson Pollock, August Wilson and Arthur Miller, Paul Robeson and Pete Seeger, Ralph Ellison and Irving Howe, Kathleen Battle and Beverly Sills, Richard Pryor and Lenny Bruce, Willie Mays and Sandy Koufax, Andre Watts and Itzhak Perlman, Jacob Lawrence and Mark Rothko, Babyface (Kenneth Edmonds) and Carole King, Thurgood Marshall and Louis Brandeis, Marvin Gaye and Bob Dylan, James Baldwin and Norman Mailer, Lorraine Hansberry and Neil Simon, Aretha Franklin and Barbra Streisand, Billy Strayhorn and Stephen Sondheim. This short and incomplete list of towering Black

and Jewish figures is neither an act of providence nor a mere accident. Rather it is the result of tremendous talent, discipline, and energy of two ostracized groups who disproportionately shape the cultural life of this country.

Furthermore, Jewish power and influence—though rarely wielded in a monolithic manner—in the garment industry, show business, medical and legal professions, journalism, and the academy—has had a major impact on the shaping of American life. We are reminded of the fundamental centrality of learning in Jewish life when we realize that as of 1989, of fifty American Nobel Laureates in the medical sciences—such as biochemistry and physiology—seventeen were Jews.

This latter point—the matter of relative Jewish zeal in business and education—is a delicate one. It does not mean that Jews are innately smarter than others or that they are involved in some secret conspiracy to control the banks and newspapers, as implied by the anti-Semitic remarks of General George Brown, Chairman of the Joint Chiefs of Staff, in a lecture at Duke University in 1974. Instead these realities reflect the dominant Jewish ways of gaining access to resources, status, and power against anti-Semitic exclusions in other spheres and over three thousand years of autonomous institution-building based on self-help and self-development around literary and mathematical skills.

African-Americans also have a rich history of business enterprise and scientific achievements—yet the entrepreneurial ethic has been set back by racist attacks (nearly two-thirds of those lynched at the turn of the century were businessmen), and exclusion from significant access to capital and credit, weak communal bonds to sustain business efforts, underfunded Black schools and colleges that downplay independent business efforts, and vicious stereotypes that undercut motivation to study math and natural sciences.

In fact, the fundamental differences between Blacks and Jews in America have been the vast impact of slavery and Jim Crow on limiting the Black quest for self-confidence in literary and scientific matters, and the containment of most Black folk in rural and agrarian areas until World War II, where access to literacy was difficult. In stark contrast, American Jews have always been primarily an urban people trying to find safe niches in industrial (and anti-Semitic) America, who fall back on strong and long traditions of independent institution-building. In this regard, the experiences of Blacks and Jews have been qualitatively different in a deeply racist and more mildly anti-Semitic America.

10   Yet, ironically, Jews and Blacks have been linked in a kind of symbiotic relation with each other. Whether they are allies or antagonists, they are locked into an inescapable embrace principally owing to their dominant status of degraded Others, given the racist and Christian character of the American past and present. First, because anti-Black and anti-Jewish waves are an omnipresent threat in this country. Second, because their support of progressive politics casts them as potential threats to the status quo in their critical and dissenting roles. And third, because both groups not only have a profound fascination with each other but also because they have much at stake in their own collective identities as a pariah and "chosen" people—be it in covenant with a God that "chooses" to side with the underdog or against a nation that "chooses" to treat them unequally or unkindly.

       When Michael Lerner—from whom I've learned so much and come to love so dearly—and I began our dialogue, we knew we had to build upon the rich legacies of Martin Luther King, Jr., and Abraham Joshua Heschel. We had to cast our exchange in such a way that we highlighted moral ideals and existential realities bigger and better than both Black and Jewish interests. We had to examine what it means to be human as Jews and Blacks and how this relates to keeping alive the best of a precious yet precarious experiment in democracy. We also had to examine the ways in which we could revitalize progressive politics in the light of prophetic traditions in the Black and Jewish heritages. This is why our Black-Jewish dialogue—much like relevant, Black-Brown, Jewish-Asian or Black-Red dialogue—is but an instance of the human struggle for freedom and democracy. And any such struggle is predicated on the democratic faith that we everyday people can critically examine our individual and collective pasts, honestly confront our difficult present, and imaginatively project an all-embracing moral vision for the future. Our courageous foremothers and forefathers as well as our innocent children and grandchildren deserve nothing less.

Analyzing Rhetorical Choices

1. West opens his essay with a series of questions. What is the effect of this strategy? Would the impact be different if he had opened with statements instead? For example, what if he had written, "Blacks and Jews in the United States are the most unique and fascinating people in modern times"?

2. What does the phrase "progressive politics" mean to you as used in the first paragraph? Why do you think West uses this phrase?
3. Like Catton, West develops part of his argument without citing sources. Is his argument nonetheless logical or credible in your opinion? Defend your point of view.

Writing About Issues and Contexts

1. In the first sentence of the second paragraph, West suggests that the decline of American civilization is a given. In the last paragraph, he writes of "keeping alive the best of a precious yet precarious experiment in democracy." What is your response to these remarks?
2. What important dialogues would you add to the list given by West in the final paragraph? Why?

R. A. Hudson *(1939–) is an emeritus professor of linguistics at University College London. An advocate of teaching more language awareness in schools, Richard Hudson is a founding member of the Committee for Linguistics in Education. His scholarly publications in-clude* Word Meaning *(1995) and* English Grammar *(1998). The excerpt in this chapter is from his 1980 text,* Sociolinguistics.

R. A. Hudson

Language Worlds

An Imaginary World

What, then, is there to say about language in relation to society? It may be helpful to start by trying to imagine a society (and a lan-guage) about which there is very *little* to say. The little world de-scribed below is completely imaginary, and most sociolinguists—per-haps all of them—would agree that it is highly unlikely that any such world either does or even could exist, given what we know about both language and society.

In our imaginary world there is a society which is clearly defined by some natural boundary, impassable in either direction. The purpose of postulating this boundary is to guarantee, on the one hand, that no members of other communities join this one, bringing their own lan-guages with them, and, on the other, that members of this community never leave it and take their language to another, thereby complicating the perfect coincidence between language and community.

Everybody in this society has exactly the same language—they know the same constructions and the same words, with the same pro-nunciation and the same range of meanings for every single word in the language. (Any deviation from such an exact identity raises the possibility of statements such as "Person A knows pronunciation M, but Person B knows pronunciation N, for the same word," which would be a statement about language in relation to society.) An obvi-ous problem is that very young members of the society, just learning to talk, must necessarily be different from everybody else. We might get round this problem by saying that child language is the domain of a branch of psychology rather than sociology, and that psychology can provide general principles of language acquisition which will allow us to predict every respect in which the language of children in this society deviated from the language of the adults. If psychology were able to provide the necessary principles, then there would be a good deal to say about language in relation to individual development, but nothing about language in relation to society. Needless to say, no psychologist would dream of claiming that this was possible, even in principle.

A consequence of the complete absence of any differences between members of this community is that language change is thereby ruled out, since such change normally involves a difference between the oldest and youngest generations, so that when the former all die only the forms used by the latter survive. Since change seems to affect every language so far studied, this makes the language of our imaginary community unique. The only way to allow for change in a totally homogeneous community is to assume that every change affects every member of the community absolutely and simultaneously: one day, nobody has the new form, the next day, everybody has it. (It is very hard to see any mechanism which could explain such change, short of community-wide telepathy!)

5   Another characteristic of the community we are considering is that *circumstances* have no influence on what people say, either with respect to its content or its form. There are no "formal" and "informal" situations, requiring different kinds of vocabulary (such as *receive* versus *get*) or different pronunciations for words (like *not* versus *-n't*). Nor are there any "discussions" and "arguments," or "requests" and "demands," each requiring not only particular forms but also particular meanings. (For instance, in an argument you *attack* the other person's position, but in a discussion you *consider* it.) Nor are there any differences between the beginnings, middles and ends of conversations, such as would require greetings and farewells. None of these differences due to circumstances exist because if they did they would require statements about society—in particular, about social interaction. Indeed, if we discount any influence of the social context, it is doubtful if speech is possible at all, since spoken messages are generally geared specifically to the needs of the audience.

Finally, we must assume that there is no connection between the culture of the postulated community and the meanings which its language (especially its vocabulary) allows it to express. The language must therefore contain no words such as *cricket* or *priest*, whose meanings could be stated only with reference to a partial description of the culture. To assume otherwise would be to allow rich and interesting statements about language in relation to society, since culture is one of the most important characteristics of society. Exactly what kinds of concepts the members of this community *would* be able to express is not clear—possibly they would only be able to assert logical truths such as "If p and q, then p," since any other kinds of word are likely to involve some reference to the community's culture.

All in all, our blue-print for a community is an uncompromising one. All the restrictions imposed on it were necessary in order to guarantee that there should be nothing to say about its language in relation to society, beyond the simple statement "Such-and-such community speak language X." However, it will be noticed that this statement is precisely the kind which is generally made by linguists (or laymen) about a language, and exhausts what they feel obliged to say about the language in relation to society. The purpose of this section has been to show that the only kind of community (or language) for which such a statement could be remotely adequate is a fictitious one.

A Real but Exotic World

We now turn to a real world, in which there is a great deal to be said about language in relation to society. It is the very exotic world of the north-west Amazon, described by A.P. Sorensen (1971) and J. Jackson (1974).

Geographically, the area in question is half in Brazil and half in Colombia, coinciding more or less with the area in which a language called Tukano can be relied on as a *lingua franca* (i.e., a trade language widely spoken as a non-native language). It is a large area, but sparsely inhabited; around 10,000 people in an area the size of England. Most of the people are indigenous Indians, divided into over twenty tribes, which are in turn grouped in five "phratries" (groups of related tribes). There are two crucial facts to be remembered about this community. First, each tribe speaks a different language—sufficiently different to be mutually incomprehensible and, in some cases, genetically unrelated (i.e., not descended from a common "parent" language). Indeed, the *only* criterion by which tribes can be distinguished from each other is by their language. The second fact is that the five phratries (and thus all twenty-odd tribes) are exogamous (i.e., a man must not marry a woman from the same phratry or tribe). Putting these two facts together, it is easy to see the main linguistic consequence: a man's wife *must* speak a different language from him.

10   We now add a third fact: marriage is patrilocal (the husband and wife live where the husband was brought up), and there is a rule that the wife should not only live where the husband was brought up, but should also use his language in speaking to their children (a custom that might be called "patrilingual marriage"). The linguistic consequence of this rule is that a child's mother does not teach her own language to the child, but rather a language which she speaks only as a foreigner—as though everyone in Britain learned their English from a foreign au-pair girl. One can thus hardly call the children's first language their "mother-tongue" except by a stretch of the imagination. The reports of this community do not mention any widespread disruption in language learning or general "deterioration" of the languages concerned, so we can assume that a language can be transmitted efficiently and accurately even under these apparently adverse circumstances, through the influence of the father, the rest of the father's relatives and the older children. It is perhaps worth pointing out that the wife goes to live in a "long-house" in which the husband's brothers and parents also live, so there is no shortage of contacts with native speakers of the father's language.

What is there to say about language in relation to such a society? First, there is the question of relating languages as wholes to speakers, assuming for simplicity that it is possible to talk usefully about "languages as wholes." For any given language X, it will first be necessary to define who are its native speakers, but since this means referring to some tribe, and tribes are in fact defined solely with reference to language, there is clearly a problem. The solution is either to list all the long-houses belonging to the tribe concerned, or to specify the geographical area (or areas) where the tribe lives. (Most tribes do in fact have their own territory, which does not overlap with that of other tribes.) However, it will have to be borne in mind that about a quarter of the native speakers of language X will be made up of the married women who are dispersed among the other tribes, and similarly about a quarter of the people living in the area designated as "language X territory" will be *non*-native speakers of X, being wives from other tribes. Indeed, any given long-house is likely to contain native speakers of a variety of languages, on the assumption that brothers need not be attracted to girls of the same "other" tribe. In addition to the native speakers of language X, there will be people who speak it as non-natives, with every degree of fluency from almost native-speaker to minimal. Thus anyone wishing to write a grammar for language X will need to say precisely for whom the grammar is claimed to be true—just for the native speakers left at home in the tribal area, or for all native speakers including those dispersed among the other tribes, or for all speakers, native or non-native, in the tribal area.

Secondly, there is the question of discourse: how is speech used in social interaction? There are questions which arise out of the number of languages available: for instance, how do people get by when they travel around within the area, as they very often do? Are they expected to use the language of the long-house which they are visiting? Apparently not—the choice of language is based solely on the convenience of the people concerned (except for the rule requiring wives to use their husbands' language when speaking to their children). If the visitor does not know the long-house language, but someone there knows his, they will use the visitor's when speaking to him. What about language itself as a subject of conversation? Here too practical needs are put first, namely the need to know as many languages as possible in order to make it easier both to travel and (for young people) to find a partner. It is quite normal to talk about a language, learning its vocabulary and phrases from it, and this continues into old age; yet people generally do not know how many languages they can speak, and do not think of language learning as a way of gaining prestige. Perhaps this is what we might expect in a society where everyone can be expected to speak *at least* (i) his father's language, (ii) his mother's language (which she will certainly have taught her children with a view to their seeking partners among her tribe) and (iii) the lingua franca, Tukano (which may also be the language of his father or his mother). However, in addition to the aspects of discourse which are directly related to multilingualism, there are many other things to be said about the relations between speech and the social circumstances in this complex Amazonian society. For instance, there is a rule that if you are listening to someone whom you respect, you should repeat after him, word-for-word, everything he says, at least for the first few minutes of his talking.

Thirdly, there is the question of the relation of language to culture, on which we have little information in the reports on the northwest Amazon referred to above, but on which we can make some safe guesses. For instance, it would be surprising if any of the languages concerned lacked a word for "long-house" or "tribe," and we might reasonably expect a word for "phratry" (though such higher-level concepts often lack names). Similarly, we may predict that most concepts relevant to the culture will have words in each language to express them, and that most words in each language will express cultural concepts, definable only in terms of the culture concerned.

In the world of the north-west Amazon there is probably nothing that a linguist could satisfactorily say about any language without at the same time making some fairly complicated statement about it in relation to society. In particular, he could not say *which* language he was describing by referring to some pre-defined community who use it (in the way in which he might feel entitled to talk about, say, "British English" or "Birmingham English"). The main source of this complexity is the rule of "linguistic exogamy," which might not be expected to be very widespread in the world. However, the other source is the amount of individual bilingualism (or, more accurately, multilingualism), which makes it hard to decide who is a speaker of a given language and who is not. This characteristic, of wide-spread multilingualism, is anything but exceptional in the world as a whole, as an armchair sociolinguist can easily deduce from the fact that there are some four or five thousand languages in the world, but only about 140 nation states. At least some states must therefore contain a very large number of languages, and probably most contain a fair number, with an average between 30 and 35. In view of the need for communication with neighbouring communities and government agencies, it is fair to assume that many members of most communities are multilingual. It is worthwhile bearing this conclusion in mind in reading the next section, since it shows that the monolingual communities familiar to many of us may in fact be highly exceptional and even "exotic" from a global perspective.

A Real and Familiar World

15   Readers are now invited to consider the world in which they themselves grew up. It is unlikely that any reader has had a background quite as linguistically exciting as the one described above, but most of us will certainly find that there is more to be said about our own sociolinguistic worlds than might be expected and much of it is surprisingly interesting.

In order to focus their thinking, readers may find it helpful to imagine themselves, reasonably fluent in Tukano, sitting in a longhouse in the north-west Amazon, telling the residents about their language, in the way that travelling Indians in the area are presumably asked to do if they reach a long-house unfamiliar with their language. The kind of information they would be expected to provide would cover both very general and very specific matters. Who else speaks the language? Where do the speakers live? Do they speak any other languages? What do they say when they first meet a stranger? What is the word meaning "phratry"? What are the meals eaten at different times of day called? Are there any special ways of talking to young children? How do you count? Is there any way of showing that you're quoting what somebody else has told you? How do you show that the thing you're referring to is already known to the addressee? Are there different ways of pronouncing any of the words according to where you come from? In answering every one of these questions, something will not only have been said about the language but also about one aspect or another of the society that uses it; and such questions could be multiplied by the inquisitive long-house residents until a complete description of the stranger's language has been provided.

The point of this exercise is to make readers aware of how much there is to say about their own language in relation to society.

Analyzing Rhetorical Choices

1. Hudson's main point is that to study language most fully, you must consider the overall society in which any language variety is spoken. Do the examples he chooses to make his case form a strong argument or not? Support your response.
2. For a lengthy piece of comparison-and-contrast writing, we would generally recommend a point-by-point rather than subject-by-subject approach. Yet Hudson seems to use the latter method to good effect. What accounts for his apparent success?

Writing About Issues and Contexts

1. Hudson mentions the custom of repeating someone's words as a show of respect. Can you think of "peculiar" rules in any of the languages you speak that are similar to this?
2. Relative to your native language, how would you answer some of the questions in Hudson's penultimate paragraph?

A widely published essayist born in San Francisco, **Richard Rodriguez** *(1944–) is an editor at Pacific News Service and a contributing editor at* Harper's Magazine, U.S. News & World Report, *and the* Los Angeles Times. *In 1997, he received the Peabody Award for his broadcast work. Rodriguez grew up in Sacramento, California, and is a graduate of Stanford and Columbia. His books include* Hunger of Memory: The Education of Richard Rodriguez *(1981),* Days of Obligation: An Argument with My Mexican Father *(1992), and* Brown: The Last Discovery of America *(2002). "Aria" is from* Hunger of Memory.

Richard Rodriguez

Aria

Supporters of bilingual education imply today that students like me miss a great deal by not being taught in their family's language. What they seem not to recognize is that, as a socially disadvantaged child, I considered Spanish to be a private language. What I needed to learn in school was that I had the right—and the obligation—to speak the public language of *los gringos*. The odd truth is that my first-grade classmates could have become bilingual, in the conventional sense of that word, more easily than I. Had they been taught (as upper-middle-class children are often taught early) a second language like Spanish or French, they could have regarded it simply as that: another public language. In my case such bilingualism could not have been so quickly achieved. What I did not believe was that I could speak a single public language.

Without question, it would have pleased me to hear my teachers address me in Spanish when I entered the classroom. I would have felt much less afraid. I would have trusted them and responded with ease. But I would have delayed—for how long postponed?—having to learn the language of public society. I would have evaded—and for how long could I have afforded to delay?—learning the great lesson of school, that I had a public identity.

Fortunately, my teachers were unsentimental about their responsibility. What they understood was that I needed to speak a public language. So their voices would search me out, asking me questions. Each time I'd hear them, I'd look up in surprise to see a nun's face frowning at me. I'd mumble, not really meaning to answer. The nun would persist, "Richard, stand up. Don't look at the floor. Speak up. Speak to the entire class, not just to me!" But I couldn't believe that the English language was mine to use. (In part, I did not want to believe it.) I continued to mumble. I resisted the teacher's demands. (Did I somehow suspect that once I learned public language my pleasing family life would be changed?) Silent, waiting for the bell to sound, I remained dazed, diffident, afraid.

Because I wrongly imagined that English was intrinsically a public language and Spanish an intrinsically private one, I easily noted the difference between classroom language and the language of home. At school, words were directed to a general audience of listeners. ("Boys and girls.") Words were meaningfully ordered. And the point was not self-expression alone but to make oneself understood by many others. The teacher quizzed: "Boys and girls, why do we use that word in this sentence? Could we think of a better word to use there? Would the sentence change its meaning if the words were differently arranged? And wasn't there a better way of saying much the same thing?" (I couldn't say. I wouldn't try to say.)

5   Three months. Five. Half a year passed. Unsmiling, ever watchful, my teachers noted my silence. They began to connect my behavior with the difficult progress my older sister and brother were making. Until one Saturday morning three nuns arrived at the house to talk to our parents. Stiffly, they sat on the blue living room sofa. From the doorway of another room, spying the visitors, I noted the incongruity—the clash of two worlds, the faces and voices of school intruding upon the familiar setting of home. I overheard one voice gently wondering, "Do your children speak only Spanish at home, Mrs. Rodriguez?" While another voice added, "That Richard especially seems so timid and shy."

That Rich-heard!

With great tact the visitors continued, "Is it possible for you and your husband to encourage your children to practice their English when they are home?" Of course, my parents complied. What would they not do for their children's well-being? And how could they have questioned the Church's authority which those women represented? In an instant, they agreed to give up the language (the sounds) that had revealed and accentuated our family's closeness. The moment after the visitors left, the change was observed. "*Ahora,* speak to us *en inglés,*" my father and mother united to tell us.

At first, it seemed a kind of game. After dinner each night, the family gathered to practice "our" English. (It was still then *inglés*, a language foreign to us, so we felt drawn as strangers to it.) Laughing, we would try to define words we could not pronounce. We played with strange English sounds, often over-anglicizing our pronunciations. And we filled the smiling gaps of our sentences with familiar Spanish sounds. But that was cheating, somebody shouted. Everyone laughed. In school, meanwhile, like my brother and sister, I was required to attend a daily tutoring session. I needed a full year of special attention. I also needed my teachers to keep my attention from straying in class by calling out, *Rich-heard*—their English voices slowly prying loose my ties to my other name, its three notes, *Ri-car-do*. Most of all I needed to hear my mother and father speak to me in a moment of seriousness in broken—suddenly heartbreaking—English. This scene was inevitable: One Saturday morning I entered the kitchen where my parents were talking in Spanish. I did not realize that they were talking in Spanish however until, at the moment they saw me, I heard their voices change to speak English. Those *gringo* sounds they uttered startled me. Pushed me away. In that moment of trivial misunderstanding and profound insight, I felt my throat twisted by unsounded grief. I turned quickly and left the room. But I had no place to escape to with Spanish. (The spell was broken.) My brother and sisters were speaking English in another part of the house.

Again and again in the days following, increasingly angry, I was obliged to hear my mother and father: "Speak to us *en inglés*." *(Speak.)* Only then did I determine to learn classroom English. Weeks after, it happened: One day in school I raised my hand to volunteer an answer. I spoke out in a loud voice. And I did not think it remarkable when the entire class understood. That day, I moved very far from the disadvantaged child I had been only days earlier. The belief, the calming assurance that I belonged in public, had at last taken hold.

Shortly after, I stopped hearing the high and loud sounds of *los gringos*. A more and more confident speaker of English, I didn't trouble to listen to *how* strangers sounded, speaking to me. And there simply were too many English-speaking people in my day for me to hear American accents anymore. Conversations quickened. Listening to persons who sounded eccentrically pitched voices, I usually noted their sounds for an initial few seconds before I concentrated on *what* they were saying. Conversations became content-full. Transparent. Hearing someone's *tone* of voice—angry or questioning or sarcastic or happy or sad—I didn't distinguish it from the words it expressed. Sound and word were thus tightly wedded. At the end of a day, I was often bemused, always relieved, to realize how "silent," though crowded with words, my day in public had been. (This public silence measured and quickened the change in my life.)

10   At last, seven years old, I came to believe what had been technically true since my birth: I was an American citizen.

But the special feeling of closeness at home was diminished by then. Gone was the desperate, urgent, intense feeling of being at home; rare was the experience of feeling myself individualized by family intimates. We remained a loving family, but one greatly changed. No longer so close; no longer bound tight by the pleasing and troubling knowledge of our public separateness. Neither my older brother nor sister rushed home after school anymore. Nor did I. When I arrived home there would often be neighborhood kids in the house. Or the house would be empty of sounds.

Following the dramatic Americanization of their children, even my parents grew more publicly confident. Especially my mother. She learned the names of all the people on our block. And she decided we needed to have a telephone installed in the house. My father continued to use the word *gringo*. But it was no longer charged with the old bitterness or distrust. (Stripped of any emotional content, the word simply became a name for those Americans not of Hispanic descent.) Hearing him, sometimes, I wasn't sure if he was pronouncing the Spanish word *gringo* or saying gringo in English.

Matching the silence I started hearing in public was a new quiet at home. The family's quiet was partly due to the fact that, as we children learned more and more English, we shared fewer and fewer words with our parents. Sentences needed to be spoken slowly when a child addressed his mother or father. (Often the parent wouldn't understand.) The child would need to repeat himself. (Still the parent misunderstood.) The young voice, frustrated, would end up saying, "Never mind"—the subject was closed. Dinners would be noisy with the clinking of knives and forks against dishes. My mother would smile softly between her remarks; my father at the other end of the table would chew and chew at his food, while he stared over the heads of his children.

My *mother!* My *father!* After English became my primary language, I no longer knew what words to use in addressing my parents. The old Spanish words (those tender accents of sound) I had used earlier—*mamá* and *papá*—I couldn't use anymore. They would have been too painful reminders of how much had changed in my life. On the other hand, the words I heard neighborhood kids call *their* parents seemed equally unsatisfactory. *Mother* and *Father; Ma, Papa, Pa, Dad, Pop* (how I hated the all-American sound of that last word especially)—all these terms I felt were unsuitable, not really terms of address for *my* parents. As a result, I never used them at home. Whenever I'd speak to my parents, I would try to get their attention with eye contact alone. In public conversations, I'd refer to "my parents" or "my mother and father."

15   My mother and father, for their part, responded differently, as their children spoke to them less. She grew restless, seemed troubled and anxious at the scarcity of words exchanged in the house. It was she who would question me about my day when I came home from school. She smiled at small talk. She pried at the edges of my sentences to get me to say something more. (What?) She'd join conversations she overheard, but her intrusions often stopped her children's talking. By contrast, my father seemed reconciled to the new quiet. Though his English improved somewhat, he retired into silence. At dinner he spoke very little. One night his children and even his wife helplessly giggled at his garbled English pronunciation of the Catholic Grace before Meals. Thereafter he made his wife recite the prayer at the start of each meal, even on formal occasions, when there were guests in the house. Hers became the public voice of the family. On official business, it was she, not my father, one would usually hear on the phone or in stores, talking to strangers. His children grew so accustomed to his silence that, years later, they would speak routinely to his shyness. (My mother would often try to explain: Both his parents died when he was eight. He was raised by an uncle who treated him like little more than a menial servant. He was never encouraged to speak. He grew up alone. A man of few words.) But my father was not shy, I realized, when I'd watch him speaking Spanish with relatives. Using Spanish, he was quickly effusive. Especially when talking with other men, his voice would spark, flicker, flare alive with sounds. In Spanish, he expressed ideas and feelings he rarely revealed in English. With firm Spanish sounds, he conveyed a confidence and authority English would never allow him.

The silence at home, however, was finally more than a literal silence. Fewer words passed between parent and child, but more profound was the silence that resulted from my inattention to sounds. At about the time I no longer bothered to listen with care to the sounds of English in public, I grew careless about listening to the sounds family members made when they spoke. Most of the time I heard someone speaking at home and didn't distinguish his sounds from the words people uttered in public. I didn't even pay much attention to my parents' accented and ungrammatical speech. At least not at home. Only when I was with them in public would I grow alert to their accents. Though, even then, their sounds caused me less and less concern. For I was increasingly confident of my own public identity.

I would have been happier about my public success had I not sometimes recalled what it had been like earlier, when my family had conveyed its intimacy through a set of conveniently private sounds. Sometimes in public, hearing a stranger, I'd hark back to my past. A Mexican farmworker approached me downtown to ask directions to somewhere. "*¿Hijito* . . . ?" he said. And his voice summoned deep longing. Another time, standing beside my mother in the visiting room of a Carmelite convent, before the dense screen which rendered the nuns shadowy figures, I heard several Spanish-speaking nuns—their busy, singsong overlapping voices—assure us that yes, yes, we were remembered, all our family was remembered in their prayers. (Their voices echoed faraway family sounds.) Another day, a dark-faced old woman—her hand light on my shoulder—steadied herself against me as she boarded a bus. She murmured something I couldn't quite comprehend. Her Spanish voice came near, like the face of a never-before-seen relative in the instant before I was kissed. Her voice, like so many of the Spanish voices I'd hear in public, recalled the golden age of my youth. Hearing Spanish then, I continued to be a careful, if sad, listener to sounds. Hearing a Spanish-speaking family walking behind me, I turned to look. I smiled for an instant, before my glance found the Hispanic-looking faces of strangers in the crowd going by.

Today I hear bilingual educators say that children lose a degree of "individuality" by becoming assimilated into public society. (Bilingual schooling was popularized in the seventies, that decade when middle-class ethnics began to resist the process of assimilation—the American melting pot.) But the bilingualists simplistically scorn the value and necessity of assimilation. They do not seem to realize that there are *two* ways a person is individualized. So they do not realize that while one suffers a diminished sense of *private* individuality by becoming assimilated into public society, such assimilation makes possible the achievement of *public* individuality.

The bilingualists insist that a student should be reminded of his difference from others in mass society, his heritage. But they equate mere separateness with individuality. The fact is that only in private—

with intimates—is separateness from the crowd a prerequisite for individuality. (An intimate draws me apart, tells me that I am unique, unlike all others.) In public, by contrast, full individuality is achieved, paradoxically, by those who are able to consider themselves members of the crowd. Thus it happened for me: Only when I was able to think of myself as an American, no longer an alien in *gringo* society, could I seek the rights and opportunities necessary for full public individuality. The social and political advantages I enjoy as a man result from the day that I came to believe that my name, indeed, is *Rich-heard Road-ree-guess*. It is true that my public society today is often impersonal. (My public society is usually mass society.) Yet despite the anonymity of the crowd and despite the fact that the individuality I achieve in public is often tenuous—because it depends on my being one in a crowd—I celebrate the day I acquired my new name. Those middle-class ethnics who scorn assimilation seem to me filled with decadent self-pity, obsessed by the burden of public life. Dangerously, they romanticize public separateness and they trivialize the dilemma of the socially disadvantaged.

20   My awkward childhood does not prove the necessity of bilingual education. My story discloses instead an essential myth of childhood—inevitable pain. If I rehearse here the changes in my private life after my Americanization, it is finally to emphasize the public gain. The loss implies the gain: The house I returned to each afternoon was quiet. Intimate sounds no longer rushed to the door to greet me. There were other noises inside. The telephone rang. Neighborhood kids ran past the door of the bedroom where I was reading my schoolbooks—covered with shopping-bag paper. Once I learned public language, it would never again be easy for me to hear intimate family voices. More and more of my day was spent hearing words. But that may only be a way of saying that the day I raised my hand in class and spoke loudly to an entire roomful of faces, my childhood started to end.

Analyzing Rhetorical Choices

1.   As arguments against bilingual education programs, how effective are the personal anecdotes Rodriguez offers?
2.   Rodriguez asserts that supporters of bilingual education are engaging in "decadent self-pity." However, he does not much develop this assertion. What, in your view, would illustrate his point more fully or count as sufficient evidence?

Writing About Issues and Contexts

1. Rodriguez believes that some cultural loss is an inevitable part of learning. Concerning his education, he reflects that "Fortunately, my teachers were unsentimental about their responsibility." How similar is your position to his? Elaborate.
2. In a similar vein, would you trade in the name Ricardo for Richard? Why or why not?

Born in Brooklyn to Irish immigrant parents, **Frank McCourt** *(1930–)*
and his brothers were taken back to Ireland by his parents when he
was four years old. He grew up in Limerick, Ireland, and returned to
the United States in 1949. Although he never attended high school,
he convinced an admissions officer to allow him to enroll at New York
University. He subsequently taught in high schools and colleges for 30
years. His 1996 memoir, Angela's Ashes, *won the 1997 Pulitzer Prize for*
biography. In 1999, he published a sequel, 'Tis: A Memoir, *from which*
the following selection is drawn.

Frank McCourt

From 'Tis: A Memoir

Teaching nine hours a week at New York Technical College in
Brooklyn was easier than twenty-five hours a week at McKee
Vocational and Technical High School. Classes were smaller, students
older, and there were none of the problems a high school teacher has
to deal with, the lavatory pass, the moaning over assignments, the
mass of paperwork created by bureaucrats who have nothing to do
but create new forms. I could supplement my reduced salary by teaching at Washington Irving Evening High School or substituting at
Seward Park High School and Stuyvesant High School.

The chairman of the English Department at the community college asked me if I'd like to teach a class of paraprofessionals. I said yes
though I had no notion of what a paraprofessional was.

That first class I found out. Here were thirty-six women, African-
American with a sprinkling of Hispanics, ranging in age from early
twenties to late fifties, teacher aides in elementary schools and in college now with government help. They'd get two-year associate degrees and, perhaps, continue their education so that someday they
might become fully qualified teachers.

That night there was little time for teaching. After I had asked the
women to write a short autobiographical essay for the next class they
gathered up their books and filed out, apprehensive, still unsure of
themselves, of each other, of me. I had the whitest skin in the room.

5   When we met again the mood was the same except for one
woman who sat with her head on the desk, sobbing. I asked what was
the matter. She raised her head, tears on her cheeks.

I lost my books.

Oh, well, I said, you'll get another set of books. Just go to the English Department and tell them what happened.

You mean I won't get throwed out of college?

No, you won't be throwed, thrown out of college.

10 I felt like patting her head but I didn't know how to pat the head of a middle-aged woman who has lost her books. She smiled, we all smiled. Now we could begin. I asked for their compositions and told them I'd read some aloud though I wouldn't use their real names.

The essays were stiff, self-conscious. As I read I wrote some of the more common misspelled words on the chalkboard, suggested changes in structure, pointed out grammatical errors. It was all dry and tedious till I suggested the ladies write simply and clearly. For their next assignment they could write on anything they liked. They looked surprised. Anything? But we don't have anything to write about. We don't have no adventures.

They had nothing to write about, nothing but the tensions of their lives, summer riots erupting around them, assassinations, husbands who so often disappeared, children destroyed by drugs, their own daily grind of housework, jobs, school, raising children.

They loved the strange ways of words. During a discussion on juvenile delinquency Mrs. Williams sang out, No kid o' mine gonna be no yoot.

Yoot?

15 Yeah, you know. Yoot. She held up a newspaper where the headline howled, Youth Slays Mom.

Oh, I said, and Mrs. Williams went on, These yoots, y'know, runnin' around slayin' people. Killin' 'em, too. Any kid o' mine come home actin' like a yoot an' out he go on his you-know-what.

The youngest woman in the class, Nicole, turned the tables on me. She sat in the back in a corner and never spoke till I asked the class if they'd like to write about their mothers. Then she raised her hand. How about your mother, Mr. McCourt?

Questions came like bullets. Is she alive? How many children did she have? Where's your father? Did she have all those children with one man? Where is she living? Who's she living with? She's living alone? Your mother's living alone and she has four sons? How come?

They frowned. They disapproved. Poor lady with four sons shouldn't be living alone. People should take care of their mothers but what do men know? You can never tell a man what it's like to be a mother and if it wasn't for the mothers America would fall apart.

20   In April Martin Luther King was killed and classes were suspended for a week. When we met again I wanted to beg forgiveness
for my race. Instead I asked for the essays I had already assigned.
Mrs. Williams was indignant. Look, Mr. McCourt, when they tryin'
to burn your house down you ain't sittin' around writin' no cawm-
po-zishuns.

In June Bobby Kennedy was killed. My thirty-six ladies wondered
what was happening to the world but they agreed you have to carry
on, that education was the only road to sanity. When they talked
about their children their faces brightened and I became irrelevant to
their talk. I sat on my desk while they told each other that now they
were in college themselves they stood over their kids to make sure the
homework was done.

On the last night of classes in June there was a final examination.
I watched those dark heads bent over papers, the mothers of two hundred and twelve children, and I knew, that no matter what they wrote
or didn't write on those papers, no one would fail.

They finished. The last paper had been handed in but no one was
leaving. I asked if they had another class here. Mrs. Williams stood
and coughed. Ah, Mr. McCourt, I must say, I mean we must say, it
was a wonderful thing to come to college and learn so much about
English and everything and we got you this little something hopin'
you'll like it an' all.

She sat down, sobbing, and I thought, This class begins and ends
in tears.

25   The gift was passed up, a bottle of shaving lotion in a fancy red
and black box. When I sniffed it I was nearly knocked over but I
sniffed again with gusto and told the ladies I'd keep the bottle forever
in memory of them, this class, their yoots.

Instead of going home after that class I took the subway to West
Ninety-sixth Street in Manhattan and called my mother from a street
telephone.

Would you like to have a snack?
I don't know. Where are you?
I'm a few blocks away.
30   Why?
I just happened to be in the neighborhood.
Visiting Malachy?
No. Visiting you.
Me? Why should you be visiting me?

35   For Christ's sake, you're my mother and all I wanted to do was invite you out for a snack. What would you like to eat?

She sounded doubtful. Well, I love them jumbo shrimps they have in the Chinese restaurants.

All right. We'll have jumbo shrimps.

But I don't know if I'm able for them this minute. I think I'd prefer to go to the Greeks for a salad.

All right. I'll see you there.

40   She came into the restaurant gasping for breath and when I kissed her cheek I could taste the salt of her sweat. She said she'd have to sit a minute before she could even think of food, that if she hadn't given up the cigarettes she'd be dead now.

She ordered the feta salad and when I asked her if she liked it she said she loved it, she could live on it.

Do you like that cheese?

What cheese?

The goat cheese.

45   What goat cheese?

The white stuff. The feta. That's goat cheese.

'Tis not.

'Tis.

Well, if I knew that was goat cheese I'd never touch it because I was attacked by a goat once out the country in Limerick and I'd never eat a thing that attacked me.

50   It's a good thing, I told her, you were never attacked by a jumbo shrimp.

Analyzing Rhetorical Choices

1.   What are all the elements compared or contrasted in McCourt's essay? Which are more important than others? Why?

2.   Unlike most texts, McCourt's piece does not include quotation marks around words we would take to be direct quotes. Why do you think he employs this method? Does it have any particular effect on you as a reader?

3.   How realistic do you find the "yoot" episode and Mrs. Williams's comments? Explain.

Writing About Issues and Contexts

1. Have you discovered that your high school and college experiences differ as McCourt describes? Is there now no moaning over assignments?

2. Concerning his students, McCourt offers that "They had nothing to write about, nothing but the tensions of their lives, summer riots erupting around them, assassinations, husbands who so often disappeared, children destroyed by drugs, their own daily grind of housework, jobs, school, raising children." What other assumptions might you make about their lives? In your eyes, would his description accurately reflect many lives today compared to 1968? Support your response.

3. Why does McCourt visit his mother when he does?

Deborah Tannen (1945–) holds the distinguished rank of University Professor and is a professor of linguistics at Georgetown University. Born in Brooklyn, New York, she became partially deaf as the result of a childhood illness. Her subsequent interest in nonverbal communication led to formal study in linguistics. She earned a Ph.D. at the University of California at Berkeley. Her numerous books include That's Not What I Meant!: How Conversational Style Makes or Breaks Your Relations with Others *(1986);* You Just Don't Understand: Women and Men in Conversation *(1990), which stayed on the* New York Times *best-seller list for almost four years;* The Argument Culture *(1998); and* I Only Say This Because I Love You: How the Way We Talk Can Make or Break Family Relationships Throughout Our Lives *(2001). The following adaptation from* You Just Don't Understand *was published in the* Washington Post.

Deborah Tannen

Sex, Lies, and Conversation

I was addressing a small gathering in a suburban Virginia living room—a women's group that had invited men to join them. Throughout the evening, one man had been particularly talkative, frequently offering ideas and anecdotes, while his wife sat silently beside him on the couch. Toward the end of the evening, I commented that women frequently complain that their husbands don't talk to them. This man quickly concurred. He gestured toward his wife and said, "She's the talker in our family." The room burst into laughter; the man looked puzzled and hurt. "It's true," he explained. "When I come home from work I have nothing to say. If she didn't keep the conversation going, we'd spend the whole evening in silence."

This episode crystallizes the irony that although American men tend to talk more than women in public situations, they often talk less at home. And this pattern is wreaking havoc with marriage.

The pattern was observed by political scientist Andrew Hacker in the late '70s. Sociologist Catherine Kohler Riessman reports in her new book *Divorce Talk* that most of the women she interviewed—but only a few of the men—gave lack of communication as the reason for their divorces. Given the current divorce rate of nearly 50 percent, that amounts to millions of cases in the United States every year—a virtual epidemic of failed conversation.

In my own research, complaints from women about their husbands most often focused not on tangible inequities such as having given up the chance for a career to accompany a husband to his, or doing far more than their share of daily life-support work like cleaning, cooking, social arrangements and errands. Instead, they focused on communication: "He doesn't listen to me," "He doesn't talk to me." I found, as Hacker observed years before, that most wives want their husbands to be, first and foremost, conversational partners, but few husbands share this expectation of their wives.

5   In short, the image that best represents the current crisis is the stereotypical cartoon scene of a man sitting at the breakfast table with a newspaper held up in front of his face, while a woman glares at the back of it, wanting to talk.

Linguistic Battle of the Sexes

How can women and men have such different impressions of communication in marriage? Why the widespread imbalance in their interests and expectations?

In the April [1990] issue of *American Psychologist,* Stanford University's Eleanor Maccoby reports the results of her own and others' research showing that children's development is most influenced by the social structure of peer interactions. Boys and girls tend to play with children of their own gender, and their sex-separate groups have different organizational structures and interactive norms.

I believe these systematic differences in childhood socialization make talk between women and men like cross-cultural communication, heir to all the attraction and pitfalls of that enticing but difficult enterprise. My research on men's and women's conversations uncovered patterns similar to those described for children's groups.

For women, as for girls, intimacy is the fabric of relationships, and talk is the thread from which it is woven. Little girls create and maintain friendships by exchanging secrets; similarly, women regard conversation as the cornerstone of friendship. So a woman expects her husband to be a new and improved version of a best friend. What is important is not the individual subjects that are discussed but the sense of closeness, of a life shared, that emerges when people tell their thoughts, feelings, and impressions.

10   Bonds between boys can be as intense as girls', but they are based less on talking, more on doing things together. Since they don't assume talk is the cement that binds a relationship, men don't know what kind of talk women want, and they don't miss it when it isn't there.

Boys' groups are larger, more inclusive, and more hierarchical, so boys must struggle to avoid the subordinate position in the group. This may play a role in women's complaints that men don't listen to them. Some men really don't like to listen, because being the listener makes them feel one down, like a child listening to adults or an employee to a boss.

But often when women tell men, "You aren't listening," and the men protest, "I am," the men are right. The impression of not listening results from misalignment in the mechanics of conversation. The misalignment begins as soon as a man and a woman take physical positions. This became clear when I studied videotapes made by psychologist Paul Dorval of children and adults talking to their same-sex best friends. I found that at every age, the girls and women faced each other directly, their eyes anchored on each other's faces. At every age, the boys and men sat at angles to each other and looked elsewhere in the room, periodically glancing at each other. They were obviously attuned to each other, often mirroring each other's movements. But the tendency of men to face away can give women the impression they aren't listening even when they are. A young woman in college was frustrated: Whenever she told her boyfriend she wanted to talk to him, he would lie down on the floor, close his eyes, and put his arm over his face. This signaled to her, "He's taking a nap." But he insisted he was listening extra hard. Normally, he looks around the room, so he is easily distracted. Lying down and covering his eyes helped him concentrate on what she was saying.

Analogous to the physical alignment that women and men take in conversation is their topical alignment. The girls in my study tended to talk at length about one topic, but the boys tended to jump from topic to topic. The second-grade girls exchanged stories about people they knew. The second-grade boys teased, told jokes, noticed things in the room and talked about finding games to play. The sixth-grade girls talked about problems with a mutual friend. The sixth-grade boys talked about fifty-five different topics, none of which extended over more than a few turns.

Listening to Body Language

Switching topics is another habit that gives women the impression men aren't listening, especially if they switch to a topic about themselves. But the evidence of the tenth-grade boys in my study indicates otherwise. The tenth-grade boys sprawled across their chairs with bodies parallel and eyes straight ahead, rarely looking at each other. They looked as if they were riding in a car, staring out the windshield. But they were talking about their feelings. One boy was upset because a girl had told him he had a drinking problem, and the other was feeling alienated from all his friends.

15   Now, when a girl told a friend about a problem, the friend responded by asking probing questions and expressing agreement and understanding. But the boys dismissed each other's problems. Todd assured Richard that his drinking was "no big problem" because "sometimes you're funny when you're off your butt." And when Todd said he felt left out, Richard responded, "Why should you? You know more people than me."

Women perceive such responses as belittling and unsupportive. But the boys seemed satisfied with them. Whereas women reassure each other by implying, "You shouldn't feel bad because I've had similar experiences," men do so by implying, "You shouldn't feel bad because your problems aren't so bad."

There are even simpler reasons for women's impression that men don't listen. Linguist Lynette Hirschman found that women make more listener-noise, such as "mhm," "uhuh," and "yeah," to show "I'm with you." Men, she found, more often give silent attention. Women who expect a stream of listener-noise interpret silent attention as no attention at all.

Women's conversational habits are as frustrating to men as men's are to women. Men who expect silent attention interpret a stream of listener-noise as overreaction or impatience. Also, when women talk to each other in a close, comfortable setting, they often overlap, finish each other's sentences and anticipate what the other is about to say. This practice, which I call "participatory listenership," is often perceived by men as interruption, intrusion, and lack of attention.

A parallel difference caused a man to complain about his wife, "She just wants to talk about her own point of view. If I show her another view, she gets mad at me." When most women talk to each other, they assume a conversationalist's job is to express agreement and support. But many men see their conversational duty as pointing out the other side of an argument. This is heard as disloyalty by women, and refusal to offer the requisite support. It is not that women don't want to see other points of view, but that they prefer them phrased as suggestions and inquiries rather than as direct challenges.

20   In his book *Fighting for Life,* Walter Ong points out that men use "agonistic," or warlike, oppositional formats to do almost anything; thus discussion becomes debate, and conversation becomes a competitive sport. In contrast, women see conversation as a ritual means of establishing rapport. If Jane tells a problem and June says she has a similar one, they walk away feeling closer to each other. But this attempt at establishing rapport can backfire when used with men. Men take too literally women's ritual "troubles talk," just as women mistake men's ritual challenges for real attack.

The Sounds of Silence

These differences begin to clarify why women and men have such different expectations about communication in marriage. For women, talk creates intimacy. Marriage is an orgy of closeness: you can tell your feelings and thoughts, and still be loved. Their greatest fear is being pushed away. But men live in a hierarchical world, where talk maintains independence and status. They are on guard to protect themselves from being put down and pushed around.

This explains the paradox of the talkative man who said of his silent wife, "She's the talker." In the public setting of a guest lecture, he felt challenged to show his intelligence and display his understanding of the lecture. But at home, where he has nothing to prove and no one to defend against, he is free to remain silent. For his wife, being home means she is free from the worry that something she says might offend someone, or spark disagreement, or appear to be showing off; at home she is free to talk.

The communication problems that endanger marriage can't be fixed by mechanical engineering. They require a new conceptual framework about the role of talk in human relationships. Many of the psychological explanations that have become second nature may not be helpful, because they tend to blame either women (for not being assertive enough) or men (for not being in touch with their feelings). A sociolinguistic approach by which male-female conversation is seen as cross-cultural communication allows us to understand the problem and forge solutions without blaming either party.

Once the problem is understood, improvement comes naturally, as it did to the young woman and her boyfriend who seemed to go to sleep when she wanted to talk. Previously, she had accused him of not listening, and he had refused to change his behavior, since that would be admitting fault. But then she learned about and explained to him the differences in women's and men's habitual ways of aligning themselves in conversation. The next time she told him she wanted to talk, he began, as usual, by lying down and covering his eyes. When the familiar negative reaction bubbled up, she reassured herself that he really was listening. But then he sat up and looked at her. Thrilled, she asked why. He said, "You like me to look at you when we talk, so I'll try to do it." Once he saw their differences as cross-cultural rather than right and wrong, he independently altered his behavior.

25   Women who feel abandoned and deprived when their husbands won't listen to or report daily news may be happy to discover their husbands trying to adapt once they understand the place of small talk in women's relationships. But if their husbands don't adapt, the women may still be comforted that for men, this is not a failure of intimacy. Accepting the difference, the wives may look to their friends or family for that kind of talk. And husbands who can't provide it shouldn't feel their wives have made unreasonable demands. Some couples will still decide to divorce, but at least their decisions will be based on realistic expectations.

In these times of resurgent ethnic conflicts, the world desperately needs cross-cultural understanding. Like charity, successful cross-cultural communication should begin at home.

Analyzing Rhetorical Choices

1. Along with R. A. Hudson, Tannen perhaps adopts the most objective and academic tone of the writers in this chapter, referring to several formal studies to develop her argument. Is her means of arguing effective? Why or why not? For example, how does she make appropriate use of psychologist Paul Dorval's tapes of same-sex conversations to draw conclusions about intersex conversations?

2. Unlike Hudson, Tannen opts for point-by-point development, proceeding, for example, through a series of gender contrasts with respect to "physical alignment," "switching topics," "staying on topic," "listener-noise," and "participatory listenership." Comment on whether this is an effective choice. Would you prefer to read about all the traits of one sex first and then about all the traits of the other? Explain your preference.

3. In making reference to males and females, Tannen sometimes lists females first (women and men) and at other times lists males first (boys and girls). What is the effect on you, if any, of these choices?

Writing About Issues and Contexts

1. How do you apply Tannen's theories to your own environment and relationships? Do you think an understanding of her arguments will help you in some of the conversations in which you participate? Support your viewpoint.
2. What is your level of optimism about the prospects of cross-cultural understanding in general, the kind that Tannen, in her closing paragraph, says the world desperately needs?

Wendell Berry (1934–), the prolific author of over 30 books, is an essay-ist, novelist, poet, and conservationist. Berry was a professor at New York University and at the University of Kentucky and is the recipient of numerous awards and honors, including Guggenheim and Rockefeller Foundation fellowships, a National Endowment of the Arts grant, and a Lannan Foundation Award. Born and raised in Kentucky, Berry cur-rently resides on a working organic farm in his home state and is an active and outspoken voice on environmental issues. "We're living, it seems, in the culmination of a long warfare—warfare against human be-ings, other creatures and the Earth itself," Berry has said of our current political and ecological climate. Works by Berry include* A Timbered Choir: The Sabbath Poems 1979–1997 *(1998),* Sex, Economy, Freedom & Community: Eight Essays *(1993), and* The Way of Ignorance and Other Essays *(2005). "The Failure of War" is taken from Berry's collec-tion of essays,* Citizenship Papers *(2003).*

Wendell Berry

The Failure of War

If you know even as little history as I know, it is hard not to doubt the efficacy of modern war as a solution to any problem except that of retribution—the "justice" of exchanging one damage for an-other, which results only in doubling (and continuing) the damage and the suffering.

Apologists for war will immediately insist that war answers the problem of national self-defense. But the doubter, in reply, will ask to what extent the *cost* even of a successful war of national defense—in life, money, material goods, health, and (inevitably) freedom—may amount to a national defeat. And national defense in war always in-volves *some* degree of national defeat. This paradox has been with us from the very beginning of our republic. Militarization in defense of freedom reduces the freedom of the defenders. There is a fundamental inconsistency between war and freedom.

In asking such a question, the doubter will be mindful also that in a modern war, fought with modern weapons and on the modern scale, neither side can limit to "the enemy" or "the enemy country" the damage that it does. These wars damage the world. We know enough by now to know that you cannot damage a part of the world without damaging all of it. Modern war has not only made it impossible to kill "combatants" without killing "noncombatants," it has made it impossible to damage your enemy without damaging yourself. You cannot kill your enemy's women and children without offering your own women and children to the selfsame possibility. We (and, inevitably, others) have prepared ourselves to destroy our enemy by destroying the entire world—including, of course, ourselves.

That many have considered the increasing unacceptability of modern warfare is shown by the language of the propaganda surrounding modern war. Modern wars have characteristically been fought to end war. They have been fought in the name of peace. Our most terrible weapons have been made, ostensibly, to preserve and assure the peace of the world. "All we want is peace," we say, as we increase relentlessly our capacity to make war.

5   And yet at the end of a century in which we have fought two wars to end war and several more to prevent war and preserve peace and in which scientific and technological progress has made war ever more terrible and less controllable in its effects, we still, by policy, give no consideration, and no countenance, to nonviolent means of national defense. We do indeed make much of diplomacy and diplomatic relations, but by diplomacy we mean invariably ultimatums for peace backed by the threat of war. It is always understood that we stand ready to kill those with whom we are "peacefully negotiating."

Our century of war, militarism, and political terror has unsurprisingly produced great—and successful—advocates of true peace, among whom Mohandas K. Gandhi and Martin Luther King, Jr., are paramount examples. The considerable success that they achieved testifies to the presence, in the midst of violence, of an authentic and powerful desire for peace and, more important, of the proven will to make the necessary sacrifices. But so far as our government is concerned, these men and their great and authenticating accomplishments might as well never have existed. To achieve peace by peaceable means is not yet our goal. We cling to the hopeless paradox of making peace by making war.

Which is to say that we cling, in our public life, to a brutal hypocrisy. In our century of almost universal violence of humans against fellow humans and against our natural and cultural commonwealth, hypocrisy has been inescapable because our opposition to violence has been selective or merely fashionable. Some of us who approve of our monstrous military budget and our peacekeeping wars nonetheless deplore "domestic violence" and think that our society can be pacified by "gun control." Some of us are against capital punishment but for abortion. Some of us are against abortion but for capital punishment. Most of us, whatever our stand on preserving the lives of the thoughtlessly conceived unborn, thoughtlessly participate in an economy that steals from all the unborn.

One does not have to know very much or think very far in order to see the moral absurdity upon which we have erected our sanctioned enterprises of violence. Abortion-as-birth-control is justified as a "right," which can establish itself only by denying all the rights of another person, which is the most primitive intent of warfare. Capital punishment sinks us all to the same level of primal belligerence, at which an act of violence is avenged by another act of violence. What the justifiers of these wrongs ignore is the fact—as well established by the history of feuds or the history of anger as by the history of war—that violence breeds violence. Acts of violence committed in "justice" or in affirmation of "rights" or in defense of "peace" do not end violence. They prepare and justify its continuation.

The most dangerous superstition of the parties of violence is the idea that sanctioned violence can prevent or control unsanctioned violence. But if violence is "just" in one instance, as determined by the state, why, by a merely logical extension, might it not also be "just" in another instance, as determined by an individual? How can a society that justifies capital punishment and warfare prevent its justifications from being extended to assassination and terrorism? If a government perceives that some causes are so important as to justify the killing of children, how can it hope to prevent the contagion of its logic from spreading to its citizens—or to its citizens' children? If you so devalue human life that the accidentally conceived unborn may be permissibly killed, how do you keep that permission from being assumed by someone who has made the same judgment against the born?

10   I am aware of the difficulty of assigning psychological causes to acts of violence. Psychological causes abound. But here I am talking about the power of example, precedent, and reason.

If we give to these small absurdities the magnitude of international relations, we produce, unsurprisingly, some much larger absurdities. What could be more absurd than our attitude of high moral outrage against other nations for manufacturing the selfsame weapons that we manufacture? The difference, as our leaders say, is that we will use these weapons virtuously whereas our enemies will use them maliciously—a proposition that too readily conforms to a proposition of much less dignity: We will use them in *our* interest, whereas our enemies will use them in *theirs*. The issue of virtue in war is as obscure, ambiguous, and troubling as Abraham Lincoln found to be the issue of prayer in war: "Both [the North and the South] read the same Bible, and pray to the same God; and each invokes His aid against the other. . . .The prayers of both could not be answered—that of neither could be answered fully."

But recent American wars, having been both "foreign" and "limited," have been fought under a second illusion even more dangerous than the illusion of perfect virtue: We are assuming, and are encouraged by our leaders to assume, that, aside from the sacrifice of life, no personal sacrifice is required. In "foreign" wars, we do not directly experience the damage that we inflict upon the enemy. We hear and see this damage reported in the news, but we are not affected, and we don't mind. These limited, "foreign" wars require that some of our young people will be killed or crippled, and that some families will grieve, but these "casualties" are so widely distributed among our population as hardly to be noticed. Otherwise, we do not feel ourselves to be involved. We pay taxes to support the war, but that is nothing new, for we pay war taxes also in time of "peace." We experience no shortages, we suffer no rationing, we endure no limitations. We earn, borrow, spend, and consume in wartime as in peacetime.

And of course no sacrifice is required of those large economic interests that now principally constitute our "economy." No corporation will be required to submit to any limitation or to sacrifice a dollar. On the contrary, war is understood by some as the great cure-all and opportunity of our corporate economy. War ended the Great Depression of the 1930's, and we have maintained a war economy—an economy, one might justly say, of general violence—ever since, sacrificing to it an enormous economic and ecological wealth, including, as designated victims, the farmers and the industrial working class.

And so great costs are involved in our fixation on war, but the costs are "externalized" as "acceptable losses." And here we see how progress in war, progress in technology, and progress in the industrial economy are parallel to one another—or, very often, are merely identical.

15   Romantic nationalists, which is to say most apologists for war, always imply in their public speeches a mathematics or an accounting that cannot be performed. Thus by its suffering in the Civil War, the North is said to have "paid for" the emancipation of the slaves and the preservation of the Union. Thus we may speak of our liberty as having been "bought" by the bloodshed of patriots. I am fully aware

of the truth in such statements. I know that I am one of many who have benefited from painful sacrifices made by other people, and I would not like to be ungrateful. Moreover, I am a patriot myself, and I know that the time may come for any of us when we must make extreme sacrifices for the sake of liberty.

But still I am suspicious of this kind of accounting. For one reason, it is necessarily done by the living on behalf of the dead. And I think we must be careful about too easily accepting, or being too easily grateful for, sacrifices made by others, especially if we have made none ourselves. For another reason, though our leaders in war always assume that there is an acceptable price, there is never a previously stated level of acceptability. The acceptable price, finally, is whatever is paid.

It is easy to see the similarity between this accounting of the price of war and our usual accounting of "the price of progress." We seem to have agreed that whatever has been (or will be) paid for so-called progress is an acceptable price. If that price includes the diminishment of privacy and the increase of government secrecy, so be it. If it means a radical reduction in the number of small businesses and the virtual destruction of the farm population, so be it. If it means cultural and ecological impoverishment, so be it. If it means the devastation of whole regions by extractive industries, so be it. If it means that a mere handful of people should own more billions of wealth than is owned by all of the world's poor, so be it.

But let us have the candor to acknowledge that what we call "the economy" or "the free market" is less and less distinguishable from warfare. For about half of this century we worried about world conquest by international communism. Now with less worry (so far) we are witnessing world conquest by international capitalism. Though its political means are milder (so far) than those of communism, this newly internationalized capitalism may prove even more destructive of human cultures and communities, of freedom, and of nature. Its tendency is just as much toward total dominance and control. Confronting this conquest, ratified and licensed by the new international trade agreements, no place and no community in the world may consider itself safe from some form of plunder. More and more people all over the world are recognizing that this is so, and they are saying that world conquest of any kind is wrong, period.

They are doing more than that. They are saying that *local* conquest also is wrong, and wherever it is taking place local people are joining together to oppose it. All over my own state of Kentucky this opposition is growing—from the west, where the exiled people of the

Land Between the Lakes are struggling to save their confiscated homeland from bureaucratic degradation, to the east, where the native people of the mountains are still struggling to preserve their land from destruction by absentee corporations.

20   To have an economy that is warlike, that aims at conquest, and that destroys virtually everything that it is dependent on, placing no value on the health of nature or of human communities, is absurd enough. It is even more absurd that this economy, that in some respects is so much at one with our military industries and programs, is in other respects directly in conflict with our professed aim of national defense.

It seems only reasonable, only sane, to suppose that a gigantic program of preparedness for national defense would be founded, first of all, upon a principle of national and even regional economic independence. A nation determined to defend itself and its freedoms should be prepared, and always preparing, to live from its own resources and from the work and the skills of its own people. It should carefully husband and conserve those resources, justly compensate that work, and rigorously cultivate and nurture those skills. But that is not what we are doing in the United States today. What we are doing, as we prepare for and prosecute wars allegedly for national defense, is squandering in the most prodigal manner the natural and human resources of the nation.

At present, in the face of declining finite sources of fossil fuel energy, we have virtually no energy policy, either for conservation or for the development of safe and clean alternative sources. At present, our energy policy simply is to use all that we have. At present, moreover, in the face of a growing population needing to be fed, we have virtually no policy for land conservation, and *no* policy of just compensation to the primary producers of food. At present, our agricultural policy is to use up everything that we have, while depending increasingly on imported food, energy, technology, and labor.

Those are just two examples of our general indifference to our own needs. We thus are elaborating a direct and surely a dangerous contradiction between our militant nationalism and our espousal of the international "free market" ideology. How are we going to defend our freedoms (this is a question both for militarists and for pacifists) when we must import our necessities from international suppliers who have no concern or respect for our freedoms? What would happen if in the course of a war of national defense we were to be cut off from our foreign sources of supply? What would happen if, in a war of national defense, military necessity required us to attack or blockade our foreign suppliers? We have already fought one energy war allegedly in national defense. If our present policies of economic indifference continue, we may face wars for other commodities: food or water or shoes or steel or textiles.

What can we do to free ourselves of this absurdity?

25   With that question my difficulty declares itself, for I do not ask it as a teacher knowing the answer. I ask it knowing that by doing so I describe my own dilemma. The news media, the industrial economy, perhaps human nature as well, prompt us to want quick, neat answers to our questions, but I don't think my question has a quick, neat answer.

Obviously, we would be less absurd if we took better care of one another and of all our fellow creatures. We would be less absurd if we founded our public policies upon an honest description of our needs and our predicament, rather than upon fantastical descriptions of our wishes. We would be less absurd if our leaders would consider in good faith the proven alternatives to violence.

Such things are easy to say. But finally we must face this daunting question, not as a nation or a group, but as individual persons—as ourselves. We are disposed, somewhat by culture and somewhat by nature, to solve our problems by violence—by maximum force relentlessly applied—and even to enjoy doing so. And yet by now all of us must at least have suspected that our right to live, to be free, and to be at peace is not guaranteed by any act of violence. It can be guaranteed only by our willingness that all other persons should live, be free, and be at peace—and by our willingness to use or give our own lives to make that possible. To be incapable of such willingness is merely to resign ourselves to the absurdity we are in; and yet, if you are like me, you are unsure to what extent you are capable of it.

It appears then that the answer to my question may be only another question. But maybe we can take some encouragement from that. Maybe, if our questions lead to other questions, that is a sign that we are asking the right ones.

Here is the other question that the predicament of modern warfare forces upon us: How many deaths of other people's children by bombing or starvation are we willing to accept in order that we may be free, affluent, and (supposedly) at peace? To that question I answer pretty quickly: *None*. And I know that I am not the only one who would give that answer: Please. No children. Don't kill any children for *my* benefit.

30   If that is our answer, then we must know that we have not come to rest. Far from it. For now surely we must feel ourselves swarmed about with more questions that are urgent, personal, and intimidating. But perhaps also we feel ourselves beginning to be free, facing at last in our own lives the greatest challenge ever laid before us, the most comprehensive vision of human progress, the best advice and the least obeyed:

"Love your enemies, bless them that curse you, do good to them that hate you, and pray for them which despitefully use you, and persecute you;

"That ye may be the children of your Father which is in Heaven: for He maketh His sun to rise on the evil and the good, and sendeth rain on the just and on the unjust."

Analyzing Rhetorical Choices

1. Berry begins the essay by stating that he knows little about history. How might this affect Berry's credibility? How does Berry's subsequent use of historical references in the essay influence your interpretation of this claim?

2. How do you interpret the phrase "The most dangerous superstition of the parties of violence is the idea that sanctioned violence can prevent or control unsanctioned violence"? How does Berry use the term *superstition*? Why is it dangerous?

3. Why do you think that Berry ends his essay with a passage from the Bible (specifically, Jesus' Sermon on the Mount)? What is the rhetorical effectiveness of this passage?

Writing About Issues and Contexts

1. In what ways do you find Berry's argument about "price" of war convincing? What do you feel are the benefits or consequences of using accounting terms to discuss war?

2. Analyze the following statement: "For about half of this century we worried about world conquest by international communism. Now with less worry (so far) we are witnessing world conquest by international capitalism." What distinctions does Berry make between the two forms of conquest? Similarities?

3. Berry asserts that the United States should rely on the resources of its own country and the skills of its own people, rather than on those of foreign countries, in order to gain economic independence. Why would this be an important first step toward national freedom? How would it affect whether or not the country engaged in war with other countries?

Strategies for Writers: Comparison and Contrast

1. Many essays in this chapter have argued, instructed, or conveyed memoir by using comparison and contrast. Jodi Kantor, Bharati Mukherjee, and Richard Rodriguez, for example, narrate their personal experiences as they make arguments about the subjects with which they are concerned. R. A. Hudson and Deborah Tannen use comparison and contrast in presentations that are scholarly. Develop a similar kind of comparison-and-contrast essay.

2. Plan a narrative or essay in which comparison and contrast would serve your purposes and be of interest to your envisioned audience. As you write, list as many relevant points of comparison and contrast as you can generate. You will probably want to decide whether you will use a dominant development pattern of subject by subject or point by point. In general, the longer your intended piece of writing, the more likely it is that you will want to use the point-by-point technique. Cornel West uses this approach admirably. Even when he expands on the point he makes about African American and Jewish contributions, he lists the 44 names he cites in Black-Jewish pairs according to their areas of achievement. For example, he writes, "Marvin Gaye and Bob Dylan, James Baldwin and Norman Mailer, Lorraine Hansberry and Neil Simon." (He does not write Marvin Gaye, James Baldwin, and Lorraine Hansberry; Bob Dylan, Norman Mailer, and Neil Simon.)

3. Decide whether your tone will be formal or informal. Do you need to sound more like Bruce Catton or Frank McCourt? In addition, consider whether you would be most effective speaking in first, second, or third person. Will you feature dialogue? Will the dialogue accurately represent the language varieties you are attempting to portray?

4. Compose your draft and share it with friends, classmates, and your instructor. Note what they consider to be strengths and weaknesses of your text and consider their comments carefully as you revise. As always, revisit questions of tone, language choice, and selection of details.

5. Consider some of the other rhetorical devices used by the authors in this chapter. For example, note the rhythm and parallelism to highlight differences that Mukherjee uses in her opening paragraph: "I am an American citizen and she is not. I am

moved that thousands of long-term residents are finally taking the oath of citizenship. She is not." You might cite other works, including the use of rhetorical questions by Wendell Berry in his essay "The Failure of War."

6. You can practice comparison-and-contrast methods by giving yourself assignments like the one that Jodi Kantor had as a reviewer for the *New York Times*. Compare and contrast two books or articles related to any of your courses.

Research and Writing Assignments

1. In the manner of Bruce Catton, compare and contrast two historical figures that interest you. Consult print and electronic sources to obtain ample information on your subjects, and integrate the relevant sources with your own observations, citing your sources carefully. Be sure to consider family background, regional origins, personality traits, personal philosophies, and significant actions.

2. Bharati Mukherjee argues that immigrants in the United States may attempt total assimilation or try to hold on completely to their native cultures. Identify and describe additional viewpoints that immigrants might hold and other methods they might use to conduct their lives. Compare and contrast your ideas with those of Mukherjee and those she attributes to her sister.

3. In "Wham! Bam! Thanks a Bunch!" Jodi Kantor considers two boxing memoirs by women. Compare and contrast Kantor's remarks and those of the authors to the arguments about boxing made by Norman Cousins (see "Who Killed Benny Paret?" in Chapter 10).

4. Name two ethnic or cultural groups other than African Americans and Jews that have made stellar contributions to the development of the United States. List at least ten achievers from each group, and try to form intergroup pairs as Cornel West does in his essay. Also compare and contrast the groups as a whole and share your overall perspective on their achievements.

5. Revisit and answer the questions that R. A. Hudson poses toward the end of "Language Worlds." Share your responses with a classmate who has also answered these questions; then write an essay in which you analyze, compare, and contrast the two

sets of answers. Include reflection about how this assignment informs your view of how language operates.

6. Richard Rodriguez and Frank McCourt make arguments either explicitly or implicitly about the best way to teach language in school. Their opinions are part of a larger conversation about policy issues such as bilingual education or the proposed English Language Amendment. Consult material on these issues, and write an essay expressing your own views. In the process, compare and contrast the suggestions or practices of Rodriguez and McCourt to one another and to your own ideas.

7. In "Sex, Lies, and Conversation," Deborah Tannen suggests that talk between men and women is like cross-cultural communication. Observe people at home, in your neighborhood, at work, or on campus to see if the characteristics concerning male and female verbal behavior that Tannen describes are evident. Write an essay detailing the differences, if any, that you notice.

8. In his essay "The Failure of War," Wendell Berry addresses the contradiction of "making peace by making war." One result of this paradox, according to Berry, is that the United States has maintained a "war economy" since the end of World War II. Based on Berry's claim, use outside research of your own to compare and contrast the benefits and the consequences of the contemporary wartime economy of the United States.

9
Cause and Effect

One of the most basic intellectual impulses is to link cause with effect, effect with cause: This fundamental intellectual operation helps us solve problems and understand actions. It rains, and the next day flowers bloom on the front lawn. A cold front blows in off the lake, and six inches of snow fall. Most of us perceive these activities as linked, even if the linkage is not always explicit. The rain may not be the direct cause of the blooming; the cold front may not be the direct cause of the snow. But the appearance of a cause/effect relationship is there, and we make the connection. Much of the time we are correct, but just because one event follows another is insufficient grounds to assume that one is the *cause* of the other. This is one of the major lessons that Brent Staples drives home in "A Black Man Ponders His Ability to Alter Space."

Even when a situation seems obvious, it is not always easy to link cause with effect. A friend might have had an auto accident that caused her minor injury, a clear case of cause and effect. Yes, the accident (cause) produced the injury (effect), but the more compelling question is what caused the accident? Bad weather? A defective auto part? Driver inattention or inexperience? Cell phone usage? A distracting passenger? The other driver? Alcohol consumption? Darkness? An unavoidable twist of fate? Making a clear connection between causes and effects is not always easy. Often it takes extensive research or scientific investigation to find the relationship, and even then that answer may be hypothetical or represent a best-guess scenario.

Perhaps the most complicated—and yet worthwhile—aspect of tracing a cause/effect relationship is determining the true or ultimate cause(s) of an effect. The current international debate about global warming points to a variety of possible causes—such as the inevitable natural cycles of weather, increased carbon dioxide in the atmosphere produced primarily by the internal combustion engine, and the loss of forested lands and especially rain forest terrain. Which causes are primary? How can we validate some potential causes and eliminate others, especially when the stakes are so high for industrialized nations like the United States? Scientific analysis is extremely helpful, but science alone has so far not proven persuasive.

Those on the environmental side of the debate have a clear view of the cause of global warming and how best to prevent it. Here, for example, is a brief analysis by EcoBridge, a Web site devoted to "the environmental education of the public."

Causes of Global Warming

Transport Sector—Choice of Vehicles

Twenty percent (20%) of U.S carbon dioxide emissions comes from the burning of gasoline in internal-combustion engines of cars and light trucks (minivans, sport utility vehicles, pick-up trucks, and jeeps). (20) Vehicles with poor gas mileage contribute the most to global warming. For example, according to the E.P.A.'s 2000 Fuel Economy Guide, a new Dodge Durango sport utility vehicle (with a 5.9 liter engine) that gets 12 miles per gallon in the city will emit an estimated 800 pounds of carbon dioxide over a distance of 500 city miles. In other words for each gallon of gas a vehicle consumes, 19.6 pounds of carbon dioxide are emitted into the air. (21) A new Honda Insight that gets 61 miles to the gallon will only emit about 161 pounds of carbon dioxide over the same distance of 500 city miles. Sport utility vehicles were built for rough terrain, off road driving in mountains and deserts. When they are used for city driving, they are so much overkill to the environment. If one has to have a large vehicle for their family, station wagons are an intelligent choice for city driving, especially since their price is about half that of a sport utility. Inasmuch as SUVs have a narrow wheel base in respect to their higher silhouette, they are four times as likely as cars to roll over in an accident. (33)

About another 10% of U.S. carbon dioxide emissions comes from trucks used mostly for commercial purposes. (20)

The gas mileage of 2000 model vehicles averaged 28.1 miles per gallon, the worst fuel economy since 1980. The main reason for the decline in gas mileage was the popularity of the SUV, garnering about 50% of car sales in 2000. If car manufacturers were to increase their fleets' average gas mileage about 3 miles per gallon, this country could save a million barrels of oil every day, while U.S. drivers would save $25 billion in fuel costs annually.

Senator Joseph Lieberman says, "If we can get 3 miles more per gallon from our cars, we'll save 1 million barrels of oil a day, which is exactly what the (Arctic National Wildlife) Refuge at its best in Alaska would produce." (81)

Transport Sector—City Gridlock

Cities are tolerating gridlock. In 1996 according to an annual study by traffic engineers (as reported in the *San Francisco Chronicle* December 10, 1996) from Texas A & M University, it was found that drivers in Los Angeles and New York City alone wasted 600 million gallons of gas annually while just sitting in traffic. The 600 million gallons of gas translates to about 7.5 million tons of carbon dioxide in just those two cities.

Electricity Generation

We burn coal and oil to power much of our electrical output. About 36% of U.S. carbon dioxide emissions stem from the burning of these fossil fuels. (7)

Deforestation

This planet is losing its forests; 34 million acres each year through burning and cutting. We are losing millions of acres of rainforests each year, the equivalent in area to the size of Italy. (22) The destroying of tropical forests alone is throwing hundreds of millions of tons of carbon dioxide into the atmosphere each year. We are also losing temperate forests. The temperate forests of the world account for an absorption rate of 2 billion tons of carbon annually. (3) In the temperate forests of Siberia alone, the earth is losing 10 million acres per year.

Methane

Levels of atmospheric methane, a powerful greenhouse gas, have risen 145% in the last 100 years. (18) Methane is derived from sources such as rice paddies, bovine flatulence, bacteria in bogs and fossil fuel production.

References

(3) Keeling, Ralph, Stephen Piper, Martin Heimann. "Global and hemispheric carbon dioxide sinks deduced from changes in atmospheric oxygen concentration" *Nature,* Vol. 381 May 16, 1996.

(7) Marland, Gregg and Angela Pippin. "United States Emissions of Carbon Dioxide to the Earth's Atmosphere by Economic Activity." Oak Ridge National Laboratory. 1990.

(18) World Wildlife Fund (WWF): "Explaining climate change/a WWF overview of the new science."

(20) Climate Action Network report. "What's New About Global Warming."

(21) Marland, Gregg. Carbon Dioxide Information Analysis Center, Oak Ridge National Laboratory, Oak Ridge, TN.

(22) Rainforest Action Network. Press Release, October 16, 1996.

(33) Taken from an article in the *San Francisco Chronicle*, December 12, 1997 originating in the *New York Times* by Keith Bradsher.

(81) During the vice-presidential debates, Joseph Lieberman mentioned this interesting statistic. October 5, 2000.

From EcoBridge's point of view, the cause/effect relationship is clear. Greenhouse gases, especially the carbon dioxide emitted in passenger vehicle exhaust, are destroying our environment. To support this contention, EcoBridge cites a variety of sources to support their cause/effect analysis, although many of them are predisposed to agree with their perspective—always a danger when analyzing a complex subject.

Is there agreement with EcoBridge concerning the causes of the problem? No, at least not according to the Heritage Foundation. Writing at the time that the United States was considering whether to sign the international Kyoto Protocol on Global Warming (the United States declined to sign), the authors of the following excerpt, Angela Antonelli, Brett D. Schaefer, and Alex Annett, find that insufficient evidence exists to link global warming with human fossil fuel consumption or other such causes.

The Road to Kyoto: How the Global Climate Treaty Fosters Economic Impoverishment and Endangers U.S. Security

. . . there is still no consensus in the scientific community either on the causes of global warming or on the extent to which it may threaten future generations. For example:

- A 1992 Gallup poll found that only 17 percent of the members of the Meteorological Society and the American Geophysical Society think global warming in the 20th century has been the result of greenhouse gas emissions, principally carbon dioxide from burning fossil fuels.[5]
- Only 13 percent of climate scientists polled in a 1992 Greenpeace survey believe that runaway global warming will occur as a consequence of continuing current patterns of energy use.[6]

- Scientists in a May 1997 article in *Science* estimated that it will be a decade or longer before they will know whether human activity is, in fact, causing climate changes.[7]

Despite such admissions from the scientific community, environmentalists continue to espouse the need to cut back on man-made emissions of greenhouse gases like carbon dioxide or face deadly consequences later. Do it, they exhort, or the atmosphere will warm to the point where melting ice caps cause devastating floods and drought-induced crop failures trigger global famine. Do it, they admonish, so that future generations will not be forced to live in a world permanently damaged by environmental recklessness and an obsession with economic growth at the expense of all else. Do it, they promise, because the costs are minimal and the benefits incalculable.

But Americans and Congress should be responding: Is it really this simple? Is the science behind the global warming phenomenon this precise? Will the economic costs really be minimal? Will countries be judged equally and fairly in the quest for "safer" skies? Who will write the new regulations? The Kyoto Protocol to the UNFCCC to be considered in December will impose economically devastating, legally binding limits on U.S. citizens and businesses. Considering the far-reaching consequences of the treaty, the facts about climate change, greenhouse gases, and international emissions regulations must be brought to light.

References
[5] H. Sterling Burnett, "Myths of Global Warming," National Center for Policy Analysis *Brief Analysis* No. 230, May 23, 1997, p. 1.

[6] Ibid.

[7] Richard A. Kerr, "Greenhouse Forecasting Still Cloudy," *Science*, Vol. 276 (May 16, 1997), p. 1042; also available on the Internet at http://www.umi.com/pqdwe...Deli=1+Mtd=2+ReqType=309.

According to this point of view, science still disagrees about the causes of global warming. Although written just a few years ago, it is worth noting that the authors cite as evidence polls taken at least five years earlier, throwing their argument somewhat into doubt. Both EcoBridge and the Heritage Foundation offer thoughtful analyses that must be evaluated according to their logic, the credibility of their sources, and the degree to which causes and effects are shown to be integrally related.

The disagreement about the causes and effects of global warming illustrates that such relationships are often complex, and it is usually the complex ones that reward the writer. Part of the problem derives from leaping to false conclusions based on misperception, contiguity, or accidental association. Science—even good and thorough scientific experimentation—can produce contradictory results. Some events occur after others, but are not necessarily caused by them. Consider superstitious practices: Does walking underneath a ladder or breaking a mirror really cause you bad luck? Sometimes effects are produced because we believe they will occur, even if they are not directly linked to the cause—an effect known as self-fulfilling prophecy.

Approaches to Writing Cause-and-Effect Essays

Like any piece of writing, the cause/effect essay can't be forced. Although you may well receive an assignment to write an essay that analyzes a cause/effect relationship, it is seldom possible to do so without spending substantial time researching your subject. As with all writing, the cause/effect essay demands knowledge and specificity that comes from knowing a subject well through research. The challenge, however, is to think about intriguing topics that exemplify this mode, topics that will interest an audience.

One strategy is to think about cause/effect relationships that are complicated and ambiguous. Such subjects often attract the attention of writers—and readers, since the less obvious the causal relationship, the more likely someone will want to read about it. That usually means that a writer does not need to spend a lot of time, for example, writing an essay explaining that a major cause of being poor is not having much money, or that getting enough sleep makes a person feel rested. Such obvious topics are boring to write about and just as boring to read. Instead, writers must ferret out more intriguing, compelling subjects such as the societal causes and effects of sexism in the workplace, or how avian flu gets transmitted from bird to bird to animal to human beings, or the possible health benefits associated from eating beets or tomato sauce. Such subjects will be worthwhile to readers if the information and conclusions are not generally known and derive from the research done by the writer.

Factual vs. Probable

Most cause/effect essays can be divided into two types: factual and probable. A factual cause/effect essay examines a subject from a scientific, historical, or otherwise factual basis. This kind of essay only makes sense to write (and read) if the subject is unfamiliar to the reader or sufficiently unknown, compelling, useful, or complex that it is worth the effort to both write and read about it. Atul Gawande's "Cold Comfort" is an excellent example of such an essay, since it sets out to explain the cause of the common cold and how best to prevent it, primarily by citing 70 years of scientific and cultural history. Part of the fascination of reading this essay is that Gawande playfully cites a wide range of research scientists while remaining aware that the common cold continues to confound them—and us. Newspapers and magazines are filled with similar examples: the effect of color on mood, the causes of inflation, the overuse of antibiotics which leads to drug-resistant diseases.

The probable cause/effect essay is more speculative, although it still requires a careful and logical analysis. It makes use of facts and research just as does the factual cause/effect essay, but its primary purpose is to speculate about the likely relationship between causes and effects, actions and consequences. What are the likely causes of racism in American society? What effect does popular music have on children's values and psychological outlook? At the heart of such an essay lies the writer's desire to draw some conclusions based on a preponderance of evidence linked together causally. Clearly many essays and articles blend these two purposes, but as a writer you need to be aware of this distinction. You must remain in control of your subject and keep its purpose in focus: You need to frame your essay so that readers can tell the difference between an analysis that is rooted in accepted fact and one that veers into opinion, speculation, and individual perspective.

Organizing Your Essay

A useful technique for planning and organizing a cause/effect essay is to divide a few blank sheets into three vertical columns. On the first sheet, write the topic on top and then label the columns "cause," "effect," and "my response." As you brainstorm about a possible subject, put your words and ideas in the appropriate category. For example, someone writing about the benefits of using only positive reinforcement for dog training might make a list like the following:

Dog Training and Positive Reinforcement

Cause	Effect	My Response
Getting rid of choke collar	Must use different techniques to teach dog how to walk	I like the idea of not causing the dog pain
Using a "haltee"	Painless way to teach dog how to walk	But you have to know how to use it and you have to be patient
Dog treats	Great for positive reinforcement	List examples!!!
Why use only positive reinforcement	Create powerful bond between dog and owner, one that is about love, not fear	Use example of my own dog, Ripley
Clicker training	Gets fast response	Explain how it works (do more research!!), how it depends on association between noise and treat
Problems	Find alternatives to painful correction	Not easy!!!
Destructive chewing	Damage (financial, emotional—Ripley destroyed my wedding shoes!)	Redirect or use hot sauce to cause discomfort
Annoying barking	Use coins-in-can to scare dog and stop behavior	Works great—but need to be consistent
Sudden noise	Dogs momentarily frightened/distracted	Great for training
Fear, intimidation	Fearful dogs lack trust, can bite, engage in bad behavior	Put this at beginning of essay

This kind of organizational brainstorming can be a great jump start for writing a cause/effect essay because it encourages a writer to think in a structured way. It also enables a writer to determine where to concentrate her efforts in terms of research, emphasis, and even how best an essay might be structured and developed. Thus the chart describes something called "clicker training," but to write about it the author needs to "do more research." Meanwhile, the chart offers a handy way to indicate that the subject of "fear/intimidation" is something the writer thinks should go at the beginning of the essay. That kind of thinking and planning is an efficient way to go about constructing a cause/effect essay.

Analyzing and Concluding

You will also want to give your cause/effect essay a meaningful conclusion, one that reinforces the cause/effect relationships at the center of the essay. At some point in the composing process, it can be useful to write a succinct statement about your primary point, the essential argument or insight that you want to impress upon the reader. The author who is planning the essay about positive reinforcement for dog training, for example, might describe her central point as, "if a person wants a loving, well-trained dog, it is essential that positive behaviors are rewarded and negative behaviors redirected or ignored. The primary effect (or end result) is a great pet, something everyone should want." By making your overall purpose clear to yourself, you can maintain a better focus, organize your essay logically, and direct the reader's attention toward particular insights and conclusions.

It might be helpful to think of writing a complex cause/effect essay in the same way as writing a mystery story or an episode of one of those popular crime scene shows on TV. Something has happened— New Orleans has flooded because the levees ruptured, Iraq has become a hotbed of insurgency, gas and fuel oil prices have skyrocketed, intelligent design is proposed to explain how the world has been created. Events like these are significant and have complex and tangled histories. Your primary purpose as a writer is to investigate their causes, just as a crime scene investigator analyzes physical evidence and tries to deduce motive. In fact, your task is typically more challenging, since in most cases there is not just one cause or effect but many causes and multiple effects. Discovering and evaluating the complex relationships between various causes and effects is one of the significant challenges and satisfactions of writing in this mode.

To analyze such relationships, the writer must consider a broad spectrum of possibilities, questions, and concerns. If writing about global warming, for example, you might want to investigate the current scientific evidence linking fossil fuel consumption and higher temperatures. Or changes over time in temperature in a specific geographic area. Or a specific element (such as the effect of water temperature on glacial melt). Or the specific conclusions of a range of experienced researchers. Or you might choose to blend personal experience, if meaningful and appropriate, with the formal analysis of others, as Sharon Begley does in "The Stereotype Trap."

Once you have completed your essay, let it rest overnight and then reread it. It should have a strong logical line running through it so your reader can see the causal relationships that produced specific effects and is persuaded that you, the writer, understand the subject. Writing such an essay provides an opportunity to find answers that resolve questions, thereby introducing clarity into your life. To write a cause/effect essay is to find the ligaments in the bones, the logical order that links multiple and complex events. To understand causes and effects is to gain some measure of control in the world.

*Atul Gawande (1966–) is a practicing surgeon and an assistant profes-
sor of surgery at Harvard Medical School. Gawande received his medical
degree from Harvard Medical School and a master's in public health
from the Harvard School of Public Health. A staff writer for* The New
Yorker, *Gawande is the author of* Complications: A Surgeon's Notes on
an Imperfect Science *(2002). He lives in Newton, Massachusetts, with his
wife and three children.*

Atul Gawande

Cold Comfort

There is, when you look into it, not a lot that makes sense about
the common cold. For one thing, there is the name. As cold experts
have pointed out, in almost all Indo-European languages one of the
words or phrases for the malady plays on the word for low temperature. In Italian, the common cold is *raffreddore,* from *freddo,* meaning cold. In Hindi, the word *sardi* denotes both being made cold and a
cold itself. The notion that a chill puts you at risk of catching a cold is
ancient and nearly universal. Yet science has found no evidence for it.
One of the first studies on the matter was led by Sir Christopher
Andrewes, of the Common Cold Research Unit, in Salisbury,
England, a half century ago. He and his team took a group of volunteers—half of whom had been kept warm and comfortable and half
of whom had been made to take a bath, stand dripping wet without a
towel in a drafty corridor for half an hour, and finally get dressed but
wear wet socks for several hours—and inoculated them with cold
virus up their noses. Despite a measurable drop in body temperature
and considerable misery, the chilled group didn't get any more colds
than the warm group. (It was work like this that earned Andrewes his
knighthood.) Follow-up experiments have since demonstrated that
being chilled has no effect on either the likelihood of catching a cold
or the severity of a cold once you've caught it. Indeed, colds are common at every latitude and longitude in the world—in the Sahara, in
Greenland, in Delhi, in Ulaanbaatar.

All the same, colds are curiously seasonal. No matter what the
temperature or how subtle the change in weather, in most parts of the
world the cold season begins with a peak in early fall, drones on

through winter, and peaks again in mid-spring. In summer, whether it's July in Vladivostok or January in Canberra, colds almost disappear. All of this raises a basic question: How do you catch a cold, anyway?

As the Canadian cold historian J. Barnard Gilmore points out in his 1998 book "In Cold Pursuit," some of the most provocative reports on the subject have come from small, isolated communities—island villages, nuclear submarines, rural trading posts. Among these is a 1931 field study of Longyear City, an Arctic coal-mining settlement on the island of Spitsbergen, midway between the Norwegian mainland and the North Pole. For seven to nine months of the year, the town's five hundred residents were iced in, and during that time colds were almost nonexistent. Legend had it, however, that the arrival in port of the first ship of summer invariably brought with it a full-blown cold epidemic. J. Harlan Paul, a physician, and H. L. Freese, a microbiologist, decided to go to Longyear City to investigate.

The two scientists arrived in September, 1930, and spent eleven months on Spitsbergen. They found, as expected, that colds died out soon after the last boat of the year departed. The long winter that followed was quiet. Then, in May, the ice began to melt and break up. And on May 23rd, at 9 P.M., the first steamer of the 1931 season arrived in port with mail and fifty new workers for the mine. The researchers made sure they boarded the steamer while it was still out in the fjord and before anyone had disembarked. They examined each of the passengers carefully. None had any signs of a cold. A new worker was evidently in an early stage of infection; within a few hours of leaving the ship he developed symptoms of a cold.

5   Less than forty-eight hours later, three townspeople developed new colds. One was a storekeeper, another an outdoor worker, and the third a miner. Paul and Freese retraced everyone's steps. They found that only the first two victims had come into close contact with any of the new arrivals. More puzzlingly, they reported, "We were unable to trace any direct contact between the man with a 'cold' who had arrived on the first boat and these three men."

Nevertheless, from that point the illness spread swiftly. Within a week, eighty-four people had come down with colds. One week later, about a hundred more caught the bug. By the end of the first month, three-quarters of the winter residents had been afflicted. Yet the researchers also discovered that there was a small but apparently hardy group of people who, despite frequent exposure, never developed the cold. A virus had travelled through town, Paul and Freese concluded, but they could not explain how.

American adults suffer an average of between two and four colds a year, and children six to eight. Although even scientists sometimes talk of "the cold virus," there is no one virus that causes colds. Since the nineteen-fifties, five families of viruses have been known to cause colds, including the coronaviruses, the parainfluenza viruses, and the adenoviruses. The most common and familiar of these is the rhinovirus family, which accounts for around forty per cent of colds and itself breaks down into at least a hundred genetically distinct viruses. The cause of approximately a third of all colds remains unknown.

Once any of these viruses get to the lining of your nose and start an infection, the miseries are pretty much the same. Symptoms usually begin from between eight and twenty-four hours after infection (though some viruses may incubate for as long as five days). On the first day of illness, you typically notice that your throat is sore or scratchy. On the second and third days, the membranes of your nose and sinuses thicken to the point of obstruction. A thin, clear secretion (made up primarily of mucoid proteins and water, but also of sloughed cells and large concentrations of virus) flows freely from the nasal lining. Inflammatory molecules in the fluid irritate the edges of your nostrils, turning them raw and red. As the cold persists, the secretions become dense and gluey. Then, after four or five days, the passages begin to open up again. For about a third of cold sufferers, a cough—caused by persistent inflammation in the upper airway—becomes the longest-lasting and most annoying problem. As a rule, cold symptoms usually go away in about a week, though for about a quarter of victims it may take two.

Antibodies from previous exposure can protect you from a particular cold-virus strain, but repeat infections are not at all uncommon. And, with so many different strains of virus circulating, you are usually an open target. Under ordinary conditions, introduction of a single rhinovirus case into the home will lead within a few days to infection in one-quarter to three-quarters of the other household members. It need not be just one virus, either. A study of Seattle families found as many as four viruses infecting a family at once.

10   Figuring out precisely how cold viruses pass between people has been particularly vexing. Researchers at the time of the First World War

were able to demonstrate what now seems obvious: you can induce a cold by taking a concentrate from the nasal secretions of someone who has an active cold and placing it directly into either the nose or the eyes of a healthy person. (The virus placed in the eye runs down into the nose via the tear ducts.) Curiously, although the technique has been perfected over the decades, even direct inoculation with purified virus doesn't uniformly succeed. A few people—under ten per cent—do not get infected, despite having no antibody to the virus. Furthermore, according to nasal specimens and antibody tests, about one out of four people will develop an active viral infection yet have no symptoms of a cold—the so-called silent cold. Biopsy studies have now shown that cold viruses generally infect only a tiny portion of the nose and do very little damage by themselves. Rather, it's the inflammatory response—the attack on the virus by white blood cells and antibodies—that causes the miserable swelling and secretions. For whatever reason, there are people who, at least some of the time, manage to rid themselves of an infection without mounting this response. They can be floridly infected, shed large amounts of virus, and pass the bug on to other people, but continue to feel fine themselves.

In the nineteen-forties, high-speed flash photographs demonstrated that an ordinary sneeze expels particles like a 12-gauge spraying bird shot—sending out droplets by the thousand from the mouth and nose at velocities approaching a hundred miles an hour. A British study published in *The Lancet* showed that a culture plate placed three feet from a sneezing subject would collect more than nineteen thousand bacterial colonies. Droplets could float for minutes, and smaller particles a few microns in diameter could hover in the air for days. The conclusion that colds were transmitted by air was taken as more or less self-evident. Proving it was another matter.

In the summer of 1950, Sir Christopher Andrewes conducted a series of experiments re-creating the isolation of Spitsbergen. He assembled a dozen volunteers and deposited them in a group of houses provided by the Duke of Sutherland, on the otherwise uninhabited island of Eilean nan Ron, off the northern coast of Scotland. After the volunteers were sequestered for ten weeks, six strangers who had recently been infected with purified rhinovirus were inserted into the group. The entrance of these "invaders" was carefully scripted. First, they spent three hours in an empty room in one of the houses, making sure they were "liberal in the way they disseminated nasal discharge," as Sir Christopher later wrote. Half an hour after they left, four of the island dwellers, designated Party A in his report, were brought in to occupy the contaminated room. The invaders then entered a second room. Here Party B was present but was separated from them by a blanket that had been stretched across the room, with space above and below to allow air to pass freely. The two groups shared the room for several hours. Testing demonstrated that fine droplets from the infected group had indeed travelled throughout the room. Finally, the invaders went to a separate house, where they lived and ate with another group, Party C, for three days, providing maximum exposure. The subjects were then closely monitored for colds over the next few days. To everyone's surprise, no one in any of the parties developed a cold. Later studies attempting to demonstrate the transmission of virus through the air were hardly more successful.

In 1984, researchers at the University of Wisconsin at Madison reported the results of their own odd series of experiments. In the first set, volunteers were infected with rhinovirus, and when they were at the peak of their colds and shedding large quantities of virus they were seated at a table in a tiny, unventilated room, three feet from healthy subjects. The researchers had everyone talk, sneeze, and, weirdly, sing during the next few hours. The result? Nine subjects were exposed; none came down with colds.

The researchers went on to conduct what became their best-known experiment. This time, they had their infected volunteers kiss the healthy test subjects, assuming that this would transmit the virus easily. Each subject was kissed on the mouth for a minimum of one minute. (Beyond this, the precise mechanics were not specified. "The donors and recipients were instructed to use the kissing technique most natural for them," the researchers reported.) The cold sufferers kissed sixteen subjects in all. The result was just one confirmed case of rhinovirus infection.

15   When they were sent home to their families, however, the experimentally inoculated people spread their colds easily and widely. The conclusion scientists drew was that a sneeze or a cough or a kiss might theoretically be capable of transmitting a cold, but it did so only rarely, and a brief exposure seemed unlikely to succeed. Some other mechanism was presumed to be more important, and this was how attention shifted to nose-wiping.

In a rather suggestive experiment, Sir Christopher's research team set up on a person's nose an apparatus with a thin tube that trickled out a clear fluid at the same rate a cold would. This fluid, however, contained an invisible fluorescent dye. With the device in place, the volunteer spent a few hours socializing with a group of people in a room—eating, chatting, playing cards. At the end, the experimenters turned out the lights and used an ultraviolet lamp to illuminate the dye. To their horror, the dye had gone everywhere—all over the person's face and hands, onto his food, onto the playing cards, onto other people's hands, and even around *their* noses. As an American observational study of an audience at a medical conference later found, in ordinary circumstances one in three adults picks his nose every hour. People rub their eyes even more frequently.

The hands had to be the culprit, and a team of scientists at the University of Virginia—Jack Gwaltney, Owen Hendley, and Richard Wenzel—provided the first persuasive evidence of this. In 1973, the team reported in the *New England Journal of Medicine* a set of studies which established a convincing chain of causation. The researchers examined ten subjects who had active colds and readily found that four had virus on their hands. When drops of extracts from their mucus were permitted to dry on nylon, wool, silk, Formica, stainless steel, wood, and other surfaces, live virus could still be recovered three hours later. This was true of virus placed on skin, too. (The virus survived well on most nonporous surfaces but hardly at all on facial tissue or cotton handkerchiefs.) If volunteers touched the contaminated surfaces—including other people's hands—the virus was picked up at least sixty per cent of the time. In another test, volunteers were asked to touch a contaminated plastic surface with a finger and immediately either rub their eyes or put their fingers up their noses. Four out of the eleven became infected. In a follow-up study, healthy volunteers were told to rub their eyes and probe their noses after holding coffee cups that had been handled by cold sufferers who had just wiped their own noses. Fifty per cent developed colds.

And so, it was concluded, contact with your hands is how a cold virus gets passed around. It need not involve direct contact with people who have a cold. Hence the familiar advice that the best way to avoid a cold is to wash your hands frequently and not touch people with colds, especially children. That's hard to put into practice, though. When Jack Gwaltney—who has now done close to forty years of research on the common cold and is recognized as the world's foremost expert on it—is asked what he does to reduce his exposure in the cold season, he says it's pretty much hopeless. "I tried to be careful about washing my hands when my grandchildren were little, especially when they had those two ropes of mucus coming down," he recalls. "But you were still going to pick them up and hug them, and they were still going to go around touching everything. There's no avoiding it."

When he feels himself coming down with a cold, Gwaltney takes ibuprofen and an antihistamine for the next week. These won't stop a cold, but they are among the few interventions reliably proven to alleviate symptoms. The ibuprofen reduces coughing and the antihistamine reduces obstruction and runniness—although you have to take an older antihistamine, like chlorpheniramine (Chlor-Trimeton) or clemastine (Tavist), the kind that you buy over the counter and that makes you drowsy. The new ones, like Allegra and Claritin, are too narrow in their effects to work for colds. Petrolatum-based ointments are thought to protect the nostrils against the inflammatory drizzle if they're used when symptoms begin, but there are no reliable studies to prove it. What about zinc? The only consistent effect that well-designed trials have reported is that it tastes bad. Antibiotics? No benefit. Vitamin C? It won't prevent colds, according to dozens of studies, but at high doses it may reduce symptoms modestly (though not as much as an antihistamine). Echinacea? Inadequately tested. How about drinking lots of fluids, as doctors always tell you to do? There's no basis for it. As one cold researcher put it, "I'm not sure it even makes sense."

20   Some drugs in the research pipeline have been gathering attention of late. A new group, known as capsid-binding agents, are designed to attach to rhinoviruses and, among other things, stop them from fastening to the cells of your nasal membranes. One of these compounds recently made headlines when two randomized trials with more than two thousand patients showed that it could reduce both the severity and the duration of a rhinovirus cold. Another new group of drugs to emerge, the 3C protease inhibitors, are designed to block replication of rhinoviruses once they've penetrated your nasal cells. There have been promising preliminary results in clinical trials of one such agent, which has now been given the unpronounceable name ruprintrivir. (Manufacturers like to give drugs unpronounceable generic names because then the only thing you'll remember is whatever brand name they eventually choose.) So far, the measurable effect of each of these drugs has been modest—perhaps reducing the duration of a weeklong cold by a day or two. Even if they come to market, they will work only for a subset of cold viruses and will have to be obtained through a doctor and started no later than the first day of a cold. They're also

bound to be expensive. It seems likely that a cure for the common cold will remain elusive.

We may have better luck stopping colds from spreading in the first place. At a recent scientific conference, Ronald Turner, formerly of the Medical University of South Carolina, announced the results of testing antiseptic skin cleansers that contained pyroglutamic acid or salicylic acid. Unlike most soaps, these cleansers not only killed cold viruses on people's hands immediately but continued to do so for hours afterward. Despite having their hands intentionally contaminated with rhinovirus and being made to probe their nostrils and rub their eyes, volunteers who had earlier washed with solutions containing one of the compounds developed fewer colds than those who used a control solution. As it turns out, pyroglutamic acid is a common ingredient in ordinary skin moisturizers, and salicylic acid is used in over-the-counter acne treatments. An effective antiviral lotion may already be on the shelves.

Will these cleansers stop viruses in the real world, though? One would think so, given all the studies about hand-spread colds. Yet there always seems to be at least one study that doesn't quite square with whatever tidy theories the scientists concoct. When it comes to colds, that study is the Wisconsin poker experiment, conducted almost twenty years ago. The cold researchers at the University of Wisconsin surmised that if the main route by which colds were spread was from hand to hand (or object to hand) and then from hand to nose or eyes, preventing people from touching their noses and eyes should stop virtually all colds. So they devised a simple but clever experiment. They took healthy volunteers and volunteers who had laboratory-induced colds and put them in a room to play a marathon session of poker from eight in the morning until eleven at night. Half of the healthy subjects were allowed to play cards normally, and the other half were restrained by devices that were designed to prevent them from touching any part of their own heads or faces as they played. Some of them wore a three-foot-wide clear plastic collar; others wore an orthopedic brace that kept their arms from bending more than forty degrees. The devices were removed only for meals and trips to the bathroom. At those times, the subjects' hands were disinfected and gloved the way a surgeon's hands would be for an operation. (Assistants were provided in the event that nose-scratching was needed.) Subjects were closely monitored for the subsequent development of colds.

The results still confound cold experts. More than half of the restrained volunteers developed colds afterward—just as many as among the unrestrained volunteers. Tests confirmed that in all cases they had caught the same virus that the sick volunteers were carrying. The scientists could not say how.

There is something almost beautifully crafty about the common cold. It knows us better than we know ourselves—living and travelling and multiplying by means of an unnoticed touch, a quick, involuntary wipe of an eye, or perhaps some tic we have not yet recognized. As every textbook that addresses the subject is forced at some point to say, "Other factors may be involved." Nonetheless, there are a few things that can be said with certainty: May will come, colds will subside, and no one will know why.

Analyzing Rhetorical Choices

1. Gawande writes an extremely factual account of the common cold, but he also occasionally indulges in wry, tongue-in-cheek expressions and ironic statements. Locate at least three such statements and discuss how they affect your response to the essay.
2. Find several instances of technical terms in the essay. How does Gawande's use of technical information affect you as a reader? Why do you think he uses terms that most laypeople would not know?
3. How does Gawande organize his essay? How would you describe the logic of his presentation?

Writing About Issues and Contexts

1. Why is writing about the common cold significant?
2. What causes a cold? How are colds transmitted? What do we know—and not know—about this common yet mysterious illness?
3. Given what Gawande reports, what is the difference between a hypothesis and a proof? Do all hypotheses require proof? What does the relationship between hypothesis and proof tell us about the relationship between cause and effect?

The eldest of nine children, **Brent Staples** *(1951–) grew up in Chester, Pennsylvania, a small town just outside Philadelphia. Staples attended a special college-prep program at Philadelphia Military College and Penn Morton College to hone his academic skills and went on to earn his undergraduate degree from Widener University and his master's and doctoral degrees in psychology from the University of Chicago. Staples is a member of the* New York Times *editorial board and has published a variety of articles and essays along with his best-selling memoir,* Parallel Time: Growing Up in Black and White *(1994). "A Black Man Ponders His Ability to Alter Public Space" recounts Staples's experience as a tall black man walking in the city, an experience that resonates with current concerns about racial stereotypes and profiling.*

Brent Staples

A Black Man Ponders His Ability to Alter Public Space

My first victim was a woman—white, well dressed, probably in her early twenties. I came upon her late one evening on a deserted street in Hyde Park, a relatively affluent neighborhood in an otherwise mean, impoverished section of Chicago. As I swung onto the avenue behind her, there seemed to be a discreet, uninflammatory distance between us. Not so. She cast back a worried glance. To her, the youngish black man—a broad six feet two inches with a beard and billowing hair, both hands shoved into the pockets of a bulky military jacket—seemed menacingly close. After a few more quick glimpses, she picked up her pace and was soon running in earnest. Within seconds she disappeared into a cross street.

That was more than a decade ago. I was twenty-two years old, a graduate student newly arrived at the University of Chicago. It was in the echo of that terrified woman's footfalls that I first began to know the unwieldy inheritance I'd come into—the ability to alter public space in ugly ways. It was clear that she thought herself the quarry of a mugger, a rapist, or worse. Suffering a bout of insomnia, however, I was stalking sleep, not defenseless wayfarers. As a softy who is scarcely able to take a knife to a raw chicken—let alone hold it to a person's throat—I was surprised, embarrassed, and dismayed all at once. Her flight made me feel like an accomplice in tyranny. It also made it clear that I was indistinguishable from the muggers who occasionally seeped into the area from the surrounding ghetto. That first encounter, and those that followed, signified that a vast, unnerving gulf lay between night-time pedestrians—particularly women—and me. And I soon gathered that being perceived as dangerous is a hazard in itself. I only needed to turn a corner into a dicey situation, or crowd some frightened, armed person in a foyer somewhere, or make an errant move after being pulled over by a policeman. Where fear and weapons meet—and they often do in urban America—there is always the possibility of death.

In that first year, my first away from my hometown, I was to become thoroughly familiar with the language of fear. At dark, shadowy intersections in Chicago, I could cross in front of a car stopped at a traffic light and elicit the *thunk, thunk, thunk, thunk* of the driver—black, white, male, or female—hammering down the door locks. On less traveled streets after dark, I grew accustomed to but never comfortable with people who crossed to the other side of the street rather than pass me. Then there were the standard unpleasantries with policemen, doormen, bouncers, cab drivers, and others whose business it is to screen out troublesome individuals *before* there is any nastiness.

I moved to New York nearly two years ago and I have remained an avid night walker. In central Manhattan, the near-constant crowd cover minimizes tense one-on-one street encounters. Elsewhere—visiting friends in SoHo, where sidewalks are narrow and tightly spaced buildings shut out the sky—things can get very taut indeed.

5   Black men have a firm place in New York mugging literature. Norman Podhoretz in his famed (or infamous) 1963 essay, "My Negro Problem—And Ours," recalls growing up in terror of black males; they "were tougher than we were, more ruthless," he writes—and as an adult on the Upper West Side of Manhattan, he continues, he cannot constrain his nervousness when he meets black men on certain streets. Similarly, a decade later, the essayist and novelist Edward Hoagland extols a New York where once "Negro bitterness bore down mainly on other Negroes." Where some see mere panhandlers, Hoagland sees "a mugger who is clearly screwing up his nerve to do more than just *ask* for money." But Hoagland has "the New Yorker's quick-hunch posture for broken-field maneuvering," and the bad guy swerves away.

I often witness that "hunch posture," from women after dark on the warrenlike streets of Brooklyn where I live. They seem to set their faces on neutral and, with their purse straps strung across their chests bandolier style, they forge ahead as though bracing themselves against being tackled. I understand, of course, that the danger they perceive is not a hallucination. Women are particularly vulnerable to street violence, and young black males are drastically overrepresented among the perpetrators of that violence. Yet these truths are no solace against the kind of alienation that comes of being ever the suspect, against being set apart, a fearsome entity with whom pedestrians avoid making eye contact.

It is not altogether clear to me how I reached the ripe old age of twenty-two without being conscious of the lethality nighttime pedestrians attributed to me. Perhaps it was because in Chester, Pennsylvania, the small, angry industrial town where I came of age in the 1960s, I was scarcely noticeable against a backdrop of gang warfare, street knifings, and murders. I grew up one of the good boys, had perhaps a half-dozen fist fights. In retrospect, my shyness of combat has clear sources.

Many things go into the making of a young thug. One of those things is the consummation of the male romance with the power to intimidate. An infant discovers that random flailings send the baby bottle flying out of the crib and crashing to the floor. Delighted, the joyful babe repeats those motions again and again, seeking to duplicate the feat. Just so, I recall the points at which some of my boyhood friends were finally seduced by the perception of themselves as tough guys. When a mark cowered and surrendered his money without resistance, myth and reality merged—and paid off. It is, after all, only manly to embrace the power to frighten and intimidate. We, as men, are not supposed to give an inch of our lane on the highway; we are to seize the fighter's edge in work and in play and even in love; we are to be valiant in the face of hostile forces.

Unfortunately, poor and powerless young men seem to take all this nonsense literally. As a boy, I saw countless tough guys locked away; I have since buried several, too. They were babies, really—a teenage cousin, a brother of twenty-two, a childhood friend in his mid-twenties—all gone down in episodes of bravado played out in the streets. I came to doubt the virtues of intimidation early on. I chose, perhaps even unconsciously, to remain a shadow—timid, but a survivor.

10   The fearsomeness mistakenly attributed to me in public places often has a perilous flavor. The most frightening of these confusions oc-

curred in the late 1970s and early 1980s when I worked as a journalist in Chicago. One day, rushing into the office of a magazine I was writing for with a deadline story in hand, I was mistaken for a burglar. The office manager called security and, with an ad hoc posse, pursued me through the labyrinthine halls, nearly to my editor's door. I had no way of proving who I was. I could only move briskly toward the company of someone who knew me.

Another time I was on assignment for a local paper and killing time before an interview. I entered a jewelry store on the city's affluent Near North Side. The proprietor excused herself and returned with an enormous red Doberman pinscher straining at the end of a leash. She stood, the dog extended toward me, silent to my questions, her eyes bulging nearly out of her head. I took a cursory look around, nodded, and bade her good night. Relatively speaking, however, I never fared as badly as another black male journalist. He went to nearby Waukegan, Illinois, a couple of summers ago to work on a story about a murderer who was born there. Mistaking the reporter for the killer, police hauled him from his car at gunpoint and but for his press credentials would probably have tried to book him. Such episodes are not uncommon. Black men trade tales like this all the time.

In "My Negro Problem—And Ours," Podhoretz writes that the hatred he feels for blacks makes itself known to him through a variety of avenues—one being his discomfort with that "special brand of paranoid touchiness" to which he says blacks are prone. No doubt he is speaking here of black men. In time, I learned to smother the rage I felt at so often being taken for a criminal. Not to do so would surely have led to madness—via that special "paranoid touchiness" that so annoyed Podhoretz at the time he wrote the essay.

I began to take precautions to make myself less threatening. I move about with care, particularly late in the evening. I give a wide berth to nervous people on subway platforms during the wee hours, particularly when I have exchanged business clothes for jeans. If I happen to be entering a building behind some people who appear skittish, I may walk by, letting them clear the lobby before I return, so as not to seem to be following them. I have been calm and extremely congenial on those rare occasions when I've been pulled over by the police.

And on late-evening constitutionals along streets less traveled by, I employ what has proved to be an excellent tension-reducing measure: I whistle melodies from Beethoven and Vivaldi and the more popular classical composers. Even steely New Yorkers hunching toward nighttime destinations seem to relax, and occasionally they even join in the tune. Virtually everybody seems to sense that a mugger wouldn't be warbling bright, sunny selections from Vivaldi's *Four Seasons*. It is my equivalent of the cowbell that hikers wear when they know they are in bear country.

Analyzing Rhetorical Choices

1. Why do you think Staples chooses to open his essay with the sentence, "My first victim was a woman—white, well dressed, probably in her early twenties"?

2. Staples begins a central section of his essay with the sentence: "Many things go into the making of a young thug." How appropriate is the word *thug?* Analyze the next two paragraphs in terms of Staples's reasoning, cause-and-effect connections, word choice, and rhetorical effectiveness. Explain whether or not he makes his argument persuasively.

3. Throughout his essay, Staples depicts himself as the fearsome force and others ("black, white, male, or female") as his victims. Yet the metaphor he evokes at the end reverses this scenario. Is Staples contradicting himself? Why do you think he makes this rhetorical move?

Writing About Issues and Contexts

1. Is the fear felt by Staples's "first victim" justified? Is Staples's anger at being thought of as a criminal justified? Explain your responses, and offer an analysis that attempts to reconcile these two points of view.

2. Staples writes, "Where fear and weapons meet—and they often do in urban America—there is always the possibility of death." Why does Staples include this statement in his essay? Does he really have to worry about being killed? Do his "victims"? Offer your own analysis of the relationships between fear, weapons, and death.

3. Offer your own analysis of Staples's solutions to his problems. Are his solutions reasonable and sensible? Can you suggest other possibilities? Is he sidestepping the problem?

Born in Englewood, New Jersey, **Sharon Begley** *(1956–) graduated from Yale in 1977 with a degree in combined sciences, with an emphasis in physics. She began her professional writing career as a science researcher at* Newsweek *in 1977, rose to senior editor for science, and was hired in 2002 by the* Wall Street Journal *to launch a featured science column. Coauthor of* The Mind and the Brain *(2002), Begley wrote many major pieces for* Newsweek, *including "Science Finds God," "Are We All a Little Crazy?" "Your Child's Brain," and "Beyond Prozac." She has received numerous awards for her work, including a Clarion Award from the Association for Women in Communications for "excellence in clear, concise communication" and a 1993 Aviation/Space Writers Association Premier Award. "The Stereotype Trap" first appeared in* Newsweek *in November 2000.*

Sharon Begley

The Stereotype Trap

The students had no idea of the real purpose of the study they had volunteered for—it is, after all, standard operating procedure in psychology to keep subjects in the dark on that little point. (If volunteers know they're being studied for, say, whether they will help a blind child cross a busy street, it tends to skew their behavior.) So when 40 black and 40 white Princeton undergraduates volunteered to play mini-golf, the psychologists dissembled a bit. This is a test of "natural ability," Jeff Stone and his colleagues informed some of the kids. This is a test of "the ability to think strategically," they told others. Then the students—nongolfers all—played the course, one at a time. Among those told the test measured natural ability, black students scored, on average, more than four strokes better than whites. In the group told the test gauged strategic savvy, the white kids scored four strokes better, the researchers reported last year. "When people are reminded of a negative stereotype about themselves—'white men can't jump' or 'black men can't think'—it can adversely affect performance," says Stone, now at the University of Arizona.

Another group of students, 46 Asian-American female undergrads at Harvard, thought they were taking a tough, 12-question math test. Before one group attacked the advanced algebra, they answered written questions emphasizing ethnicity ("How many generations of your family have lived in America?"). Another group's questionnaire subtly reminded them of their gender ("Do you live on a co-ed or single-sex dorm floor?"). Women who took the math test after being reminded of their Asian heritage—and thus, it seems, the stereotype that Asians excel at math—scored highest, getting 54 percent right. The women whose questionnaire implicitly reminded them of the stereotype that, for girls, "math is hard," as Barbie infamously said, scored lowest, answering 43 percent correctly.

The power of stereotypes, scientists had long figured, lay in their ability to change the behavior of the person holding the stereotype. If you think women are ninnies ruled by hormonal swings, you don't name them CEO; if you think gays are pedophiles, you don't tap them to lead your Boy Scout troop. But five years ago Stanford University psychologist Claude Steele showed something else: it is the *targets* of a stereotype whose behavior is most powerfully affected by it. A stereotype that pervades the culture the way "ditzy blondes" and "forgetful seniors" do makes people painfully aware of how society views them—so painfully aware, in fact, that knowledge of the stereotype can affect how well they do on intellectual and other tasks. Now, with half a decade of additional research under their belts, psychologists are discovering the power of stereotypes not only over blacks, but over women, members of ethnic minorities and the elderly, too. And the research is shedding light on such enduring mysteries as why black kids, even those from middle-class families and good schools, often score lower than white kids on standardized tests.

In their seminal 1995 study, Steele and Joshua Aronson, now at New York University, focused on how the threat posed by stereotypes affects African-Americans. They reasoned that whenever black students take on an intellectual task, like an SAT, they face the prospect of confirming widely held suspicions about their brainpower. This threat, the psychologists suspected, might interfere with performance. To test this hunch, Steele and Aronson gave 44 Stanford undergrads questions from the verbal part of the tough Graduate Record Exam. One group was asked, right before the test, to indicate their year in school, age, major and other information. The other group answered all that, as well as one final question: what is your race? The results were sobering. "Just listing their race undermined the black students' performance," says Steele, making them score significantly worse than blacks who did not note their race, and significantly worse than all whites. But the performance of black Stanfordites who were not explicitly reminded of their race equaled that of whites, found the scientists.

5   You do not even have to believe a negative stereotype to be hurt by it, psychologists find. As long as you care about the ability you're being tested on, such as golfing or math, and are familiar with the stereotype ("girls can't do higher math"), it can sink you. What seems to happen is that as soon as you reach a tough par 3 or a difficult trig problem, the possibility of confirming, and being personally reduced to, a painful stereotype causes enough distress to impair performance. "If you are a white male and you find yourself having difficulty, you may begin to worry about failing the test," says psychologist Paul Davies of Stanford in an upcoming paper. But "if you are a black male . . . you begin to worry . . . about failing your race by confirming a negative stereotype." It's a sort of "oh God, they really are right about people like me" reaction.

You don't outgrow it, either. Becca Levy of Yale showed over-60 volunteers subliminal messages (through words flashed quickly on a monitor) and then tested them on memory. Seniors who saw words like "Alzheimer's," "senile" and "old" always scored worse than seniors who saw words like "wise" and "sage"—in some tests, 64 percent better. Does it matter? In a follow-up, Levy used the same subliminal priming. But this time she asked the volunteers whether they would accept life-prolonging medical intervention. Those seniors primed with positive stereotypes usually said yes; those reminded of senility and frailty said no. "What's so frightening," says Levy, "is that the stereotype, at least in the short run, overwhelms long-held beliefs."

Stereotypes seem to most affect the best and the brightest. Only if you're black and care about academics, or female and care about math, will you also care if society thinks you're bad at those things. A girl whose sense of self-worth is tied up in her poetry, for instance, is less likely to freeze up when her facility with calculus is belittled. To test the effect of the "bimbo" stereotype, scientists at the University of Waterloo in Ontario showed men and women undergrads TV commercials with and without gender stereotypes. (In one, a student says her primary goal in college is to meet "cute guys.") Then the students, who all said they were good at math and that it mattered to them, took a standardized test. Women who saw the commercials with female stereotypes not only did worse on the math problems than did women who saw gender-neutral commercials, as well as worse than men: they actively avoided math problems in favor of verbal ones. But the effect of stereotypes didn't end there. Women who saw stereotyped ads expressed less interest in math-based careers like financial analysis and physics afterward, and more interest in math-free fields like writing. "Exposure to stereotypic commercials persuades women to withdraw" from fields like math and science where they are the targets of stereotypes, Davies says. Of course, if the stereotype is positive, it can induce you to persist in something you're supposed to be good at even if you're not. Steele admits sheepishly that he keeps playing sports (even though he's no Tiger Woods) because, as a black man, he's told by society that he's a natural.

The power of stereotypes may explain the persistent gap between black and white kids on standardized tests even when the black kids come from middle and upper socioeconomic classes. Tellingly, that gap widens with age. Little kids have comparable scores on standardized tests, but by sixth grade, black kids lag by two full grade levels in many districts. It is around sixth grade, Steele points out, that "race becomes a big factor in the social organization of school"—and hence a more powerful reminder of which group you belong to.

Can the pernicious effects of stereotypes be vanquished? If no one reminds you of a negative stereotype, your performance doesn't suffer. It can actually improve if instead you think of a positive stereotype—Steele recommends bellowing something like "You are Stanford students!" but clearly that has limited applicability. Deception helps, too: if women are told that a difficult math test reveals no gender differences, finds Stephen Spencer of Waterloo, they perform as well as men. Otherwise, women score much lower. While such manipulations may weaken the brutal power of stereotypes, at the end of the day they remain manipulations. But until stereotypes fade away, that may be the best we can hope for.

Analyzing Rhetorical Choices

1. Begley begins this report by summarizing two independent scientific studies, each of which is focused on the consequences of stereotypes on behavior, athletic behavior in the one case and academic behavior in the other. Why is this an effective way to begin?

2. Begley uses some descriptive words and phrases and at times adopts something of a breezy tone. Some examples include, "If you think women are ninnies ruled by hormonal swings," "the 'bimbo' stereotype," "ditzy blondes," "the best and the brightest," "freeze up," and so on. What effects do these kinds of zippy, and at times commonplace, phrases have on the report—on its tone, seriousness, readability, and overall effectiveness?

3. Speaking of word choice, in the third paragraph, Begley uses the phrase "with half a decade of additional research under their belts." She could have written instead, "with five years of additional research under their belts." Why do you think she chooses the former and not the latter? Examine the essay for other usage choices that similarly reinforce the kind of tone and perspective that Begley wants to impart to the reader.

4. That this piece was written for *Newsweek*, a popular news magazine with a national audience, obviously affected how and why it was written. What ways do you think its being written for *Newsweek* shaped it in terms of style, length, complexity, and structure?

Writing About Issues and Contexts

1. To what groups does the title "The Stereotype Trap" refer? Who gets stereotyped? Who gets trapped? Why? How?

2. Begley reports that "You do not even have to believe a negative stereotype to be hurt by it." How is that possible? What accounts for the power of negative stereotyping? And why is it that negative stereotypes seem to affect "the best and the brightest"?

3. Why are the effects of negative stereotyping important? What long-term direct and indirect influence do they have on those groups (Asians, blacks, women, short people, whomever) that are a frequent target of negative stereotyping?

4. Begley does not provide much analysis of positive stereotyping. Can you provide some examples that you have either witnessed or indulged in? If positive stereotypes have a positive effect on performance, does this mean that stereotyping is not necessarily a bad thing? How should we respond to this issue of stereotyping in society?

A graduate of the University of California at Berkeley, **Eric Hansen**
*(1948–) has spent much of his life traveling and writing. In 1975, he
spent a year living in villages along the border of Nepal and Tibet, and in
1982 he traveled extensively in the Borneo rain forest and lived with a
small group of nomadic hunters and gatherers known as Penan. As he
recounts in an interview, "At the time, these people had never seen
tinned food, a telephone, or the ocean, and they had little knowledge of
life beyond the forest." Hansen is the author of several books, including*
Stranger in the Forest *(1988), from which this selection is taken, and*
Orchid Fever *(2000). Hansen had hoped that orchid cultivation would
allow the Penan to continue to live in the Borneo rain forest, after their
hunting grounds were largely destroyed through cultivation, but that
proved impossible. He continues to be interested in the rural and traditional people of Asia and the Asian rim, including the nomadic goat
herders of Mongolia and the wool traders of Western Tibet, Nepal, and
Northern India.*

Eric Hansen

The Bali Saleng

"The people are afraid," Pa Biah warned me. "Don't travel by
yourself; it is not safe. The people know you have come to the valley.
They may hurt you if they see you alone in the jungle."

The red glow from Pa Biah's cheroot gradually faded, and as he
coaxed the fire back to life with his foot, we sipped hot bitter tea from
chipped enamel mugs. Ibu Iting, his wife, sat nearby. She was making
thread by pulling strands of cotton from the edge of an old piece of
fabric. While holding the ends of two strands in her left hand, she
twisted them together by rubbing them between her right hand and
thigh. She threaded her needle and continued to listen to our conversation as she patched a well-worn pair of trousers.

"Last year," Pa Biah continued, "*bali saleng* was described as a
brown-skinned man with long black hair and pointed teeth. He wore
a powder blue, short-sleeved, military-type shirt with matching
shorts. He had a special set of spring-powered shoes that enabled him
to jump four meters in the air and ten meters away in a single bound.
He could spring through the air to cover long distances quickly and
capture people by surprise. After tying up his victim with strips of rat-

tan, he would take the blood from the wrist or the foot with a small knife and rubber pump. The corpse would then be hoisted with vines up into the jungle canopy so that searchers could not find it."

Listening attentively, I tried to imagine a police department's composite sketch of such an individual. The image of *bali saleng* was still too farfetched for me to take seriously.

5   "A *bali saleng* cannot be killed by man," Pa Biah continued. "Bullets bounce off him, spears cannot pierce his body, and when he gets old he will take on a young man without family and train him."

Pa Biah went on to tell me that the year before a pregnant woman was reported to have been killed by a *bali saleng* near the village of Long Ampung. Pregnant women are considered prime targets because they contain the blood of two people.

That night the people of Long Nawang locked themselves into their family quarters and did not open their doors until daybreak.

I listened to Pa Biah's stories with interest, but I failed to recognize my own imminent danger. I was placing too much confidence in my knowledge of the language and too little importance on the power of fear. Instead of accepting the people's beliefs as something real and adjusting my behavior accordingly, I was relying on a false sense of security. With nearly eighteen hundred jungle miles behind me, I had become careless.

The next morning I got up and left at dawn—alone. I didn't get far. Four hours up the valley, as I followed the Kayan River southeast from Long Nawang, I was attacked in the village of Long Uro. The first thing I heard was the frantic pounding of children's feet along hardwood planks of the longhouse porch. There were a few startled cries from the women then the sound of men's voices. It all happened very quickly. It took me a moment to realize that I was the cause of the commotion.

10   A group of about two dozen men, some armed with spears, came down to the trail where I was standing. After some excited questioning and gesturing (not all of which I understood), I felt their hands on me. I was stripped of my pack and forced to the ground. I didn't resist. I sat in the dirt with my back to a drainage ditch as the men formed a tight semicircle in front of me. For the next two hours they fired accusations at me in Indonesian. I was repeatedly questioned and crossexamined. My mind became alert, and I was careful not to show my fear. They wanted to know why I was by myself, why I didn't have a cooking pot, what I was doing in the Kayan River valley, and how I had come over the mountains from Sarawak. My answers didn't

sound very convincing, and I soon realized how vulnerable I was. The experience of facing so many frightened people was intimidating. My belongings were ransacked; shotgun shells, diaries, salt, clothing, and half-finished letters to friends littered the ground. I was repeatedly asked about the contents of my pack. After two men had gone through everything, I realized that they had been looking for spring-powered shoes, the small blood knife, and the rubber pump.

Over and over they repeated two questions: "Why do you walk by yourself?" and "Why aren't you afraid of *bali saleng?*"

The fact is that no one in Borneo walks by himself in the jungle. It is too easy to fall down or to get lost or sick. Every year people disappear in the rain forest without a trace. Solo travel isn't done except by the spirits. It was difficult to explain to these villagers why I had no fear. By now hours had passed, and I felt my energy fading. These frightened, angry people, with their excited sing-song manner of speaking, were exhausting me. Here in a village of practicing animists was a middle-class Westerner arguing about evil spirits in their jungle. By consistently basing my answers on logic and reasoning, I was only making the situation worse. I would have merely increased their suspicions if I had claimed not to believe in spirits. How could I possibly be convincing? I asked myself. It became irrelevant and unimportant to me whether they understood who I really was. By this time I wanted only one thing: to be able to leave the village safely. I realized that I had to accept their fear and deal with it on their terms. It was absurd for me to try to convince them that one of their greatest fears was unfounded. A solution came to me unexpectedly.

The Kenyah, as do all the inland people, have a tradition of amulets, charms, and spell-breakers. The collective term for these items is *jeemat*. A *jeemat* can be made from a wide assortment of materials; the most common are seedpods, bones, wood shavings, crushed insects, beeswax, cowrie shells, and odd-shaped black pebbles known as hook stones. A *jeemat* can be made by man or found, but the most powerful ones (the hook stones) are given by a spirit or ghost. Directions for their use are revealed during a dream. It is very bad luck to lose or give away a charm that has come from the spirits. *Jeemats* are usually worn around the neck or wrist and are an important part of one's personal adornment. They are visible proof of one's faith in the power of the spirit world.

With this in mind, I remembered I was wearing a small, stuffed fabric banana pin that a friend had given me before I started my trip. The pin was about three inches long and had a bright yellow, polka-dot peel. The banana was removable. It could be dangled at the end of a short safety string. Until that moment in Long Uro, I had used the pin only to amuse people.

15   "This," I said, gesturing to the pin, "is my *jeemat*. It protects me from *bali saleng*." It caught them off guard; it also aroused their interest. One of the men came forward to touch the banana, but I cautioned him not to. He stopped three feet away from me.

"It has very strong *obat*," I said. *Obat* has many definitions: magic, power, or medicine. "Be careful, this charm was made especially for me by a spirit. That is why I'm not afraid to walk alone in the jungle." The mood of the interrogation changed as interest shifted to my banana pin.

"Where did it come from?" "What is it made of?" "Do you have more?" "How much would one cost?" they wanted to know.

I did not concoct my banana-pin story because I thought my tormentors were simple-minded or childish. Quite the opposite. The Kenyah have a highly developed relationship with the spirit world. I couldn't think of any other story they might believe. From generations of experience, they know how to coexist with both good and bad spirits. Firmly rooted in the twentieth century, I certainly didn't have anything to teach them. I was the outsider, the ignorant one. I had great respect for all the inland people. With their unique forms of architecture, social organization, and sophisticated farming techniques, they have established themselves in an incredibly difficult environment. The decision to present the banana pin as a powerful charm not only helped save me in this situation, but also forced me to reconsider how I was responding to the people. I stopped being the observer and began to accept their supernatural world, and my journey was never the same. In that single moment I grew much closer to my experiences.

The tension eased after I had revealed the power of the banana-pin charm. A few obstinate older men insisted on going over the fine points of my story, but the rest seemed to think I was probably harmless. I was flushed with relief. The blood and adrenaline pounded through my body and made my fingertips and toes ache. I felt lightheaded and blessed to have survived this incident unharmed.

20   I was free to go, but it was too late to continue up the valley to my original destination—Long Sungai Barang. I had to spend the night in Long Uro. Dozens of eyes stared at me through knotholes and cracks in the rough wooden walls as I ate a miserable and lonely dinner. I was served half-rotten fish pounded in a mortar, bones and

all. Having finished my meal, I strung my mosquito net in a filthy corner, unrolled my mat, and escaped into an exhausted sleep.

During the night there must have been more discussion because in the morning, just after I left the village, I came upon a young man standing at the side of the pathway. He was barefoot, well muscled, and dressed in blue shorts. He wore white gloves and held a large unsheathed parang at his side. He didn't respond to my greeting as I approached, but as I passed he fell into step a few feet behind me. I continued on for a short while then decided it would be better to confront him. I turned to speak, but he had vanished into the undergrowth. I knew that he could be no more than fifty feet from where I stood, but I couldn't see him. For months this jungle had seemed so benign and giving. How quickly it had become frightening. It was clear to me that at any moment I might be ambushed and killed.

Farther up the valley I passed abandoned farm huts and stopped briefly in the village of Lidung Payau to ask directions to the village of Long Sungai Barang. On the far side of Lidung Payau, I saw what I soon realized was a cage fashioned out of logs six inches in diameter. The structure was raised off the ground and had a slat floor that let excrement out and the flies in. The cage measured six feet by five feet by four feet and had a shingled roof. It was "home" not to an animal, but to a man. There were no doors or windows. I later learned that the inhabitant, barely visible between the gaps in the horizontal logs, had lived in the cage for more than two years. I don't know what his crime was. The cloud of furiously buzzing blackflies must have driven him mad. I looked upon this wretched man as a fellow sufferer, but when I tried to speak with him, he moved to the far side of his cage, and I could sense his fear of my presence.

I no longer had my sense of security and self-confidence. I lost track of time. As my anxiety mounted, a few hundred yards began to seem like miles. My thinking became erratic and unsound. There was no turning back, and for the first time since leaving Long Sungai Anai three days earlier, I began to panic. I sensed that I was being watched. Soaked in perspiration, I paused frequently to look over my shoulder and listen for the sound of human voices or of jungle knives slashing through the undergrowth. I scanned the surrounding walls of impenetrable green and brown foliage, but I could detect nothing. There were only the normal sounds of the jungle: the wind, the flutter of leaves, dripping water, and rubbing branches. I could see black hornbills perched nearby, so I called to them. I wanted to hear something friendly and reassuring, but their calls came back to me sounding like strangled pleas.

I hurried on to Long Sungai Barang, hoping that word of the incident in Long Uro hadn't preceded me. I wanted a fresh start. I now realized the full extent of my naiveté, my incredible stupidity. I was completely alone and vulnerable. I didn't know what else to do except to keep walking and to try to relax. I stopped frequently, considered going back, couldn't decide, then continued on. Whenever I sat down to rest and clear my mind, a new wave of anxiety would engulf me.

25   I knew that Long Sungai Barang was the last village in the upper Kayan River valley. If the people there weren't friendly, I would be trapped. Four hundred miles of primary rain forest separated me from the most accessible coast.

It was late afternoon by the time I entered the longhouse at Sungai Barang. I was disoriented and confused, and my legs were bleeding freely from leeches and barbed vines. I was led to the headman's room. While he was being summoned, I was surrounded by about a dozen Kenyah men. I could feel the deep, painful grooves that the straps of the rattan pack had cut into my shoulders. My shirt was pasted to my back from the heat of the day. The men seemed relaxed and curious, but I felt they looked right through me and sensed my uncertainty.

We talked about the approaching rice harvest for perhaps ten minutes; then to my left I heard the familiar creak and slam of a sapling-powered hardwood door. In midsentence I looked up, expecting to see the headman, but there before me stood a young, white-skinned woman with golden hair. She was dressed in a flowered sarong and a blouse. She was barefoot, pretty, and smiling. I was completely unnerved. It just wasn't possible for her to be there. I became incredulous and even more confused. Finally I just smiled back and felt my pent-up fears and anxieties begin to dissolve.

The first thing I noticed as she stood there was the fragrance of her skin. It wasn't the scent of soap or perfume; it was the scent of another culture, another world, a fresh, wonderful smell that made me question my attraction to smoky jungle campfires and eating wild animals. We spoke Indonesian. There was no urgency to our voices. In Kenyah fashion we began with trivial matters in order to mask the real intent of our conversation, and gradually we led up to the important questions. More people came into the room. They sat quietly, watched, and listened. Eventually the temptation to speak our own language was overwhelming. The woman smiled again and in perfect English said, "I'm Cynthia. I live next door. The headman won't be back until late tonight. Would you like to come over to my place for a visit?"

Analyzing Rhetorical Choices

1. In what ways is it effective to open with the direct statement of Pa Biah? Why does Hansen mention that he "tried to imagine a police department's composite sketch of such an individual"? What is the point of introducing this notion of a Western police department here?

2. How do Hansen's language choices reinforce his sense of fear and anxiety?

3. Explain what Hansen means by writing that the "young, white-skinned woman with the golden hair" has a skin fragrance that was "the scent of another culture, another world, a fresh, wonderful smell that made me question my attraction to smoky jungle campfires and eating wild animals." What has happened here, both in terms of the narrative and the style? What are the causes and effects of this sudden change?

Writing About Issues and Contexts

1. Is Hansen right to make light of the *bali saleng*? What, if anything, should Hansen be afraid of?

2. What is the root cause of the villagers' fear? What underlies their belief system? Is their belief system more or less primitive than Hansen's?

3. Hansen writes, "For months this jungle had seemed so benign and giving. How quickly it had become frightening." What accounts for this sudden, dramatic shift?

4. Reconsider Orwell's "Shooting an Elephant" (Chapter 2) in light of Hansen's essay. How does each reveal the potential for conflict when different cultures meet?

Louise Erdrich (1954–) is perhaps best known for her novel Love Medicine *(1984) as well as other works that focus on the experience of Native Americans:* The Beet Queen *(1986),* Tracks *(1988), and* The Bingo Palace *(1994). In contrast, her novel* The Master Butchers Singing Club *(2003) focuses on the immigrant-German-father side of her family. Part Chippewa Indian, Erdrich was raised in North Dakota where her parents worked at the Bureau of Indian Affairs boarding school, which she attended. She received a bachelor's degree from Dartmouth in 1976 and a master's in creative writing from Johns Hopkins in 1979. Her fiction has appeared in many magazines and reviews; "Sister Godzilla" appeared first in* The Atlantic Monthly.

Louise Erdrich

Sister Godzilla

The door banged shut, and then the children were alone with their sixth-grade teacher. It was the first day of school, in the fall of 1963. The habits of Franciscan nuns still shrouded all but their faces, so each of the new nun's features was emphasized, read forty times over in astonishment. Outlined in a stiff white frame of starched linen, Sister's eyes, nose, and mouth leaped out, a mask from a dream, a great rawboned jackal's muzzle.

"Oh, Christ," Toddy Crieder said, just loud enough for Dot to hear.

Dot Adare, a troublemaker, knew Toddy was in love with her and usually ignored him, but the nun's extreme ugliness was irresistible.

"Godzilla," she whispered.

5   The teacher's name was Sister Mary Anita Groff. She was young, in her twenties or thirties, and so swift of movement, for all her hulking size, that walking from the back of the room to the front, she surprised her students, made them picture an athlete's legs and muscles concealed in the flow of black wool. When she swept the air in a gesture meant to include them all in her opening remarks, her hands fixed their gazes. They were the opposite of her face. Her hands were beautiful, as white as milk glass, the fingers straight and tapered. They were the hands in the hallway print of Mary underneath the cross. They were the hands of the Apostles, cast in plastic and lit at night on the tops of television sets. Praying hands.

Ballplayer's hands. She surprised them further by walking onto the graveled yard at recess, her neckpiece cutting hard into the flesh beneath her heavy jaw. When, with a matter-of-fact grace, she pulled from the sleeve of her gown a mitt of dark mustard-colored leather and raised it, a thrown softball dropped in. Her skill was obvious. Good players rarely stretch or change their expressions. They simply tip their hands toward the ball like magnets, and there it is. As a pitcher, Mary Anita was a swirl of wool, as graceful as the windblown cape of Zorro, an emotional figure that stirred Dot so thoroughly that as she pounded home plate—a rubber dish mat—and beat the air twice in practice swings, choked up on the handle, tried to concentrate, Dot knew she would have no choice but to slam a home run.

She did not. In fact, she whiffed, in three strikes, never ticking the ball or fouling. Purely disgusted with herself, she sat on the edge of the bike rack and watched as Sister gave a few balls away and pitched easy hits to the rest of the team. It was as if the two had sensed from the beginning what was to come. Or, then again, perhaps Mary Anita's information came from Dot's former teachers, living in the red-brick convent across the road. Hard to handle. A smart-off. Watch out when you turn your back. They were right. After recess, her pride burned, Dot sat at her desk and drew a dinosaur draped in a nun's robe, its mouth open in a roar. The teeth, long and jagged, grayish-white, held her attention. She worked so hard on the picture that she barely noticed as the room hushed around her. She felt the presence, though, the shadow of attention that dropped over her as Mary Anita stood watching. As a mark of her arrogance, Dot kept drawing.

She shaded in the last tooth and leaned back to frown at her work. The page was plucked into the air before she could pretend to cover it. No one made a sound. Dot's heart beat with excitement.

"You will remain after school," the nun pronounced.

10   The last half hour passed. The others filed out the door. And then the desk in front of Dot filled suddenly. There was the paper, the carefully rendered dinosaur caught in mid-roar. Dot stared at it furiously, her mind a blur of anticipation. She was not afraid.

"Look at me," Mary Anita said.

Dot found that she didn't want to, that she couldn't. Then her throat filled. Her face was on fire. Her lids hung across her eyeballs like lead shades. She traced the initials carved into her desktop.

"Look at me," Mary Anita said to her again, and Dot's gaze was drawn upward, upward on a string, until she met the eyes of her teacher, deep brown, electrically sad. Their very stillness shook Dot.

"I'm sorry," she said.

15   When those two unprecedented words dropped from her lips, Dot knew, beyond reason and past bearing, that something terrible had occurred. She felt dizzy. The blood rushed to her head so fast that her ears ached, yet the tips of her fingers fell asleep. Her eyelids prickled and her nose wept, but at the same time her mouth went dry. Her body was a thing of extremes, contradicting itself.

"When I was young," Sister Mary Anita said, "as young as you are, I felt a great deal of pain when I was teased about my looks. I've long since accepted my . . . deformity. A prognathic jaw runs in our family, and I share it with an uncle. But I must admit, the occasional insult, or a drawing such as yours, still hurts."

Dot began to mumble and then stopped, desperate. Sister Mary Anita waited, and then handed her her own handkerchief.

"I'm sorry," Dot said again. She wiped her nose. The square of white material was cool and fresh. "Can I go now?"

"Of course not," Mary Anita said.

20   Dot was confounded. The magical two words, an apology, had dropped from her lips. Yet more was expected. What?

"I want you to understand something," the nun said. "I've told you how I feel. And I expect that you will never hurt me again."

The nun waited, and waited, until their eyes met. Then Dot's mouth fell wide. Her eyes spilled over. She knew that the strange feelings that had come upon her were the same feelings that Mary Anita had felt. Dot had never felt another person's feelings, never in her life.

"I won't do anything to hurt you," she blubbered passionately. "I'll kill myself first."

"I'm sure that will not be necessary," Sister Mary Anita said.

25   Dot tried to rescue her pride then, by turning away very quickly. Without permission, she ran out the schoolroom door, down the steps, and on into the street, where at last the magnetic force of the encounter weakened, and suddenly she could breathe. Even that was different, though. As she walked, she began to realize that her body was still fighting itself. Her lungs filled with air like two bags, but every time they did so, a place underneath them squeezed so painfully that the truth suddenly came clear.

"I love her now," she blurted out. She stopped on a crack, stepping on it, sickened. "Oh, God, I am *in love*."

Toddy Crieder was a hollow-chested, envious boy whose reputation had never recovered from the time he was sent home for eating tree bark. In the third grade he had put two crayons up his nose, pretend tusks. The pink one got stuck, and Toddy had to visit the clinic. This year, already, his stomach had been pumped in the emergency room. Dot despised him, but that only seemed to fuel his adoration of her.

Coming into the schoolyard the second day, a bright, cool morning, Toddy ran up to Dot, his thin legs knocking.

"Yeah," he cried. "Godzilla! Not bad, Adare."

30   He wheeled off, the laces of his tennis shoes dragging. Dot looked after him and felt the buzz inside her head begin. How she wanted to stuff that name back into her mouth, or at least Toddy's mouth.

"I hope you trip and murder yourself!" Dot screamed.

But Toddy did not trip. For all of his clumsiness, he managed to stay upright, and as Dot stood rooted in the center of the walk, she saw him whiz from clump to clump of children, laughing and gesturing, filling the air with small and derisive sounds. Sister Mary Anita swept out the door, a wooden-handled brass bell in her hand, and when she shook it up and down, the children, who played together in twos and threes, swung toward her and narrowed or widened their eyes and turned eagerly to one another. Some began to laugh. It seemed to Dot that all of them did, in fact, and that the sound, jerked from their lips, was large, uncanny, totally and horribly delicious.

"Godzilla, Godzilla," they called under their breath. "Sister Godzilla."

Before them on the steps, the nun continued to smile into their faces. She did not hear them—yet. But Dot knew she would. Over the bell her eyes were brilliantly dark and alive. Her horrid jagged teeth showed in a smile when she saw Dot, and Dot ran to her, thrusting a hand into her lunch bag and grabbing the cookies that her mother had made from whatever she could find around the house—raisins, congealed Malt-O-Meal, the whites of eggs.

35   "Here!" Dot shoved a sweet, lumpy cookie into the nun's hand. It fell apart, distracting Sister as the children pushed past.

The students seemed to forget the name off and on all week. Some days they would move on to new triumphs or disasters—other teachers occupied them, or some small event occurred in the classroom. But then Toddy Crieder would lope and careen among them at recess, would pump his arms and pretend to roar behind Sister Mary Anita's back as she stepped up to the plate. As she swung and connected with the ball and gathered herself to run, her veil lifting, the muscles in her shoulders like the curved hump of a raptor's wings,

Toddy would move along behind her, rolling his legs the way Godzilla did in the movie. In her excitement, dashing base to base, her feet long and limber in black laced shoes, Mary Anita did not notice. But Dot looked on, the taste of a penny caught in her throat.

"Snakes live in holes. Snakes are reptiles. These are Science Facts." Dot read aloud to the class from her Discovery science book. "Snakes are not wet. Some snakes lay eggs. Some have live young."

"Very good," Sister said. "Can you name other reptiles?"

Dot's tongue fused to the back of her throat.

40   "No," she croaked.

"Anyone else?" Sister asked.

Toddy Crieder raised his hand. Sister recognized him.

"How about Godzilla?"

Gasps. Small noises of excitement. Mouths agape. Admiration for Toddy's nerve rippled through the rows of children like a wind across a field. Sister Mary Anita's great jaw opened, opened, and then snapped shut. Her shoulders shook. No one knew what to do at first. Then she laughed. It was a high-pitched, almost birdlike sound, a thin laugh like the highest notes on the piano. The children all hesitated, and then they laughed with her, even Toddy Crieder. Eyes darting from one child to the next, to Dot, Toddy laughed.

45   Dot's eyes crossed with urgency. When Sister Mary Anita turned to new work, Dot crooked her arm beside her like a piston and leaned across Toddy's desk.

"I'm going to give you one right in the breadbasket," she said.

With a precise boxer's jab she knocked the wind out of Toddy, left him gasping, and turned to the front, face clear, as Sister began to speak.

Furious sunlight. Black cloth. Dot sat on the iron trapeze, the bar pushing a sore line into the backs of her legs. As she swung, she watched Sister Mary Anita. The wind was harsh, and the nun wore a pair of wonderful gloves, black, the fingers cut off of them so that her hands could better grip the bat. The ball arced toward her sinuously and dropped. Her bat caught it with a thick, clean sound, and off it soared. Mary Anita's habit swirled open behind her. The cold bit her cheeks red. She swung to third, glanced, panting, over her shoulder, and then sped home. She touched down lightly and bounded off.

Dot's arms felt heavy, weak, and she dropped from the trapeze and went to lean against the brick wall of the school building. Her

heart thumped in her ears. She saw what she would do when she grew
up: declare her vocation, enter the convent. She and Sister Mary Anita
would live in the nuns' house together, side by side. They would eat,
work, eat, cook. To relax, Sister Mary Anita would hit pop flies and
Dot would catch them.

50   Someday, one day, Dot and Mary Anita would be walking, their
hands in their sleeves, long habits flowing behind.

"Dear Sister," Dot would say, "remember that old nickname you
had the year you taught the sixth grade?"

"Why, no," Sister Mary Anita would say, smiling at her. "Why, no."

And Dot would know that she had protected her, kept her from
harm.

It got worse. Dot wrote some letters, tore them up. Her hand
shook when Sister passed her in the aisle, and her eyes closed, automatically, as she breathed in the air that closed behind the nun.
Soap—a harsh soap. Faint carbolic mothballs. That's what she
smelled like. Dizzying. Dot's fists clenched. She pressed her knuckles
to her eyes and very loudly excused herself. She went to the girls'
bathroom and stood in a stall. Her life was terrible. The thing was,
she didn't want to be a nun.

55   "I don't want to!" she whispered, desperate, to the whitewashed
tin walls that shuddered if a girl bumped them. "There must be another way."

She would have to persuade Mary Anita to forsake her vows, to
come and live with Dot and her mother in the house just past the edge
of town. How would she start, how would she persuade her teacher?

Someone was standing outside the stall. Dot opened the door a
bit and stared into the great craggy face.

"Are you feeling all right? Do you need to go home?" Sister Mary
Anita was concerned.

Fire shot through Dot's limbs. The girls' bathroom, a place of secrets, of frosted glass, its light mute and yet brilliant, paralyzed her. But
she gathered herself. Here was her chance, as if God had given it to her.

60   "Please," Dot said, "let's run away together!"

Sister paused. "Are you having troubles at home?"

"No," Dot said.

Sister's milk-white hand came through the doorway and covered
Dot's forehead. Dot's anxious thoughts throbbed against the lean
palm. Staring into the eyes of the nun, Dot gripped the small metal
knob on the inside of the door and pushed. Then she felt herself

falling forward, slowly turning like a leaf in the wind, upheld and buoyant in the peaceful roar. It was as though she would never reach Sister's arms, but when she did, she came back with a jolt.

"You *are* ill," Sister said. "Come to the office, and we'll call your mother."

65   As Dot had known it would, perhaps from that moment in the girls' bathroom, the day came. The day of her reckoning.

Outside, in the morning schoolyard, after mass and before first bell, everyone crowded around Toddy Crieder. In his arms he held a wind-up tin Godzilla, a big toy, almost knee-high, a green-and-gold replica painted with a fierce eye for detail. The scales were perfect overlapping crescents, and the eyes were large and manic, pitch-black, oddly human. Toddy had pinned a sort of cloak on the thing, a black scarf. Dot's arms thrust through the packed shoulders, but the bell rang, and Toddy stowed the toy under his coat. His eyes picked Dot from the rest.

"I had to send for this!" he cried. The punch hadn't turned him against Dot, only hardened his resolve to please her. He vanished through the heavy wine-red doors of the school. Dot stared at the ground. The world went stark, the colors harsh in her eyes. The small brown pebbles of the playground leaped off the tarred and sealed earth. She took a step. The stones seemed to crack and whistle under her feet.

"Last bell!" Sister Mary Anita called. "You'll be late!"

Morning prayer. The pledge. Toddy drew out the suspense of his audience, enjoying the glances and whispers. The toy was in his desk. Every so often he lifted the lid and then looked around to see how many children were watching him duck inside to make adjustments. By the time Sister started the daily reading lesson, the tension in the room was so acute that not even Toddy could bear it any longer.

70   The room was large, high-ceilinged, floored with slats of polished wood. Round lights hung on thick chains, and the great rectangular windows let through enormous sheaves of radiance. This large class had been in the room for more than two years. Dot had spent most of every day in the room. She knew its creaks, the muted clunk of desks rocking out of floor bolts, the mad thumping in the radiators like the sound of a thousand imprisoned elves, and so she heard and immediately registered the click and grind of Toddy's windup key. Sister Mary Anita did not. The teacher turned to the chalkboard, her book open on the desk, and began to write instructions for the children to copy.

She was absorbed, calling out the instructions as she wrote. Her arm swept up and down, it seemed to Dot, in a frighteningly innocent joy. She was inventing a lesson, some way of doing things, not a word of which was being taken in. All eyes were on the third row, where Toddy Crieder sat. All eyes were on his hand as he wound the toy up to its limit and bent over and set it on the floor. Then the eyes were on the toy itself, as Toddy lifted his hand away and the thing moved forward on its own.

The scarf it wore did not hamper the beast's progress, the regular thrash of its legs. The tiny claw hands beat forward like pistons and the thick metal tail whipped from side to side as the toy moved down the center of the aisle toward the front of the room, toward Sister Mary Anita, who stood, back turned, immersed in her work at the board.

Dot had gotten herself placed in the first row, to be closer to her teacher, and so she saw the creature up close just before it headed into the polished open space of floor at the front of the room. Its powerful jaws thrust from the black scarf; its great teeth were frozen, exhibited in a terrible smile. Its painted eyes had an eager and purposeful look.

Its movement faltered as it neared Mary Anita. The children caught their breath, but the thing inched forward, made slow and fascinating progress, directly toward the hem of her garment. She did not seem to notice. She continued to talk, to write, circling numbers and emphasizing certain words with careful underlines. And as she did so, as the moment neared, Dot's brain finally rang. She jumped as though it were the last bell of the day. She vaulted from her desk. Two steps took her across that gleaming space of wood at the front of the room. But just as she bent down to scoop the toy to her chest, a neat black boot slashed, inches from her nose. Sister Mary Anita had whirled, the chalk fixed in her hand. Daintily, casually, she had lifted her habit and kicked the toy dinosaur into the air. The thing ascended, pedaling its clawed feet, the scarf blown back like a sprung umbrella. The trajectory was straight and true. The toy knocked headfirst into the ceiling and came back down in pieces. The children ducked beneath the rain of scattered tin. Only Dot and Mary Anita stood poised, unmoving, focused on the moment between them.

75 Dot could look nowhere but at her teacher. But when she lifted her eyes this time, Sister Mary Anita was not looking at her. She had turned her face away, the rough cheek blotched as if it had borne a slap, the gaze hooded and set low. Sister walked to the window, her back again to Dot, to the class, and as the laughter started, uncomfortable and groaning at first, then shriller, fuller, becoming its own

animal, Dot felt an unrecoverable tenderness boil up in her. Inwardly she begged the nun to turn and stop the noise. But Sister did not. She let it wash across them both without mercy. Dot lost sight of her unspeakable profile as Mary Anita looked out into the yard. Bathed in brilliant light, the nun's face went as blank as a sheet of paper, as the sky, as featureless as all things that enter heaven.

Analyzing Rhetorical Choices

1. Erdrich begins with an opening that has considerable shock value when she writes that "Sister's eyes, nose, and mouth leaped out, a mask from a dream, a great rawboned jackal's muzzle." How does this description set the tone for what follows?
2. Erdrich describes Toddy Crieder as "a hollow-chested, envious boy." What does the phrase "hollow-chested" imply about Crieder, especially in relation to his emotions?
3. Erdrich sometimes uses short phrases that function as sentences: "Praying hands." "Ballplayer's hands." "Gasps." "Small noises of excitement." "Mouths agape." "Furious sunlight." "Black cloth." What rhetorical effect do these sentences have? Why do you think Erdrich uses them so frequently?
4. Explain the significance, to you, of the last sentence of this story: "Bathed in brilliant light, the nun's face went as blank as a sheet of paper, as the sky, as featureless as all things that enter heaven."

Writing About Issues and Contexts

1. Why is it significant that Mary Anita Groff is a nun?
2. How would you describe this love that an 11- or 12-year-old girl has for a grown woman, one who is so physically grotesque?
3. What is the significance of Sister Mary Anita's hands? Why does Erdrich dwell on them to so great an extent?
4. At the heart of this story is the complex emotional dynamic among three key individuals: Dot, Sister Mary Anita Groff, and Toddy Crieder. How would you describe both the causes and the effects that lie at the heart of this story?
5. The other children play the role of spectators, but they are not impartial or sympathetic toward Sister Mary Anita. What perspective does Erdrich offer concerning the children? Are they innocent? What is their relationship to their teacher, to Toddy Crieder, and to the event that climaxes the story?

---

*A national writer for the Associated Press, **Pauline Arrillaga** (1970–)
reveals the human aspect beneath the news stories on which she reports.
Arrillaga's work covers politics, the United States space program, and issues of immigration along the Mexican-American border. Arrillaga was
awarded the 2005 Livingston Award for Young Journalists for her story
"Doors to Death," in which she examines the illegal smuggling of human beings across the border. In addition to being named a 2005–2006
Racial Justice Fellow at the University of Southern California, Arrillaga
received the 1996 Associated Press Managing Editors' top feature writing prize; she is also the recipient of awards from the Press Club of
Dallas and the Texas Associated Press Managing Editors group. "One
by One" originally appeared as an editorial in the "Crossroads" section
of the* Milwaukee Sentinel Journal *in June of 2004.*

Pauline Arrillaga

One by One

They used to gather in a cavernous hotel ballroom, tables packed
with bankers and shopkeepers rubbing elbows with politicians. Those
were the days when downtown Phoenix was booming, and the Downtown Lions Club boomed right along with it.

In the 1970s, it wasn't unusual for 150 members to show up at
the weekly lunch meetings to catch up with colleagues and friends.
Nor was it unusual for a boss to pay his employee's dues, since the
club bred leaders and, sometimes, more commerce.

Amid the camaraderie, issues were discussed, ideas debated, ref-
erendums rehashed—a proposed highway project, perhaps, or ways
to keep litter off the streets. Lions Club luncheons were an arena for
political engagement, one that drew dozens of ardent participants.

Now, in 2004, Meredith Stam gets "flak for coming here.
Totally." Stam, a 26-year-old paralegal, is completely out of place at a
21st-century Lions Club lunch.

5   The group meets now in a cramped conference room. Its membership has plummeted to 30, though, on a recent afternoon, only a
third of them congregated over fish and fruit plates to hear a spiel
against a proposed light rail project.

Stam was one of four without white hair or wrinkles.

Her friends roll their eyes at her Lions affiliation. When they come together, it's more likely to be for a game of volleyball or flag football. Civic involvement, Stam observes, isn't much of a national pastime anymore.

"We're sitting on the sidelines," she says.

Twenty-first-century America is not the nation of joiners that amazed Alexis de Tocqueville in the 1830s; it is not a place where citizens engage constantly to assemble democracy's quilt. The very groups that once promoted citizenship have seen their membership rates dwindle, groups like the Grange, Masons, American Legion, Boy Scouts and Girl Scouts.

10   "Bowling alone," is what Harvard University political scientist Robert Putnam calls it—a reference to an intriguing statistic that finds Americans bowling as much as ever but participation in leagues down sharply.

"There has been, at least over the past 40 years, a pretty strong downward movement in most forms of political participation," he says.

He cites Roper polls that indicate the number of Americans who worked for a political party fell 42% between 1973 and 1994; who attended a public meeting fell 35%; who wrote to a representative fell 23%; who signed a petition fell 22%.

In America today, many of us sit back and watch others do the grunt work that was once widely regarded as a citizen's duty and privilege.

We have become, it seems, a nation of bystanders.

When ordinary citizens are not engaged in civic life, a democratic
15 society becomes unbalanced. The minority that speaks out is heard; the majority that doesn't is ignored. For example, older Americans tend to be more outspoken than younger Americans.

The result? "We're not having the same kinds of debates about student loans and national service and training for a first job as we are about Social Security and Medicare," says William Galston, director of the University of Maryland's Center for Information and Research on Civic Learning and Engagement.

"If a lot of citizens drop out of the system, then the ones who stay in will have disproportionate influence. Some issues get debated actively and taken seriously, and others not," he says.

Historically, this was not an issue in a nation where civic participation was once as much a part of the landscape as its mountains and plains.

Organizations, some as old as the country itself, brought citizens together to solve problems locally and press issues nationally; political parties recruited the masses to help spread their message; civil protest was a viable means to political and social change.

20   Everyday Americans had a voice, and the nation's leaders listened because they depended on them—whether as citizen soldiers, taxpayers or volunteers.

For government leaders, "popular support was the currency of power," write political scientists Matthew A. Crenson and Benjamin Ginsberg in their book "Downsizing Democracy."

Somewhere along the way, Americans grew less interested in being active citizens. What happened? The "old-timers" of the Phoenix Downtown Lions offer some ideas:

- "The problem," says 71-year-old Gene Hardin, "is people die."

One factor is the loss of the "long civic generation"—those who came of age during the Depression and World War II, spurred into action by hard times (and not yet distracted by television and the Internet). They were more inclined to vote, attend a meeting, join a group.

25 - "Things change," suggests 82-year-old Helen Tibken, "and we change with it."

Putnam, the political scientist, points to social and technological developments. Over the last 50 years, as the golden age of civic engagement lost some sparkle, suburban sprawl brought lengthier commutes; women, once a backbone of organizations, entered the workplace; television went from a diversion to a fixation; and the Internet made face-to-face contact unessential.

- "People say they're just too busy," adds Allen Nahrwold, 65, "and they really are."

Roderick Hart, director of the Annette Strauss Institute for Civic Participation at the University of Texas, agrees that a lack of time—whether perceived or real—is partly to blame. Today, with single-parent households or two-parent families in which both mom and dad must work to make ends meet, civic duties can become expendable.

For many, some experts say, check writing has replaced active political participation. It takes less time and energy to write a check to the Sierra Club than to hoist a picket sign protesting oil drilling in Alaska.

30   "Civic participation and efficiency don't go well together," says Hart, "and we crave efficiency more than anything else."

Political scientist Theda Skocpol has another theory: Too many organizations are dominated by managers who can, and do, succeed without members doing anything.

Between 1959 and 1999, the total number of national organizations listed in the Encyclopedia of Associations grew almost fourfold, from about 6,000 to near 23,000. But membership rolls didn't. One study found that in 1962, the median size of groups listed in the index was about 10,000 members. In 1988, it was 1,000.

Call it the great irony of modern-day citizenship.

"America's organizing groups like never before," says Skocpol, author of the book "Diminished Democracy: From Membership to Management in American Civic Life." "They just aren't joining them."

35   Whereas mobilizing citizen supporters was once the most effective way to bring visibility and clout to an organization and its concerns—consider the boycotts, marches and sit-ins of the civil rights era—today's advocacy groups have found other, oftentimes more expedient, avenues.

Member organizations have been superseded by professionally managed groups with paid staff members focused on drafting policy rather than people. They hire researchers to write legislation, lobbyists to sway congressional staffs and public affairs specialists to pitch to the media.

Putnam illustrates the difference this way: Many of the nation's older member organizations have headquarters in places like Irving, Texas (Boy Scouts); Tulsa, Okla. (Jaycees); and Oak Brook, Ill. (Lions)—where they are close to their participants.

Dozens of today's advocacy associations (Common Cause, the National Organization for Women, and the Wilderness Society, among them) do business from Washington, D.C. Even AARP, the advocacy group for older Americans, is located only blocks from the Capitol rather than somewhere like Arizona or Florida, where many of the nation's retirees live.

These groups do have members. AARP is one of the biggest, with some 35 million dues-paying constituents. But these "members" don't meet weekly to devise policy strategies; they pay $12.50 annually to hire someone else to do it and receive newsletter updates by mail.

40   The group's own data show that most Americans who join AARP do so for the benefits they can receive by flashing their membership card.

That's not to say there aren't some "chapters," where group members can come together for some old-fashioned, face-to-face fellowship. But those are few and far between. Arizona, with 720,000 AARP members, had 31 local chapters eight years ago. Now, there are 19.

The community groups "are having difficulty staying afloat," says Curtis Cook, an associate state director for AARP Arizona. "It's just not a thing that people care to do very much in today's modern society, with all of the attractions and allurements elsewhere."

But the decline of mass political participation is not simply a consequence of the decay of civil society brought on by TV, suburbanization and busy lives, argue Crenson and Ginsberg in "Downsizing Democracy."

Starting in the Progressive Era of the early 20th century, they write, the government established regulatory commissions to serve as watchdogs on special interests. The outcome, Crenson and Ginsberg suggest, was twofold: Citizens became less vigilant and involved, and interests like the banks and railroads came to control the very commissions that were supposed to work on behalf of the public good.

45   Another recent change: statutes and judicial rulings that made advocacy by litigation commonplace, taking them out of the political arena. Name your issue: smoking, the environment, gay marriage— with only one name under the heading "plaintiff," a lawsuit can effect change for millions of Americans through the action of but one.

Consider the decade's most infamous court case: Bush vs. Gore.

There were no mass demonstrations as the case that would decide the 2000 presidential election wound its way to the Supreme Court, Crenson and Ginsberg note. Neither candidate went out of his way to elicit public support.

"The absence of political ferment was said . . . to indicate the maturity of American democracy and Americans' profound respect for the rule of law," write the authors.

Instead, they argue, "Americans failed to become agitated because most knew the political struggle they were witnessing did not involve them."

50   If Americans are to experience a civic reawakening, experts insist, the nation's leaders need to sound the alarm.

As recently as 1960, John F. Kennedy famously challenged Americans to "ask not what your country can do for you—ask what you can do for your country."

But somewhere along the way, leaders became less enthusiastic about challenging the citizenry. After Sept. 11, 2001, George W. Bush urged Americans to "get about the business of America" by shopping and traveling.

Skocpol notes that the Sept. 11 attacks caused a surge in patriotism and feelings of community connectedness, but those attitudes weren't often accompanied by action "because there weren't a lot of places to go to do things."

"It's tempting to think everything's changed because people have changed. If there were more organizations asking us to do things," she says, "my guess is a lot of people would respond to that."

Analyzing Rhetorical Choices

1. What rhetorical strategies does Arrillaga use to motivate her readers to action? Evaluate whether you think the strategies are successful.

2. Arrillaga begins her essay with a description about the way things used to be, using phrases such as "Those were the days" and "Amid the camaraderie." What is the effect of this description on readers? How might this description invoke a sense of nostalgia in readers?

3. To whom or what does the title of Arrillaga's essay refer? How does the title relate to the issues discussed in the essay?

Writing About Issues and Contexts

1. According to Arrillaga, elements such as television, the Internet, and "suburban sprawl" have caused many Americans to become inactive in their civic duties. What other causes of inaction do you see in your community? Among your peers?

2. What effect does the lack of civic involvement have on the American political system? How has the political environment changed over the years due to nonparticipation by citizens?

3. Arrillaga states that "check writing has replaced active political participation." Do you agree with the author that writing a check is not equivalent to being actively involved? Can check writing be beneficial to the individual or the organization? Explain your answers.

Born in Pittsburgh, Pennsylvania, **Michael Davitt Bell** *(1941–1997)
earned a bachelor's degree from Yale University and a Ph.D. from
Harvard, where he specialized in American literature. Beginning in 1981,
he served as J. Leland Miller Professor of American History, Literature,
and Eloquence at Williams College. Most of his scholarly work is in
nineteenth-century American fiction. His books include* Hawthorne and
the Historical Romance of New England *(1971),* The Development of
American Romance: The Sacrifice of Relation *(1980), and* The Problem
of American Realism: Studies in the Cultural History of a Literary Idea
*(1993). He died in 1997, shortly after the following essay was published
in* The Atlantic Monthly.

Michael Davitt Bell

Magic Time: Observations of a Cancer Casualty

For four years I've been battling (as they always say) cancer, and
now I've lost. I'm told I have the proverbial six months to live—which
I might, with luck and additional chemotherapy, be able to stretch to a
year. The sarcoma that appeared in my right thigh in the summer of
1992, that first metastasized in my lung in 1994 and cost me a kidney
a year later, has now spread all through my lungs. Beyond doubt I'm
dying. Nothing unusual here, of course—except that I find I not only
am reconciled to my fate but also have achieved a strange kind of happiness that's new in my experience.

In 1979 I had another cancer, a melanoma that was removed in a
simple outpatient procedure and did not recur. But by the end of my
first year of treatment for the sarcoma, with chemotherapy, radiation,
surgery to remove the original tumor, more chemotherapy, I had descended into a depression so severe that all sense of self was gone, all
desire, except for a persistent, repetitive series of affect-free fantasies
of specific and detailed ways I might kill myself.

I doubt that I can account fully for the level of happiness, even eu-
phoria, I've now reached, three years later and in the face of much
worse news. But some of it comes, I'm sure, from the fact that since the
cancer's appearance in my lung in the summer of 1994 revealed that
the original treatment hadn't eliminated the disease, and thus the sta-

tistical odds of my surviving were close to nil, I have determined to be open and honest with other people about my disease and my prognosis. I think this has also allowed me to be open and honest with myself.

My relationships with friends and family—above all with my two daughters, now in their twenties, whose mother and I divorced when they were small—have thus taken on an emotional openness and intensity almost inconceivable for someone who, like me, grew up in an upper-middle-class WASP family in the Midwest, a family in which the word "love" was never spoken or heard except, perhaps, to express admiration for an object or article of clothing ("I just *love* the way that sweater looks on you!"). So I find I'm not overcome with remorse or anger, or with terror of the fate awaiting me; instead I'm cherishing each moment, each mundane experience I have left. This is, for me, a magic time.

5   My own experience may be quite different from the experience of others in similar circumstances, or of those who love and care for them. But the general point here, a lesson I can share, is that for me over the past four years, after the traumas of treatment and of confronting my own death, the experience of dying of cancer may have been fundamentally about etiquette, about how one deals socially with people who don't have cancer and don't, for excellent reasons, really want to talk about it. Doctors, famously, need to keep professionally distant from their dying patients, and some even see such patients as a reproach, a token of failure. Friends and family don't want to seem intrusive or insensitive, and we are inevitably an unwelcome reminder of their own mortality. Nor are we who are about to die innocent of evasions and avoidance. I'd even guess that the popularity of cancer support groups stems from the chance not only to talk about common fears and experiences but also to be in a setting where this particular problem of etiquette, of figuring out how to talk to people who don't have cancer, who aren't dying, is for the moment suspended. Between the living and the dying a kind of wall seems to persist, a barrier of fear, shame, and perhaps most of all embarrassment.

I remember reading, back in the 1970s, a sociological study of paranoid behavior. Instead of analyzing the supposed paranoids for clinical symptoms, the researchers interviewed them *and* the people with whom they were routinely in contact: family, friends, fellow workers. What became evident was that when the supposed paranoids entered a room, these others actually did feel embarrassed and change the subject; they *had* been talking about the supposed paranoids behind their backs. So it is, perhaps, with the problem of etiquette for the dying.

Nevertheless, the wall can be breached; lines of communication can be kept open. As I say, I believe that my determination to keep breaching the wall accounts for my success in achieving acceptance and happiness in the face of my impending death. And this determination has extended even to strangers. People I've never met before—people I run into in stores, or at roadside rest stops where I'm walking my dog—ask what happened to the leg that was permanently stiffened by the removal of the original tumor. I don't put them off with "surgery" or "I hurt it." Briefly, I tell them what happened—describing the tumor, the surgery, sometimes even mentioning my current prognosis—and they're interested, concerned. Mindless pleasantry is transformed into actual conversation.

"Thanks for asking," I say to them, and I mean it.

"Hey," they reply. "Good luck!"

10   Worse things could happen.

To speak of manners in the context of cancer and dying may seem jarring, even insincere, but it shouldn't. For as the great novelists of manners, the Jane Austens and the Henry Jameses, all knew, the etiquette of communication and miscommunication, the comedy of understanding and misunderstanding, is not only deeply fascinating and entertaining but also profoundly significant. These novelists knew that once the misunderstandings have been cleared up, just before the ending, the possibility of love and of true communication has come to exist. And much more love, more interesting love, is possible than if no difficulties and misunderstandings had occurred in the first place. After all, you can't have the satisfying resolution of the ending if you don't start with conflict and crisis.

We who are about to die have relationships with our doctors, of course, and here, too, the etiquette of communication, what one might call bedside manners, raises interesting problems and complications.

My oncologist read an earlier version of this essay, and we discussed it over lunch. Although he liked it for the most part, he had one suggestion. "Don't you think," he said, "you should say more about your doctors?"

All right. With one exception my doctors have been wonderful. Again and again they've saved my life, or at least prolonged it, and I've been lucky to have prescribed for me the latest, least invasive procedures. Drastic as the treatment of my sarcoma seemed, it could have been much worse. Ten years ago the recommended procedure would have been to remove my leg at the hip.

15   Why, then, had I said so little about my doctors? What my oncologist may not have understood is how small a part doctors play in our *experience* of having cancer. We wait in hallways or antechambers for our appointments, often for a long time, and when at last we see our doctors, the consultations are understandably brief. In the hospital, where doctors govern everything we do, our direct experience of them is even more marginal: we're patients twenty-four hours a day, and our doctors' appearances on their rounds seem a matter of nanoseconds, something we might miss entirely if we were to blink. What's weirdest of all in this experience is the stark contrast between our doctors' pervasive power and their absence. Perhaps this is like the believer's experience of the deity.

Early in my treatment for sarcoma, in 1993, PBS broadcast Bill Moyers's series *Healing and the Mind*—programs about alternative, holistic methods for treating life-threatening diseases. Moyers avoided, I thought, one of the less agreeable implications of holistic approaches to illness: if you can help yourself get better by developing a more positive attitude, then it's your fault if you're not getting better, or are in fact dying.

Healing and the Mind did touch on another standard implication of the mind-body approach. At the heart of this approach is a familiar indictment of American medicine: that our doctors are educated to treat diseases rather than people, taught to deal with us impersonally, as carriers of symptoms, rather than holistically, as suffering individuals. This complaint is in some measure justified, to be sure. But as early as during my first hospital stay for chemotherapy I realized that this may be exactly what we want our doctors to do. We have far more at stake than they do in keeping everything but the clinical, technical details at bay. In such circumstances we may *want* to think of ourselves as sets of symptoms, as meat that's being fixed, rather than as people whose very souls are being sucked into our sickness. And then, while our doctors are doing their best to cure us, we blame them for our own denial.

Speaking of doctors, I finally decided recently that I should read the best seller by Sherwin B. Nuland, M.D., *How We Die*. Am I wrong, or has American taste in best sellers been getting weirder? *How We Die*: the ultimate self-help book—the last one you'll ever need! I've long fantasized that one might make the charts with a book called *Health Tips for the Dead*—or, even better, *More Health Tips for the Dead*.

I'm imagining myself here as a standup comic, or maybe a standup-while-I-can-still-stand (or while-you-can-still-stand-me) comic. I can't see if you're really out there—it's so dark, and I've got these stage lights in my eyes, and my jokes are getting no response, not a sound, not even the clink of ice in a glass, an idle cough or two.

20   "Hey!" I want to shout into the darkness, the silence. "Hey! Help me out! I'm *dying* up here!"

I know I'm being flippant. What's more important, I know why. We who are about to die (or at least this has been true in my case) sometimes focus on our relations with others in order to deny the most difficult and terrifying aspect of what I might call terminal etiquette: keeping open our lines of love and communication with ourselves. This is what I lost utterly during my terrible first year of treatment; I lost touch with who I was, with all sense of desire or purpose, and thus lost, as well, all sense of my connection to others, even my daughters.

From November through early February of that year I lived alone in an apartment in Boston, where I had had to move for treatment. I underwent two rounds of chemotherapy, in November and December, and then six weeks of radiation, beginning immediately after Christmas. I remember that late in January my younger daughter, who was then still in college, came up to stay for a week on her break between semesters. One night, as we played gin rummy before going to bed, I tried desperately to hide from her the shaking in my hand that left me barely able to hold my cards. I was that scared of the empty and meaningless hours looming in my future, of the sleepless night awaiting me, of the fact that I had no idea whatever of how I would spend the coming day. And this happened every night, with or without visitors. During the days I was numb, seeing everything as if from a great distance. I had lost the ability to cry. Although I had bought a portable stereo to console me in my exile, I had pretty much stopped listening to music. I tried, but I simply couldn't remember my life before the beginning of all this horror, what it had been like to be the person I had been. And I couldn't imagine ever returning to that life once my treatment was completed; I would never again be that person, or any person; nor would I be able to rediscover the emotional basis of my love for my friends or my daughters.

Once my definitive death sentence was upon me, I determined that this would not happen to me again, that I would not lose my ability to love and communicate with myself, and with it my ability to love others. For within ourselves is the highest wall, with its grim towers and parapets. On the near side stands the self that still functions in the sunny world of the mundane, the self so little different from you, my reader. On the far side lurks and slouches the unbearable, almost gothic knowledge of what is soon to happen: the awful pain, the progressive loss of personal autonomy and control of bodily function, and then (what will, of course, happen in time to all of us) the absolute and irrevocable annihilation of our very selves. In this process I will lose myself for sure, at the end; but I must not do so in the way I did during that terrible first year of treatment.

The popular name of this wall is Denial, and even to think of breaching it, of peering over at the dark and tangled wilderness on the other side, teeming with creatures of unspeakable disproportion, seems almost more than anyone should have to bear. Nevertheless, and often to the horror of my friends, I chose to read Nuland's book, to read the chapters devoted to exactly how one dies of cancer. If I was to love myself, to accept myself sufficiently to maintain my open love for those most dear to me, I just had to know.

25   Nuland describes, in considerable detail, the physical processes of dying from the most common forms of disease and trauma. He wants to dispel, he writes, the "scenarios" we compose about death—notably "the longed-for ideal of 'death with dignity.'" A story he tells at the outset identifies both his main purpose and his principal target audience—people whose loved ones are dying. The story is about a woman he had almost certainly cured of breast cancer, whose mother had then died of the same disease. The daughter had been horrified by the process. "Dr. Nuland," she had protested in despair, "there was no dignity in my mother's death!" Nuland reports that he offered her comfort by telling her, from his own expert perspective, that this was not unusual, that he had not often seen much dignity in the process by which we die.

Nuland's purpose seems clear enough. People about to go through the death of a loved one will be cured of their despair, much as all those mothers who turned to Dr. Spock in the 1950s were cured of their potential guilt: by being assured that what terrifies them is perfectly "normal." (Nuland's other great fifties touch—recalling to me my admiration as a teenager for James Dean in *Rebel Without a Cause*—is his extended description of cancer cells as "the juvenile delinquents of cellular society," as a "mob of maladjusted adolescents raging against the society from which it sprang." Could I start *identifying* with this disease?)

Fine, I thought, as I read Nuland's story of the woman horrified by her mother's hideous death; she's reassured. But what's in this story for his other potential audience: people who are themselves about to die, like me? Are we supposed to feel better about the agony we anticipate—the loss of independence and bodily function, the on-set of disintegration and pain? Are we supposed to feel better about all of this because it's *normal?*

And why all the detail? "When we are familiar with the patterns of the illness that afflicts us," Nuland answers, "we disarm our imag-inings." So I read about the details of cancer, and how it finally kills you, as I sat on the deck of my country house on a radiant afternoon in early summer, with my yellow Labrador retriever lying at my side.

"Unrestrained and patternless growth," I read,

> enables a cancer to force its way into nearby vital structures to engulf them, prevent their functioning, and choke off their vitality. By this means, and by destroying the organs from whose stem cells they are made, the masses of cancer cells kill the gradually sickening person after feasting on the nutrients that were to have sustained him.

30   My dog shifted herself out of the sunlight and back into the slowly moving shadow cast by the deck umbrella, and I read about how tumors expand so rapidly that they exhaust the available blood supply. "The result," Nuland explains,

> is that a portion of an enlarging tumor may die, literally of malnutri-tion and oxygen lack. It is for this reason that cancers tend to ulcer-ate and bleed, sometimes producing thick, slimy deposits of necrotic tissue (from the Greek *nekrosis,* meaning "becoming dead") within their centers or at the periphery. . . . This is precisely why the an-cients referred to *karkinoma* as the "stinking death."

A hummingbird hovered above the bright-red feeder I had filled with sugar solution, and then darted for the woods across my lawn. The air was almost completely still. "Pneumonia and abscesses," I read,

> along with urinary and other infections, are frequently the immediate causes of death of cancer patients, and sepsis is their common termi-nal event. The profound weakness of severe cachexia [nutritional de-pletion] does not permit effective coughing and respiration, increas-ing the chances of pneumonia and inhalation of vomitus. The final hours are sometimes accompanied by those deep, gurgling respira-tions that are one of the forms of the death rattle.

Whew! I guess my response should have been *What a relief!* As if my undisarmed imaginings could ever have come up with anything *this* bad. "Stinking death" indeed! I thought of Lauren Bacall's account, in the autobiography she published years ago, of what Bogart smelled like as he neared death, with so much of the tissue in his body already dead and rotting. I thought of the young widow who told me, shortly after the melanoma had been removed from my back, that by the time her husband had finally died from the spread of *his* melanoma, he'd lost half his body weight—and something like 80 percent of what remained had been cancer or necrotic tissue.

But Nuland is right, of course: it's essential to know just what to expect—or at least this has turned out to be true for me. And he's right, too, about the most urgent reason for this. "Real control," he observes, "requires one's own knowledge about the ways of sickness and death."

I'm not convinced that we can reach such knowledge without direct experience, but for me, at all events, it has seemed crucial to stay in touch with some concrete, if imaginary, pre-vision of my near and inevitable future. And for me the key word is "control." I want the story of my dying, however painful and disgusting it may be, to be *my* story, *my* "scenario," at least as much as possible. After all, it's the only story I have left.

Analyzing Rhetorical Choices

1. How does Bell stimulate the reader's interest in the opening two paragraphs?

2. Critique Bell's account of his response to Sherwin Nuland's book. He states that he is being flippant, but is that flippancy effective here? Why or why not?

3. At one point, Bell writes, "We who are about to die have relationships with our doctors." Why do you think he chooses this phrasing and places it so prominently in the essay? To what historical image or scene is he rhetorically linking himself?

4. When Bell writes, "My dog shifted herself out of the sunlight and back into the slowly moving shadow cast by the deck umbrella, and I read about how tumors expand so rapidly that they exhaust the available blood supply," is he simply stating facts or foreshadowing his own fate? Explain your viewpoint.

Writing About Issues and Contexts

1. What has allowed Bell to be open and honest with himself about cancer and human mortality?

2. What is Bell saying here about the kind of etiquette that surrounds someone who is dying of cancer? Why is this particular form of etiquette difficult for him? How is this problem reinforced by his anecdote about the sociological study of paranoid behavior?

3. What has Bell's losing struggle with cancer taught him? What lesson(s) does he want to teach us?

4. How do you read Bell's final paragraph? What does he mean by stating that he wants "the story of my dying, however painful and disgusting it may be, to be *my* story, *my* 'scenario' "?

David Ropeik (1951–) is an instructor of risk peception and risk communication at the Harvard School of Public Health, where he studies how humans interpret and react to risks. Ropeik believes that humans make decisions about risks from an emotional standpoint rather than one based on factual evidence. Ropeik is a commentator on risk issues for the program "Morning Edition" on National Public Radio, and he frequently lectures to various government, corporate, and consumer groups worldwide. Ropeik was a 1994–1995 Knight Science Journalism Fellow at MIT, as well as a 1999 National Tropical Botanical Garden Fellow. A two-time recipient of the DuPont-Columbia Award, which is considered the "Pulitzer Prize" of television journalism, Ropeik is the coauthor of Risk: A Practical Guide for Deciding What's Really Safe and What's Really Dangerous in the World around You *(2002). "What Really Scares Us" appeared in* Parade *magazine in March 2003.*

David Ropeik

What Really Scares Us

The list of things to be afraid of seems to grow daily: Terrorism. Snipers. Child abductions. West Nile virus. According to a number of public-opinion surveys, many people thnik it's more dangerous to be living now than it ever has been.

But those fears fly in the face of evidence that, in many ways, things are better than they've ever been. The average American life expectancy in 1900 was about 47 years. Now it's nearing 80. Diseases that plagued us—polio, smallpox, tuberculosis—have been all but eradicated in the U.S. In 1960, out of every 1000 babies born, 26 did not survive their first year. That number is now down to seven.

So why this disconnect between the facts and our fears? Well, it turns out that when it comes to the perception of risks, facts are only part of how we decide what to be afraid of and how afraid to be. Another huge factor—sometimes the most important factor—is our emotions.

Why do humans perceive risks this way if our highly advanced brain gives us the power to reason? It's because our brains are biologically built to fear first and think second. Which, in the end, is a pretty good strategy for survival.

5   Say you're walking through the woods and see a line on the ground, and you're not sure if it's a snake or a stick. The visual information goes to two parts of the brain. One is called the prefrontal

cortex, behind your forehead. That's the area where we do a lot of our reasoning and thinking. The other area is called the amygdala, which is the brain's key emotion center.

Because of the way the brain is constructed, the information gets to the amygdala before it gets to the prefrontal cortex. So, before the reasoning part of the brain has had a chance to consider the facts, the fear center is saying, "Jump back, you dummy! It *could* be a snake!"

But how does the brain turn raw sensory information into fear? Apparently our brains have built-in patterns for interpreting sensory information that help us subconsciously filter incoming messages, making us more afraid of some things than others. Psychologists have identified many of the specific emotional characteristics of risks that are likely to make us more, or less, afraid.

Emotional Factors That Determine Our Fears

Control. Imagine that you're driving down the highway, feeling pretty safe because you're behind the wheel. Now switch seats with your passenger. You're probably a little more nervous, maybe even turning into a full-fledged backseat driver. Not because the risk has gone up—the annual odds of being killed in a motor vehicle crash are 1 in 6700—but because you no longer are in control.

Trust. We trust certain sources more than others. We're less afraid when a trusted doctor or scientist, such as the head of the Centers for Disease Control and Prevention explains anthrax than when a politician explains it.

Newness. When a risk first shows up, we treat it more like a snake until we've lived with it for a while and our experience lets us put the risk in perspective. We are more afraid of West Nile virus when it first shows up in our area than after it has been around for a few years. (Odds of dying from West Nile virus: 1 in 1,000,000.)

Choice. We're more afraid of risks that are imposed on us than risks we take by choice. Imagine that you're driving along, talking on your cell phone. In the next lane, some other guy is driving and using *his* cell phone. Though both of you are in danger, the risk from the motorist next to you feels greater, because it's being imposed on you.

Dread. Things that can kill us in really awful ways seem riskier. We're more afraid of being eaten alive by a shark (odds, 1 in

281,000,000) or dying in a plane crash (1 in 9,000,000) than of dying from heart disease (1 in 300).

Me or Them. If the risk is to you, it's worse than if that same risk only threatens somebody else. We're *all* worried about terrorism, now that we know it can happen here too, to us. A one in a million risk is too high if we think *we* could be that "one."

Is it hard to understand? The more complicated a risk is, the less we can understand it—and the more we treat it like a snake, just to be safe. For example, we're concerned about ionizing (nuclear) radiation, but we're not worried about infrared radiation, which we know simply as heat.

Natural or manmade? If it's natural, we're less afraid than if it's man-made. We're more frightened of nuclear power accidents (odds, 1 in 200,000) than of solar radiation. Yet sun exposure causes an estimated 1.3 million new cases of skin cancer in America per year, 7800 of which are fatal.

Several of these factors are often at work on the same risk at the same time, some making us more afraid and some less. The effect of these factors changes over time. Also, individual fears vary based on individual circumstances. For instance, women fear breast cancer more than men, while men fear prostate cancer more than women.

10   While it's understandable that we perceive risks this way, it also can be dangerous. Some people, afraid to fly because they lack control or because the risk of terrorism is new and feels high, choose instead to drive—a much bigger risk. It may make them *feel* safer, but overreacting this way raises their risks.

Underreacting can be dangerous too. People who aren't concerned about the risk of the sun—because it's natural and because of that nice glowing tan—raise their cancer risk by not taking the danger of sun exposure seriously enough to slap on sunscreen or wear a hat.

In the end, the best way to reduce the danger of any given risk is to arm yourself with some basic facts from a reliable, neutral source, so the rational side of your perceptions can hold its own in the contest against your natural emotions. The better you can do at keeping your perception of risks closer in line with what the risks actually are, the happier *and* safer you'll be.

Analyzing Rhetorical Choices

1. How does the use of statistical information contribute to the overall effectiveness of Ropeik's argument?

2. Ropeik states that factual reasoning is only one part of how we perceive risk, and that emotional characteristics override our capacity to reason when we are faced with danger. What advice does Ropeik offer to alleviate the effect of these emotional characteristics? Do you agree with his advice? Explain your answer.

3. Analyze the persuasive elements used by Ropeik, particularly at the end of the essay. How would you describe his tone, style, and word choice? In what way do these stylistic and rhetorical devices contribute to the success of the persuasive elements?

Writing About Issues and Contexts

1. Cite at least three cause-and-effect relationships described by Ropeik. How does he use these cause-and-effect relationships to help alleviate his readers' perception of risk?

2. According to Ropeik, we are less afraid of something if it is natural as opposed to manmade: "We're more frightened of nuclear power accidents (odds, 1 in 200,000) than of solar radiation." Why do you think that people are more afraid of manmade accidents than of natural dangers? In addition to sun overexposure, what other examples can you give of natural dangers that people tend to downplay or overlook?

3. What connections does Ropeik make between our sense of control over situations and our fear of danger? How might taking too much control over a situation, in the form of overreaction, cause more danger?

Strategies for Writers: Cause and Effect

1. The mode of cause and effect, more than most ways of organizing your essays, is closely tied to logic. Think of several mishaps that have occurred to you or that you've seen on television. With your classmates, discuss the causes and the ultimate effects of these mini-disasters. Then think of other effects and trace their causes, particularly in relation to people featured in the media. Some possibilities: Jackie Mason, Michael Jackson, Tonya Harding, Gary Hart, Ingrid Bergman. How did these figures become the object of public scorn? How, if at all, did they alter that public perception?

2. Cause-and-effect relationships also connect very directly to argument. Fallacious reasoning has its root in poorly conceived cause and effect. Rigorous thinking directly connects an effect with its real cause, not simply something that is associated with the effect. Many superstitions, for example, have their foundations in false cause-and-effect relations. Eric Hansen's discussion of superstition, for example, draws on this apparent relation between a consequence and its supposed cause. How does his account compare with Sharon Begley's in "The Stereotype Trap"? What other misuses of cause and effect have you noticed? Consider the self-fulfilling prophecy: An effect can actually be created, even if you or someone else has merely invented the cause. ("I am female; therefore, I am not good at math," or "She's Asian American; therefore she must be good at math.")

3. Debate with your classmates whether poor writing is a result of not knowing grammar or whether using a particular language variety is evidence of poor writing ability or lack of intelligence. Why are some varieties of language more acceptable than others? Consider engaging in library research on this controversial topic. How do we use or misuse cause and effect to reinforce our stereotypes of various people and groups in terms of their language use?

4. In "One by One," Pauline Arrillaga addresses how America has become "a nation of bystanders." How compelling is her argument regarding the immediate effects of citizens lacking the desire to become involved in civic duties? What possible, perhaps more serious effects could result from such inaction?

5. The cause-and-effect relationships in Louise Erdrich's story, "Sister Godzilla," are far more ambiguous than one would usually expect. What is the cause-and-effect relationship between the nun's grotesque appearance and the various effects this has on her students? One of the fascinating things about cause-and-effect relationships is the way in which we are often left to speculate, rather than having the relationship spelled out in formulaic fashion. What other essays in this section evoke this sense of ambiguity? Why? What might be another subject that allows you to engage in this type of rich analysis?

6. Both Atul Gawande and David Ropeik draw on highly scientific frameworks to explore their subjects. In what ways does their reliance upon empirical research influence the way they develop and present their subjects? How effective are these two presentations? What kinds of readers do they anticipate by writing the way they do?

Research and Writing Assignments

1. Atul Gawande uses his medical school background and understanding of the scientific method to analyze the causes of the common cold. He posits a hypothesis, examines the scientific experiment that is set up to test that hypothesis, and then reports the results. What is particularly striking, however, is that this scientific method fails to solve the two basic questions that concern Gawande—namely, what causes a cold and how best to prevent one. In an essay, examine the strengths and weaknesses of the scientific method, especially when it comes to health issues. During the past 30 or so years, the medical establishment has issued recommendations and advisories concerning eggs, butter, margarine, fen-phen, hormone supplements, preservatives, and herbal remedies, among others. Choose a specific subject, research what the scientific establishment has reported, and write an essay that weighs the strengths and weaknesses of their methods and conclusions. What can we learn from scientific analysis? What are the strengths and limits of this kind of inquiry?

2. "A Black Man Ponders His Ability to Alter Public Space," "The Stereotype Trap," and "Sister Godzilla" explore the consequences of stereotypes and superficial judgments based on physical characteristics, both those we apply to others and

those we (sometimes unconsciously) apply to ourselves. In an essay that draws on both personal history and library research, offer your views on the power, both negative and positive, of stereotyping and how we might best disrupt the harmful cause-and-effect relationship negative stereotyping creates. How do we distinguish between positive and negative stereotyping? (Is there such a thing as positive stereotyping?) Can we have one without the other? How do we overcome negative stereotypes? How can we get beyond superficial impressions rooted in misunderstanding? If stereotyping is impossible to eliminate, how do we control it within our personal and professional lives? There are enough questions and issues here to form the subject of a book, so focus your essay on a particular kind of stereotyping or a specific incident. You might want to reread related selections by Toni Cade Bambara, Countee Cullen, and Henry Louis Gates, Jr. (Chapter 5); Frederick Douglass (Chapter 7); and Cornel West (Chapter 8).

3. Eric Hansen's account of traveling in the Borneo countryside explores two competing ways of understanding cause and effect: a Western way that honors scientific logic and a more native way that honors a religious, mythic, and spiritual logic. We are often tempted to call the latter superstition. In an essay that draws on library research, explore the subject of superstition by examining one such practice among native people in America, Africa, Europe, or Asia. You might want to focus on forms of behavior that center on certain major rites of passage: birth, adolescence, marriage, or death. What forms of logic prevail? How does this particular practice make sense within this culture? What insights does it provide in terms of some of our own "superstitious" practices?

4. Both Malcom Gladwell (Chapter 6) and David Ropeik (this chapter) use cause-and-effect relationships to analyze how people tend to rely on a false sense of security when it comes to avoiding danger and taking risks. According to both authors, we subconsciously allow our emotions to dictate when to be fearful and to what extent. Drawing on this consideration, write an essay that further explores the extent to which our emotions have the ability to create situations of increased danger. How could the danger be avoided with rational reasoning as opposed to emotional factors? You should use scientific research to support your argument.

5. Michael Davitt Bell writes, "Beyond doubt I'm dying. Nothing unusual here, of course—except that I find I not only am reconciled to my fate but also have achieved a strange kind of happiness that's new in my experience." Using this statement as a departure point, write an essay addressed to the general public that considers how we can best make sense of the inevitability of death. Certainly, many religions are concerned with death (and a possible afterlife), but in your essay, be aware that many readers (including religious ones) do not share this view. How do you think all of us can make sense of death and integrate this thinking into our lives in useful and productive ways, as Bell apparently did?

6. A possible cause of civic inactivity among citizens is efficiency and lack of time. Consider two possible causes as outlined by Pauline Arrillaga in "One by One": People do not have time to do much more than write out a check to an organization, and the organizations have found "more expedient" forms of getting their messages to the media. In your essay, analyze the cause-and-effect relationship between citizens and civic organizations. What has caused the organizations to relocate farther away from their members and participants? What are some possible long-term effects of this distance? Do you agree that if more organizations asked people to actively participate, they would? Why or why not?

10
Argument

The Importance of Argument

It might be said that the world moves forward primarily through two modes: narration and argument, the modes that open and close this book. Narration can act as a powerful mode for change: Through the telling of stories, people often attempt to change each other's ideas, views, and values—think of the Bible and other religious and mythic accounts, novels and illustrative stories, films and television. From inspirational biographies of people like Gandhi or the seven astronauts who died aboard the shuttle *Columbia,* to the wringing confessions we hear in the popular media such as on "Oprah" and "Dr. Phil," to the imaginative tales we enjoy in *Harry Potter* and *The Lord of the Rings*—the narratives we hear change us, sometimes profoundly.

At least as important as narration, however, is argument, that other life-changing mode. Unlike narration, which appeals strongly to the imagination, argument appeals to the logical part of our minds, for it depends upon the presentation of proof, evidence, and clear reasoning in order to push us toward a specific conclusion, often while showing the inadequacies of another perspective. While narration depends on character, conflict, motion, and setting to move us forward, argument depends on logic, empirical evidence, abstract thinking, and formal analysis. Although argument can be expressed in a variety of modes, including narration, the arguments highlighted in this section are generally founded on rhetorical principles that are *presentational* and *expositional* in character. These are the kinds of arguments we hear when, for example, Colin Powell made a presentation to the United Nations General

Assembly arguing that Saddam Hussein possessed weapons of mass destruction, was concealing them, represented a threat to his neighbors and the world, and therefore must be removed from power, either by the UN, an international coalition, or by the United States acting largely alone. They are also the kinds of arguments we hear when lawyers present their cases to the Supreme Court about gun control, abortion rights, or capital punishment; when legislators advocate for specific forms of legislation centered on tax reform or universal health coverage; when salespeople in an appliance store try to persuade customers to buy the latest model of television or a snappy new personal digital assistant.

Argument is thus a vitally important mode, one with universal value in our culture. To argue well is to find ways to persuade others to change their minds and actions; thus argument and persuasion are closely bound up with each other. Persuasion is the means by which skilled writers and speakers make their arguments effective by choosing the best examples, excellent wording and phrasing, and the most artful and sophisticated ways to present their evidence. Rather than create artificial distinctions between *argument* and *persuasion,* we'll consider argument to include that famous dictum, "all the available means of persuasion." A good argument draws upon all those persuasive elements that have been discussed and illustrated throughout this book. Further, we will restrict this discussion to arguments that have an ethical basis, thus excluding propaganda, diatribes, and physical intimidation from our discussion. No doubt rants and threats alter behavior, but they have little to do with the careful, considered reasoning that is most prized in academic settings.

Even when the subject is focused in this way, it is perhaps not surprising that argument is often viewed negatively by many people. "Don't give me an argument about that," one friend might say to another. "She's got a lot of ideas but is way too argumentative," someone might say about an acquaintance. "Every time we get together, all he does is argue with me," another complains. Few of us look forward to getting into an argument, and most of us would rather not spend time with someone who is argumentative. That said, our intention in this chapter of *Rhetorical Choices* is to rehabilitate the term *argument*, especially in the context of academic writing. Writing a good argument essay is considered by many teachers and students to be the most challenging assignment of all because it is the most complex and abstract in terms of form and structure. In many academic disciplines, learning how to engage in constructive argument is the litmus test for accomplishment: It is the chief way one demonstrates mastery of a subject. Offering a hypothesis and developing forms of proof in a science class on genetic engineering or advocating for the universality of individual civil liberties in a political science class are both forms of advanced argumentation. English, philosophy, history, sociology, and many other disciplines require students to develop a specific perspective and develop the means to support it through careful research and analysis. This chapter introduction itself offers a series of brief arguments *about* argument, thus reinforcing how ubiquitous it is to our thinking and being in the world.

"It's the Economy, Stupid"

The best way to illustrate how argument works is to analyze it in operation. Printed below are two short opinion essays on the economy, specifically on tax cut legislation. Although focused on the Bush tax cut proposals put before Congress in 2003, they have a timeless quality: Economists, politicians, and everyday Americans are continually debating the role of the federal government, local/state/federal autonomy, how best to fuel the nation's economy, whether federal tax dollars should be increased or decreased, and whether tax dollars should be allocated to the poor in order to improve their lives and fund social programs, or to wealthier Americans in order to fuel investment and individual savings. Here are two perspectives that offer contrasting arguments on these timeless and complex concerns.

Tax Cuts Alone Cannot Shrink Government

Without reform, government spending threatens to eliminate the economic benefits of last year's tax cut.
by Wayne T. Brough, Ph.D.

The U.S. Treasury recently announced that the government is running a deficit of $66.5 billion for the first seven months of the fiscal year. Increased government spending coupled with a downturn in revenues has pushed the federal government back into deficit spending. Despite this dramatic swing in fiscal balances, the federal budget continues to flounder in Congress, with the Senate unwilling or unable to even establish parameters to limit federal spending. Indeed, the congressional urge to spend is threatening to eliminate the economic benefits of lower taxes.

With time running short, Senate Majority Leader Tom Daschle (D-SD) has yet to bring a budget resolution to the floor. The resolution is an important step in the budgetary process, because it provides over-all guidelines for spending. Without the resolution, there are fewer constraints on the appropriations process and more room for mischief when bills come to the floor. Some have suggested the House and Senate adopt "deeming resolutions" or extend the expiring budget caps to constrain appropriators, but with the Senate unwilling to adopt a budget resolution, it is not evident that the alternatives would fare any better.

While Republicans attribute the deficit's return to the war on terrorism and Democrats blame it on President Bush's tax cut, the simple fact remains that Congress lacks the fiscal discipline to live within its means. The growth of government is well chronicled. The recent $190 billion farm bill dropped all pretense of attempting a more market-based approach to agriculture. In addition, Congress is moving forward with a supplemental spending bill of almost $30 billion, along with a budget that includes $768 billion in discretionary spending.

Government spending not only means a greater burden for American taxpayers, it also has an impact on the economy's performance. A study by Professors Richard K. Vedder and Lowell E. Galloway demonstrates that throughout the 20th century, as the size of government grew, the economy suffered. Conversely, the greatest economic growth occurred as the role of government in the economy receded. The study also suggests that it is not surprising that surpluses have turned to deficits. Since World War II, increased federal spending has quickly dissipated any surpluses.

True to form, Congress continues to spend at a pace that diverts resources from productive uses in the private sector to redistributive uses by the government. Discretionary spending has increased significantly, much of it not related to defense. At the same time, Congress has repeatedly failed to address ailing entitlement programs that are a significant strain on the fiscal budget. This budget year, Social Security, Medicare, and Medicaid have been the largest drain on federal revenues and should warrant serious federal oversight. Each of these programs is staving off failure; outdated policies, changing demographics, and simple waste, fraud, and abuse are chronic problems. Without much-needed reform, these entitlement programs will continue to increase pressure on the federal budget.

President Bush ran on a platform of lower taxes, and Congress passed the legislation enacting those tax cuts. Voting for the tax cut meant more than a tax rebate for constituents; it was an important vote about the size and scope of government. The American people opted for a smaller government. Unfortunately, Congress has yet to deliver. It is important to remember that tax cuts alone cannot boost the economy—government spending must follow suit. If the government does not alter its behavior, resources will continue to flow from the private sector to government coffers.

When Congress continues spending in the wake of a tax cut, the bill eventually comes due, and the federal government will need to have the wherewithal to pay. The government has three options, none of which is conducive to economic growth. The first option is to print money. However, as the 1970s demonstrated, inflation can have a debilitating effect on economic growth. The second option is to borrow. The federal government can seek to raise money in the financial markets, which, again, has adverse effects on economic growth. While deficits may not directly translate into higher interest rates, many government programs have marginal, or even negative, rates of return, so excessive government spending will result in lower economic growth than if resources were left in the more productive private sector. Finally, a Congress determined to spend can simply abandon tax cuts, which many in Congress appear willing to do; opting instead to generate more revenues to satisfy profligate policies.

Sadly, Congress has done little to heed the call for a more limited government. The Senate used procedural rules to block a permanent reduction in taxes, leaving all of the Bush tax cuts to expire after ten years. The Death Tax, which is costly to administer and a poor source of revenue, is up for repeal, but the Senate leadership is playing games to minimize the chances of actually eliminating the tax. And Congress continues to spend in the face of burgeoning deficits. For many in Congress, it seems to be business as usual, which suggests that further reforms may be necessary to secure the benefits of tax cuts. Institutional reforms that make it more difficult to raise taxes or increase spending levels may be an important element of efforts to limit the size and scope of government. In the past, Congress has successfully avoided balanced budget amendments, supermajorities for tax increases and other restraints on congressional behavior. But in the face of renewed government expansion and rising deficits, it may be time to revisit ways to impose fiscal discipline on Congress.

Trickle Down Again
by Matthew Rothschild

George W. Bush's stimulus program is a stimulus for the country club set.

This year, according to the Citizens for Tax Justice, the top 1% of Americans—those making $374,000 or more—stand to gain $30,000 each, while the lowest 20% will get only a $6 tax cut. Go buy yourself a cheeseburger and a beer on George!

Looking at it another way, the top 5% will get 47% of the benefits, while the bottom 60% will get only 8% of the benefits.

What's more, eliminating the dividend tax is permanent, while other tax breaks in the plan are temporary.

Aside from being grossly skewed toward his golfing buddies, Bush's plan is not a smart way to jump-start the economy.

First of all, it is back-loaded. Robert Greenstein, executive director of the Center on Budget and Policy Priorities, notes, "It would cost $674 billion through 2013 but would put out only $102 billion in the first year, the period when the stimulus is needed."

And secondly, it is geared precisely to the population that is least likely to spend the money right away. The wealthy traditionally save more than the poor and the middle class, who have pressing needs that they are waiting to meet but can't afford.

A tax cut to the poor and middle class would be spent on vital things in a hurry, thus injecting money into the economy and spurring growth. But just fattening a wealthy person's bank balance would not do much for the economy.

There are obvious things that would help: exempting the first $10,000 or $20,000 of payroll taxes, or giving states more money to make up for the deficits they face, as the Democrats proposed. (Instead, Bush's abolition of the dividend tax will hurt states because they won't collect their own share of dividend taxes, and tax-free state bonds will no longer be as attractive to investors who would now invest in stocks giving tax-free dividends.)

Bush did propose a few things that might help, like upping the child care credit, extending unemployment benefits, and offering retraining grants to up to 1.2 million workers.

And Bush is right to be worried about the lagging economy, and to be willing to go deeper into deficit to try to dig us out. The Republicans make strange Keynesians, but that doesn't mean they're wrong here. The U.S. deficit as a percentage of GDP has been falling, so the United States is not about to go bankrupt. And the economy needs an injection of spending to ward off a recession and a crisis of overcapacity leading to deflation.

Deficits are not the serious problem they are made out to be. But Republicans have been playing games with this issue forever. When the budget used to be in a deficit, they moaned and groaned and said there was no room for any spending on urgent social programs. Now, when the budget is again in deficit, they say they can give away $674 billion in taxes and run up an Iraq war bill that may be anywhere from $50 billion to $200 billion. (There is always money for war, corporations, and the rich, it seems, and never for health care, housing, or the elimination of hunger and poverty.)

Democrats are right to call Republicans hypocrites here, but they shouldn't be advocating less spending. They should be advocating spending that is fairer and more productive.

For Bush's part, I can't imagine why he would want to propose such a lopsided tax program.

I guess he just couldn't resist sending early Valentines presents to all his friends.

Each of these authors writes with passion, has a clear focus or central idea that he wants to develop, and possesses knowledge about his subject. Brough and Rothschild are not writing in opposition to each other, although if put on a panel they might well disagree about how best to allocate taxes and to define the role of the federal government. Let's examine each essay more closely and then ask a series of questions that would help us determine the strengths and weaknesses offered by each of these arguments.

Brief Summary, Wayne T. Brough, "Tax Cuts Alone Cannot Shrink Government": Brough believes tax cuts are generally beneficial because, he contends, the smaller the size of the government, the stronger the economy. He states that "as the size of government grew, the economy suffered. Conversely, the greatest economic growth occurred as the role of government in the economy receded." He further states that the American people support this view (they supported Bush's tax cut proposal in 2000), and once we cut taxes, the only way to improve the economy is for Congress to curb spending.

Brief Summary, Matthew Rothschild, "Trickle Down Again": Rothschild believes that the Bush tax cut proposal for 2003 is unfair and unjust. He makes that point in his first sentence: "George W. Bush's stimulus program is a stimulus for the country club set." He does not address the issue of government spending or the size of the federal government. Rather, his focus is on the scope and nature of the tax cut, which in his view puts money into the wrong hands: "A tax cut to the poor and middle class would be spent on vital things in a hurry, thus injecting money into the economy and spurring growth. But just fattening a wealthy person's bank balance would not do much for the economy." To end the recession, spur the economy, and serve specific social interests, Rothschild wants the tax cuts to go to the poor and to improve health care, housing, and hunger relief for low- and middle-income families.

Analyzing Arguments

How effective are Wayne Brough and Matthew Rothschild in making their respective arguments? We'll examine various strategies of each, although the following discussion is not intended to be exhaustive. We invite you to engage in a further discussion about the various rhetorical strategies that they employ—and how effective they are in persuading you of their different positions.

State Thesis Early

Brough puts his thesis into the title and subtitle of his essay. The argument is explicit: Government must reform itself by shrinking (its size and its spending) in order to solidify the benefits of the 2001 tax cuts (and any future tax cuts enabled by federal legislation). Rothschild implies his argument in his title (tax cuts that go primarily to the rich are known as "trickle down" proposals because the financial benefits slowly trickle down to the middle and working class). His first sentence states his thesis and the rest of the essay expands on that idea.

Establish Your Authority

Rothschild is a regular columnist for *The Progressive*, the periodical that published this review. His credentials are well known to his readers, who follow his columns regularly in that magazine. Like any author who writes a column for a newspaper or magazine, he establishes trust in his readers by speaking with authority and knowledge over time. Brough writes for an organization known as the Citizens for a Sound Economy, who sponsor his column. He also puts the abbreviation "Ph.D." after his name, to signal his academic credential.

Cite Facts and Statistics

Brough's essay, which was written for the Internet, embeds a URL link (underscored) to support his assertion about the $66.5 trillion deficit. He discusses specific details of the budget and the Congress: the $190 billion farm bill, Congress's supplemental spending bill, overall congressional spending, Daschle's and Bush's actions. Rothschild's essay, which was written for a specific printed magazine, cites specific statistics (and the sources for those statistics) along with specific budget details.

Cite Knowledgeable/Trustworthy Authorities

Rothschild cites reputable sounding people and organizations: Citizens for Tax Justice and Robert Greenstein, the director of the Center on Budget and Policy Priorities. Brough cites the study by Professors Vedder and Galloway (note that they also presumably have doctorates, as he does) and includes a URL link to that study.

Create a Persuasive Rhetorical Persona

Brough creates a formal persona: He is "Wayne T. Brough, Ph.D." and his choice of language has few individualistic elements in terms of word choice, phrasing, tone, or style. His paragraphs tend to be about 80–170 words long, suggesting that he concentrates on his subject in some depth. Rothschild, on the other hand, uses highly individualistic words and phrases, his tone is colloquial, and his personal views about his subject get expressed immediately. His paragraphs are very short, often just one sentence, suggesting that he sees no need to develop his subjects in great detail, perhaps because he thinks his audience already agrees with him.

End with a Strong Statement That Reflects the Major Argument

Rothschild closes with a cheeky one-sentence paragraph that returns us to his opening statement about a stimulus program for the "country club set." Brough's final sentence reminds us of his thesis, namely that it may now be necessary to "impose fiscal discipline on Congress." Both essays close with statements that evoke their opening statements and major arguments.

We could focus on many more strategies for writing successful argument essays, but we hope the preceding discussion provides you a starting point. By including two very different perspectives written in very different styles to quite different audiences, we hope to indicate that argument is a supple mode that is open to a variety of approaches. More than almost any other mode, however, an argument essay must be written with a keen awareness of audience. After all, the entire thrust of an argument is to persuade, to change someone's values and views. Your argument will be particularly effective if you take into account the potential assumptions, perspectives, and objections of your audience. In their different ways, both Brough and Rothschild do this effectively. This does not mean that a writer distorts or subverts his or her point of view, but it does mean a writer must find ways to state that point of view so that it gets carefully considered by readers.

In this chapter we see how another accomplished writer expresses her awareness of audience in "It's a Jungle Out There." Camille Paglia begins with a specific thesis (or proposition), stating it dramatically and boldly:

Rape is an outrage that cannot be tolerated in civilized society. Yet feminism, which has waged a crusade for rape to be taken more seriously, has put young women in danger by hiding the truth about sex from them.

She then supports her thesis by discussing date rape, the nature of young men, and the politically interested nature of feminism, using a variety of sources to support her position. This is the same pattern we see in the Brough and Rothschild essays—and in many other argument essays.

Because the mode of argument depends substantially on forms of evidence and logic, it can be undermined by false thinking. Certain kinds of false thinking occur so often that they have been categorized into fallacies. We list some of the more prominent ones here so that you can guard against them.

- **The false binary:** assuming that a subject must be analyzed in terms of two opposing notions (black or white, yes or no). "If the Congress raises federal income taxes, the result will be either economic inflation or economic depression."
- **Argumentum ad hominem:** directing criticism toward the character or personality of the individual making the argument rather than the argument itself. Ad hominem fallacies are often intended to be insulting since they damage someone's character. "Wayne Brough argues for Congress to impose limits on its own spending because he is insensitive and possesses not a whit of sympathy for the working poor."
- **Non sequitur:** making a statement that does not follow logically from the statements (premises) that precede it. Non sequitur (which means "does not follow" in Latin) is a form of disjointed logic. "If we raise taxes, we could resolve some of the racial tensions in this country."
- **Begging the question:** assuming that the statement to be proven is already true or factual. Begging the question sidesteps logical analysis because, incorrectly, the speaker/writer makes an assumption that what is being proven is already true. "The nation's economy matters to all politicians—and to all Americans—because it is so important."
- **False analogy:** making a false claim that one idea or object is like another. Analogies can be powerful, but false analogies distort the claim an author is making. "The economy is like a balloon: if it over-inflates, it will pop!"

- **Hasty generalization:** offering a sweeping conclusion or making a major assertion without first assessing all the evidence. "No Congressperson has ever voted to cut subsidies to voters in his or her own district."
- **Post hoc, ergo propter hoc:** assuming a false cause/effect relationship just because one event follows another. The phrase comes from Latin and means "after this, therefore on account of this" and describes the logical fallacy that just because B follows A, B was caused by A. "The last time federal spending was reduced, American productivity decreased by 14 percent."
- **Weak, poor, or inadequate authority:** citing authorities who either have little factual knowledge or lack authority to support the thesis being developed. "My roommate said the Republican tax proposal would help college students" or "Lots of people agree that the Democratic tax plan would improve our prosperity."

It is difficult to guard against these fallacies, but one of your best protections is to remain aware of the kind of thinking that you are doing.

Most logical thinking falls into one of two broad categories: inductive or deductive. *Inductive thinking* examines the particulars, looking for similarities that allow the writer to move from the specific to the general (without, of course, drawing hasty generalizations). *Deductive thinking* moves from the general to the specific, with an emphasis on how a general set of principles or a general idea will lead to a specific result. Matthew Chapman offers an excellent example of inductive thinking in this chapter, since he forms his essay on specific facts, assertions, and observations. Camille Paglia mostly uses deductive thinking in her essay, since she makes assertions and then elaborates on them and offers specific examples.

Whether you use inductive or deductive reasoning, it is important to remain aware that the mode of argument demands that you analyze your assumptions, formulate your thesis carefully, find persuasive forms of proof, take stock of your audience, and create a persuasive rhetoric that fuses style with form with clear thinking. No wonder so many students and teachers find argument to be the most challenging mode of all.

*A prolific writer noted for his politically conservative viewpoint, **William F. Buckley, Jr.** (1925–), is equally known for an acerbic wit tempered with charm. Buckley has written more than 20 works on politics and government, along with several novels and books on sailing. His first book,* God and Man at Yale, *was published in 1951, after Buckley graduated from that institution. The founding editor of the* National Review, *a politically conservative magazine, Buckley was awarded the Presidential Medal of Freedom in 1991. From 1966 to 1999, Buckley hosted "Firing Line," a weekly program televised throughout the United States. Buckley recently published his autobiography,* Miles Gone By: A Literary Autobiography *(2004).*

William F. Buckley, Jr.

The Conflict over the Unusual Word

I am perhaps too stubbornly defiant of the strictures of such estimable critics as James Jackson Kilpatrick, who wars against the use by journalists of words not recognized immediately by everybody.

The editor [of *Sky* magazine], Duncan Christy, having bombarded his readers for eleven months with words judged "unusual" taken from my opera,* has decided to end his regular blurts in his magazine and has invited me to write in general about words ("I hope such an essay would be an encomium to words, alloyed with some direct observations about why we should not let words like 'encomium' and 'belletristic' and 'valedictory' go.")

---

*DEAR SIR: What does he mean, "opera"? As in *Madame Butterfly?* CURIOUS

DEAR CURIOUS: He means "works." The word is the plural of *opus*—"a creative work." Best, ED.

DEAR SIR: Well, why didn't he *say* "taken from my works"? CURIOUS AND ANNOYED

DEAR C&A: He was asked to write an essay about *words,* so you shouldn't be surprised if he starts out by using an unusual word. Let's hear him out, okay? ED.

Well sure, so let me get a few things off my chest, since the question of me and words has come up before.

1. Two people of the same approximate age and similar education won't have identical vocabularies. John will know the meaning of maybe one hundred words that Jane doesn't know. But Jane will know an equivalent number of words that puzzle John, when and if he runs into them.

2. The reader's attitude toward an unusual word often depends on the context in which it is used. Two stories hang on this point. Years ago a classmate took me delicately to one side and said, Bill, *National Review* would have a much larger circulation if you would just forbid the use of so many arcane words. I told him it was his imagination that so many such words congested my magazine, and I made him a bet. Sight unseen—I said—here's ten dollars that says the next issue of *Time* magazine will have more words you judge unfamiliar than you can target in any back issue, you take your pick, of *National Review*.

Well, you can guess I would not be telling you this story if I had lost the bet. Question: Why was my friend under an illusion that cost him ten bucks?

5   Explanation. If a sentence or paragraph of prose is analytical in nature, an unusual word springs out at you. But when the identical word appears in a passage in which the writer is describing something, or telling a story, the eye leaps over a word otherwise arresting. Since *National Review* is a journal of opinion, most of its articles and features are, as one would expect, analytical and critical. An unusual word, in a verbally demanding environment, comes at you more aggressively.

An example.

"*She was a ravishing beauty, from the sunlit hair to the limpid eyes to the full lips, sparkling teeth, and curious, tectonic smile.*" What kind of a smile? The reader doesn't know, exactly, and isn't going to ask, not unless whatever the writer goes on to say about the beautiful lady can't be understood without knowing exactly what it is that makes up a "tectonic" smile, whatever the hell that is.

"*In that plane the practiced eye can discern the tectonic disruptions of an early geological age.*" The word "tectonic" ("Relating to, causing, or resulting from structural deformation of the earth's crust") reaches out at you, and you see in its eyes the candid stricture: Buddy, unless you know what a tectonic disruption is, you can't swing with me on this one. Go read something else, or—if you want to—stick with me and see if you can follow what comes next.

The context often establishes whether the unusual word can coast by without interrupting the reader's thought.

10   3. The law of the advantage of flexing your muscles. The following episode is my all-time favorite, though I have never set it down before.

Thirty-five years ago my hosts took me, prelecture, to dinner at the large hotel in Garden City, New York. Our waiter, a man of about fifty, was visibly excited by my presence. At the end of the meal he drew me to one side to disclose the reason. He belonged, it turned out, to a militant labor union to which he was required to pay dues. Every month the union newsletter featured proudly the union's most recent political activities on behalf of its membership. They are *terribly* Democratic," he complained, "and I am a *Goldwater Republican.* So when I saw you come in I really cheered."

I thanked him, and then he leaned over and whispered into my ear. "Let me tell you something, Mr. Buckley. I subscribed to *National Review* just a month ago. Now if you would do something about all those long words, you will"—he stretched out his arms expansively— "double . . . no, *triple* your circulation."

My friend Swifty Lazar was a very famous and, all bald-pated five feet of him, instantly recognizable mogul movie agent. He could not patronize a fancy restaurant without running the risk that somebody, usually a young pretty woman—maybe a patron, maybe a waitress— would corner him and beg for an audition. "Can I call you at your office?" she would typically ask.

"*Always say yes,*" counseled the worldly Irving Lazar, "to that or *any other* request. . . . There isn't any civil alternative. You're not going to be able to explain to the applicant, in the middle of a restaurant, why, in the world we live in, and the way the world works, you can't just agree to give auditions, etc. etc. etc., every time somebody asks for one. So, just say yes, and let her nudge up against reality when she actually calls the office for an appointment."

15   "*Do you agree with me, Mr. Buckley?*" the waiter persists.

"Yes, sure," I reply. "We'll certainly try to do something about those words."

Flash forward, one year. Same dining room, same waiter (different speech). He beams when I come in. Both his hands close on my right hand. "You took my advice. It's made the magazine! Everybody can read it now!"

I was carried away by the underlying meaning of it all and smiled back exultantly. I thanked him. "It was *very* good advice you gave me."

The moral here is really liberating. The unused muscle begins to work out. In January it hurts awfully, looking at all those unfamiliar words—like the first day of skiing, or tennis. In February, the incidence of such unknown and offensive words is a little less, and you feel the relief.

20   In March it still happens to you, but only now and again. By June?—yes! You feel no pain at all. It isn't necessarily that your vocabulary has increased at a geometric rate. It is that the words you used to think of as alien and intimidating are less and less that, as they continue to crop up, and your mind and imagination are gradually including them in your immediate visibility range. If you are assigned the job of sportswriter (my sister Priscilla was, age twenty-two, by United Press), you gradually become comfortable with any number of words you simply could not have defined before. Exactly the same thing happens, or has happened, to the reader of the sports section. Or of the financial section. After a while you feel quite at home.

4. It's fair to distinguish between different categories of unusual words. I like the late Dwight Macdonald's nomenclature. Some words, he wrote in a celebrated review of Webster's Third, belong in the "zoo section" of the dictionary. I.e., the words do exist, but the need for them is so remote, you can—and should—keep them caged up in the zoo until it is absolutely necessary to take one out, which may be never. I know a word that describes the feeling you have in the roof of your mouth when peanut butter sticks to it, but I will never use it; in fact, I decline to disclose it.

On the other hand, it is important to remember that every word berthed in the dictionary is there because at some point one of three things happened. Either an objective thing or a concept or abstraction came on the scene which hadn't been descried before and now just had to be given a name ("cyberspace"); or an artistic hand closed in on what had been a void and the new word survives the infidelity of the season, earning its way into the dictionary ("seakindly"); or an authoritative writer simply uses the word and such is his prestige that his mere enunciation of it validates its legitimacy ("tushery").

Leading to my conclusion, 5., which is that while one can be very firm in resisting people who spout zoo words, one should be respectful and patient with those who exercise lovingly the wonderful opportunities of the language. I went downtown some years ago to hear a black pianist about whom the word had trickled in that here was something really cool and ear-catching, besides which his name rolled about the tongue releasing intrigue and wry amusement, and so I heard Thelonious Monk. He struck some really sure-enough *bizarre* chords, but you know, it would never have occurred to me to walk over and say, Thelonious, I am not familiar with that chord you just played. So cut it out please.

Analyzing Rhetorical Choices

1. How would you describe Buckley's tone in this essay? Is he humorous, annoyed, calm, thoughtfully reflective? In a short paragraph, describe the tone and cite a few specific phrases to support your view.

2. Look closely at Buckley's use of language—for instance, when he writes, "The moral here is really liberating. The unused muscle begins to work out." What do his choices say about his assumptions regarding audience? What kind of persona does he create with his word choices?

3. How does Buckley end this essay? Why do you think he tells us about the Thelonius Monk episode?

Writing About Issues and Contexts

1. How would you describe Buckley's method of arguing? Does he appeal to emotion? To reason? How does he incorporate humor? What means does he use to try to persuade us of his central argument about changing our attitude toward uncommon or unusual vocabulary?

2. Buckley relates the story of a waiter who approached him years ago and suggested that he reconsider using "long words" in his publication; a year later, that same waiter thanked Buckley for taking his advice, although Buckley did not implement the changes requested by the waiter. Buckley recounts that he was "carried away by the underlying meaning of it all." How does this episode support Buckley's argument? What larger point is he making with this statement?

3. Comment on Buckley's statement that "while one can be very firm in resisting people who spout zoo words, one should be respectful and patient with those who exercise lovingly the wonderful opportunities of language." Do you agree with Buckley's perception of language use? Why or why not?

A writer of both fiction and nonfiction, **Joy Williams** (1944–) is a graduate of the University of Iowa Writers' Workshop. She has written four novels, including State of Grace, which was nominated for the National Book Award, The Changeling, Breaking and Entering, and The Quick and the Dead, which was nominated for a Pulitzer. She has also published numerous stories, essays, and articles. Williams has been described as a writer with fierce passions who has a deep interest in conservation issues. Both the passion and the love for wildlife are evinced in the following selection.

Joy Williams

The Killing Game

Death and suffering are a big part of hunting. A big part. Not that you'd ever know it by hearing hunters talk. They tend to downplay the killing part. To kill is to put to death, extinguish, nullify, cancel, destroy. But from the hunter's point of view, it's just a tiny part of the experience. *The kill is the least important part of the hunt,* they often say, or, *Killing involves only a split second of the innumerable hours we spend surrounded by and observing nature . . .* For the animal, of course, the killing part is of considerably more importance. José Ortega y Gasset, in *Meditations on Hunting,* wrote, *Death is a sign of reality in hunting. One does not hunt in order to kill; on the contrary, one kills in order to have hunted.* This is the sort of intellectual blather that the "thinking" hunter holds dear. The conservation editor of *Field & Stream,* George Reiger, recently paraphrased this sentiment by saying, *We kill to hunt, and not the other way around,* thereby making it truly fatuous. A hunter in West Virginia, one Mr. Bill Neal, blazed through this philosophical fog by explaining why he blows the toes off treed raccoons so that they will fall down and be torn apart by his dogs. *That's the best part of it. It's not any fun just shooting them.*

Instead of monitoring animals—many animals in managed areas are tagged, tattooed, and wear radio transmitters—wildlife managers should start hanging telemetry gear around hunters' necks to study their attitudes and listen to their conversations. It would be grisly listening, but it would tune out for good the *suffering as sacrament* and *spiritual experience* blather that some hunting apologists employ. *The unease with which the good hunter inflicts death is an unease not merely with his conscience but with affirming his animality in the midst of his struggles toward humanity and clarity,* Holmes Rolston III drones on in his book *Environmental Ethics.*

There is a formula to this in literature—someone the protagonist loves has just died, so he goes out and kills an animal. This makes him feel better. But it's kind of a sad feeling-better. He gets to relate to Death and Nature in this way. Somewhat. But not really. Death is still a mystery. Well, it's hard to explain. It's sort of a semireligious thing . . . Killing and affirming, affirming and killing, it's just the cross the "good" hunter must bear. The bad hunter just has to deal with postkill letdown.

Many are the hunter's specious arguments. Less semireligious but a long-standing favorite with them is the vegetarian approach: you eat meat, don't you? If you say no, they feel they've got you—you're just a vegetarian attempting to impose your weird views on others. If you say yes, they accuse you of being hypocritical, of allowing your genial A&P butcher to stand between you and reality. The fact is, the chief attraction of hunting is the pursuit and murder of animals—the meat-eating aspect of it is trivial. If the hunter chooses to be *ethical* about it, he might cook his kill, but the meat of most animals is discarded. Dead bear can even be dangerous! A bear's heavy hide must be skinned at once to prevent meat spoilage. With effort, a hunter can make okay chili, *something to keep in mind,* a sports rag says, *if you take two skinny spring bears.*

5   As for subsistence hunting, please . . . Granted that there might be one "good" hunter out there who conducts the kill as spiritual exercise and two others who are atavistic enough to want to supplement their Chicken McNuggets with venison, most hunters hunt for the hell of it.

For hunters, hunting is fun. Recreation is play. Hunting is recreation. Hunters kill for play, for entertainment. They kill for the thrill of it, to make an animal "theirs." (The Gandhian doctrine of nonpossession has never been a big hit with hunters.) The animal becomes the property of the hunter by its death. Alive, the beast belongs only to itself. This is unacceptable to the hunter. *He's yours . . . He's mine . . . I decided to . . . I decided not to . . . I debated shooting it, then I decided to let it live . . .* Hunters like beautiful creatures. A "beautiful" deer, elk, bear, cougar, bighorn sheep. A "beautiful" goose or mallard. Of course, they don't stay "beautiful" for long, particularly the birds. Many birds become rags in the air, shredded, blown to bits. *Keep shooting till they drop!* Hunters get a thrill out of seeing a plummeting bird, out of seeing it crumple and fall. *The big pheasant folded in classic fashion.* They get a kick out of "collecting" new species. *Why not add a unique harlequin duck to your collection?* Swan hunting is satisfying. *I let loose a three-inch Magnum. The large bird only flinched with my first shot and began to gain altitude. I frantically ejected the round, chambered another, and dropped the swan with my second shot. After retrieving the bird I was amazed by its size. The swan's six-foot wingspan, huge body, and long neck made it an impressive trophy.* Hunters like big animals, trophy animals. A "trophy" usually means that the hunter doesn't deign to eat it. Maybe he skins it or mounts it. Maybe he takes a picture. *We took pictures, we took pictures.* Maybe he just looks at it for a while. The disposition of the "experience" is up to the hunter. He's entitled to do whatever he wishes with the damn thing. It's dead.

Hunters like categories they can tailor to their needs. There are the "good" animals—deer, elk, bear, moose—which are allowed to exist for the hunter's pleasure. Then there are the "bad" animals, the vermin, varmints, and "nuisance" animals, the rabbits and raccoons and coyotes and beavers and badgers, which are disencouraged to exist. The hunter can have fun killing them, but the pleasure is diminished because the animals aren't "magnificent."

Then there are the predators. These can be killed any time, because, hunters argue, they're predators, for godssakes.

Many people in South Dakota want to exterminate the red fox because it preys upon some of the ducks and pheasant they want to hunt and kill each year. They found that after they killed the wolves and coyotes, they had more foxes than they wanted. The ring-necked pheasant is South Dakota's state bird. No matter that it was imported from Asia specifically to be "harvested" for sport, it's South Dakota's state bird and they're proud of it. A group called Pheasants Unlimited gave some tips on how to hunt foxes. *Place a small amount of larvicide* [a grain fumigant] *on a rag and chuck it down the hole . . . The first pup generally comes out in fifteen minutes . . . Use a .22 to dispatch him . . . Remove each pup shot from the hole. Following gassing, set traps for the old fox who will return later in the evening . . .* Poisoning, shooting, trapping—they make up a sort of sportsman's triathlon.

10   In the hunting magazines, hunters freely admit the pleasure of killing to one another. *Undeniable pleasure radiated from her smile. The excitement of shooting the bear had Barb talking a mile a minute.*

But in public, most hunters are becoming a little wary about raving on as to how much fun it is to kill things. Hunters have a tendency to call large animals by cute names—"bruins" and "muleys," "berry-fed blackies" and "handsome cusses" and "big guys," thereby implying a balanced jolly game of mutual satisfaction between the hunter and the hunted—*Bam, bam, bam, I get to shoot you and you get to be dead.* More often, though, when dealing with the nonhunting public, a drier, businesslike tone is employed. Animals become a "resource" that must be "utilized." Hunting becomes "a legitimate use of the resource." Animals become a product like wool or lumber or a crop like fruit or corn that must be "collected" or "taken" or "harvested." Hunters love to use the word *legitimate*. (Oddly, Tolstoy referred to hunting as "evil legitimized.") *A legitimate use, a legitimate form of recreation, a legitimate escape, a legitimate pursuit.* It's a word they trust will slam the door on discourse. Hunters are increasingly relying upon their spokesmen and supporters, state and federal game managers and wildlife officials, to employ the drone of a solemn bureaucratic language and toss around a lot of questionable statistics to assure the nonhunting public (93 percent!) that there's nothing to worry about. The pogrom is under control. The mass murder and manipulation of wild animals is just another business. Hunters are a tiny minority, and it's crucial to them that the millions of people who don't hunt not be awakened from their long sleep and become antihunting. Nonhunters are okay. Dweeby, probably, but okay. A hunter *can respect the rights* of a nonhunter. It's the "antis" he despises, those *misguided, emotional, not-in-possession-of-the-facts, uninformed zealots who don't understand nature . . . Those dime-store ecologists cloaked in ignorance and spurred by emotion . . . Those doggy-woggy types, who under the guise of being environmentalists and conservationists are working to deprive him of his precious right to kill.* (Sometimes it's just a *right;* sometimes it's a *God-given* right.) Antis can be scorned, but nonhunters must be pacified, and this is where the number crunching of wildlife biologists and the scripts of *professional resource managers* come in. Leave it to the professionals. They know what numbers are the good numbers. Utah determined that there were six hundred sandhill cranes in the state, so permits were issued to shoot one hundred of them. Don't want to have too many sandhill cranes. California wildlife officials reported "sufficient numbers" of mountain lions to "justify" renewed hunting, even though it doesn't take a rocket scientist to know the animal is extremely rare. (It's always a dark day for hunters when an animal is adjudged *rare*. How can its numbers be "controlled" through hunting if it scarcely exists?) A recent citizens' referendum prohibits the hunting of the mountain lion in perpetuity—not that the lions aren't killed anyway, in California and all over the West, hundreds of them annually by the government as part of the scandalous Animal Damage Control Program. Oh, to be the lucky hunter who gets to be an official government hunter and can legitimately kill animals his buddies aren't supposed to! Montana officials, led by K. L. Cool, that state's wildlife director, have definite ideas on the number of buffalo they feel can be tolerated. Zero is the number. Yellowstone National Park is the only place in America where bison exist, having been annihilated everywhere else. In the winter of 1988, nearly six hundred buffalo wandered out of the north boundary of the park and into Montana, where they were immediately shot at point-blank range by lottery-winning hunters. It was easy. And it was obvious from a video taken on one of the blow-away-the-bison days that the hunters had a heck of a good time. The buffalo, Cool says, threaten ranchers' livelihoods by doing damage to property—by which he means, I guess, that they eat the grass. Montana wants zero buffalo; it also wants zero wolves.

Large predators—including grizzlies, cougars, and wolves—are often the most "beautiful," the smartest and wildest animals of all. The gray wolf is both a supreme predator and an endangered species, and since the Supreme Court recently affirmed that ranchers have no constitutional right to kill endangered predators—apparently some God-given rights are not constitutional ones—this makes the wolf a more or less lucky dog. But not for long. A small population of gray wolves has recently established itself in northwestern Montana, primarily in Glacier National Park, and there is a plan, long a dream of conservationists, to "reintroduce" the wolf to Yellowstone. But to please ranchers and hunters, part of the plan would involve immediately removing the wolf from the endangered-species list. Beyond the park's boundaries, he could be hunted as a "game animal" or exterminated as a "pest." (Hunters kill to hunt, remember, except when they're hunting to kill.) The area of Yellowstone where the wolf would be restored is the same mountain and high-plateau country that is abandoned in winter by most animals, including the aforementioned luckless bison. Part of the plan, too, is compensation to ranchers if any of their far-ranging livestock is killed by a wolf. It's a real industry out there, apparently, killing and controlling and getting compensated for losing something under the Big Sky.

Wolves gotta eat—a fact that disturbs hunters. Jack Atcheson, an outfitter in Butte, said, *Some wolves are fine if there is control. But there never will be control. The wolf-control plan provided by the Fish and Wildlife Service speaks only of protecting domestic livestock. There is no plan to protect wildlife . . . There are no surplus deer or elk in Montana . . . Their numbers are carefully managed. With uncontrolled wolf populations, a lot of people will have to give up hunting just to feed wolves. Will you give up your elk permit for a wolf?*

It won't be long before hunters start demanding compensation for animals they aren't able to shoot.

Hunters believe that wild animals exist only to satisfy their wish to kill them. And it's so easy to kill them! The weaponry available is staggering, and the equipment and gear limitless. *The demand for big boomers has never been greater than right now,* Outdoor Life *crows, and the makers of rifles and cartridges are responding to the craze with a variety of light artillery that is virtually unprecedented in the history of sporting arms . . .* Hunters use grossly overpowered shotguns and rifles and compound bows. They rely on four-wheel-drive vehicles and three-wheel ATVs and airplanes . . . *He was interesting, the only moving, living creature on that limitless white expanse. I slipped a cartridge into the barrel of my rifle and threw the safety off . . .* They use snowmobiles to run down elk, and dogs to run down and tree cougars. It's easy to shoot an animal out of a tree. It's virtually impossible to miss a moose, a conspicuous and placid animal of steady habits . . . *I took a deep breath and pulled the trigger. The bull dropped. I looked at my watch: 8:22. The big guy was early. Mike started whooping and hollering and I joined him. I never realized how big a moose was until this one was on the ground. We took pictures . . .* Hunters shoot animals when they're resting . . . *Mike selected a deer, settled down to a steady rest, and fired. The buck was his when he squeezed the trigger. John decided to take the other buck, which had jumped up to its feet. The deer hadn't seen us and was confused by the shot echoing about in the valley. John took careful aim, fired, and took the buck. The hunt was over . . .* And they shoot them when they're eating . . . *The bruin ambled up the stream, checking gravel bars and backwaters for fish. Finally he plopped down on the bank to eat. Quickly, I tiptoed into range . . .* They use decoys and calls . . . *The six point gave me a cold-eyed glare from ninety steps away. I hit him with a 130-grain Sierra boattail handload. The bull went down hard. Our hunt was over . . .* They use sex lures . . . *The big buck raised its nose in the air, curled back its lips, and tested the scent of the doe's urine. I held my breath, fought back the shivers, and jerked off a shot. The 180-grain spire-point bullet caught the buck high on the back behind the shoulder and put it down. It didn't get up* . . . They use walkie-talkies, binoculars, scopes . . . *With my 308 Browning BLR, I steadied the 9X cross hairs on the front of the bear's massive shoulders and squeezed. The bear cartwheeled backward for fifty yards* . . . *The second Federal Premium 165-grain bullet found its mark. Another shot anchored the bear for good* . . . They bait deer with corn. They spread popcorn on golf courses for Canada geese and they douse meat baits with fry grease and honey for bears . . . *Make the baiting site redolent of inner-city doughnut shops.* They use blinds and tree stands and mobile stands. They go out in groups, in gangs, and employ "pushes" and "drives." So many methods are effective. So few rules apply. It's fun! . . . *We kept on repelling the swarms of birds as they came in looking for shelter from that big ocean wind, emptying our shell belts* . . . A species can, in the vernacular, be *pressured by hunting* (which means that killing them has decimated them), but that just increases the fun, the *challenge.* There is practically no criticism of conduct within the ranks . . . *It's mostly a matter of opinion and how hunters have been brought up to hunt* . . . Although a recent editorial in *Ducks Unlimited* magazine did venture to primly suggest that one should *not fall victim to greed-induced stress through piggish competition with others.*

15   But hunters are piggy. They just can't seem to help it. They're overequipped . . . insatiable, malevolent, and vain. They maim and mutilate and despoil. And for the most part, they're inept. Grossly inept.

Camouflaged toilet paper is a must for the modern hunter, along with his Bronco and his beer. Too many hunters taking a dump in the woods with their roll of Charmin beside them were mistaken for white-tailed deer and shot. Hunters get excited. They'll shoot anything—the pallid ass of another sportsman or even themselves. A Long Island man died last year when his shotgun went off as he clubbed a wounded deer with the butt. Hunters get mad. They get restless and want to fire! They want to use those assault rifles and see foamy blood on the ferns. Wounded animals can travel for miles in fear and pain before they collapse. Countless gut-shot deer—*if you hear a sudden, squashy thump, the animal has probably been hit in the abdomen*—are "lost" each year. "Poorly placed shots" are frequent, and injured animals are seldom tracked, because most hunters never learned how to track. The majority of hunters will shoot at anything with four legs during deer season and anything with wings during duck season. Hunters try to nail running animals and distant birds. They become so overeager, *so aroused,* that they misidentify and misjudge, spraying their "game" with shots but failing to bring it down.

The fact is, hunters' lack of skill is a big, big problem. And nowhere is the problem worse than in the new glamour recreation, bow hunting. These guys are elitists. They doll themselves up in camouflage, paint their faces black, and climb up into tree stands from which they attempt the penetration of deer, elk, and turkeys with modern, multiblade, broadhead arrows shot from sophisticated, easy-to-draw compound bows. This "primitive" way of hunting appeals to many, and even the nonhunter may feel that it's a "fairer" method, requiring more strength and skill, but bow hunting is the cruelest, most wanton form of wildlife disposal of all. Studies conducted by state fish and wildlife departments repeatedly show that bow hunters wound and fail to retrieve as many animals as they kill. An animal that flees, wounded by an arrow, will most assuredly die of the wound, but it will be days before he does. Even with a "good" hit, the time elapsed between the strike and death is exceedingly long. *The rule of thumb has long been that we should wait thirty to forty-five minutes on heart and lung hits, an hour or more on a suspected liver hit, eight to twelve hours on paunch hits, and that we should follow immediately on hindquarter and other muscle-only hits, to keep the wound open and bleeding,* is the advice in the magazine *Fins and Feathers.* What the hunter does as he hangs around waiting for his animal to finish with its terrified running and dying hasn't been studied—maybe he puts on more makeup, maybe he has a highball.

* * *

"Quality" hunting is as rare as the Florida panther. What you've got is a bunch of guys driving over the plains, up the mountains, and through the woods with their stupid tag that cost them a couple of bucks and immense coolers full of beer and body parts. There's a price tag on the right to destroy living creatures for play, but it's not much. *A big-game hunting license is the greatest deal going since the Homestead Act,* Ted Kerasote writes in *Sports Afield. In many states residents can hunt big game for more than a month for about $20.* It's cheaper than taking the little woman out to lunch. It's cheap all right, and it's because killing animals is considered *recreation* and is underwritten by state and federal funds. In Florida, state moneys are routinely spent on "youth hunts," in which kids are guided to shoot deer from stands in wildlife-management areas. The organizers of these events say that these staged hunts *help youth to understand man's role in the ecosystem.* (Drop a doe and take your place in the ecological community, son . . .)

Hunters claim (they don't actually believe it but they've learned to say it) that they're doing nonhunters a favor, for if they didn't *use* wild animals, wild animals would be useless. They believe that they're just *helping Mother Nature control populations (you wouldn't want those deer to die of starvation, would you?).* They claim that their tiny fees provide *all* Americans with wild lands and animals. (People who don't hunt get to enjoy animals all year round while hunters get to enjoy them only during hunting season . . .) Ducks Unlimited feels that it, in particular, is a selfless provider and environmental champion. Although members spend most of their money lobbying for hunters and raising ducks in pens to release later over shooting fields, they do save some wetlands, mostly by persuading farmers not to fill them in. *See that little pothole there the ducks like? Well, I'm gonna plant more soybeans there if you don't pay me not to* . . . Hunters claim many nonsensical things, but the most nonsensical of all is that they *pay their own way.* They do not pay their own way. They *do* pay into a perverse wildlife-management system that manipulates "stocks" and "herds" and "flocks" for hunters' killing pleasure, but these fees in no way cover the cost of highly questionable ecological practices. For some spare change . . . *the greatest deal going* . . . hunters can hunt on public lands—national parks, state forests—preserves for hunters!—which the nonhunting and antihunting public pay for. (Access to private lands is becoming increasingly difficult for them, as experience has taught people that hunters are obnoxious.) Hunters kill on millions of acres of land all over America that are maintained with general taxpayer revenue, but the most shocking, really twisted subsidization takes place on national wildlife refuges. Nowhere is the arrogance and insidiousness of this small, aggressive minority more clearly demonstrated. Nowhere is the murder of animals, the manipulation of language, and the distortion of public intent more flagrant. The public perceives national wildlife refuges as safe havens, as sanctuaries for animals. And why wouldn't they? The word *refuge* of course *means* shelter from danger and distress. But the dweeby nonhunting public—they tend to be so literal. The word has been reinterpreted by management over time and now hunters are invited into more than half of the country's more than 440 wildlife "sanctuaries" each year to bang them up and kill more than half a million animals. This is called *wildlife-oriented recreation.* Hunters think of this as being no less than their due, claiming that refuge lands were purchased with duck stamps (. . . *our duck stamps paid for it . . . our duck stamps paid for it . . .*). Hunters equate those stupid stamps with the mystic, multiplying power of the Lord's loaves and fishes, but of 90 million acres in the Wildlife Refuge System, only 3 million were bought with hunting-stamp revenue. Most wildlife "restoration" programs in the states are translated into clearing land to increase deer habitats (so that too many deer will require hunting . . . you wouldn't want them to die of starvation, would you?) and trapping animals for restocking and study (so hunters can shoot more of them). Fish and game agencies hustle hunting—instead of conserving wildlife, they're killing it. It's time for them to get in the business of protecting and preserving wildlife and creating balanced ecological systems instead of pimping for hunters who want their deer/duck/pheasant/turkey—animals stocked to be shot.

20   Hunters' self-serving arguments and lies are becoming more preposterous as nonhunters awake from their long, albeit troubled, sleep. Sport hunting is immoral; it should be made illegal. Hunters are persecutors of nature who should be prosecuted. They wield a disruptive power out of all proportion to their numbers, and pandering to their interests—the special interests of a group that just wants to kill things—is mad. It's preposterous that every year less than 7 percent of the population turns the skies into shooting galleries and the woods and fields into abattoirs. It's time to stop actively supporting and passively allowing hunting, and time to stigmatize it. It's time to stop being conned and cowed by hunters, time to stop pampering and coddling them, time to get them off the government's duck-and-deer dole, time to stop thinking of wild animals as "resources" and "game," and start thinking of them as sentient beings that deserve our wonder and respect, time to stop allowing hunting to be creditable by calling it "sport" and "recreation." Hunters make wildlife *dead, dead, dead.* It's time to wake up to this indisputable fact. As for the hunters, it's long past check-out time.

Analyzing Rhetorical Choices

1. How do you explain the use of italics in this essay? What, exactly, do they represent, and how effective are they in helping Williams support her argument?

2. Discuss Williams's tone in this essay. What kinds of tonal shifts do you detect and on what basis do you think she makes them?

3. Where does Williams make her argument explicit? Evaluate the effectiveness of the argument in terms of its placement. In what ways, if any, would the essay's effectiveness be altered if the argument were placed somewhere else?

4. Why do you think Williams published this essay in *Esquire* magazine, a publication noted predominately for its male readers?

Writing About Issues and Contexts

1. Evaluate at least three of the statements by hunters that appear in this essay in terms of their logic and persuasiveness. How do you evaluate Williams's perspective and analyses of these prohunting statements?

2. What parallels does Williams draw between wild animal predators and hunters?

3. What is Williams's primary purpose in the long paragraph beginning, "Hunters believe that wild animals exist only to satisfy their wish to kill them." Analyze the effectiveness of this paragraph in terms of how she critiques the hunters' perspective, and discuss in what ways it sets up the short paragraph that follows.

4. In what ways is this essay an effective argument against hunting? In what ways is it less successful? Another way of thinking about this is to ask whether this essay has altered your perspective about hunting. Whatever your answer, explain it by making reference to specific sections of this essay that you find either effective or ineffective.

*Born in Kansas City and with degrees from the University of Missouri
and Yale, **Paul Shepard** (1925–1996) became one of the founders of the
American ecology movement. His teachings and writings have influenced
many, including the well-known nature writers Barry Lopez and Peter
Matthiessen. For the last 20 years of his life, he held the position of
Avery Professor of Natural Philosophy and Human Ecology at Pitzer
College and the Claremont Graduate School. His published works include* The Tender Carnivore and the Sacred Game *(1973) and* Man in the
Landscape *(1967, 1991). The selection that follows is an excerpt from
the latter book and explores the complex relation between human beings
and nature, with a special focus on the volatile subject of hunting. It is
worth noting that Shepard loved the outdoors, was an avid birder, and
was a hunter and fisherman as well.*

Paul Shepard

Hunting and Human Values

Killing animals for the meat industry or for scientific research can
be rationalized to the satisfaction of all but a few, but hunting for
sport is frequently regarded as morally indefensible. Some of my ac-
quaintances class hunting with war and murder. They are humane
and humanist, with broad literary knowledge, articulate and very
keen, as it were, in the slaughter of the advocates of hunting. In a debate in *The Saturday Review,* for instance, Joseph Wood Krutch
carved up his hunter opponent and served him to the readers, steam-
ing in his own juices.

Hunting has been defended by the fiction that sporting activity in
the field somehow prepared a young man for a higher plane of conduct in human affairs. But whatever validity this idea had became obsolete with the end of aristocratic social structure. It has been held
that the hunt promotes character, self-reliance, and initiative—an un-
tenable Theodore Roosevelt belief. The development of leadership
does not depend on killing. Assertions are sometimes made about instinctive needs and vague primitive satisfactions and psychological
benefits, but the sharpest opponents of hunting appear simply not to
have forgiven Darwin and Freud to begin with. To suggest that hunt-

ing has psychic or evolutionary values only infuriates. Others claim that the hunter is really attempting to escape the roar and friction of civilization, to squeeze out of society's trammels for a few hours of recuperation. The outraged response is, of course, that hunting with a camera is equally rewarding and more uplifting. According to the Faulkner and Hemingway interpretation, hunting is a manipulation of symbols for proving one's virility or otherwise coping with the erosion of the human personality and the decadence of civilization.

Opposition to hunting for sport has its accusing finger on the act of killing. Determinism gives no out. We cannot plead that we are bipedal carnivorous mammals and damned to kill. We must discover what it means to search for an equilibrium between the polarities of nature and God. We find that to share in life is to participate in a traffic of energy and materials, the ultimate origin of which is a mystery, but which has its immediate source in the bodies of plants and other animals. As a society, we may be in danger of losing sight of this fact, kept vividly before us in hunting.

The condemnation of killing wild animals assumes that death is the worst of natural events, that order in nature is epitomized by living objects rather than the complex flow patterns of which objects are temporary formations. The implication is that carnivorous predation as a whole is evil. The anti-hunters face a paradox of their own making. Dr. Schweitzer, who did not believe in hunting for sport, sprinkled his jungle writings with accounts of righteous killing of predators. Europeans and Americans in the same *Zeitgeist* have always destroyed predators, the big cats, eagles, wolves, bears, and pests such as rodents, insects, and birds.

5   Joseph Wood Krutch condemns the hunter for killing, claiming that the distinction between life and death is one of the most absolute boundaries which we know. But this is not so. Life has atomic as well as planetary dimensions. The most satisfactory definitions and descriptions of life are in physical and chemical terms of events and processes which, occurring in a certain harmony, produce what we call life. The organic and the inorganic are mingled inextricably in the living body.

The traditional insistence upon the overwhelmingly tragic and unequivocal nature of death ignores the adaptive role of early death in most animal populations. It presumes that the landscape is a collection of *things*. In this view the dissolution of body and personality are always tragic and disruptive, and do not contribute to the perfection of an intelligible world. But death, as transformation in a larger system, is an essential aspect of elegant patterns which are orderly as well as beautiful: without death growth could not occur, energy could not flow beyond plants, nutrient substances would be trapped forever. Without death the pond, the forest, the prairie, the city could not exist. The extremely complicated structure of living communities has yet to be fully explored, but constitutes a field pattern. Plants and animals participate in them without question in an attitude of acceptance which in human terms would be called faith.

The unfortunate social and economic misapplication of Darwin's theory in the late nineteenth century can still be seen in reluctance to accept evolution as a significant factor in man's highest as well as his more primitive activities. Evolutionary theory also had the curious effect on some people of making nature seem more chaotic instead of less. Evolution is unrelated to the fate of individuals. We have projected our notions of ethics and our terror of death into our perception of all life. Animals die before they have lived out their potential life span; that is characteristic of the natural world and essential to our understanding of it.

A moral criterion is sometimes offered for killing limited to the necessity for food and defense. This logically opposes the sportsman and approves of the slaughterhouse. Under primitive conditions killing meant something quite different than it does in the modern slaughterhouse or by the broadscale application of chemical pesticides. The events of daily life in a hunting society are permeated with universal significance immediate to every individual. No activity of life is regarded as "merely" physical, but always related to a whole, partly unseen. We cannot now adopt animistic superstition nor regain that kind of consciousness, but we admire the poignant sense of the interpenetration of man and nature which primitive life ritualizes and we may seek its results. Primitive ways are nearly gone but we acknowledge that such reverence for life is more reverent and is better ecology than a fanatic emphasis on fear of death and the attempt at godship by judging all instances and causes of death among animals. To our repugnance for soil (dirt), parasitism (disease), and decay (slime) we add predation. We condemn it as though it were murder, and extend "justice" into biotic realms where it is meaningless, incorporating democracy with its protection of the "weak" and containment of the "strong." Man dominates some parts of nature, but there is no process known by which this vindicates extending his social ethics, his democracy, or any other ideological or moral system into the adaptations of populations or the interrelations of species.

Does the hunter not interfere in natural patterns and upset nature's balance? Yes and no. Man is not a demigod operating above and outside nature. But nature is in him as well as he in it. Nature's balance is always slightly upset.

10   Individuals are important. The taking of a life, so evanescent in a cosmic scheme, is nonetheless profoundly moving to us as individuals. Killing an animal probably obliterates an awareness somewhat similar to our own consciousness. As sympathetic and vulnerable humans, we are confronted with mystery by the death of any creature. This is why the tension over killing is so incisive and urgent. Our sympathy for a fellow creature is felt intensely at the crucial moment of death. Yet that emotion fulfills a cultural and personal necessity for evidence of our connection to large-scale processes in a moment of profound intensity. If the death is so experienced our response may be regarded as a form of behavior which unites men with nature rather than alienating them.

Mental well-being is defined by a model of cultural behavior. Culture is an interface between man and his environment. Collective dreams and myths, apprehended symbolically, change slowly with the healthy functioning of society and the psychic security of its members. There is in literary and pictorial arts an iconography of hunting. With its artistic heritage, hunting is much more than a wanton vestige of barbarism. It is intimately associated with social order and with love. "Venery" is an archaic term meaning both sexual pursuit and hunting game—the foundation of love. The origins of human compassion belong to the hunters of old.

Hunting may be an inherent behavior, but it is not *only* an instinct. It is a framework of organization which acknowledges an extra-human context. Killing is not justified simply as indigenous or venerable. But it is a historical part of the activity of a people. It has a place in the total fabric of what they have become, a mode of their relationship to nature. For perhaps 95 percent of their history men and "near-men" have been hunters. Primitive peoples ritualize hunting except where hunting societies and the technological world have collided, where cultural deterioration has reduced customary inhibition to wanton killing.

Probably the richest collection of the ceremonies of propitiation of wild spirits by hunters is Sir James G. Frazer's *The Golden Bough*. If anthropologically obsolete, Frazer's perspective and genius for collecting remain nonetheless monumental. To judge from *The Golden Bough*, hunting has been universally bound by ceremonial preparation and epilogue. When British Columbian Lillooet Indians dispose of the bones of their kill in a certain way, saying, "See! I treated you respectfully. Nothing shall defile you! May I be successful in hunting and trapping!" they are not only seeking to perpetuate their food supply. They do more than solicit success and spiritual acquiescence. Their ceremony makes less distinction between subject and object than we assume in the orthodox sense of magic. Even Frazer's view of ritual as coercive and petitionary was perhaps too restrictive. The ceremony is also an affirmation and participation, not only manipulative but attuning, assimilative, and confrontative. Imitative magic is prototechnological and prescientific, but that part emphasizing "wehood" and the participating in a larger whole are religious.

Both magic and religion in primitive ritual reveal fundamental components of the hunter's attitude. The organized ceremony simultaneously serves a magic and a religious purpose, and ecological and social functions as well. The ceremony is aimed at maintaining equilibrium in the total situation. The whole of life, corporeal and spiritual, is affected. The prey, or parts of it, are killed ritually and eaten sacramentally. By following the prescribed style the hunters sacrifice the prey in evocation of events too profound for conscious understanding. By its own self-imposed limitations the ritual hunt renounces further killing in favor of a larger context of interrelationship. If the preliminary solicitation is effective and the traditional procedure is followed, the hunt is successful. Unlike farmers who must labor in the fields and who earn by their sweat a grudging security within nature, the primitive hunter gets "something for nothing." The kill is a gift. Its bestowal depends on the conduct of the hunters. Without this gift the hunter will die. As Malinowski says, "food is the main link between man and his surroundings" and "by receiving it he feels the forces of destiny and providence." Of all foods meat is the gift *par excellence* because shortage of protein, not shortage of food *per se,* is the essence of starvation. The elusiveness of the quarry explicitly symbolizes the continuing dependence of human life on powers beyond human control. Hunting provides the logical nucleus for the evolution of communal life with its celebrations of a biosocial participation mystique and the sharing of the kill.

15   What do the hunt and kill actually do for the hunter? They confirm his continuity with the dynamic life of animal populations, his role in the complicated cycles of elements, his sharing in the sweep of evolution, and his place in the patterns of the flow of energy and in the web of his own society.

It may at first seem irrelevant to seek present values for us in the strongly schematized hunting behavior of primitive man. But "our deepest experience, needs, and aspirations are the same, as surely as the crucial biological and psychic transitions occur in the life of every human being and force culture to take account of them in aesthetic forms," says Richard V. Chase. Many anthropologists report that there is widespread belief in the immortality of the spirits of all living things, a point of view which we may be too barbaric to share. Frazer wrote, about the time Schweitzer was conceiving of "Reverence for Life," "If I am right in thus interpreting the thought of primitive man, the savage view of the nature of life singularly resembles the modern scientific doctrine of the conservation of energy." The idea of organic interrelationship which ecologists explore may spring not from inductive science at all, but from a rather fundamental human attitude toward the landscape. In these terms, the hunt is a singular expression of our identity with natural processes and is carried on with veneration appropriate to the mystery of those events.

This concept transcends particular economic situations. Men in all sorts of societies—primitive, pastoral, agricultural, and technical—continue to hunt fervently. The hunt has ceased to be the main source of food, but remains the ritual symbol of a larger transaction. The prey represents all that is received, whether from a host of animal gods, an arbitrary god, or from the law of probability.

It is sometimes said that hunters are cruel, insensitive, and barbaric. In fact, however, the hunter may experience life and death deeply. In a poem called "Castles and Distances" Richard Wilbur writes:

> *Oh, it is hunters alone*
> *Regret the beastly pain, it is they who love the foe*
> *That quarries out their force, and every arrow*
> *Is feathered soft with wishes to atone;*
> *Even the surest sword in sorrow*
> *Bleeds for its spoiling blow.*
>
> *Sometimes, as one can see*
> *Carved at Amboise in a high relief, on the lintel stone*
> *Of the castle chapel, hunters have strangely come*
> *To a mild close of the chase, bending the knee*
> *Instead of the bow, struck sweetly dumb*
> *To see from the brow bone*
>
> *Of the hounded stag a cross*
> *Grown, and the eyes clear with grace. . . .*

In urban and technological situations hunting continues to put us in close touch with nature, to provoke the study of natural history, and to nourish the idea of conservation. Even royalty is subject to the uncertainty of the gift. From the Middle Ages we have numerous examples of the values of the hunt. Its forms coincided with social structure in complex royal households and its practice stimulated first-hand observation at a time when hearsay and past authority were the main sources of information. The unique work of Frederick II in thirteenth-century ornithology is an example, an advance in the understanding of birds gathered during hunting trips afield. A more recent example is the work of the late Aldo Leopold. A hunter and a forester, his career was a living documentation of the slow sensitizing of a man to his environment through the medium of gun and dog. In postulating a "split rail value" for hunting, Leopold observed that hunting is a reenactment of a historically important activity when contact with the natural environment and the virtues of this contact were less obscured by modern urban life.

Civilization extends the means of food and energy distribution and of storage against lean years. The ultimate origin of food in the soil is no longer apparent to the average person, as even agriculture is a closed industrial process. In this engineered and insulated atmosphere the natural world has become a peripheral relic, a strange, sometimes entertaining, sometimes frightening curiosity. What has become of *the gift?* It has receded from view except for those who seek it. They may be found in the open country trying their luck. By various arbitrary limitations, both behavioral and mechanical, the hunter curbs his technological advantage. This peculiar assemblage of legal, ethical, and physical restraints constitutes sportsmanship, a contemporary ritual. The hunt is arbitrarily limited. The hunter brings to focus his whole physical and spiritual attention on the moment of the kill. He expects to eat the quarry, even though economically it is dietetically irrelevant. Yet he will cook and eat it in a mood of thoughtful celebration known only to hunters.

20   It follows that hunting is not just an excuse to get out of doors. Killing and eating the prey are the most important things that hunters do. The successful hunt is a solemn and yet glad event. It places man for a moment in vital rapport with a universe from which civilization tends to separate him by its fostering of an illusion of superiority and independence. The natural environment will always be mysterious, evoking an awe to be shared among all men who take the trouble to see it. If modern sportsmanship is a shallow substitute for the complex mythology or unifying ceremony of other cultures, we must acknowledge that only a part of the society hunts, that ritual forms of

this technological era are still young and poorly defined, and that we are part of an age which may be said to be living on the accumulated capital—cultural and biological—of a million years of hardship, death, effort, and invention. Given a hard-earned margin magnified by machines, human society may behave irresponsibly for a time and forget the ties that bind it to the world.

Regardless of the technological advance, man remains part of and dependent upon nature. The necessity of signifying and recognizing this relationship remains, though it may not seem so. The hunter is our agent of awareness. He is not only an observer but a participant and receiver. He knows that man is a member of a natural community and that the processes of nature will never become so well understood or controlled that faith will cease to be important.

Analyzing Rhetorical Choices

1. Discuss Shepard's opening sentence, "Killing animals for the meat industry or for scientific research can be rationalized to the satisfaction of all but a few, but hunting for sport is frequently regarded as morally indefensible." What assumptions lie behind this statement? In what ways is this an effective opening to this essay?

2. Analyze the tone that Shepard adopts. How would you describe it, and how do Shepard's diction and sentence structure reinforce it?

3. Why do you think Shepard includes the lines from Richard Wilbur's poem, "Castles and Distances," and why is it placed at this point in the essay? Discuss its effectiveness in helping Shepard reinforce his argument.

4. What does Shepard mean by calling the natural world "a gift" and hunting "a ritual"? How do these word choices affect your response to Shepard's perspective?

Writing About Issues and Contexts

1. What rationalizations for hunting does Shepard offer? Analyze their persuasiveness in terms of logic and ethical justification.

2. Outline the structure of Shepard's argument. How does he build his case for the place of hunting within contemporary human society?

3. Shepard writes that "The hunt has ceased to be the main source of food, but remains the ritual symbol of a larger transaction." What does he mean by the phrase "larger transaction"? Who—or what—are involved in this transaction, and what exactly is being exchanged?

4. Offer your views concerning whether "The hunter is our agent of awareness" by analyzing two or three key arguments that Shepard makes concerning the human and the natural.

Born in Union City, New Jersey, **Norman Cousins** *(1915–1990) was a
graduate of the Teacher's College of Columbia University. A writer for
the* New York Evening Post *and* Current History *magazine, he joined the
Saturday Review in 1940. He became editor of the* Review *in 1942 and
served until 1978. Cousins lectured widely on world events and wrote a
number of books that supported the power of positive thinking to combat illness, as in* Anatomy of an Illness, *published in 1979. He served as
an adjunct professor of psychiatry at the UCLA medical school.*

Norman Cousins

Who Killed Benny Paret?

Sometime about 1935 or 1936 I had an interview with Mike
Jacobs, the prizefight promoter. I was a fledgling reporter at that time;
my beat was education but during the vacation season I found myself
on varied assignments, all the way from ship news to sports reporting.
In this way I found myself sitting opposite the most powerful figure in
the boxing world.

There was nothing spectacular in Mr. Jacobs' manner or appearance; but when he spoke about prize fights, he was no longer a bland
little man but a colossus who sounded the way Napoleon must have
sounded when he reviewed a battle. You knew you were listening to
Number One. His saying something made it true.

We discussed what to him was the only important element in successful promoting—how to please the crowd. So far as he was concerned, there was no mystery to it. You put killers in the ring and the
people filled your arena. You hire boxing artists—men who are adroit
at feinting, parrying, weaving, jabbing, and dancing, but who don't
pack dynamite in their fists—and you wind up counting your empty
seats. So you searched for the killers and sluggers and maulers—fellows who could hit with the force of a baseball bat.

I asked Mr. Jacobs if he was speaking literally when he said people came out to see the killer.

5   "They don't come out to see a tea party," he said evenly. "They
come out to see the knockout. They come out to see a man hurt. If
they think anything else, they're kidding themselves."

Recently, a young man by the name of Benny Paret was killed in
the ring. The killing was seen by millions; it was on television. In the

twelfth round, he was hit hard in the head several times, went down, was counted out, and never came out of the coma.

The Paret fight produced a flurry of investigations. Governor Rockefeller was shocked by what happened and appointed a committee to assess the responsibility. The New York State Boxing Commission decided to find out what was wrong. The District Attorney's office expressed its concern. One question that was solemnly studied in all three probes concerned the action of the referee. Did he act in time to stop the fight? Another question had to do with the role of the examining doctors who certified the physical fitness of the fighters before the bout. Still another question involved Mr. Paret's manager; did he rush his boy into the fight without adequate time to recuperate from the previous one?

In short, the investigators looked into every possible cause except the real one. Benny Paret was killed because the human fist delivers enough impact, when directed against the head, to produce a massive hemorrhage in the brain. The human brain is the most delicate and complex mechanism in all creation. It has a lacework of millions of highly fragile nerve connections. Nature attempts to protect this exquisitely intricate machinery by encasing it in a hard shell. Fortunately, the shell is thick enough to withstand a great deal of pounding. Nature, however, can protect man against everything except man himself. Not every blow to the head will kill a man—but there is always the risk of concussion and damage to the brain. A prizefighter may be able to survive even repeated brain concussions and go on fighting, but the damage to his brain may be permanent.

In any event, it is futile to investigate the referee's role and seek to determine whether he should have intervened to stop the fight earlier. That is not where the primary responsibility lies. The primary responsibility lies with the people who pay to see a man hurt. The referee who stops a fight too soon from the crowd's viewpoint can expect to be booed. The crowd wants the knockout; it wants to see a man stretched out on the canvas. This is the supreme moment in boxing. It is nonsense to talk about prizefighting as a test of boxing skills. No crowd was ever brought to its feet screaming and cheering at the sight of two men beautifully dodging and weaving out of each other's jabs. The time the crowd comes alive is when a man is hit hard over the heart or the head, when his mouthpiece flies out, when the blood squirts out of his nose or eyes, when he wobbles under the attack and his pursuer continues to smash at him with pole-ax impact.

10   Don't blame it on the referee. Don't even blame it on the fight managers. Put the blame where it belongs—on the prevailing mores that regard prizefighting as a perfectly proper enterprise and vehicle of entertainment. No one doubts that many people enjoy prizefighting and will miss it if it should be thrown out. And that is precisely the point.

Analyzing Rhetorical Choices

1. How does Cousins attempt to persuade? Is he successful? Why does Cousins begin with his interview with Mike Jacobs? Why is it significant that Jacobs is a fight promoter?

2. Cousins uses a number of strategies throughout his argument, including direct quotation, a switch to second person in the third paragraph, and an explicit description of boxing's brutal effects in paragraph nine, among others. Analyze the effectiveness of such strategies in persuading you that Cousins is right.

3. Does Cousins appear to be targeting a particular audience for this essay? What evidence from the text might indicate this?

Writing About Issues and Contexts

1. What does this article say about human nature? What evidence supports your contention? Do you agree that "the only important element in successful promoting" is "how to please the crowd"? Why or why not?

2. Explain the reaction of the New York State Boxing Commission, the district attorney, the governor of New York, and others to the death of Benny Paret. Do you think their responses were sincere? Cynical? Troubled?

3. Who does bear responsibility for the death of Benny Paret? Explain your answer by referring to Cousins.

Born in Atlanta and a graduate of Morehouse College, Crozer Theological Seminary, and Boston University (where he earned his Ph.D.), **Dr. Martin Luther King, Jr.** *(1929–1968) is possibly the most admired civil rights leader of his or any other time. He achieved national prominence in 1955 as a result of his personal courage and oratorical skills as he led the boycott against segregated buses in Montgomery, Alabama. In 1957, King and other southern black ministers founded the Southern Christian Leadership Conference, through which King emphasized the goal of black voting rights. He published his first book in 1958,* Stride Toward Freedom: The Montgomery Story. *Known particularly for his advocacy of nonviolent strategies to bring about change, King's renown grew as he became* Time *magazine's Man of the Year in 1964, and in the same year, the recipient of the Nobel Peace Prize. King wrote "Letter from Birmingham Jail" in response to "A Call for Unity," a letter written by eight Birmingham clergymen and published in a local newspaper. King was assassinated in April 1968.*

Martin Luther King, Jr.

Letter from Birmingham Jail

My Dear Fellow Clergymen:

While confined here in the Birmingham city jail, I came across your recent statement calling my present activities "unwise and untimely." Seldom do I pause to answer criticism of my work and ideas. If I sought to answer all of the criticisms that cross my desk, my secretaries would have little time for anything other than such correspondence in the course of the day, and I would have no time for constructive work. But since I feel that you are men of genuine good will and that your criticisms are sincerely set forth, I want to try to answer your statement in what I hope will be patient and reasonable terms.

I think I should indicate why I am here in Birmingham, since you have been influenced by the view which argues against "outsiders coming in." I have the honor of serving as president of the Southern Christian Leadership Conference, an organization operating in every southern state, with headquarters in Atlanta, Georgia. We have some eighty-five affiliated organizations across the South, and one of them is the Alabama Christian Movement for Human Rights. Frequently we share staff, educational, and financial resources with our affiliates. Several months ago the affiliate here in Birmingham asked us to be on call to engage in a nonviolent direct-action program if such were deemed necessary. We readily consented, and when the hour came, we lived up to our promise. So I, along with several members of my staff, am here because I was invited here. I am here because I have organizational ties here.

But more basically, I am in Birmingham because injustice is here. Just as the prophets of the eighth century B.C. left their villages and carried their "thus saith the Lord" far beyond the boundaries of their home towns, and just as the Apostle Paul left his village of Tarsus and carried the gospel of Jesus Christ to the far corners of the Greco-Roman world, so am I compelled to carry the gospel of freedom beyond my own home town. Like Paul, I must constantly respond to the Macedonian call for aid.

Moreover, I am cognizant of the interrelatedness of all communities and states. I cannot sit idly by in Atlanta and not be concerned about what happens in Birmingham. Injustice anywhere is a threat to justice everywhere. We are caught in an inescapable network of mutuality, tied in a single garment of destiny. Whatever affects one directly, affects all indirectly. Never again can we afford to live with the narrow, provincial "outside agitator" idea. Anyone who lives inside the United States can never be considered an outsider anywhere within its bounds.

5   You deplore the demonstrations taking place in Birmingham. But your statement, I am sorry to say, fails to express a similar concern for the conditions that brought about the demonstrations. I am sure that none of you would want to rest content with the superficial kind of social analysis that deals merely with effects and does not grapple with underlying causes. It is unfortunate that demonstrations are taking place in Birmingham, but it is even more unfortunate that the city's white power structure left the Negro community with no alternative.

In any nonviolent campaign there are four basic steps: collection of the facts to determine whether injustices exist; negotiation; self-purification; and direct action. We have gone through all these steps in Birmingham. There can be no gainsaying the fact that racial injustice engulfs this community. Birmingham is probably the most thoroughly segregated city in the United States. Its ugly record of brutality is widely known. Negroes have experienced grossly unjust treatment in the courts. There have been more unsolved bombings of Negro homes and churches in Birmingham than in any other city in the nation. These are the hard, brutal facts of the case. On the basis of these conditions, Negro leaders sought to negotiate with the city fathers. But the latter consistently refused to engage in good-faith negotiation.

Then, last September, came the opportunity to talk with leaders of Birmingham's economic community. In the course of the negotiations, certain promises were made by the merchants—for example, to remove the stores' humiliating racial signs. On the basis of these promises, the Reverend Fred Shuttlesworth and the leaders of the Alabama Christian Movement for Human Rights agreed to a moratorium on all demonstrations. As the weeks and months went by, we realized that we were the victims of a broken promise. A few signs, briefly removed, returned; the others remained.

As in so many past experiences, our hopes had been blasted, and the shadow of deep disappointment settled upon us. We had no alternative except to prepare for direct action, whereby we would present our very bodies as a means of laying our case before the conscience of the local and national community. Mindful of the difficulties involved, we decided to undertake a process of self-purification. We began a series of workshops on nonviolence, and we repeatedly asked ourselves: "Are you able to accept blows without retaliating?" "Are you able to endure the ordeal of jail?" We decided to schedule our direct-action program for the Easter season, realizing that except for Christmas, this is the main shopping period of the year. Knowing that a strong economic-withdrawal program would be the by-product of direct action, we felt that this would be the best time to bring pressure to bear on the merchants for the needed change.

Then it occurred to us that Birmingham's mayoral election was coming up in March, and we speedily decided to postpone action until after election day. When we discovered that the Commissioner of Public Safety, Eugene "Bull" Connor, had piled up enough votes to be in the run-off, we decided again to postpone action until the day after the run-off so that the demonstrations could not be used to cloud the issues. Like many others, we wanted to see Mr. Connor defeated, and to this end we endured postponement after postponement. Having aided in this community need, we felt that our direct-action program could be delayed no longer.

10   You may well ask, "Why direct action? Why sit-ins, marches, and so forth? Isn't negotiation a better path?" You are quite right in calling for negotiation. Indeed, this is the very purpose of direct action. Nonviolent direct action seeks to create such a crisis and foster such a

tension that a community which has constantly refused to negotiate is forced to confront the issue. It seeks so to dramatize the issue that it can no longer be ignored. My citing the creation of tension as part of the work of the nonviolent-resister may sound rather shocking. But I must confess that I am not afraid of the word "tension." I have earnestly opposed violent tension, but there is a type of constructive, nonviolent tension which is necessary for growth. Just as Socrates felt that it was necessary to create a tension in the mind so that individuals could rise from the bondage of myths and half-truths to the unfettered realm of creative analysis and objective appraisal, so must we see the need for nonviolent gadflies to create the kind of tension in society that will help men rise from the dark depths of prejudice and racism to the majestic heights of understanding and brotherhood.

The purpose of our direct-action program is to create a situation so crisis-packed that it will inevitably open the door to negotiation. I therefore concur with you in your call for negotiation. Too long has our beloved Southland been bogged down in a tragic effort to live in monologue rather than dialogue.

One of the basic points in your statement is that the action that I and my associates have taken in Birmingham is untimely. Some have asked: "Why didn't you give the new city administration time to act?" The only answer that I can give to this query is that the new Birmingham administration must be prodded about as much as the outgoing one, before it will act. We are sadly mistaken if we feel that the election of Albert Boutwell as mayor will bring the millennium to Birmingham. While Mr. Boutwell is a much more gentle person than Mr. Connor, they are both segregationists, dedicated to maintenance of the status quo. I have hoped that Mr. Boutwell will be reasonable enough to see the futility of massive resistance to desegregation. But he will not see this without pressure from devotees of civil rights. My friends, I must say to you that we have not made a single gain in civil rights without determined legal and nonviolent pressure. Lamentably, it is an historical fact that privileged groups seldom give up their privileges voluntarily. Individuals may see the moral light and voluntarily give up their unjust posture; but, as Reinhold Niebuhr has reminded us, groups tend to be more immoral than individuals.

We know through painful experience that freedom is never voluntarily given by the oppressor; it must be demanded by the oppressed. Frankly, I have yet to engage in a direct-action campaign that was "well timed" in the view of those who have not suffered unduly from the disease of segregation. For years now I have heard the word "Wait!" It rings in the ear of every Negro with piercing familiarity. This "Wait" has almost always meant "Never." We must come to see, with one of our distinguished jurists, that "justice too long delayed is justice denied."

We have waited for more than 340 years for our constitutional and God-given rights. The nations of Asia and Africa are moving with jet-like speed toward gaining political independence, but we still creep at horse-and-buggy pace toward gaining a cup of coffee at a lunch counter. Perhaps it is easy for those who have never felt the stinging darts of segregation to say, "Wait." But when you have seen vicious mobs lynch your mothers and fathers at will and drown your sisters and brothers at whim; when you have seen hate-filled policemen curse, kick, and even kill your black brothers and sisters; when you see the vast majority of your twenty million Negro brothers smothering in an airtight cage of poverty in the midst of an affluent society; when you suddenly find your tongue twisted and your speech stammering as you seek to explain to your six-year-old daughter why she can't go to the public amusement park that has just been advertised on television, and see tears welling up in her eyes when she is told that Funtown is closed to colored children, and see ominous clouds of inferiority beginning to form in her little mental sky, and see her beginning to distort her personality by developing an unconscious bitterness toward white people; when you have to concoct an answer for a five-year-old son who is asking "Daddy, why do white people treat colored people so mean?"; when you take a cross-country drive and find it necessary to sleep night after night in the uncomfortable corners of your automobile because no motel will accept you; when you are humiliated day in and day out by nagging signs reading "white" and "colored"; when your first name becomes "nigger," your middle name becomes "boy" (however old you are) and your last name becomes "John," and your wife and mother are never given the respected title "Mrs."; when you are harried by day and haunted by night by the fact that you are a Negro, living constantly at tiptoe stance, never quite knowing what to expect next, and are plagued with inner fears and outer resentments; when you are forever fighting a degenerating sense of "nobodiness"—then you will understand why we find it difficult to wait. There comes a time when the cup of endurance runs over, and men are no longer willing to be plunged into the abyss of despair. I hope, sirs, you can understand our legitimate and unavoidable impatience.

15   You express a great deal of anxiety over our willingness to break laws. This is certainly a legitimate concern. Since we so diligently urge

people to obey the Supreme Court's decision of 1954 outlawing segregation in the public schools, at first glance it may seem rather paradoxical for us consciously to break laws. One may well ask: "How can you advocate breaking some laws and obeying others?" The answer lies in the fact that there are two types of laws: just and unjust. I would be the first to advocate obeying just laws. One has not only a legal but a moral responsibility to obey just laws. Conversely, one has a moral responsibility to disobey unjust laws. I would agree with St. Augustine that "an unjust law is no law at all."

Now, what is the difference between the two? How does one determine whether a law is just or unjust? A just law is a man-made code that squares with the moral law or the law of God. An unjust law is a code that is out of harmony with the moral law. To put it in the terms of St. Thomas Aquinas: An unjust law is a human law that is not rooted in eternal law and natural law. Any law that uplifts human personality is just. Any law that degrades human personality is unjust. All segregation statutes are unjust because segregation distorts the soul and damages the personality. It gives the segregator a false sense of superiority and the segregated a false sense of inferiority. Segregation, to use the terminology of the Jewish philosopher Martin Buber, substitutes "I-it" relationship for an "I-thou" relationship and ends up relegating persons to the status of things. Hence segregation is not only politically, economically, and sociologically unsound, it is morally wrong and sinful. Paul Tillich has said that sin is separation. Is not segregation an existential expression of man's tragic separation, his awful estrangement, his terrible sinfulness? Thus it is that I can urge men to obey the 1954 decision of the Supreme Court, for it is morally right; and I can urge them to disobey segregation ordinances, for they are morally wrong.

Let us consider a more concrete example of just and unjust laws. An unjust law is a code that a numerical or power majority group compels a minority group to obey but does not make binding on itself. This is *difference* made legal. By the same token, a just law is a code that a majority compels a minority to follow and that it is willing to follow itself. This is *sameness* made legal.

Let me give another explanation. A law is unjust if it is inflicted on a minority that, as a result of being denied the right to vote, had no part in enacting or devising the law. Who can say that the legislature of Alabama which set up that state's segregation laws was democratically elected? Throughout Alabama all sorts of devious methods are used to prevent Negroes from becoming registered voters, and there are some counties in which, even though Negroes constitute a majority of the population, not a single Negro is registered. Can any law enacted under such circumstances be considered democratically structured?

Sometimes a law is just on its face and unjust in its application. For instance, I have been arrested on a charge of parading without a permit. Now, there is nothing wrong in having an ordinance which requires a permit for a parade. But such an ordinance becomes unjust when it is used to maintain segregation and to deny citizens the First-Amendment privilege of peaceful assembly and protest.

20   I hope you are able to see the distinction I am trying to point out. In no sense do I advocate evading or defying the law, as would the rabid segregationist. That would lead to anarchy. One who breaks an unjust law must do so openly, lovingly, and with a willingness to accept the penalty. I submit that an individual who breaks a law that conscience tells him is unjust, and who willingly accepts the penalty of imprisonment in order to arouse the conscience of the community over its injustice, is in reality expressing the highest respect for law.

Of course, there is nothing new about this kind of civil disobedience. It was evidenced sublimely in the refusal of Shadrach, Meshach, and Abednego to obey the laws of Nebuchadnezzar, on the ground that a higher moral law was at stake. It was practiced superbly by the early Christians, who were willing to face hungry lions and the excruciating pain of chopping blocks rather than submit to certain unjust laws of the Roman Empire. To a degree, academic freedom is a reality today because Socrates practiced civil disobedience. In our own nation, the Boston Tea Party represented a massive act of civil disobedience.

We should never forget that everything Adolf Hitler did in Germany was "legal" and everything the Hungarian freedom fighters did in Hungary was "illegal." It was "illegal" to aid and comfort a Jew in Hitler's Germany. Even so, I am sure that, had I lived in Germany at the time, I would have aided and comforted my Jewish brothers. If today I lived in a Communist country where certain principles dear to the Christian faith are suppressed, I would openly advocate disobeying that country's anti-religious laws.

I must make two honest confessions to you, my Christian and Jewish brothers. First, I must confess that over the past few years I have been gravely disappointed with the white moderate. I have almost reached the regrettable conclusion that the Negro's great stumbling block in the stride toward freedom is not the White Citizen's Counciler or the Ku Klux Klanner, but the white moderate, who is more devoted to "order" than to justice; who prefers a negative peace which is the absence of tension to a positive peace which is the presence of justice; who constantly says, "I agree with you in the goal you seek, but I cannot agree with your methods of direct action"; who paternalistically believes he can set the timetable for another man's freedom; who lives by a mythical concept of time and who constantly advises the Negro to wait for a "more convenient season." Shallow understanding from people of good will is more frustrating than absolute misunderstanding from people of ill will. Lukewarm acceptance is much more bewildering than outright rejection.

I had hoped that the white moderate would understand that law and order exist for the purpose of establishing justice and that when they fail in this purpose they become the dangerously structured dams that block the flow of social progress. I had hoped that the white moderate would understand that the present tension in the South is a necessary phase of the transition from an obnoxious negative peace, in which the Negro passively accepted his unjust plight, to a substantive and positive peace, in which all men will respect the dignity and worth of human personality. Actually, we who engage in nonviolent direct action are not the creators of tension. We merely bring to the surface the hidden tension that is already alive. We bring it out in the open, where it can be seen and dealt with. Like a boil that can never be cured so long as it is covered up but must be opened with all its ugliness to the natural medicines of air and light, injustice must be exposed, with all the tension its exposure creates, to the light of human conscience and the air of national opinion, before it can be cured.

25   In your statement you assert that our actions, even though peaceful, must be condemned because they precipitate violence. But is this a logical assertion? Isn't this like condemning a robbed man because his possession of money precipitated the evil act of robbery? Isn't this like condemning Socrates because his unswerving commitment to truth and his philosophical inquiries precipitated the act by the misguided populace in which they made him drink hemlock? Isn't this like condemning Jesus because his unique God-consciousness and never-ceasing devotion to God's will precipitated the evil act of crucifixion? We must come to see that, as the federal courts have consistently affirmed, it is wrong to urge an individual to cease his efforts to gain his basic constitutional rights because the quest may precipitate violence. Society must protect the robbed and punish the robber.

I had also hoped that the white moderate would reject the myth concerning time in relation to the struggle for freedom. I have just received a letter from a white brother in Texas. He writes: "All Christians know that the colored people will receive equal rights eventually, but it is possible that you are in too great a religious hurry. It has taken Christianity almost two thousand years to accomplish what it has. The teachings of Christ take time to come to earth." Such an attitude stems from a tragic misconception of time, from the strangely irrational notion that there is something in the very flow of time that will inevitably cure all ills. Actually, time itself is neutral; it can be used either destructively or constructively. More and more I feel that the people of ill will have used time much more effectively than have the people of good will. We will have to repent in this generation not merely for the hateful words and actions of the bad people, but for the appalling silence of the good people. Human progress never rolls in on wheels of inevitability; it comes through the tireless efforts of men willing to be co-workers with God, and without this hard work, time itself becomes an ally of the forces of social stagnation. We must use time creatively, in the knowledge that the time is always ripe to do right. Now is the time to make real the promise of democracy and transform our pending national elegy into a creative psalm of brotherhood. Now is the time to lift our national policy from the quicksand of racial injustice to the solid rock of human dignity.

You speak of our activity in Birmingham as extreme. At first I was rather disappointed that fellow clergymen would see my nonviolent efforts as those of an extremist. I began thinking about the fact that I stand in the middle of two opposing forces in the Negro community. One is a force of complacency, made up in part of Negroes who, as a result of long years of oppression, are so drained of self-respect and a sense of "somebodiness" that they have adjusted to segregation; and in part of a few middle-class Negroes who, because of a degree of academic and economic security and because in some ways they profit by segregation, have become insensitive to the problems of the masses. The other force is one of bitterness and hatred, and it comes perilously close to advocating violence. It is expressed in the various black nationalist groups that are springing up across the nation, the largest and best-known being Elijah Muhammad's Muslim movement. Nourished by the Negro's frustration over the continued existence of racial discrimination, this movement is made up of people who have lost faith in America, who have absolutely repudiated Christianity, and who have concluded that the white man is an incorrigible "devil."

I have tried to stand between these two forces, saying that we need emulate neither the "do-nothingism" of the complacent nor the hatred and despair of the black nationalist. For there is the more excellent way of love and nonviolent protest. I am grateful to God that, through the influence of the Negro church, the way of nonviolence became an integral part of our struggle.

If this philosophy had not emerged, by now many streets of the South would, I am convinced, be flowing with blood. And I am further convinced that if our white brothers dismiss as "rabblerousers" and "outside agitators" those of us who employ nonviolent direct action, and if they refuse to support our nonviolent efforts, millions of Negroes will, out of frustration and despair, seek solace and security in Black-nationalist ideologies—a development that would inevitably lead to a frightening racial nightmare.

30   Oppressed people cannot remain oppressed forever. The yearning for freedom eventually manifests itself, and that is what has happened to the American Negro. Something within has reminded him of his birthright of freedom, and something without has reminded him that it can be gained. Consciously or unconsciously, he has been caught up by the *Zeitgeist,* and with his black brothers of Africa and his brown and yellow brothers of Asia, South America, and the Caribbean, the United States Negro is moving with a sense of great urgency toward the promised land of racial justice. If one recognizes this vital urge that has engulfed the Negro community, one should readily understand why public demonstrations are taking place. The Negro has many pent-up resentments and latent frustrations, and he must release them. So let him march; let him make prayer pilgrimages to the city hall; let him go on freedom rides—and try to understand why he must do so. If his repressed emotions are not released in nonviolent ways, they will seek expression through violence; this is not a threat but a fact of history. So I have not said to my people, "Get rid of your discontent." Rather, I have tried to say that this normal and healthy discontent can be channeled into the creative outlet of nonviolent direct action. And now this approach is being termed extremist.

But though I was initially disappointed at being categorized as an extremist, as I continued to think about the matter I gradually gained a measure of satisfaction from the label. Was not Jesus an extremist for love: "Love your enemies, bless them that curse you, do good to them that hate you, and pray for them which despitefully use you, and persecute you." Was not Amos an extremist for justice: "Let justice roll down like waters and righteousness like an everflowing stream." Was not Paul an extremist for the Christian gospel: "I bear in my body the marks of the Lord Jesus." Was not Martin Luther an extremist: "Here I stand; I cannot do otherwise, so help me God." And John Bunyan: "I will stay in jail to the end of my days before I make a butchery of my conscience." And Abraham Lincoln: "This nation cannot survive half slave and half free." And Thomas Jefferson: "We hold these truths to be self-evident, that all men are created equal. . . ." So the question is not whether we will be extremists, but what kind of extremists we will be. Will we be extremists for hate or for love? Will we be extremists for the preservation of injustice or for the extension of justice? In that dramatic scene on Calvary's hill three men were crucified. We must never forget that all three were crucified for the same crime—the crime of extremism. Two were extremists for immorality, and thus fell below their environment. The other, Jesus Christ, was an extremist for love, truth, and goodness, and thereby rose above his environment. Perhaps the South, the nation, and the world are in dire need of creative extremists.

I had hoped that the white moderate would see this need. Perhaps I was too optimistic; perhaps I expected too much. I suppose I should have realized that few members of the oppressor race can understand the deep groans and passionate yearnings of the oppressed race, and still fewer have the vision to see that injustice must be rooted out by strong, persistent, and determined action. I am thankful, however, that some of our white brothers in the South have grasped the meaning of this social revolution and committed themselves to it. They are still all too few in quantity, but they are big in quality. Some—such as Ralph McGill, Lillian Smith, Harry Golden, James McBridge Dabbs, Anne Braden, and Sarah Patton Boyle—have written about our struggle in eloquent and prophetic terms. Others have marched with us down nameless streets of the South. They have languished in filthy, roach-infested jails, suffering the abuse and brutality of policemen who view them as "dirty nigger-lovers." Unlike so many of their moderate brothers and sisters, they have recognized the urgency of the moment and sensed the need for powerful "action" antidotes to combat the disease of segregation.

Let me take note of my other major disappointment. I have been so greatly disappointed with the white church and its leadership. Of course, there are some notable exceptions. I am not unmindful of the fact that each of you has taken some significant stands on this issue. I commend you, Reverend Stallings, for your Christian stand on this past Sunday, in welcoming Negroes to your worship service on a non-segregated basis. I commend the Catholic leaders of this state for integrating Spring Hill College several years ago.

But despite these notable exceptions, I must honestly reiterate that I have been disappointed with the church. I do not say this as one of those negative critics who can always find something wrong with the church. I say this as a minister of the gospel, who loves the church; who was nurtured in its bosom; who has been sustained by its spiritual blessings and who will remain true to it as long as the cord of life shall lengthen.

35 When I was suddenly catapulted into the leadership of the bus protest in Montgomery, Alabama, a few years ago, I felt we would be supported by the white church. I felt that the white ministers, priests, and rabbis of the South would be among our strongest allies. Instead, some have been outright opponents, refusing to understand the freedom movement and misrepresenting its leaders; all too many others have been more cautious than courageous and have remained silent behind the anesthetizing security of stained glass windows.

In spite of my shattered dreams, I came to Birmingham with the hope that the white religious leadership of this community would see the justice of our cause and, with deep moral concern, would serve as the channel through which our just grievances could reach the power structure. I had hoped that each of you would understand. But again I have been disappointed.

I have heard numerous southern religious leaders admonish their worshipers to comply with a desegregation decision because it is the law, but I have longed to hear white ministers declare: "Follow this decree because integration is morally right and the Negro is your brother." In the midst of blatant injustices inflicted upon the Negro, I have watched white churchmen stand on the sideline and mouth pious irrelevancies and sanctimonious trivialities. In the midst of a mighty struggle to rid our nation of racial and economic injustice I have heard many ministers say: "Those are social issues, with which the gospel has no real concern." And I have watched many churches commit themselves to a completely otherworldly religion which makes a strange, un-Biblical distinction between body and soul, between the sacred and the secular.

I have traveled the length and breadth of Alabama, Mississippi, and all the other southern states. On sweltering summer days and crisp autumn mornings I have looked at the South's beautiful churches with their lofty spires pointing heavenward. I have beheld the impressive outlines of her massive religious-education buildings. Over and over I have found myself asking: "What kind of people worship here? Who is their God? Where were their voices when the lips of Governor Barnett dripped with words of interposition and nullification? Where were they when Governor Wallace gave a clarion call for defiance and hatred? Where were their voices of support when bruised and weary Negro men and women decided to rise from the dark dungeons of complacency to the bright hills of creative protest?"

Yes, these questions are still in my mind. In deep disappointment I have wept over the laxity of the church. But be assured that my tears have been tears of love. There can be no deep disappointment where there is not deep love. Yes, I love the church. How could I do otherwise? I am in the rather unique position of being the son, the grandson, and the great-grandson of preachers. Yes, I see the church as the body of Christ. But, oh! How we have blemished and scarred that body through social neglect and through fear of being nonconformists.

40   There was a time when the church was very powerful—in the time when the early Christians rejoiced at being deemed worthy to suffer for what they believed. In those days the church was not merely a thermometer that recorded the ideas and principles of popular opinion; it was a thermostat that transformed the mores of society. Whenever the early Christians entered a town, the people in power became disturbed and immediately sought to convict the Christians for being "disturbers of the peace" and "outside agitators." But the Christians pressed on, in the conviction that they were "a colony of heaven," called to obey God rather than man. Small in number, they were big in commitment. They were too God-intoxicated to be "astronomically intimidated." By their effort and example they brought an end to such ancient evils as infanticide and gladiatorial contests.

Things are different now. So often the contemporary church is a weak, ineffectual voice with an uncertain sound. So often it is an archdefender of the status quo. Far from being disturbed by the presence of the church, the power structure of the average community is consoled by the church's silent—and often even vocal—sanction of things as they are.

But the judgment of God is upon the church as never before. If today's church does not recapture the sacrificial spirit of the early church, it will lose its authenticity, forfeit the loyalty of millions, and be dismissed as an irrelevant social club with no meaning for the twentieth century. Every day I meet young people whose disappointment with the church has turned into outright disgust.

Perhaps I have once again been too optimistic. Is organized religion too inextricably bound to the status quo to save our nation and the world? Perhaps I must turn my faith to the inner spiritual church, the church within the church, as the true *ekklesia* and the hope of the world. But again I am thankful to God that some noble souls from the ranks of organized religion have broken loose from the paralyzing chains of conformity and joined us as active partners in the struggle for freedom. They have left their secure congregations and walked the streets of Albany, Georgia, with us. They have gone down the high-ways of the South on tortuous rides for freedom. Yes, they have gone to jail with us. Some have been dismissed from their churches, have lost the support of their bishops and fellow ministers. But they have acted in the faith that right defeated is stronger than evil triumphant. Their witness has been the spiritual salt that has preserved the true meaning of the gospel in these troubled times. They have carved a tunnel of hope through the dark mountain of disappointment.

I hope the church as a whole will meet the challenge of this deci-sive hour. But even if the church does not come to the aid of justice, I have no despair about the future. I have no fear about the outcome of our struggle in Birmingham, even if our motives are at present misun-derstood. We will reach the goal of freedom in Birmingham and all over the nation, because the goal of America is freedom. Abused and scorned though we may be, our destiny is tied up with America's des-tiny. Before the pilgrims landed at Plymouth, we were here. Before the pen of Jefferson etched the majestic words of the Declaration of Independence across the pages of history, we were here. For more than two centuries our forebears labored in this country without wages; they made cotton king; they built the homes of their masters while suffering gross injustice and shameful humiliation—and yet out of a bottomless vitality they continued to thrive and develop. If the in-expressible cruelties of slavery could not stop us, the opposition we now face will surely fail. We will win our freedom because the sacred heritage of our nation and the eternal will of God are embodied in our echoing demands.

45   Before closing I feel impelled to mention one other point in your statement that has troubled me profoundly. You warmly commended the Birmingham police force for keeping "order" and "preventing vi-olence." I doubt that you would have so warmly commended the po-lice force if you had seen its dogs sinking their teeth into unarmed, nonviolent Negroes. I doubt that you would so quickly commend the policemen if you were to observe their ugly and inhumane treatment of Negroes here in the city jail; if you were to watch them push and

curse old Negro women and young Negro girls; if you were to see them slap and kick old Negro men and young boys; if you were to observe them, as they did on two occasions, refuse to give us food because we wanted to sing our grace together. I cannot join you in your praise of the Birmingham police department.

It is true that the police have exercised a degree of discipline in handling the demonstrators. In this sense they have conducted themselves rather "nonviolently" in public. But for what purpose? To preserve the evil system of segregation. Over the past few years I have consistently preached that nonviolence demands that the means we use must be as pure as the ends we seek. I have tried to make clear that it is wrong to use immoral means to attain moral ends. But now I must affirm that it is just as wrong, or perhaps even more so, to use moral means to preserve immoral ends. Perhaps Mr. Connor and his policemen have been rather nonviolent in public, as was Chief Pritchett in Albany, Georgia, but they have used the moral means of nonviolence to maintain the immoral end of racial injustice. T. S. Eliot has said, "The last temptation is the greatest treason: To do the right deed for the wrong reason."

I wish you had commended the Negro sit-inners and demonstrators of Birmingham for their sublime courage, their willingness to suffer, and their amazing discipline in the midst of great provocation. One day the South will recognize its real heroes. They will be the James Merediths, with the noble sense of purpose that enables them to face jeering and hostile mobs, and with the agonizing loneliness that characterizes the life of the pioneer. They will be old, oppressed, battered Negro women, symbolized in a seventy-two-year-old woman in Montgomery, Alabama, who rose up with a sense of dignity and with her people decided not to ride segregated buses, and who responded with ungrammatical profundity to one who inquired about her weariness: "My feets is tired, but my soul is at rest." They will be the young high school and college students, the young ministers of the gospel and a host of their elders, courageously and nonviolently sitting in at lunch counters and willingly going to jail for conscience' sake. One day the South will know that when these disinherited children of God sat down at lunch counters, they were in reality standing up for what is best in the American dream and for the most sacred values in our Judaeo-Christian heritage, thereby bringing our nation back to those great wells of democracy which were dug deep by the founding fathers in their formulation of the Constitution and the Declaration of Independence.

Never before have I written so long a letter. I'm afraid it is much too long to take your precious time. I can assure you that it would have been much shorter if I had been writing from a comfortable desk, but what else can one do when he is alone in a narrow jail cell, other than write long letters, think long thoughts, and pray long prayers?

If I have said anything in this letter that overstates the truth and indicates an unreasonable impatience, I beg you to forgive me. If I have said anything that understates the truth and indicates my having a patience that allows me to settle for anything less than brotherhood, I beg God to forgive me.

50   I hope this letter finds you strong in the faith. I also hope that circumstances will soon make it possible for me to meet each of you, not as an integrationist or a civil-rights leader but as a fellow clergyman and a Christian brother. Let us all hope that the dark clouds of racial prejudice will soon pass away and the deep fog of misunderstanding will be lifted from our fear-drenched communities, and in some not too distant tomorrow the radiant stars of love and brotherhood will shine over our great nation with all their scintillating beauty.

Yours for the cause of Peace and Brotherhood,
MARTIN LUTHER KING, JR.

Analyzing Rhetorical Choices

1. Why would King have chosen the form of a letter for this response rather than asking for a column in the newspaper that had published the "A Call for Unity"? What effect does this have? What might this indicate about King's purpose?

2. Toward the middle of the essay, King writes, "I must make two honest confessions to you . . ." Why does he wait so long to directly address the clergy to whom he writes this letter? What is the effect of this strategy? What aspects of the letter would have changed had King written this first? How?

3. Look carefully at King's choice of words. For instance, what situation does he evoke when he says that in the South, people "live in monologue rather than dialogue"? Why would King say that we must break unjust laws "openly" and "lovingly"? How do choices such as these fit with King's overall strategy for the letter?

4. King makes various religious and other contextual references in the letter. Why? To what effect? What assumptions, then, does King seem to be making about his readers?

Writing About Issues and Contexts

1. Explore the various definitions of *civil disobedience* and the extent to which King's letter exemplifies them. Does King justify his argument that civil disobedience in some cases is justified?

2. What is the difference between a legal responsibility and a moral responsibility?

3. King states, "Oppressed people cannot remain oppressed forever." Assess this statement in terms of your historical knowledge of oppressed people. As part of your response, define the term *oppressed people*.

*One of America's most distinguished architectural critics, **Paul Goldberger** (1950–) graduated from Yale University in 1972. Goldberger was architecture critic and cultural news editor at the* New York Times *for 25 years before becoming chief architecture critic for* The New Yorker *in 1997. A Pulitzer Prize winner in 1984, Goldberger's published works include* The City Observed *(1979),* The Skycraper *(1981), and* Up from Zero *(2004), on the redevelopment of the World Trade Center site. "Building Plans" represents a subtle form of argument at a time when the practical implications of tragedy bring other implications to the fore. It appeared in a special issue of* The New Yorker *devoted entirely to the September 11 attacks and published on September 26, 2001.*

Paul Goldberger

Building Plans: What the World Trade Center Meant

There have been skyscrapers in New York for more than a century, and we are accustomed to seeing the bigger, stronger buildings crowd out the smaller, weaker ones. Height is our most potent architectural currency. The Metropolitan Life campanile reigned once, then the Woolworth Building and, briefly, the Chrysler Building, then the Empire State Building and the World Trade Center towers, those two vertical lines that anchored the composition of the skyline for twenty-five years. The towers were not beautiful buildings. They were gargantuan and banal, blandness blown up to a gigantic size. But size was the point, and the people who stood in line to visit the hundred-and-seventh-floor observation deck or eat at Windows on the World and buy little souvenir snow globes with the towers inside understood this, just as real-estate developers did, and as the terrorists who rammed their planes into the towers last week did.

With the invention of the passenger elevator in the mid-nineteenth century and the steel frame two decades later, an intimate connection was forged between the tallest tower in the city and the biggest corporation, the richest bank, or whatever financial entity wanted to be seen as running the place. Before there were skyscrapers, the horizon in most cities was dominated by church steeples. (In New York, the tallest thing was Richard Upjohn's Trinity Church, built in 1846.) The earliest skyscrapers wrested control of the skyline from God and gave it to Mammon, where it has pretty much remained. In 1913, a fawning minister called the Woolworth Building the "cathedral of commerce," in celebration of the triumph of corporate power that Cass Gilbert's lyrical Gothic skyscraper represented. It is a pretty straight line from the Woolworth Building to the World Trade Center. The architectural dressing changed, but the basic idea of building as high as you could to express power became a convention in almost every city, first in this country and then, by the nineteen-eighties, around the world.

The urge to make buildings higher and higher has been fading for the last few years, for purely practical reasons. Constructing towers of a hundred stories or more isn't much of a challenge technologically today, but it is not particularly economical, either. It never was. The space on the lower floors that is given up to make room for elevator shafts to the upper floors cuts into rentable space. The World Trade Center was a dinosaur in this sense, although the economics of the place got a lot better over time, and just two months ago the Port Authority concluded a deal to lease the towers for $3.2 billion to the developer Larry Silverstein, who then hired David Childs, of Skidmore, Owings & Merrill, to upgrade the complex. Childs has designed several new towers in New York, including the A.O.L. Time Warner Center that is going up at Columbus Circle. Silverstein hoped to fix up the Trade Center's image and turn it into a kind of downtown Rockefeller Center.

The very tallest buildings have usually been put up by people more interested in attention-getting value than in immediate financial return. That was the motivation of Governor Nelson Rockefeller and the Port Authority in the nineteen-sixties, when the World Trade Center was conceived, and it is the motivation for the entrepreneurs who have built or plan to build tall buildings in cities like Shanghai, Hong Kong, and Kuala Lumpur, where the Petronas Towers, the tallest skyscrapers in the world at the moment, were built in 1998. The destruction of the World Trade Center may well put an end to this kind of thing. "I think many of our clients would not want to build such a visible symbol, that they will want to build not so iconic and not so tall, the way the wealthy in Mexico started driving around in Volkswagens instead of Jaguars," David Childs said a few days ago.

5   The Trade Center was structurally innovative. Earlier skyscrapers were supported by complex frames of steel or concrete columns and

beams. Their exteriors were a "curtain wall" of metal, glass, or masonry hung from the frame, and their interiors were broken up by the grid of columns and beams. The Trade Center was more like a vast tube. Its exterior walls were a kind of steel mesh that supported most of the building's structural weight, freeing the interior floors from the usual maze of columns. The architects, Minoru Yamasaki and Emery Roth & Sons, and the engineer, Leslie Robertson, did not invent this tubular system. It was used earlier by Fazlur Khan and Myron Goldsmith, of Skidmore, Owings & Merrill, for an apartment house in Chicago finished in 1965. But the use of it at the Trade Center towers, which at the time of their construction were the tallest buildings in the world, represented an enormous advance. It was part of a tendency toward lightness in the design of almost everything—from cars and telephones to buildings.

Lighter does not mean weaker, of course. The relative lightness of the twin towers compared with, say, the Empire State Building, which has a steel frame and limestone cladding, does not appear to have been a factor in their collapse. Nothing about the design of the buildings seems to be intrinsically at fault. The towers withstood the assaults. They did not fall over, and their tops did not slice off. It was the explosions of the jet fuel that did the buildings in, not the impact of the jetliners themselves, and the buildings did not collapse until some time after the crashes—well over an hour for one tower, just under an hour for the other. Steel softens and melts under tremendous heat—it is, after all, created by the heat of the forge—and it was only a matter of time before the extraordinary heat of the fire would take its toll. The Trade Center was "amazingly robust," said Bill Baker, an engineer at the Skidmore firm who has designed the structural systems for several new skyscrapers. "It took a large commercial jet and the explosion, and it still stood, which is a lot to ask of any building." Fireproofing, Baker explained, "is really just a matter of buying time, and the building did buy time. There was basically an hour and forty minutes, and while a lot of people didn't make it out, a lot of people did."

The structural system of a skyscraper is designed to support the mass of the building itself—so that it does not collapse of its own weight—and to protect it from natural forces such as earthquakes and wind. Wind affects every skyscraper. The taller a building is, the greater the forces of wind pummelling it. Engineers have become so good at handling this that buildings don't fall down and they don't usually sway noticeably, either. But there isn't any building, except maybe the Pyramids, that could withstand the consequences of an enormous jetliner smashing into it with a full load of fuel. "You can't design for that, just like you can't design for the epicenter of an earthquake," David Childs said. William Pedersen, of Kohn Pedersen Fox, the architect of the new financial center planned for Shanghai, which would be slightly taller than the towers in Kuala Lumpur, says that when his firm was designing that building, there were no discussions of planes fully loaded with fuel flying into it. "If there is a physical way to protect a building from this, which I doubt, it would be prohibitive in cost, and the natural light would disappear."

Architecture doesn't usually work symbolically until it has been around for a while. The Woolworth Building went up less than a decade after the Wright Brothers took their first flight at Kitty Hawk. It still stands, just a few blocks to the east of the site of the World Trade Center, and it looked tiny in the televised shots of lower Manhattan last week, a delicate, dignified artifact.

Many of our greatest urban symbols achieve their meaning by connecting monumentality with the business of everyday life. Unlike cities such as Washington, D.C., New York has few pure monuments, with no purpose other than to inspire. There is the Statue of Liberty, but almost every other symbol of New York combines architectural ambition with the prosaic. People drive and walk across the Brooklyn Bridge every day. They ride their bicycles in Central Park, they board trains at Grand Central, and they go to work in Rockefeller Center or the Empire State Building. The Eiffel Tower is vastly more beautiful than the Trade Center was—so, for that matter, is the Empire State Building—but it is not part of life in Paris in quite the same way that the skyscrapers are part of life in New York. When the Eiffel Tower was built, a gaggle of artists and writers protested that it had nothing to do with Paris. No one could make that point about our skyscrapers. They were part of the city's essence from the day they went up.

10   We count on our urban symbols to be present. They are not supposed to evaporate. When buildings go away, they go almost as slowly as they came, piece by piece. The architect Cesar Pelli estimates that if the World Trade Center had been demolished conventionally it would have taken two years to dismantle. Pelli, who designed the World Financial Center, four squat towers next to the Trade Center, said to me that he thought of his buildings as "a set of foothills beside the mountain, and now the mountain is gone." It was an enormous familiar presence. As the years passed, it seemed to take on the quality of a huge piece of minimalist sculpture, and its dullness

was almost a virtue. Now that the Trade Center has become a martyr to terrorism, I suspect that architectural criticism of it will cease altogether. It has become a noble monument of a lost past. It is no more possible to know what will replace it as a symbol than it is to know what, if anything, will be built someday where the towers stood. But when the biggest thing in a city that prizes bigness becomes the most fragile thing, and the void has more weight than the solid, the rules of city-building change.

Analyzing Rhetorical Choices

1. How does Goldberger use expert testimony to reinforce and support his argument? Evaluate the effectiveness of this strategy.

2. Analyze and comment on Goldberger's use of examples—particularly as they relate to architectural history and the Twin Towers themselves. What purposes do these details serve?

3. Comment on Goldberger's rather matter-of-fact tone and largely straightforward declarative sentences. Does this style diminish or enhance the implications of his essay? What effects does his tone have on this subject?

Writing About Issues and Contexts

1. How does Goldberger communicate the larger and symbolic value of the World Trade Center? For what purpose?

2. Comment on Goldberger's statement that the Trade Center "seemed to take on the quality of a huge piece of minimalist sculpture, and its dullness was almost a virtue," contrasted with its having "become a martyr to terrorism." How does this essay move beyond the architectural details it provides?

3. Goldberger writes, "We count on our urban symbols to be present. They are not supposed to evaporate." What might be the implications of this statement—that is, beyond architecture?

Although very much a political feminist, **Camille Paglia** *(1947–) inspires controversy with her outspoken challenges and critiques of feminism. Born in upstate New York and educated at the State University of New York at Binghamton and Yale, Paglia has published several books, including* Sexual Personae: Art and Decadence from Nefertiti to Emily Dickinson *(1990), her best-selling scholarly work;* Sex, Art, and American Culture *(1992), from which the following essay is taken;* Vamps and Tramps *(1994); a book analyzing Alfred Hitchcock's* The Birds *(1998); and most recently,* Break, Blow, Burn: Camille Paglia Reads Forty-three of the World's Best Poems *(2005). "It's a Jungle Out There" appeared first in* Newsday, *a Long Island, New York, newspaper.*

Camille Paglia

It's a Jungle Out There

Rape is an outrage that cannot be tolerated in civilized society. Yet feminism, which has waged a crusade for rape to be taken more seriously, has put young women in danger by hiding the truth about sex from them.

In dramatizing the pervasiveness of rape, feminists have told young women that before they have sex with a man, they must give consent as explicit as a legal contract's. In this way, young women have been convinced that they have been the victims of rape. On elite campuses in the Northeast and on the West Coast, they have held consciousness-raising sessions, petitioned administrations, demanded inquests. At Brown University, outraged, panicky "victims" have scrawled the names of alleged attackers on the walls of women's rest rooms. What marital rape was to the '70s, "date rape" is to the '90s.

The incidence and seriousness of rape do not require this kind of exaggeration. Real acquaintance rape is nothing new. It has been a horrible problem for women for all of recorded history. Once fathers and brothers protected women from rape. Once the penalty for rape was death. I come from a fierce Italian tradition where, not so long ago in the motherland, a rapist would end up knifed, castrated, and hung out to dry.

But the old clans and small rural communities have broken down. In our cities, on our campuses far from home, young women are vulnerable and defenseless. Feminism has not prepared them for this.

Feminism keeps saying the sexes are the same. It keeps telling women they can do anything, go anywhere, say anything, wear anything. No, they can't. Women will always be in sexual danger.

5 One of my male students recently slept overnight with a friend in a passageway of the Great Pyramid in Egypt. He described the moon and sand, the ancient silence and eerie echoes. I will never experience that. I am a woman. I am not stupid enough to believe I could ever be safe there. There is a world of solitary adventure I will never have. Women have always known these somber truths. But feminism, with its pie-in-the-sky fantasies about the perfect world, keeps young women from seeing life as it is.

We must remedy social injustice whenever we can. But there are some things we cannot change. There are sexual differences that are based in biology. Academic feminism is lost in a fog of social constructionism. It believes we are totally the product of our environment. This idea was invented by Rousseau. He was wrong. Emboldened by dumb French language theory, academic feminists repeat the same hollow slogans over and over to each other. Their view of sex is naive and prudish. Leaving sex to the feminists is like letting your dog vacation at the taxidermist's.

The sexes are at war. Men must struggle for identity against the overwhelming power of their mothers. Women have menstruation to tell them they are women. Men must do or risk something to be men. Men become masculine only when other men say they are. Having sex with a woman is one way a boy becomes a man.

College men are at their hormonal peak. They have just left their mothers and are questing for their male identity. In groups, they are dangerous. A woman going to a fraternity party is walking into Testosterone Flats, full of prickly cacti and blazing guns. If she goes, she should be armed with resolute alertness. She should arrive with girlfriends and leave with them. A girl who lets herself get dead drunk at a fraternity party is a fool. A girl who goes upstairs alone with a brother at a fraternity party is an idiot. Feminists call this "blaming the victim." I call it common sense.

For a decade, feminists have drilled their disciples to say, "Rape is a crime of violence but not of sex." This sugar-coated Shirley Temple nonsense has exposed young women to disaster. Misled by feminism, they do not expect rape from the nice boys from good homes who sit next to them in class.

10 Aggression and eroticism are deeply intertwined. Hunt, pursuit, and capture are biologically programmed into male sexuality. Generation

after generation, men must be educated, refined, and ethically persuaded away from their tendency toward anarchy and brutishness. Society is not the enemy, as feminism ignorantly claims. Society is woman's protection against rape. Feminism, with its solemn Carry Nation repressiveness, does not see what is for men the eroticism or fun element in rape, especially the wild, infectious delirium of gang rape. Women who do not understand rape cannot defend themselves against it.

The date-rape controversy shows feminism hitting the wall of its own broken promises. The women of my '60s generation were the first respectable girls in history to swear like sailors, get drunk, stay out all night—in short, to act like men. We sought total sexual freedom and equality. But as time passed, we woke up to cold reality. The old double standard protected women. When anything goes, it's women who lose.

Today's young women don't know what they want. They see that feminism has not brought sexual happiness. The theatrics of public rage over date rape are their way of restoring the old sexual rules that were shattered by my generation. Because nothing about the sexes has really changed. The comic film *Where the Boys Are* (1960), the ultimate expression of '50s man-chasing, still speaks directly to our time. It shows smart, lively women skillfully anticipating and fending off the dozens of strategies with which horny men try to get them into bed. The agonizing date-rape subplot and climax are brilliantly done. The victim, Yvette Mimieux, makes mistake after mistake, obvious to the other girls. She allows herself to be lured away from her girlfriends and into isolation with boys whose character and intentions she misreads. *Where the Boys Are* tells the truth. It shows courtship as a dangerous game in which the signals are not verbal but subliminal.

Neither militant feminism, which is obsessed with politically correct language, nor academic feminism, which believes that knowledge and experience are "constituted by" language, can understand preverbal or non-verbal communication. Feminism, focusing on sexual politics, cannot see that sex exists in and through the body. Sexual desire and arousal cannot be fully translated into verbal terms. This is why men and women misunderstand each other.

Trying to remake the future, feminism cut itself off from sexual history. It discarded and suppressed the sexual myths of literature, art, and religion. Those myths show us the turbulence, the mysteries and passions of sex. In mythology we see men's sexual anxiety, their fear of women's dominance. Much sexual violence is rooted in men's sense of psychological weakness toward women. It takes many men to deal with one woman. Woman's voracity is a persistent motif.

Clara Bow, it was rumored, took on the USC football team on weekends. Marilyn Monroe, singing "Diamonds Are a Girl's Best Friend," rules a conga line of men in tuxes. Half-clad Cher, in the video for "If I Could Turn Back Time," deranges a battleship of screaming sailors and straddles a pink-lit cannon. Feminism, coveting social power, is blind to woman's cosmic sexual power.

15   To understand rape, you must study the past. There never was and never will be sexual harmony. Every woman must take personal responsibility for her sexuality, which is nature's red flame. She must be prudent and cautious about where she goes and with whom. When she makes a mistake, she must accept the consequences and, through self-criticism, resolve never to make that mistake again. Running to Mommy and Daddy or the campus grievance committee is unworthy of strong women. Posting lists of guilty men in the toilet is cowardly, infantile stuff.

The Italian philosophy of life espouses high-energy confrontation. A male student makes a vulgar remark about your breasts? Don't slink off to whimper and simper with the campus shrinking violets. Deal with it. On the spot. Say, "Shut up, you jerk! And crawl back to the barnyard where you belong!" In general, women who project this take-charge attitude toward life get harassed less often. I see too many dopey, immature, self-pitying women walking around like melting sticks of butter. It's the Yvette Mimieux syndrome: Make me happy. And listen to me weep when I'm not.

The date-rape debate is already smothering in propaganda churned out by the expensive Northeastern colleges and universities, with their overconcentration of boring, uptight academic feminists and spoiled, affluent students. Beware of the deep manipulativeness of rich students who were neglected by their parents. They love to turn the campus into hysterical psychodramas of sexual transgression, followed by assertions of parental authority and concern. And don't look for sexual enlightenment from academe, which spews out mountains of books but never looks at life directly.

As a fan of football and rock music, I see in the simple, swaggering masculinity of the jock and in the noisy posturing of the heavy-metal guitarist certain fundamental, unchanging truths about sex. Masculinity is aggressive, unstable, combustible. It is also the most creative cultural force in history. Women must reorient themselves toward the elemental powers of sex, which can strengthen or destroy.

The only solution to date rape is female self-awareness and self-control. A woman's number one line of defense is herself. When a real rape occurs, she should report it to the police. Complaining to college committees because the courts "take too long" is ridiculous. College administrations are not a branch of the judiciary. They are not equipped or trained for legal inquiry. Colleges must alert incoming students to the problems and dangers of adulthood. Then colleges must stand back and get out of the sex game.

Analyzing Rhetorical Choices

1. How would you describe Paglia's "voice"? Cite several passages in which you clearly identify this voice, and describe how it affects you as a reader.

2. How effective are Paglia's ways of backing up her central argument, which intertwines a critique of feminism with outrage against rape? Which strategies are more effective than others? Are her arguments complete? Reductive? Effective, despite any shortcomings?

3. Paglia's argument is both forthright and humorous. How so? How might she infuriate some and enlighten or educate others?

Writing About Issues and Contexts

1. If you are not familiar with them, look up Paglia's various references. What is the usefulness of her references to popular culture and historical and literary figures? How do they add to or detract from her argument?

2. Is Paglia correct that academic feminists are emboldened by "dumb French language theory"? That feminists have "drilled their disciples to say, 'Rape is a crime of violence but not of sex'"? What research would you need to do to determine the validity of these statements?

3. What is your response to Paglia's description of college men? How much of her argument depends on the accuracy of this depiction?

*Lani Guinier (1950–) has written extensively on issues related to civil
rights. Her work led President Bill Clinton to nominate her in 1993 for
the post of assistant attorney general for civil rights. Conservative politicians attacked her ideas, and, in the eyes of many, misinterpreted her legal writing, leading to Clinton's withdrawal of her nomination. Since
then, Guinier has authored several books, including* The Tyranny of the
Majority: Fundamental Fairness in Representative Democracy *(1994),
from which this excerpt is taken. The book outlines Guinier's proposals
for ensuring fairness in voting and governing processes, a stance inspired
in part by the work of John Stuart Mill. In 1998, she published* Lift
Every Voice: Turning a Civil Rights Setback into a New Vision of Social
Justice, *in which she discusses her unsuccessful nomination. Guinier is
considered by many to be a "scholar and activist of unparalleled stature
in the field of civil rights."*

Lani Guinier

The Tyranny of the Majority

I have always wanted to be a civil rights lawyer. This lifelong ambition is based on a deep-seated commitment to democratic fair
play—to playing by the rules as long as the rules are fair. When the
rules seem unfair, I have worked to change them, not subvert them.
When I was eight years old, I was a Brownie. I was especially proud
of my uniform, which represented a commitment to good citizenship
and good deeds. But one day, when my Brownie group staged a hat-
making contest, I realized that uniforms are only as honorable as the
people who wear them. The contest was rigged. The winner was assisted by her milliner mother, who actually made the winning entry in
full view of all the participants. At the time, I was too young to be
able to change the rules, but I was old enough to resign, which I
promptly did.

To me, fair play means that the rules encourage everyone to play.
They should reward those who win, but they must be acceptable to
those who lose. The central theme of my academic writing is that not
all rules lead to elemental fair play. Some even commonplace rules
work against it.

The professional milliner competing with amateur Brownies stands as an example of rules that are patently rigged or patently subverted. Yet, sometimes, even when rules are perfectly fair in form, they serve in practice to exclude particular groups from meaningful participation. When they do not encourage everyone to play, or when, over the long haul, they do not make the losers feel as good about the outcomes as the winners, they can seem as unfair as the milliner who makes the winning hat for her daughter.

Sometimes, too, we construct rules that force us to be divided into winners and losers when we might have otherwise joined together. This idea was cogently expressed by my son, Nikolas, when he was four years old, far exceeding the thoughtfulness of his mother when she was an eight-year-old Brownie. While I was writing one of my law journal articles, Nikolas and I had a conversation about voting prompted by a *Sesame Street Magazine* exercise. The magazine pictured six children: four children had raised their hands because they wanted to play tag; two had their hands down because they wanted to play hide-and-seek. The magazine asked its readers to count the number of children whose hands were raised and then decide what game the children would play.

5   Nikolas quite realistically replied, "They will play both. First they will play tag. Then they will play hide-and-seek." Despite the magazine's "rules," he was right. To children, it is natural to take turns. The winner may get to play first or more often, but even the "loser" gets something. His was a positive-sum solution that many adult rulemakers ignore.

The traditional answer to the magazine's problem would have been a zero-sum solution: "The children—all the children—will play tag, and only tag." As a zero-sum solution, everything is seen in terms of "I win; you lose." The conventional answer relies on winner-take-all majority rule, in which the tag players, as the majority, win the right to decide for all the children what game to play. The hide-and-seek preference becomes irrelevant. The numerically more powerful majority choice simply subsumes minority preferences.

In the conventional case, the majority that rules gains all the power and the minority that loses gets none. For example, two years ago Brother Rice High School in Chicago held two senior proms. It was not planned that way. The prom committee at Brother Rice, a boys' Catholic high school, expected just one prom when it hired a disc jockey, picked a rock band, and selected music for the prom by consulting student preferences. Each senior was asked to list his three favorite songs, and the band would play the songs that appeared most frequently on the lists.

Seems attractively democratic. But Brother Rice is predominantly white, and the prom committee was all white. That's how they got two proms. The black seniors at Brother Rice felt so shut out by the "democratic process" that they organized their own prom. As one black student put it: "For every vote we had, there were eight votes for what they wanted. . . .[W]ith us being in the minority we're always outvoted. It's as if we don't count."

Some embittered white seniors saw things differently. They complained that the black students should have gone along with the majority: "The majority makes a decision. That's the way it works."

10   In a way, both groups were right. From the white students' perspective, this was ordinary decisionmaking. To the black students, majority rule sent the message: "we don't count" is the "way it works" for minorities. In a racially divided society, majority rule may be perceived as majority tyranny.

That is a large claim, and I do not rest my case for it solely on the actions of the prom committee in one Chicago high school. To expand the range of the argument, I first consider the ideal of majority rule itself, particularly as reflected in the writings of James Madison and other founding members of our Republic. These early democrats explored the relationship between majority rule and democracy. James Madison warned, "If a majority be united by a common interest, the rights of the minority will be insecure." The tyranny of the majority, according to Madison, requires safeguards to protect "one part of the society against the injustice of the other part."

For Madison, majority tyranny represented the great danger to our early constitutional democracy. Although the American revolution was fought against the tyranny of the British monarch, it soon became clear that there was another tyranny to be avoided. The accumulations of all powers in the same hands, Madison warned, "whether of one, a few, or many, and whether hereditary, self-appointed, or elective, may justly be pronounced the very definition of tyranny."

As another columnist suggested in papers published in Philadelphia, "We have been so long habituated to a jealousy of tyranny from monarchy and aristocracy, that we have yet to learn the dangers of it from democracy." Despotism had to be opposed "whether it came from Kings, Lords or the people."

The debate about majority tyranny reflected Madison's concern that the majority may not represent the whole. In a homogeneous society, the interest of the majority would likely be that of the minority also. But in a heterogeneous community, the majority may not represent all competing interests. The majority is likely to be self-interested and ignorant or indifferent to the concerns of the minority. In such case, Madison observed, the assumption that the majority represents the minority is "altogether fictitious."

15   Yet even a self-interested majority can govern fairly if it cooperates with the minority. One reason for such cooperation is that the self-interested majority values the principle of reciprocity. The self-interested majority worries that the minority may attract defectors from the majority and become the next governing majority. The Golden Rule principle of reciprocity functions to check the tendency of a self-interested majority to act tyrannically.

So the argument for the majority principle connects it with the value of reciprocity: You cooperate when you lose in part because members of the current majority will cooperate when they lose. The conventional case for the fairness of majority rule is that it is not really the rule of a fixed group—The Majority—on all issues; instead it is the rule of shifting majorities, as the losers at one time or on one issue join with others and become part of the governing coalition at another time or on another issue. The result will be a fair system of mutually beneficial cooperation. I call a majority that rules but does not dominate a Madisonian Majority.

The problem of majority tyranny arises, however, when the self-interested majority does not need to worry about defections. When the majority is fixed and permanent, there are no checks on its ability to be overbearing. A majority that does not worry about defectors is a majority with total power.

In such a case, Madison's concern about majority tyranny arises. In a heterogeneous community, any faction with total power might subject "the minority to the caprice and arbitrary decisions of the majority, who instead of consulting the interest of the whole community collectively, attend sometimes to partial and local advantages."

"What remedy can be found in a republican Government, where the majority must ultimately decide," argued Madison, but to ensure "that no one common interest or passion will be likely to unite a majority of the whole number in an unjust pursuit." The answer was to disaggregate the majority to ensure checks and balances or fluid, rotating interests. The minority needed protection against an overbearing majority, so that "a common sentiment is less likely to be felt, and the requisite concert less likely to be formed, by a majority of the whole."

20   Political struggles would not be simply a contest between rulers and people; the political struggles would be among the people themselves. The work of government was not to transcend different interests but to reconcile them. In an ideal democracy, the people would rule, but the minorities would also be protected against the power of majorities. Again, where the rules of decisionmaking protect the minority, the Madisonian Majority rules without dominating.

But if a group is unfairly treated, for example, when it forms a racial minority, *and* if the problems of unfairness are not cured by conventional assumptions about majority rule, then what is to be done? The answer is that we may need an *alternative* to winner-take-all majoritarianism. In this book, a collection of my law review articles, I describe the alternative, which, with Nikolas's help, I now call the "principle of taking turns." In a racially divided society, this principle does better than simple majority rule if it accommodates the values of self-government, fairness, deliberation, compromise, and consensus that lie at the heart of the democratic ideal.

In my legal writing, I follow the caveat of James Madison and other early American democrats. I explore decisionmaking rules that might work in a multi-racial society to ensure that majority rule does not become majority tyranny. I pursue voting systems that might disaggregate The Majority so that it does not exercise power unfairly or tyrannically. I aspire to a more cooperative political style of decisionmaking to enable all of the students at Brother Rice to feel comfortable attending the same prom. In looking to create Madisonian Majorities, I pursue a positive-sum, taking-turns solution.

Structuring decisionmaking to allow the minority "a turn" may be necessary to restore the reciprocity ideal when a fixed majority refuses to cooperate with the minority. If the fixed majority loses its incentive to follow the Golden Rule principle of shifting majorities, the minority never gets to take a turn. Giving the minority a turn does not mean the minority gets to rule; what it does mean is that the minority gets to influence decisionmaking and the majority rules more legitimately.

Instead of automatically rewarding the preferences of the monolithic majority, a taking-turns approach anticipates that the majority rules, but is not overbearing. Because those with 51 percent of the votes are not assured 100 percent of the power, the majority cooperates with, or at least does not tyrannize, the minority.

25   The sports analogy of "I win; you lose" competition within a political hierarchy makes sense when only one team can win; Nikolas's intuition that it is often possible to take turns suggests an alternative

approach. Take family decisionmaking, for example. It utilizes a taking-turns approach. When parents sit around the kitchen table deciding on a vacation destination or activities for a rainy day, often they do not simply rely on a show of hands, especially if that means that the older children always prevail or if affinity groups among the children (those who prefer movies to video games, or those who prefer baseball to playing cards) never get to play their activity of choice. Instead of allowing the majority simply to rule, the parents may propose that everyone takes turns, going to the movies one night and playing video games the next. Or as Nikolas proposes, they might do both on a given night.

Taking turns attempts to build consensus while recognizing political or social differences, and it encourages everyone to play. The taking-turns approach gives those with the most support more turns, but it also legitimates the outcome from each individual's perspective, including those whose views are shared only by a minority.

In the end, I do not believe that democracy should encourage rule by the powerful—even a powerful majority. Instead, the idea of democracy promises a fair discussion among self-defined equals about how to achieve our common aspirations. To redeem that promise, we need to put the idea of taking turns and disaggregating the majority at the center of our conception of representation. Particularly as we move into the twenty-first century as a more highly diversified citizenry, it is essential that we consider the ways in which voting and representational systems succeed or fail at encouraging Madisonian Majorities.

To use Nikolas's terminology, "it is no fair" if a fixed, tyrannical majority excludes or alienates the minority. It is no fair if a fixed, tyrannical majority monopolizes all the power all the time. It is no fair if we engage in the periodic ritual of elections, but only the permanent majority gets to choose who is elected. Where we have tyranny by The Majority, we do not have genuine democracy.

Analyzing Rhetorical Choices

1. Why does Guinier choose to begin her essay as she does, with a personal story? What effect does this have?
2. Why does Guinier alternate other personal stories with her theoretical argument? For what purpose? In what ways is the anecdote about her son Nikolas effective or ineffective as a means of conveying her argument?

3. In what ways can you guess, by her prose style and method of arguing, that Guinier has a legal background?

Writing About Issues and Contexts

1. What is Guinier saying about the ways in which "we construct rules that force us to be divided into winners and losers when we might have otherwise joined together"?
2. After describing the episode at Brother Rice High School, Guinier writes, "In a way, both groups were right." How is this possible?
3. What is Guinier's "positive-sum, taking-turns" approach? How does it tie together the personal stories and legal sources she uses in delineating her argument? To what effect?

The great-great-grandson of famed evolutionist Charles Darwin,
Matthew Chapman *(1950–) was born in England and now resides in
the United States. A Hollywood screenwriter with the movie* Runaway
Jury *among his credits, Chapman is also the author of* Trials of the
Monkey *(2001), which is a highly personal, idiosyncratic excursion
through his life and actions as he confronts issues of faith, love, alcoholism, and self-fulfillment. Salon, which affectionately describes
Chapman as boozy and girl-crazy early in the book, has stated about*
Trials of the Monkey: *"With keen observation, self-deprecating humor
and a confessional style that boils away the sentimental fat, Chapman
has managed to create an unconventional memoir of the collision between his weighty legacy and his quixotic life."*

Matthew Chapman
God or Gorilla

In the case of *Kitzmiller* v. *Dover Area School District*, eleven
parents sued to remove intelligent design from the curriculum. The
defendants brought in some of the leading lights in the intelligent design movement to defend it as science and elucidate the gaps in evolution. The plaintiffs brought in experts on evolution to explain it and
refute intelligent design.

That's the basic story, but if you think you know everything there
is to know about this, you are wrong. Only I know the truth.

Dover lies a mere thirty miles from the Three Mile Island nuclear
plant, and the meltdown of its core and subsequent leak in the
Seventies is responsible for the weird behavior now seen in the locals.

I have no evidence for this belief, and my lack of evidence is a
matter of pride.

5   Having said that, I suppose I should declare my bias at the start.
My great-great-grandfather was Charles Darwin. This was not something I thought much about growing up in England. Evolution was
fully accepted. Darwin was a historical figure. If I did think about my
connection to him, it was only negatively. The pressure to succeed academically and the unlikeliness of doing so in comparison to my ancestor was such that I decided to turn my back on academia and pursue a
course of willful ignorance. When I finally moved to Hollywood in the
early Eighties, I had gone about as far as I could in that direction.

I then discovered that many Americans not only rejected the theory of evolution; they reviled it. I had come here in part because I never felt comfortable in England. I hated the snobbery and thought of America as being less weighed down by its past, more advanced. Sir Francis Drake might have been the first man to sail around the world, but it was an American who first set foot on the moon. Now here I was in the New World faced with a willful ignorance that went far beyond anything I had ever attempted.

True, I did not know much about evolution, but a quick study of the subject showed that 99 percent of scientists believed in it. Why would one doubt them? Did the pedestrian question the theory of gravity? Did the farmer who went to the doctor question his diagnosis? Why in this one area of science did nonexperts feel compelled to disagree with those who clearly knew better?

Dover's population, with an influx of people who commute to nearby towns, is approaching 2,000. The Dover Area School District, however, covers a largely rural population of about 24,000, and Dover Senior High School has about 1,000 students.

In June of 2004, reporters Joe Maldonado and Heidi Bernhard-Bubb, working respectively for the *York Daily Record* and the *York Dispatch*, covered a school board meeting in Dover. Under consideration was a new edition of *Biology: The Living Science*, by Kenneth Miller and Joseph Levine. The chair of the curriculum committee was Bill Buckingham, an ex-cop and corrections officer and self-confessed OxyContin addict. According to Joe and Heidi, he told the meeting that he was disinclined to purchase the book because it was "laced with Darwinism." He went on to say, again according to the reporters, that "it's inexcusable to teach from a book that says man descended from apes and monkeys." The separation of church and state, he continued, was "mythical," and he wanted a book that included views of creationism as well as evolution. When asked after the meeting what consideration he intended to give to other religions, he said, "This country wasn't founded on Muslim beliefs or evolution. This country was founded on Christianity, and our students should be taught as such."

10   The following Monday, at another meeting, Buckingham apologized for his comments but went on to grumble that "liberals in black robes" were taking away the rights of Christians. Bill, who, from the record, seemed to be alternately menacing and self-pityingly apologetic, finally cried out, "Two thousand years ago someone died on a cross! Can't someone take a stand for him?" Fellow creationist and

school board president Alan Bonsell, owner of a nearby radiator and auto-repair shop, supported Buckingham's ideas in a more reasonable tone, and conflict ensued. There were accusations of atheism and un-Americanism, and many tears were shed.

But Buckingham and Bonsell were undeterred and soon fixed on the intelligent design screed *Of Pandas and People* as the book they wanted the ninth-grade students to have in order to get some "balance" in their science education. There were votes and more votes (and more tears), and finally *Pandas* was voted out. But someone still wanted the book to be available to the students, and an anonymous donation of sixty books was made to the Dover High library.

It was eventually agreed that a statement would be read to the ninth-grade science students before they began studying evolution that read in part:

> Because Darwin's Theory is a theory, it continues to be tested as new evidence is discovered. The Theory is not a fact. Gaps in the Theory exist for which there is no evidence. A theory is defined as a well-tested explanation that unifies a broad range of observations.
>
> Intelligent Design is an explanation of the origin of life that differs from Darwin's view. The reference book, *Of Pandas and People*, is available for students who might be interested in gaining an understanding of what Intelligent Design actually involves.

The science teachers refused to read this, so Superintendent Richard Nilsen and Assistant Superintendent Mike Baksa went from classroom to classroom and made sure every ninth grader got to hear it.

On December 14, 2004, eleven Dover parents, represented by the Pennsylvania ACLU, Americans United for Separation of Church and State, and the powerful Philadelphia law firm Pepper Hamilton, filed suit in Federal District Court in Harrisburg.

15 The Comfort Inn, where I stayed during the six weeks of the trial, is in downtown Harrisburg. It overlooks the Susquehanna River and a series of beautiful bridges that cross it. A cooling breeze blows off the river but never enters the hotel. The windows are sealed shut. Your climatic choices are limited to Off, Fan, Low Heat, High Heat, Low Cool, and High Cool. This became, to my mind, a perfect metaphor for the debate.

The case was a civil suit without a jury, so members of the press were given the jury box to sit in. Placed on one side of the modern courtroom, these were the best seats in the house, comfortable leather chairs affording great views of a screen upon which exhibits would be displayed. To our left was the witness box, and beyond it, the bench occupied by Judge John E. Jones III, a good-looking man of fifty. In front of him sat the clerk of the court and the stenographer. Right in front of us was the lectern from which the lawyers asked their questions. To our right were the spectators in the back of the court on two rows of uncomfortable wooden pews.

The plaintiffs made their case first. Seeking to keep the judge—a Bush appointee—engaged, both sides cut back and forth between the loftier theses and the human beings who drove them.

During the first two days of the trial, for example, Ken Miller, a professor of biology at Brown University, co-author of the biology textbook now used at Dover High, and an expert on "the coupling factor on the thylakoid membrane," was followed by office manager Tammy Kitzmiller, a pretty, divorced mother of two, whose name was attached to the suit because one of her daughters was actually in the ninth grade.

I eventually got to meet Tammy and her teenage daughters. The daughters had numerous piercings in their ears. Tammy had a belly ring. I did not interview Ken Miller, but I suspect he does not have any piercings; however, if you read his testimony (available on the National Center for Science Education website), you'll get a pretty good overview of the nature and function of science. Like many of the plaintiffs' witnesses, Miller, a practicing Catholic, had no trouble believing in both evolution and God.

20   On the third day of testimony, Robert Pennock took the stand and was questioned by Eric Rothschild, the lead attorney for the plaintiffs. Rothschild is a man in his late thirties with a balding head shaved close. He has a deceptively cherubic face; but it's a dark face too, with the air of someone keeping a secret. One might imagine that as a geeky child he had encountered some bullying and was not about to let it continue into adulthood.

Pennock, an enthusiastic man with a beard, is a professor at Michigan State University. He has a B.A. in biology and philosophy and a Ph.D. in the history and philosophy of science. His primary appointment is in the College of Natural Sciences, but he's also in the Department of Philosophy, the College of Engineering, the Computer Science and Engineering Department, and the Graduate Program in Ecology, Evolutionary Biology, and Behavior.

He spoke of how evolution is "a great exemplar of the scientific method. It's a well-confirmed interlinked series of hypotheses," and is useful not just in and of itself but as a way of learning how to think. "One needs to know it with regard to medicine, and even with regard to engineering applications. . . . So there's practical applications to evolution right now. You can get a job at Google if you know something about evolution."

We next received a lesson on the history of methodological naturalism, going back as far as Hippocrates, who refused to see epilepsy, then known as "the sacred disease," as divine possession but instead looked for natural causes.

This was followed by a critique of intelligent design with particular attention to William Dembski, a big cog in the movement. Pennock read from an article of Dembski's entitled "What Every Theologian Should Know About Creation, Evolution, and Design":

> The view that science must be restricted solely to purposeless naturalistic material processes also has a name. It's called methodological naturalism. So long as methodological naturalism sets the ground rules for how the game of science is played, IDT has no chance.

25   And later:

> In the words of Vladimir Lenin, "What is to be done?" Design theorists aren't at all bashful about answering this question. The ground rules of science have to be changed.

Rothschild paused a moment and then said, "And I have to admit I didn't know until I read that that Vladimir Lenin was part of the intelligent design movement, but putting that aside . . ."

Soon after this, he received an Internet proposal of marriage.

Pennock's cross-examination was by a man named Patrick Gillen, of the Thomas More Law Center, which had offered its services pro bono for the defense. This seemed like a logical inconsistency from the start. Run by Richard Thompson, a Catholic and former Michigan prosecuting attorney who made a name for himself by trying to put Jack Kevorkian in prison, its stated mission is "Defending the Religious Freedom of Christians," "Restoring Time-honored Family Values," and "Protecting the Sanctity of Life," which, as a biblical literalist myself, I take to mean defending such freedoms as the biblically mandated right to capture women in battle, shave their heads, lock them up for a month, rape them into matrimony (Deuteronomy 21:10), and then deny them the right to an abortion afterward.

All well and good, but if the defense thesis was that intelligent design was merely another scientific theory, what were these Catholic activists doing in court?

30 One of my chief defects is an inability to hate people I violently disagree with once I get to know them. In Gillen's case, my sympathy was ignited by the contrasts in his face. A tallish man in his mid-thirties, with a long head topped with thinning hair, he had excellent teeth, revealed frequently in a blazing grin; but from the middle of his nose up, he wore an expression of extreme anxiety, his brows furrowed, his eyes filled with concern.

Before getting into Gillen's cross of Pennock, I should paint a brief portrait of the two legal teams.

On the plaintiffs' side, apart from Rothschild, a lawyer who up until now had spent most of his life in the corporate environment of reinsurance law, was another lawyer from Pepper Hamilton, Stephen Harvey. The third lawyer, Witold "Vic" Walczak, was from the ACLU. Now and then another lawyer from Pepper Hamilton, Thomas Schmidt, was used to cross-examine defense witnesses who were so clearly feeble-minded or old that the sharp-elbowed style of the other three might actually render them unconscious.

Lending intellectual heft to this legal phalanx were Katskee and Matzke. Richard Katskee, a lawyer from Americans United for Separation of Church and State, was an expert in constitutional law. Nick Matzke, from the National Center for Science Education, provided the science.

But the team did not end here. There were two legal assistants and the unsung hero of the plaintiffs' case, Matthew McElvenny, Technology Specialist, the faultless Wizard of Oz whose computer held all the necessary exhibits—drawings of bacteria, excerpts from books and articles, depositions, even news video—and projected them up on the screen.

35 As anyone will tell you who has covered a trial, sleep is the slyest and most persistent enemy, but when the Wizard of Oz was on, highlighting and scrolling without a single mistake, one inevitably perked up.

Here then was a team of highly skilled professionals operating in an atmosphere of frictionless amiability. Here was a collegiate machine.

On the defense side, one was reminded more of a dysfunctional family with a frequently absent father.

Richard Thompson, who, in profile at least, bore an uncanny resemblance to William Jennings Bryan, was the star, and it was hard to imagine that any case in the history of his Thomas More Law Center had ever been as important as this one. For the first few days, he attended court dutifully, once or twice cross-examining a witness in an odd combative style, often turning toward the jury box (filled with an unsympathetic jury of reporters), then turning back to point his finger at a witness to ask a question whose substance seemed to bear no relationship to the tone in which it was asked. Then he would sit down and rock back and forth in his chair, staring up at the ceiling as if contemplating weightier matters—and then he'd disappear for a week.

Next among the defendants' lawyers—though some say first among them—was Robert Muise. He is a tall, sturdy man, quietly resolute, with a faint Boston accent. Always willing to talk, as unfailingly polite as Gillen and Thompson, he seemed to be a tough guy underneath but worn down, becoming a victim. Perhaps this had nothing to do with politics and religion: he and Gillen, though both only in their late thirties or early forties, had seventeen kids between them, one nine, the other eight. Thompson, perhaps too busy pursuing Doctor Death, had produced a scant three.

40   For a while there was a legal assistant, but she went the way of Thompson. Sometimes it was nine against one, Gillen alone, smiling dutifully, fumbling for his own documents. By prior arrangement or out of simple human (humanistic?) decency, the plaintiffs' machinery was put at his disposal so that he could display his documents on screen.

Gillen began by asking Pennock questions designed to show that just because a theory (such as the Big Bang) confirms some people in their religious beliefs, it is not necessarily unscientific. Pennock quickly sliced this up into its constituent parts and disposed of it. People could believe what they wanted; that was neither his business nor particularly interesting: all that counted was the evidence.

Gillen now moved in on the Ancestor, a computer program that Pennock and three colleagues had designed to demonstrate natural selection. Self-replicating computer organisms are dropped into an artificial digital "life system." The "viruses," if you like, are then seen to mutate and develop, those that adapt best surviving, those that don't dying.

"They evolve things," said Pennock, waving his hands around, "where the programmer would think, 'Why, I would never have even thought to do it that way!' "

Gillen began to ask another question, but Pennock, leaning even farther forward in his chair, now bouncing with enthusiasm, was too full of gusto to be stopped. "And the other thing about it is—sorry, I get excited about this . . . we can keep track of the full evolutionary history! So we have a *complete fossil record*, if you will!" He beamed at the courtroom, which responded with supportive laughter.

45 Gillen collected himself and pushed on, trying to extract the obvious: all this might be true, but if anyone looked at one of the resulting "organisms," he would actually be correct if he inferred that there was an intelligent designer behind it—four of them, in fact. Pennock would have none of it. Neither he nor Darwin was interested in who created the original organism (this, of course, was a tough concept for Gillen, who clearly had a pretty good idea who He was and had to bite his tongue not to mention Him by name), only in the *mechanism* of its *development*.

When court finished for the day, I asked Pennock if I could come and see these organisms, hoping that there would be some Pac-Man-like creatures to view, but was disappointed to be told that they do not exist in visible form.

I had only one problem with Pennock—and in fact with all the scientists who spoke: their use of unnecessarily obscure words. As if the science wasn't hard enough to follow, Pennock would use a word like "qua" instead of "as" or "by virtue of being." For example, he said, "Sometimes people will speak qua scientist, and sometimes they will speak about something from their own personal views." I found myself wondering if he talked to his wife like that: "Listen, honey, this place is a mess, and I'm not just saying that qua husband."

One night during the trial, a local preacher named Reverend Groves put on a show at the Dover firehouse that consisted of him showing a DVD entitled "More Reasons Evolution Is Stupid." The producer and star of the DVD is a man named Kent Hovind, an ex-science teacher, a.k.a. Doctor Dino, who owns a creationist theme park down in Pensacola, Florida. Hovind would throw up an aspect of evolution (that apes and man share a common ancestor, say), with the addition of enough complex-sounding science to make himself seem well-informed, and then dismiss it with the line "That's stupid!" or "I'm sorry, boys and girls, but that's not common sense, that's just stupid!"

When this endless clay-pigeon shoot was done, and the DVD turned off, a man named Burt Humburg, a medical resident at Penn State, calmly raised up a table-top document stand and started to defend evolution. Within moments, a woman, suffering from dental defects that would do an Appalachian proud, was standing in the middle of the hall shouting, "You've been brainwashed in college!" There were grunts and murmurs of agreement, and Burt, although he struggled on manfully for a while, was silenced. I would catch up with him later and find, increasing my admiration, that he was raised in some charismatic division of the church where they spoke in tongues but had been washed clean by the H_2O of science and born again in reason.

50 A few days later I interviewed Reverend Groves for a documentary film I was shooting. A wiry little homo-hater in his late fifties, dressed in tightish pants and cowboy boots, he had an insinuating manner that belied his courage. Every Halloween he joins the parade in York, putting on one of those gruesome anti-abortion shows so beloved of the breed, smashing blood-filled dolls and displaying graphic photographs of aborted fetuses and so scaring the children that in 2002 he was actually arrested by the local police. He sued, however, on the basis of free speech, won, and is now a parade fixture, albeit at the rear.

By this time, it was public knowledge that I was an offspring of Darwin, and in the course of the interview it became apparent to me, really for the first time, how hated the poor old codger is. People such as Groves believe that Darwin marks a point in history from which materialism sprang, bringing with it Hitler, Stalin, Pol Pot, pot, sex, prostitution, abortion, homosexuality, and everything else nasty in the word.

"The moral condition of America," said Groves, "is a result of taking steps away from the Bible and away from God over the past fifty to one hundred years, since evolution was introduced . . . you cast yourself on the sea of nothingness as far as the moral code goes. And every man does that which is right in his own eyes, as the Bible said. And when you do that, you—it's like a moral free-for-all. And that's what's happened in America. We no longer have religious freedom in America, we have a religious free-for-all in America. America was not that way, was not that immoral when it stayed to its Christian roots originally. . . . And now we're in the purge, with the ACLU, with legal organizations such as that, to purge our whole society from anything Christian."

It occurred to me how lucky we are that Darwin lived such a dull monogamous life. Had he been an adulterer, his theory would be dead and buried. Or maybe not. Joseph Smith, a contemporary of Darwin's and the polygamous founder of the Mormons, simply stated that his "truth" was handed to him on a set of golden plates that then mysteriously disappeared. Perhaps if Darwin had done the same he'd have avoided all this controversy.

According to a recent U.S. poll, 54 percent of American adults now dispute that man developed from earlier species, which is a 10 percent increase since the last poll, in 1994. Scientists must bear some responsibility for this: they just don't seem able to provide entertainment the way the other side can. When did you last hear a scientist come up with anything as fun or contentious as man of God Pat Robertson calling for the assassination of Hugo Chavez? Why haven't we seen a man of science on TV asking Bush to explain why God, being such a great pal, gave him such lousy intelligence on the WMDs, or demanding an explanation for all the gaps and contradictions in the biblical record?

55   As Groves had shown no restraint in taking a whack at my ancestor, I felt no compunction in whacking back and asked him some of the questions Darrow asked Bryan at the end of the Scopes trial. Was Jonah really swallowed by a whale? Yes. How did Joshua "command the sun to stand still" when we know that the earth goes around the sun and that stopping it would be disastrous? That's what a miracle is. Were the six days of creation literal days, and how old is the earth? Bryan, when pushed, conceded that perhaps the six days could have been symbolic, and on the subject of the age of the earth pleaded a pathetic ignorance. "I have been so well satisfied with the Christian religion," Bryan said, "that I have spent no time trying to find argument against it." But Groves was made of sterner stuff. He was unashamed of a literal reading of Genesis and an earth that was only 6,000 to 10,000 years old. Carbon dating was nonsense. And that was that.

When I visited Groves in his cinder-block church, he had set up his own video camera to film me filming him. He told me it was just to keep a record of the event, and I did not object. At the end of my interview, he asked me if I was an atheist, and I replied that, no, I was an agnostic, believing that faith even in nothing was too much faith. I finished by observing how odd it was that a country as riddled with Christian faith as America has so little regard for its poor, sick, and imprisoned.

Two days later, two reporters told me they had visited the church in search of local color and found me booming from a TV on the altar, declaring my agnosticism to many gasps of horror. Apparently, the consensus was that I'd end up in hell, probably to find Great-Great-Grandpa sitting at the Devil's side.

When I upbraided Groves about this—he had not told me I was to be used in this way—he shrugged off my objections and told me it had been "educational." He and his flock concluded that I had a different understanding of Christianity. Coming from Europe, mine was "more socialistic," while his was more concerned with "individual salvation."

The first defense witness, Michael Behe (father of nine), looks like the archetypal professor, bearded, vague, tweed-jacketed. Author of *Darwin's Black Box*, he is a biochemist and professor of biology at Lehigh University in Bethlehem, Pennsylvania. Bethlehem, it turns out, is the birthplace of the expression "irreducible complexity." Bethlehem!

60   Behe's shtick, if I may so characterize it, is largely to do with the irreducible complexity of the bacterial flagellum. It is slightly more than this, but if you can understand that flagellum argument, you can understand it all.

Although the concept of irreducible complexity is sold as "brand new," it is in fact more "like new." It began with religious philosopher William Paley's 1802 argument about someone finding a watch and inferring that there had to be a watchmaker. The argument now also includes reaching the same conclusion while looking at Mount Rushmore or seeing "John Loves Mary" written in the sand.

The bacterial flagellum is, however, an amazing thing. Without a diagram, it's more or less impossible to describe. Behe had one, at which he pointed with a laser pointer. In fact, he pointed at everything with a laser pointer. Even when there was only text on the screen, often stuff he had written himself, a red dot danced distractingly across the words. Here he is describing the flagellum:

> The bacterial flagellum is quite literally an outboard motor that bacteria use to swim. . . .This part here, which is labeled the filament, is actually the propeller of the bacterial flagellum. The motor is actually a rotary motor. . . . It spins the propeller, which pushes against the liquid in which the bacterium finds itself and, therefore, pushes the bacterium forward through the liquid.
>
> The propeller is attached to something called the drive shaft by another part which is called the hook region which acts as a universal joint. . . . The drive shaft is attached to the motor itself which uses a flow of acid from the outside of the cell to the inside of the cell to power the turning of the motor, much like, say, water flowing over a dam can turn a turbine. . . . It's really much more complex than this. But I think this illustration gets across the point of the purposeful arrangement of parts. Most people who see this and have the function explained to them quickly realize that these parts are ordered for a purpose and, therefore, bespeak design.

I often encountered Behe outside the courtroom. He was a likable man, and when he found out I was a Darwin descendant he was delighted, stating later in a newspaper article that I was a friendly fellow and my presence in the courtroom was a comfort to him. But I could not get past two thoughts. If an intelligent designer had made the bacterial flagellum, it was logical to assume he had made everything else, and if he had, wasn't this by definition God? One day, I was having this debate with him when another man weighed in, suggesting that since complex machines like the space shuttle are designed by a team, wasn't it probable that the flagellum was also made by a team?

Behe smiled tolerantly and shrugged: he himself believed in a single designer, that was his personal opinion; we could believe what we wanted.

65   My second thought was that if you looked back at the history of science, you could point to any number of things that, given our knowledge at the time, seemed possible only through the intervention of God but that later turned out to have natural explanations even Behe accepted. I missed the point, he told me—and told Rothschild later during cross: the bacterial flagellum is not only complex, it is *irreducibly* complex. In other words, if you removed one element of it, none of the others had function, and so the whole could not have developed by natural selection but must have been abruptly created with all its parts in place. In this context, the mousetrap was often cited.

On the stand, Behe sat forward in his chair, earnest and concentrated. Only once did I see him lose his composure. This was when Rothschild revealed that Behe's own department at Lehigh had issued a statement saying it fully supported evolutionary theory and that

> The sole dissenter from this position, Professor Michael Behe, is a well-known proponent of intelligent design. While we respect Professor Behe's right to express his views, they are his alone and are in no way endorsed by the department. It is our collective position that intelligent design has no basis in science, has not been tested experimentally, and should not be regarded as scientific.

Behe put his hands behind his head and leaned back in his chair, smiling defiantly. He looked like a naughty child who had told his mother he'd seen a ghost and wouldn't budge from the story no matter what. I couldn't help wondering what Behe would be without intelligent design. The scientific community may despise him, but he is beloved on the other side. He gets invited to talk all over the country, and he has sold a lot of books.

Outsiders such as myself were in a froth of anticipation for the testimony of the pugnacious, OxyContin-addicted crusader Bill Buckingham.

By this time many of the plaintiffs had taken the stand and confirmed press reports of Buckingham's outlandish statements. They had been a diverse group, funny, angry, simple, complicated, intelligent, rich, poor, some eloquent on the Constitution, all but a few of them believers, but all having a clear respect for learning and fairness. A picture had slowly come into focus of an arrogant, brutish fundamentalist who would hold to his beliefs no matter what the consequences.

70   But when he arrived, walking with a cane, he seemed old, tired, and subdued. If, as Samuel Johnson said, "Patriotism is the last refuse of a scoundrel," Buckingham was upping the ante with his lapel pin, an American flag wrapped around a cross. He had been through two stints of rehab to kick his addiction, and one wondered if another drug had been prescribed to keep him from making outrageous statements in court.

Knowing that Stephen Harvey was about to question him, one almost felt pity. Harvey, a prematurely gray-haired man in possession of the best suits at the trial—and a Republican, it would turn out—was a man whose considerable personal charm and boyish smile disappeared entirely during cross-examination and was replaced by a cold intensity that was almost frightening to behold.

Buckingham, a 1973 graduate of the Penn State Police Academy, had attended the FBI criminal-investigation school. Before he retired, he was a supervisor at York County Prison.

He testified in a low, mildly surly voice, a whine of self-pity always present underneath. He was unashamedly ignorant and utterly devoid of curiosity. He believed, he stated, in a literal reading of the Book of Genesis. He knew almost nothing about evolution except that "it's happenstance, it just happened," and soon revealed an equal ignorance of intelligent design. "I just know that it's another scientific theory that we thought would be good to have presented to the students."

Worse even than his ignorance were his lies. The most important part of his testimony, and the source of one of the most dramatic moments in court, was his contention that neither he nor board president Alan Bonsell had ever used the word "creationism" in the afore-reported school board meetings. They had been fixed on the scientific theory of intelligent design from the start. Their intent had never been religious. The reporters had lied.

75   "Now," Harvey countered, "it's your testimony that at neither meeting no one on the board ever mentioned creationism, isn't that right?" "That's true." "You're very clear on that point, correct?" "Absolutely, because it's just something we didn't do."

Harvey asked him if he'd mind looking at exhibit P-145. The Wizard of Oz tapped a few buttons and there was Buckingham being interviewed by a local TV news reporter outside a school board meeting at which the current biology book had just been discussed.

"The book that was presented to me," Buckingham said on the video, "was laced with Darwinism from beginning to end. It's okay to teach Darwin, but you have to balance it with something else, such as creationism."

Buckingham looked both irritated and put-upon, and claimed that "when I was walking from my car to the building, here's this lady and here's a cameraman, and I had on my mind all the newspaper articles saying we were talking about creationism, and I had it in my mind to make sure, make double sure, nobody talks about creationism, we're talking intelligent design. I had it on my mind, I was like a deer in the headlights of a car, and I misspoke. Pure and simple, I made a human mistake."[1]

During this testimony, if you looked to the back of the court you could see Bonsell, president of the school board, grinning as Buckingham screwed things up. It hardly seemed to matter to him. Their case could not be damaged. God was on their side.

80 The two local reporters, Heidi Bernhard-Bubb and Joe Maldonado, were called to testify to the truthfulness of their articles. A new lawyer for the defense, Edward White III, came forward to cross-examine them.

White is famous for defending anti-abortion activists who listed doctors' personal information, in the form of "wanted" posters, on an Internet site called the "Nuremberg Files." Three doctors listed on the site were killed in the Nineties, and at one time, I am told, there were "X"s over their faces. The site is now shut down, but if you

---

[1]Neither Buckingham nor his lawyers could be reached for comment. Later in the trial, the plaintiff's attorneys were able to shed light on what he was trying to hide: namely, that a conscious decision had been made to replace any mention of "creationism" with the phrase "intelligent design." Whether this was Buckingham's idea or Bonsell's—or in fact was suggested by, say, the Thomas More Law Center or The Discovery Institute, a creation-science "think tank"—is anyone's guess. Buckingham did admit on the stand, though, that he had received legal advice from both organizations at or around the time of the board meetings.

search the web for Christians of this persuasion you can still find sites listing the names of the three murdered doctors.

White's face was not one within which I could find anything to like. In repose, his head was tilted back in petulant defiance. A superior sneer worked his mouth, and his eyes were arrogant and cold. But he was rarely in repose. Every few minutes, his hand would reach up to scratch his nose, then readjust his watch, his glasses, the knot of his tie; now a jacket-shrug, a chin-scratch, a neck-scratch, then back to the glasses, the tie, and this cycle would repeat two or three times before he settled. This was not a man at ease in his own skin.

When he cross-examined Bernhard-Bubb, White questioned the accuracy of her note-taking and suggested that since meetings sometimes lasted three hours, she might have missed things while going to the bathroom. He suggested as well that she had reason to distort her articles in order to please her editors.

Maldonado received even harsher treatment. A handsome man in his thirties, half Hispanic, tough looking, hair shaved close to his head, a fashionable goatee on his chin, Maldonado was polite in an almost military fashion—"Yes, sir," and "That is correct"—and indeed it was soon revealed that he had served in the Air Force for almost seven years. Like Bernhard-Bubb, he was only a part-time writer for the *York Daily Record*. The rest of the time he was the owner-operator of a sandwich shop.

85   White went through a brief version of his previously described preening ritual, then turned his contemptuous eye on the witness. "Your primary occupation is running the sandwich shop?" Maldonado replied that it was a toss-up between the sandwich shop and his writing. "You don't have any formal training though, correct?" "No, sir." "And freelancing, I know you love to write, but it's also a way to supplement your income, correct?" "That is correct." "And depending on where the article appears in the paper determines the amount of money you're paid per article, right?" "Yes." "So a front-page story gets you about $65?" "$67.50." "And then if it runs on a cover of one of the sections, the local sections, it's about $60?" "$62.50." "And then just your average story is around $50, right?" "Somewhere in that ballpark, yes." "And it is the editors who decide where in the newspaper your stories will run, correct?"

It was apparent where he was going with the line of questioning—namely, that the York paper was biased against intelligent design, and therefore it was to Maldonado's economic advantage to lie in order to get his stories onto the front page. Objections were raised and sustained, and the line of questioning died.

There was something so moving to me in this exchange—the idea of a man running a sandwich shop and working a double shift as a reporter to "supplement" his income with $50 articles for the local paper—that I decided the very next day to pay him a visit.

PBJJ's, Maldonado's sandwich shop, is in the old Central Market in York, one of those cavernous spaces given over to stands selling crafts and bric-a-brac. Joe is rightfully famous for his "Mojo Chicken" sandwich. Hanging above the counter are two American flags. With him that day was the younger of his two sons, fourteen-year-old Jaryid. His older son, Alex, is at Penn State studying meteorology, and there was a jar on the counter for his college fund. Next to this was a book of poems Maldonado had written.

Jaryid had had open-heart surgery when he was seven months old, which caused some developmental delays. A couple of years ago, Maldonado and his wife, Julie, although appreciative of the teacher's efforts, could see he was suffering in regular school. "It was so much for him, it was just overwhelming to go from one subject to the other, and I never got the sense that he was mastering one lesson before he'd move on to the next one." So they took him out. By "supplementing his income" with the sandwich shop in the mornings and reporting in the evenings, Joe is free to devote every afternoon to educating his son.

90   Not only had Maldonado—the liberal reporter—been in the military ("I'm proud to say I served my country"); he had also spent his first year of higher education at Jerry Falwell's Liberty University.

As a Christian, he had been forced to think a lot about the issues raised by the trial. He told me that his faith was so deeply embedded in him, it was very hard to lose God from the equation. To him, the more significant question was whether intelligent design was "ready-for-prime-time science." He spoke eloquently on the subject and referred to the fact that Darwin had spent over two decades collecting evidence before he presented his theory.

Before I left the shop, I bought a copy of Maldonado's book, which he inscribed, "And the Lord said, 'Let there be . . .' Where's the science in that? Joe." Later that night, I opened it with some trepidation and discovered that Joe wrote beautiful poems full of yearning and eroticism and a keen sense of sin. It occurred to me that perhaps Ed White had somehow got hold of a copy, and that when he said, "I know you love to write," he was toying with the idea of reading a few poems in court.

I also went to visit Bernhart-Bubb. She lives in the upper apartment of a nice house in York. She has two children, Ulysses and Bronwyn, both below school age. Here the liberal reporter was found to be a practicing Mormon. While studying at Brigham Young, however, she had been in a band, which she described as being a little like Franz Ferdinand. When her son, in order to impress the guest, started to say "Fuckie, fuckie, fuckie, fuckie," she remained unruffled. She was intelligent, funny, likable, and disagreed with her church on such issues as gay marriage.

Things are not what they seem. Or perhaps, more accurately, only on the outer edge do you find the authentic clichés, and when you find them, if you are me, those that you hate often turn out to be more poignant than repellent.

95 Heather Geesey, a school board member who supported Bonsell and Buckingham, fell squarely into the repellent category, however, without mitigation. I found her the most terrifying of all the witnesses. A woman who seemed to think—against all evidence—that everything she did or said was astonishingly cute and funny, she clearly relished being on the same team as "President Alan," as she referred to Bonsell, and grinned relentlessly throughout.

Cross-examining her was ACLU lawyer Vic Walczak. Vic had the weary but pugnacious demeanor of a man who had devoted his life, for little pay, to defending the Constitution but knew that the only questions he would ever be asked related to the ACLU's defense of NAMBLA (the North American Man Boy Love Association) and the Ku Klux Klan.

He asked Geesey if she supported the teaching of intelligent design. "Yes." "Because it gave a balanced view of evolution?" "Yes." "It presented an alternative theory?" "Yes." "And the policy talks about gaps and problems with evolution?" "Yes." "Yes. You don't know what those gaps and problems refer to, do you?" "No." "But it's good to teach about those gaps and problems?" "That's our mission statement, yes." "But you have no idea what they are?" "It's not my job, no." "Is it fair to say that you didn't know much about intelligent design in October of 2004?" "Yes." "And you didn't know much about the book *Of Pandas and People* either, did you?" "Correct." "So you had never participated in any discussions of the book?" "No." "And you made no effort independently to find out about the book?" "No.". . . "And no one ever explained to you what intelligent design was about." "No." This went on for quite a while, Geesey grinning throughout as if her ignorance was just the cutest thing, until finally, still smiling happily, she stated that she had relied on the curriculum committee—Bill Buckingham and Alan Bonsell—to make the decision. "And do you know whether Mr. Buckingham has a background in science?" "No, I do not." "Do you know that in fact he doesn't have a background in science?" "I don't know. He's law enforcement, so I would assume he had to take something along the way."

So this was the genesis of the whole thing: an auto repairman appointed an OxyContin-addicted biblical literalist without a shred of knowledge to decide which books the kids should learn from, and a woman who had no curiosity about anything, even her own most deeply held beliefs, seconded the whole idea.

And unless one doubted two seemingly decent professional reporters and a host of other witnesses, she would happily lie.

100   Judge Jones had practiced law for several years before being picked by then Governor Tom Ridge to chair the state liquor-control board. He had thus far been fair and amiable and funny. One day an objection was raised as to the admissibility of a question put to a witness. A long debate followed with lawyers on both sides giving it their all. When Jones finally ruled the question legitimate, and it was asked again, the witness said, "I don't know." "After all that!" said Jones.

On another occasion when a witness was criticizing the press by saying he didn't pay much attention to people who bought "ink by the bucket," Jones caught my eye and raised his eyebrows.

Soon after this, I visited him in chambers, and he proved to be everything he appeared in court—civilized, thoughtful, and funny. He read extensively. He was more than polite, he was courteous, a gentleman, a man who seemed to treat everyone around him with equal respect. When I complimented him on his humor, he smiled briefly and expressed the hope that it helped relax tension, though he tried never to be cruel. As a lawyer he had experienced cruelty from the bench and was determined never to abuse his power in that way.

He never did while I was there, though Geesey seemed to test the limits of his patience. In her deposition, she had said that she could not remember when the words "intelligent design" had first been used at school board meetings. On the stand she was very clear that it was in June. Perhaps sensing trouble, Gillen asked her if there was anything that had come up since her deposition that allowed her to "date with somewhat more precision" when she first heard the term "intelligent design" being used. Geesey explained that what jogged her memory were two letters written to local newspapers, one of which was authored by her.

As she was about to leave the witness stand, Jones stopped her, saying he was confused. "So am I," responded Geesey in typical perky fashion. "Well," said Jones, "it's more important that I'm not confused than you're not confused." He pointed out that neither letter mentioned intelligent design. Eventually, Walczak was able to establish that she'd been shown her letter at her deposition and in fact had been questioned about it rigorously.

105   When contacted later about whether she had perjured herself on the stand, Geesey insisted that she had told the truth, calling the lawyers' attempts to discredit her "a big old lie."

Alan Bonsell took the stand a short while later. He is a good-looking, gum-chewing man somewhere in his late thirties or early forties. With the relaxed, entitled, slightly contemptuous manner of a politician or an athlete, he had, throughout the trial, which he visited most often in the afternoons, lounged on the uncomfortable pews, arms stretched out behind him, head back, the grin in place, the mouth chewing. He reminded me of George Bush, in that he exuded a confidence unwarranted by the facts. He had a degree in business management from York College, and I often wondered, and never concluded, whether he was a worse ideologue than Buckingham (because smarter) or just a man of similar personal faith trying to reach a managerial compromise between his friend's more extreme views and those of the rest of the board.

He had a habit of repeating the questions asked of him with added emphasis and a slight upward lilt on the last word or two. "Did I ever think about it? I think about a lot of things."

He admitted that his own personal views about the universe were based on the first two chapters of Genesis but said that at no time had he tried to get creationism into the science class. He believed evolution should be taught, but "when they don't include, you know, problems with it or gaps in a theory, I mean, and you teach it, it almost sounds like they're teaching it as fact."

When asked to come up with an example, he said he'd "seen things on different subjects of how bears turn into whales, you know, this was a natural scientific theory, which I just thought was absurd. There's also statistical things that I've read about how the statistical probability of life happening by itself was basically impossible." I couldn't help wondering what the statistical probability was of God's slapping it all together in six days.

110   One of the mysteries in the case (aside from who created the universe) was who had anonymously donated the sixty copies of *Of*

Pandas and People to the school library. At various times, but most importantly in their depositions, both Buckingham and Bonsell claimed they had no idea who this could be. In court, however, Buckingham admitted that he had gone to his church and asked for donations in order to buy them. He had then given the money to Bonsell's father, who had bought the books and given them to the school.

Steve Harvey, who had the plum job of cross-examining Bonsell, now took him back to his deposition. It soon became abundantly clear that Bonsell knew—and had known at his deposition—the exact provenance of the books. He had lied under oath.[2]

The exact motivation for lying in the first place never became entirely clear to me, but whatever it was, it did not cause the judge to be happy. When Harvey had finished his cross, Judge Jones asked to see Bonsell's deposition, specifically the section about the donation of the books. He then proceeded to grill Bonsell about the inconsistencies: "The specific question was asked to you, sir: 'You have never spoken to anybody else who was involved with the donation?' And your answer was, 'I don't know the other people.' That didn't say, 'who donated.' That said, 'who was *involved* with the donation' . . . now, you tell me why you didn't say Mr. Buckingham's name."

Bonsell stumbled, and Judge Jones became increasingly irritated. Why, furthermore, had Bonsell's father been used in the transaction at all? No clear answers were forthcoming. Bonsell was obviously rattled. He had come onto the stand for the early part of his testimony chewing gum. That had gone soon after Harvey started in on him. Gone too was the swagger and the backward tilt of the head. He walked rather humbly back to the pews.

Within an hour or so, both the pose and the gum were back.

115 Perhaps I'm naïve, or perhaps I have forgotten something, but the Christianity I was raised on had a high regard for truth. How then to explain all this lying? Not just the smaller lies—who bought the books? was the word "creationism" used?—but the larger, insistent lies, the distortion of quotes, the denial of evidence.

Might it all indeed come back to Three Mile Island? The fruit of science, after all, is not just knowledge but technology. Is it because our technology has become so dangerous and baffling that knowledge

---

[2]Bonsell, of course, denied that he had lied about anything. Whether he or Buckingham or Geesey will be charged with perjury remains unknown.

itself must also be feared? Do the ignorant even recognize a distinction between one and the other?

Forsaken in the shadow of those monstrous cooling towers, perhaps Buckingham and Bonsell cannot be blamed for seeking whatever light and dignity is still available to them: belief in a God who loves them individually, God their father. Where we come from is who we are: I will not be mistaken for a Texan; they will not be mistaken for an ape.

One thing I know is that this small crusade in Pennsylvania was not a narrow assault on ninth-grade science education; it was a war on the scientific method and the value of evidence. What was being said, not just by Buckingham and Bonsell but by the President and countless others, is that when the evidence is overwhelming and you don't like it, ignore it.

What natural selection will ultimately do with all of us remains to be seen, but in the Dover school board election that took place shortly after the trial, it eliminated nearly all those who supported intelligent design. Only Heather Geesey, who was not up for reelection, survived. Bonsell got fewer votes than anyone.

120   On December 20, 2005, Judge Jones ruled that the defendants' intelligent design policy violated the Establishment Clause of the First Amendment. In a withering 139-page opinion, he found that the goal of the intelligent design movement is religious in nature, that intelligent design is not science and cannot be taught in Dover schools, and that the board's claimed reason for including intelligent design in the curriculum—solely because it was good science—was a "sham." In referring to board members, he used such words as "striking ignorance" and "breathtaking inanity." Additionally, he wrote that Buckingham and Bonsell "had either testified inconsistently, or lied outright under oath on several occasions," and that "It is ironic that several of these individuals who so staunchly and proudly touted their religious convictions in public, would time and again lie to cover their tracks and disguise the real purpose behind the ID policy." Amen.

When I returned to the Comfort Inn on the last day of the trial, I did not know that I had one more treat in store. Sitting outside the hotel was a man named Scott Mehring.

While covering this story, I was in the habit of asking anyone who looked interesting what they thought of the issues being discussed. Generally speaking, the answers were as limited and predictable as the temperature settings in my hotel room, with by far the largest group opting for the "Off" setting: "Don't know, don't care." But I thought I should ask one last person. Perhaps, finally, I'd find someone who had something new to say on the subject.

Mehring, of Mechanicsburg, Pennsylvania, is forty-eight years old, the onetime owner of a business that had something to do with performance cars. He wore a tight leather motorcycle jacket with no visible shirt underneath and had a Rod Stewart haircut. He liked to party, he told me, and was ready to go out and party hard, but because he'd lost his license for various reasons he had no car and his cab had not yet arrived. So, sure, he'd be happy to share his views with me. I took out my recorder.

"If you go back to the Big Bang," he said, speaking rapidly, "the elements, I'm not sure exactly what they actually were, but whatever the elements were—the atom, the neutron, the proton neutron, whatever it was that created the Big Bang—*where* did that stuff come from? Spontaneous generation is a dead theory—at one time they thought it was true—left a piece of meat on the ground maggots appeared, they thought the maggots came out of the meat, but actually they just came out to eat the food, so you can't say spontaneous generation created it. . . . Now if you believe in physics, you got the eleventh dimension—it's a new theory, the eleventh dimension—and inside the eleventh dimension they say that there's an infinite number of universes. So my take is that if you die on the earth, we just somehow hop over to the eleventh dimension, and hop from universe to universe to universe forever inside the eleventh dimension. So that means the Bible could be right with everlasting life after we die. *But*, okay, the elements that started the Big Bang, if that was an intelligent designer? Then you've got another complication. If there was, like, one dude somewhere at the very top that created everything? Well, *where did he come from?* Who created him? And who created the God who created God? It gives me goose bumps. It's a loop, like in computer programming—it's an endless loop."

125 He paused and shook his head. His cab had arrived.

"If you think about this too much," he concluded, "you can go insane."

Analyzing Rhetorical Choices

1. In his second paragraph, Matthew Chapman writes, "That's the basic story, but if you think you know everything there is to know about this, you are wrong. Only I know the truth." What rhetorical

effect(s) do you think he is trying to achieve here? Is he being arrogant? Is he insulting his readers—and if so, why? What relation does his statement have to the subject of his essay?

2. Why is it important that his great-great-grandfather is Charles Darwin? What rhetorical effect(s) does the statement and restatement of this fact make in his reporting and his relationship to his subject and those he interviews?

3. What does he mean by saying that the settings on his motel air ventilation system became "a perfect metaphor for the debate"? Find examples in the essay of each of the settings and explain your choices.

4. Define Chapman's tone and cite two examples from the essay that best illustrate it. How does that tone affect his treatment of this trial and its various witnesses and testimony? Is Chapman a trustworthy reporter? Why or why not?

5. Explain the ending of this essay. Why do you think Chapman chooses to end his essay with that brief interview with Scott Mehring?

Writing About Issues and Contexts

1. What is Chapman's argument? How does he support it?

2. In what ways does Chapman not only make an argument about evolution but also evaluate the effectiveness of various arguments about evolution, creationism, and intelligent design? Analyze the ways Chapman offers evidence to support his argument—and how effective that evidence is in making his case.

3. Do you agree with the judge's decision? Explain your position based on the evidence presented in this trial as reported by Matthew Chapman.

4. Chapman provides a lot of impressions in this essay, impressions about the lawyers, the witnesses, the judge, the reporters, and so forth. Is that information helpful? Is it insightful? Prejudicial? Does this essay offer an effective argument about evolution? Explain your response.

5. Do you think Chapman takes this trial seriously? Explain why or why not, based on your reading of this essay.

Strategies for Writers: Argument

1. As you determine what you will argue, you may want to reread some of the essays in this chapter—as well as those elsewhere in this book. For instance, Paul Goldberger's argument is a subtle, implicit one; Martin Luther King, Jr.'s, more explicit. As with the other modes presented in this book, it is also important to consider your audience. Would a more implicit or explicit argument work best?

2. Will you argue inductively or deductively? William F. Buckley, Jr., for instance, argues inductively, using specific instances to make a broader argument. Joy Williams also primarily uses an inductive form of argument, citing specific passages from magazines and articles and then critiquing them. Paul Shepard and Martin Luther King, Jr., on the other hand, work deductively, establishing principles and positions and then arguing from them. Some essays blend both forms of argument, at times moving from the particular to the general, and at other times from the general back to the particular. Which method will work best for your subject and your individual style?

3. Will you employ Rogerian techniques? By that we mean persuasive strategies named after the psychologist Carl Rogers who emphasized the value of finding common ground in an argument in order to achieve consensus and agreement. Martin Luther King, Jr., Matthew Chapman, and Paul Shepard might be said to argue in a Rogerian fashion, encouraging readers to appreciate viewpoints that might counter their own. Both assume friendship and goodwill on the part of their readers, even those who might potentially object. This strategy emerges from their own ethical relationship to their audiences, their view that argument is not about pounding an opponent into submission but rather engaging in meaningful dialogue and mutual consideration. (Contrast this approach to the perspectives taken by Joy Williams and Camille Paglia, for example.) Will a Rogerian approach work best for your essay?

4. How will you select your evidence? A good argument depends on specific examples—as you can see in Paul Goldberger's essay on architecture and in Matthew Chapman's essay on the Dover trial centered on evolution and intelligent design. An audience of your peers will have a different set of expectations than,

say, an audience of business persons or college professors. What evidence will be most useful to you? Will you use library sources, the Internet, personal interviews, statistical data, or other forms of research to help you demonstrate your knowledge and authority?

5. Debate the various facets of your argument with your classmates. Check the logic of your arguments against the fallacies outlined at the start of this chapter. Have you unknowingly fallen victim to fallacious reasoning? Once you have checked for fallacies, the next step is to determine if your classmates find your arguments effective and your evidence useful in proving your argument. In classroom discussions, try to develop an ear for good argument. Do you notice logic operating differently in different cultural contexts? Are you or your classmates responding to arguments on the basis of logic, emotion, friendship, identification?

6. What really persuades you to someone else's position? Do you see patterns in the ways you and your classmates respond to certain issues and questions? Does the way someone uses language affect the ways you respond to that argument or whether you take it seriously? Is Matthew Chapman more able to write about the issues that concern him because he is the great-great-grandson of Charles Darwin? Is Camille Paglia able to write about rape more effectively because she is a woman? Discuss these arguments—and the issues that surround arguments—in conversation and as you exchange drafts.

7. It is worth remembering that many writers begin the writing process because they have a particular argument or perspective that they believe in. Then they read, engage in research, talk to colleagues, and often find that their views change, that what they believed before no longer holds true for them. As you move through the research and writing process, is this same phenomenon happening to you? Have you modified or even reversed your arguments as you have researched and written? Do you need to revise substantially so that your essay reflects your more considered perspective?

Research and Writing Assignments

1. In "Letter from Birmingham Jail," Martin Luther King, Jr., offers a passionate defense of civil disobedience, stating that "I would be the first to advocate obeying just laws . . . . Conversely, one has a moral responsibility to disobey unjust laws." Likewise, Camille Paglia's "It's a Jungle Out There" also relies to some extent on a common assumption that individuals need to take charge of their own lives and assume responsibility for their own actions. In an essay that cites one or more of these essays closely, develop an argument about civil obedience, and the relationship between law, morality, and religion. To make this essay manageable, focus on a specific issue or concern that brings these contending forces into focus, and then engage in library research on a topic such as civil rights conflicts in 1960s America, antiwar protests during a time of national conflict (Vietnam, Iraq), violating anticensorship laws, the history of women's suffrage, or conscientious objectors to war during the 1940s. How can we best decide when laws are just and when they are unjust? Who gets to decide such questions? How do we best take responsibility for our own actions?

2. Lani Guinier critiques one of the major principles of democracy, the tenet that the majority rules. "Where we have tyranny by The Majority," Guinier writes, "we do not have genuine democracy." In an essay that makes consistent use of Guinier's essay, write a proposal for how decision making in American public life can be structured so that decisions are made most fairly. If you decide to adopt Guinier's proposal of "taking turns," explain how that would work in practical terms. If you decide that the majority should rule, offer an explanation that takes into account the views of minority groups in this country. You might want to read some of the works of James Madison and Alexis de Tocqueville, both of whom have made important contributions to our thinking about democratic forms of government.

3. Dialogue is often difficult between two individuals with opposing perspectives, yet true, meaningful dialogue should always be a goal for those engaging in argument. Create such a dialogue between two individuals meeting at a coffee shop or

some other calm setting, one who agrees with Joy Williams that hunting is cruel and should be banned and the other who agrees with Paul Shepard that hunting is an elementary part of nature and the wilderness experience. Although these two individuals hold very different views, create a dialogue that allows them genuinely to speak and to listen. Your dialogue may or may not offer a resolution to this ongoing debate about hunting, but it should draw on the works of both Williams and Shepard—and it should not result in fist-pounding, red-faced pontificating.

4. Each of the essays in this section to some extent challenges or critiques a dominant public perception. For instance, Matthew Chapman takes Americans to task for privileging religious belief over scientific thinking. Chapman does this by offering a reportorial description of the Dover, Pennsylvania, trial in which he uses the technique of the interview and the citation of various "experts'" testimony to develop an argument about the contrasting positions of intelligent design versus the theory of evolution. Write a follow-up essay to Chapman's in which you engage in research that challenges another misconception or inequality—one related to popular belief, race, gender, class, family, or academic life—that has a personal meaning for you. One possibility is to think about a group around whom stereotypical views have formed (freshmen, blacks, women, men, bratty brothers, absent fathers), then search for sociological studies that illuminate your subject, and finally write an essay that argues for a reconception of that stereotype based on your research.

5. In his essay, Paul Goldberger writes about buildings as iconographic symbols. Choose a building on your own campus or in your own neighborhood and analyze it in terms of how its design, function, and meaning relate to one another. How do the aesthetics of the building reinforce or counteract its intended use? How do you interpret the various design features of the building: its windows, its entryways, its towers, its use of internal and external space? In what ways, if any, can the building be seen as a tool, an art object, an expression of educational or economic philosophy, or a symbol or cultural expression, like the World Trade Center? In your essay, be sure to include frequent mention of specific design features, and be sure to tie those features to an overall structure that assesses its meaning and value.

6. In their essays, Norman Cousins, Joy Williams, and Paul Shepard are all concerned with violence. Since both boxing and hunting are forms of recreation and sport, the question arises: When, if ever, do such entertainments cross the line and become inappropriate or even immoral and destructive to society? In an essay that carefully analyzes the arguments made by Cousins, Williams, and Shepard, offer your perspective about this controversy. Should boxing or hunting be outlawed? Should dogfighting or deer hunting (or violent video games) be banned? In your essay, develop some specific criteria that you think can be applied to help in thinking about this issue.

Credits

Index

Additional Penguin Titles of Interest

Note to Instructors: Bundle any of the titles listed below with *Rhetorical Choices* and your students will receive a special discount of up to 60% off the retail price of the Penguin book! Contact your Allyn & Bacon/Longman sales representative for details on how to create a Penguin-Longman Value Package.

Allison, Dorothy, *Bastard Out of Carolina*

Alvarez, Julia, *How the García Girls Lost Their Accents*

Austen, Jane, *Pride and Prejudice*

Bellamy, Edward, *Looking Backward*

Chopin, Kate, *The Awakening and Selected Stories*

Coraghessan Boyle, T., *The Tortilla Curtain*

DeLillo, Don, *White Noise*

Douglass, Frederick, *My Bondage and My Freedom*

Du Bois, W.E.B., *The Souls of Black Folk*

Equiano, Olaudah, *The Interesting Narrative and Other Writings*

klin, Benjamin, *The tobiography and Other ings*

Howard, *Black Like Me*

wrence K., *The Republic*

der, *The Federalist*

igrant Voices: tives of n the Life

emoir e of

King Jr., Martin Luther, *Why We Can't Wait*

Lavin, Mary, *In a Café: Selected Stories*

MacArthur, Brian, *The Penguin Book of Twentieth-Century Speeches*

McBride, James, *The Color of Water: A Black Man's Tribute to His White Mother*

Morrison, Toni, *The Bluest Eye*

Naylor, Gloria, *The Women of Brewster Place*

Parker, Dorothy, *The Portable Dorothy Parker*

Plato, *Great Dialogues of Plato*

Postman, Neil, *Amusing Ourselves to Death*

Rose, Mike, *Lives on the Boundary*

Rose, Mike, *Possible Lives*

Rushdie, Salman, *Midnight's Children*

Silko, Leslie Marmon, *Ceremony*

St. Augustine, *The Confessions of St. Augustine*

Thoreau, Henry David, *Civil Disobedience*

Thoreau, Henry David, *Walden*

Twain, Mark, *The Adventures of Huckleberry Finn*

Various, *The Portable Beat Reader*

Wilde, Oscar, *The Picture of Dorian Gray*

Williams, Juan, *Eyes on the Prize: America's Civil Rights Years 1954–1965*